WINE LABELS
1730 - 2003

MADEIRA, James Hyde, London 1798. RUM, Ann Robertson, Newcastle *c.*1810. CLARET, James Hyde, London *c.*1790. CURASCOA, Charles Reily & George Storer, London 1849. TOKAY, Silver-gilt, John Reily, London 1817. PORT, Battersea enamel, London 1753-56. HOCK, Benjamin Smith, London 1807. RUM, Yapp & Woodward, Birmingham 1846. RIVESALT, enamel, English *c.*1780. CURRANT, mother-of-pearl, English *c.*1800. VODKA, silver-gilt border, Stuart Devlin, London 1987. SHERRY, Wyard Druitt, London *c.*1972. CLARET, Thomas Phipps & Edward Robinson, London 1806.

WINE LABELS
1730 - 2003
A WORLDWIDE HISTORY

Edited and co-authored by
John Salter
M.A.(Oxon.), F.C.M.I., F.C.I.W.M., F.R.G.S., F.R.S.A., A.C.I.Arb.

Antique Collectors' Club
in association with
The Wine Label Circle, 2004

DEDICATION

Sadly, since writing the Introduction and just before the Circle's Exhibition at the Fine Art and Antiques Fair at Olympia, London, in November 2003, Captain Sir Thomas Barlow Bt., D.S.C., R.N. (Retd) died. He was the longest serving Honorary Secretary of the Wine Label Circle and indeed Father of the society, just nearing his ninetieth year. He was the anchorman of the Book Committee, he was the fount of all knowledge about labels and, as an old boy of Copthorne School (of which I was a Governor for some seventeen years and given a decanter (fig. 59) appropriately upon retiring), and a Wykehamist, he was the master wordsman in guiding the efforts of the Book Committee in the production of this work.

Accordingly, at the Circle's AGM held in November 2003 in Alnwick Castle, it was decided, as a tribute to his outstanding contribution to the work of the Circle, that this book should be dedicated to him. Our President, Peggy Pullan, expressed the thoughts of members when she said: 'Tom will be hugely missed by members of the Circle and by many other friends. To so many of us he was a mentor as well as a greatly respected and much-loved friend. It could be said that he personified the Wine Label Circle; he was a member for forty-two years, joining in 1961, President in 1978-79 and Secretary from 1987 to 2003. His profound and scholarly knowledge was encylopaedic and encompassed virtually every aspect of wine label collecting.'

The Circle also wishes to put on record by publishing this book the notable work of other members of the Circle who sadly have passed on, including our former President Brian Beet, who so kindly wrote the Foreword shortly before he died.

John Salter, January 2004

Published 2004 by Antique Collectors' Club
Sandy Lane, Old Martlesham, Woodbridge, Suffolk
in association with
The Wine Label Circle
Website: http://www.winelabelcircle.org

ISBN 1 85149 459 6

Copyright © 2004 John Salter and The Wine Label Circle

This publication is protected by International Copyright Law and the right of John Salter and the other contributors to be identified as authors of this work has been asserted by them in accordance with the Copyright, Designs and Patents Act, 1988.

All rights reserved. No part of this publication may be reproduced in any material form (including photocopying or sorting it in any medium by electronic means and whether or not transiently or incidentally to some other use of this publication), stored in a retrieval system or transmitted in any form or by any means, without the prior written permission of the copyright owner.

British Library Cataloguing in Publication Data is available from the British Library.

Salter, J.R. (John R.), 1932-
Wine Labels
Includes bibliographical references and index

Printed in England

Editor and Contributor

Professor John R. Salter
President 1986-87, and Hon. Solicitor 1982-, Wine Label Circle

Other Contributors Past and Present

Captain Sir Thomas Barlow Bt., D.S.C., R.N. (Retd)
President 1978-79, and Hon. Secretary 1987-2003, Wine Label Circle

Kevin A. Barrington

Gwen Baxter

John Beecroft
President 1973-74 and Hon. Editor, Wine Label Circle Journal, 1959-2001
Wine Label Circle

Brian Beet
President 1990-91, Wine Label Circle

John Carss
President 1994-95, and Hon. Librarian 2001-, Wine Label Circle

Theo Dalder

Jack Davis

Anthony Dove

Dr Jack Edwards
President 1996-97, Wine Label Circle

Patrick Gaskell-Taylor
President 1984-85 and Hon. Treasurer 1976-, Wine Label Circle

Andrew Gilmour
President 1988-89, Wine Label Circle

Betty Harris

Richard Hodgson

Sir Geoffrey Hutchinson, Q.C.

Bruce Jones
President 2001-02 and Joint Hon. Editor Wine Label Circle Journal 2002-

Commander Gustav Lind
Royal Swedish Navy

Dr Conor O'Brien

Colin Paul

Rasmus Reeh

Dr John Rocyn-Jones
President 1992-93, Wine Label Circle

Ian Smart

Keith Thacker

Dr Bernard M. Watney, F.S.A.
President, 1980-81, Wine Label Circle

Dr Richard Wells

The Rev. Eric Whitworth
President, 1976-77 and Hon. Secretary 1963-87, Wine Label Circle

Labelled decanters for PORT and BRANDY were in vogue in the Prince of Wales's establishment at Carlton House. See page 20.

Figure 6. The Dinner Party, *by Jules Alexandre Grun (1868-1934). See page 23.*

The Book Committee

The President, *Ex Officio*
Patrick Gaskell-Taylor, *Chairman*
Tom Barlow
Brian Beet
John Carss
Jack Edwards
Andrew Gilmour
John Salter

CONTENTS

Dedication by John Salter 4
Acknowledgments 12
Foreword by Brian Beet 13
The Wine Label Circle 14
Introduction by Tom Barlow 15

Chapter 1 Development of the Wine Label 17
- Part 1 Early Documentary Evidence by Tom Barlow and John Salter 17
- Part 2 Contemporary Illustration by Patrick Gaskell-Taylor 19
- Part 3 The Wakelin Ledgers by Bruce Jones ... 23
- Part 4 Evolution and Early Development, 1735-1760 by Tom Barlow and Andrew Gilmour 26
- Part 5 The Neo-classical Period, 1760-1800 by John Carss 28
- Part 6 The Regency Period, 1800-1837 by John Carss 31
- Part 7 The Victorian Period, 1837-1901 by John Carss 33
- Part 8 The Twentieth Century by Patrick Gaskell-Taylor 38

Chapter 2 Shapes and Designs 45
- Part 1 Escutcheons by Andrew Gilmour 45
- Part 2 Rectangles by Tom Barlow 49
- Part 3 Scrolls by Tom Barlow 54
- Part 4 Ovals by Andrew Gilmour 57
- Part 5 Crescents by John Carss 61
- Part 6 Stars and Buttons by Tom Barlow 64
- Part 7 Sun in Splendour by John Rocyn-Jones and Tom Barlow 66
- Part 8 Bottle Collars and Neck Rings by Brian Beet 66
- Part 9 Single Letters and Cut-out Words by Tom Barlow 70
- Part 10 Bacchic Revellers by Tom Barlow 74
- Part 11 Barrels by John Rocyn-Jones and John Salter 78
- Part 12 Anchors by Tom Barlow 80
- Part 13 The Balloon Label by Tom Barlow and Conor O'Brien 82
- Part 14 Bugles by Tom Barlow 83
- Part 15 Crowns by John Rocyn-Jones and John Salter 84
- Part 16 Harps by John Rocyn-Jones, Tom Barlow and Conor O'Brien 85
- Part 17 Hearts by John Rocyn-Jones and Tom Barlow 86
- Part 18 Goblets by John Rocyn-Jones and Tom Barlow 87
- Part 19 Shells by Tom Barlow 88
- Part 20 Vine and Other Leaves as Labels by Tom Barlow 89
- Part 21 Armorial Labels and Labels from Royal Palaces, Universities and Corporate Bodies by Tom Barlow 94
- Part 22 Commemorative Labels by Tom Barlow 104
- Part 23 Military and Naval Labels by Tom Barlow 106

Chapter 3 Making 108
- Part 1 Making and Decorating in Silver by Ian Smart 108
- Part 2 Gilding by Andrew Gilmour 117
- Part 2 Condition by Brian Beet 119
- Part 4 Fakes and Conversions by Brian Beet 122
- Part 5 Revivals and Reproductions by Tom Barlow and Brian Beet 123
- Part 6 Caring and Cleaning by Tom Barlow 124

Chapter 4 Marks 125
- Part 1 Hallmarks on Early Labels by Tom Barlow 125
- Part 2 The Sterling Lion by Tom Barlow 127
- Part 3 Plate Duty Marks by Anthony Dove .. 129
- Part 4 The Britannia Marks by John Salter ... 135
- Part 5 Makers' or Sponsors' Marks by Tom Barlow 136
- Part 6 Tally Marks by John Salter and Tom Barlow 138

Chapter 5 Makers 139
- Part 1 Sandylands Drinkwater by Andrew Gilmour 139
- Part 2 John Harvey by Brian Beet 143
- Part 3 The Batemans by Brian Beet 144
- Part 4 The Binleys by John Beecroft 149
- Part 5 The Hyde Family by Brian Beet 152
- Part 6 John Reily and his Successors by Brian Beet 154
- Part 7 Charles Rawlings and William Summers by Brian Beet 157
- Part 8 Paul Storr by Gwen Baxter 159
- Part 9 Rundell, Bridge and Rundell by Kevin Barrington 161
- Part 10 The Phipps Family by Tom Barlow ... 165
- Part 11 Susanna Barker by John Rocyn-Jones 169
- Part 12 John Rich by Tom Barlow 175
- Part 13 Women Silversmiths by Tom Barlow .. 178
- Part 14 Makers' Locations by Bruce Jones 179

CONTENTS

Chapter 6	**Names** **184**	**Chapter 9**	**Labels from Outside the British Isles and Ireland** **342**
Part 1	Unusual Wine Label Names by Tom Barlow and Bruce Jones 184	Part 1	Australia by Brian Beet 342
Part 2	Reversible Wine Labels (Palimpsests) by Tom Barlow and John Salter 192	Part 2	Belgium by Brian Beet and Tom Barlow 344
Part 3	Drinks in Vogue at Different Periods by Brian Beet 194	Part 3	Burma by Brian Beet 346
		Part 4	Canada by Brian Beet 347
Chapter 7	**The Provinces** **201**	Part 5	China by Brian Beet 348
Part 1	Chester and District by John Salter and Tom Barlow 201	Part 6	Denmark by Rasmus Reeh 349
Part 2	Exeter and District by Patrick Gaskell-Taylor 208	Part 7	Finland by Gustav Lind 352
		Part 8	France by Kevin Barrington 352
Part 3	Bristol and Bath by Tom Barlow 221	Part 9	Germany by Patrick Gaskell-Taylor ... 355
Part 4	Newcastle and District by Brian Beet 223	Part 10	India by Brian Beet 356
Part 5	York by Tom Barlow and Patrick Gaskell-Taylor 229	Part 11	Malaysia and Singapore by Brian Beet 357
Part 6	Birmingham by Jack Davis 240	Part 12	Malta by Tom Barlow 357
Part 7	Sheffield by Jack Edwards and Tom Barlow 246	Part 13	The Netherlands by Theo Dalder 360
		Part 14	Norway by Rasmus Reeh 363
Part 8	Edinburgh by John Salter 254	Part 15	Poland by Gustav Lind 364
Part 9	Glasgow, Greenock and Paisley by John Salter 256	Part 16	Portugal by Gustav Lind 364
		Part 17	Russia by Gustav Lind 365
Part 10	Scottish Provincial by John Salter 265	Part 18	South Africa by Tom Barlow and Brian Beet 366
Part 11	Ireland by Conor O'Brien 273		
Part 12	The Channel Islands by Tom Barlow 281	Part 19	Spain by John Salter 368
Chapter 8	**Labels from Other Materials than Silver** **282**	Part 20	Sweden by Gustav Lind 368
		Part 21	United States of America by Brian Beet 372
Part 1	Old Sheffield Plate by John Carss 282		
Part 2	Other Metals by Brian Beet 288	Part 22	Other Colonial Territories by Brian Beet and John Salter 374
Part 3	Battersea Enamels by Geoffrey Hutchinson and Bernard Watney 292	**Chapter 10**	**Patterns of Ownership** **375**
Part 4	Non-Battersea Enamels by Eric Whitworth, John Salter and Richard Wells 298	Part 1	Early Collectors by John Carss 375
		Part 2	Notable 18th-century Families by Tom Barlow 382
Part 5	Bin and Barrel Labels by Colin Paul, Keith Thacker and John Salter 305	**Appendices** **385**
Part 6	Electroplate by Ian Smart 314	Appendix 1	Names of Wines, Spirits, Liqueurs and Alcoholic Cordials 385
Part 7	Mounted Corks by Richard Hodgson 326	Appendix 2	Makers of Wine Labels 400
Part 8	China, Pottery, Glass and Celluloid by Patrick Gaskell-Taylor and John Salter 331	Appendix 3	Glossary 419
		Appendix 4	Bibliography 421
Part 9	Mother-of-pearl by Brian Beet 333	**Notes** **426**
Part 10	Other Organic Materials by Brian Beet 337	**Index** **435**

SHERRY, MADEIRA, Susanna Barker, London 1786-89. RED, Stuart Devlin, London 1980. CLARET, Benjamin Smith, London 1835. CURRANT WINE, George McHattie, Edinburgh c.1825. BUCELLA, John Reily, London 1808.

Figure 2. A Portrait of Members of the Society of Dilettanti from 1777 to 1779 *by Sir Joshua Reynolds (see page 19).*

ACKNOWLEDGEMENTS

Figs. 1, 3 and 478. © The British Museum
Fig. 2. The Society of Dilettanti.
Fig. 7. Reproduced by permission of Messrs Garrard & Co. and the Picture Library of the Victoria and Albert Museum.
Figs. 16-20. John Carss Esq.
Fig. 483. From the Parish Register of St Botolph, Aldersgate, by kind permission of the Guildhall Library, City of London MS 3854/5.
Figs. 582 and 583. Guildhall Library, Corporation of London, MS 6495/1.
Figs. 704-709. Executors of Sir Thomas Barlow dec.
Figs. 1022-1049. © Christies Images Ltd 2004.
The Book Committee is most grateful to The Worshipful Company of Goldsmiths, The Worshipful Company of Vintners, the late Brian Beet and Messrs. Bonhams for their support for this publication and to the Antique Collectors' Club for its design and production.

Illustrations

The figure numbers are attributed from left to right, top row downwards. Most illustrations are life size, but some have been enlarged or reduced.

FOREWORD

This is the first major book to be published on the subject of wine labels since Norman M. Penzer's ground breaking *The Book of the Wine Label* (1947). It contains, therefore, over half a century's worth of subsequent research, almost all of which has been produced by members of the Wine Label Circle. The Circle was founded by Edward J. Pratt in 1952 to promote the appreciation and knowledge of labels. Since its inception, it has published a twice-yearly journal – the *Wine Label Circle Journal (WLCJ)*.

It is easy to understand why wine labels have long enjoyed an enthusiastic following. They have been produced in a fascinating variety of materials for the last 250 years and so reflect many of the changes in decorative fashion and manufacturing techniques to have occurred during that time. They also provide a canvas for the evolution of drinking habits. As a subject for collection, moreover, wine labels have two particularly strong attractions: they can still be found in some quantity and, compared with many other fields, they are relatively inexpensive.

As with all areas of collection and research, there remain questions to be answered. With wine labels the most perplexing problem is why they should first have appeared in the 1730s. There was obviously a need for such an article from the time dark green glass wine bottles began to be made (around 1660), and it would also be quite logical if they had first appeared in the 1760s when clear glass decanters, silver coasters and wine funnels started to become fashionable; but the 1730s do not appear to have seen any major innovation that might have provoked the introduction of the wine label. Such puzzles can only serve to stimulate interest and, perhaps, the publication of this book will elicit the answer!

Brian Beet, December 2002

Above. Dust jacket for Dr Penzer's book published in 1947.

The Wine Label Circle

In April 1952 Mr E.J. Pratt, the Secretary, writing from Taunton, Somerset, affirmed that 'the Wine Label Circle is now established. It has started in a small and unobtrusive way with a few members [in fact twenty-three] and its first publication [its Journal] is launched'. Honorary Members were André Simon and Norman Penzer. The cover of the Journal was designed by its first Honorary Editor, Jean Rhodes. Pratt thought that in due course the Circle should have an 'Overseas Section'. In the event many collectors from all round the world have joined. Sidney Bell did the legal work, Patrick Sandeman represented the wine trade, and all three became Life Members.

The Pratt Collection formed the basis of Harvey's Wine Museum in Bristol, now closed and its contents auctioned by Bonhams. It had many visitors, the attraction being the beauty and craftsmanship of wine labels, which inspires collectors and is exemplified by the six Ravenet labels shown on this page. The Journal is now in its eleventh volume, having run to some one hundred and eleven issues. The Circle mounted an exhibition of decanter labels, for both wines and sauces, at Olympia in November 2003.

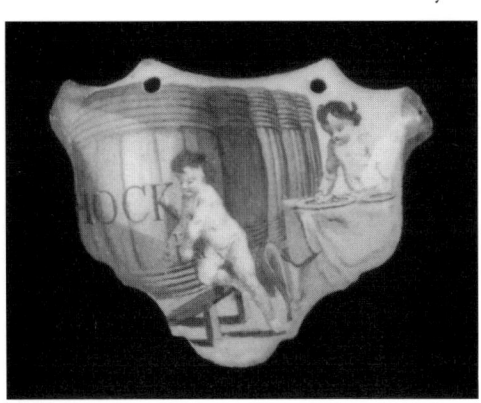

The Circle celebrated its Golden Jubilee year with its published work on *Sauce Labels* now followed by its companion work on *Wine Labels*. Its next task will be to publish on the subject of *Medicinal and Toilet Box Labels*. The Society maintains records of titles and publishes in the Journal regular updates of the material contained in the books. The Society can be accessed through its website:

http://winelabelcircle.org

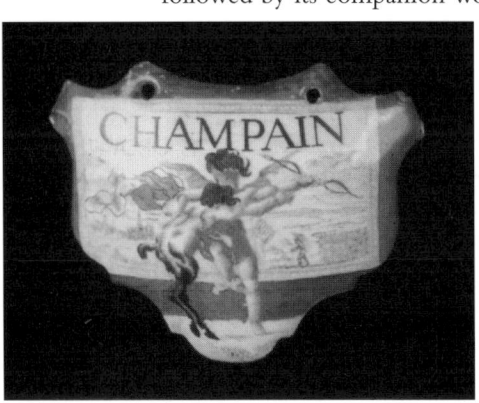
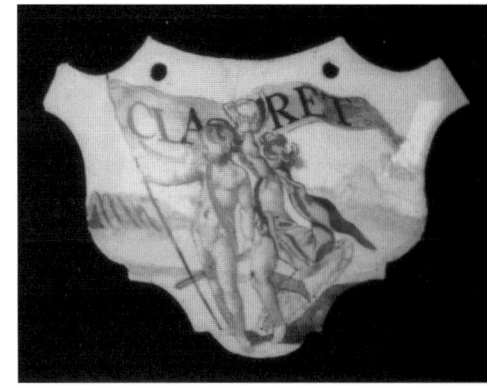

INTRODUCTION

This book has been written to supplement, but not to replace, Dr Norman Penzer's *The Book of the Wine Label*, which was published in 1947. It does not revisit the historical antecedents of the wine label, which he explored so thoroughly, but takes its start from 1735 when bottle-tickets began to adorn the dining rooms of society. From there it goes more thoroughly into some of the aspects of their development which Penzer did not cover.

The story of this book's production dates back to 1960, only a few years after the Wine Label Circle was founded, when it was already becoming clear that a new and revised edition of Penzer's work would be justified to put on record the wealth of new information that research by members of the Circle was bringing to light: the hitherto unknown designs that were being discovered, and the range of unsuspected wine names that these labels bore. No action was taken at the time, but in 1964 Mr Pratt, the Circle's founder, proposed that this research should be included in a completely new book. At the same time, Mrs Penzer kindly transferred to the Circle the copyright of her late husband's work, in order to facilitate the project. Details of how the book should proceed were left vague in the hands of a succession of authors, culminating with the well-known authority on silver, Miss Judith Banister. She made some progress, but ill health and her other commitments compelled her to relinquish the task and it languished until 1985. The project was then taken over by a committee of the Wine Label Circle, with a remit to establish a proper format for the book, allocate subjects to selected authors and invite contributions from outside experts. But fresh discoveries were being made all the time and, without a firm date to work to, the process of fitting them into chapters in preparation or already written seemed likely to go on for ever. A line had to be dawn and a definite programme established for contributors to adhere to. In 1996 John Salter, a long-standing member of the Circle, and currently its Honorary Solicitor, accepted the appointment of editor-in-chief to the project. He produced the first text of the book and drew up a timetable to take the work through its concluding stages, leading to its publication.

The book starts by searching contemporary literature and early tradesmen's ledgers and the records of the assay offices for references to bottle-tickets or wine labels, and by examining paintings, drawings and prints for illustrations of them. Chapter 1 continues with general treatises on labels and their development from their earliest days through Georgian, Neo-classical, Regency and Victorian periods to modern times when the need for them declined and they began to enter the collector's field. An account is given of some of the early collectors, predecessors of the enthusiasts who eventually founded the Wine Label Circle.

In Chapter 2 the designs that silversmiths have employed in making wine labels, based on the prevailing fashions of the day, are described; the standard types are covered and some of the less common designs, conspicuous for some particular aspect of their appearance, or for rarity, are also mentioned. Next, manufacturing processes are examined, and an explanation is given of some of the marks that may be found on labels, but are not sufficiently clarified in other books of reference, such as Jackson. Further chapters contain brief accounts of the better known silversmiths who specialised in wine label manufacture to some degree, and some of the unusual names found on labels are discussed. An updated list of names and makers of labels may be purchased from the Circle – see its website at http://www.winelabelcircle.org. An account is given of the country's provincial assay offices and of the labels produced by the silversmiths who used them. There are chapters on labels made in other countries than Britain and made of materials other than silver. The appendices include a bibliography of wine label related literature and a glossary of useful terms. Inevitably a book compiled from articles by so many different hands will contain a large variety of styles. An attempt has been made to harmonise the general effect, with valuable help from Slaney Begley but, as the main purpose of the book is to record the last half-century's accumulation of wine label knowledge rather than to present a literary *tour-de-force*, individual authors' words remain largely as they wrote them.

Wine Labels is a companion volume to *Sauce Labels* published in 2002 and written by John Salter in celebration of the Circle's Golden Jubilee. It is hoped to publish regular updates on both wine and sauce labels in the *Wine Label Circle Journal*, available to members of the Circle.

Tom Barlow, October 2003

Figure 1.

CHAPTER 1

DEVELOPMENT OF THE WINE LABEL

PART 1 – EARLY DOCUMENTARY EVIDENCE

There was evidently nothing so significant in contemporary eyes about the bottle-ticket, when it first made its appearance in society dining rooms in the mid-1730s, that it led writers of the time to introduce it into their novels or for it to be mentioned in any other literature. There was a lot of drinking and talking, as shown by the political wags meeting at their tavern club in 1797 (see fig. 1). The Chairman is the essayist John Courtenay M.P. He is addressing Col. Hanger (Georgey), who has Sheridan on his left, drinking BRANDY. On the Chairman's right is Michael Angelo Taylor drinking MUM (said[1] to be a popular German beer, brewed of barley, malt and wheat, originally from Brunswick) and on his left is Fox drinking CHAMPANE.

This is not to say that eminent writers did not follow the social trend and acquire bottle-tickets, as Jonathan Swift's will of 1740 makes clear (see below). However, whilst Dr Johnson, a lover of wine, in his famous *Dictionary* of 1755 refers to a 'bottle-friend' and a 'bottle-companion', he makes no mention of a bottle-ticket. Pepys noted in 1699 in his *Diary* that he went to a Mr Rawlinson's 'and saw some of my new bottles with my crest upon them, filled with wine, about five or six dozen'. Wine was kept in dark glass bottles at this time to protect it from the damaging effects of light. Presumably, the owner had to remember what was put in them!

The *Oxford English Dictionary* (1888-1927)[2] does not have an entry for 'bottle-ticket' and its authority for 'wine label' is a quotation from 1848, by which time, of course, they were standard items of a silversmith's stock. The reference is, in fact, taken from H.B. Forster's Stowe Catalogue of that year. It is consequently not surprising that the earliest documentary references are to be found in the ledgers of the firms that manufactured these (at the time) novelties and retailed them to their clients. One of the earliest is an entry in the Gentlemen's (Clients') Ledger of George Wickes (see fig. 7 and Chapter 1, Part 3: The Wakelin Ledgers) of 9 May 1737, charging Lord Lymington £1.10s.0d. for '6 Bottle Ticketts'.[3]

Even earlier is an account rendered on 21 March 1737 by Paul de Lamerie[4] to Earl Fitzwalter[5] charging him £0.4s.6d. for 'mending and adding silver to three pieces with chains to hang on bottles of wine'. This record is of particular interest for several reasons. It provides a pointer towards the date when labels were 'invented'. If this trio had to go back to be mended in 1737, then they were presumably in use before that date. It is to be noted, too, how de Lamerie describes them by their function, indicating that there was as yet no generally recognised term for the labels. This supports a view expressed by Penzer[6] that he could not determine when the word 'bottle-ticket' came into use, or when 'decanter label' and 'wine label' began to supplant it. It does, however, confirm that the first intended purpose of the article was to hang around the neck of a bottle rather than to adorn a decanter. Thirdly, and most tantalisingly for the collector, is the fact that it was Paul de Lamerie's workshop (if not the great man himself) that carried out the order. No label bearing de Lamerie's mark has ever been seen, but he was active into the 1740s, by which time the demand for labels was growing. As de Lamerie was asked to repair the labels, it is quite possible that he had made them in the first place. Earl Fitzwalter appears again in May 1738, when he paid 'Edward, silversmith in Lombard Street, for 14 tickets, silver, for wine bottles, at 5s. and 6d. each'.[7]

Dean Jonathan Swift, who died in 1745, made his will in May 1740. In it he bequeathed to the Earl of Orrery 'the enamell'd silver plates to distinguish bottles of wine by, given me by his Excellent Lady'. In his article on Irish wine labels (see Chapter 7, Part 11) Dr Conor O'Brien surmises that the gift was probably made in August 1739, indicating, perhaps, that bottle-tickets were becoming better known by then, but yet made an interesting and unusual present. The word 'enamell'd' in this context probably means black wax (niello) filled. Again, the description of the items is strictly functional – neither the word 'ticket' nor 'label' is used. On the other hand, one of the early Wakelin Ledger volumes does contain two entries for 'lables' [*sic*]: 'To five lables for bottles, 2ozs 16dwts, £1.10s.0d. – The Earl of Malton, debtor' is dated 9 April 1738 while an entry for November 1743 reads 'To two lables for Bottles, Mr Westphaly, 12s.'. William Westphaly was Yeoman of the Pantry in the household of 'His Royal Highness, the Prince of Wales, Debtor'.[8]

From 1748 we have a nearly continuous record for twenty years of the labels that one firm, Parker and Wakelin, was supplying to its clients (see Chapter 1, Part 3), and doubtless other silversmiths had similar entries in their ledgers, which unfortunately have not survived. There is still nothing in the books of the period, or even casual mention in magazines or gazettes before the 1770s.[9] For any other contemporary evidence that is extant we have to look elsewhere. One important source, that has been somewhat overlooked and not yet properly researched, is the inventories of plate in town and country houses compiled by the families who lived in them. Examples of two well-documented 'family' collections of plate that included wine labels, formed from the first half of the eighteenth century and described in Chapter 10, are those of the 2nd Earl of Warrington at Dunham Massey in Cheshire and the Sykes family at Sledmere near Hull. There are certain to be similar records in other archives around the country, perusal of which would bring to light further early references.

Finally, there are the registers and other records held by assay offices – some now closed, others still functioning. The structure of the registers at the Goldsmiths' Hall in London is well documented, with smallworkers and largeworkers entered in separate volumes from 1697 to 1773 and thereafter in one volume.[10] They show the names and marks of silversmiths who used the London office and their date of entry, but they do not give details of the work they sent for assay. This information has not been published and we have to search elsewhere to discover which silversmiths actually made wine labels. Bucklemakers, plateworkers, casemakers and other specialist crafts are listed by category, but wine labels evidently did not require a trade description of their own (although we know that several silversmiths did specialise in them and must have been recognised by retailers and clients as leaders in that field). Sadly, two vital registers are missing: those listing the smallworkers between 1739 and 1758, and the largeworkers between 1758 and 1773, just the period when labels were emerging from infancy into full bloom. This gap seriously handicaps our ability to link specific makers to labels that clearly belong to these early days.

The records of English provincial assay offices are likewise incomplete, but they all have some books that for some years of the eighteenth century show items that were sent for assay, wine labels amongst them. These registers, duty books and other documents are listed in the chapters on the provincial offices and in the bibliography.

Wine labels did not reach Scotland until the latter years of the eighteenth century and so there is nothing concerning them in such early records of the Edinburgh Assay Office as have survived. In Ireland, too, where the Dublin registers are more complete as regards the craftsmen who were entered there than any others, no details of the articles they made have survived earlier than around 1787.[11]

PART 2 – CONTEMPORARY ILLUSTRATION

Part 1 has shown that the general literature of the eighteenth century contains scant references to wine labels. Painters and illustrators were quicker to take note of these new and eminently portrayable devices. One of the earliest illustrations, in a painting attributed to Stephen Slaughter of about 1745, shows a gentleman seated in front of a punch bowl, surrounded by three bottles with suspended labels CLARET, BURGUNDY and (perhaps) CHAMPAGNE.[12] Perhaps the best known reference in painting is William Hogarth's *An Election Entertainment*, of 1754-55.[13] A drunken party is in progress, to woo electors, and on the tables are several squat bottles, two of which have paper or parchment labels around their necks. The names CHAMPAIGN and BURGUNDY are written in script on these labels. Labels of this type are too ephemeral to have survived until the present era.

Another painting is a still life by Moses Haughton (senior), which shows a bowl of punch, some bread and other comestibles, and a bottle with a white crescent enamel label for CLARET hung about its neck.[14] The painting is signed and dated 1773. Haughton (1734-1804) was a well-known Birmingham enameller, who later took up still-life painting and was elected to the Royal Academy in 1788.

The Society of Dilettanti in London owns another painting in which a wine label is specifically delineated. Sir Joshua Reynolds painted *A Portrait of Members of the Society* from 1777 to 1779. It shows seven members admiring Greek vases, drinking wine and conversing. To the right of the picture (see fig. 2, page 11), a dark glass decanter in shade is clearly hung with an escutcheon-shaped label – the horn at one side is visible – with, unusually, a rounded base instead of the usual point; perhaps Reynolds was using artistic licence. In other respects the label is similar to Sandylands Drinkwater labels of the 1750s. It is not possible to decipher a name, but the commentary to the 1986 Royal Academy *Reynolds* exhibition noted a relish for vintage claret among the Dilettanti. The painting is one of a pair possibly intended to record the reception into the Society in 1777 of Sir William Hamilton, noted diplomat and collector of antiquities. The second painting also indicates bottles; they have highlights from reflections of windows, which can at first glance be mistaken for labels, but close examination of the painting disproves this.[15]

In cartoons wine labels are represented not so much as objects in their own right, as they are in a painting, but rather as a means of indicating the contents of vessels that themselves are part of the message of the cartoon. Hence the labelling of contents can be either as a conventional label – often a crescent, or as a scroll of paper diagonally around a bottle, recalling the paper labels in the Hogarth

Development of the Wine Label

Figure 3.

painting – or simply as script on the vessel. The best-known cartoonists who depicted labels were James Gillray (1756-1815) and George Cruikshank (1792-1878), both London men. The cartoons described below featuring labels are a few examples in a wide field.[16]

The son of an evangelical sexton in Chelsea, James Gillray's birth coincided roughly with the genesis of political caricature in England, the etchings of current topics after drawings by George Townshend. Gillray's life spanned the four decades between the American Revolution and the Battle of Waterloo, often described as the golden age of the English political cartoon. He was apprenticed in his early teens to an engraver and publisher of banknotes, before entering the Royal Academy in 1778. After various forays into political satire – between illustrating and portraiture – he turned his full energies to caricature when aged about thirty.

One of his relatively early caricatures to depict labels (see page 6), published by H. Humphrey, was the 1792 *A Voluptuary under the Horrors of Digestion*, which commented on the tastes and habits of the Prince of Wales.[17] The prince is seen in a first floor room of Carlton House amid a litter of food, bottles, medicines and unpaid bills held down by a chamberpot. On the table are two pear-shaped decanters with crescent labels for PORT and BRANDY. A gilded caster is labelled CHAIN, meaning cayenne pepper.

In 1793 there were reports of the French invasion of Holland by a General Demouriez, leading to speculation about his other activities. In another cartoon[18] treacherous members of the English Opposition dining at St James's on 15 May 1793, dressed as *sans-culottes* waiters, bring platters to the general's table with the roast head of Pitt, ecclesiastical pudding, and a stewed crown liberally garnished with frogs. On the table, completing the bizarre meal, is a decanter with a crescent label for VIN DE PARIS, hardly a name that collectors of wine labels are ever likely to encounter.

A Decent Story, a cartoon dated 4 November 1795 (fig. 5), is more of an illustration than a political satire. Etched from a sketch by John Sneyd, it shows three men and two women seated around a table, having a lively and good-humoured conversation.[19] The only accoutrements on the table are wineglasses and a stoppered decanter, with crescent labels for PORT, placed within a coaster.

Development of the Wine Label

Figure 4.

A 1797 cartoon[20] of five members of the Opposition seated at a table enjoying a wild night at their tavern club includes three dumpy carafes with crescent labels for BRANDY, CHAMPANE *(sic)* and MUM illustrated in fig. 1, page 17.

England's Hanoverian connections around the turn of the eighteenth century and the political twists and turns in the numerous small principalities that then comprised Germany provided many opportunities for caricaturists. Gillray's well-known *Germans eating Sour-Krout* of 1803 shows five German men, looking more like monsters, ferocious of visage, either rakishly thin or grossly obese, gorging themselves on huge mounds of soured cabbage.[21] Also on the table to complete the message is a squat stoppered flask bearing a narrow diagonally placed label, possibly paper, for VINEGAR.

Thus it can be seen that the bottle-ticket, generally in the form of a crescent, was familiar to the upper and middle classes and so could be used by Gillray to reinforce the message of his cartoon. It could therefore be a significant element of the picture rather than an incidental part of the illustration.

Gillray's old age was overlapped by the youth of another of the Regency era's great cartoonists: George Cruikshank. Cruikshank produced more than 10,000 images during a working life of seven decades. His father was an etcher and draughtsman and the boy learnt at his father's knee; he must have been a talented pupil – his first paid work was at the age of eleven. Cruikshank could hardly have had any professional connections with James Gillray, owing to the latter's madness during his last years, but he clearly knew the older cartoonist's work. His efforts were at first directed against similar targets – politicians and others in high places – but in 1847 he took the pledge as a teetotaller after repeated drinking binges and thereafter a good deal of his work was in support of the campaign for teetotalism.

A relatively early caricature is *Qualification: the prince, in love and in drink and o'ertoppled by debt* of 1820. This shows how familiar Cruikshank must have been with Gillray's work, for the composition is strikingly similar; today he would be accused of plagiarism. The prince, somewhat older and more of a human wreck, is slumped in a chair beside a table with two decanters, one fallen and the other standing with a crescent label, by this date less fashionable than in the 1790s. The floor is littered with overturned bottles, gaming dice and a player's mask. Instead of a background of Carlton

Development of the Wine Label

Figure 5.

House, a screen with orgiastic scenes stands behind the torpid Regent. The cartoon was used in a satirical pamphlet later that year, once the prince had succeeded to the throne, concerning the steps he was taking as George IV to divorce Queen Caroline.[22]

In 1841, still some years before Cruikshank took the pledge, the *Comic Almanack* published (see fig. 3) *December: a Swallow at Christmas – Rara Avis in Terra*.[23] This publication was launched about 1810, towards the end of Gillray's life, and was less a politically satirical journal than an opportunity for the contributors to pursue zany and surreal ideas. The cartoon shows the face of a glutton into whose mouth are marching along a plank a stream of anthropomorphised delicacies – fish, turtle, plum pudding, turkey, ham, mince pies and more. Also heading for his mouth is a crate of seventeen assorted bottles, decanters and foaming tankards. The stoppers have faces and the first three or four bottles are already levitating towards the mouth. All the containers except the tankards are identified with various types of label – crescent, scroll, curved rectangle and star – or have the name applied direct on to the glass. The names are quite varied too: SHRRY *(sic)*, COLD PUNCH, MADEIRA, HOCK, CHAMPAGNE, MOSELLE, CLARET, PORT, BURGUNDY, RUM, WHISKEY, GIN and O.D.V. These are mostly fairly common names, some in lower case lettering, but Cold Punch and O.D.V do not occur among the names recorded on silver bottle-tickets to date.

Another Cruikshank cartoon showing a number of labels is his *Wines in a Ferment and Spirits in Hot Water* (see fig. 4). This shows about a score of containers – decanters, bottles, casks, tankards – again in anthropomorphic form, on and around a table. They are mostly labelled with bottle-tickets, the majority of which are crescents, some elongated and hanging diagonally. The names include BRANDY, PORT, SHERRY, WHISKEY, CLARET, CHAMPAGNE, RUM, ARRACK, ALE, PORTER, XXX STOUT, SMALL BEER and OLD TOM. Most of the containers have speech bubbles above them declaiming pro-drink slogans. For example, the PORT decanter is saying 'Gentlemen, the man must be mad to refuse a glass of generous Port!', and the small lidded tankard of SMALL BEER is announcing 'He must be a spooney to be afraid of me!'.

In Cruikshank's *Mr John Bull in a Quandary or the Anticipated effects of the Railway Calls*, which is lampooning railway speculators in trouble as they face calls for more funds, a horrified and obese John Bull is being set upon by a myriad of Lilliputian midgets who are pulling him about and making off with all his goods, including a large elegant decanter with a crescent label for PORT. In this scene the wine label is merely incidental, rather than being an important part of the message.

However, in H. Humphrey's *A Decent Story*, published in 1805, PORT is shown as the essential ingredient of good mixed company (see fig. 5).

These examples of wine labels depicted in cartoons are but a small sample of a fairly large population that might come to light if print and cartoon archives were thoroughly researched. The population of names would be even larger if all drink names on vessels, not limited to those in bottle-ticket form, were also included. As far as the caricaturists were concerned, there was no distinction for their purpose between a bottle-ticket and any other identifier. An anonymous French cartoon of 1784 has stoppered bottles, one with a paper label for FRONTIGNAC and another with an escutcheon-shaped, probably paper label for CLOS DE VOGUE; a large wine jug is inscribed VIN DE LAFITTE.

The cartoon illustrations of wine labels do not of course cover the range of designs of the real artefacts; they are only representational. Nor do they seem to follow the fashions of the real thing – the crescent of the 1780s seems to be the standard type right through to the middle of the nineteenth century. The range of names that appear on wine labels in cartoons is greater, however. Paper labels feature in significant numbers, which seems to confirm that they were in general used to mark the contents of bottles well before they had to be so labelled following the legislation of 1861.

The Dinner Party, by Jules Alexandre Grun (1868-1934), reminds us of elegant dining at the stage of coffee and liqueurs (fig. 6, page 7). Even in modern times the tradition of using the wine label as a cipher occasionally recurs, as in the *Independent on Sunday* in 1992, when Riddell's view through a keyhole shows British Chancellor of the Exchequer Norman Lamont as an alchemist mixing up an economic brew from flasks with paper labels and bottle-tickets for STERLING, HOUSE PRICES, MARKET INTEREST RATES and similar economic factors.[24] At about the same time the weekly journal *The Spectator* carried a cartoon by Peter Brookes after Gillray's 1792 *A Voluptuary under the Horrors of Digestion* (again!), this time with Norman Lamont in the scorned prince's chair, the crescent wine label for PORT being clearly visible.[25]

PART 3 – THE WAKELIN LEDGERS

The Wakelin Ledgers, now in the Victoria and Albert Museum, London, are the account books of an eighteenth-century firm of silversmiths, founded by George Wickes in 1722. Edward Wakelin became a partner in 1747 and appears to have taken control of the manufacturing side, with George Wickes concentrating on retailing. In 1760 Edward Wakelin registered a joint mark with John Parker and these two continued together until 1776, when the firm was taken over by Edward's son, John Wakelin, and William Taylor. Robert Garrard joined in 1792 and the firm ultimately became Garrard and Co.

There are two basic types of ledger surviving from these partnerships: the 'Gentlemen's Ledgers', which show sales to members of the public (see fig. 7, page 25); and the 'Workmen's Ledgers', which show dealings with other silversmiths. The ledgers cover the whole business of this major firm, from ambassadorial plate through pieces such as tureens to smaller items of domestic silver, including wine labels.

The Gentlemen's Ledgers show numerous sales of wine labels to the upper echelon of society. The Workmen's Ledgers have accounts of purchases of labels between 1748 and 1760 by George Wickes from Edward Wakelin, the former apparently acting as retailer, the latter as manufacturer. The partnership also purchased labels from another firm, James Ansill and Stephen Gilbert, from 1766 to 1772, as well as a few labels from Margaret Binley in 1767.

The entries from a selection of these ledgers have been analysed, not from the totality of the ledgers. The analysis that follows does not therefore provide a complete picture of the firm's dealings in wine and sauce labels, but does give some flavour of this part of their business.

Looking first at wine labels, a summary of the relevant transactions in the ledgers is shown in Table 1 below. The value in the Gentlemen's Ledgers is much higher, as the customer – the Gentleman – paid the full retail price. By contrast, in the Workmen's Ledgers the silversmith, who commissioned the work, provided the silver and the manufacturing silversmith – the workman – was paid only for the workmanship.

Table 1. Wine label purchases and sales

Gentlemen's Ledgers (sold retail)	Number	£. s. d.	Average no. per year
1747-60	226	67 03 4	16
1771-79	572	158 16 9	64
1780-90	377	109 17 5	34
TOTAL RETAIL	**1175**	**335 17 6**	**35**
Workmen's Ledgers (trade)	Number	£. s. d.	Average no. per year
Sold to Geo Wickes 1748-60	938	59 07 1	72
Bought from Ansill & Gilbert/Binley 1766-72	261	13 07 8	37

In the first period (1747-60), retail sales averaged sixteen labels each year, though in the years 1751-55 no sales were recorded. However, Edward Wakelin was busy in this period with the manufacture of labels for George Wickes, for whom he made a total of 938 labels in thirteen years, an average of seventy-two labels a year between 1748 and 1760. In our analysis there is a ten year gap in the 1760s before any further details of retail sales are recorded. Similarly, there are no details of label manufacture for George Wickes. This may reflect the absence of the ledgers, or an imbalance in the sampling of entries. There are, however, entries in the Workmen's Ledgers from 1766 to 1772 of 261 labels made for the firm by Ansill and Gilbert and by Margaret Binley.

Details of retail sales resume in 1771 and 572 labels were sold in the period 1771-79, an average of sixty-four per year. In the third period, covering 1780-90, retail sales continued steadily until 1784, 335 labels being recorded between 1780 and 1784, an average of sixty-seven each year. Thereafter the number of labels falls away sharply. It is likely that this apparent decline is due to the absence again of certain ledgers. The details available in the Gentlemen's Ledgers do appear to indicate that demand in the 1770s was stronger than in the 1740s and 1750s. The decline after 1784 is unexpected and probably not typical. The high level of labels supplied to George Wickes in the 1750s is also an unexpected feature.

The ledgers are account books, and we have exact details of the prices paid for 1171 of the 1175 labels. Over the whole period 1747-90, 1171 labels were sold for a total sum of £335.17s.6d., an average of 5s.9d. per label. This average price was very steady over the forty years, partly due perhaps to low inflation at the time. In addition, labels after 1760 generally became lighter and required less workmanship. Surprisingly, the imposition of duty in 1784 did not affect the price per label. In the Workmen's Ledgers, the prices shown are payment only for workmanship, and average between 1s. and 1s.3d. per label. The value of the silver, supplied by Wakelin, was about 1s.3d making a cost to Wakelin of 2s.3d. per label. However, the average retail price of labels sold by Wakelin was 5s.9d., suggesting a substantial retail mark-up of around 3s.6d.

The Gentlemen's Ledgers also show how many labels were purchased by customers on each occasion a purchase was made. There were 277 occasions when separate entries appear in the ledgers for the 211 customers, some customers making purchases on more than one occasion. Table 2 shows, for instance, in the first line, that on 141 of the 277 'purchasing occasions' between one and three labels were bought. This represents fifty-one per cent of all entries in the ledgers, but accounts for only 244 of the 1175 labels sold, or twenty-one per cent of all labels sold.

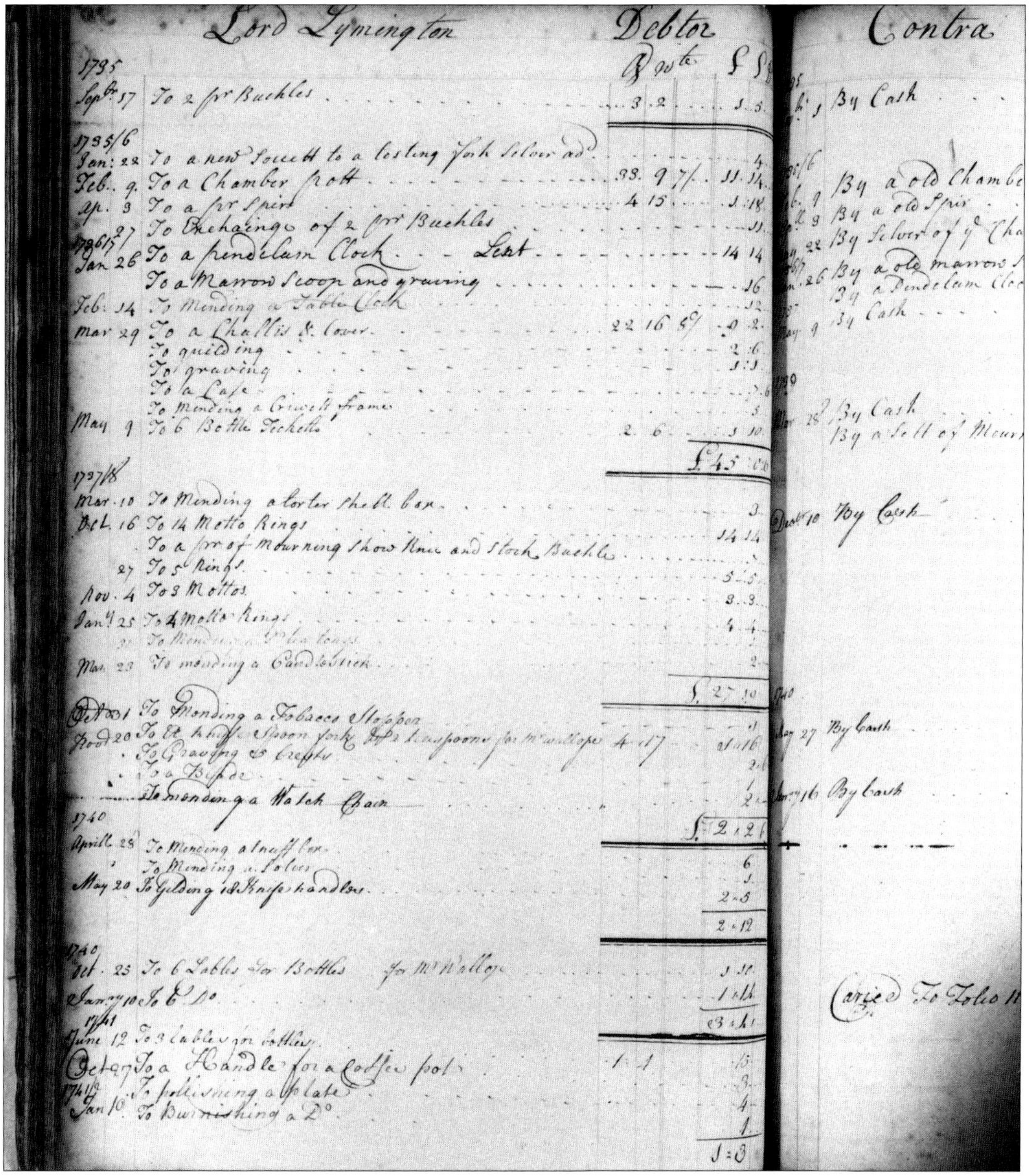
Lord Lymington Debtor Contra
1735 Sepr 17 To 2 pr Buckles
Feb. 9 To a Chamber Pott
Jan 26 To a pendelum Clock
Mar 29 To a Challis & Cover
May 9 To 6 Bottle Tickets
Oct. 16 To 14 Motto Rings
Nov. 4 To 3 Mottos
1740 Oct. 25 To 6 Lables for Bottles
By Cash

Figure 7.

<u>Table 2. Number of labels purchased on each occasion (Gentlemen's Ledgers)</u>

Size of set purchased (labels)	No. of purchasing occasions		Labels purchased	
	No.	**%**	**No.**	**%**
1-3	141	51	244	21
4	35	13	140	12
5	15	5	75	6
6	30	11	180	15
More than 6	56	20	536	46
TOTAL	**277**	**100**	**1175**	**100**

The main conclusion to emerge from Table 2 is that the majority of the labels were sold in fairly large sets. While sixty-four per cent of the entries refer to purchases of between one and four labels, this covers only thirty-three per cent of all labels. Put another way, two-thirds of all labels were sold in sets of more than four labels (that is, five or more), and sixty-one per cent in sets of six or more. In the early period (1747-60), only twelve per cent of labels were sold in sets of less than four. Judging by the number of labels now seen as single labels or in pairs, it is apparent how dispersed the original groups have become.

Other entries in the ledgers include the sale of decanter corks, 163 appearing in the ledgers between 1771 and 1786 at an average price of 4s.10d. per cork; the provision of chains for labels (usually 1s. a chain); mending labels (this most commonly cost 1s. too); polishing; alteration of names (thirteen instances, costing between 1s.6d. and 2s. per label); and blacking the names (2d. to 3d.). The ledgers also show that the firm gave credit to customers who 'traded-in' old wine labels, the credit being only for the silver content. There were 200 such labels, quite a high number when compared with the 1175 sold by the firm in the same period.

Of the 211 customers who are mentioned in the Gentlemen's Ledgers for buying wine labels, seventy-eight were titled, including seventeen earls, fifteen honourables and sixteen baronets. The most numerous single group were, however, the 105 esquires. The clergy accounted for eight customers and there were seventeen female customers. The titled customers tended to spend rather more on labels than their untitled counterparts. Among the more famous names appearing in the ledgers as purchasers of wine or sauce labels are three first ministers – Waldegrave, Grafton and North. Other political customers included the famous Speaker Arthur Onslow, the first Viscount Melbourne, the 4th Duke of Marlborough and the fashionable 5th Earl of Carlisle. Leading naval officers were prominent, and royalty were represented by Frederick Louis, Prince of Wales, and by the Duke of Cumberland, brother of George III.[26]

PART 4 – EVOLUTION AND EARLY DEVELOPMENT, 1735-1760

It is not possible to state precisely when wine labels were invented, but it must have been around 1735, during the reign of George II. A more accurate date cannot be given because there was no legal requirement for wine labels to be hallmarked or assayed at that time. Nevertheless, there are a number of pointers as to why they came in and when they first began to be used. Dr Penzer's account of the evolution of the wine label is still satisfactory, as regards the general story, and amendments to it since he wrote it in 1947 mainly result from our greater knowledge of the working lives of the silversmiths who made the early labels and the marks they used. For instance, his attribution of certain early marks to S. Dell, J. Holland II and, later, to S. Bradley, whose working dates led him to arrive at an earliest date, have since been discarded in favour of Sandylands Drinkwater, John Harvey, James Hyde or perhaps Thomas Heming, mistaking his script 'T' for Harvey's script 'J', and Susanna Barker (see Chapter 5, Parts 1, 2 and 11). Labels by Sandylands Drinkwater are now known with his first mark, entered in 1735, and the lion passant, which was in use until 1739; the labels must, therefore, have been made between these dates. Likewise, Harvey's earliest labels can be dated to 1738. This puts Penzer's date for the appearance of the wine label back from the early 1740s to the mid-1730s. An early escutcheon label for CLARETT (see fig. 8) has the maker's mark 'I•L' with a star above it (see fig. 15), attributed by Grimwade[27] to an unidentified maker known by candlesticks dated 1735 and an inkstand of 1737 (but who may, of course, have continued to be active after those years). This may be as near an actual date as we shall get, given the absence of any other marks, but further evidence comes from tradesmen's ledgers (see Chapter 1, Part 1), which start to mention bottle-tickets and wine labels at about this time.

Penzer attributes the need for labels partly to the introduction of clear glass decanters, some years before 1737, which allowed a wine decanted from an unmarked, dark coloured bottle brought up from the cellar to be better identified and also enabled it to be shown off to better effect than had been possible in those bottles or through the opaque glass of early containers. This is largely true, and it certainly accounts for the speedy emergence of designs such as escutcheons and 'two puttis' that were suited to grace the dinner table, but it does not satisfactorily explain another group, usually considered to be equally early. These are a cross between an escutcheon and a rectangle with waved sides and small indented corners (see figs. 8-14 and Chapter 1, Parts 1 and 2). They usually have the name of the wine

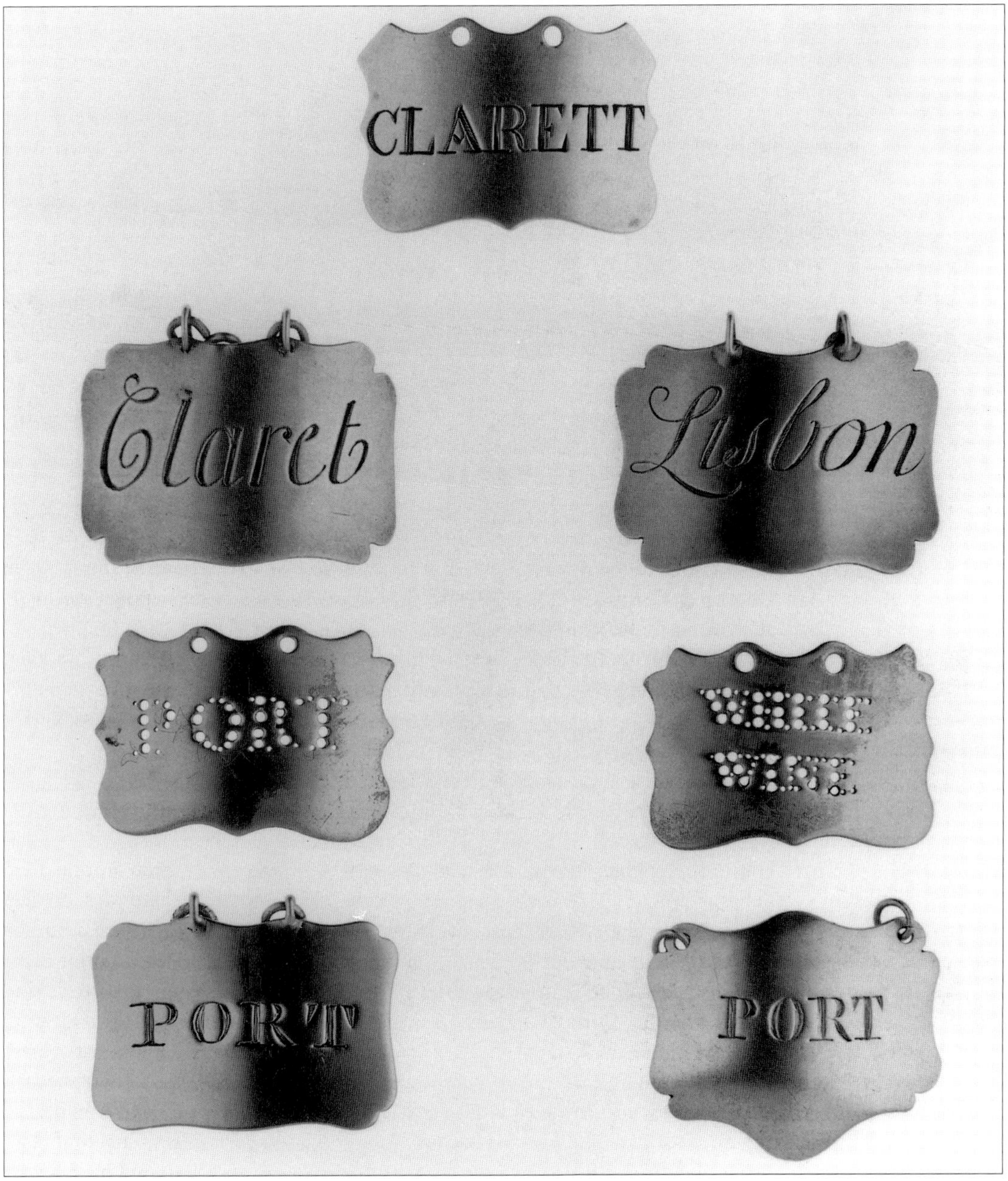

Development of the Wine Label

Figures 8-14.

engraved in large script letters (see figs. 9 and 10), and the wines are those in vogue in the second quarter of the eighteenth century: CLARETT and Claret (see figs. 8 and 9), Lisbon (see fig. 10), Madeira, PORT (see figs. 11, 13 and 14) and WHITE WINE (see fig. 12). As Penzer points out, when bottles were used to store wine in the cellar they would have been unmarked, or perhaps had a strip of parchment with the name on it (in script letters?), glued to the side. So it would be logical to suggest that, when the bottle came to the sideboard, a simple detachable strip of some material (rectangular in shape) would have sufficed to identify the contents. A rectangle would have been the logical shape for it but, if that is indeed what happened, the surviving evidence would be labels or tickets such as these. If there were others they have not survived. This is not surprising, as when they went out of fashion they would have been melted down and converted into something more up-to-date. This group, then, is well suited to the term 'bottle-tickets', as wine labels were first known.

Figure 15.

Some early decanters had wine names engraved upon them, including for ALE, BEER, BURGUNDY, CHAMPANE, CLARET, OLD HOCK, LISBON, MADEIRA, MOUNTAIN, WHITE PORT, RED PORT, PORT, SHERRY, WHITE WINE, W. WINE and WHITE.

27

Development of the Wine Label

Figures 16-20.

About 1760 the Beilby family were painting on glass in coloured or white enamel. There are known to be a few decanters that were decorated by them with flowers or fruiting vine and wine names, beautiful work and most ornamental, with names such as CLARET, PORT, ALE, W. WINE, MADEIRA and MOUNTAIN.

There is another type of label decanter that was chiefly used for spirits. It was usually made of coloured glass – blue as a rule, though green and red decanters are also known, including a very few that were red flashed only in soda glass. The 'label' consisted of an imitation chain and label in gilt, nowadays very much worn. Gilt labels on clear glass are also known. The titles include BRANDY, SHRUB, HOLLANDS, GIN, RUM and, in clear glass, PUNCH and WHISKEY.

Pairs of labelled decanters are shown in figs. 16-20 for the Modern, Victorian, Regency, Neo-Classical and Early periods (detailed in the Circle's Olympia Exhibition Catalogue, Case J, November 2003).

As regards design, this was the age of the rococo and, as has been stated above, the favourite shapes were escutcheons of ogee outline cut from plate, and cast, flowing concoctions (such as by John Harvey), composed of C-scrolls, rocaille, leaves and grapes, or embodying putti, Dionysus or, in an example by Thomas Heming, a goat's head (see fig. 21). It is noticeable that the taste for chinoiserie, so evident in furniture and porcelain, did not permeate the field of the wine label. Towards the end of George II's reign there appears a large, heavy, broad rectangle, twice the length of the group described above, with a gadrooned or feathered border. A conspicuous feature of these labels, as of most early escutcheons, but not of 'two putti' and plumed rococo designs, is the lettering of the name in large Roman capitals. In addition to Drinkwater and Harvey, mentioned above, other silversmiths who made labels in the early years were Thomas Rush, Louis Hamon and Edmund Medlycott, but strangely the names of Paul de Lamerie and George Wickes are absent. In the provinces labels were being manufactured in Newcastle from at least 1750 and in Chester a few years later, while some Irish labels can be attributed also to this time (see Chapter 7).

PART 5 – THE NEO-CLASSICAL PERIOD, 1760-1800

During the mid-eighteenth century there was a growing interest in classical archaeological sites of the Roman States and Greece, and in their excavation for architectural evaluation and analysis. Some earlier digging had taken place at Herculaneum, but work did not start at Pompeii until 1748. Publications about the finds there soon reached England and France, where they proved to be of great interest in both academic circles and to society as a whole. The discoveries began to influence the styles of new houses being built and the contents with which they were filled, including wine labels, which had become accepted dining room accoutrements.

Among those who travelled from Britain to the sites were artists and architects who returned to London with drawings that emphasised the basic simplicity and beautiful proportions of the

Development of the Wine Label

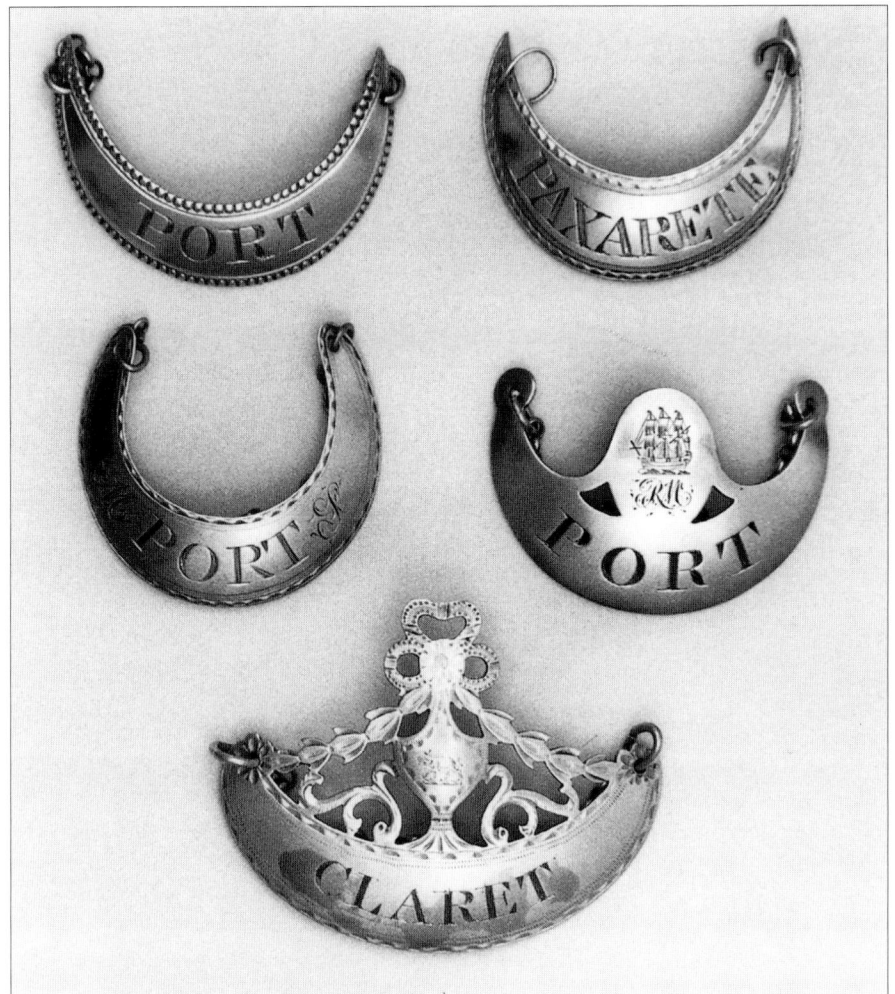

Figures 22-26.

Figure 21.

buildings and artefacts thus revealed. They showed classical stone columns and porticoes, urns and vases (see figs. 27 PEPPERMINT, 28 PORT, 29 FRONTINIAC, 30 BRANDY, 22 PORT, 23 PAXARETE, 24 PORT, 25 PORT and, in particular, 26 CLARET by John Sherwin, *c.*1790), some decorated with laurel wreaths and festoons, acanthus and anthemion and a variety of scroll borders. Important amongst these travellers was the Scottish architect Robert Adam who visited Rome from 1755 to 1757.

Soon after his return Adam set up business in London with his brother James and other family members. They were at the forefront of developing this new classical style, or neo-classical as it is now frequently termed.

The concept of the neo-classical style was quick to mature. By the early 1760s not only had Robert Adam developed the style for the architecture of his buildings, but also for their complete furnishing and contents. One of the best known of these is Osterley Park in Middlesex, where Robert Adam carried out a complete external and interior refurbishment between 1761 and 1780. These influences were taken up by men such as Josiah Wedgwood, who quickly adapted the classical shapes for his ceramics and eventually copied those being excavated to produce his black basalt Etruscan and relief wares. Adam Style has, in fact, become a sub-term used to describe the designs of this period.

The simplicity of the neo-classical style, as evidenced in such items as urns, vases and cartouches (see figs. 27 PEPPERMINT, 28 PORT, 29 FRONTINIAC and 30 BRANDY), was readily adaptable to silver design in general and to wine labels in particular by incorporating swags and festoons. Components could be made using the new mechanical processes, which were then hand assembled and finished. Whilst the Adam Brothers' company did not make their own silver, they

Development of the Wine Label

Figures 27-30.

worked in close co-operation with manufacturers, including Boulton and Fothergill of Birmingham and later with similar high-class companies in Sheffield.

The second half of the eighteenth century saw the growth of the industrial revolution, and with it the rise of a new wealthy class of entrepreneurs, manufacturers and merchants. This new layer of society had different ideals and attitudes from the established aristocratic and upper classes and was highly receptive to the developing neo-classical style. It symbolised their business, manufacturing and entrepreneurial success, and a wider acceptance of education and technology. Products in the new neo-classical taste were required in large quantities to satisfy the demands and rising standards of the new members of society. Luxury articles, such as table silver, were particularly sought after, but wine labels were, at first, an exception.

Analysis of surviving silver labels of this period shows that fewer were made between 1760 and 1775 than in the preceding and following years, and those that were produced did not adapt to the new neo-classical designs until the early 1770s. This drop could be attributed to a temporary fashion for enamel and ceramic labels, and to the arrival of 'label decanters' with their gilded titles, but this cannot be the sole reason.[28]

When wine label designers did start to adapt neo-classical thinking, their greatest exponent was Hester Bateman, who used urns and vases, with or without festoon and drapery, to great effect. A label by Hester Bateman, dating from around 1775 and marked for PORT, is based on the crescent shape, has an urn above with an open corded festoon and bottom border. A similar Old Sheffield Plate (OSP) label marked for CLARET has foliate garlands to the urn and drapery below the crescent. The Hester Bateman label typifies the hand-worked London-made label with engraving and piercing of that time, and the OSP label of a similar or slightly later date is a good example of the mass-production die-stamping that was slowly being introduced in Sheffield and Birmingham. John Sherwin in Ireland in the 1790s adopted the Hester Bateman design (see CLARET, fig. 26). The crescent shape was also adopted by James Hyde (for PORT, fig. 22) and Benjamin Taitt (also for PORT, fig. 24) at this time. Turn of the century examples are shown for PORT (see fig. 25 by Peter and Ann Bateman, 1800) and for PAXARETE (see fig. 23 by Elizabeth Morley, 1811).

New items from the classical world continued to be uncovered, to fuel neo-classical culture. However, later designs were often overworked and elaborate, having lost the earlier simplicity of shape, line and adornment. With this trend grew criticism of the direction in which the neo-classical style was moving. An artistically stimulated society sought redirection under the influence of new architects and the Prince of Wales, later to become Prince Regent. These aspirations and re-evaluation of the classical world signalled the way for the next chapter in style and design, the Regency period.

PART 6 – THE REGENCY PERIOD, 1800-1837

As the eighteenth century drew to a close, a number of factors were already in place to influence the styles and fashions of the 1800s. Political changes, at home and abroad, were leading to a rethink of old values, and paving the way for new ideas and designs. After forty years the first neo-classical interpretation of the ancient Greek and Roman styles was being reviewed to give greater emphasis to their purity and structure, and to adhere more strictly to the archaeological aspects from which it was felt later neo-classical designs were departing, and to which the current French Empire style did not aspire.

In the latter years of the eighteenth century, prominent architects and designers were travelling extensively in Europe – and particularly in Italy – and important works on design were published by them on their return. One of the most influential authors was Charles Heathcote Tatham (who worked under the architect Henry Holland). He published works on design reviewing and re-thinking Italian and Roman architecture.

It proved to be an era subject to many varied influences, which, as would be expected, led to a complexity of styles. Specific influences had different effects in different areas, such as architecture, house interior and furniture design, on silver and, to a lesser extent, fine art. To the Roman and Greek classicism were added styles and motifs from Egyptian antiquity. French exploration of the Nile in 1798 brought views and description to Europe never before considered. In the area of furniture design the effect was often dramatic.

Another influence was that, in modest ways, liberal ideas were beginning to be established. There was a more relaxed way of living and a new ease and elegance in houses compared with the grandeur of the neo-classical time.

By the early nineteenth century the industrial base of the country was established and abroad British supremacy, particularly at sea, was creating the foundation for imperial expansion. The potential for change and for forward thinking existed and began to be realised.

Perhaps the final factor in the change from the neo-classical to the Regency style was the influence and force of the Prince of Wales, future Prince Regent, himself. He was to be the first and to date the last energetic royal patron of the arts since Charles I. His dynamism, enthusiasm and expenditure on buildings, furniture and collecting were extensive and a critical influence on the court and the nobility with whom he associated and for whom he set matters of taste.

In London, in addition to carrying out extensive work on his own property, Carlton House, the Prince Regent took the initiative in encouraging much public building and major urban planning. This included the construction of Regent's Street, Regent's Park and the Nash Terraces, together with smaller but important private developments, such as Burlington Arcade. It was due to his gift to the nation, as George IV, of his father's library that work began on the British Museum.

Charles Heathcote Tatham's ideas on design and style had the support of architects such as Henry Holland, James Wyatt and John Nash, but most importantly were encouraged by the Prince Regent. In 1806 Tatham published *Designs for Ornamental Plate*, which led to the production of large ornamental pieces of silver to a high standard of detail and finish. Only the major silversmiths of the day could achieve this standard, but it helped set the style and the basis of design for the era.

Silver style and design were a complex combination based on historical background, newly introduced features and contemporary methods of production. The preceding neo-classical period

Development of the Wine Label

Figure 31.

Figure 32.

had drawn inspiration for applied decoration from Greek and Roman artefacts. The Regency period saw these artefacts reproduced in their own right, but to them, where suitable, were added embellishment and motifs drawn from such wide sources as nature, Egyptian antiquity and classical mythology. With the overall shape based on classical design, acanthus leaves, shells, masks and grapes, vines and tendrils began to adorn silver items of all sizes.

One of the most renowned manufacturing firms of supreme quality silver of the Regency era was Rundell, Bridge and Rundell, whose designs were particularly influenced by late eighteenth-century French silver design. The French Revolution brought to England many refugees from France, along with their jewellery and silver plate. Rundell, Bridge and Rundell saw and acquired much of this silver, which inspired the early strains of naturalism and the revival of rococo style. Both Paul Storr and Benjamin Smith carried out work for this firm who produced much silver plate for the Prince Regent.

The motifs and embellishments of the Regency era, in particular the grape vine and tendril, wreaths, lions' masks and figures of wine mythology, were highly adaptable to wine label design. Unlike earlier times, it is of particular interest to note that the major silversmiths of the Regency era were practically all responsible for the manufacture of wine labels of particular and often unique design. Storr and Benjamin Smith, together with other famous silversmiths such as Digby Scott and Edward Farrell, produced large and fine wine labels in this period.

As an instance and of specific interest is the origin of one of them. A unique vase was discovered at Hadrian's Villa near Tivoli in 1770. This marble vase was purchased by the Earl of Warwick in 1774 and named after him. Engravings of *The Warwick Vase* were first published in 1778 and then in 1800. The lion's pelt detail on the vase led to the famous Storr label of this name, which was first produced in 1812. An example by Paul Storr for CHAMPAIGNE, dated 1818, is shown in fig. 31.

Apart from other London silversmiths, Birmingham and Sheffield were soon to start their mass-production by die-stamping labels with designs based on the decoration adorning the items manufactured by the leading silversmiths.

In many ways the Regency era proved to be a transition period. It provided a base for the individual design used in embellishment and decoration to be developed and established as identified styles in the following Victorian period, often of simpler form and more readily mass-produced. To illustrate this in wine labels, the vine and tendril border of the Regency period, for example a fine London pierced title for BRONTE label of 1830 (see fig. 32), evolved into the individual vine leaf labels introduced in about 1824 by Charles Rawlings, and labels of both pure rococo and gothic revival were produced.

As the nineteenth century progressed, many of the influences that brought about the Regency era declined to be replaced by new political, social and industrial factors. By 1830 these new factors were becoming predominant in the design and manufacture of silver in general and of wine labels in particular.

PART 7 – THE VICTORIAN PERIOD, 1837-1901

By the end of the third decade of the century, tastes and social attitudes were changing again, but the selection of a particular year to denote the end of the Regency era and the beginning of the Victorian one has to be an arbitrary choice. Certainly changes were becoming apparent several years before Queen Victoria's accession in 1837, so that for the purposes of discussing the evolution of wine labels during this period the end of George IV's reign in 1830 is an appropriate a year to begin as any. During the next seventy years, enormous social changes took place. Graceful, aristocratic Georgian living faded; a new bustling middle class became established. Alterations to the state of the economy, changes in shopping habits, commercial procedures, new methods of manufacture, even the growth of Free Trade, affected the way in which people lived, and so how they regarded even such small artefacts as wine labels, their design and their use.

Wine label designs changed accordingly, reflecting a fresh attitude to decorative art, as well as to new methods of manufacture. The festoons of grapes and vine leaves, which had started to overflow in Regency labels, took on a more subdued appearance. In an age that was becoming ever more mechanised, designers and craftsmen working in silver turned to geometrical shapes, and based their designs on architectural styles. Representations of nature became less realistic, even though a hankering for it was still there. As an example, one popular manufacturer of the period, Sampson Mordan and Co. (a firm specialising in innovative articles), took advantage of the drive for Free Trade to market a label commemorating the political moves in that direction of the middle years of the century. It is a label of typical Victorian manufacture, employing die-stamping processes, while its decoration includes cornucopia, wheat sheaves, modern boxed merchandise, and a banner emblazoned with the word 'Free', and is illustrated by PORT (see fig. 33, c.1846).

Wages were still low, but rising labour costs were beginning to make the old casting method of manufacture unattractive and uneconomic for small objects, such as wine labels, which were not going to attract mass purchase: Die-stamping was commercially more viable and quantity production could be adapted to meet demand. But above all new electroplating processes were resulting in a much cheaper product, which thus became available to a much wider public. Label production reached its maximum in the second quarter of the nineteenth century. After that it began to decline. Before 1830 labels had been for the aristocracy and then slowly for the rich merchants who were beginning to aspire to social standing. Then, as the Victorian age advanced and the middle classes grew in numbers, a much wider market developed. These new classes of society were split between those who wished to show their financial success and those who held and fostered austere and non-conformist attitudes to life. A decline in demand and popularity of silver wine labels during the Victorian period can be attributed partly to the attitudes of the latter group.

During the early Victorian period improvement in the production of wine enabled it to be served straight from the bottle, thereby reducing the use of decanters and their accompanying silver labels. It also helped make practicable legislation, introduced by Gladstone, in 1860.

Before this date the retailing of wines and spirits was restricted to hotel keepers, publicans and wine merchants. The new legislation allowed wines and spirits to be purchased from shops for consumption at home. It brought about the arrival of 'Off Licences', and at the same time individual bottles were required to be labelled to identify the contents under the so-called 'Single Bottle Act'. Printed paper labels became commonplace, and this furthered the decline in the need for, and consequently the use of, silver wine labels.

It is noticeable that the silver labels of the latter half of the nineteenth century that exist are mainly for fortified wines and spirits, which could stay in decanters on the sideboard; the only label for wine

Development of the Wine Label

that commonly occurs is for claret. An explanation for this is, of course, that this wine is best decanted. Its importation, and that of other French wines, into Great Britain was affected temporarily by the Franco-Prussian War of 1870-71. The popularity of the three-bottle spirit decanter frame, usually made by the newly-introduced method of electroplating a base metal with silver, helped to perpetuate the use of the hanging bottle-ticket around decanters with such names as brandy, whisky and gin, sometimes accompanied by sherry and/or port.[29]

Members of the new, prosperous level of society who were creating a market for small silver items such as wine labels demanded cheap, mass-produced items with which to emulate the established richer strata. The development of electroplating with silver enabled these to be made in styles that were frequently based on previous popular designs, particularly the chased escutcheon and single vine leaves.

The spectacular and flamboyant innovations and extremes of design otherwise seen in the mid- and late Victorian eras did not influence the design and production of wine labels. Of the architectural and furniture styles that did influence label designs, probably the most noticeable was that of the gothic revival, although both the rococo revival and the introduction of the rustic style are evident. The Arts and Crafts movement and Art Nouveau, starting in the latter part of the nineteenth century, had no major representation as by that time few labels were in production.

Although some handmade labels were still being produced in Birmingham during the early decades of the nineteenth century, by about 1820 most labels were machine made. As a generalisation, the manufacture of labels can be split into the mass-produced, cheaper items, mainly of the Birmingham silversmiths, and the more individual and hand-worked items from the London firms. One specialist area that Birmingham did continue to occupy was that of the beautiful and elaborate pierced and engraved wine label. Fig. 50 is an interesting example engraved for BRANDY, part of a set of three spirit decanter bottle labels made by Hilliard and Thomason, hallmarked in Birmingham for 1861. The number of wine labels assayed at other offices, including Edinburgh and Sheffield, was comparatively small. A very minor production of labels occurred in the countries of the Empire; of these India was the main source.

In order to assess the styles of wine labels of the Victorian era, three overlapping periods of time can be identified. The first of these is from 1830 to the middle of the century and is largely an evolution of preceding styles. The highly successful die-stamped vine leaf label, first introduced in the early 1820s and associated with Charles Rawlings, continued in production with declining quality in Birmingham examples. Of the good examples that were made, a particularly attractive variation was a three-leaf label introduced in the 1840s. A fine example, pierced for PORT, made by Reily and Storer in 1845, is shown in fig. 34. Many grape, vine and tendril designs based on Regency themes were made by die-stamping and casting (see for details Part 1 of Chapter 3) and by electroplating (see for details Part 6 of Chapter 8). The famous Birmingham manufacturers, Elkington and Co., made labels of this style; fig. 36 is an example of such a label, pierced for BRANDY and marked on the face of the label for 1859. This company typifies the industrial growth and innovation of the Victorian era. Founded in the early years of the century, it is best known for the introduction of the silver electroplating process and produced many high quality and elaborate items by this means. Examples of electroplating are CLARET (see figs. 54 and 55, c.1880), WHISKY by John Gilbert (see fig.45, c.1880) and GLENDRONACH by Thomas Prime and Son (see fig. 46, c.1870).

A popular rectangular label with a vine and tendril border was introduced early in the period. Fig. 37 is an example and is a heavy cast label pierced for PORT, made by Reily and Storer in 1837. The design of the label is commonly known as a 'five bar gate' and was popular for about thirty years. It was copied in smaller scale for some sauce labels.[30] Taylor and Perry of Birmingham also used a vine and tendril design to give interest to their LISBON label (see fig. 35) of 1840.

The re-introduction of the mid-eighteenth-century chased escutcheon label, in both chased and die-stamped form, by the Birmingham manufacturer George Unite (the maker in 1846 of fig. 41 for GIN), typifies the reproduction of earlier label styles. Whilst some of these were of average quality, not one carries the finish of the earlier handmade items. An exception to the development or re-introduction of previous label designs is an original style based on rococo scrolls, typical of styles of one hundred years earlier, but contemporary with a rococo revival in both architecture and furniture.

Development of the Wine Label

Figures 33-46.

Fig. 39 is a fine cast example made by John S. Hunt, hallmarked in 1849 and pierced for CLARET. This maker was part of the famous company of Hunt and Roskell, with its origins going back to Storr and Co. in the Regency period.

Also at this time the more simple and symmetrical style, typifying Thomas Chippendale's reverse 'C' scrolls, appeared in a number of label designs. Chippendale's simple, clean and uncluttered lines were taken as a base for the label. Fig. 38 shows a very heavy cast escutcheon shaped example, pierced for MOSELLE by another celebrated maker, Benjamin Smith IV, in 1838. The design was not a reproduction of a previous style. This innovation was a move away from the heavily ornate labels of the previous decades, and is more a forerunner of the ideas and considerations of the period to follow.

The mid-Victorian period for wine labels can be considered as starting during the early 1850s and running for about twenty years. It was a time when new and innovative styles were being applied throughout the design field, but particularly in the areas of architecture and furnishings. These contemporary movements were reflected in the design of labels – particularly by the means of cutting and piercing the flat plate to produce the design. The new designs were often accompanied by a new appreciation of quality, both of manufacture and style. The influence of designers such as Augustus Pugin was reflected in the gothic revival wine labels. These incorporated the characteristic gothic decorative motifs of tracery, cusping, finials and trefoils. Many variations of this style exist. An example, made by William Smiley in 1863 and marked for MADEIRA, is shown in fig. 42. A further new design of similar shape is the label shown in fig. 43 marked for WHISKEY, the design consisting of a series of entwined rings. This label is also by William Smiley, dated 1875; variations of it exist with coloured enamel infill, and in different sizes. Another interesting gothic revival example is shown in fig. 46. It is marked for GLENDRONACH and is an electroplated label of about 1870 with the maker's mark of Thomas Prime and Son. Other architectural compositions are shown for SHERRY by Hilliard and Thomason, Birmingham, 1880 (see fig. 53); for CLARET (see fig. 57) in 1838, MARSALA (see fig. 40) in 1853 by E. and J. Barnard (who also made in 1856 the PORT illustrated in fig. 58) and for WHISKEY in Sheffield by an undecipherable maker in 1891 (see fig. 44).

The production of silhouetted, cut-out letters as wine labels occurred over a large part of the era, but this middle period can be associated with their peak in popularity and some of their most satisfactory designs. These items were manufactured by most methods of working and a particularly large number are Edinburgh hallmarked, especially those made from flat plate with engraved and pierced detail. The quality of manufacture is generally high and the design of some cast items includes many of the details found in late Georgian labels. A letter S made by Marshall and Sons of Edinburgh (undated, c.1840), with both engraved and pierced details, is shown in fig. 47. Another single letter label, showing the quality and ingenuity of Victorian design, incorporated Mr Punch and his dog entwined with a gothic shaped letter S (see fig. 49). Such unusual designs, as through the history of wine labels, were usually specially commissioned. This label, part of a set of initial letters, was made by Rawlings and Summers and hallmarked in 1847. A later initial letter for W by William Summers, London, 1868, is shown at fig. 48.

The development of electroplating with silver (see Chapter 8, Part 6) became increasingly popular during the second part of the nineteenth century and was used on pierced, intricate and cut-out name design with great effect. A gothic revival example similar to GLENDRONACH mentioned above is a WHISKY in electroplating made by John Gilbert (see fig. 45) around 1880. Fig. 55 shows a CLARET label with cut-out name supported by a cord held between the beaks of two birds, and a similar elaborate design in fig. 54, again marked for CLARET, is a typical turn of the century label formed from a tied ribbon.

Much use came to be made of materials other than silver or electroplate during the Victorian period, an age associated with the days of Empire, and in particular with India, whence came labels consisting of tiger claws and boar tusks mounted in silver (see Chapter 8, Part 10). Fig. 56 is an example of the former, of Indian manufacture, marked for SHERRY, c.1870.

The late Victorian period started in about 1870 and produced few labels. Typical of this time is the cut-out name, produced in sterling silver but more frequently in electroplate or low grade silver.

Development of the Wine Label

Figures 47-58.

These labels, as with individual letters, often incorporated the gothic and rustic styles that were in use elsewhere at this time. In particular, fig. 51 shows a SHERRY label dated 1885 by Hilliard and Thomason and is a good example of this type of label and of the rustic variation of detail. The label for CLARET in fig. 52, hallmarked in 1875, illustrates one of the better quality and more unusual examples of cut-out name. It was manufactured in Sheffield by J.R. Rhodes and is a variation that is more frequently found without the pierced foliate sprays above and below.

By the latter part of the nineteenth century the silver wine label had become an accessory and form of decoration rather than an item of need to identify the contents of a bottle or decanter. Although still found as part of a spirit decanter set or labelling a decanted bottle of claret or port, by 1880 the everyday use of this varied and fascinating item of the silversmith's art had passed.

PART 8 – THE TWENTIETH CENTURY

The first fifty years of the twentieth century saw little activity in the field of wine labels, but there has been a minor boom in craftsman-designed labels in recent years, stimulated by *The Goldsmith and The Grape* exhibition of 1983, which took place at Goldsmiths' Hall, and at the beginning of the twenty-first century it is perhaps not inappropriate to attempt a short survey of the output of wine labels since about 1900. The 1985 Annual General Meeting of the Wine Label Circle was held at the premises of Stuart Devlin, contemporary master craftsman and designer (see fig. 87 for RED).

Examples of labels have occurred in a number of the early years of the twentieth century, but, perhaps surprisingly, there seems to have been no record of British Art Nouveau labels. A number of noted silversmiths were active at that time, as is evidenced by the work of Omar Ramsden, whose mark has been recorded on a small number of labels (see SHERRY, fig. 65, 1937), and the Liberty designers and William Davenport in Birmingham (see BRANDY, fig. 82, 1902), but the only Art Nouveau labels known are American and Continental, including German slot labels. An example is fig. 88, a Danish label for MADEIRA, which is marked only with a hieroglyphic and 830s.[31] Some of the other labels clearly derive from earlier styles. For example, fig. 89, for WHISKEY,[32] is a reproduction by Garrards in 1902 of Paul Storr labels; fig. 90, for PORT and by the Goldsmiths and Silversmiths Company in 1911,[33] has a Regency flavour; fig. 91, for ITALIAN VERMOUTH and by Emmanuel in 1915,[34] has cut-out letters; and fig. 93, for OLD J, produced by Mappin and Webb, London, in 1920, is in gothic style. Very few labels were made between 1915 and the 1930s; although the Sheffield firm of James Dixon carried labels in its catalogue of 1925, many of their designs had not changed since 1870.[35]

The Art Deco 1930s are represented by the attractive silver and enamel labels made by Turner and Simpson of Birmingham (see figs. 63 for RYE, 1960, and 71 and 72 for BRANDY and GIN, 1933),[36] the James Dixon label shown at fig. 94 (OPORTO)[37] and Charles Boyton's simple triangle in 1937 (see fig. 92, for GIN).[38] The 1940s seem to be more or less blank, which is unsurprising in view of the stringency of the war years. From the 1950s to the present day there seems to have been a gradual increase in output, spurred on by state occasions, such as Queen Elizabeth II's Coronation, Silver Jubilee and Golden Jubilee.

Commemorative labels are one of the four basic types into which it seems reasonable to classify twentieth-century labels. The other three are labels with an advertising purpose; mass-produced general labels; and, most importantly, individually designed labels that are produced in small quantities. These categories need not be mutually exclusive, as is clear from the examples illustrated.

Among the advertising labels noted are LATOUR (see fig. 62) made by Michael Wyard Druitt and Co. Ltd in 1973 depicting the tower standing in the vineyard of Château Latour, LA INA in 1969,[39] the Harvey label made by Vanders and sponsored by J. Harvey and Sons for BRISTOL CREAM in 1961 (see fig. 68),[40] and WHITE HORSE made by Elkingtons in 1915.[41] A further example is the Laymont and Shaw label engraved with the triple spires of Truro Cathedral, which was made by C. Shapland of High Holborn and has the 1981 date letter. This Truro wine firm specialises in the import of Spanish wines and so the labels are engraved with MOUNTAIN or SHERRY.[42] Another example

Figure 59.

is taking RYE on board Concorde (see fig. 66) made by Troika Designs Ltd in 1986 and sponsored by British Airways (mark BA) to commemorate ten years of operation of the mode of transport. The International Wine and Food Society were quite discrete in commissioning Michael Druitt's gourmet label (see fig. 67 for CLARET – compare with fig. 1223 from Belgium, 1814-1831).

This review touches only lightly on the mass-produced general labels; examples are the Dixon labels[43] and the reproductions of early designs that can be seen in shops. Possibly the 1911 PORT (see fig. 90) falls into this class, but the design seems to be original.

Some commemorative labels were produced in considerable quantity, such as the Roberts and Belk Sheffield 1977 Silver Jubilee labels (see fig. 85 for GIN),[44] the VERMOUTH[45] by SJR and the Vander reproduction of the Bateman scroll with Prince of Wales feathers made for the Royal Wedding in 1981;[46] these would all be regarded as mass-produced. Others were made in moderate runs, such as the Wine Label Circle's own label by John A. Donald in 1967 commemorating its 100th member (see fig. 83 for LONDON on an annular ring and fig. 86 for PLYMOUTH, a slot-in name strip),[47] Alex Styles' attractive Prince of Wales feathers design, produced by Garrards in 1981 for the Royal Wedding (see fig. 75 for PRINCE OF WALES PORT)[48] and the Irish EEC (as it was

Development of the Wine Label

Figures 60-70.

Figures 71-74.

Development of the Wine Label

Figures 75-86.

known) commemorative by William Egan in 1973 (see fig. 81, for SERCIAL);[49] all these have the individual designer flavour, as do the Durbin[50] and Crichton[51] Coronation labels (see figs. 78 and 84). An example of the truly individual commemorative label is John Flitton's MEAD for the 1977 Silver Jubilee (see fig. 74).[52] The London Society, founded in 1912, honoured its treasurer, Mr Theodore Durrant, on retirement in 1985 by adorning a gifted decanter with a John Flitton oval label decorated with flowers and leaves and engraved for DURRANT'S SHERRY.[53] To celebrate the hallmarking of platinum, Michael Druitt produced a peacock label in this material in 1973 (see fig. 76 for PORT, based on the CLARET of 1796 made by P. and A. Bateman).

Development of the Wine Label

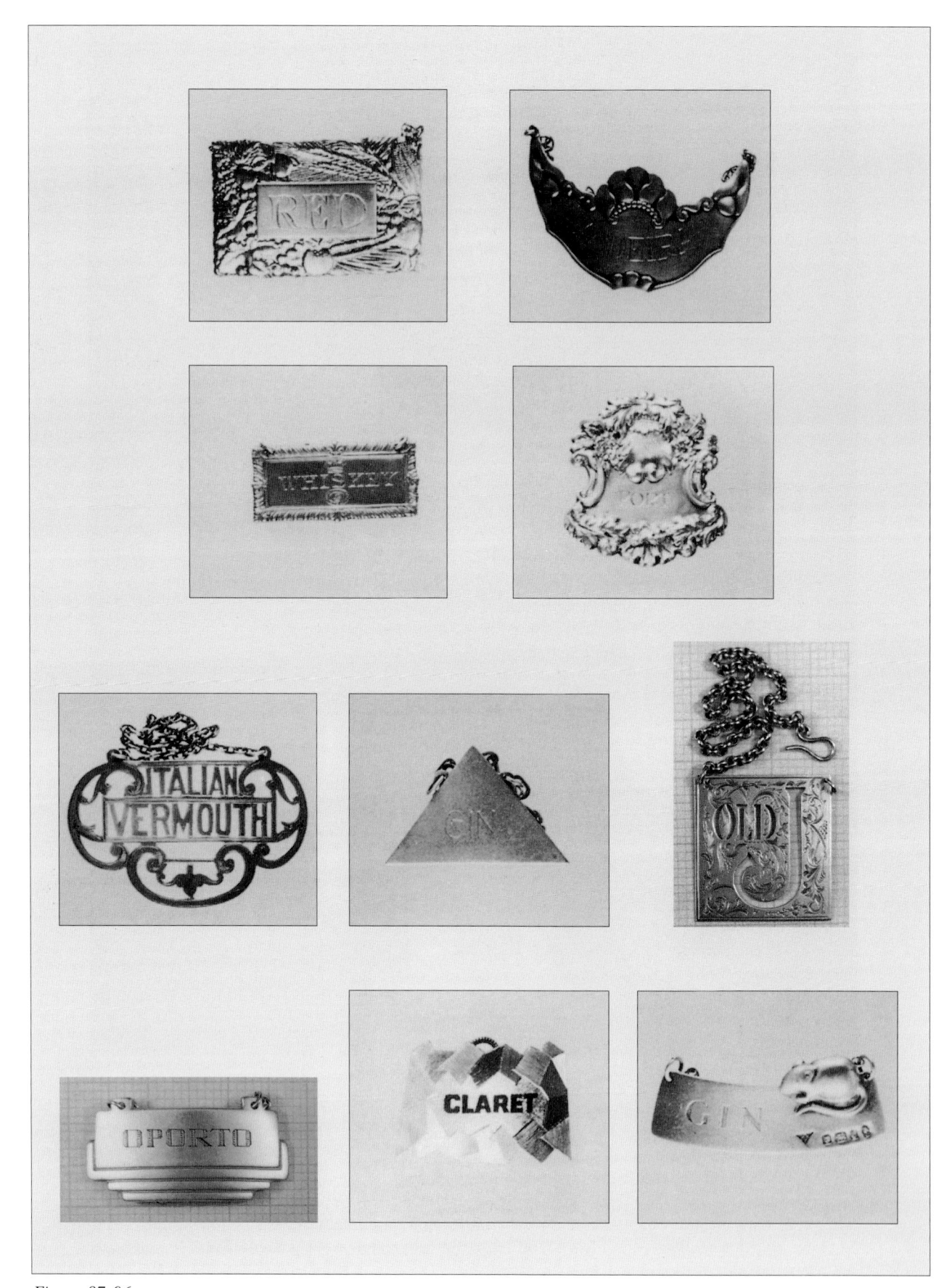

Figures 87-96.

Development of the Wine Label

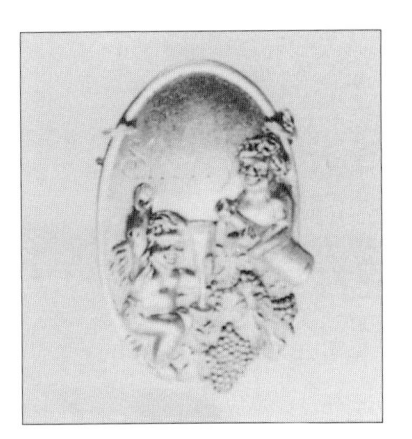

Figures 97-99.

To celebrate the 550th anniversary of their charter, the Worshipful Company of Vintners, a City of London Livery Company, commissioned in 1987 from Sarah Jones labels comprising the arms of the Company (see BURGUNDY, fig. 77 and see further Chapter 2, Part 22). To celebrate the 350th anniversary of their charter, the Company of Goldsmiths of Dublin in 1987 commissioned T. Weir of Dublin to make a label comprising a harp supported by shamrock (see WHISKEY, fig. 80). Some commemorative labels were limited by the availability of materials from which they were made, as might have been the case for MARSALA (fig. 79), which was made from a piece of the Zeppelin shot down in 1916 at Goodwin Sands and therefore is unmarked.

The individual designer labels, like antique labels, vary widely in terms of design and its success in aesthetic and utilitarian terms. The most satisfactory are those by John Flitton in 1978 (see fig. 74) and by the Reece-Goldsworthy Studio in 1983 (see fig. 95, for CLARET).[54] These labels are original – strikingly so in the case of the angular CLARET – pleasing, and would look appropriate around a decanter. Is it simply coincidental that these labels were designed wholly or partly by engravers, or is it that the engraver is used to conceiving a complete design on a small scale and so is particularly suited to wine labels? Another interesting feature of modern labels is the use of parcel gilt, by makers such as Reece-Goldsworthy and Stuart Devlin (see fig. 87 for RED). This is a technique that was presumably available to the makers of antique labels, but not used by them. However, a treatment not available in those days, oxidised silver, has been used on recent wine labels, such as those by John Donald in 1967 (see fig. 83) and Lexi Dick.[55]

As on early labels, so in recent times natural history has a role in the design of some labels, for example Brian L. Fuller's glis-glis (see fig. 96, for his GIN in 1977, and compare with his PORT, fig. 61, in 1985),[56] Mirjam Hirsch's flowers on a small label for WHITE in 1980,[57] Stuart Devlin's foliage, fruit and vegetables (see fig. 87, for RED) in 1980, Sarah Jones's swan,[58] John Flitton's labels, and Lexi Dick's snake (see fig. 69 for her FINO of 1983). However, in the case of Stuart Devlin and Lexi Dick the type of natural element used seems to be original. Another example of harking back to concepts used by the designers of antique labels is Anthony Elson's 1977 variant on the two cupids theme (see fig. 97, for SHERRY).[59] A kind of trelliswork supports Stuart Devlin's VODKA of 1987 (see fig. 64), giving the oval frame an almost jewel-like appearance.

This review would not be complete without reference to sets of individually produced labels commissioned by Wine Label Circle members and previously illustrated in the *Journal*. In the 1960s Jimmy Sanders commissioned twenty different labels from Frank Clark, based on contemporary themes found on paper labels from bottles of wines and spirits such as Sandeman's Sherries, VAT 69 and Long John Whisky.[60] In the early 1970s Malcolm Gray commissioned Alison Richards to make a set of labels to commemorate his silver wedding in the form of his family crest, an anchor.[61] Another individual commission was the 1971 label by Michael Driver (see fig. 70, for XERES); its pair was used for a wedding present.[62] In 1959 Lady Sachs commissioned Collingwoods of Conduit

43

Development of the Wine Label

Figures 100-101.

Street in London to produce a boar's head BURGUNDY (see fig. 98) and AMONTILLADO to celebrate their silver wedding as a gift for her husband Sir Eric Sachs. These examples remind us how important patronage is to the craftsman-designers of today, just as it was two hundred years ago. They rely not only on the great institutions who often commission grand pieces such as maces, rose bowls and salvers (however, the London Stock Exchange recently commissioned wine labels from Anthony Elson – see fig. 99 WHISKY and the WHISKY and BRANDY displayed on Stock Exchange decanters in figs. 100-101),[63] but equally on the individual friends of the art and lovers of silver.[64]

Finally, mention must be made of the Circle's own Golden Jubilee decanter label by Wendy Marshall, a postgraduate student at Bishopsland – a stunning design, see fig. 59 for MADEIRA – with the help of the Oliver Makower Trust, produced in 2002 and bearing H.M. The Queen's Golden Jubilee mark, and of the Circle's own Presidential label produced by Vanders following a design competition commissioned by the Circle and won by M. Fitzpatrick from the Medway School of Art (it was reproduced for Circle members and is illustrated by fig. 60 for PORT).

CHAPTER 2

SHAPES AND DESIGNS

PART 1 – ESCUTCHEONS

An escutcheon was originally a shield upon which a coat of arms was displayed. In the course of time it came to mean any shield-shaped device or ornament, including the key plates on furniture. The word is used as the general term for a class of labels whose shape vaguely resembles a key plate.

The outline is normally symmetrical and achieved by a succession of convex and concave curves, generally with a pair of 'horns' at the top of the label and an ogee shape at the base with a point in the centre. The curvature of the outline varies considerably from maker to maker, so that the ultimate appearance may be either angular or smoothly rounded. Almost invariably, however, the outline does not contain a straight edge except rarely at the top, which is usually concave between the suspension ring holes. In contrast to the outline, the name on the label is engraved or, more rarely, pierced in a straight line boldly across the centre of the label.

There are three basic shapes: the somewhat angular design (see fig. 104, PORT, by Richard Binley, c.1760), the flattened triangular shape (see fig. 103, CLARET, by John Jacobs, c.1740) and the 'standard escutcheon' (see fig. 107, LISBON by Henry Bickerton, c.1760). All these shapes are among the earliest recorded and from them evolved the later variants as illustrated.

A further distinct group of early labels that is not uncommon is the 'square escutcheon' (also mentioned in Chapter 2, Part 2). It is broadly rectangular in outline, without the ogee base; it has curved edges and incurved corners that resemble table tops and toilet mirrors of the period (see fig. 102, MEDEARY, unmarked, c.1735). The letters of the title on these square escutcheons are almost invariably engraved in script. They are usually unmarked and have always been presumed to date from around 1735. However, a few marked examples are to be found, the earliest bearing an unidentified mark,[1] 'I L' with star above of 1735/37. One by Sandylands Drinkwater has his second mark of post-1739 with the title in Roman capital letters, and another is by an unidentified IR of around 1755.[2]

Escutcheons can be positively established as being the earliest design of labels made in any numbers datable with certainty to pre-1739.[3] Since in the early days they were virtually the sole design they must have been made in large quantities to judge by the number that have survived, the design varying little from the start in say c.1735 until they waned in popularity from 1760 to 1780.

As to the decoration on the label, this is generally by flat chasing. However, since they were very

Shapes and Designs

definitely functional, the main fact that strikes one is the boldness of the lettering of the title, which is clear and large. Broadly speaking escutcheons tend to have larger letters relative to their overall size than other designs and the earlier the label the larger the lettering. Chased labels occur more frequently than plain and, although each label is individually chased by hand, it is surprising to find how standard is the design consisting, since the earliest days, of a pattern of vine leaves, grapes and tendrils. Normally one finds four vine leaves above and four below the title linked by stems and tendrils with bunches of grapes disposed between the leaves.[4] There is evidence that some early escutcheons had fewer vine leaves than later ones. The chased decoration stops short of the edge of the label and may be outlined by a single thin line of reeding round the edge of the decoration. The ground may also be punched, which enhances the overall appearance (see fig. 105 for CYDER by Robert Lucas, *c*.1740, and fig. 110 for CHAMPAIGN by Edmund Medlycott, *c*.1760). Very occasionally a crest is to be found on escutcheons, usually on plain labels below the wine name, and also (very rarely) incorporated in a cartouche within the usual chased decoration (see fig. 106 for MADEIRA, unmarked, possibly Edinburgh, *c*.1800 and fig. 108 for PORT by John Harvey, *c*.1750).

Plain versions (see fig. 109 for W. WINE unmarked but attributed to Thomas Hyde II, *c*.1784) usually have no border and engraved titles, but are occasionally pierced (see fig. 104). Some makers, such as Margaret Binley (see fig. 113 for LISBON, *c*.1770) and William Abdy I (see fig. 111 for CLARET, *c*.1786), applied a feather-edging. Sandylands Drinkwater also incorporated this effect in his rare 'lipped' design (see below), while John Jacobs (see fig. 103) and Richard Richardson II of Chester used a single reeded line.

Escutcheons enjoyed enormous popularity in the period 1730-60, but later examples are quite common because fashion in the provinces tended to lag behind London or because replacement labels were needed for sets because the originals had become lost or worn, to add new names as fashion in wines changed, or as deliberate reproductions of an older style. Fig. 122 illustrates QUINTA DE PORTE and (fig. 122a) a paper label for QUINTA DO PORTO.

Since they were made in such numbers over a relatively long period many makers' marks are to be found on escutcheons. First and foremost, however, is Sandylands Drinkwater, whose work is covered in another chapter. He must be pre-eminent as regards the numbers he made, and surely sets the standard for others in terms of quality. Other notable early makers were Thomas Rush (1724-1733), James Slater (*c*.1725-*c*.1750) and Louis Hamon (1736-*c*.1753). After Drinkwater the most prolific maker of escutcheons was John Harvey I (1738-*c*.1760, see fig. 108). His labels tend to be of uniformly good quality, as are those of Edmund Medlycott (1748-1773, see fig. 110 – a label of outstanding quality). Other makers with characteristic escutcheons were the Bickerton brothers, late in the life of escutcheons, Henry (1762-1796) and Benjamin (1762-1796, died 1808),[5] whose labels tend to be rather flattened and elongated (see fig. 107). John Humphris (1760-1770) also made an unusual elongated escutcheon in around 1762.[6]

Richard and Margaret Binley must be mentioned. Richard, having been apprenticed to and worked for Sandylands Drinkwater, took over his business in 1760 and died in 1764. His escutcheons are rare (see fig. 104) and he is better known for the pedestrian solid broad rectangles with heavy feathered edges, also found with Drinkwater's mark, which perhaps herald the decline of the escutcheon and the rise of the rectangular label. Margaret Binley took over her husband Richard's business and here we see the evolution of the escutcheon with feathered edge as in fig. 113 and a changed shape to a lip-like outline (as in fig. 114). This shape was further modified into a shaped rectangular label with gadrooned borders that must be considered a variant of the basic escutcheon shape.

Another late variant of the escutcheon is frequently found unmarked. It is known with an armorial below the title made by Thomas Hyde I (*c*.1784). It differs from other escutcheons in that the name is not engraved in a straight line. It was also made by Thomas Hyde II to whom the unmarked W. WINE (see fig. 109) is attributed (*c*.1784).

Escutcheons were not made exclusively in London. Indeed, they are known from all the provincial centres where, as hinted at earlier, they continued for longer than their London versions.

Shapes and Designs

Figures 102-114.

In England, outside London, Newcastle seems to have produced the greatest number of escutcheons and with characteristic features only found on Newcastle labels. Foremost is the large heavy 'quiffed' or plumed escutcheon made in turn by Isaac Cookson, by John Langlands and by Langlands and Robertson, believed to date from around 1750.[7] Isaac Cookson also made a triangular

Shapes and Designs

Figures 115-120.

escutcheon and he too varied the basic shape so that the 'horns' closed over at the top of the label to give the effect of two round 'eyes'. This is characteristic of Newcastle only. Furthermore the chasing is idiosyncratic and unique. Newcastle also has the distinction of having the earliest known fully hallmarked labels[8] by Robert Makepeace II date lettered from 1751 to 1754.

Chester also produced escutcheons. Mention has been made of Richard Richardson II's reeded version and Joseph Walley also produced escutcheons in around 1775-80.

Still in the north of England, competent escutcheon makers were Stephen Buckle (c.1748)[9] and Hampston and Prince of York dating from *c.*1776. Standard escutcheons are known from Scotland and Ireland. An outstanding variant of the escutcheon is illustrated at fig. 106 which, although unmarked, is presumed to be from Edinburgh. Irish escutcheons tend to be of somewhat eccentric shape and the letters tend to be smaller than normal – see fig. 114 for a Cork example by William Reynolds for CLARET dating from around 1765.[10] Note also, two mid-eighteenth century Irish triangular labels for CLARETT [*sic*] and WHITE WINE, by a maker IH, not positively identified, but probably from Cork.[11] An escutcheon is recorded with the mark of Guillaume Henry of Guernsey, who died in 1767, but it is possible that this was a London label exported and marked there.

Escutcheon labels were not only made in silver. Indeed, the most beautiful, colourful, coveted and expensive escutcheons are the Ravenet enamel labels from Battersea, 1753-55. These and other enamel labels from Staffordshire of this period are described in the chapter on enamels.[12] Other

Figure 121.

Figure 122.

Figure 122a.

escutcheons are known in mother-of-pearl, made perhaps in the Birmingham area. Copperback Old Sheffield Plate (OSP) escutcheons are known (see figs. 115-121) with interesting titles such as MOUNTAIN, LISBON, CYDER and RHENISH dating from around 1746 until somewhere between 1763 and 1770 when plating on both sides began.[13] These too must have been made in reasonable numbers and are found with nineteen or more titles,[14] the design of the decoration reflecting the title of the label. Much more rare are gilt metal or pinchbeck escutcheons, as are brass labels bearing traces of silvering.

The escutcheon was reinterpreted around 1825 by John Reily in foliate form and die-stamped. It was widely copied by other makers and is found in OSP and in electroplate.

Finally, returning to silver escutcheons, they enjoyed a belated revival by George Unite of Birmingham. The labels, while of conventional escutcheon shape, are a pale reflection of the eighteenth-century label and have acid etched decoration consisting of arabesques.

PART 2 – RECTANGLES

Rectangular labels have been made in a wide range of shapes from square, through all sorts of oblong, to narrow strips. They vary in length from less than 2.25cm (1in.) to nearly 6cm (2½in.), and in depth from 0.8 cm (¼in.) to 4.5cm (1¾in.). By strict definition the sides of rectangular labels ought to be straight, but for the purposes of this chapter it is intended to include all labels that have a generally rectangular outline, even when the sides are curved, waved or indented. The definition will cover, too, labels with humps and domes, and those that have shields or plaques above the panel, even when that device dominates the overall appearance of the label.

It would surpass the task of Sisyphus to try to describe every different variety of rectangle (and it would not help him quench his thirst). It is by far the commonest shape and it is found over the whole period during which labels have been manufactured. Some twenty-seven examples are shown – see figs. 123-149.

One design of rectangle that is usually considered to be very early (see fig. 123) is an almost square shape, with wavy sides and little indentations at the corners (see also Part 1 of this chapter); it is always entirely plain and it usually has the name in script letters. Sandylands Drinkwater made some that have his second mark, entered in 1739 and in use until at least the mid-1760s, but they do not have a sterling lion to help in pinning them down more accurately. Other known examples of this shape by an unidentified IR and John Rich are certainly later, but although the earliest date for the design cannot be accurately ascertained, it seems reasonable to suggest that it had arrived by the mid-1740s. To be more sure of a date for a rectangle we have to move on to the late 1750s, when rectangular labels by the Bickerton brothers (Benjamin and Henry) appear, possibly made before they registered their marks. This shape of label was also being made by Drinkwater, both with and without the lion of 1756, though not, as far as is known, with the preceding lion of 1739. Richard Binley, an apprentice of Drinkwater's, was turning out this shape from this period until his death in around 1764, while William Cafe's WHITE (see fig. 125) could date from around 1758. Rectangles of this period are usually large, 5.7 x 3.2cm (2¼ x 1¼in.); the titles are engraved in large Roman capitals that fill the panel and they nearly always have a thick-feathered border (see fig. 124 for VYDONIA). A smaller version has also been recorded.

Rectangle designs did not, of course, remain static. They moved with the times to take, for example, the decorated borders currently in fashion. Many makers of this period are unidentified, because the registers that should contain their names are missing, but one whom we do know of was Margaret Binley, widow of Richard (see above); she continued his business for some fifteen years after his death in 1764, introducing several new and up-to-date shapes and borders (see figs. 126 and 127). An interesting variation is shown at fig. 128. The design can be classed as rectangular, because that is the shape that the broad rococo motif surrounding the ribbon-like panel produces. Nineteen of these labels came from Belton House, sold in 1984. Ten of them are unmarked and the remainder have the marks of James Hyde (dated 1799), T. and J. Phipps (1819) and J. Reily. The

Shapes and Designs

Figures 123-137.

design, with its rococo motif, and the style of the engraving of the names could reasonably be attributed to the mid-1760s, and the unmarked examples may well date from then, the ones with makers' marks being made later to add to the set. Normally, all rectangles of this period have sharp corners; the practice of rounding them, or cutting the corners diagonally, came later.

The next alteration to the shape was to extend the upper edge to form a dome or recessed space in which a floral decoration or a plaque was placed (see figs. 150-155). Hester Bateman introduced this design at the beginning of the 1770s, to be followed later in the decade by Susanna Barker. It can be argued that the so-called cushion shape (see figs. 156-166) is really an extension of the rectangle, but here it is treated as a separate class, appearing in the mid-1760s.

The next major change did not come, in fact, for another twenty years, when makers began to cut the corners diagonally (see figs. 135-137, 147 and 149). The practice seems to have started in about 1787. A handful of cut-cornered examples are recorded with the incuse duty mark of 1784-6, or without any duty mark. These are discussed below, but there are plenty that have just the cameo king's head and lion passant, indicating a date between 1786 and 1791. The absence of earlier examples does not prove conclusively that none was made before 1787, but the sudden adoption of the style by such well-known makers as Hester Bateman, James Hyde and the Phipps and Robinson partnership, all at about the same time, does make it reasonable to suggest that this was when the fashion started.

Let us consider the few labels of this class that could be earlier than 1787. There is a long

Shapes and Designs

Figures 138-149.

rectangular one for MADEIRA, with very pronounced cut corners, which has only the maker's mark of Susanna Barker, as used from 1780. It appears to be a pair with one for CLARET (see fig. 137), which has the same maker's mark, but is accompanied by the cameo king's head duty mark and lion passant, which suggests a date of *c*.1787. It is certainly possible that the MADEIRA is earlier – *c*.1780 to 1783, but it is more likely to be of the later date, incompletely marked. A label for BRANDY by the Sheffield manufacturers Henry Tudor and Thomas Leader, which has the incuse duty mark, has been recorded. It is undated, but Jackson says that this incuse mark has been noted with the date letter for 1786/87; the label could, therefore, be as late as July 1787. Finally there is a SHERRY label of largish size with a beaded border by John Rich, which has the incuse head duty mark and lion passant. It is in any case a hard label to explain, because the beaded border is seldom found as late as this, and not on labels of this size. From its marks it should be earlier than May 1786, but from its decoration it is not much later than 1780, in which case it is considerably earlier than any other cut-cornered label.

After the introduction of the cut corner further relaxation from the hard contours of the early shape continued. Rounded corners and fully rounded ends appear within the next few years, followed by other variations, such as inward curving corners and sides bowed both inwards and outwards. The very pretty medium-sized rectangle with cut-out border of rosettes, made by T. Phipps and E. Robinson, John Whittingham and others, dates from this period.

51

Shapes and Designs

Figures 150-155.

After about 1790 it became the almost universal practice in London to shave the corners in some way or other, and sharp corners were very much the exception. This is true for English provincial makers as well, but not for Scotland or Ireland, where sharp corners persisted well into the nineteenth century. To some extent the treatment of the corners and sides is linked to the style of border decoration. The feathered edge fitted the old sharp-cornered shape well. The beaded edge, which John Rich used for the SHERRY label noted earlier, does not really look right (which may be why he did not repeat it). The reeded edge, either single or double, seems to be more suitable for cut or rounded corners than sharp ones.

The first extrusion of the upper edge was made to provide space for extra decoration, as in the so-called 'domed rectangle' (see figs. 150-155).[15] Sometimes the space was used to contain a plaque for initials, as in an example by Samuel Meriton. From about 1790 it became quite common to place a shield or plaque above the rectangular panel, occasionally standing on its own, but usually supported by swags or stays. This sometimes transforms the overall appearance of the label from something roughly rectangular to something much more complex.[16] It should be noted that crescents had been taking shields and plaques between their horns much earlier than this, and scrolls surmounted by shields are found from the mid-1770s, as Part 3 of this chapter shows.

In the nineteenth century the demand for fairly simple indicators of a decanter's contents increased to meet the requirements of a society whose standards were rising, but whose pockets did not stretch to the extremes of ostentation developed during the Regency period. The production of straightforward rectangular labels, mainly plain with reeded borders, was prodigious, and the range of names, as more and more wines and liquors arrived in the country, was enormous. The shape was now static, and it is true to say that the rectangular concept produced no innovatory

Shapes and Designs

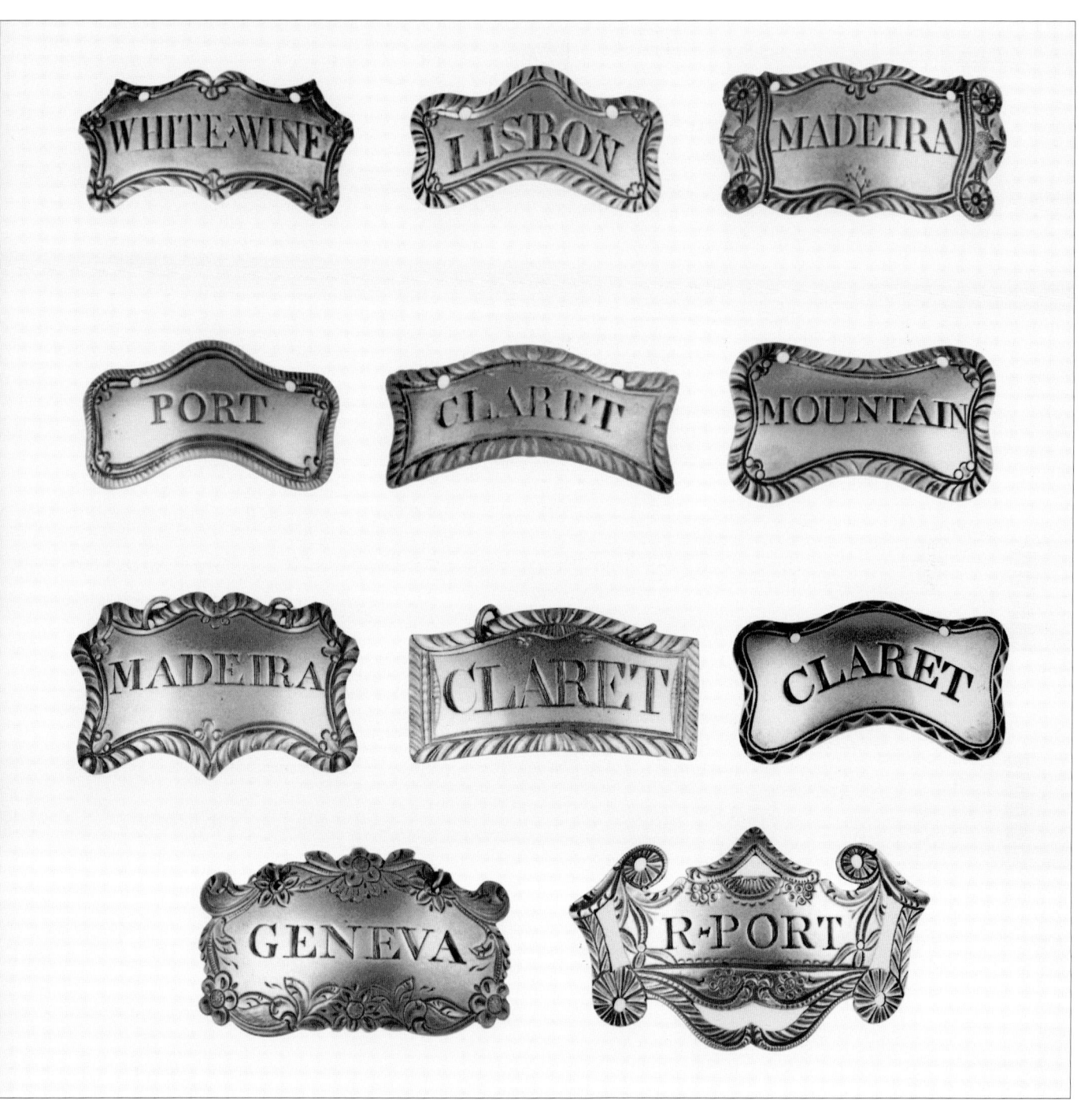

Figures 156-166.

design after the turn of the century, except with regard to border decoration. The nineteenth century witnessed an explosion of borders, cast, stamped, pierced and engraved, open or solid, the most common of which were fruiting vines, with many variations reflecting the taste or invention of the silversmith.

One other variation of the rectangle, which arrived during the third and fourth quarters of the eighteenth century, must be mentioned. Hester Bateman produced this attractive design, which can be described best, perhaps, as a curved rectangle, flanked by sprays and surmounted by the Prince of Wales' feathers (see fig. 134 for PORT). It is more logical to give the rectangle as its derivation, rather than the crescent; it is a rectangle, bent upwards and with features added, rather than a crescent from which the horns, which are the essence of that design, are taken away. It dates from

53

Shapes and Designs

c.1775, and was copied by all Hester Bateman's family after her, down to William Bateman in 1815. It almost seems that the family acquired some sort of prescriptive right over the design, because the only other London maker to copy it, until C. Reily and G. Storer in the 1840s, was Thomas Morley (husband of Elizabeth Morley), who has a version dated 1794. It was, however, copied by Dorothy Langlands in Newcastle and by Hampston and Prince in York. There are also versions from Glasgow and Edinburgh by Robert Gray, while the Anderson Collection in the Vintners' Hall has an intriguing example with unidentified marks that have a colonial appearance (see further below, Chapter 9, Part 21 and fig. 1439 by Louis Boudo of Charleston, South Carolina).

In Scotland, the particularly distinctive feature that Edinburgh makers introduced in the development of the rectangle was to add loops above the upper edge to take the chain. The rectangle in Ireland developed a shape with characteristic curved sides (see Chapter 7, Parts 10 and 11).

The offshoot of the simple rectangle, referred to above, which became the cushion shape (see figs. 156-166), must have evolved around 1760. Its characteristics are bowed or waved sides, an upper edge that is often humped, and corners rounded or shaped to take roundels. Edmund Medlycott entered his mark in 1748; his label for WHITE-WINE, shown at fig. 156, has the lion passant of 1756, so was probably made in around 1760. Richard Binley's LISBON (see fig. 157) must be earlier than 1764, the year of his death, and his widow, Margaret, was responsible for several variations of the design during the next ten years. James Phipps' first mark has been seen on cushions between 1767 and 1772, and Hester Bateman's marks from around 1770. Other makers who used the design were William Barrett I, Susanna Barker, John Humphris and H.J. Walther.

The cushion shape began to lose popularity towards the end of the 1770s, hardly any examples being recorded until Henry Chawner and John Rich briefly revived versions of it in 1791 and 1792. After that it disappears from London workshops except for deliberate copies made in the next century. An early Birmingham use of the design was that of Boulton and Fothergill in 1775. The design spread to Ireland and was used by Samuel Teare in the 1790s, as well as by a maker not positively identified but who may be Darby Kehoe, active from the 1770s. A single Scottish example has the mark of William Ferguson from Elgin, active c.1828.

Nearly all cushion-shaped labels have the broad feathered border (see fig. 495, MADEIRA, by Hester Bateman) that flourished in the 1760s. Hester Bateman and Susanna Barker made use of beaded borders. A cushion shape by Hester Bateman of c.1790 has a bright-cut border, and a semi-revival by Henry Chawner of 1792 has rosettes at the lower corners with acanthus leaves and flowerheads around the edge. A domed cushion shape by Hester Bateman (see fig. 505) follows the cushion shape of Richard Binley (see fig. 157).

PART 3 – SCROLLS

A scroll is, accurately, a roll of paper, usually long and narrow, which takes up a serpentine form when partially unrolled, leaving the rolled ends curled up behind and in front, and offering a suitable space on which to write a message or display the name of a wine. In pre-wine label days bottles lying in the cellar had parchment or paper stuck on them to indicate the contents, so it is not surprising that the parchment concept transformed into a silver 'ticket' when the time came for the bottle, or later the decanter, to appear on the sideboard. Sandylands Drinkwater's cut-out grape and tendril WHITE-WINE of around 1745 (see fig. 168) and Edmund Medlycott's BURGUNDY of around 1750 (see fig. 167) have the name on a scroll, clearly identifiable in the casting. Some twenty years later, under rococo influence, label makers took the scroll out of its frame and made it into a wrought or stamped label on its own (see fig. 493, MADEIRA, Hester Bateman, c.1775, fig. 169, PORT, James Hyde, c.1778 and fig. 753, WHISKEY, Christian and David Reid, c.1830). The 'unrolled' paper concept is not given much emphasis, because it is difficult to convey a curled effect satisfactorily on a flat surface. Makers tended to formalise the extremities into a roundel, a flowerhead or a beaked point (see fig. 170, SHERRY, J. Phipps, c.1775).[17] This asymmetrical scroll shape could be left plain (see fig. 171, CLARET, H. Bateman, c.1775), but was well adapted to take

Shapes and Designs

Figures 167-178.

a border decoration, and this was how the majority were treated. Early examples have the feather edge, which predominated in the late 1760s and early 1770s (as PORT above), but as zigzag and bright cutting became popular they were introduced to good effect, particularly by the Phipps family partnerships, the Batemans, James Hyde, Susanna Barker and others (see fig. 172, WHITE•WINE, William Barrett I, *c.*1771; fig. 173, MOUNTAIN, Susanna Barker, *c.*1778). Hester Bateman used a saw-tooth border on her HOCK label (*c.*1775) with dramatic effect (see fig. 174), and her LISBON (see fig. 175) of the same date, in scroll form but with straight sides instead of the usual curly ends, is likewise strikingly original in design.[18]

Shapes and Designs

Figures 179-187.

 A feature that soon emerged from the single scroll was the addition of a shield or plaque supported by stays placed above the upper edge to display a crest (see fig. 176, CLARET, John Rich, c.1770). Another development that appeared at this time is best described as a double (or symmetrical) scroll. It can be likened to the volutes of an Ionic capital, a scroll viewed sideways,[19] but without portraying the scroll ends realistically. These labels have incurving rounded ends or pendent lobes (see fig. 178, CLARET, Margaret Binley, c.1770/75; fig. 179, HOCK, T. Phipps and E. Robinson, c.1783; and figs. 490 for RED·PORT and 497 for SHERRY by Hester Bateman of this period), and incorporate the plaque with its supporting stays above the name panel as an integral part of the design. Initially, they had a convex profile, curving downwards towards the extremities (as CLARET does). Later versions (HOCK) tend to curve upwards from the middle. The majority of single scrolls sweep upwards from left to right. Only rarely do they descend in the opposite direction (see fig. 181, BRANDY, William Sloden, Bristol, 1791; fig. 740, PORT, Thomas Wigan, Bristol, c.1763-70; and fig. 175, Hester Bateman's LISBON).

 Single and double scrolls made by makers outside London, in addition to those mentioned above, have occasionally been noted. A double scroll by Henry Tudor and William Leader of Sheffield is fully marked for 1779 and, as remarked upon in Chapter 7 (Sheffield), the same design is also known in OSP. An unmarked plated label for RUM is illustrated (see fig. 189).[20] From Newcastle, a single scroll label was made by William Stalker and John Mitchison at about the same time, while from York comes a double scroll, based on the Phipps and Robinson version (see fig. 179), by J. Hampston and J. Prince, c.1780. The only known Exeter scroll, a plain single design, is much later by Isaac Parkin, dated 1825. None has been noted by Chester makers. It is slightly surprising that

Shapes and Designs

Figure 188.

Figure 189.

no scrolls were made in Birmingham during the period of the design's popularity in the late 1770s and 1780s. It appears on the name panel on a stamped cartouche shape for SHERRY by Matthew Linwood II, dated 1819 (see fig. 182), but not as a scroll on its own until mid-Victorian times when T. Harwood and Sons produced a very realistic version of the single type (see fig. 183, GIN, 1865).

There was, as explained elsewhere, no demand for wine labels in Scotland before the 1780s (see fig. 180, by Adam Graham, Glasgow, *c.*1784). No other single scrolls are known than this group from Glasgow, but much later MacKay and Chisholm produced a small version with pronounced curly ends and rarely seen (see fig. 184, CURACOA, Edinburgh, 1865). William Ritchie of Perth made a set of three of the double scroll type in around 1810, and Robert Naughton made one in Inverness around 1825. Scrolls do, moreover, feature on the name panels of rectangular-shaped labels with 'C-scroll' edges made by J. MacKay of Edinburgh (*c.*1810/20, see fig. 185, TENERIFFE) and W. Ziegler. Early Irish labels of the period when scrolls were fashionable are equally scarce. One exciting example of a single scroll has been seen, made by Robert Calderwood, who died in 1765 (see Ireland). It is plain, without border decoration, but it has other distinctive features, and must have been made at the same time that the design first appeared in England. Two rather similar unmarked examples are also known, which are likely to be contemporary with it, or slightly later, but no others until 1818, when Peter Godfrey produced a version (see fig. 186, MOSELLE), which also has distinctive features and, interestingly, an identical counterpart that sweeps in the opposite direction, downwards from left to right. The intriguing serpentine MARSALA (see fig. 187) by an unidentified 'TW' may also be Irish or possibly by Thomas Wallis (1773-1801).

The single scroll largely disappears in England in about 1780-83, but its double symmetrical version lasted for another ten or fifteen years. It re-emerged briefly in the next century, towards the end of the Regency period, in the elaborate cast, oak-leaf bordered label by John Reily (see fig. 188, 1823), and equally elaborate designs by C. Rawlings and W. Summers and by the Barnard family.

PART 4 – OVALS

Oval and eye-shaped labels originated as products of early neo-classical thinking and their period of popularity spanned the heyday of late eighteenth-century wine label production. Together with crescents they supplanted escutcheons as the most favoured shape of the mid- to late eighteenth century. They were only overtaken in the popularity stakes by the ubiquitous rectangle at the turn of the century. Ovals vary in shape from elongated (see fig. 204, James Hyde's WHITE•WINE, *c.*1789 and fig. 202, William Barrett I's GENEVA, *c.*1789) and pointed (eye-shaped, such as fig. 205, Smith and Hayter's PORT, 1792) through pure ovals (see figs. 203 and 206, Phipps and Robinson's LISBON, *c.*1780, and RASPBERRY BRANDY, 1799) to one that is nearly round (see fig. 211 for Wallis and Hayne's VIDONIA of 1818). Judging by the quantity that have survived, they must have been made in large numbers, and indeed it is the most common label to be found with the incuse king's head duty mark of 1784/86 (as on Susanna Barker's MADEIRA, fig. 196, William Abdy's SHERRY, fig. 197, and Susanna Barker's CHAMPAGNE, fig. 201).

Since the outlines of these labels are so simple in shape, they generally rely upon the border to provide a sense of individuality, and these may be shaped, engraved or attractively pierced.

An addition to the simple oval with its decorated border is provided by a class of 'embellished ovals' – where the basic shape is an oval but surmounted by a cartouche for an armorial or initials,

Shapes and Designs

Figures 190-201.

contained by swags that fall downwards, or stays to support it. Examples are fig. 190 for SHERRY, fig. 191 for HOLLANDS and fig. 192 for WHITE-WINE both by James Hyde, and fig. 194 for MADEIRA by Phipps and Robinson in 1794. The cartouche varies from vertical oval, to horizontal oval, to shield shape, and the pendant swags vary in shape and thickness to either good effect or sometimes bad, as that which looks like a spider or octopus. Generally these embellished ovals do not have pierced borders, and rely on engraving and bright cutting. A further group of labels may be termed 'suspended ovals', which have the panel containing the name of the wine suspended within a border that may be both solid or pierced in a cable design. Examples are fig. 193, Richard Evans overstriking Peter and Ann Bateman, 1791, for CURRANT; fig. 195, Samuel Knight overstriking William Abdy II, 1817, for CLARET; fig. 198 by James Hyde for BRANDY, c.1790; and the Irish labels in figs. 214 and 215 by J. Sherwin and B. Taitt respectively.

The oval typifies the neo-classical with all its elegance, lightness of touch and labour intensive workmanship. There was therefore no room for this concept with the advent of industrialisation, which brought the plain rectangle to prominence at one end of the market and, at the upper end,

Shapes and Designs

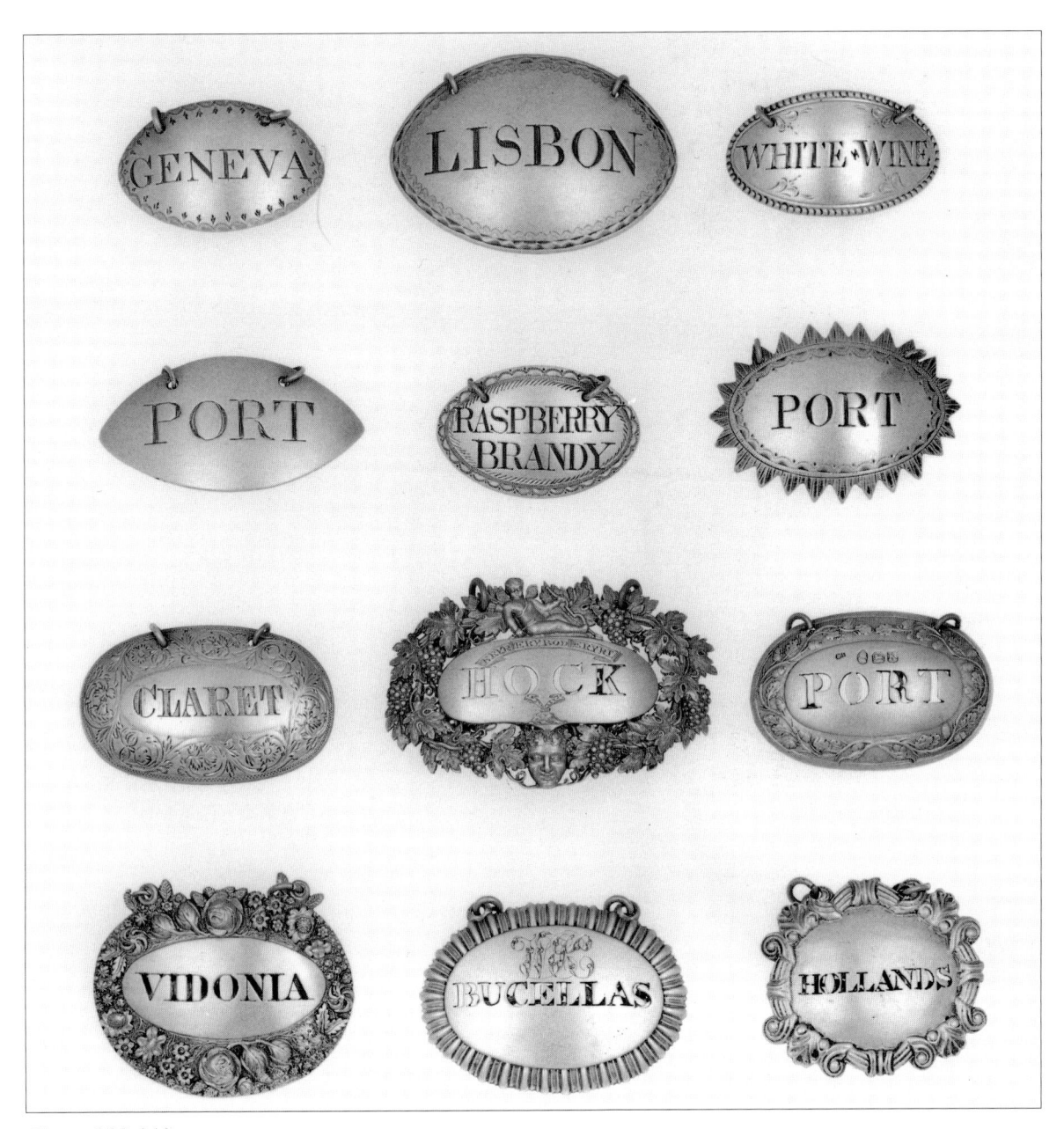

Figures 202-213.

the last cast labels of the Regency. In consequence, the end of the eighteenth century saw the demise of this small, elegant, restrained label in its original concept. The oval did however continue into the nineteenth century, commonly as more flamboyant die-stamped labels of fussy design and decoration and often inferior quality. A few cast ovals of the Regency period are also known but, while the workmanship is good, they have lost the lightness of touch of the neo-classical. Regency labels are represented by Alexander Field's CLARET of 1802 (see fig. 208), Solomon Hougham's PORT of 1805 (see fig. 210), Wallis and Hayne's VIDONIA of 1818 (see fig. 211), Abstainando King's HOLLANDS of 1820 (see fig. 213), George Pearson's HOCK of 1821 (see fig. 209) and William Elliott's BUCELLAS of 1824 (see fig. 212).

Nearly all eighteenth-century manufacturers of wine labels made ovals. Some should be singled out on account of their innovative designs or the outstanding quality of their work.

First of these was Susanna Barker (1778-93), who made a speciality of ovals with varying borders, both pierced and engraved.[21] Others were James Hyde (1777-99), John Rich (1765-1810), William Abdy II (1784-1823), Hester Bateman (1761-90), Peter and Anne Bateman (1791-1800), James

Shapes and Designs

Figure 214.

Figure 215.

Phipps (1767-83) and Thomas Phipps and Edward Robinson (1783-1810). Thomas Chawner (1773-1802), not noted as a wine label producer, must be mentioned for his oval designs with eighteen or twenty-four waved or pointed borders (his SHERRY of c.1783 is shown in fig. 200), as must Henry Chawner (1786-96), who made a label with a curious engraved border with a meander of vine leaves, grapes and tendrils (his SHERRY of c.1795 is shown in fig. 199).[22]

As to the borders encountered, they are too numerous to list in full; however on plain ovals (not pierced) the following deserve mention:

1. Plain – no decoration at all – rare[23] – fig. 205.
2. Reeded edge – fig. 194.
3. Engraved, bright cut and wriggle work – in varying degrees of elaborateness with floral engraving also sometimes present – this is the most common design – fig. 192.
4. Milled edge – rare.[24]
5. Beaded edge – common – fig. 204.
6. Feathered edge – rare.
7. Gadrooned edge – very rare – fig. 212.
8. Punched and prick dotted border – rare[25] – fig. 207 by Phipps and Robinson.
9. Foliated or scroll surmounts – a design of James Hyde[24,25] – figs. 191-192.
10. Swags – rare[24] – figs. 190 and 192.
11. Petal border – rare[24] – fig. 207 by Phipps and Robinson.
12. Waved concaved border – rare[24] – fig. 200.

Pierced borders include:

1. Pales with bright-cut or beaded or double beaded (S. Barker) edges.[23] This is the most common type of pierced borders.
2. Trefoils with bright-cut edge (Irish).[24]
3. Flowerheads with bright-cut edge (Irish).
4. Vitruvian scroll with beaded or bright-cut edge – perhaps the most attractive borders.[23]
5. Alternating small ovals and slanted leaves to create the appearance of Vitruvian scroll border – a rare, but pleasing border.
6. Double pierced border of paired trefoils, probably an exclusive design of William Abdy.[25]
7. Ovals linked by swags, probably an exclusive design of William Abdy.[25]
8. Conjoined ovolo design, probably an exclusive design of William Abdy.[23]

Many provincial makers produced oval labels, but the Irish were particularly noted for their own characteristic types. Mention has been made above of the pierced bordered oval by John Sherwin. His W-WINE of *c.*1790 is illustrated in fig. 214. This label and similar pierced bordered ovals by William Law, George Nangle and John Teare all tend to be larger than the London-made labels, but the gauge of the silver used is thinner and becomes progressively thinner towards the end of the eighteenth century. Another label, almost exclusively of Irish design, has a sharply-pointed oval surmounted by a barrel astride which a putto sits clutching a bottle in each hand; from the barrel are appended leafage or ribbons stretching towards the pointed ends of the oval. This design originated with John Teare in around 1790; later William Law made an extremely thin example (see Chapter 2, Part 11). Smaller die-stamped and rather inferior versions were made in England by W. Troby and T. Ballam in 1824. Before leaving Irish ovals, mention should be made of the famous ballooning label made by Benjamin Taitt in about 1785. It may be classed as an oval as the balloon, which is, of course, its principal feature, and the name panel are enclosed within an oval border of Irish character and design. It is described in Part 13 of this chapter. Benjamin Taitt also made around 1785 the label illustrated by fig. 215 for the misspelt MADERIA.

While Irish makers seemed to prefer pierced borders, Scottish makers made more restrained plain ovals with the exception of William Davie, Edinburgh c.1785, whose oval had a 'chain' border. Other north of England centres, such as Newcastle and York, made plain, rather unremarkable ovals and here examples are known by Langlands and Robertson, as well as their eccentric octopus-like label mentioned earlier; Hampston and Prince from 1784-5 and William Etherington c.1790, both of York, made plain ovals. Ovals were also made at Sheffield and Birmingham but of rather plain designs.

Oval wine labels were made of materials other than silver, but are not common. As one would expect, they are to be found in OSP with reeded, beaded, double beaded and pierced and chased borders and even one with a pseudo bright-cut border. They are also occasionally found in mother-of-pearl – a particularly attractive example for 'EST EST', with a pierced border, is in the Victoria and Albert Museum collection.[25]

PART 5 – CRESCENTS

Crescent shaped labels are in an elegant yet most basic style that was first in use in about 1750.[26] The shape was particularly popular and subject to innovations over the following sixty years. They are one of the earliest and most common shapes portrayed in contemporary illustrations, and were produced by most of the well-known label makers of the eighteenth century.

The basic shape consists of the segment formed by two intersecting circles. It has horns (points) at each end, and its shape ranges from flat and open ended, through tall with pointed tips, to virtually circular with tips nearly touching. Examples occur with slight variations to the line of the outer or inner edge, or with additional decoration to the shape, usually above the centre. The labels are generally worked from flat plate, and either left plain or provided with hand worked decoration.

The earliest form is a large plain label whose two points nearly touch; it generally has a width of about 5cm (2in.). The label was cut from flat plate with the crescent points wide apart and was formed by bending the plate back to bring the points close together, which at the same time produced the characteristic sloping face to the label. This method of manufacture was probably adopted to make economic use of the plate. The placing of the eyes that take the chains of crescent labels has always presented a problem – how to ensure that the chain does not catch in the tips of the horns. A characteristic method used by early designers was to put small, semicircular extrusions on the top of the outside edges to take the eyelets. Both Sandylands Drinkwater and Louis Hamon did this, and an example by Louis Hamon for LISBON is illustrated in fig. 218.

The next development was to apply a feather edged border, at first to large labels of the early plain design, but without extruding eyelets, as in the case of CLARET by Margaret Binley, c.1765 (see fig. 216), and then to smaller examples, as produced by J. Phipps c.1770 and several other makers soon afterwards, such as James Hyde and John Rich. Beaded, bright-cut and reeded borders were used as fashions changed.

Bright cutting first appears as a border for crescents in about 1770 and undoubtedly produces an extremely fine and effective result, as examples by James Phipps, T. Phipps and E. Robinson and the Batemans clearly show. It remained popular for twenty years. An example marked for SHRUB by Peter and Ann Bateman dated 1795 is shown in fig. 223. Two larger examples are shown in figs. 23 and 24 above. PAXARETE (see fig. 23) is a late example by Elizabeth Morley in 1811 and PORT (see fig. 24) is an Irish label of horseshoe shape, typical of Irish crescents, by Benjamin Taitt in around 1790. It also occurs with a reeded edge.

Shapes and Designs

Most crescent labels were London made, but examples carrying the hallmarks of the other manufacturing cities are found. Sheffield crescent labels, usually of simple outline with either beaded or reeded borders, are found in both sterling and OSP and examples of the latter occur with fruiting vine infill above the crescent. They are all of a die-stamped manufacture. Langlands and Robertson of Newcastle made the deep crescent label for MADEIRA with a high pointed cusp, illustrated in fig. 221 around 1780, an early date for this development.

Another extremely effective example of the crescent design is the rare pierced label illustrated by CLARET in fig. 222. This label, together with its pair for PORT, is extremely finely executed and probably of Irish origin. They have maker's marks only, R.E., stamped twice. The wheat husk and rosette pierced borders, common on eye-shaped Irish labels, were also used on crescent shapes. The labels are usually large, wide examples and the design is most effective on the simple crescent outline. An example dating from about 1790 and pierced for TENERIFFE is known. An Irish label for CLARET with urn or vase and scroll above and wheat husk garlands by John Sherwin, *c*.1790, is shown at fig. 26 above.

Both reeded and beaded edges were used to enhance the crescent shape during the latter part of the eighteenth century. James Hyde produced labels of the beaded style. An illustration of one marked for SHERRY with an incuse head duty mark is shown in fig. 220, and of one *c*.1790 marked for PORT is shown at fig. 22 above. Examples of OSP crescent labels with reeded edges are shown in illustrations accompanying Part 1 of Chapter 8 (below). The pierced saw-tooth elaborate border work, generally associated with scroll labels, is rare on crescents but, when used as it was by some of the important late eighteenth-century makers, it produces a very fine design. An example of 1799 marked for SHERRY by Phipps and Robinson is shown in fig. 224.

The crescent, though elegant enough in its basic form, readily lent itself to embellishment, particularly with features from the neo-classical style associated with Robert Adam. The space between the horns was eminently suitable for lodging urns, plaques and shields, which in turn could be supported by swags, stays and festoons, and they could be further extended above or under the basic label, or the horns could be turned inwards and a device placed to rest on them (the so-called enclosed crescent). These developments transform the crescent from its original purity and simplicity into something much more elaborate, almost a separate design in its own right. All these variations described above came into use during the last quarter of the eighteenth century, but they were not compatible with the fashions of the next century and did not stay in production for long after 1800. The best-known exponent of this development of the crescent was certainly Hester Bateman. Her children's partnerships continued her designs, while other leading manufacturers, including Phipps and Robinson, James Hyde and John Rich, either imitated them or introduced their own variations.

These labels were all formed from flat plate using the basic skills of cutting out, piercing and surface finish to embellish the basic design. Two examples of the neo-classical style of crescent are illustrated: they are PORT *c*.1775, fig. 226, and FRONTINIAC *c*.1790, fig. 225, both by Hester Bateman (although the latter is overstruck T.A.). A fine example of a more restrained, but similar label by Hester Bateman is BRANDY illustrated in fig. 227.

The general move in design at the end of the eighteenth century to plainer styles in furniture and houses was reflected in wine labels. The elaborate edge finishes and neo-classical adornments gave way to simpler shapes and more restrained finishes. The labels produced at this time based on the crescent shape and described below do not appear to have been produced in large numbers and are usually individual designs associated with one area of manufacture and often with one maker. A variation of the crescent label typical of this period was the addition to the basic shape of a cusp to the top edge. A design using double reeding to enhance the clean lines was particularly made by the Bateman family; Peter and Ann, Peter, Ann and William, and then Peter and William all produced examples of this label around the latter part of the eighteenth and early nineteenth centuries. An example by Peter and William for RUM in 1805 is shown in fig. 217.

The cusped shape was also used on two other particular labels. The bright-cut Langlands and Robertson label has been previously mentioned. The second is a label produced only in Sheffield. It is formed as a drape or festoon held by a ring or button, and spreading downwards to the top

Shapes and Designs

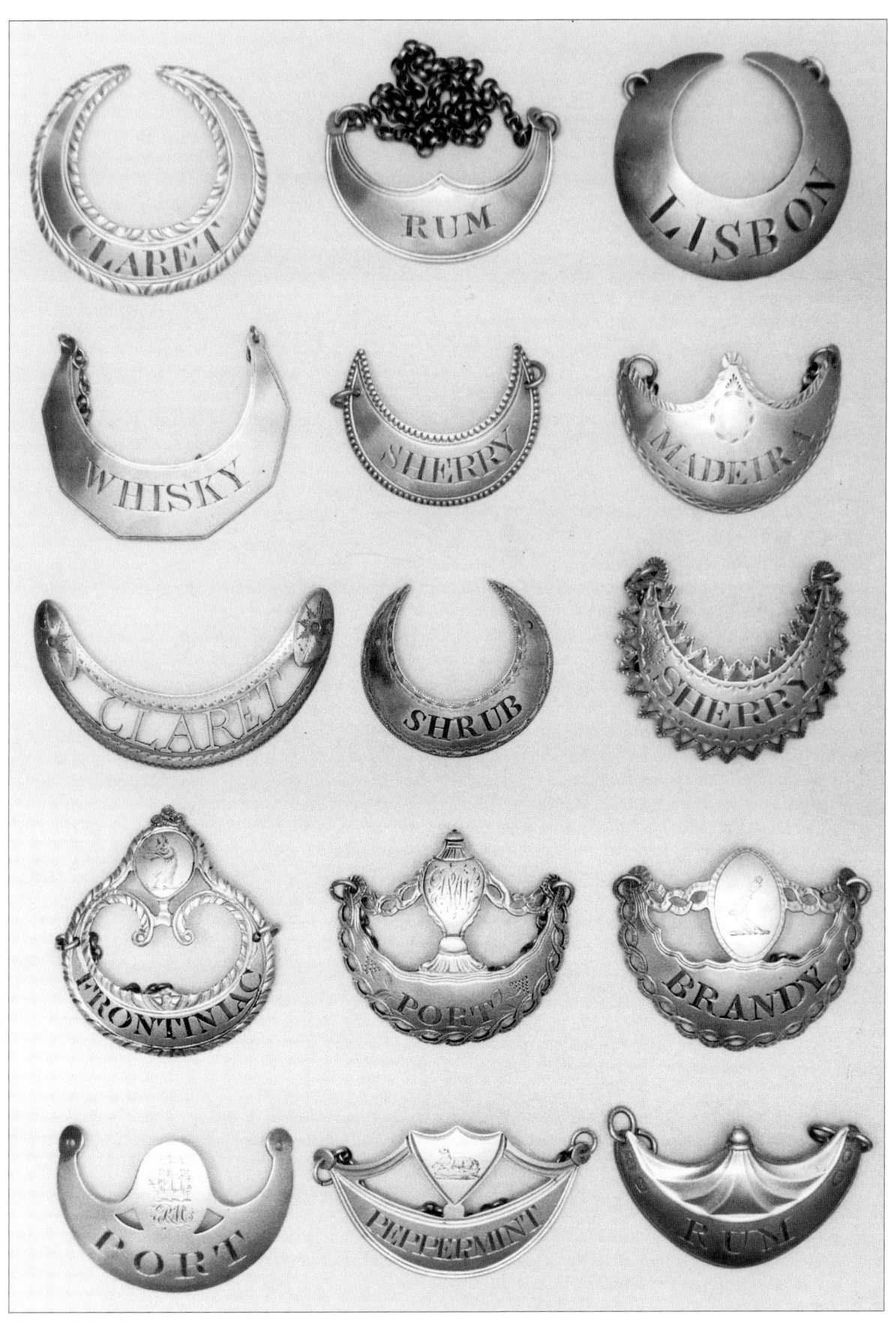

Figures 216-230.

Shapes and Designs

edge of the crescent. It comes with a number of small variations and an example engraved for RUM, hallmarked 1797, Thomas Law & Co., is shown in fig. 230. The variations are all pressed labels and occur in both sterling silver and OSP (see below, Chapter 8, Part 1).

The design of another label was greatly enhanced by reeding, which emphasised the simple and clean style of this time. This is the crescent with shield and supporters above and is worked from flat plate. The crescent label marked for PEPPERMINT shown in fig. 229, dated 1794, is a fine example made by Phipps and Robinson. Another variation of this style for PORT by Peter and Ann Bateman in 1808 is shown in fig. 228.

Again an effective and simple enhancement of the crescent shape occurred at this time with the shaping of the outside edge to a series of facets. Examples are usually with Edinburgh hallmarks and a label by William Auld *c.*1800, engraved for WHISKY, is illustrated in fig. 219, but it is possible that these labels were in fact manufactured in Sheffield as the label also occurs in OSP (see below, Chapter 8, Part 1).

The characteristically clean lines of the crescent were not compatible with the ornate and flamboyant styles[27] that developed in the early nineteenth century so, although reproductions were made throughout the nineteenth century, its use as a basic concept for a wine label had ceased.

PART 6 – STARS AND BUTTONS

Star-shaped labels can be considered as embellished circular or button shapes or as a class on their own. Either description is suitable for this design, which made its appearance during the middle years of the 1780s. Button shapes are also first recorded at about the same time.

The principal maker of stars was Susanna Barker (see fig. 231, MADEIRA, *c.*1787, and CALCAVELLA and SHERRY similar). Her contemporary Hester Bateman, who introduced so many new designs and who, with her family, has enjoyed more lasting fame, did not take up this particular design. Indeed, the only other London silversmith of the period who did make them was William Abdy I (see fig. 232, PORT, *c.*1787, and RUM and MADEIRA similar). His stars are marginally smaller than Susanna Barker's. Both are cut from a sheet of plate, but whereas Barker used an old form of suspension, eyes soldered to the back of the label (c.f. the suspension of early 'square' rectangles, Chapter 2, Parts 1 and 2), Abdy has conventional eyelet holes in two of the star's rays. They differ, too, in the way the name is engraved. Susanna Barker's titles are usually placed straight across the centre of the panel; Abdy's are curved under the upper edge, and have a pair of crossed feathers balancing the title in the lower half.

Abdy's version spread to Scotland, where two Dundee makers used it. In a set of six labels of *c.*1795-1800, five have the mark of Edward Livingstone, with the Dundee town Pot of Lilies mark, and the sixth has J. Douglas's mark, with town marks associated with Dundee. Douglas moved from Edinburgh to Dundee in around 1800. His label (*c.*1810) has the title WHISKY, which is a very early example of this name anywhere, but particularly so in Scotland (see fig. 894).

The design is not recorded by Irish makers. The only English provincial example is by R. Morton and Co. of Sheffield, and is hallmarked for 1786/87. It is an attractive version, with the rays having a curved outline that resembles flower petals.

In 1808, T. Phipps and E. Robinson made a set of six stars. They are more like Susanna Barker's design than Abdy's, but are larger. As only one set is known, it may have been made to a special order. Indeed it is possible, given how scarce they are, that all star labels were specially commissioned. In any case, the fashion for them was short-lived. The shape is not recorded again until 1819, when J. Jackson made a set of three very large labels with twelve rays – 6.5cm (2½in.) in diameter – for the Blount family of Sodington in Worcestershire with their family crest of an armed foot within a sun in splendour engraved above the name of the wine (see fig. 233, SHERRY, 1819). They are cut from an extremely thin gauge sheet of metal, whereas earlier labels made for the Blount family were cast.

A pair of large size stars by William Elliott, dated 1838, has been recorded and the picture is completed with a plated, copper-backed example, which may be dated to the early years of the

Shapes and Designs

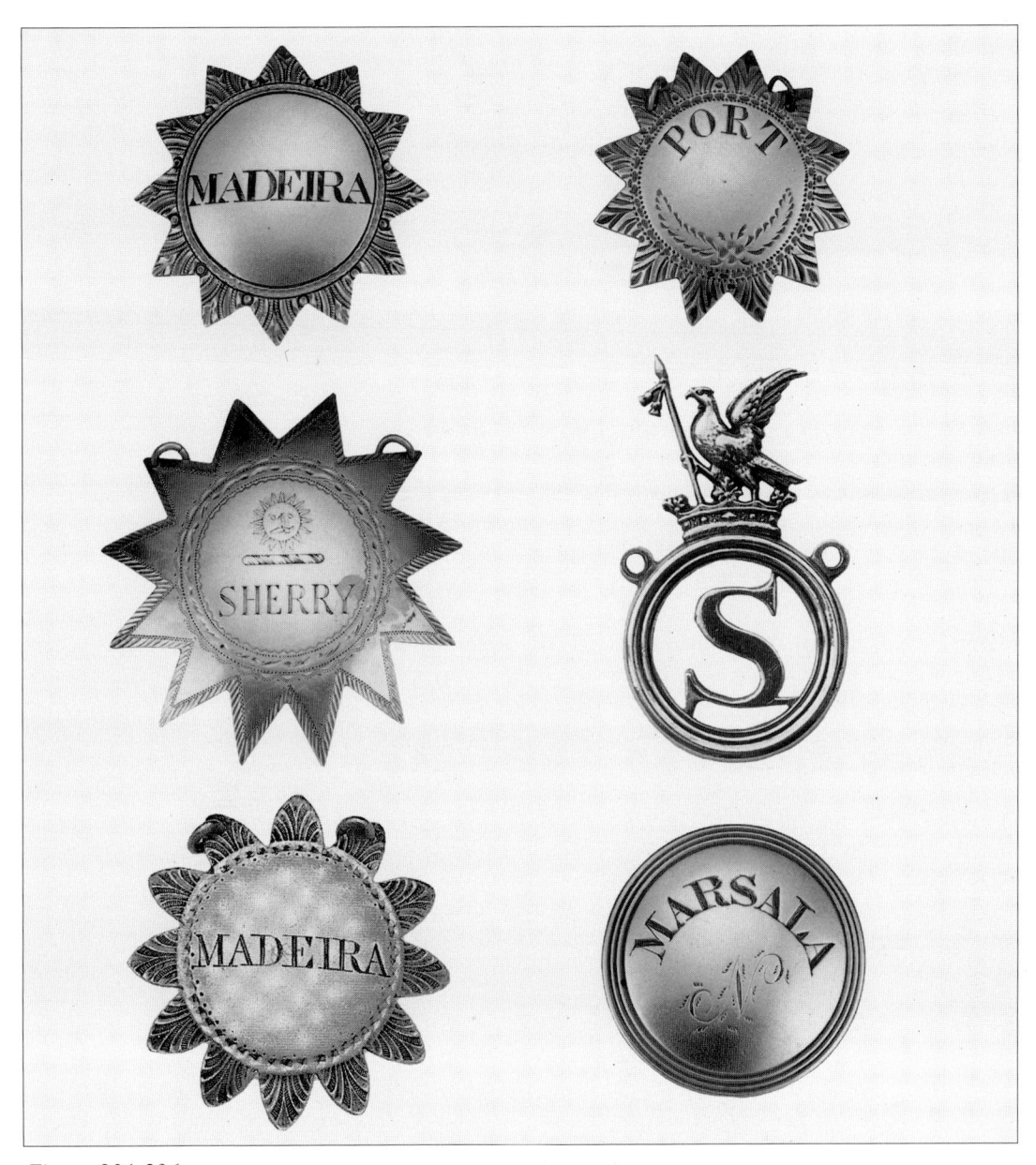

Figures 231-236.

century, and with a rather special star known as the sun in splendour (see Part 7 below).

Button-shaped labels are also scarce, their period of popularity coinciding generally with the age of the star. Robert Barker (see fig. 236 for MARSALA in 1793) made some during the few short years (1793-94) that he was active after Susanna Barker's retirement or death; she did not make any button-shaped labels herself. A button label has been recorded with the marks of T. Graham and J. Willis of Bath, *c*.1795. One for HOLLAND with initials on its face is by Francis Parsons and Benjamin Goss of Exeter, *c*.1797 (see fig. 715), in a set with RUM and BRANDY. Another has a Newcastle mark, attributed by M. Gill to G. Lewis and J. Wright, with a probable date of 1818. One by Charles Rawlings in 1827 is shown at fig. 273. A label that has a claim to be included in this family is an annular circle, containing the single letter 'S' surmounted by a crest of an eagle holding a lance, by C. Reily and G. Storer (1829 – see fig. 234). There are also the 'polo' design for WHITE•WINE, rather like the mint with the hole in it, and the larger filled in circular design, for GIN, with a broad matted border. All these were probably made, like the stars, to special order.

A rare variety of the button (which is usually circular) is the plain oval with an initial letter. Around 1801 W. Welch of Exeter made one with the letter 'B' engraved (see fig. 718).

65

Shapes and Designs

Figures 237-239.

PART 7 – SUN IN SPLENDOUR

This wine label was originally modelled as the sun with twenty-four rays, alternately straight and wavy, the face of the sun enclosed by a garter upon which the title is incised and charged with a slipper. HOCK and WHITE WINE, both unmarked, are illustrated in figs. 238 and 237. MADEIRA completes the set of three, although there may have been others.

This cast heraldic label, some 4.5cm (1¾in.) in diameter,[28] was presumably made for Sir Walter Blount, 6th Baronet, perhaps on the occasion of his marriage in 1766. The crest is that of the Blount family, baronets, of Sodington in Worcestershire. It represents an armed foot within a sun in splendour.[29]

A slightly smaller version was made by John Rich in London in 1792. It is illustrated at figs. 239/672 engraved for PORT. Perhaps it was made to add to the set of three mentioned above. In 1819 J. Jackson made a set of three wine labels (see fig. 233), perhaps for a Blount set of three decanters, modelled as a sun with twelve rays, and very large, being 6.5cm (2½in.) in diameter. These were made for the Blount family, the armed foot armorial being engraved above the name of the wine (see further Parts 6 and 21 of this chapter, concerning stars and buttons and armorial labels).

Figure 240.

PART 8 – BOTTLE COLLARS AND NECK RINGS

Although it is obviously convenient to deal with these two types of label together, there is a basic distinction that separates them: a bottle collar (see fig. 240 for CLARET by John Bridge of Rundell, Bridge and Rundell in 1828) is a circular hoop that rests on the neck or shoulders of a bottle or decanter, while a neck ring is a label that is suspended from a wire loop instead of a chain. Both enjoyed their main period of popularity between 1790 and 1830. The earliest known neck ring (*c*.1750) by Sandylands Drinkwater for ETNA is shown at fig. 477.

Bottle collars are found as frequently, if not more so, in OSP, such as for PORT (*c*.1880) and CHAMPAIGN (*c*.1800), and ivory, such as for GIN (*c*.1810), as they are in silver. Other materials,

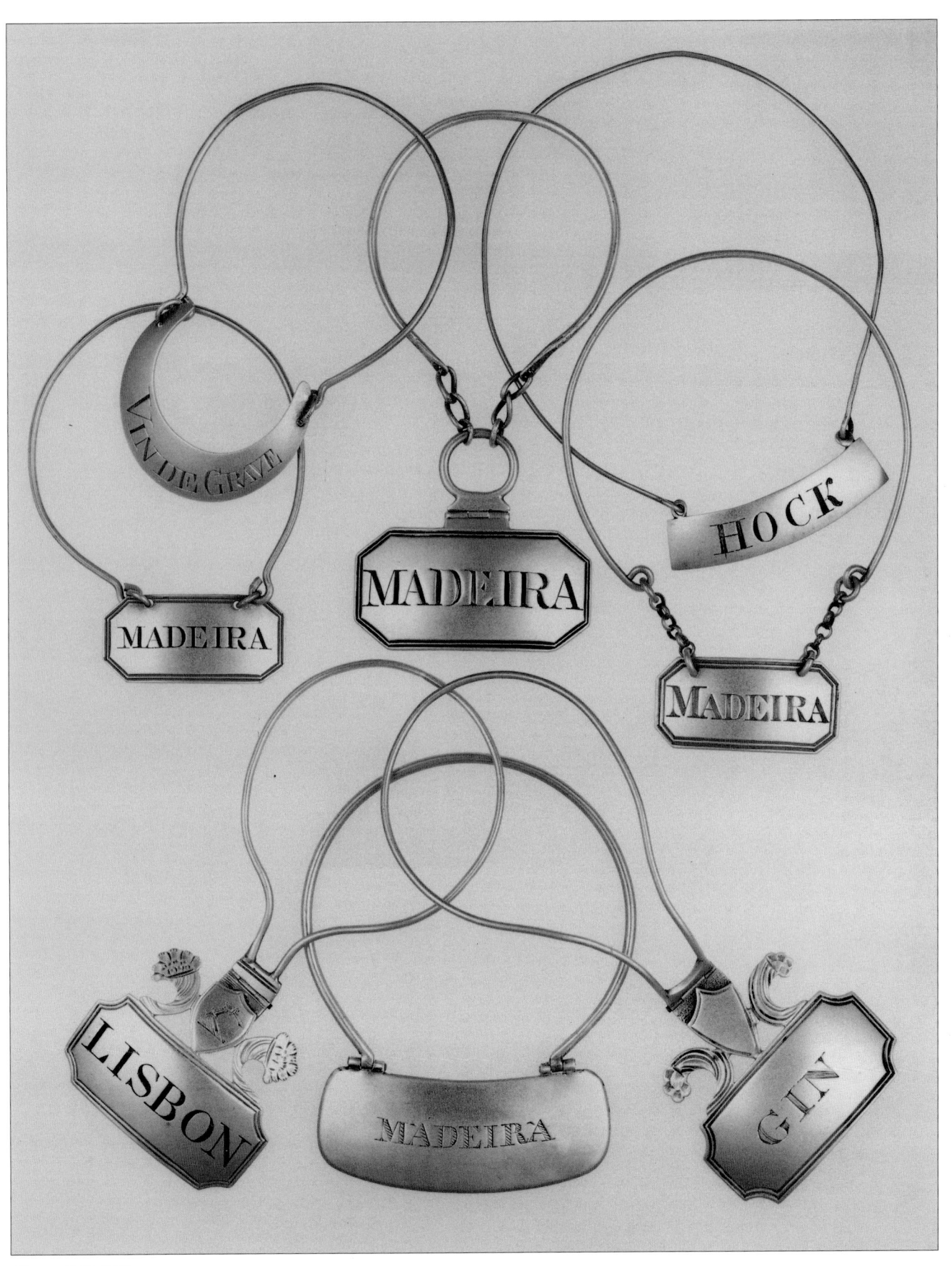

Figures 241-248.

Shapes and Designs

for instance mother-of-pearl, as for SHERRY (*c*.1800), leather with silver mounts and electroplate are rarely encountered. The angle of their slope varies from the near vertical to the almost flat, reflecting the shape of the bottle or decanter on which they were intended to fit. Most commonly they are completely plain or have simple reeded borders, but other decoration, such as beaded or rope-work borders, as used by John Reily in London in 1808 for a silver-gilt MADEIRA, piercing and bright-cutting, was occasionally employed. Ornately stamped or cast bottle collars are rare. Given the overwhelming modesty of form and material, and the fact that it is not unusual to find them engraved with the names of humble or esoteric beverages, it is not unreasonable to speculate that they were mostly intended for use on bottles rather than decanters.

Of the more elaborate forms, an OSP example for PORT (*c*.1880) is particularly noteworthy in that the 'bright-cut' decoration has been achieved by hand-stamping with a diamond-shaped punch (see fig. 257). A very large and ornate die-stamped collar for HOCK by Samuel Jackson, London, 1829, was made in silver-gilt as well as silver and is also unusual in the rear latching of the loop so that it can be opened to pass over a large lip before being fixed in place. A cast collar for IRISH WHISKEY falls well outside the core period, being made by William Comyns, London, in 1898. It has an open back spanned by a hooked chain and was probably fashioned for the oval, ring-handled jugs that were popular at the time (see fig. 258).

The greatest of designs in this group, however, must be the cast, silver-gilt example (see fig. 240) for CLARET by Rundell, Bridge and Rundell (sponsor's mark of John Bridge), London, in 1828. Superbly cast with integral lettering, the upper border represents a baron's coronet while the lower border of strawberry leaves suggests a ducal coronet. It is later engraved with the monogram B-C below a baron's coronet for Angela Burdett-Coutts, heiress of the famous banking business, who was created a baroness in 1871 for her considerable charitable works and whose stepfather was the Duke of St Albans. Much as the iconography fits her circumstances, it cannot have been made for her as she would then have been a mere fourteen years old and forty-three years away from her personal title. At the time of writing it is the only known example of its type and the mystery about its original commissioner continues. It weighs 2oz 14dwt and is 9.53cm (3¾in.) wide. Also in silver-gilt, rather like a napkin ring with cable borders, is John Reily's MADEIRA, distinctive because of its interesting inscription (see below, Chapter 5, Part 6, John Reily).

A late type of bottle collar consists of a small crescent open at its top so that it can be slipped over the neck of a bottle. These were a speciality of William Summers in the 1870s and usually have a lower border pierced with pales.

Neck rings are more an alternative means of suspension than a distinctly different type of design. At their simplest they merely have a wire loop instead of a chain and are connected to two holes, with or without jump rings, at the top of the label – see fig. 244 for MADEIRA by Phipps and Robinson in 1795, fig. 241 for VIN DE GRAVE, unmarked, *c*.1810, in the style of labels attributed to Hugh Gordon of Fortrose in Scotland, and fig. 243 in similar style by 'I.C' with 'key' mark for HOCK. Slightly more practical in use are those labels with a circular wire loop attached to the label by a jump ring to a single, central hole. An early example of this type is John Langlands' HOCK, Newcastle, *c*.1760 (fig.250). More often than not this latter type is rectangular with a dome above, usually pierced out, in which form it was frequently made by the Whitfords, the Knights, Robert Garrard, and the maker who used a small IT punch, all London and all in the first third of the nineteenth century. See fig. 249 for SHERRY by Rawlings and Summers, 1833, and fig. 251 for MADEIRA by Phipps, Robinson and Phipps, 1811.

The most sophisticated version of this method of suspension was to attach the wire loop to the label by means of a hinge. This approach was particularly favoured by Phipps and Robinson (see fig. 255 for HOCK, 1793, fig. 242 for MADEIRA, 1794, fig. 246 for LISBON, 1798 and fig. 256 for CHAMPAGNE by Phipps, Robinson and Phipps in 1812), but Joseph Pearson of Dumfries (working *c*.1795-1817) was possibly unique in employing a wire hinged at both ends to either side of the top of a label for MADEIRA, *c*.1800 (see fig. 247).[30] The hinge was also

Shapes and Designs

Figures 249-256.

Shapes and Designs

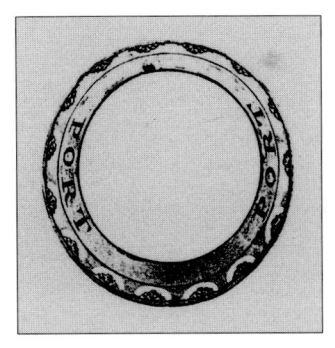

Figures 257-258.

used by Thomas Heming in making his sophisticated GIN in 1791 (see fig. 248).

Some loops were connected to the label by chains. Illustrated are figs. 242 for MADEIRA by Phipps and Robinson (1794) and Cattle and Barber's MADEIRA, York, 1808 (see fig. 245). Some labels were slot (see fig. 252, F. Fenech, Malta, c.1820), initial (see fig. 253, Charles Rawlings, 1824) or decorative (see fig. 254, William Simpson I, Banff, c.1825).

Having said that both bottle collars and neck rings were mostly made between 1790 and 1830, it must be noted that neck rings, though very rare, were made at an earlier date. Examples are known by Sandylands Drinkwater before 1757 (see fig. 477)[31] and by John Langlands I of Newcastle (see fig. 250) between 1758 and 1778.[32] There is, too, an early reference from the Wakelin Ledgers of 1 January 1756 for two large bottle tickets with soldered loops, costing 2s.6d. for workmanship, and weighing 11.5dwts.[33]

PART 9 – SINGLE LETTERS AND CUT-OUT WORDS

A fashion for using the initial letter of a wine on a label instead of the full title arose towards the end of the eighteenth century and single letters are to be found thereafter, in one form or another, for as long as the demand for wine labels persisted. What started the fashion is not clear. Some people, filled with a sense of their own importance, may have felt that the single letter displayed a refinement that showed their superiority over those who used the whole title. Others may have felt just the opposite, a desire not to be ostentatious. Yet again, it may just have been an economy. In all probability all three motives were at work. Certainly someone with pretensions of grandeur must have commissioned the huge 'C' made by Smith and Gamble in Dublin in 1829/30 (see fig. 272) and the elaborate cast 'B' that J.S. Hunt made for a London client in 1849 (see fig. 262), but whether it was modesty or economy that led to the little gothic 'C' (one of a set made by C. Reily and G. Storer in 1831, see fig. 275) is hard to say. None of these examples can claim great artistic merit and this is a criticism that can be levelled at all single letters. They are not subjects that readily become labels of distinction, but it is nevertheless fair to say that some makers made the best out of a difficult task. Moreover, as an early article in the *Wine Label Circle Journal* points out, with twenty-six designs to choose from there is at least variety, and it is indeed the case that every letter of the alphabet has been made into a label.[34]

Penzer defines six variants on the single letter theme,[35] but here they are divided into just two classes. The first and earlier design is simply a label of standard shape, usually a rectangle, but occasionally an oval or button, with the single letter on the panel instead of the full wine name. The letter is usually an engraved or pierced Roman capital: gothic and script letters have been recorded and very occasionally the letter is embossed. The best known and apparently the earliest form of this type is the so-called 'Postage Stamp', introduced by T. Phipps and E. Robinson in the late 1790s (see fig. 268, 'W', 1797). Another early example is a narrow rectangle with pronounced cut corners, a set of three labels for 'B', 'G' and 'R' by Peter, Ann and William Bateman, dated 1802 (see fig. 274 for 'G'). The Phipps family partnerships went on to develop the postage stamp design further as the nineteenth century advanced. They gave it a plain bevelled edge instead of a reeded border, and an applied floral border to suit Regency tastes. Several of their contemporaries took up the design, including John Rich, Elizabeth Morley, John Atkins, Charles Rawlings and John Whittingham. John Egan (Dublin) used it in 1812, and Peter Grierson (Glasgow) devised a version in 1818. The heavy

Shapes and Designs

Figures 259-276.

cast cartouche containing a letter 'P', made by T. and J. Phipps (see fig. 264, 1818) shows Regency exuberance at its height. Also from Glasgow is a possibly unique set of six large rectangular labels made by Robert Gray and Sons in 1828 (see fig. 263, 'S'), which have letters, formed as lengths of rope, embossed on a matted background. Fig. 273 shows a button-shaped label by Charles Rawlings, pierced for 'M', a variant of the usual rectangle, made in 1827.

Outside London, English provincial assay offices showed little interest in this style of label. In Newcastle, the Reid family partnerships produced some sturdy examples, and a few have been seen by Exeter makers. Surprisingly there are very few from Birmingham and none from Sheffield, Chester or York. In Edinburgh it was not until the second basic form of single letter – the cut out or 'silhouette' – made its appearance, that the silversmiths of that city took up the concept.

This new concept first appears (with one exception, discussed below) towards the end of the second decade of the nineteenth century. The letter becomes the whole label, sometimes cast, sometimes cut from sheet and sometimes stamped. It can be entirely plain, as the Roman capital 'M' by C. Rawlings and W. Summers (see fig. 266, 1852), it can be engraved on the face or, as is the cast letter 'C' made by Paul Storr in 1827 (see fig. 271), decorated in relief with scrolls and flowerheads. A particularly strong demand arose in Edinburgh, where J. McKay, G. McHattie, W. and P. Cunningham and others produced large numbers of heavily engraved and relief-decorated versions from the early 1820s onwards. Strangely, they do not occur in other Scottish cities, except Glasgow. Illustrated at fig. 277 is Marshall and Sons' of Edinburgh profusely chased Celtic type decorated with a single letter 'R' of *c.*1845. The letter rests on crouching beasts!

Script lettering gave a little more scope for artistry than did Roman capitals, as Peter Aitken's single 'W' (see fig. 270, Glasgow, 1820) shows. Gothic letters were adopted during the 1830s as the influence of (for example) Pugin spread to domestic articles. A gothic 'H' marked for James Barber of York (see Chapter 7, Part 5) is a London design of Emes and Barnard.

Two London firms in particular specialised in single cut-out letters: Charles Rawlings and William Summers, and Charles Reily and George Storer. For twenty-five years from 1829, when both firms started, they produced a large variety of designs, ranging from plain Roman capitals to quaintly embellished pieces, such as Punch and his dog Toby on a pair for 'P' and 'S' (see fig. 281 for 'P'), made by C. Rawlings and W. Summers in 1845 (see also fig. 265). C. Reily and G. Storer combined the new cut-out with a fine armorial in their plain 'S' surmounted by the crest of an eagle holding a lance above a ducal crown (see fig. 234, 1829). Actually the credit for the earliest recorded single letter cut-out must go to Birmingham, from where the earlier style of single letter label is hardly known. In 1820, Joseph Willmore created a design (see fig. 276, 'H') that has the head of Dionysus in relief among flowerheads and acanthus leaves (see Part 10 below on Bacchic Revellers).

In the 1860s the cut-out took a further step as makers brought single letters together to form the whole name again, thus coming full circle to the original form of title. Penzer notes six methods of performing the operation, but they are all variations of the same principle.[36] R. Garrard's cast cartouche for CLARET (see fig. 261, 1861) shows one way of doing it, while H.W. Dee used a rope to string the letters together (see fig. 259, MADEIRA, 1864). In 1871 W. Summers, surviving partner of the Rawlings and Summers partnership, produced a long set of cut-out names with letters held together by bars (see fig. 260, CAPRI). At least eight other names are recorded, ranging from GIN to FALERNO. Two exceptions to the 1860s or later dating for the cut-out word design must be noted. A label for CLARET, with the letters held in a double frame, by Hampston, Prince and Cattles of York, is shown in Chapter 5, Part 7. It appears to be a 'one-off' piece, and its date of *c.*1804 is some fifteen years earlier than the next known example of this technique. A thin, plain rectangular label for BURGUNDY, which has the Roman capital letters attached to the upper and lower sides of a slot in the panel, was made by an unidentified, probably Scottish, maker 'HF', in all probability in *c.*1830. Throughout England a very large number of cut-out word labels were made during the latter years of the nineteenth century. They were sometimes of silver (unmarked), but more often were plated or electro-formed. They usually employ script or italic letters, which are easier to hold together, and none can be said to be of great artistic significance.

Shapes and Designs

Figure 277.

As has been stated earlier, every letter of the alphabet has been recorded as a label. The initials of the commoner wines and spirits are, as might be expected, the most plentiful, and are, indeed, the only ones found on the first type, where the letter is engraved or pierced on a standard shape. The usual letters are those for spirits: 'B', 'G', 'H', 'R' and 'W', together with 'C' (CLARET), 'M', 'P' and 'S'. With the advent of the cut-out label, all the other letters of the alphabet arrive, though it is hard to speculate what practical use some of them could have been put to ('J', for instance, to say nothing of 'Q', 'X' or 'Z'). It has been suggested that clients might have been encouraged to acquire a complete set, simply as something to collect and put on show, rather than for actual use on a decanter.

Finally, mention must be made of a set of three cut-out letters that do not fit into the chronology outlined above, but which are among the most attractive designs known, and may indeed be the earliest recorded. The set consists of 'B', 'G' and 'R' in elaborate script lettering (see fig. 267, 'B', c.1786-91). They have the mark of T. Phipps and E. Robinson (1783-1810), accompanied by the lion passant and King's head cameo duty mark, in use after May 1786. The front of the label has a simple acanthus leaf and dot decoration; the back is plain. They are not moulded into their form, or wire-drawn, but cut from a thin sheet, and they certainly belie the observation made above that single letter labels lack artistic merit. They have no date letter, because they pre-date 1791 when full hall-marking for labels became compulsory, and there is certainly space for one alongside the other marks, if the makers had wished to include it. The marks are consistent with those that the partnership was using on other articles between 1786 and 1791 on other articles. So it seems reasonable to date these labels accordingly. This, however, does put them six to eleven years earlier than the next single letters, the postage stamps produced by the same firm in the late 1790s, and, of course, before any other known cut-out letters. Even if, for some reason, a date letter was deliberately omitted, they still cannot be later than 1810, when the Phipps and Robinson partnership ended, and that is still several years before the design is seen again. Furthermore, the pair were meticulous in obeying the hallmarking regulations and one is left to conclude that there is no good reason for supposing that the labels do not indeed date from 1786-1791 and that the design was then, for some unexplained reason, dropped. They were time-consuming and expensive objects to make, and fragile, too. Perhaps they were a special order, and when the concept next came up, engraving the letter on a small rectangle – the postage stamp – would have seemed more economical.

To end this section, attention can be drawn to the extremes of size that single letters reached. The huge 'C' of Smith and Gamble (see fig. 272) is 7cm (2¾in.) high. The crest is that of several Irish families, but which one commissioned the label is not known. A tiny unmarked label for 'S' (see fig. 269) measures only 1.5 x 1cm (⅝ x ⅜in.), and was not for a wine but intended for a soy sauce.[37]

Shapes and Designs

Figures 278-280.

PART 10 – BACCHIC REVELLERS

When a desire to demonstrate opulence and taste became as important a feature of the wine label as that of simply indicating what was in the decanter, scenes such as are found on this class of label were an obvious source for designers to draw upon. 'Bacchic Revellers' include humans and semi-humans – boys, 'putti', cherubs, satyrs – and deities in whatever form they manifested themselves (see for examples fig. 285 for CLARET or fig. 286 for PORT, both unmarked). The archetypal label has two naked boys, one holding a goblet and a flask, the other a basket of grapes, supporting a scroll-shaped name panel in a cartouche of grapes and vine leaves. Beneath the name panel is a bearded face. It is, with the escutcheon,[38] the earliest shape of label to be noted or, at any rate, to have survived. Some are known bearing the first mark of Sandylands Drinkwater, which he entered in 1735, together with the lion passant in use between 1729 and 1739. They can therefore be dated after 1735 and before 1738 when Drinkwater entered his second mark (see fig. 278 for PUNCH). The design was also used by his contemporary, John Harvey, from about 1738, and both men continued with it throughout their careers. It was taken up by other makers, and there is, indeed, evidence of its popularity throughout the remainder of the eighteenth century and well into the first half of the nineteenth. It was copied by Isaac Cookson in Newcastle (*c*.1747), but not elsewhere in England until later. The Phipps and Robinson partnerships developed the design, making the boys taller and more upright. Their labels are cast, as were those of other eighteenth-century workshops, but when Birmingham (J. Willmore) and Sheffield (R. Gainsford and W. Tucker) took up the design in the first decade of the next century, dies were used, producing some elegantly crisp examples (see fig. 279 for SHERRY), but also during this period, it has to be said, some less

Figures 281-283.

Shapes and Designs

Figures 284-286.

distinguished work. It spread to Ireland (J. Teare) in the early 1800s, and to Scotland (G. McHattie and J. Macdonald) ten years later. As befits one of the earliest shapes, and one of the most long lasting, it was one of the first to be described in all its styles and varieties in the *Wine Label Journal*.[39]

The origin of the design is obscure, though boys as cupbearers date back to classical times. They are depicted performing this service on the walls of a villa at Pompeii, and on numerous Etruscan and Greek vases. The cupbearer to the gods on Olympus was the youth Ganymede. It is not surprising, therefore, that he came to be incorporated into the wine label in classically-minded eighteenth-century England. Penzer describes the boys as Cupids, but this they cannot be. There was only one Cupid, the Roman god of love, winged and armed with bow and arrow, and not linked in any way with wine, other than for its notorious assistance to amorous pursuit. Nor can they be cherubs, as was once asserted. Cherubs are essentially biblical creatures. Originally winged guardians of the Tabernacle, they became transformed into human figures during the sixteenth century, when the term came to be applied to a child with wings, or sometimes just a child's face. Although the figures on these labels are neither of these, unexpectedly both Cupid and cherubs do appear elsewhere (see below). Our figures are just boys, or 'putti', to adopt the Italian word used to describe them in classical art.

The bearded head below the scroll has been variously ascribed to Dionysus, Pan, Silenus and a satyr. The first is most likely. Pan should have a goat's ears and horns, and some labels are claimed to show these features, but neither he nor his cult are particularly associated with wine. Silenus was old, pot-bellied and ugly; he did, indeed, teach Dionysus the art of viticulture, but that does not seem sufficient to account for his appearance on wine labels. The satyrs were wild men who

Figures 287-288.

Shapes and Designs

Figures 290-292.

accompanied Dionysus and Silenus on their travels. Dionysus himself fits the picture much better. The offspring of Zeus and Semele, he had his origins in Phrygia or Thrace, whence his cult spread to Greece and later to Rome. Dionysian orgies involved much drinking and he became to all intents the god of wine. To the Romans he was Bacchus and, from being a bearded rather dissolute figure, he became a handsome youth. For both of them the mode of transport was a chariot drawn by panthers, and Dionysus is found in his Greek form, reclining in one, with a putto offering him a cup of wine, on a label by T. Phipps, E. Robinson and J. Phipps of 1809 (see fig. 280 for CLARET). This design is interesting, because it is clearly taken from a much earlier Irish version attributed to Stephen Walsh,[40] which has been shown to have Dublin marks for 1747/48. It might be thought unusual for such a design to have originated in Ireland, and strange, too, that no other example has come to light from intervening years. Perhaps there was an English prototype, which has disappeared.[41] There was indeed an English prototype of the boy advancing behind a scroll panel, made by John Harvey around 1746, which was also made in Ireland by Stephen Walsh in around 1750. In Edinburgh, G. McHattie used the reclining Dionysus design in *c.*1820, and adapted it a few years later as an award for the Caledonian Horticultural Society presented for 'Excellent CURRANT WINE'. It was also used by John Reily in 1809, Daniel Hockley in 1816, Charles Rawlings in 1821 and Sebastian Crespel II in 1826.

Labels featuring a single putto are found almost as early. In John Harvey's version, mentioned above, the boy holds the usual goblet and flask, and is shown advancing behind the scroll panel. An Irish example, dating from around 1750, by Stephen Walsh,[42] and a set by Edmund Medlycott, *c.*1755, are known (of which BURGUNDY is illustrated in fig. 293). A century later, it was taken

Figures 293-295.

Figure 296.

Figure 297.

up by E. Farrell. Another intriguing label of this class for CLARET has a distinctly somnolent child lying behind the panel, clutching it with one hand and holding a bunch of grapes with the other. The label is unmarked, but can be dated *c*.1760 (see fig. 294).

In a design of 1823 the inappropriately named London silversmith Abstainando King portrays a rather small putto supporting a rather large panel, and adds an amusing touch with a panther's head peering round one end of the panel, and its tail hanging out at the other end. Penzer illustrates[43] similar style labels for CORTON and PIERRY. Digby Scott and Benjamin Smith made a cast cartouche-shaped SHERRY label in 1804 (see fig. 283) that has a large face as its most prominent feature. It is wreathed with leaves, and so may be intended as the Roman Bacchus, since putti are usually bare-headed or crowned with curly locks of hair. Another version is that of S. Mordan and Co. in 1839, see fig. 284 for HOCK, in which three putti are sitting or leaning on the panel and two more are holding it up.

In all the designs described so far, whether cast or die-stamped, the face or figure has been moulded to give depth, but in the only label embodying putti from the Bateman family workshop, he is engraved. The partnership of Peter, Ann and William has a design of 1799 that shows the boy, visible to the waist, holding a swag in front of himself, containing the name (see fig. 295 for BRANDY).

A swag for the name also appears on a plated label illustrated by Penzer[44] shown in his figure 8. The label is peculiar because the figure holding the swag, a winged boy, is undoubtedly a cherub. Cherubs, as was noted above, have no real association with wine. So, although the subject makes for an attractive label, it can only be described as a case of mistaken identity. Penzer also illustrates a label with two winged cherubs holding up festooned drapery for SHERRY.

It was stated earlier that Cupid, like the cherub, does also appear on wine labels, despite having no connection with the grape. The reclining youth, winged and armed with bow and arrow, who lies at the top of a very fine design by George Pearson in 1821 (see figs. 209 and 287), can only be him, but the reason for him being there is not clear. The face below the panel is not a typical putto, but a more adult youth and, as in the Scott and Smith label (see fig. 283), is crowned with leaves, so perhaps again the Roman Bacchus is intended.

Dionysus appears again as a bearded face or mask on a series of single letters produced by J. Willmore in Birmingham in the second and third decades of the nineteenth century (see fig. 288 for 'M' in 1830). He is placed against a background of acanthus leaves, and sometimes there is a putto as well. Eleven letters have been recorded – B, C, G, H, M, P, R, S, T, V and W.[45]

It may be questioned whether the winged female bust, originally introduced by Charles Rawlings, which surmounts W. Summers' later label of 1878 (see fig. 282 for CLARET), is either truly Bacchic or a reveller, but she deserves to be mentioned. Sometimes, for obvious reasons, she has been called Lady Bountiful, but actually there is no knowing who she is meant to be. She has a double pair of wings, which are veined, and her inordinately long arms are stretched out over the name panel, but do not hold it. Below is a panther's head. The label is found in two sizes; the one shown here is the larger one.

Shapes and Designs

The Boy or Girl on the Barrel (see fig. 290) originated as a label in Dublin between 1773 and 1786.[46] The theme is a familiar one as an 'inn' sign outside German wine *stuben*. J. Teare and G. Nangle both have labels in which a large barrel is the main feature, with the boy sitting astride it. The example illustrated here (see fig. 292) is a less distinguished version, die-stamped for GIN, by W. Troby (1824). The tubby infant on his diminutive cask is almost swamped by the surrounding matted vine leaves and grapes (see also Part 11 below on Barrels).

Some other revellers are the five Dutchmen depicted by E. Farrell using a design of the Dutch artist W. Teniers, who take up various attitudes around the name panel, drinking, smoking, and certainly enjoying themselves (see fig. 291 for SHERRY). A set of four of these labels is recorded, dated 1817.

Bacchus peers over bunches of grapes surrounding a PORT label (see fig. 296) made by Robert Garrard II in London in 1854 which is fully marked on its face.

Item 270 in the Royal Inventory of 1914 reads as follows: 'Forty-six Large Wine Labels, with richly chased Bacchanalian Devices, and Head of Jupita Ammon', who had a bearded ram's-horned head.[47] Forty-five of these were made by Paul Storr in 1809-10. One for RED BURGUNDY is shown at fig. 386.[48] The forty-sixth label was made by Philip Rundell in 1821.[49] There are also fifty-five labels depicting the head of a Bacchante (see below, Part 21, Labels from Royal Palaces).

Last of all, to bring the tradition of revellers into the twentieth century, is the gentleman seated at his table, laden with fish, fowl and drink (see fig. 297). This label was commissioned in 1973 by the International Food and Wine Society from M.W. Druitt to commemorate their anniversary. It is copied from a label of the second quarter of the nineteenth century that has Belgian hallmarks (see below under Belgium, fig. 1308).

If the figures that feature on these labels over two and a half centuries from 1735 are looked at as a whole, they can be said to move from the mythological to the vaguely indeterminate classical, and, from the middle of the nineteenth century, to the simply representational. In the eighteenth century the classes commissioning wine labels understood classical allusions as a matter of course, and so indeed did the label designers. In the nineteenth century this was no longer really the case, and strict accuracy may have seemed less important. If a winged Cupid looked more attractive than a bearded Dionysus, then that is how the label turned out, and if the artist crowned his putto with leaves, the embellishment did not necessarily turn him into a god. It is perhaps better not to try to analyse the details too critically, but to concentrate on a label's quality and its effectiveness for its main purpose, which is to add delight to the contents of the decanter. In this respect revellers, as a class, succeed as no other design of label has ever done.

PART 11 – BARRELS

This would appear to be an exceptionally rare shape. One of the earliest recorded examples is by Richard Richardson of Chester and dates from around 1765. This label is 5cm (2in.) high and has the name PORT. The design differs from that shown at fig. 298 for MADEIRA by Susanna Barker; it is formed as a typical cask for port, with realistic staves and hoops.

The silver example by Susanna Barker is fully marked and dated 1792. It is from a large set as other examples have been recorded with other names.

The shape appears in a different design, with the barrel lying flat rather than upright, incised for TERRANTEZ. It was made in 1826 by Emilio Critien, a Maltese silversmith. It appears to have been a single label and is shown in fig. 299.

A barrel lying on its side with surrounding vines and tendrils was made in 1805 by Peter, Ann and William Bateman.[50] It bears the title of PORT (see fig. 303). Though in silver this shape is uncommon, there exist many examples of a variation made in electroplate in which the barrel is surrounded by fruiting vines. An example is shown in fig. 300 for GIN, the reverse of which bears the Patent Office Design Registry mark for May 1867.

There appear to be at least two variations on this theme in which the design has been laboriously

Shapes and Designs

Figures 298-306.

cut out and worked by hand out of sheet nickel. The base metal was then electroplated with pure silver by means of the method patented by G.R. Elkington and his cousin Henry in 1840. An electroplated upright barrel with fruiting vine for BRANDY has on it the design registration mark (a diamond) for 19 May 1866 (see fig. 301).[51]

A plated sideways barrel surmounted by a sign for WHISKEY is illustrated, fig. 302,[52] and its companion PORT (see fig. 1208) is discussed below (see Chapter 8, Part 6, Electroplate).

The Irish examples of a boy or girl sitting astride a barrel above eye-shaped labels abound. Those for CLARET and SHERRY by Benjamin Taitt, for CLARET by William Law *c.*1796 (see fig. 911), for SHERRY by George Nangle *c.*1790 (see fig. 912), for PORT by J. Teare *c.*1800 and for CLARET by John Osborne[53] are discussed elsewhere.[54] Illustrated are a MADEIRA (see fig. 304) and CLARET (see fig. 306) and a sketch for SHERRY (see fig. 305).

A twentieth-century barrel by J.F. Kikkert of Amsterdam (1906-23) is shown at fig. 1368 in Chapter 9, Part 13, The Netherlands.

79

Shapes and Designs

PART 12 – ANCHORS

Anchors, both proper and 'foul', occur occasionally as family crests, and are to be found engraved on labels of many types that embody plaques or shields, but anchors that stand alone as labels in their own right are scarce. The foul anchor has been the traditional emblem of the Board of Admiralty since the beginning of the seventeenth century and in all likelihood dates from much earlier. It is still in use today and it appears on naval buttons and cap badges. It was therefore a totally appropriate device for naval officers to turn into a wine label, and functional, too, as the stock provided a suitable panel on which to put the name of the wine.

Correctly the stock of an anchor is fixed on the shank perpendicular to the line of the arms, and the flukes lie at right angles across the ends of the arms, so that the anchor will hold securely in the ground, but the badge, intended for display on an ensign or letterhead, has them all in the same plane, for obvious practical reasons, and wine labels follow suit. The anchor is 'foul' when it has a length of cable (cordage) wound from the ring around the stock, shank and arms.

The majority of anchor labels are not of top quality workmanship, perhaps implying manufacture by local craftsmen. Virtually all are unmarked, and their origins are therefore unknown, but most of them appear to date from the last part of the eighteenth century, judging by the type of anchor they portray. A rather far-fetched suggestion has been put forward that their often rough finish is because they were made by silversmiths who had been press-ganged into the Navy, though there is absolutely no evidence to support this theory. Indeed it is confuted by a well-documented entry to be found in the Wakelin Ledgers (q.v.)[55] in September 1774, for 'ten anchor bottle tickets with plaited wire for cable' commissioned for Admiral Sir Hugh Palliser, at that time Controller of the Navy (Third Sea Lord, in charge of ship construction and supplies). The label shown at fig. 307, unmarked for SHERRY, could be one of this set. Unfortunately the ledger does not give the name of the workman who made the labels.

Figure 307.

Figure 308.

Figures 309-311.

A handsome, well-made label, illustrated at fig. 308 (MADEIRA), has the mark of T. Phipps and E. Robinson and the date of 1799.[56] It is notable for the stock lying acockbill (i.e. aslant across the shank), and this happens to be a feature, likewise, of the only other recorded marked example, an anchor of a different shape by Edward Jay, dated 1793. Flukes, arms and stock are to be found in several shapes, and the braided wire, which represents the cable, varies too. The Phipps and Robinson version differs in having the 'foul' cable cut from the same sheet of metal as the body of the anchor, instead of being a separate length attached to it. The label chain is unusual in that it consists of links of studless chain cable, which is led to two eyes at the ends of the stock instead of to the anchor ring, something that would obviously be impossible in practice. Cables formed of forged iron links were only just being introduced to replace hemp cordage as anchor chains at this date, so finding it as part of a wine label of 1799 is strange indeed. Jay's label of six years earlier has a conventional label chain suspension led to the anchor ring.

The design did not survive into the nineteenth century, or perhaps not long after the Napoleonic Wars ended. A set of eight smallish examples may date from this period, while two later labels have been seen with the initials 'WS' and the date 1883 on them, which may be Scottish but are of doubtful provenance. In the present century, the well-known silversmith Alison Richards was invited in 1973 to make a set of labels (see figs. 309-311) formed as anchors which were the family's crest.[57] Unfortunately they were later stolen and trace of them has been lost.

This scarcity of such an obvious maritime artefact might seem strange for an allegedly maritime nation. Sailors do, of course, like their drink, but it should be remembered that they were never well-off, even when prize money was plentiful, nor, as a profession, have they been in the habit of ostentatiously displaying such wealth as they had.

Shapes and Designs

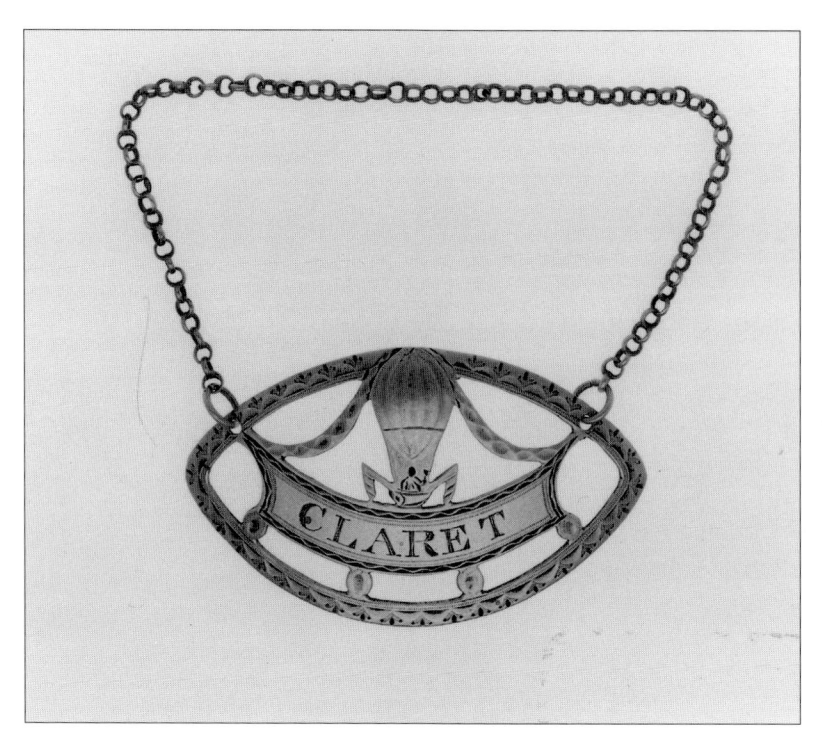

Figure 312.

PART 13 – THE BALLOON LABEL

Only one example of this design is recorded (see fig. 312), made by Benjamin Taitt, for CLARET. He registered his mark in Dublin in 1784, as required by the Act of the previous year, and made this label a year later.[58] It appears to commemorate the first ascent of a balloon in Ireland. The balloonist was a Mr Crosbie, and he took off from the Ranelagh Gardens in Dublin on 19 January 1785. The representation of the navigator in the basket holding two flags, and the striped pattern material of the balloon, is similar to an engraving published at the time showing Crosbie's ascent from the grounds of the Duke of Leinster's house in Dublin in July 1785 in a vain attempt to cross the Irish Sea. The enormous size of the crowds that assembled to witness the event was no less a rare phenomenon for those times than the remarkable flight itself. A rival to Crosbie, one James Dinwiddie, had planned a balloon ascent over Belfast, also in July 1785, timing it to coincide with the week of Belfast's Volunteers Review when much larger crowds would have gathered from across the province than would usually have been expected in Dublin. In the event the ascent was not made. Six months later Richard Crosbie went up again, attempting to cross St George's Channel to England, but his balloon fell into the sea.

The label consists of an eye-shaped frame,[59] not unlike the design developed by James Sherwin a few years later, in which the balloon sits with a festoon of rigging securing it to the curved rectangular name panel. The balloonist is in a basket below the balloon, waving the two flags, while the name panel is attached to the frame by four globules that may be intended to represent bags of ballast for the balloonist to jettison if the need arose.[60]

The first manned ascent was by J-F.P. de Rozier in an anchored Montgolfier hot-air balloon on 15 October 1783. The first free manned flight was by de Rozier with a passenger on 21 November 1783 and lasted twenty-five minutes. The ornate balloon was 70 feet high and 43 feet wide. The first solo flight was by Professor Charles in a smaller hydrogen balloon on 1 December 1783, and before Crosbie's flight in 1785 four flights were undertaken in 1784, including Paolo Andreani's from Milan in February, Vincenzo Lunardi's from Moorfields in London in September and James Sadler's from Birmingham in October of that year.

Figures 313-315.

PART 14 – BUGLES

The correct name for a bugle, as it is represented in the form of a wine label, is bugle-horn. 'Bugle' was a mediaeval word for a buffalo or wild ox, from whose horns hunting horns (bugle horns) were once made. It has long been the emblem of Light Infantry regiments, which, tradition has it, were originally recruited from hunters and foresters. St Hubert is their patron saint, and he had a bugle horn as his ecclesiastical crest. The officers of Light Infantry regiments may, indeed therefore, have commissioned wine labels for their messes in the form of their regimental emblem, but it might be expected that if they did, the labels would have some specific wording on them to indicate the military association.

An alternative origin is to be found in the Archery Societies that were springing up all over the country in the latter part of the eighteenth century. There had been such bodies for centuries before then, from the time when the country's security depended on having men well trained in drawing a longbow. The prizes awarded for archery contests in the eighteenth century included badges of bugles. Toxophily was not the only pursuit of such societies, however; they were also social affairs, with dances and dinners at which wine flowed. The bugle horn was an obvious device to turn into a wine label for their decanters.

The bugle horn, as developed into a musical instrument for military bands, was more like a trumpet, with a straight tube. As an instrument for passing orders to soldiers in the field it was given a more practical shape by bending the tube back on itself, making it shorter, and easier to carry. In this form it has not been seen on a wine label; the labels illustrated here all date from the nineteenth century and are clearly bugle horns of the old traditional shape. They are likely to have been made for Archery Societies.

Fig. 313, for SHERRY, is one of a pair with PORT, cast, and marked with the Victoria duty mark and mid-nineteenth century Edinburgh thistle town mark of *c*.1860. There is no maker's mark. Their date is probably *c*.1860.[61] Fig. 314 for MADEIRA is one of a set with PORT and WHISKEY by George Unite with Birmingham marks for 1857.[62] Fig. 315 for RUM is by T. Wallis with London marks for 1802, and is the earliest known bugle.

Shapes and Designs

Figures 316-318.

PART 15 – CROWNS

This shape, examples of which are shown in figs. 316-318, is known as a crown, although it is actually based on the strawberry leaves and balls of a marquis's coronet, and should really be described as a 'ducal' or crested coronet, which is not indicative of rank.[63] It is a rare shape, first made by Alexander Kelty (see fig. 316 for MADEIRA, a pair with PORT) between 1803 and 1811 in Newcastle. Kelty arrived there from London in 1802 and retired in 1812. Copies were made in London later by Thomas Edwards (see fig. 317, SHERRY, 1824, a pair with CLARET) and E. Edwards II (see fig. 318, RUM, 1831).[64]

Crowns and coronets are often incorporated into a design. A design consisting of a viscount's coronet on an octagonal shield above a large single capital letter (see fig. 319) was made by Smith and Gamble in Dublin in 1829.[65] The single letters concerned are 'B', 'S', 'L' and one other. Rawlings and Summers around 1829 decorated their MADEIRA with an appropriate coronet (see fig. 320).

An electroplated CLARET (see fig. 1220) with its companion PORT display the Imperial Crown over laurel wreaths. It has been suggested that these labels were intended to mark Queen Victoria's 1887 Golden Jubilee (see below, Chapter 8, Part 6, Electroplate).

The Swedish crown appears over the title DISTILLED BRANDY (or in Swedish DISTILERADT BRANVIN), an aquavit produced by E. Sathersten (see fig. 1229 below, Chapter 8, Part 6, Electroplate).

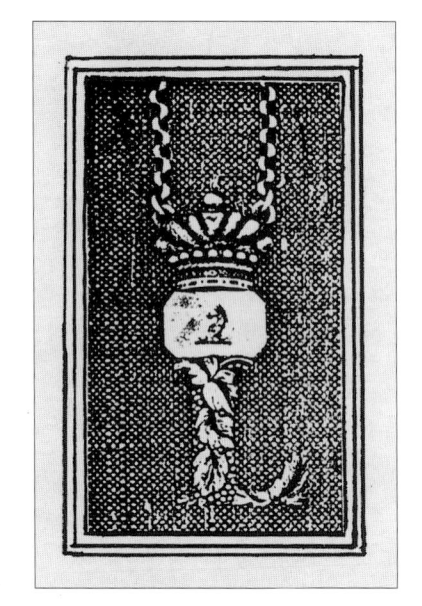

Figure 319.

Figure 320.

84

Shapes and Designs

PART 16 – HARPS

A very rare design of which only four examples may exist consists of an 'Irish' harp surmounting a scroll bearing the name of the wine (see fig. 321). Three are by James Phipps I, with his second mark, entered in 1772 (see fig. 321a) and in use until he retired in around July 1783. The fourth is by Benjamin Taitt, whose Dublin mark was registered in 1784, but he may well have been in business before that (see fig. 322). On the reverse of the labels is the inscription (see fig. 321a) in script letters 'It's New Strung And WILL be Heard'. They clearly have an Irish association and were presumably made to special order.

The three Phipps labels are for SHERRY, WHITE WINE and PORT. These labels are almost identical to the Taitt MADEIRA example, except that there is a very slight variation in the way that the decorated borders are executed.

This slogan and harp symbol is very similar to the insignia adopted on the proposal of Dr William Drennan at the foundation meeting of the Society of United Irishmen in Dublin in October 1791. However, a date some years prior to 1791 for this label is indicated by the existence of these identical but earlier examples bearing the mark of this London maker, James Phipps the elder, 1772-83. We do not know when Drennan's slogan was coined[66] but that the sense of it was in circulation at least as early as 1785 is indicated by a reference to 'new strings to the Irish Harp' in Drennan's widely read *Letters of Orellana, an Irish Helot* first published in the *Belfast Newsletter* in 1785 and later that year in Dublin as a Volunteer pamphlet. The labels were obviously intended to lend colour to political discussion at the dinner table and were more than likely commissioned by a wealthy Hibernian patriot enjoying residences in both England and Ireland. Thus the sense of it was known amongst the United Volunteer Movement in the 1780s, struggling to restore authority to the Irish Parliament, which had been restricted by Poynings' Law in the time of Henry VII. The slogan was adopted by the Society of United Irishmen whose intention was to unite Catholics and Protestants through the ideals of the French Revolution in 1791, but, as we have shown, the labels pre-date this organisation. Poynings' Law was repealed in 1782 and the Irish Parliament re-established in 1783.

The dating of these four labels has posed quite a conundrum. It has been suggested that the set of three labels was made in London not long after 1783 and that the fourth was made in Dublin to match them a few years later. The logical explanation is that the labels were commissioned to

Figures 321 and 321a.

Shapes and Designs

Figure 322.

commemorate the above-mentioned event, but whether the Irish label came first, and was copied in London, or vice versa, cannot be certain. Thus this label did not relate to the revolutionary Society of United Irishmen. History informs us that this movement was quelled a few years after the death of the founder, Theobald Wolfe Tone, in 1798, in which year he accompanied the French invasion of Ireland, was captured, was condemned to death and slit his own throat when in prison.

Much later, in 1897, the Worcestershire Regiment was presented with a set of labels formed from an Irish harp, which it had been granted as its regimental crest to commemorate active service in Ireland a hundred years earlier in 1748.[67]

In 1987 the Company of Goldsmiths of Dublin wished to commemorate the 350th anniversary of the granting to them of their royal charter by Charles I in 1657. They accordingly commissioned a wine label for the occasion in the form of a harp flanked by shamrocks.[68] The maker was Thomas Weir.

PART 17 – HEARTS

There was a short-lived vogue for labels shaped as hearts during the 1750s and 1760s. One by Sandylands Drinkwater for BURGUNDY (see fig. 324) has his second mark of 1739 (see fig. 325), flat chased with grapes and vine leaves. If it can be accepted that the design is an attempt to break away from the standard escutcheon, a date of between 1750 and 1755 can be reasonably suggested. There is a similar label in the Cropper Collection at the Victoria and Albert Museum.

Another heart for CLARET, unmarked,[69] is illustrated (see fig. 323). It is rather thin, with a decoration of incised grapes, and used to be in the Sachs Collection.

A slightly smaller version, plain with a feathered border, was made in a set of four by Thomas Hyde at about the same time and bears his first mark, 1747-c.70.

Another of the same shape has a single reeded border and the unidentified mark 'T:R', while a pair of rather larger entirely plain examples for LISBON and MOSELLE are by 'I R', also unidentified. Heart-shaped enamels, probably from Staffordshire, have also been recorded.

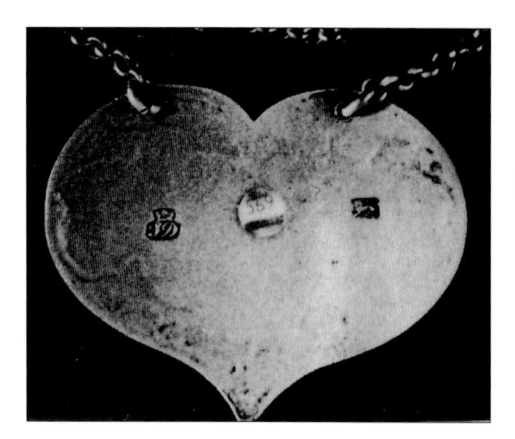

Figures 323-325.

Figure 326.  *Figure 327.*

PART 18 – GOBLETS

The neo-classical revival led to objects such as goblets and urns becoming natural sources of inspiration for makers of wine labels. Examples of the former, wide lipped with a short flat foot, start to appear in the late 1770s. Hester Bateman made small free-standing goblet shaped labels (see fig. 326, *c.*1781, for WHITE WINE and fig. 328 for BRANDY) and surrounded them with foliate swags, bows and wreaths (see figs. 329/670 for a version by John Rich).[70] Thomas Phipps and Edward Robinson devised a more stylised form and the Birmingham maker Joseph Taylor later brought out a simpler, but still effective version with a large shield above it. His LISBON of 1820 is illustrated in fig. 327. The design spread to Ireland where the Cork silversmith J. Carden, and his later partnership with Jane Williams, gave it an Irish touch.

Another variation of the swagged and bowed design has an urn, covered or uncovered, replacing the goblet, and providing a suitable space for a crest or its owner's initials. It is often found on crescent labels and proved to be an extremely popular design that lasted for many years.

Thus there were basically two types of goblet: the wide, flat-topped type with a short foot, and the narrow, upright oval type, which is sometimes called a 'lidded urn'. The first type can be found completely plain or with bright-cut borders, but its most common form is with a large bow and swags of foliate garlands above and a crescent of foliate garland below. This is a particularly pleasing design and one that was obviously a great commercial success in its day. The lidded urn is usually found on crescents, both upward and downward turned, with pierced cable festoons either side. This may have been the inspiration for John Sherwin's CLARET of around 1790, illustrated above in fig. 26, and for William Sloden's SHERRY, 1791, illustrated below in fig. 730.

Goblets also appear in OSP designs, see figs. 956, 958 and 975.

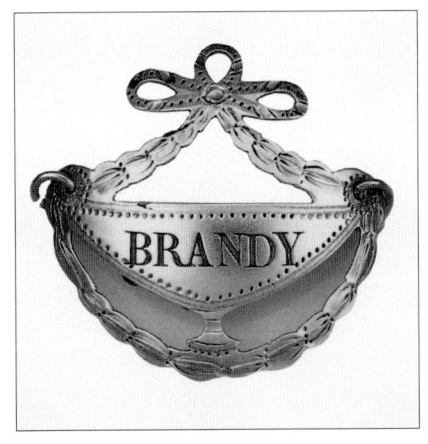

Figure 328.  *Figure 329.*

Shapes and Designs

Figures 330-332.

PART 19 – SHELLS

Wine labels formed as shells, and shells as part of the decorative motif on the borders of wine labels, started to appear during the first decade of the nineteenth century. No valid reason can be suggested for the attention that then began to be paid to this style of ornament, as shells have no identifiable association with wine in mythology or ancient history. Poseidon and Triton were depicted blowing conches, and shells featured in many types of rococo motif, but not on the wine labels of that period. Shells had no place in the general scheme of neo-classical design, as found on labels, but when reeded borders became common on simple rectangles, makers looked for a device to relieve their plainness and found it by placing scallop shells at the corners and mid-points of the sides (see fig. 335, TINTA, Phipps and Robinson; fig. 336, PORT, Emes and Barnard, 1813). At the same time leading goldsmiths, such as Paul Storr and Benjamin Smith II, produced single shell labels based on scallops, heavy cast labels that appealed to their Regency clientele (see fig. 331, WHITE HERMITAGE, B. Smith II, 1808), while Birmingham firms J. Taylor, J. Willmore, M. Linwood and others followed with die-stamped versions, usually smaller in size (see figs. 333 and 334, RUM and HOLLANDS, M. Linwood II, 1809, and fig. 332, PORT, M. Linwood II, 1811), as did some Irish makers, notably J. Teare II (see fig. 330, HOCK, c.1815).

The scallop was the type of shell that found most favour, but pectens were also popular. The former were manufactured in several sizes, ranging from Paul Storr's cast labels, 5.5cm (2¼in.) in diameter, down to sauce labels of half that size. The Edinburgh maker J. McKay produced a set of cast sauce labels that were 4.5cm (1¾in.) in diameter; these are unusually large for sauce labels.

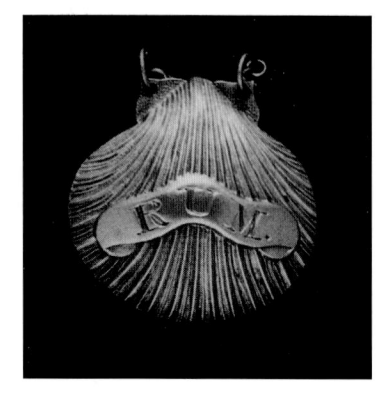

Figure 333. 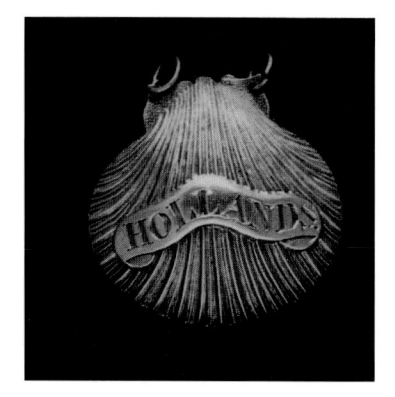   *Figure 334.*    *Figure 335.*

Shapes and Designs

Figure 336.

Figure 337.

Figure 338.

Pecten-shaped labels are usually by Irish or Birmingham makers, die-stamped and measuring 5cm (2in.) in diameter.

Regency designers of the 1810s and 1820s went on to incorporate shells into the already exuberant edges of their cartouche shapes, but the fashion for the whole shell did not last beyond the first quarter of the century. As part of the border of reeded, feathered and gadroon edged labels, shells persisted up to the middle of the century on London, provincial and Irish labels, and on a few Scottish provincial labels (William Hannay of Paisley, for instance, *c.*1820-30).

Scallop shells have been recorded with minor modifications to their natural shape to suit designers' individual requirements; pectens, however, always seem to adhere to their correct shape. The only other type of shell that has been seen as a label is the tridacna. Raphael Weed, the celebrated American collector, had two of different sizes, which came from a larger set made by J. Mortimer and J. Hunt in 1840.[71]

A famous set of 'Seventeen Shell Wine Labels', being No. 271 in the Royal Inventory of 1914, belongs to the Grand Service, which owed its inception and continued growth to the Prince Regent. Ten of these were made by Benjamin Smith in 1807, designed from the scallop shell, the name plate with a pierced title being soldered to the ribbed back of the shell, of which PORT and CHAMPAGNE are illustrated (see figs. 337 and 338).

PART 20 – VINE AND OTHER LEAVES AS LABELS

Vine leaves have always been an important motif for decorating wine labels, so it is not surprising that it was a vine leaf that first became a whole label. Labels modelled as vine leaves came into fashion in the early 1820s. Foremost among the silversmiths who introduced them was Charles Rawlings, working on his own until 1829, and then in partnership with William Summers (see fig. 339, INDIA MADEIRA, 1825). Another maker who was prominent in this field was Charles Reily, who adopted an asymmetrical version made by his father, John Reily, just before John's death in 1826. Charles produced vine leaf labels first in partnership with John's widow, Mary (see fig. 341, SHERRY, 1826), and then with George Storer (see below). A third firm to become interested was J. Cradock and W.K. Reid, and the latter produced the symmetrical design at fig. 340 (BUCELLAS, 1828) when he set up on his own.

Although *c.*1823 appears to mark the beginning of real popularity for this design, the first recorded date for a single leaf design may be 1818, in which year two sets of four silver-gilt labels are attributed to a John Baddeley, who entered his mark as a plateworker in that year. The mark was at one time attributed to John Bridge, who registered it in 1823, but may have been using it earlier. The leaves of one set are symmetrical, with no stalks, and have the name in embossed letters on a banner applied across the front of the label.[72] An identical but much later label for SHERRY in the Cropper Collection at the Victoria and Albert Museum is by R. Garrard II and is dated 1845.[73] The second set has asymmetrical leaves, similar to INDIA MADEIRA (above), but suspended so that the stem runs diagonally, as in G. McHattie's also much later label for SHERRY (see fig. 344,

89

Shapes and Designs

c.1830).[74] No other labels by Baddeley have been recorded, and the present whereabouts of these two sets are unknown.

Between 1818 and 1823 there was a gap, but single leaves then began to appear in large numbers. The great majority were stamped from dies, but Philip Rundell and Benjamin Smith III produced elegant cast symmetrical leaf labels (see fig. 342, BURGUNDY, B. Smith III, 1827). Other makers who took up the theme, basing their designs on those of the original three firms, were Thomas Edwards, William Ellerby, Thomas Holland and the Lias brothers. Their labels are usually smaller than those of the first manufacturers, perhaps in order to fit the decanter better. It is also interesting to note that all but one of them were entered as plateworkers, rather than small workers, as indeed were Cradock, Reid, Storer, Baddeley and, originally, Rawlings.

For the earliest use of vine leaves on labels we go back to their first days, as noted above, but, of course, long before they had been an obvious motif to apply to any artefact connected with the service of wine, from classical times onwards. On the first labels, engraved on escutcheons for instance, leaves are just part of the decoration, not the main theme, and so are outside the scope of this section.[75] Under neo-classical influence, the taste for objects such as vine leaves tended to disappear (but there remained a place for the acanthus leaf; note also Hester Bateman's laurel wreath design of the 1780s).[76] With the new century, natural themes revived and became exuberant in Regency times. The vine leaf re-emerged and played a more significant part in label design, until it eventually became, as we have seen above, the whole label.

Large leaf labels continued to enjoy popularity for some twenty-five years, a long time when other fashions were changing rapidly. Throughout this period Rawlings and Summers seem to have remained content with their asymmetrical leaf. Reily and Storer, however, the other London firm specialising in the leaf, ventured further, and introduced various combinations, using two and three leaves (see fig. 343, MADEIRA, 1831; fig. 347, CLARET, 1847; fig. 348, MADEIRA, 1849).

Outside London, Birmingham makers were quick to adopt the design, using die-stamping processes to turn out vine leaves in large quantities. Labels by Joseph Willmore II are recorded from 1825, and by the partnership of J. Taylor and J. Perry from a few years later (see fig. 345, MARSALA, J. Willmore, 1829). George Unite, the most prolific maker of them all, also started work at this time, with a design incorporating two leaves, and his workshop was still producing the same label (see fig. 346, RUM, 1843), in silver and gilded versions, in the mid-1860s. Further north, in Sheffield, R. Gainsford made a single-leaf label, based on a design of Rawlings and Summers and characterised by its own style of tooling of the surface. Vine leaves are not found in York or Chester, nor did they find favour in the West Country. The fashion did not spread to Scotland. A version by G. McHattie of c.1830 has been mentioned above, and the only other known Scottish example is a copy of Reid's symmetrical design in smaller size by A. Edmondson of Edinburgh, also c.1830. In Ireland a few asymmetrical leaves were made by R.W. Smith of Dublin (c.1830) and in partnership with J. Gamble (c.1835). The mark of Phineas Garde (Cork and Dublin) has also been recorded on a label of later date.

Further afield, vine leaf labels have been noted with the marks of firms working in Calcutta. One, by Hamilton and Co, is cast and dates from c.1830 (see fig. 355); another, larger and stamped, is by Pittar and Co., a little later.[77] Maltese craftsmen produced conventional vine leaves for their English clientele, and one design, a vine leaf of unusual shape, displayed horizontally across the tendril, which is unique to the island. They date from the mid-1820s to the mid-1840s.[78] A vine leaf with the title PORTWIJN by a Dutch maker has been seen, probably from the second half of the nineteenth century. No leaves have been recorded from Scandinavia or the Americas.

Apart from the vine, the leaf most often met with as a decorative motif is the acanthus. From classical times its shapely leaves have featured as an architectural adornment, and on all manner of Greek and Roman artefacts. Its use on labels is appropriate, but as it has not formed a whole label it is not discussed further here. So, too, the leaves of several other plants, shrubs and trees that have been incorporated into borders – sometimes recognisably, as for instance roses and beech, but more often stylised and unidentifiable – are dealt with elsewhere.

Shapes and Designs

Figures 339-346.

Shapes and Designs

Figures 347-352.

Shapes and Designs

Leaves that form part of heraldic crests and military badges are sometimes found in the labels that their owners or regiments commissioned. In one case, at least, the leaf is the whole label. The 22nd (Cheshire) Regiment of Foot, whose emblem was an acorn and oak leaf, had a set of oak leaf labels made for their officers' mess by Rawlings and Summers in 1855 (see fig. 351, SHERRY).[79] An earlier use of oak leaves as border can be seen in a massive label by John Reily.[80] A garland of bay leaves used to be placed on the head of 'Victor Ludorum' and Roman emperors demonstrated their godhood with a laurel wreath around their forehead. One of Hester Bateman's most effective designs, also produced by T. Phipps and E. Robinson, has elegant sprays of laurel flanking an oval containing its proud owner's crest above a banner.[81] Ivy, also, was used in ancient times to wreathe Bacchic brows. It has not been seen as a border motif, but a single cast ivy leaf label for CLARET was made by J.C. Edington in 1828 (see fig. 350). It is beautifully veined on the back as well as the front.[82] He was yet another plateworker, and had been apprenticed to W.K. Reid.

One other design requires special mention, the cast four-leaf clover made by Benjamin Smith II in 1807 (see fig. 349, SHERRY). The inspiration for the design is not known: it could be heraldic. It seems to stand apart from the general single leaf category and, indeed, claims to precede the vine leaf as the first single leaf. A cast four-leaf clover sauce label has been noted to match this decanter label. The claim of a fern leaf, which has also been seen, to be included in the single leaf category may have to be discarded for a different reason. It is unmarked and has the title MADEIRA in Roman capitals applied across the fronds along the stem. It would look very attractive without the name as a lady's brooch, and there is some evidence that it may have been converted from such a piece of jewellery.

As might be expected, plated labels formed as single leaves started to be produced very soon after their silver prototypes appeared, and electro-formed examples were made well into the second half of the nineteenth century. Designs were at first direct copies of the original versions, but as time passed they tended to become cruder and rather clumsy.

Names on leaf labels are usually pierced in a curve; where the letters run straight across, as on the late example for MANZANILLA by S. Smith (see fig. 352, 1875), the result is not so attractive. The titles to be found are usually for those wines and spirits that might be expected for the period, but MOKA on a single vine leaf by Reily and Storer of 1849 (see fig. 353) and MT on a single vine leaf by Nathaniel Mills of Birmingham in 1831 (see fig. 354) are hard to explain, while BEER on a plated middle of the century vine leaf seems inappropriate as well as very late in time. Single vine leaf sauce labels have been seen. Presumably the leaf matched similar labels on decanters, but had no relevance to the contents of the cruets.

Single leaves fell out of fashion, in London homes in the middle of the nineteenth century, but Birmingham makers continued to find customers for them for another ten years at least, until, in fact, the general demand for labels began to decline during the 1860s. That they remained in demand for so long may seem strange, as they were not an easy shape to manipulate, particularly in the large size in which they first appeared. Furthermore they cannot be considered as outstanding examples of label design. Size was, of course, a measure of the owner's importance and opulence, and this doubtless helped to retain their popularity, as did the paucity of imagination that was overtaking label design by then, and the lack of any shape more attractive. All in all these representations of *Vitis vinifera* and *Vitis sylvestris* can claim to have made a significant contribution to the world of wine labels.

Figure 353.

Figure 354.

Figure 355.

Shapes and Designs

PART 21 – ARMORIAL LABELS AND LABELS FROM ROYAL PALACES, UNIVERSITIES AND CORPORATE BODIES

In this section are described labels based on the heraldic devices found on coats of arms, those of individual families, corporate bodies, city livery companies and universities, and the labels that belong to the Crown in royal palaces.

Armorial labels

Families entitled to coats of arms have displayed them on their possessions, and particularly on their plate, for centuries, and so they put them on their wine labels as a matter of course when they came into existence. At a time when ostentatious exhibition of your wealth and standing was customary, the more visible the arms were the more important the owner must be. Usually it is the crest from the full coat of arms that is found on labels, cast, wrought or stamped, to form the whole label, but more often simply engraved above or below the name of the wine. They start to appear in the 1750s.

In the Cropper Collection at the Victoria and Albert Museum is a set of four labels by Sandylands Drinkwater, cast as a mailed arm embowed and holding an arrow (see fig. 479), which can be dated to around 1750.[83] Two more examples from early in the second half of the century are shown at fig. 356 (CHAMPAGNE, crest of Egerton, and CLARET, not illustrated but with cornet on top) and fig. 357 (OLD HOCK, crest of Agnew). All are unmarked, and presumably come from longer sets, commissioned to a special order, which would mean that not being 'set' (intended) for sale, they were not required to be marked.

Sir Walter Blount's set of cast suns in splendour, an armed foot within (see Part 7 of Chapter 2), c.1766, were likewise unmarked. Imposing labels such as these were primarily, of course, for the rich and powerful, but anyone who possessed arms could make a show of some sort just by having them engraved on a label of standard design. Sometimes they put them on the back of the label, though the reason has to be wondered at, unless it was to serve as some sort of security in the case of theft or loss. The designers of labels assisted the fashion by adding plaques and shields to labels on which to accommodate the emblems.

It is often now difficult to establish for whom the label was originally made, because the crest may be common to a number of families and, unless it has an identifying feature, or perhaps a motto, or the date of the label provides a clue, there is no way of being sure which branch of a family, or which of several different families, it belonged to. A few examples will serve to show the pattern: BURGUNDY, by R. Barker, 1793, possibly arms of Campbell of Lochiel (see fig. 371); SHERRY, by C. Rawlings and W. Summers, 1829, possibly arms of Andrews or Fane (see fig. 372); and LISBON, by I. and H. Lias, 1847, possibly arms of Bertram (see fig. 375).

More common than abstract heraldic devices are the animals that families have adopted as their crests and turned into a label. Stags predominate (see fig. 380 for SHERRY by J. Garrard, 1841) together with lions in various poses, while cats, dogs, wolves, bears and even an elephant are also known. An elephant was manufactured by E. Farrell in 1819 for an untraced destination. Some others are illustrated here (see fig. 359, MADEIRA, a Talbot proper, C. Rawlings and W. Summers, 1833, arms of Talbot of Malahide; fig. 360, PORT, a lion rampant, M. and C. Reily, 1826, arms untraced; fig. 361, WHISKEY (and also HOLLANDS and MADEIRA), a fox sejant, C. Rawlings and W. Summers, c.1845, arms of Holland; fig. 362, BEER (and also LISBON), a lion passant, unmarked, c.1769, arms untraced). A dolphin has emerged from the sea to lodge within the arms of a crescent for LISBON in 1799 by Phipps and Robinson (see fig. 383),[84] but of all species that have been turned into labels birds have been the commonest. Eagles, falcons, hawks, owls,[85] swans, a peacock (for CLARET, 1796, by P. and A. Bateman, see fig. 381) and an ostrich are some that have been recorded (see fig. 364, a demi-eagle, R. Emes and E. Barnard, 1852, arms of Vansittart; fig. 367, PORT, an ostrich proper, C. Rawlings and W. Summers, 1856, following an earlier version of 1840 for SHERRY, see fig. 382, by the same makers, arms of Coke, Earl of Leicester).

Whether a sphinx counts as an animal can be argued, but even if it, or she, is only a myth, there

Shapes and Designs

Figures 356-367.

95

Shapes and Designs

Figures 368-369.

Figure 370.

are certainly labels made in its likeness. They are unmarked and it has to be said there is some doubt whether they really started their existence as wine labels. The same sceptical attitude must be taken of a notorious trio of farm animals (a pig, a sheep and a cow), made by C.T. and G. Fox in 1851, which puzzled collectors in the 1950s when they first appeared, until they were convincingly shown to have been taken from the plinth of an agricultural trophy and had wine titles added. A goat's mask, however, which surmounts the name panel on a label of around 1757 by T. Heming is happily authentic as part of the original design, though symbolic rather than heraldic.[86] The goat was associated with Dionysus in ancient Greece and Thrace.

Hunting has provided inspiration for many labels that incorporate pursuer and pursued in their design. A die-stamped cartouche-shaped label for BUCELLAS (see fig. 365, T. Johnson, 1829) depicts a boar's head surrounded by instruments of the chase. Two Scottish labels by J. McKay (c.1818) are modelled as a horse with its rider (see fig. 368), and a greyhound (see fig. 369), standing on panels engraved for CLARET and MADEIRA. A third label, a hare, is believed to exist to complete the coursing trio.[87] A rather similar label, also Scottish, by Daniel Sutherland of Glasgow (c.1820), consists of a running fox with streaming brush (see fig. 366). The fox has already been mentioned in its heraldic context (see fig. 361, above); he also appears on labels based on Aesop's fable of the fox and the grapes. One example has a pair of foxes sitting one at each end of the name panel, gazing upwards. (This label is sometimes referred to by collectors as the 'singing foxes'; actually, of course, they are looking longingly up at the grapes above their heads.) Another by R. Garrard II, for CLARET, 1829 (see fig. 363) has Reynard crouched over the top of the name panel, with the grapes he covets almost within his grasp. A PORT label (see fig. 358) shows a running fox and TALLIOO.

Beasts of heraldic origin have not been the only inhabitants of the animal kingdom to have mutated into label form. The crowned lions of the splendid royal labels described below must principally be a demonstration of royal supremacy; a much smaller and much less imposing version was adopted for his labels by the Marquess of Shrewsbury (see fig. 379 for SHERRY, 1817, by John Reily). The magnificent 'big cat' mask, usually gilded, by Paul Storr and also by Benjamin Smith III in Regency years,[88] and one of the most desirable labels a collector can meet, has sometimes been called a lion's or leopard's mask, but in fact he is surely a panther. Dionysus, god of wine, employed a panther to haul his chariot, and this association makes this attribution the most appropriate.

Shapes and Designs

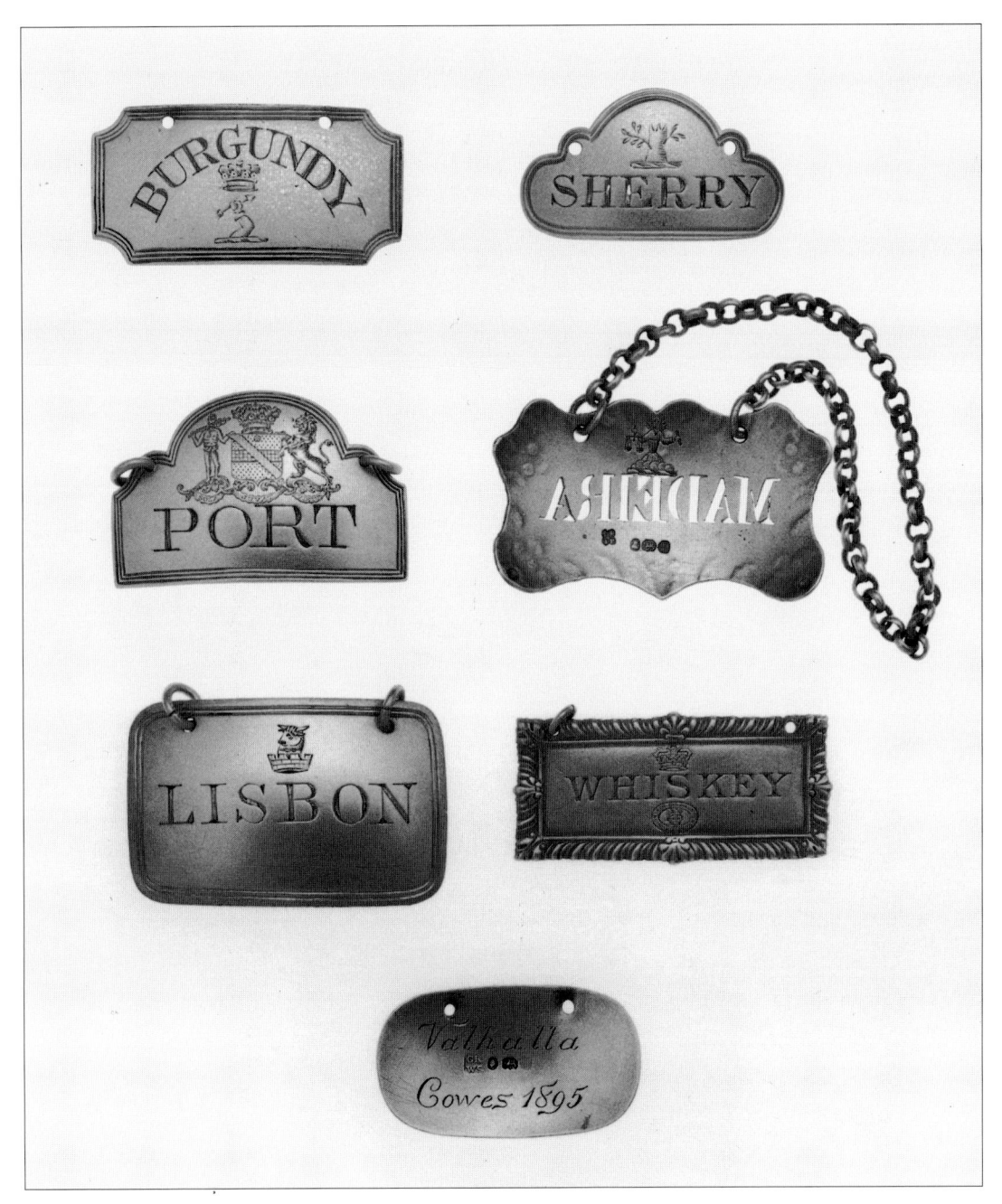

Figures 371-377.

François Ravenet shows a panther in one of the designs he produced for the enamel labels made by the Battersea factory between 1753 and 1756, though in another it is a tiger being cuddled by a dangerously suicidal child.[89] Other eighteenth- and nineteenth-century silversmiths, too, have had a panther in their designs. T. Wallis and J. Hayne incorporated a panther's mask in a cast cartouche of 1812. The Knights, George, Samuel and William, made a smaller version between 1816 and the mid-1820s, a variety of which is discussed more fully in the section below on commemorative labels. Abstainando King has yet another amusing version (in 1828), in which the head of the panther peers round one end of the name panel, while his tail emerges at the other end. There is a squirrel devouring nuts on a mid-nineteenth-century plated label (see fig. 370 for GIN), and in the twentieth century a mouse[90] and 'glis glis' (the edible dormouse, delicacy of ancient Roman feasts, and now a species found wild in the Chilterns) adorn labels made by Brian Fuller (*c*.1978).

As wine labels have spread to the far corners of the globe, so local fauna has found a place on them.

Shapes and Designs

Figures 378-385.

Dating probably from the late years of the nineteenth century, bats have become labels in at least three sizes. These labels are nearly always unmarked, but one has been recorded with a Shanghai mark, and a Far Eastern origin for the whole colony seems probable. In China the bat is a symbol of longevity and happiness, so its outstretched wings are therefore well-suited for displaying the name of the wine that leads to these desirable achievements. There is a heart-shaped design, too, of Chinese origin containing a single letter ('P' and 'M' have been recorded), surrounded by a trio of flying bats. By far the most common beast to come out of China, however, is the dragon. Many versions of him exist: usually he is shown guardant and passant within the horns of an open crescent, the labels often having the marks of Shanghai and Hong Kong silversmiths of the late nineteenth century.[91] Also from the East, perhaps from Burma or Malaya, have come lions, a dolphin, a pair of mythical birds with crests and long tails, and dancing human figures.[92] The tusks, claws and teeth of the animals hunted mainly in India, which have been turned into labels, are described in another chapter.[93]

Shapes and Designs

Royal labels

The labels at Buckingham Palace and Windsor Castle that belong to the Crown were fully described by Dr N.M. Penzer in an article in *The Connoisseur* in July 1961 (later circulated in the *Wine Label Circle Journal* (June 1962).[94] In his article Penzer followed the order in which the various services containing the labels appear in the Royal Inventory of 1914, and he included only the 409 labels that are in that inventory. He did not include labels that are kept in other royal residences or that are the property of other members of the royal family. The summaries below are given in chronological order of the labels' manufacture or their acquisition in these services.

The earliest labels are five in the Coronation Service made by John Rich and dating from 1794; two more are by John Salkeld and one by John Reily (1800-1804) and there is a later one by John Reily of 1819. They are all rectangles of plain design, and there seems to be no clear pattern in their assemblage, but there can be no doubt that there were once many more of them. Several labels of this design, by the same and other makers, which date from the same years and have on their reverse side the sovereign's crown or the garter motif and a serial number – as do the labels still in the Coronation Service – have found their way through salerooms into private collections. The explanation may be the 'Ambassadorial Theory', discussed below, or more simply that they were disposed of when more up-to-date and fashionable styles were acquired. Two sharp-cornered rectangles by Susanna Barker are known, which must be earlier than 1793, and several by John Rich, most of them dated 1794. One is also known with the mark of Thomas Hyde of *c.*1790.

The absence of any labels, either in the inventory or saleroom examples, from the earlier years of George III's reign (1760-*c.*1790), despite these being years of immense label productivity, might suggest that it was not until his son, the Prince of Wales, with his strong views on what was fashionable, began to exert an influence on affairs, that they came to be taken seriously in the royal household. The plainness of these early labels is very noticeable compared with what was then available in the then prevalent neo-classical style, and in the light of the prince's flamboyant tastes, and so is the choice of makers. The palace did not go either to the leading label manufacturing firms – the Batemans, the Hydes and the Phipps and Robinson partnership (except for the Prince of Wales Service labels, see below) – or to Parker and Wakelin, who were the leading purveyors of labels for the aristocracy. Instead the orders went predominantly to John Rich, and then to John Reily; the latter certainly in the Hyde tradition by marriage, but the former less well known.

In addition to the labels already mentioned, Rich executed two in a set of six double-reeded cut corner rectangular labels in the Prince of Wales Service at Buckingham Palace. Four are by T. Phipps and E. Robinson, and all are dated 1794. They have pierced titles for KINGS CUP, whose ingredients are not known, and they have specially constructed long chains to be hung around jugs.

Figure 386.

Figure 387.

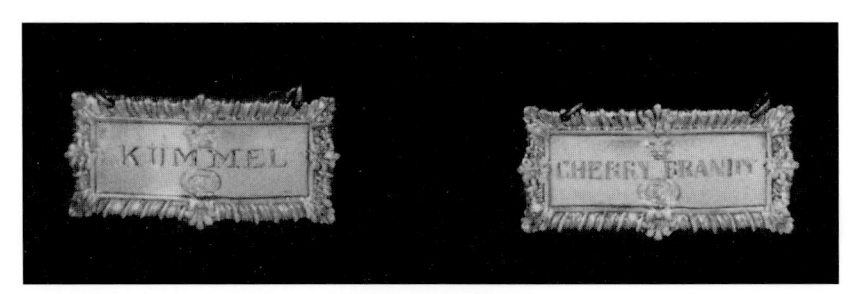

Shapes and Designs

Figures 388-389.

The Royal crown is engraved on the reverse of the labels.

The year when the Royal Collection of labels began to take shape does seem to be 1794. No good reason for this can be thought of. It was the year in which the Prince's long dalliance with Mrs Fitzherbert was drawing to a close, as he prepared to marry Princess Caroline of Brunswick, but that provides no explanation. There may, however, be a clue in two contemporary labels that feature prominently the Prince of Wales' feathered plumes in their designs, one of which he may have seen, and the other would certainly have been brought to his notice. Hester Bateman introduced her celebrated curved rectangular design with Prince of Wales' plumes in the mid-1770s and it was extremely popular throughout the last quarter of the century.[95] It is not known to have had any links with the Prince, but a rather similar shape, which appeared in Ireland in the next decade, certainly did have association with him. In this version the feathers are quite realistic and there is often a crown lodged in them as well.[96] They were produced by several Irish makers, George Nangle, Benjamin Taitt and John Teare, for the Prince's Irish supporters who wanted him to be crowned king while George III was suffering from his first bouts of madness (as it was then diagnosed). Whether they helped his cause can be doubted, but at least he must surely have become aware of the existence of these dining room accessories.

Before leaving the Coronation Service of plate, mention should be made of an explanation for the appearance in salerooms of labels that must surely once have been part of it, which has been suggested as more probable than the theory given above that they were simply disposed of when they became out of fashion. It has been claimed that it was the practice of the monarch to make loans of plate from the royal household to the noblemen that he appointed as his ambassadors to courts abroad. They were presumably expected to return these items when their appointments ended, but this did not always happen, at any rate in so far as small items like wine labels were concerned, and, in the course of time, subsequent generations of the ambassador's family might reasonably enough have let them go. Later on, in the nineteenth century, it is known that Queen Victoria made gifts that included wine labels to visiting guests and dignitaries and these, too, may well eventually have found their way on to the market.

The largest and most complete of the services of royal plate is the Grand Service, which the Prince of Wales – by now the Prince Regent – began to commission in the opening years of the

Figure 390.    *Figure 391.*    *Figure 392.*

nineteenth century from the firm of Rundell, Bridge and Rundell, intending it primarily for his lavish entertainments at Carlton House. The wine labels in the service consist of five designs, which Penzer describes very fully in the order in which they appear in the 1914 inventory. Here they are placed in the chronological order of their manufacture, with the name of the maker and a very brief description to aid identification. The numbers shown for each type of label are those in the inventory. If it is assumed that the original orders were for round dozens, one can see the extent to which the maker contracted out the work he could not carry out himself. They also may help to indicate how ambassadorial loans, royal gifts and losses from other causes have depleted them.

Date	Description
1807-9	6 large scallop shells by B. Smith II. (One replacement by Garrards, the Crown Jewellers, in 1900.) See figs. 337 and 338. This shell design was very popular for a few years: nearly all known examples date between 1806 and 1812. It has been suggested that they were supplied from Smith's stock to meet urgent demand before the later specially commissioned designs were ready.
1809-10	46 heads of Jupiter Ammon in vine leaf cartouches, 45 by Paul Storr. Very large – 7.6 x 8.9cm (3 x 3½in.). One addition by P. Rundell, 1821. See fig. 386 for RED BURGUNDY. An apparently unique design. Not recorded except in this set.
1811	33 Imperial Lions by Paul Storr. 7.6 x 7.6cm (3 x 3in.) and one replacement by Garrards, 1889. Massive, unique labels. Illustrated is MOSELLE by Paul Storr, 1811, in the Royal Collection (see fig. 387). Lesser lions on different mountings are known.
1812	45 narrow rectangular with raised border by Paul Storr (7 more by Paul Storr in 1820, 3 by J. Bridge in 1821, 119 late Victorian and Edwardian by Garrards). Figs. 388 and 389 in Buckingham Palace by Paul Storr in 1812. Fig. 376 by S. Garrard in 1902 for WHISKEY in a private collection has a lion standing on a crown within a garter inscribed HONI SOIT QUI MALY PENSE. Fig. 391 for CLARET in a private collection omits the garter.
1812-14	23 heads of a Bacchante in festooned drapery by Paul Storr, 2 by William Bateman I added in 1813, 13 by J. Bridge added in 1827, 16 with no maker's mark added in 1829, and 1 by W. Bateman II added in 1831. See fig. 390 (open background with slip chain), fig. 392 (filled in background). An apparently unique design, but a rather similar one without the Bacchante head is also known by Paul Storr.
1816-18	5 heavy cast crescent labels with shell borders by Paul Storr (1816-18) were presented to King Edward VII. See figs. 393-397.

The titles on the labels in the four major sets are for the usual wines to be expected for the period, for brandy, for a large range of liqueurs and, after around 1820, for whiskey and gin. The names on the long rectangular set duplicate those on the more elaborate labels.

If one can attempt to summarise further the history of the Crown's labels, it can be said that before the last decade of the eighteenth century there were none. In that decade a random assortment of mainly standard rectangular labels was acquired, the majority by John Rich, a competent designer but not one of the outstanding silversmiths of the period. In 1803 the Prince Regent began discussions with the leading firm of Rundell, Bridge and Rundell for the manufacture of plate in the latest and most opulent taste (including wine labels) from the leading silversmiths of the day: Paul Storr, Digby Scott and Benjamin Smith.[97] This took about ten years to assemble, and when he came to the throne in 1820 he proceeded to add to it. In between whiles he seems to have diverted himself with minor orders for his yacht *Prince Regent* (see below). The

Shapes and Designs

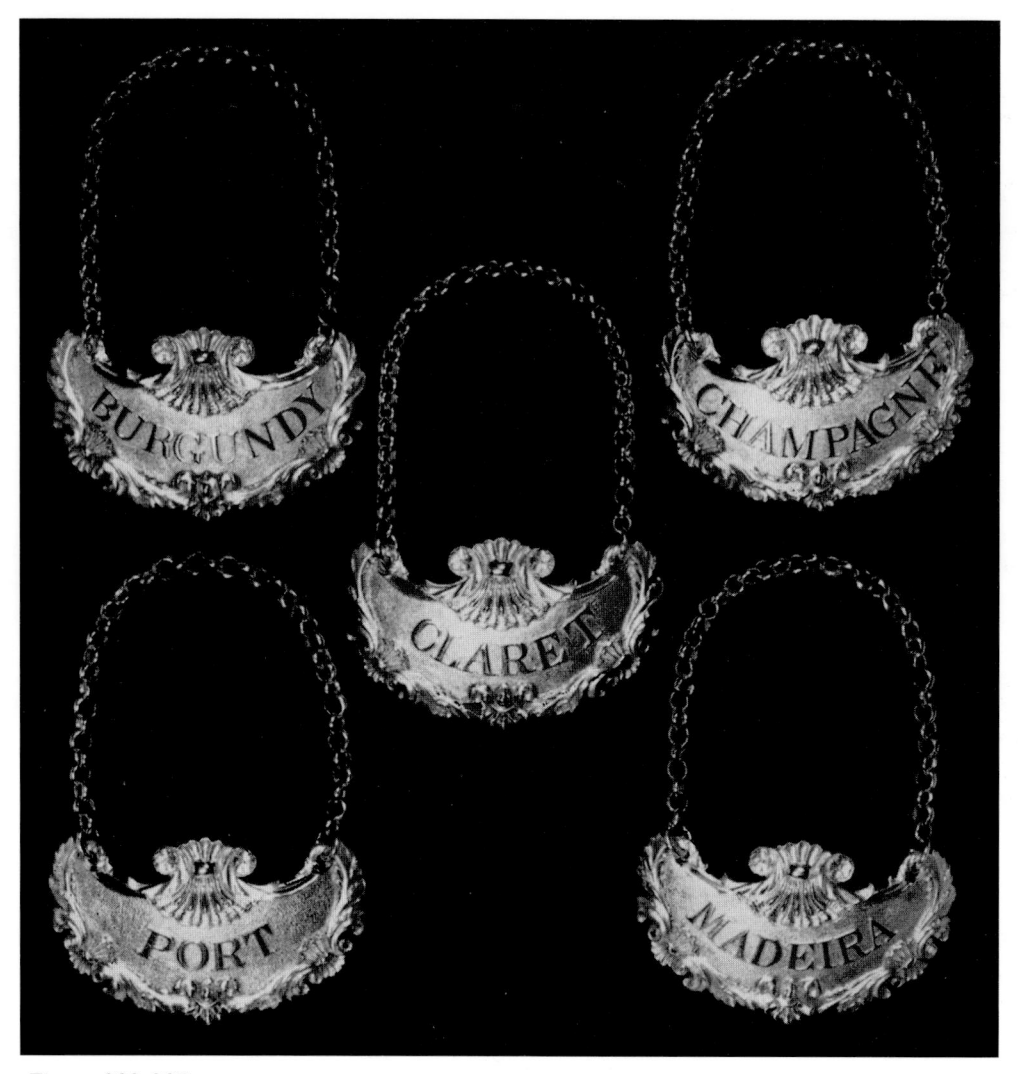

Figures 393-397.

situation remained unchanged throughout William IV's reign, and most of Queen Victoria's reign. In her closing years the long set of rather pedestrian rectangular labels was trebled in size, and replacements were ordered to bring the original sets back to their original numbers. In the twentieth century no wine labels were ordered. It should finally be stressed that the above comments cover only the labels that are in the 1914 inventory of plate at Buckingham Palace and Windsor Castle. It may well be that other royal residences contain labels from the above sets, particularly the early ones, and that others are still unrecorded. It should further be stressed that labels which do not belong to the Crown but to individual members of the royal household are private possessions and very properly have no place here.

Wine labels of universities and corporate bodies

As might be expected, collegiate establishments have, in the course of years, laid down wines to aid their discussions and their relaxations, and have then required labels to identify them in the decanter. In the universities, several colleges have listed wine labels in the inventories of their plate. Fig. 398 shows a label for SHERRY by C. Rawlings and W. Summers, dated 1829, which has on it the arms of Trinity Hall, Cambridge, on a plaque forming part of the label. Fig. 373 for PORT shows the arms of a city livery company, the Mercers, engraved above the name. It was made by J. Ash in 1804. MADEIRA (see fig. 374) by T. and J. Phipps in 1820 and SHERRY by Phipps and Robinson,[98] 1806, were made for the Goldsmiths' Company, and have its arms engraved on the back. Another livery company, the Vintners, commemorated their 550th anniversary in 1987 with a cast design of their

Figures 398-402.

emblem, two swans, commissioned from Sarah Jones (see fig. 403, BURGUNDY and CLARET). The Irish Company of Goldsmiths chose an Irish harp (see figs. 404, 405, WHISKEY, by T. Weir, Dublin, 1987) to mark the 350th anniversary of the granting of their charter by Charles I in 1637. The label also has their arms included in the hallmark. The Worshipful Company of Ironmongers[99] in the City of London placed their crest either side of DRY PORT and FRUITY PORT, each named twice on electroplated bottle rings. The Worshipful Company of Stationers[100] acquired in February 1825 at a cost of £11.4s.0d. a set of 16 'Unwin pattern' wine labels made by Emes and Barnard in 1824 in shaped oval format with shell, rose, pear and fruiting vine border, with pierced titles including SHERRY, LISBON and MADEIRA. The Worshipful Company of Distillers used labels, curiously unmarked and quite beautiful, depicting the Company's arms with the addition underneath of a reclining nude in a somewhat provocative pose.[101]

Several city corporations' plate includes sets of wine labels. The Corporation of Newcastle ordered escutcheons surmounted by a lion holding a banner above a castle from T. Watson in 1819 (see fig. 401, MADEIRA). The City of Chester had labels made by G. Lowe, the leading silversmith in the city during the nineteenth century, rectangular in shape, as most labels made in Chester were, with their arms, three wheatsheaves and a sword engraved above the wine name.

Members of Inns of Court were not known for their abstinence. A fine CHAMPAGNE cork label has engraved on the reverse 'Inner Temple' and the crest of that society appears on the rim as Pegasus, the flying horse.

PART 22 – COMMEMORATIVE LABELS

In this section the labels to be considered were made to mark special occasions or to convey some message that the originator wished to perpetuate. They vary from very elaborate representations of emblems connected with the occasion to words or messages placed on a label of standard design. Many wine labels made in the twentieth century were for commemorative purposes, and reference for details of these should be made to Chapter 1, Part 8, above.

An early example of the first type is the famous Balloon label (see fig. 312) made by B. Taitt in Dublin in 1784.[102] Another example, also Irish, is a set of four labels, Irish harps, made by J. Phipps in London (see fig. 321) and B. Taitt in Dublin (see fig. 322) in around 1783, which probably hailed the revival of the Irish parliament in that year.[103] Another eighteenth-century label that may have been intended as a political or historical reminder is an escutcheon of around 1750 attributed to J. Lamb of Whitehaven in Cumbria. Instead of the usual chased grapes and vine leaves around the name – WHITE – are engraved a large rose, flanked by two smaller ones, emblems seen on Jacobite wine glasses and associated with the Old Pretender and his two sons. There were certainly Jacobite supporters in Cumbria after the failure of the 1745 rebellion, but this interpretation of the decoration on the label must remain conjectural. There is a well-known design, first made by Hester Bateman in the 1770s (referred to above), which features a plume of three feathers above a curved rectangular panel.[104] This plume is, of course, the emblem of the Prince of Wales, but at that time George III's eldest son was still too young to have developed political ambitions or cultural tastes. His years of scheming against his father's political notions were yet to come, and so was his emergence as a leader of fashion. The design may therefore be no more than an artistically inspired decorative motif. Across the Irish Sea, however, as has been explained above, matters were different. The political significance of the crown lodged in the Prince of Wales' feathers that surmount the open 'Irish crescents' made by Dublin silversmiths in the late 1780s and 1790s is absolutely clear,[105] and indeed, the conveying of political meaning in this way followed the pattern of the harp labels described above.

In the nineteenth century, during the 1830s, S. Mordan and Co. produced a set of labels that portray cornucopia of fruit, wheatsheaves, a rake, a scythe and what might be a baking tin containing loaves of bread, with the word FREE stamped twice (see fig. 400, WHISKEY). The label may be linked to the repeal of the Corn Laws in 1832, or perhaps to the early moves towards free trade. An interesting set of labels in electroplate commemorates the battle of Navarino in 1827. They were probably commissioned by Admiral Codrington, who commanded the English, French and Russian ships that defeated a Turkish and Egyptian fleet, thus setting the path for the independence of Greece.[106] It must be conceded, however, that the admiral was more interested in perpetuating the summit of his own naval career than in marking that country's restoration as a nation. From about the same date, however, a label made by all three members of the Knight family, Samuel, George and William, featured three of the national flowers of the United Kingdom: the rose of England, the thistle of Scotland and the shamrock of Ireland (see fig. 399, MADEIRA, 1820). This was a time of patriotic fervour, following the defeat of Napoleon, when a display of national emblems would certainly have seemed appropriate. The picture is slightly complicated by the incorporation into the design of two panthers' heads, which seem to have no connection with the national flowers, but one appropriate for a wine label.

A Scottish label of the 1820s by D.C. Rait of Glasgow has musical instruments surrounding the name panel. Their association with wine in the decanter is not apparent, but presumably they marked some occasion of musical significance now forgotten. More recently, in 1973, the Irish Company of Goldsmiths commissioned a special label from W. Egan and Co. to mark the entry of Ireland into the European Economic Community (see fig. 402). It is a representation of an ancient Irish gold collar (the Glenisheen Collar) of around BC700, now in the National Museum of Ireland in Dublin.

Another kind of commemoration found on labels consists of a simple inscription, a sentence or words, engraved on a conventional label shape, which provides space for the message. One such is

Shapes and Designs

Figure 403.

inscribed 'The Abbott's Bottle'; another has 'A BLAMIRE bottle 100 years old'. Another rectangular label, re-engraved for CLARET, has 'VALHALLA, Cowes, 1895' on the back (see fig. 377). *Valhalla* was a big, luxurious steam yacht and Cowes is, of course, the principal annual racing and social event of the yachting world. At another level, a label made of aluminium has been noted, whose inscription on the back relates that it was part of the first Zeppelin to be shot down over England in 1917 (see figs. 989b and 989c). The wine name is MARSALA.[107]

In the twentieth century there has been something of a fashion for celebrating royal occasions with specially designed wine labels. Several silversmiths marked the Coronation of Queen Elizabeth in 1953 in this way. One design by L.A. Crichton, commissioned by the Wine Label Circle, is illustrated in Chapter 1, Part 8, fig. 84. (It also commemorated the year of the Circle's foundation.) Leslie Durbin produced a design based on the royal arms – the lion and the unicorn. In 1977 the celebrations for the Queen's Silver Jubilee produced several designs of quality, and others, which, it has to be said, were more for the souvenir trade than the collector's cabinet. A few years later in 1981, when Prince Charles married Lady Diana Spencer, the occasion was marked by Garrard and Co. by a label based on his three feathers and a heart (see Chapter 1, Part 8, fig. 75).

Mention should be made of label designs that have been adapted to bear inscriptions only faintly linked to a label's real purpose, or sometimes not at all. A version of the 'Reclining Dionysus' design (see Chapter 2, Part 10) was adapted by G. McHattie in Edinburgh to take an inscription awarding

Figure 404.

Figure 405.

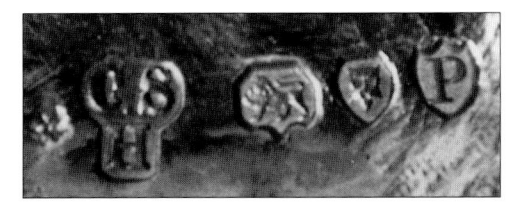

Figure 407.

Figure 406.

105

Shapes and Designs

Figure 408. 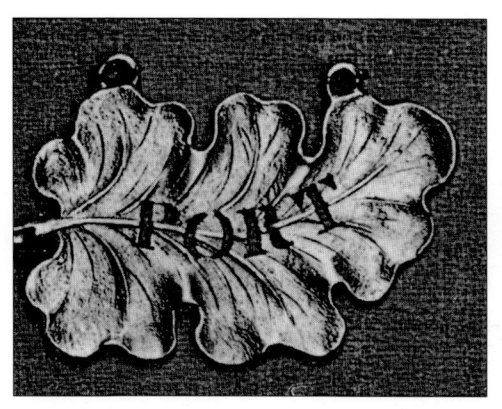 *Figure 409.*  *Figure 410.*

it by the Caledonian Horticultural Society for the best currant wine; another is known for the best gooseberry wine. It could, of course, be argued that as examples of this conversion sometimes still have their chains they were intended for the decanter into which the prize-winning wine was poured, and so deserve to be included as wine labels, but other designs that commemorate athletic champions, for example, or are simply tokens of remembrance between friends, have no reference to wines and no relevance to the subject of the present work.

Finally, under this heading, no better form of commemoration could there be than the general exhortation to take wine at any opportunity, recorded on a crescent-shaped label made by P., A. and W. Bateman in 1800.[108] The original title, RAISIN, has been erased and replaced by three lines of Latin hexameters:

> Si bene quid memini causae sunt quinque bibendi;
> Hoapitas adventus, praesens sitis atque futura,
> Aut vini bonitas, aut quaelibet altera causa.

A rough doggerel translation might read:

> If, for a drink, you sometimes sigh,
> Remember well five reasons why:
> To greet a guest, or feeling dry,
> Or since you may be, by and by,
> Good wine, or any other reason why.

The label has later had a crudely formed PORT, composed of strips of silver, placed between the horns of the crescent.

PART 23 – MILITARY AND NAVAL LABELS

A recent comprehensive survey of silver plate belonging to the country's armed forces by Roger Perkins has little mention of wine labels.[109] Most of the silver acquired by the regiments of the army does not date back further than the mid-nineteenth century, by which time wine labels were beginning to lose some of their importance. The ships of the Royal Navy led too troubled an existence at sea until the Napoleonic Wars ended for wardrooms to have had any use for such articles, and even during more stable Victorian times, naval and Royal Marine officers afloat were not used to sitting round a circulating decanter after dinner. By the time that the Royal Air Force was furnishing its officers' messes in the years between the two World Wars, wine labels were no longer essential.

In olden days regiments took the major items of plate that they needed from their central depots in England to wherever in the world they were stationed. Small garrisons may well have had no occasion to take minor items such as wine labels, and in India, where much of the army spent a lot of time, and formality in the officers' mess was the norm, these articles could be obtained locally, often made up from tusks and claws. A Royal Naval ship commissioned for two or three years

Figures 411-414.

would draw such silver as she or her predecessors had acquired from a central trophy store for the duration of the commission. These would normally be ceremonial and other important pieces, and not minor items such as wine labels.

The only labels known to bear a ship's name are a set that was presented to H.M.S. *Bristol* by Messrs Harvey, the Bristol wine merchants, when she was first commissioned in 1973. The wardrooms of naval shore establishments, the training and specialist schools and holding barracks, did not take permanent shape until the mid-nineteenth century and they evidently did not use their limited funds on wine labels, nor, so it seems, is there a record of wine labels in the depots of the Royal Marines.

The definitive work on military silver by Roger Perkins mentioned above illustrates two examples of regimental wine labels. One is fashioned as an oak leaf, emblem of the 22nd Foot, later the Cheshire Regiment (see fig. 409, PORT) from a set made in two sizes by C. Rawlings and W. Summers in 1855. The other is a plain rectangular label by F. Powell (1818), for MADEIRA, which has an emblem of three plumes above the wine name and '77th' engraved below the name, for the 77th Foot, later the East Middlesex Regiment. Other recorded labels include a pair for PORT and SHERRY showing the sphinx emblem of the 4th Lincolnshire Regiment, made by Deakin and Francis, assayed in Chester in 1893. Another example, bearing the name of the 9th Bengal Native Infantry, was made by C.S. Harris in London in 1890 (see fig. 406 and fig. 407 for the reverse). A set made as field guns, with the wine name on narrow panels hanging below the gun, are unmarked, and were probably made in India for an artillery unit stationed there in the mid-nineteenth century, possibly the Madras Artillery for whom other mess silver has been noted. Another example (see fig. 410) for SHERRY, made in 1897 by W. Gibson and J. Langman, shows part of the crest of the Worcestershire Regiment. A further example (see fig. 408) is the Barnard Brothers' MADEIRA, on a curved scroll surmounted by a dragon mounted on a wooden stand, which has an oval badge applied engraved with the insignia of the 38th Grenadiers.

A design that clearly has naval associations is the single foul anchor, illustrated and discussed in Chapter 2, Part 12. These late 18th-or early nineteenth-century labels cannot be linked to any particular ship, but they were presumably made for naval officers, perhaps when they retired and 'swallowed the anchor', or while still serving, from their prize money. Another version, with the anchor viewed in profile, has been noted, engraved on labels made by J. Reily in 1818 for the Prince of Wales (later George IV) for use on board his yacht the *Prince Regent* (see figs. 411-414, BRANDY and PORT with ANCHOVY and SOY, and Part 21, Royal labels, above).[110]

CHAPTER 3

MAKING

PART 1 – MAKING AND DECORATING IN SILVER

With the exception of workshop manuals, almost all modern writing about gold and silver wares concentrates on famous makers and changing styles. Yet style and technique are always each other's prisoners. Neither can reach its goal without conforming to the other. Understanding how wine labels and their designs have developed over time, therefore, requires an awareness of the silversmith's changing methods and equipment, as well as knowledge of his and his patrons' changing tastes. Looking at some of the more exuberant products of the 1850s, erupting in high relief and intricate piercing, we need to remember that their makers' predecessors in the 1750s, even had they conceived them, would have found them daunting to make (see fig. 415, taken from Diderot's *Encyclopaedia* or '*Dictionnaire raisonné des sciences, des arts et des métiers, par une société des gens de lettres*', Paris, 1751).

Although they became increasingly elaborate during the nineteenth century, wine labels remained a group of essentially two-dimensional objects, principally because they were always called upon to communicate in only one direction, as adjuncts to the surface of a three-dimensional container. Even neck rings rarely displayed more than a single title. Thus their makers as well as their designers had to deal with only a few basic features: a two-dimensional profile, an identifying title, probably some element of surface decoration, and finally some means of attachment. All the problems of designing, forming and embellishing 'in the round' as with, say, a coffee pot, or of assembling securely an inventory of components to make something like a candlestick, were almost entirely irrelevant. When the cosmetics are pared away, the silver wine label is a flat and simple artefact.

There are in any case few things a silversmith can do to his raw material. How he does them – and how well – is another matter. Faced with a piece of unworked silver, and setting aside colouring, he can only cut it, solder it, melt it, hit it, stretch it or bend it. Thus the question is how each of those possibilities bears upon the evolution of silver wine labels, whether as a servant of their design or as one of its ineluctable constraints.

Bending and soldering can be set apart, though not entirely dismissed. Both are important to the making of silver chain, the most frequent attachment of the wine label to a decanter or a bottle, but neither has figured largely in the making of labels themselves. We are left, therefore, with cutting, melting, hitting and stretching. Of these, hitting and stretching silver are closely associated processes. There are several ways to stretch it by other means, notably by squeezing it through rollers or in a press. Traditionally, however, the silversmith's special skill has resided in shaping his malleable material by stretching it with blows of his hammer over a suitably formed support. That skill has

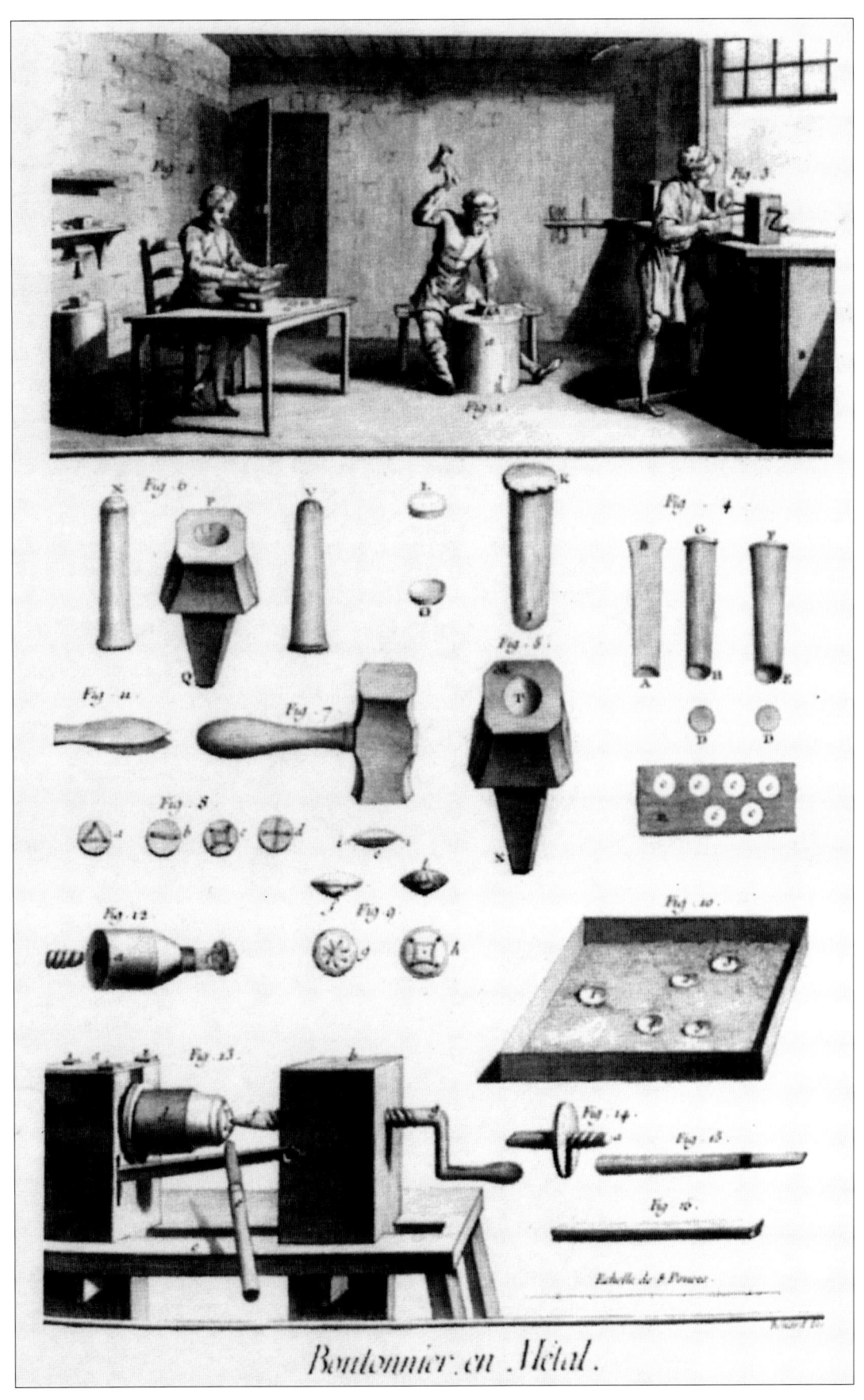

Figure 415.

Making

played little part in shaping wine labels. At most, 'doming' a label to match the curve of a bottle needs only a few gentle mallet blows over a depression in a wooden block. In working the profile of the label, therefore, the choice of hand methods has always been between melting and freezing the metal – that is, casting it – and cutting it: between a method, in other words, that begins by raising the temperature of silver to that of a liquid and one that depends on working from a solid sheet of silver at room temperature.

As far as decoration is concerned, cutting and casting are again important techniques, but hitting is also significant: first on the rare occasions when a hammer has to be used with punches to express from the back of a blank some embossed *repoussé* detail of an embellishment, second and more often to chase a pattern into the front, again with punches, and third to cut through the metal from front to back with small chisels. More importantly, stretching, with a press rather than a hammer, joins casting as a significant means of producing decoration in relief. To begin with, however, the label must have an outline.

Today, when deciding how to shape the profile of a label, the choice between cutting and casting may seem straightforward. Historically, however, this was more difficult. The first silver wine labels in the 1730s had simple enough profiles: a plain or slightly shaped rectangle, a narrow crescent, at most an echo of the escutcheon already familiar from brass furniture fittings. Such shapes might have been cast. The skills and tools needed were certainly available. Realistically, however, that would have been a wastefully complicated way to make a flat metal version of the thin parchment labels already in use down in the cellar (see Chapter 1, Part 4). The obvious course was to cut a blank outline from a piece of silver sheet. Unfortunately, neither procuring nor cutting sheet silver was a simple matter in the 1730s.

There is evidence of metal being rolled into sheet in Nuremberg before the middle of the sixteenth century. However, commercial-scale mills for rolling out iron, and thereafter non-ferrous metals, such as silver and copper, began to appear in Britain only in the 1720s. Ten or even twenty years later, few of the smiths making wine labels would have had access to a suitable mill. Accurate rollers able to produce smoothly finished sheet need very hard but tenacious steel, formulated to take and keep an unusually high polish. Steel of that standard was simply not available in quantity at an acceptable price until Benjamin Huntsman developed his crucible casting process early in the 1740s. Before then, the sheet from which the profile of a silver wine label was to be cut could only be hand forged as 'battery silver' from a solid cast ingot – a process not only laborious in itself but also entailing several interruptions to relieve the stress and hardening caused by a forging hammer by annealing the metal on the hearth. In some cases, the workshop, before it could cast the ingot to be forged, would have had to alloy pure silver with copper by melting them together to produce metal of an acceptable sterling or 'Britannia' assay. Although the evidence is scanty, that task seems to have fallen increasingly to specialised refiners in large centres, such as London, but it was unlikely to have been so in a city such as Newcastle, where the matter would have been left to the individual silversmith.

A 'battery' sheet having been forged, the 1730s silversmith faced another difficulty in cutting such a profile as an escutcheon from it, a difficulty again attendant upon the primitive state of steel technology. To cut that profile by hand today, or at any time during the last two centuries, the worker would reach for a hard-toothed saw blade as little as 0.25 mm (1/100 in.) thick and only 0.5 mm (1/50 in.) wide. His predecessor of the early 1730s could do no such thing. Indeed, it would be another thirty years before the generality of jewellers and goldsmiths or silversmiths had at their disposal the thin, strong and durably sharp steel blades essential to an accurate and fast-cutting jeweller's piercing saw. Until then a sheet wine label's profile had to be roughed out with hand shears, worked down patiently with small chisels and finished with a succession of files. All these tools, as well as punches and gravers, although later also made of Huntsman's cast steel, were substantial enough to be made in 1730 by carburising and thus hardening the surface of wrought iron. Fine saw blades were not. As a result, it was only when a suitable steel became generally available in the 1760s that silversmiths found themselves with saws fit to cut delicate shapes from their metal.

Given a profiled blank, the early eighteenth-century smith could choose to decorate his label or not, but he (or the retailer after him) would certainly need to add a title, whether for stock or to order. For either purpose he had three obvious options: to cut shaped holes from the blank with chisel, file or saw; to remove material from its surface with graver or scorper; or to pattern its surface by depressing or displacing parts of it with hammer and punch to form letters or decorative motifs – in all cases working freehand. In other words, the choice lay between piercing, engraving and flat chasing.

Lacking suitable saw blades, piercing a blank in the very early years, even more than cutting its outline, was time-consuming work – and time, as always, was money. It meant hammering through silver sheet with small chisels and punches, or using small files to enlarge holes drilled with a hardened iron bit in a bow drill. Even at the substantial retail prices quoted in the later 1730s – 3s.6d. to 5s.6d. a label – it could hardly have been worth so much effort to letter or embellish by piercing when the simpler alternatives of flat chasing and engraving were at hand. Not surprisingly, therefore, only a few of the silver labels that date to those years have pierced decoration or titling. Most feature instead scratch-engraved letters on a ground either left plain or decorated with flat chasing.

Neither engraving nor chasing needed new or elaborate equipment. A graver was (and is) a short thin rod of hardened and tempered metal, round, oval or quadrilateral in section, with one end set into a palm-fitting wooden handle and the other ground at an angle and sharpened to provide a shaped cutting face. Using only hand pressure, it removed a curl of silver, creating a groove of variable width on the front of a label while leaving no trace of name or design on the back. A chasing punch was a similar rod but without a handle, slightly rounded at one end to receive the blows of a light hammer and meticulously carved, filed and polished at the other end to form whatever shape it was meant to impress into or express from a metal surface, inevitably leaving some trace on the other side. In either case, the work had to be supported on a material adhesive strong enough to hold it in position, firm enough to maintain its overall shape, but yielding enough to accommodate the intended displacement of metal. That material was traditionally chaser's pitch – a mixture of bitumen, tallow (or wax) and brick or tile dust – but for so small an object as a wine label even a patch of leather on wooden backing might suffice.

During the eighteenth century, intricate engraving and large-scale chasing became, as they still are, jobs for specialists. By the 1770s, for example, there appeared the highly skilled form of engraving known as bright-cutting, in which a craftsman cuts silver to produce reflective surfaces, or facets, making decoration on a piece such as a wine label sparkle in sunlight or candlelight. At the same time, changing fashion was beginning to create a demand for more florid decoration: a demand that chasing from the back of a wine label could help to satisfy by raising vine leaves, grapes or other motifs into high relief on its front surface. Closely related but rarer was a process known as pouncing, in which part of a surface was effectively hammered back, leaving the remainder standing proud: a technique so far noted among marked wine labels only on examples from the workshop of Paul Storr.[1]

In the early eighteenth century, however, all that lay in the future. Meanwhile, such a simple task as scratch-engraving a name or flat-chasing a few vine leaves on the front of a wine label was well within the scope of any silver workshop, as was chasing a feather-edged, gadrooned or ovolo border. So, of course, was producing from sheet the few basic label shapes on the market in the early 1730s. Silver wine labels were still a novelty, rather than a well-established feature of the polite dining room. Jostling for fashionable favour was still to come.

Things began to change during the 1740s. The service of wine at table once the ladies had withdrawn was becoming more formal, as evidenced by the appearance of silver bottle coasters. Improved glass-making techniques, coupled with the introduction in 1745 of a glass excise tax levied by weight, were encouraging a move to lighter, but more elegantly decorated, clear decanters. The net result was a demand for more consciously decorative wine labels to complement the new styles. London silversmiths such as Louis Hamon and Sandylands Drinkwater responded by offering in parallel with their plain escutcheons and crescents a range of heavier silver labels in patterns that echoed more nearly the mature rococo of other contemporary tableware. One such pattern combined vine leaves, grapes and C-scrolls around a central ribbon (see fig. 471). Another, more frequent and destined to be longer lived, added two infant putti and a mask of Dionysus (see fig. 468) – a pattern[2] known more recently as 'two cupids' (which the infants in this case were certainly not). Both these patterns called for a more massive, three-dimensional effect, and thus much higher relief than either engraving or flat chasing sheet silver could deliver. In practice, that meant turning to the other decorative technique already established in precious metal working, casting – a method rarely used for wine labels before 1745, increasingly frequent thereafter, but reaching its apotheosis only in the next century.

During the second half of the eighteenth century, the great majority of labels continued to be formed from sheet, increasingly often rolled, and to fall within a familiar and relatively narrow range of shapes, albeit with progressively more sophisticated engraved or chased embellishment. The introduction of casting notwithstanding, conservative continuity was more evident than change, in method as well as design. In any case, casting, which had been used by silversmiths for more than two thousand years, from Egypt and Scythia through Greece and Rome, was no more a technical novelty than engraving or chasing. Theophilus described all of the processes in twelfth-century Germany, and Cellini and Biringuccio in sixteenth-century Italy. Nevertheless, the appearance of cast wine labels marked a profoundly important departure. It was not so much that these were the first labels made other than from sheet, but rather that they were the first to be made by a process adapted to the serial production of identical copies from a single model.

The possibility of production in series by casting seems to have been exploited only haphazardly during the next thirty or forty years. Although the unknowable odds against survival make it impossible to be certain, it appears that a handful of makers cast a few copies from a very limited number of patterns. What is more, surviving specimens argue that casting was a technique used during the eighteenth century only by wine label makers in London. Yet the Industrial Revolution was gathering pace, not only breeding and disseminating new technology but also spawning new centres of affluence (and not only in Britain) populated by men eager for such minor luxuries as fashionable table silver. With a market of that kind growing in the metropolis and spreading to the provinces, serial production was clearly the requirement of the future, and indeed the only way to satisfy a new race of customers who expected to buy ready-made rather than bespoke. What wine label makers were coming to need, therefore, was an economical method of turning out relatively small batches of identically decorated blanks, say twenty at a time, while keeping pace with the demand for more adornment in design. Titles could then be added to order, by their own workmen or in the retailer's back room. Casting was an obvious solution.

As to the process itself, casting was a structural and decorative method – or rather a suite of methods – already established in every London workshop. Indeed it had been instrumental in creating the glories of European gold and silver for more than four hundred years. Yet, despite the fact that it was one of the means by which the finest examples were produced during the century from 1750, its application to making wine labels has sometimes been misunderstood and remains a question in need of systematic study. There seems to be no evidence, for instance, that wine labels were ever cast in a rigid closed mould, as spoons might be cast in two-part moulds of bronze. This was presumably because the variety of sizes and patterns needed to serve the foibles of so many different customers would have made this method, which was designed for long production runs, uneconomical.

Nor does it seem that wine labels were cast during the eighteenth century by the lost wax (*cire perdue*) process, in which a wax model is encased ('invested') in a plaster-like mixture, usually of gypsum and silica, from the hardened matrix of which the wax can thereafter be melted out to leave a cavity fit to receive molten metal such as silver. It is conceivable that some of the largest and grandest of the nineteenth-century labels were made in that way – another matter inviting investigation – but even that seems unlikely. Firstly, the ceramic mould could not be reused, and secondly each copy to be produced by lost wax casting meant carving a new wax master. The latter problem might have been avoided by carving a more durable model, and then making that rather than the mould the dominant element. One such process, known at least since the sixteenth century, involves pressing a metal original into or between fine-grained cuttlefish bones, leaving a compacted indentation ready to receive molten silver. But that still had the fatal disadvantage that the cuttlefish mould was good for only a single casting.

Two-part metal moulds could only have been justified by an implausibly long production run, while the lost wax and cuttlefish methods allowed no run at all. What remained in the 1750s was sand casting, and it was certainly by one version or another of this process that all, or almost all, cast wine labels were thereafter produced in that and the following century.

The conventional processes of sand casting are fairly straightforward. If a unique product is needed, a caster may sometimes use his hand and eye to carve an intaglio version of it directly into the casting medium. The use of a negative image is of no help, however, when several copies are required of a finely detailed object such as a wine label. If this is the case, the mould needs to be formed around a positive model. A positive master of the object, carved in metal or wood, or even the original object to be copied, is pressed into a bed of tightly packed casting sand (which is actually slightly oiled clay powder) confined within the lower section – the 'drag' – of a two-part frame or 'flask', creating an exact negative. If the original is 'in the round', with details on both or all the faces to be reproduced, it will be sunk only half way, so that it can be removed at the proper time without disturbing that obverse impression.[3] The upper section of the frame – the 'cope' – can then be put in place, packed from the top with more sand to record a reverse impression, lifted away to allow removal of the master, and finally clamped back on to the drag to form a complete three-dimensional mould, meticulously aligned and having been provided also with channels cut in the sand for molten metal to enter and gases to escape. If, however, all the relevant detail of the master is on the obverse face, and thus recorded by the impression in the drag section – as is almost invariably the case with a wine label – the packed sand in the cope will remain undisturbed when the master is withdrawn, and a flat-backed copy will result.

The advantage of sand casting for a short production run of wine labels is obvious. One model in a sufficiently durable material – such as lead or even wood – or alternatively one original label to be copied, can be used repeatedly without sustaining damage. Moreover, subject only to clearing away and replacing a little burnt material on the surface of an impression, both casting sand and flask can be reused indefinitely.

Many cast wine labels were probably made in sand, and rarely – if ever – would they have involved making a reverse impression in the cope of a flask. Thus they would have emerged, like the original, flat-backed. However, a large number of eighteenth- and nineteenth-century cast labels were not flat-backed. Instead, while their obverse faces were crisply cast in relief, their reverse faces – their backs – were irregularly concave. Moderately high magnification, moreover, often shows a reverse surface not smoothly compacted, as would be expected to emerge from a closed sand mould, but marked with microscopic pitting and low contours in sinuous patterns more reminiscent of a viscous liquid. This is exactly the sort of pattern found on the free surface of a silver ingot or a block of pewter or lead cast in an open mould. Especially in combination with an overall concavity – a sign of shrinkage of an exposed surface in cooling – it argues that wine labels similarly patterned on the reverse were also cast in open moulds, either of sand freshly impressed to make each copy or of some semi-permanent solid material such as charcoal, silica-rich plaster or a soft stone like slate or steatite, or conceivably even of a metal such as bronze.

Distinctively patterned reverse concavity can be seen on a wide variety of cast silver labels. In some cases the concavity is so considerable and the initially frozen shell of poured metal so evident that the result suggests the possibility of a further technical refinement known as 'slush casting'. This involves swiftly pouring back the unfrozen residue of semi-molten metal into the crucible, considerably reducing the weight of silver needed for each copy of the original. In such a case, the first metal poured into the open mould freezes quickly, covering the whole surface with a solid skin. Provided any further molten metal is withheld or removed quickly enough, that skin may be thin enough to reproduce on its reverse surface the basic contours of the mould itself, in which case the effect may be almost as though the copy had been incompetently stamped rather than competently cast.

Open casting of the kinds described is not now a usual silversmithing technique. It can only be done by hand, and it requires the nicest judgment as to the temperature of the mould as well as the metal. However, it was widely used in the eighteenth and nineteenth centuries, when casting pewter and brass (as it still is today). Moreover, an open process has regularly been used for casting not only ingots of precious and other metals but also pigs of iron, a metal with a much higher melting point than silver. There is no obvious reason, therefore, why it should not have been used to cast wine labels in the century from 1740. Indeed, evidence from the surviving labels themselves makes it reasonable to conclude that it was. All that remains is to find an example of an eighteenth- or nineteenth-century open wine label mould.

However conducted, casting wine labels in and after the 1740s represented an important enrichment of the manufacturing methods available. Whereas working from the sheet entailed a sequence of activities — including battering or rolling, rough cutting, filing, flat chasing and engraving — casting could in principle produce a complete copy, including relief decoration and titling as well as profile, from a single process stage. In practice it did not. Both profile and decoration had to be tidied after casting, using chisels and files to remove the web around an outline and punches and gravers to chase up and sharpen details of the relief decoration. What was important about casting, therefore, was less a reduction of the labour required for a single label than the ability to multiply a master twenty-fold, coupled with an almost limitless increase in the range and richness of the patterns attainable. Plants, animals and birds, fairies and fantasies, drapery and debauchery: casting could and did record them all — and in series.

The fact remained that casting, although a serial method, was fit only for relatively short production runs and, because of the need for 'tidying', remained relatively labour intensive. This was deemed acceptable in the 1750s, 1760s and 1770s, when it was used to supplement the labels made from sheet metal, but soon demand began to outstrip production and new methods were called for.

The crucial limitations were, as ever, economic. For relatively austere patterns of wine label — rectangles, octagons, crescents and escutcheons, soon to be joined by new-fangled ovals — hand working from the sheet remained an acceptable process, especially now that both profile cutting and decorative piercing were made so much easier and quicker by the arrival of fine steel blades. In fact, from the early 1770s the role of hand working was enlarged by the movement of fashionable taste away from rococo exuberance and towards the restrained elegance of Adam designs, well suited to saw piercing and to the low-relief effects of engraving and flat chasing. Against that, however, the introduction of more varied and intricate borders to highlight the Adam elegance — feather-edging, beading, compound gadrooning, ovolo or, above all, bright-cutting — imposed countervailing penalties of time and cost. At the same time, despite its obvious merits, casting of small pieces such as wine labels was proving less well adapted than might have been hoped to either changing taste or the economics of a growing market. It was not merely that it offered scope for only limited production runs, involving relatively high labour costs for chasing up copies and remaking moulds. It was also that, even with slush casting, it tended to consume more silver per label than sheet working, and thus to bring higher material costs as well. Casting produced some uncommonly fine labels in the 1750s and 1760s, and its day would come again with the revival of rococo extravagance for a luxury market in the next century. As the 1780s dawned, however, makers of wine labels needed another method that would allow them to reproduce economically numerous copies of patterns more intricate or in higher relief than those for which hand-worked sheet was a natural choice, and at a cost, therefore, much lower than casting could offer.

As with casting itself forty years earlier, the method was already at hand in the form of what is now called die-stamping. Indeed, versions of that process had been used to shape gold, silver, copper and its various alloys for over three thousand years, making it an even older method than casting. A special and important role for die-stamping had long been the minting of coins and medallions, commonly by pressing or hammering two separate intaglio dies on to the opposite sides of a metal blank. With that exception, however, die stamping had been a one-sided 'single-die' technique, used to reproduce a single image on one surface of a decorative item such as a classical patera or the boss of a medieval chalice. Thus we have from Ptolemaic Egypt 'negative' intaglio dies of bronze, into which thin sheets of beaten gold covered with a pad of soft lead were hammered to produce a 'positive' image. And thereafter, from seventh-century Byzantium, the twelfth-century Germany of Theophilus and the pre-Colombian Americas, we learn of exactly the same technique, save only that the intaglio die of bronze or iron was sometimes hammered directly on to the blank, with a block of lead beneath.

That same method of single die-stamping by hand was still in use, especially to shape trinkets or 'toys' from thin metal, when the father of the great engineer Matthew Boulton, another Matthew, was apprenticed to a Birmingham master stamper in about 1710. By the time wine label makers were reaching for larger volume at lower cost, some seventy years later, techniques in the stamping trade were already changing radically. The eventual result, compared with the simple methods of 1710, was revolutionary. Nevertheless, the aim and achievement of later eighteenth-century European silver workers was not to revolutionise the essence of the stamping method, but rather by stages to mechanise it, until it became the first truly industrial system of silver manufacturing. Thus they first substituted for hammering by hand a variety of simple man-powered machines: foot- or hand-operated drop presses, screw presses and spiralling fly presses. At the same time, for bronze dies they substituted hardened iron and then steel intaglios. Huntsman's cast steel was in time to serve that purpose, as also for the piercing dies increasingly used with fly presses to form intricate tracery patterns in items such as cake baskets. By the mid-century, therefore, there was available a faster, more economical and more effective means of stamping both openwork patterns and surface designs in imitation of flat chasing.

Wine label makers working in silver showed little inclination at first to exploit this opportunity. Few if any silver labels shaped or decorated by die-stamping can be attributed with confidence to the 1750s or 1760s. However, their colleagues (and competitors) working from that time in the novel fused or 'Sheffield' plate seized eagerly upon the mechanisation of die-stamping as a means not only of decorating their 'copper-back' products – suitable fruit and foliage stamped on escutcheons, or decorative borders on rectangles and crescents – but also of titling and even (and importantly) of cutting complete profiles from rolled sheet.

The first experiments with die-stamping silver labels seem to have been limited to the lettering of titles. Use for that purpose took two forms: stamping out individual letters to form a pierced title, or using similar dies with less force to mark the outlines of letters for subsequent scratch engraving. Both uses are sometimes said to have originated in the Bateman workshop during the 1770s. They were certainly general there from about that time. Whether they began there is much less clear. Lettering on some of the labels made as early as the 1740s, for example by Sandylands Drinkwater, has very much the appearance of die-stamping and piercing. However, the more ambitious and important use of die-stamping for the relief decoration of silver labels came somewhat later, and not in the London of either Drinkwater or the Batemans. Instead it was the newer and more highly mechanised centres to the north that took the lead.

From the 1780s, the more affluent or ambitious Birmingham and Sheffield makers began to use mechanised decorative stamping for goods that included silver as well as plated wine labels. Earlier work with small hand-operated presses had used single intaglio dies to strike blanks lying on a flat bed of suitable metal – soft lead for embossing, hard iron or steel for cutting. The newer technique began to substitute for that bed a 'positive' cameo die, precisely carved in steel by the die sinker, using better steel tools, to match the familiar intaglio image. By offering a longer working life for the equipment, that 'double-die' method, which may have been developed earlier to stamp out fused plate, promised much longer production runs. Moreover, in concert with the thinner and more homogeneous silver sheet emerging from better-engineered rolling mills, now, like the larger presses, driven in the major workshops by water power and soon to be driven by steam, the new method yielded products, including wine labels, that were die-stamped in higher relief and sharper detail than ever before.

The large screw presses and water-powered stamping presses coming into service towards the end of the eighteenth century were a whole world away from the painstaking hand stamping of Matthew Boulton's father. They could stamp out complete bowls or dishes. Alternatively, fed with much heavier sheet than hitherto, they could produce a fair imitation of casting, notably for the elaborately patterned flatware then becoming fashionable. In the case of wine labels, however, it was their ability, fed with thinner sheet, to turn out an indefinitely large quantity of finely detailed copies from one set of dies, immediately encompassing profile, decoration and sometimes even titling, which constituted the true revolution.

As in the classical past, that revolution owed much to the state's need for a finer and more secure coinage. Boulton installed his new coining press at the Soho Works in Birmingham in 1783. By the time he died in 1809, eight machines, fed by an integral rolling mill, were pouring out 30,000 to 40,000 copper coins an hour. The market for wine labels hardly called for such numbers. Even within a smaller compass, however, mechanised die-stamping marked the beginning of a new era, both technically and economically. Because the new machinery used thinner sheet while producing finer detail, it reduced material costs. Because the presses needed only one or two men to keep them running, and the copies they stamped needed none of the 'tidying' required by castings and only a little polishing, the system cut labour costs as well. And then, having increased demand by producing cheaper goods, mature die-stamping technology could turn out as many copies as customers wanted.

Mechanised stamping brought wine labels into the mainstream of the Industrial Revolution. As with so many other expressions of that revolution, however, it also opened something of a gulf between the different centres of their manufacture. During the nineteenth century, we continue to see labels being hand worked from sheet in Sheffield and Birmingham, the two main centres of 'industrial' silversmithing, but they were by and large confined to plain octagons and rectangles and became increasingly uncommon. Cast labels are not found from those cities (which, in justice, had produced very few such specimens previously). Instead, die-stamping established there something akin to a monopoly, being used to produce not only relief decoration but also excellent piercing, enhanced sometimes by equally fine hand engraving. At the same time, moreover, relatively simple die-stamped labels in both the older-fashioned and newer Adam patterns began to figure more largely among those marked in Scotland, and even in Dublin, suggesting that some at least had been bought in as blanks from the English factories.

In contrast, most London label makers continued throughout to concentrate on casting for the grander, more highly decorated products aimed at a metropolitan elite, and hand working from the sheet for the run of simple outlines directed to a less affluent middle class. The few makers in Exeter and York followed this latter example. There were exceptions, such as the Barnards, who made good use of stamping, while Sampson Mordan produced some of the most finely stamped labels of all. In the main, however, London silversmiths seem to have scorned mechanised double die-stamping as a way to make wine labels, with the notable exception of vine leaves (and one might well ask where the stamped blanks for some of those originated). The full implications of that technical and industrial divide were not apparent until the twentieth century, but the economic writing, even within the small world of wine labels, was on the wall. London and its satellites still had the craftsmen and the metropolitan market, but the Midlands and the North had the machines.

A final word needs to be said about methods of attaching wine labels to decanters. A neck ring, usually formed by soldering together the ends of a wide rolled silver strip, presented no problem, since it was merely dropped on to the decanter's shoulder. In all other cases, however, some supplementary system of suspension was needed. One of those used, albeit rarely, was to form a length of silver wire 1mm or 2mm (about $\frac{1}{32}$ or $\frac{1}{16}$ in.) in diameter into a ring, which was then either soldered on to the upper edge of the label or more elaborately attached to it by some type of hinge. By far the most frequent method, however, was to use a length of handmade silver chain fitted at each end with a divided 'jump' ring, which could thus be attached to the label to form a suspension loop. The attachment might sometimes be by means of fixed rings, stamped or cast into or soldered on to the label itself. Most often, however, it was merely a matter of drilling or punching two small holes into the label to accept the 'jump' rings. The only special skill lay, therefore, in making the chain needed. To minimise tangling, chain for wine labels was usually made of double links, each formed by soldering together two small rings of narrow rolled strip in such a way that their planes were fixed at right angles to each other. That meant simultaneously closing the two rings, joining them to each other at the correct angle and linking the result to the previous pair, all in a single soldering pass, using an oil lamp for heat and a crude blowpipe to provide the draught. Manufacturing such chain by hand was thus by no means the least of the crafts embedded in the eighteenth- or nineteenth-century wine label.

With that, the history of wine label making and decorating techniques comes almost to an end. Silversmithing at large had many things still to learn: more efficient heat sources and temperature control; the uses of electricity, for power but also for electroplating, not least of base metal wine labels; the more varied and refined chemistry of alloys, abrasives and adhesives; above all, perhaps, the much larger use of rotary machines for spinning, turning and polishing. None of that, however, touched the making of silver wine labels more than tangentially. There were, of course, changes and improvements of detail after 1800, such as the introduction in London soon thereafter of cast-in lettering, but the general case is that all the nineteenth century methods were in place by the end of the eighteenth century: hand working from the sheet, casting in its various forms, and now the truly industrialised process of stamping. Even in the twentieth century (ignoring more or less minor aberrations such as machine engraving), the only significant innovation to record is the use of coloured enamelling in the 1920s and 1930s to reflect the Art Deco style then in vogue, and that itself served only a limited audience for a short time. As far as solid silver labels are concerned, all development during the last two hundred years has been a matter for the designers rather than the makers – which is only to say that, from its birth in the London of George II and de Lamerie, it needed little more than half a century for the technique of the silver wine label to reach full maturity.

PART 2 – GILDING

There is no doubt that gilding can enhance the appearance of some labels. Two methods were used to apply the gold. Fire gilding, the oldest method, involves applying a paste of gold and mercury to the surface, which is then heated until the mercury vaporises. A very thin coating of gold is left adhering (amalgamated) to the underlying silver. After polishing the effect is of a gold surface with a slight tinge of lemon yellow, but the colour can be deepened by repeating the process. Because mercury vapour is very injurious to the lungs, the process was superseded by an electrolytic method of depositing the gold. Gilding was very popular during the Regency period. Gilt labels with earlier date letters than 1810 may have been gilded after original manufacture. Some examples, however, were probably produced during the earliest days of wine labels. These are very rare.

The earliest known gilt labels are a 'two putti' set by Sandylands Drinkwater, bearing his first mark (1735-39). A gilded rococo label by John Harvey of 1739-45 is also known, as are other gilt metal escutcheons. In all these instances the gilding appears original, but today one cannot be absolutely certain that they were not gilded at a later date.

That gilded labels were in use in the eighteenth century is further confirmed by entries in the Wakelin Ledgers of 1779-80, which not only refer to the supply of gilt labels but also to gilding. The practice in the eighteenth century was to refresh the gilding on plate from time to time. Wine labels followed the fashion of other plate in use at the time.

Gilt labels start to appear in greater numbers in the early nineteenth century, and reach a peak of splendour and magnificence in the heyday of the Regency. At this time large, fashionable, ostentatious services of plate were all gilded and quite obviously the wine and sauce labels had to follow suit. It is not surprising then to find the large ornate labels of Paul Storr, Digby Scott, and Benjamin and James Smith to be gilded.

It may be that some plain labels were gilded at a later date, when such decoration was fashionable – during the rococo (1740-60) and Regency (1805-25) periods for instance. Silver gilt was out of fashion during the neo-classical period, so it is not surprising that one does not encounter any gilt labels by the Batemans or Phipps and Robinson, for example, whose main style was for neo-classical urns, swags and bright cut decoration. Gilding was also used to hide repairs or changes of name. In these instances the label often appears worn beneath the gilding and traces of a change of name tend to show through the gold.

Making

Figure 416.

If the hallmarks were struck on a label after it had been gilded, but before it was finally buffed or polished, then they will appear crisp and fresh. However, sometimes a customer would ask to have a silver label gilded. In this case the gilding would be done after hallmarking, the marks would not be as crisp, but the gilding would still be contemporary with the label. Certain well-known designs of Regency labels, such as Paul Storr's 'lion's pelt' and the large wreath of vine leaves with a banner across by Digby Scott and Benjamin Smith (see fig. 416, London, dated 1806), appear in equal numbers gilt and not gilt and again there seem to be some occasions when they were hallmarked before and sometimes after gilding. It is impossible to detect reliably with the naked eye whether gilding on a label is contemporary or indeed to tell whether it has been fire gilt with mercury and gold or whether it has been gilded electrolytically. Therefore pre-Regency silver gilt labels should be viewed with suspicion; they may be perfectly genuine or they may have been gilt a few years or decades after manufacture; there is no simple way of telling.

PART 3 – CONDITION

Condition is always a major consideration when contemplating a purchase. The standard advice is only to buy specimens in perfect condition. While this is sound enough in theory, especially if the acquirer justifies a purchase partly as an investment, it must be remembered that some of the rarer types might never become available or affordable in perfect condition. Thus, if an example is required, it may have to be imperfect. It must also be remembered that, for research purposes, a slightly defective example may have as much to say as a pristine one. Isaac Robert Cruikshank's *High Life Below Stairs* (see fig. 417), published by S.W. Fores of Piccadilly, London, shows the Prince Regent enjoying chicken and CURACOA in 1819 with his aide waving around a labelled decanter, which indicates that labels might often need repair. The decision on which criteria to adopt is obviously one for the individual concerned. In this part the main problem areas will be discussed.

With the exception of some of the very rarest designs that have only survived in a damaged or worn state, such as John Reily's oval 'oak garland', silver labels in poor condition are best avoided. When inspecting a label for the first time, as much attention should be given to the back as to the face. Begin by looking for obvious physical damage, such as splits, parts missing, holes and excessive wear. The degree of wear is very much in the eye of the beholder, but if it has been sufficient for some of the finer elements of the decoration to have been lost, then it must count as serious.

Holes occur chiefly on die-stamped labels where the higher points of the design have been worn through. They have also been perpetrated by some early collectors who wished to pin up their trophies and drilled one or two holes to facilitate the process. In cast designs holes and splits can have occurred at the time of manufacture because insufficient metal was put into the mould or because the cooling was uneven. This should not be considered too serious unless it is disfiguring. Holes can also occur naturally if the engraving of the wine name has met one of the hallmarks on the reverse, either because one or the other was done too deeply or because the metal was too thin. Again this should not be regarded too seriously unless the holes are large. Usually they are mere pin-pricks. Sometimes such perforations are hidden by blacking in the letters; so always look for it seeping into the marks on the reverse. Holes in the lettering can also be a sign of re-engraving, which is discussed later.

Missing parts should be detectable quite easily either by rough edges or by an imbalance in the design. However, some designs can be converted into others if parts are lost. For instance, a 'goblet and festoon' that has lost part of the festooning can have the rest removed so that it appears to be a 'goblet'. Such conversions are not always easy to assess and there is no substitute for a thorough knowledge of design.

Having inspected a label for damage, the next logical step is to look for repairs. The most frequently encountered will be repairs of splits and breaks. Old repairs may have been done with lead solder, which is a duller colour than silver and was usually applied too liberally, leaving a definite blob. More recently, silver solder will have been employed. While closer in colour, silver solder still has a yellowish tinge and shows up clearly when breathed upon. Unless very skilfully applied, there will be a slightly convex and shiny surface to the repaired area. Missing parts may have been restored and soldered on, in which case the same points apply. Sometimes the label may have been plated over to disguise the repair and this problem will be covered below.

The most common defect from which labels suffer is the re-engraving of the wine name. This has almost always been done quite genuinely by owners whose tastes changed. Thus a family in the late eighteenth century who started drinking sherry instead of mountain would take their MOUNTAIN labels to the silversmith to have them re-engraved rather than go to the expense of buying new ones. The growing fashion for whisky in the nineteenth century was probably responsible for more re-engraving than any other single cause and the presence of this name on any label made before 1820 is a prime reason to suspect re-engraving.

There are four methods of changing the wine name on a label and, in order of frequency of encounter, they are filling-in, erasure, cutting-out and covering-over. As regards the first method, the old lettering will be filled in with solder before the new name is engraved. This can be detected in the same way as soldered repairs. The reason why breathing on silver shows up solder is that vapour condenses at a different rate because of the difference in conductivity between the two metals. The same effect is achieved by putting the object in the fridge for a few minutes or by applying photographic dulling spray. If the work has not been done skilfully, there will also be a slight pitting on the surface of the solder. As with repairs, the tell-tale signs can be disguised by electroplating, which is discussed below.

With the second method, that of erasure, detection is much easier. A significant quantity of metal will have been removed, so there will be a definite thinness of gauge in the affected area. Frequently the metal has been left so thin that the new lettering goes right through in places or hits the hallmarks on the reverse, thus creating holes. In the case of heavier gauge labels, there will be a dishing or a flattening of the surface, which will be clearly discernible when looked at along the side plane. Sometimes the metal is beaten out from the back to get over this problem, but this leaves an obvious hammered out trough on the reverse, which will also have flattened the hallmarks if placed there. In most cases of erasure, parts of the design or decoration surrounding the name tablet will have been taken away as well.

The last two methods of removing an old wine label are less common. In the case of cutting-out, the engraved area is removed and a fresh piece of silver inserted. This will leave a solder line around the new silver and frequently involves the hallmarks being lost in the process. Apparently unmarked labels should always be inspected for such surgery. In the case of covering-over, a new piece of silver will have been soldered over the old name. While this can usually be recognised instantly, it can be difficult to see in the more involved designs where the name tablet takes the form of a distinct reserve. However, the soldered line will still be there and the tablet area will be thicker in gauge than the rest of the label. Whichever method has been employed to change the name of the label, it will usually result in the piercing or engraving of the wine name being fresher and sharper than the rest of the design.

The presence of solder resulting from repairs and some methods of re-engraving can be hidden by electroplating the whole label. This involves coating the piece with a layer of pure silver and will leave the surface brighter and whiter than is normal for sterling silver, which is only 92.5 per cent pure. However, a similarly unnatural bright and white surface can be the effect of over cleaning, especially if Silver Dip has been used excessively, as this product burns off all the impurities on the surface of silver. The whiteness of new plating can also be toned down by oxidising agents, such as domestic bleach, but a plated surface will still retain a slightly oily feel and be sensitive to finger prints.

A similar problem that may be encountered is the habit of some early collectors of coating their labels in lacquer or having them plated with rhodium in order to save themselves the chore of cleaning. Old lacquer yellows with age and should be quite evident. It is easily removed with paint stripper. Rhodium, however, is an inert white metal that bonds with the silver and cannot be removed. It has a steely blue tone and, if suspected, can be tested for by placing a dot of domestic bleach on the back of the label. If the metal in contact with the bleach blackens within a couple of minutes, it is untreated. If the metal does not react, it has been rhodium plated.

A few hours should be spent studying the surface of old silver under a strong glass, so that the deep patina of accumulated wear and cleaning can be appreciated. This surface is impossible to recreate. So, if the surface of an antique object under magnification appears mirror smooth, or if the pattern of scratches is all of the same depth or tends to follow the same direction, alarm bells should start to ring. At best the label has been over cleaned. More likely it has been interfered with in some way.

OSP labels are more vulnerable to wear than those in other materials because the copper base will begin to be exposed as the silver coating wears through. A little copper showing through at the highlights should not be regarded as a detraction. Indeed most collectors of this material find it natural and attractive. The amount of copper that a person finds acceptable varies. Significant wear should be reflected in the price. Given this problem, however, it is necessary to be constantly on one's guard against re-plating. All of the points made above about the colour and feel of re-plated silver apply here, but there are a couple of further indications. Firstly, if the finer points of the design are worn but the copper is not showing through, then this is a definite sign that the item has been

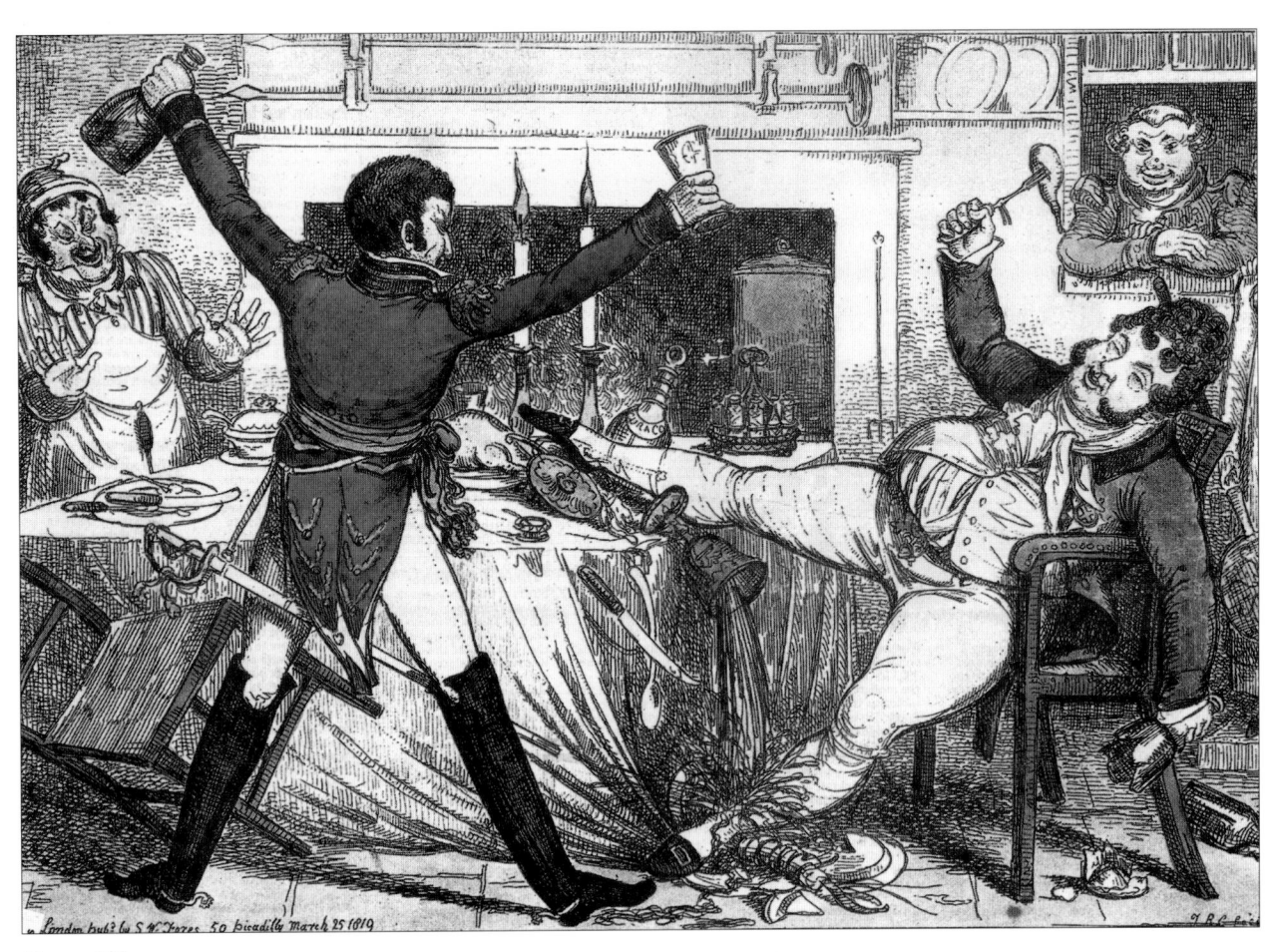

Figure 417.

re-plated. Secondly, a sound knowledge of construction will enable the viewer to detect edges that should be bare or soldered, but which have been covered when the label was electroplated.

Unless there is an obvious disparity between the degree of wear to the design and the condition of the plating, it is impossible to tell if an electroplate label has been re-plated.

Enamel labels of the eighteenth century will very rarely be encountered in absolutely perfect condition. Being a form of glass, enamel is too delicate and brittle to survive prolonged use without some damage. Added to this, it will expand and contract at a different rate from its copper base, leading inevitably to some cracking of the surface. Once the surface has been cracked, the copper base will become vulnerable to oxidisation, which will further loosen the hold of the enamel. For this reason enamel labels should never be washed in water, let alone in warm water. The degree of acceptable damage varies with the individual, but, because of its high incidence, restoration is common. Old restoration will have discoloured and be quite evident, but recently it has become more skilful. Modern restoration entails the object being refired, which will give it a glassy appearance and feel that is easily recognised with practice. An inspection of surface patination under a strong glass, as described above for silver, is also a sure test.

Enamel labels were extensively reproduced from the late nineteenth century onwards, principally by the Paris firm of Samson. Their products often bear a mark of crossed S's on the reverse. Later reproductions also show a tendency for green copper oxidisation to seep into the edges of the white enamel on the back, which will also frequently fall a little short of the edge of the label. There is little published guidance on enamel labels, other than those made by the short-lived Battersea factory (see Chapter 8, Parts 3 and 4), so the collector has to develop his or her own understanding of palette, motifs and construction in order to distinguish between the products of the eighteenth, nineteenth and even twentieth centuries.

Making

PART 4 - FAKES AND CONVERSIONS

The sort of mirror-smooth surface described earlier as a clear warning that something undesirable has happened to a label could also be evidence that it is a complete fake. These are fortunately quite rare, but there was a short spate of fakes in the early 1980s, often made from pieces of old silver bearing genuine hallmarks. The metal was usually unnaturally thin, and all had absolutely mint engraving. A few examples from this workshop are also known with fake Scottish provincial marks, the most noteworthy of which was a confection putatively from Perth in the form of the city arms.

A second, and equally rare, form of fake is the conversion of a genuine silver object into a wine label by engraving it with a wine name and fitting it with a chain. Badges and insignia were the most popular forms for such conversions, most of which seem to date from the 1950s and 1960s. These cases are not easy to prove absolutely. The best advice is to remain well on the side of caution when confronted by a highly unusual design on which the wine name does not sit happily (see fig. 574).

The final type of fake that may be encountered is a label that has been recast from an original. These are easily identified as the hallmarks have a coarse, grainy appearance that stands out when compared with genuinely struck marks. The same grainy texture can often also be detected in the deeper parts of the design. Some of the more common Bateman designs have been subjected to this form of reproduction, as has the elephant of Daniel Hockley. Examples of the latter have been found in India, and it could be that they were produced by contemporary manufacturers seeking to satisfy local demand by the quickest and cheapest method.

A few incidences have been noted of 'mother-of-pearl' gaming counters being converted to wine labels by engraving a wine name, drilling a couple of holes and attaching a chain. Fish shaped counters are the most frequent subject (see figs. 418, 420-423, 427-429).

Imitations of English hallmarks, known as pseudo hallmarks (see fig. 433), were often employed by silversmiths in the British colonies, China and the USA, mostly in the first half of the nineteenth century. These pseudo hallmarks are not regarded as fakes or forgeries. Few would fool a modern collector and they are accepted as genuine marks of the various locations and silversmiths where

Figures 418-426. Mother-of-pearl labels.

Making

Figures 427-432. Mother-of-pearl labels.

this practice was followed. They are discussed in Chapter 4, Part 1 and in several parts of Chapter 9. Pseudo marks can occasionally be found on electroplated labels and these are discussed in Chapter 8, Part 6 (see also fig. 1195 for GIN in electroplate with imitation sterling silver marks shown in fig. 1231).

PART 5 – REVIVALS AND REPRODUCTIONS

From time to time labels appear whose design is out of context with their date. Usually they are reversions to an older period and there can be several reasons for them, other, of course, than the deliberate misrepresentations considered above (see Chapter 3, Part 4, above) or the retention of designs in the provinces for many years after they had gone out of fashion in London.

One such category can be classed as a 'continuation piece', where the owner of a cherished set has added later labels of the same design for new wines in his cellar. He could have had one of the existing labels in the set re-engraved (see Chapter 3, Part 4, above), or he could have had another label made, perhaps by the same firm if it was still active, or else by its successor. An indication of this would be a set of labels of the same design with different dates, or with a later mark of the original firm. There is clearly no intention to deceive, here, but rather a laudable desire by the owner to harmonise the silver on his table.

The next class to consider is of labels manufactured in a style and design that has come back into fashion many years later – a genuine revival of an older taste. It could be argued that neo-classicism was based on a reversion to more ancient classical styles, but its appearance led to genuinely new designs and is not, therefore, the same thing. More germane is the reaction that followed Regency exuberance and that led to a revival of rococo style decoration (with its naturalistic embellishments, flowers, shells and leaves) and then to neo-gothic styles in the 1830s and 1840s. Examples can be seen in escutcheons, crescents and gadroon-edged rectangles made by C. Reily and G. Storer and many other makers during these years in London, while in Birmingham G. Unite was producing escutcheons that had machined floral and Jacobean-style decorations.

The third class consists of deliberate reproductions or copies of early labels (see fig. 76), but it then becomes necessary to ask when a revival becomes a reproduction. There is, perhaps, no firm or universal answer, but a guiding rule might be that a label continuing a set, or the reappearance of a design after a gap of years, are conscious observances of a certain taste or culture, whereas reproductions have a different purpose. They are likely to be of more recent date, to be modelled on rarer, and possibly unique, originals and to appear at any time, not dependent on a change of culture. They may not appeal to the collector of antiques, but they copy designs that have stood the test of time and, as they are likely to be less expensive than the originals, they are accessible to a wider clientele. Deciding if they are successful has to be a matter for individual judgement.

PART 6 – CARING AND CLEANING

Writing in 1745 Dr Jonathan Swift (fig. 434) advised the butler that when polishing the silver he should leave some of the polish in the crevices to prove that he had been assiduous in his task. This may not appeal to today's collector, who wants the chasing to be clear and the areas behind the putto's ears to be as unblemished as a child's after his or her bath. It must, however, be remembered that all polishing is abrasive and corrosive in its action, physically or chemically, and repeated polishing will eventually wear away the metal. The use of solid or liquid polish should therefore be restrained; when either is used the label should be washed well afterwards and left to dry.

Washing in warm soapy water is, in fact, the best way of keeping labels clean, followed by a gentle rub with a soft cloth. The best way of dealing with ordinary tarnish, the dullness of appearance from which all silver exposed to the air naturally suffers – and the more polluted the air, the more quickly it happens – is to apply a 'foam' polish (which comes as a solid, in a tin) with a sponge, or immerse the label in a liquid cleaner for not more than a few minutes, then wash it in clean water and repeat the process if necessary. Both these substances depend on chemical reaction to remove the blackened or dull surface, and will affect the metal if used in excess. If they are applied sparingly, however, and the label is thoroughly washed afterwards, no harm will be done. Polishing with a soft dry cloth will bring back the natural patina. One form of liquid cleaner on the market is styled 'long term'. It contains an inhibitor that slows down the tarnishing process and so makes cleaning necessary less often.

If a maker's mark or hallmark is badly blackened, obscured by dirt or old polish, so that the details are hard to distinguish, and if they do not respond to warm soapy water, immerse them in the cleaner and use a toothbrush (bristle, not nylon) or a toothpick, being careful not to probe too hard and risk scarring the silver. The engraved letters of a name can become blackened too, but be careful that it is tarnish or dirt that you are attacking and not the remains of black-wax filling. The letters of many engraved titles used to be black-wax filled, and in the course of time the filling has partially disintegrated. The traces can be considered unsightly and some claim that their removal is justified, but this may involve heavy physical pressure and consequent risk of damage. It seems preferable to leave them as they are, and not to tinker with what age and long usage have brought about.

Another method of preservation is to coat the label so that the metal has no contact with the air. The coating material must, of course, be transparent and colourless. It must not 'yellow' or otherwise lose its transparency with time, temperature or air condition. There are lacquers (acrylic are best) that fulfil these conditions, but they have to be carefully applied to avoid leaving brushmarks or an uneven surface. It is important, too, before embarking on this process, to know how to remove the lacquer without damage, if this becomes desirable (see Part 4).

There was a fashion some years ago for giving labels a rhodium coating (see Part 3). Because rhodium fuses chemically with silver, it is practically impossible to remove without damaging the label. Although it produces a shiny appearance that lasts forever, and only requires an occasional rub with a soft cloth to keep it bright, it hides the natural marks that arrive with age and use, the overall effect is unnatural and it is not as attractive as the real patina of old silver. Many collectors discount labels that have been so treated and the practice should be discouraged.

There are also on the market liquid 'silver solutions' that can be applied with a brush to areas of wear. The process is, in effect, a form of silver-plating. A disadvantage is that, being very thin, the patch will wear away under subsequent cleaning. In any case, it is hard to match the colour of the patch with that of the original surface. It is not suitable for labels, particularly OSP or electroplated ones.

Silver or plated labels should not be stored so that they are left in contact with rubber (for example, a rubber band). Rubber leaves an indelible black stain on the metal and erodes it seriously.

CHAPTER 4

MARKS

PART 1 – HALLMARKS ON EARLY LABELS

In order to understand what hallmarks the early manufacturers of wine labels, or bottle-tickets, in England and Wales were expected to put on when, in the mid-1730s, the demand first arose for these 'devices for marking bottles by', to quote Dean Jonathan Swift (fig. 434) in his will of 1740,[1] we must go back to 1697, when an Act of William III brought in the new higher standard for silver, the Britannia standard (95.8 per cent fine) in lieu of the sterling standard (92.5 per cent fine). The new standard does not, of itself, really concern us, because it ceased to be compulsory before wine labels were invented and silver of this standard was rarely used for manufacturing labels (see below, Part 4, The Britannia Marks). One provision of the Act did have an impact as regards their hallmarking: the Act laid down that all articles of wrought plate had to be hallmarked, granting exemption only to 'silver wire and things which in respect of their smallness are incapable of receiving a mark'.[2] It was only, in fact, making explicit what had been implied in general terms in previous legislation, but it opened a loophole. It did not define such items precisely, nor did another Act, passed the following year, which once more ordered all workers in small wares to put their own mark on them and added that shopkeepers were not to retail items that did not have the touch of the Hall or a maker's mark. The intention, presumably, was to clarify the two earlier pieces of legislation that, until then, had been the main regulators of the system. One of these was the Act of 1363, which had instituted the maker's mark or sign and ordered it to be put on all articles 'which ought to be touch'd' after they had been assayed. The second was the Act of 1478, which forbade the setting for sale of any article 'which would bear the Touch' until it had been assayed and received the mark of the maker.

Silversmiths manufacturing small items such as wine labels could therefore have reasonable grounds for confusion as to where they stood. There was no exact definition of 'small items' and

Figure 433. Pseudo hallmarks – see Chapter 3 Part 4.

Figure 434. Dr. Swift.

Figure 435. James Slater.

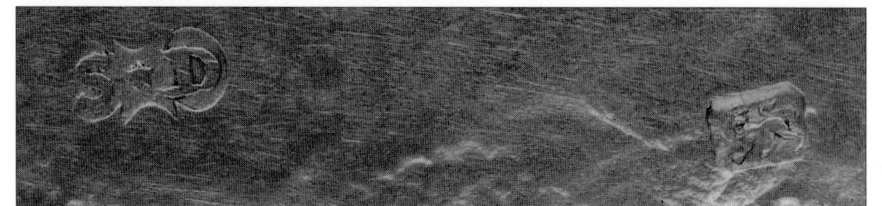

Figure 435a. Sandylands Drinkwater.

vagueness as to the articles which 'the Touch' applied to. Furthermore, there was some uncertainty as to how to describe and categorise labels, which were small and light in weight but usually capable of bearing a mark. To add to the confusion, if they were not being offered for sale through the usual commercial channels, but were made to a client's special order, it could be construed that the labels were not liable for assay, a factor that assumed extra importance from laws passed in 1716 and 1720.

The law of 1716 enabled Goldsmiths' Hall to charge a levy for carrying out the assay, that of 1719 enabled English provincial assay offices to adopt the lion passant as a device, and that of 1720, when restoring the old standard makers' marks, imposed a duty, payable at the time of assay, on articles of silver 'which should be, or ought to be touch'd'. Label manufacturers clearly had an incentive for claiming that their wares fell outside these regulations, but in practice they took the line of caution and self-interest. They did not send their labels for assay, but they put their own mark on to ensure that work was credited as theirs, and they sometimes had the lion passant mark put on as well. This mark, as explained in Part 2 of this chapter, was the mark of the Goldsmiths' Company and indicated the sterling quality of the silver. Although by the 1730s it was not yet an obligatory part of the assay, label manufacturers could take the view that if its presence helped to convince the customer of the label's integrity, it was clearly sensible to have it there.

Clearly there was much latitude as to how the legislation was to be interpreted, and the government had other causes for concern too. Duty dodging was leading to considerable loss of revenue and the range of 'small items' which were avoiding marking was increasing continually. So in 1738 the Plate Offences Act was introduced in an attempt to remove these anomalies and simplify the whole hallmarking procedure. The two types of makers' marks that had distinguished old and new standards of silver were abolished, and henceforth silversmiths were to use one new mark (see Part 5, below). Further, the application of the lion passant was to be compulsory. The Act also clarified the confusion about 'small wares' by naming specifically those that were to be exempt, but then recreated confusion by allowing a general exemption to 'such other things as by reason of smallness or thinness are incapable of receiving the mark, or not weighing 10dwt.'.

Neither wine labels nor bottle-tickets are listed and Penzer surmised that this was because they were still unknown. This is only partially correct, as we now know that the earliest mention we have for them is in March 1737.[3] The officers of the Hall must have decided which articles were to be included in the new Act. Labels existed, but they were not in common circulation and had no firm description, so they escaped consideration. This seems a more likely explanation for not listing them by name as exempt than to argue that labels were known but deliberately not put on the exempt list because they were clearly capable of being hallmarked. If the latter had been the case, the government would surely not have allowed the ambiguity as to the application of the Act, which the manufacturers invoked, to continue without clarification until 1790.

Before May 1739, then, when the Plate Offences Act became law, labels might be expected to have the maker's old standard mark, accompanied sometimes by the lion passant in use between 1729 and 1739. After May 1739 they will have the new form of the maker's mark, and, for a few months, the same lion). We do not know exactly when the next version of the sterling lion was introduced, but it was probably in about August of that year, after which both marks are in new form. There does not seem to be any consistency as regards the application of the lion passant mark on labels, even after it had supposedly become obligatory, nor can any strict rule be deduced as to how the maker's mark should be struck. Sometimes it is struck once, and sometimes twice. It has been suggested that this double striking was done simply to provide a proper number of stamps, in order to satisfy a public that had no real understanding of hallmarking law. Fig. 435 shows the mark of James Slater, entered between October 1725 and January 1728 (Grimwade reference 1647), struck once on a wine label.

By the mid-1750s it was usual for a label to have some marks, but a considerable number of labels of earlier date have no mark at all. Some manufacturers may have felt that as they believed these articles to be exempt from assay there was no need to mark them. It may be, too, that some yielded to temptation and used substandard silver, though random inspection of unmarked labels does not support this. It does appear, however, from ledgers, invoices and early inventories, that many early orders for labels were for multiple sets, and in these cases the manufacturers may have taken the view that it was sufficient only to put their marks on one of the set. In the course of time the sets have been broken up and the link between the marked and unmarked members of it have been lost. Some intact sets seem to lend weight to this theory.

PART 2 – THE STERLING LION

The origins of the lion passant guardant as a mark guaranteeing the standard of silver have been well explored by Jackson[4] and, so far as the appearance of this mark on wine labels is concerned, further clarified by Penzer.[5] The lion passant guardant was adopted by Goldsmiths' Hall as an indication that the silver was of sterling standard, hence the name by which it is known. It has also been thought of as a mark denoting London, but this is incorrect, as legislation referring to the lion mark after the Act of Union with Scotland generally applies to Great Britain. The sterling lion is an important aid, however, in identifying limiting dates for early labels by London makers, and it can be a useful guide for provincial labels as well. Three of these Goldsmiths' Hall lion marks cover the main period of wine labels.

The earliest London assay office lion that is likely to be found on a wine label is the lion passant of 1729-39. The punch is a plain oblong rectangle containing a smooth bodied lion with a large head (see fig. 435). The outline of the punch is generally rectangular with slightly rounded, or lightly clipped corners. Obviously a large number of different punches were in use at one time, so allowance must be made for slight variation in die-cutting and wear and tear. This lion ceased to be used at some time during the Goldsmiths' Company year 1739-40. Jackson shows two different punches for the date letter 'd' of this year. The first was taken into use in May, when the Company's year started, but the records do not show when the second one, in the different punch which continued for the remainder of the cycle, replaced it some months later. Makers' marks changed, too, in May 1739, to comply with the legislation of the previous year, so when their new marks are found on labels that have the 1739-39 lion the date can be fixed to within a few months with real certainty. An example of this anomalous combination is a label by Sandylands Drinkwater (see fig. 435a), which has his second 'new' mark with the 'old' (1729-39) lion. Fig. 325 shows his new mark with the new lion. Fig. 436 shows his old mark with the old lion.

The London lion of 1739-50 is similar to that of 1729-39, but the outline of the punch is distinctive in that it follows the outline of the lion and has three indentations at the base and sides of the shield. Variations have been noted in the number and positioning of the indentations, but these may be attributed to the whims of the punch cutter. The lion of 1751-56 is similar, but instead of having three indentations at the base it has two blips.

Marks

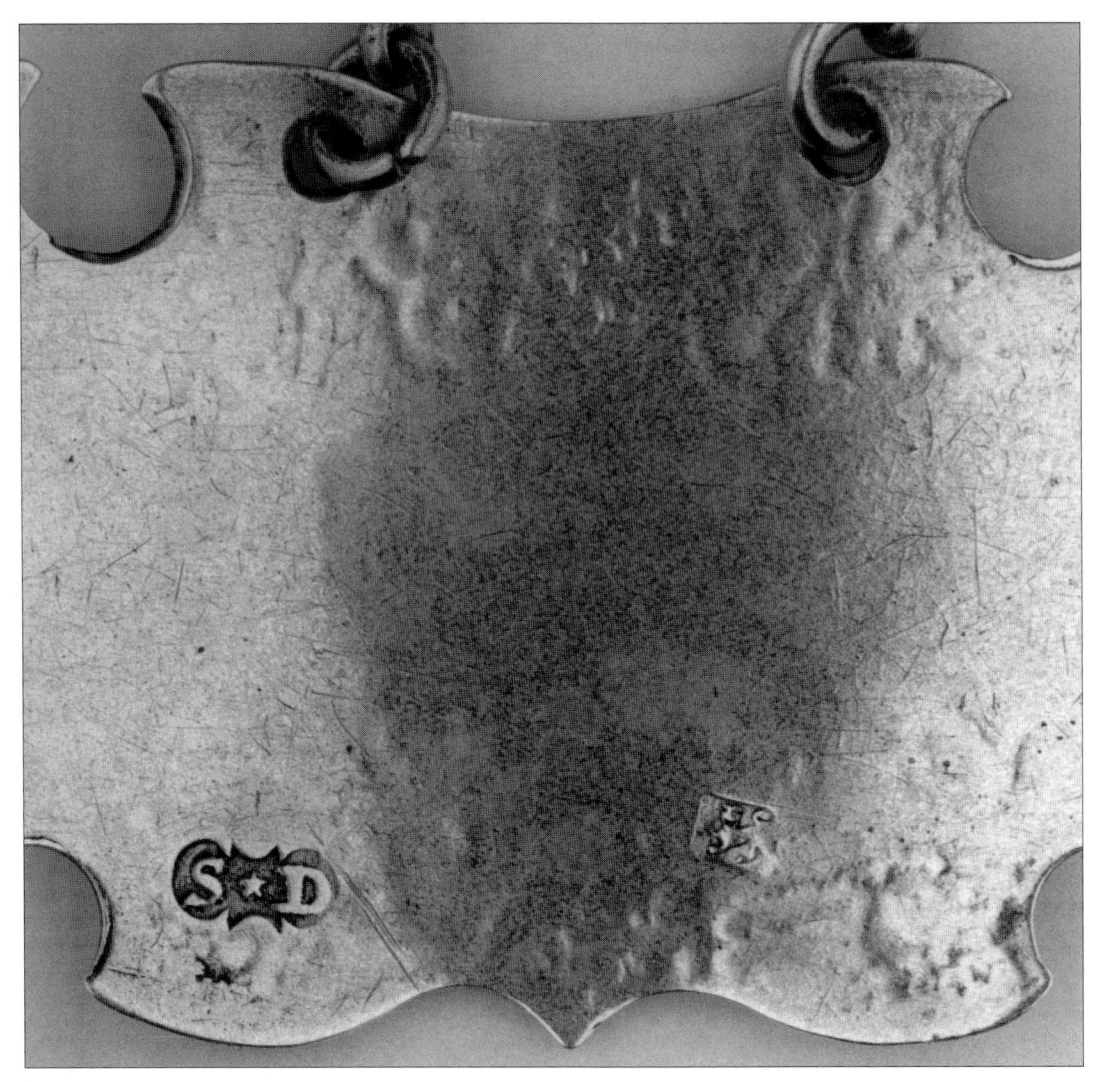

Figure 436.

The London lion of 1739 has not been recorded on hallmarked silver with a date letter of the cycle that started in May 1756, so the lion of 1756 presumably came in at the same time as the date letter change. Labels were still then exempt from assay, so that the lion, when present, can provide a 'cut-off' date – before or after 1756. The lion is still guardant, but different from the previous animal, having a large head with flowing mane and hairy legs. The outline of the punch is rectangular with the top corners slightly clipped and an ogee base coming to a pronounced point. It stayed in use until 1790, with minor variations to the size and shape of the punch, especially after 1776.

After 1790 labels were no longer exempt from assay and full hallmarking, so that the post-1790 London lion becomes relatively less important as an aid for dating purposes. Its appearance did alter in that year, as did the punch, to a frame with more pronounced cut corners. It stayed in this form, with further minor variations, until 1821. In that year it ceased to be guardant in London, and the punch became smaller. It remained thus until the end of the century. In the twentieth century the frame tended to change with each new cycle of date letters.

The lion passant marks used in the provincial assay offices have, in general, kept step with the London prototype, though changes in their introduction date have not always coincided with London. The animal himself, and the shape of the frame that contains him, vary sufficiently from office to office to provide a useful guide to identification. A particular aberration has been recorded on some labels from Newcastle and York of the last quarter of the eighteenth century, which have the lion progressing to the right. This is possibly explained as a mistake by the punch cutter.

PART 3 – PLATE DUTY MARKS

As noted above, duty was first imposed on wrought silver plate on 1 June 1720 at 6d. per ounce, but did not involve a mark on items assayed.[6] In 1758 it was replaced by a dealers' licence of £2. From 1 December 1784 plate duty was re-introduced (in addition to the licence), at 6d. per ounce on silver and 8s. per ounce on gold, to pay for the American War of Independence, and now its payment had to be recorded by a mark.

This 'duty' mark was used at all the assay offices (including Edinburgh, but not necessarily the Scottish provincial incorporations who used deacons to approve marking and hence did not technically have 'assay offices')[7] administered by the Commissioners of Stamps, who had jurisdiction over the new tax. It consisted of the reigning sovereign's head in profile and at first was an intaglio (incuse) of George III, facing left, in a rectangular outline with clipped corners (see fig. 437, on a spoon; fig. 443, R:PORT by Hester Bateman; fig. 444, RUM by John Lee II; and fig. 445, PORT by Thomas Watson overstriking Hester Bateman's mark). It was used between 1 December 1784 and 29 May 1786 in London and until later in the provinces. Wine labels were exported and an exportation mark (see figs. 461 and 461a) might have been applied, in use at all assay offices in 1784-85, known as the 'duty drawback' (see below, Part 4, The Britannia Marks).

Figure 437.

In 1786 it was decided that, at the start of the next annual date letter of the London assay office on 29 May 1786, the duty mark should be merged with the others in a block. Known at the time as a 'stub', this was intended for use in a machine press. It was impractical to have an incuse mark with others that were in cameo, so the duty mark was changed to conform, and was put in an oval frame with the head facing right (see figs. 438 and 446 RUM by Elizabeth Morley).

It is not generally appreciated that the only purpose of the sovereign's head mark was to act as a receipt for the payment of duty and as such was intended to be struck before the assay took place. This is illustrated very clearly on a London label by Elizabeth Morley, where the stub overstrikes the duty mark and was therefore punched after it, and on an Edinburgh spoon (see fig. 439). As London was held responsible for the collection of this tax from all the other assay offices, the despatch of these punches was carefully controlled from Goldsmiths' Hall. Until the first quarter of the nineteenth century, the provincial offices had the duty mark as a separate punch, but those assay offices that used the stub had it sent to them with the sovereign's head already engraved, the other assay marks being made locally.

These provincial offices were sent their new cameo punches by the Commissioners of Stamps late in 1786, with specific instructions that they were not to be used before 1 January 1787. It is therefore possible to find provincial incuse heads used in conjunction with a 1786 date letter. Examples have been noted from Birmingham and Newcastle.

The sovereign's head mark was thus a clear indication that duty had been properly paid. The penalties for improper use were horrific, so although labels appeared to be still legally excepted from assay, many manufacturers of them had doubts and preferred to be cautious, sending their labels in and accepting the payment of the duty (which they could then pass on to the customer). It became increasingly common, therefore, after 1 December 1784 to find the duty mark on wine labels,

Marks

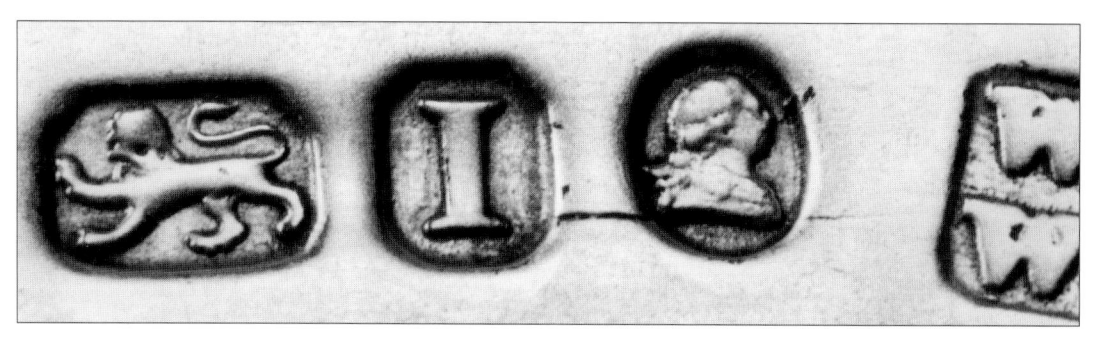

Figure 438.

Figure 439.

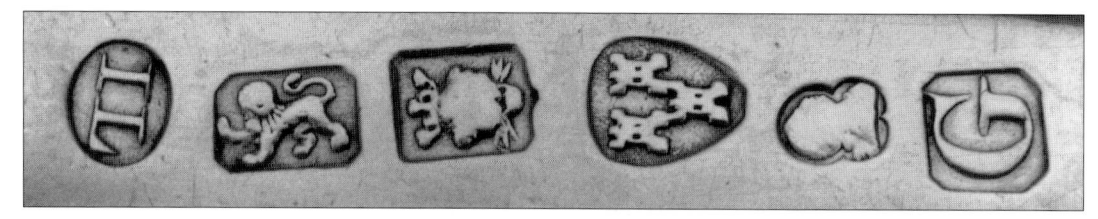

Figure 440.

accompanying the maker's mark and the lion passant guardant.

The next and culminating event affecting the marks on labels was the Marking of Silver Plate Act of 1790,[8] which removed all doubts about their status and nomenclature. The Act stated that wine labels were not exempt from assay. This meant that after May 1790 all London assayed labels should be marked with the leopard's head, the maker's mark, an alphabetical date letter, the lion passant and the sovereign's head duty mark. In practice, however, they seldom had all five until much later. The maker's mark was invariably the main item; the date letter became a regular feature; and the leopard's head, crowned or uncrowned, was not used until the nineteenth century. The alterations to the lion passant are covered in the previous section of this chapter, while the punch that contained the sovereign's head and variations to it are discussed below.

Variations occur in the outline shape of the oval duty mark on plate assayed at London in the years 1797, 1804 and 1815, in each of which additional duty had to be paid. In the years immediately following the shape reverted to a plain oval, so it is evident that these variations were not intended to represent a new rate of duty *per se*, but rather to show that the *increase* had been paid for that year. The other assay offices used the three-cusped or trefoil mark in 1797, and apparently indiscriminately thereafter, until the late 1820s.

The first increase in duty was from 5 July 1797 when it doubled on both silver and gold to 1s. and 16s. per ounce respectively. The London assay office denoted this by the use of two cusps in the outline of the punch. The placing of these cusps depends on the position of the duty mark relative to the others in the stub – see figs. 462 (left-hand cusp) and 463 (right-hand cusp) and fig. 447 (on a wine label, WHITE by Thomas Ollivant overstriking Hester Bateman's mark) all used in 1797. A third variation is the three-cusped mark used at the provincial assay offices (see fig. 440). Thus the normal duty mark has two cusps,

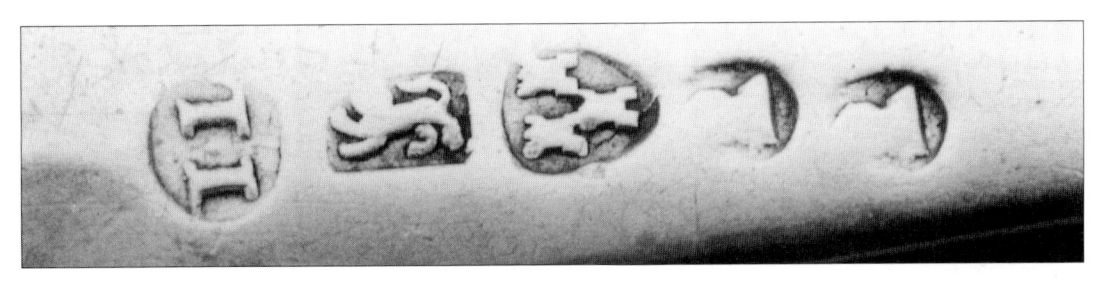

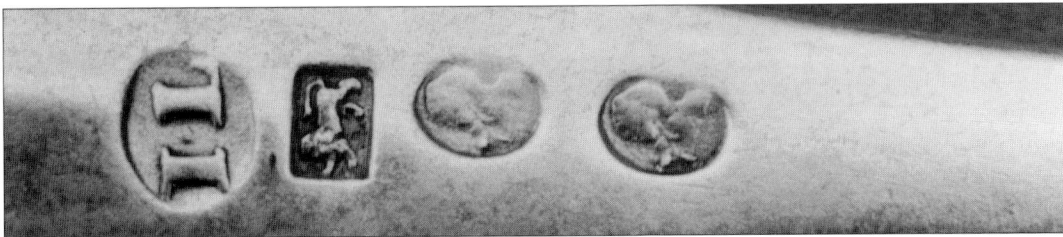

Figure 441.

namely a basal cusp and, if the duty mark appears on the right end of the stub, a right-hand cusp; if the duty mark is on the left-hand end of the stub, the second cusp is a left-hand cusp.

These new punches were used in London from 5 July 1797, but there was evidently a delay before they arrived at the provincial offices. Offices were requested by the Stamp Office to strike the current oval duty mark twice (see fig. 441, giving two examples in use at Newcastle) until the trefoil punch was received. The assay offices at Birmingham, Newcastle, Sheffield and York are all known to have used this double head mark, but no examples have been noted on wine labels. In Scotland, Edinburgh was the only burgh using the sovereign's head duty mark at the time. It used the trefoil, as prescribed, in 1797 and for a few years afterwards.

The next increase was effective from 10 October 1804, when the duty on silver rose to 1s.3d. per ounce, while that on gold remained unchanged. The London assay office used only one variation this year, namely a single basal cusp (see fig. 442). Two examples of the pre-11 October 1804 oval duty mark on wine labels are illustrated (see fig. 448, PORT, by John Reily and fig. 449, PORT, by Peter, Ann and William Bateman) and four examples of post-10 October 1804 cusped duty marks (see fig. 450, MADEIRA, by Phipps and Robinson; fig. 451, MALAGA, by HL/SD; fig. 452, MADEIRA, by Elizabeth Morley; and fig. 453, CLARET, by James Atkins).

Dublin, responsible for exacting duty in Ireland, was not liable to do so until 1807 and so was unaffected by the two earlier increases. From 1807 makers of Dublin-assayed silver paid 'the full amount of duty payable to His Majesty', namely 1s.3d. per ounce. There was a great variety in the outline shape of Irish duty marks over the years but, with one exception mentioned below, these had no relevance to the changes in duty.[9]

In 1815 there were two alterations to the duty, resulting in two variations to the shape of the punch from the standard oval that was in use at the beginning of the year (see fig. 454). On 14 June the extra levy, which English silver imported into Ireland had had to pay, was standardised with the

Figure 442.

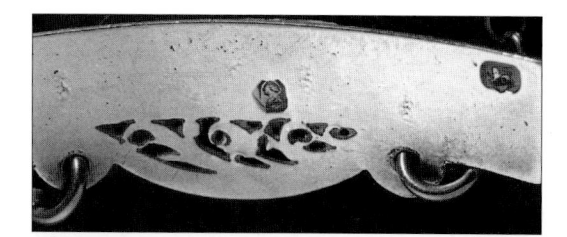

Figure 443.

Figure 444.

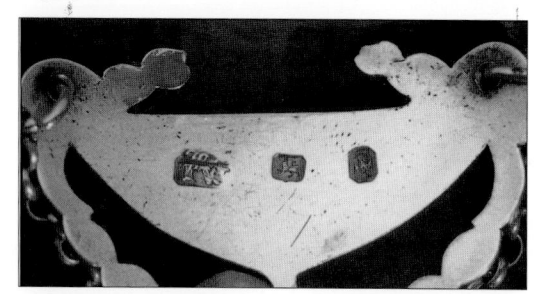

Figure 445.

Figure 446.

Figure 447.

Figure 448.

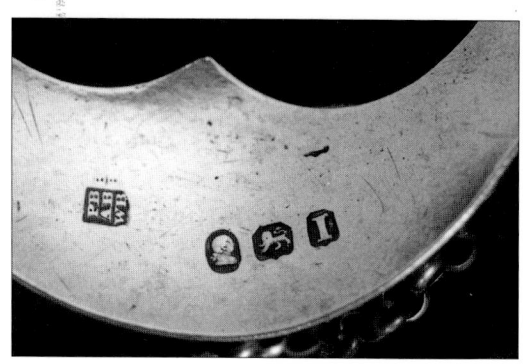

Figure 449.

Figure 450.

duty payable in Great Britain and a variant of the oval punch was introduced to mark silver assayed after that date. It had a single basal cusp similar to that used for the 1804 increase (see figs. 455 and 456), and it was only used in London, never in the provinces. On 31 August the duty was increased again to 1s.6d. for silver and 17s. for gold. This increase was marked by a further variant, a punch with a flattened base (see figs. 457 and 459), which was applicable throughout the country and remained in use until May 1816.

In Edinburgh, the Incorporation of Goldsmiths was requested to bring forward the start date of their year from 16 September to 1 September to match the start of payment at the new rate, which they agreed to do (see fig. 458).

By the 1830s all the assay offices,[10] with the exception of York, were using the stub method of

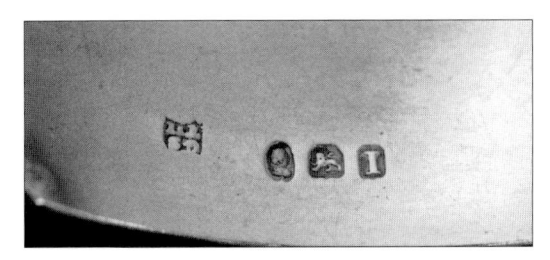

Figure 451.

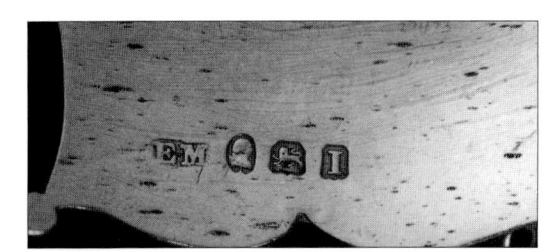

Figure 452.

Figure 453.

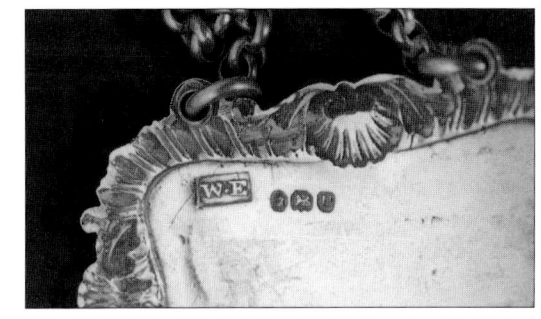

Figure 454.

marking, except where this was not practical, for example, where excessive curvature of a label prevented its use. The death of George III in 1820 did not automatically lead to a change of sovereign's head. As this was only a receipt of duty, the Stamp Office appeared to be content for out-dated punches to be used for some years.

The use of duty marks seen on York silver between 1820 and 1840 was erratic to say the least, that of George III being used as late as 1838, but George IV correctly used in 1824. The appearance of a trefoil-shaped punch for the head of George IV is very curious and is not known at any other assay office. It might imply that the previous rigorous control of these marks by the London Goldsmiths had lapsed somewhat.

The outline of Queen Victoria's head, from 1838 in London but not until various later dates in the provincial offices, was in a plain oval, facing left, unlike her three predecessors who faced right. Her profile remained the same until the abolition of duty in 1890, although the heads on her coinage aged with her.

Following Queen Victoria's accession to the throne in June 1837 there was a delay in the cutting and bringing into use at assay offices of new dies. John Smith, the Goldsmiths' Company's engraver

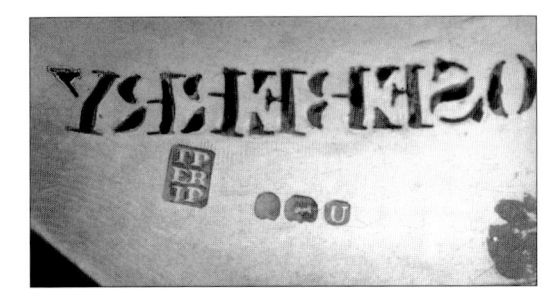

Figure 455.

Figure 456.

Figure 457.

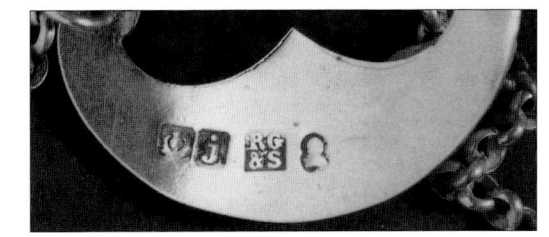

Figure 458.

Marks

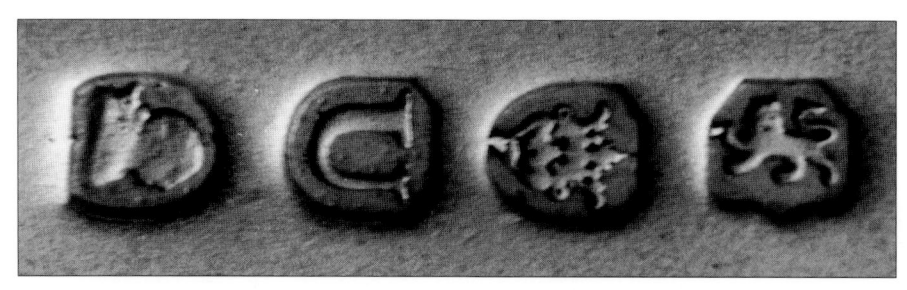

Figure 459.

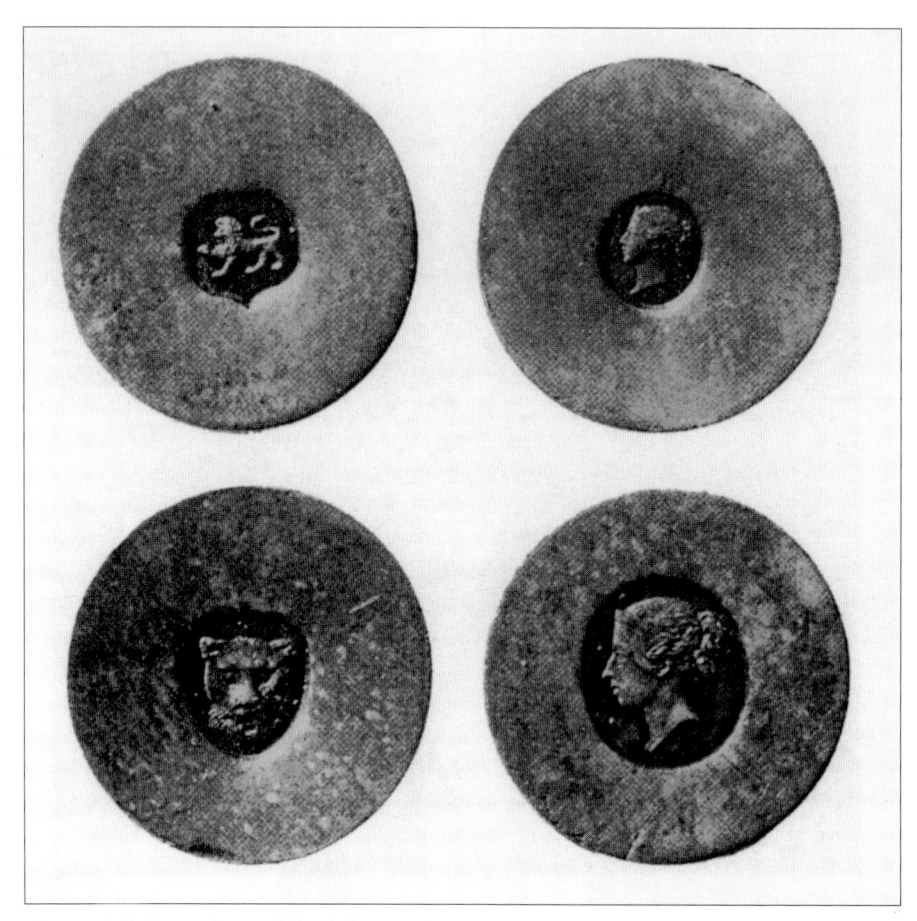

Figure 460 (originals one fifth of this size!).

at this time, suffered from deteriorating eyesight. He should not have continued working as an engraver, but he had four young children to support. At first the Court of the Company was sympathetic and reversed a decision to replace him.[11] It was generally agreed, however, that Smith's first duty mark of 1838/39 and second duty mark of 1839/40 were of poor quality,[12] so in July 1839 the Wardens invited a number of engravers (including Smith) to produce dies as specimens of their talent. At a Court Meeting held on 20 November 1839 impressions were inspected and it was unanimously resolved that those struck on circular pieces of silver be approved (see fig. 460 for the submitted impressions). In each case (leopard's head, lion passant and duty marks) the dies selected were the work of 'Mr. Wyon of Her Majesty's Mint'.[13] William Wyon was born in 1795. In 1828 he became the Chief Engraver to the Royal Mint. His work was much admired, particularly his engraving of a diademed head of Victoria for the 1838 Queen's Medal for the Royal Society. After November 1839 he was appointed to the office of engraver at Goldsmiths' Hall, a job he retained until his death in 1851. This anecdote may partly explain why it took so long for the new duty mark to reach the provincial offices.

PART 4 – THE BRITANNIA MARKS

To put her into her historical perspective, an image of the female warrior Britannia appears on the coinage of Roman Britain. Later, on coinage in 1577, she kneels before Elizabeth I and in 1604 she is shown presiding over oceans (or so it was claimed).

Until 1697 the silver used by the Mint and jewellers was equally pure – the silver content had to be at least 92.5 per cent. To stop silversmiths from melting down coins, a new standard was introduced. Known as the Britannia standard because its mark was the figure of Britannia, it stipulated that all silver objects other than coins had to be 95.8 per cent fine, equivalent to 23 carats. The Britannia standard was legally imposed from 27 March 1697 (officially 25 March, but the punches unsurprisingly arrived two days late). However, the higher standard silver was found to be easily damaged and too soft to take hallmarks well, and its use was made optional in 1720.

The Britannia mark has not been seen on eighteenth-century wine labels. Possible makers using this standard include John Harvey, a noted pioneer, who entered a 'new style' (Britannia) mark in January 1739, but the earliest labels known by Harvey bear his old style mark, entered in February 1738, and his third (sterling) mark of June 1739. Two nineteenth-century Britannia stamped labels have been noted, however: one made by George Knight in 1825 and the other (a sauce label) by William Knight II in 1831. Both are presumed to have been made to special order.

Britannia also appears as a duty drawback mark in a different format (see figs. 461 and 461a). When wrought plate was exported, duty could be reclaimed by virtue of a drawback clause in the Plate Duty Act of 1784. The repayment was initially indicated by a stamp referred to in the London Goldsmiths' Company records as the exportation mark. It consisted of an intaglio standing figure of Britannia holding a spear and shield.[14] It was only in use from 1 December 1784 to 24 July 1785, when it was withdrawn because of the damage it caused to finished articles. Thereafter drawback could still be claimed on production of a customs document.

Very occasionally the duty drawback mark has been recorded on wine labels. The scarcity of examples in Britain has probably added to its obscurity. Some makers may have preferred to pay the duty and forgo the drawback, rather than risk having their work damaged. Furthermore, since these articles were being exported, it is reasonable to suppose that the majority of them are still abroad. There was an overseas market for wine labels among purchasers of English silver in Europe and expatriate colonies, and firms with permanent offices abroad. A second reason for the mark being so little known is its absence from the original Jackson, which is curious since nearly all other books on hallmarks do have references to it.

Figure 461.

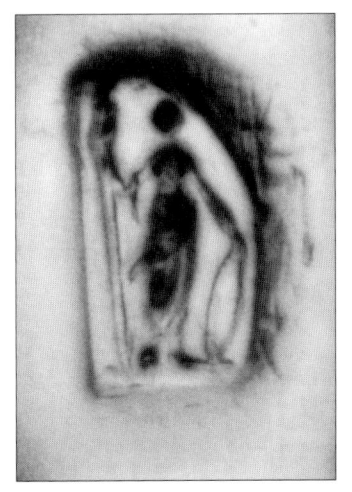

Figure 461a.

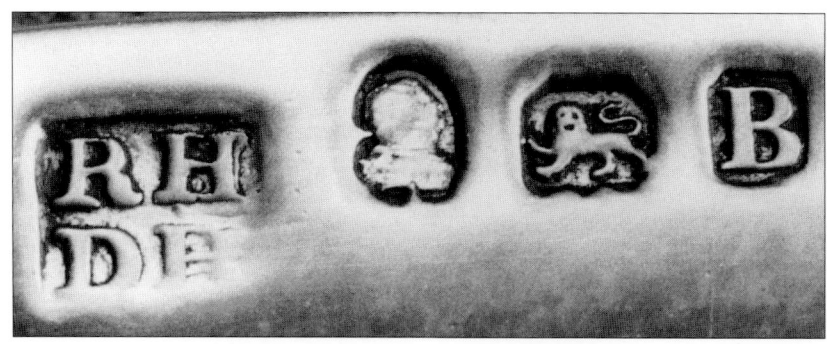

Figure 462.

Figure 463.

PART 5 – MAKERS' OR SPONSORS' MARKS

Silversmiths have been subjected to laws controlling the practice of their craft certainly since 1238. At first these laws mainly concerned the standard of gold and silver to be used, and set up provisions for assaying finished articles before they could be sold. In 1363 an Act of Edward III established the first regulation concerning makers' marks: every silversmith was to have his own mark, which was to be applied to every article, or part of an article, that he made, after it had been assayed. The purpose was to protect the customer against fraud, the use of substandard metal, by identifying the man who used it and enabling him to be brought to book. The law has been re-enacted, in one form or another, many times down the centuries since 1363. In time, happily, it was no longer necessary to regard it principally as a means of catching offenders against the law, though its purpose always remained the protection of the customer.[15] It has come to be a badge by which a craftsman can proudly distinguish his work and, as the attention paid to antique silver has grown, the maker's mark has assisted greatly in the study of that subject, particularly in the field of wine labels.

The legislation has always made it clear that maker's mark regulations applied throughout the country, to the provincial assay offices, to Scotland and to Ireland, as well as to London, though there have been occasions when they were observed more in the breach than in the observance. Recently, as the country has become more closely affected by European legislation, it has become necessary to comply with European attitudes and in 1973 the Hallmarking Act made great changes. The law that had made the maker's mark compulsory had to be abolished, but firms and individuals can still apply their mark if they wish and fortunately, in this country, the majority still do (see also below).

We must now return to the eighteenth century to consider the form that the maker's mark took when wine labels began to appear and how the silversmiths of the day applied the law as regards marking them. We start, as in Part 1 above, with the Act of William III of 1697, which brought in the new (Britannia) standard for silver and made compulsory new makers' marks to replace those for old standard silver, which by that time usually consisted of the first letters of the Christian and surname.[16] As explained in Part 1 above, the use of old standard silver was allowed again in 1720 and the old standard marks were restored. In the mid-1730s, therefore, two styles of makers' marks were to be found, but, in practice, little Britannia standard silver was being used and certainly no labels made to it have been recorded. It is worth mentioning that the precise style of the old standard marks was nowhere laid down, but it had become customary to use letters from the silversmith's name instead of the original emblems or signs of previous centuries as literacy became more general. For the silversmith and for the public the existence of two types of mark belonging to one manufacturer was bound to be confusing and it was one of the anomalies that the Plate Offences Act of 1738 was meant to remove. As stated above, this Act required the old makers' punches to be destroyed and new ones to be made. They were to consist, still, of the first letters of the Christian and surnames, but they were to be in a different form, and they were, of course, compulsory. They were to be registered at Goldsmiths' Hall in London, or at the appropriate assay office elsewhere, helping to ensure that no two makers' marks were alike, though in fact some are very difficult to tell apart. The shape and size of the punch was not laid down; the type of lettering (capitals, italics, script, etc.) could vary and the mark could incorporate a crown, a coronet, acorn, pellet or other device. It has not been found necessary to alter or amend the regulation since it became law in May 1739 and indeed it still applies on the voluntary basis described elsewhere.

Consider, next, the process of applying the mark. When it was first introduced in the fourteenth century, the goldsmith was the sole manufacturer of a piece and the mark he struck was clear evidence of his own workmanship and responsibility for an article. He may have had apprentices learning to do some of the work, but it was he who finished it and supplied it to the customer. As the eighteenth century advanced, workshops grew larger and more workmen were employed; apprentices stayed on with their masters, fully trained, for many years after they had gained their freedom, as did sons with their fathers, undoubtedly making some of the firm's products entirely themselves, but still stamping it with the mark of the head of the firm. Thomas Hyde, for example, son of Thomas Hyde senior, became free in 1770, but seems to have stayed on in his father's shop, using his father's mark, for his whole life and probably never entered his own mark at all. Hester Bateman employed a large workforce, and her children started off in her shop, too, before entering their own marks. There were clearly people in her employ carrying out every stage of manufacture, and indeed it has been said that she never herself engaged in actual silversmithing, but it is her mark that distinguishes all the firm's products. Richard Binley's story is slightly different. He worked for Sandylands Drinkwater, his master, for many years after obtaining his freedom in 1749, before registering his own mark in 1760. There is evidence, however, that Binley had had his own mark for several years previously, as it has been seen on labels with the pre-1756 lion passant, yet all the output of Drinkwater's workshop, in which Binley was employed, has only Drinkwater's mark.

There were, of course, still many silversmiths working alone, applying their own marks to their pieces and marketing them, but, as the industry grew, those who were retailers as well as manufacturers took to buying in part of their requirements – some of it marked by the firm from which they bought it, some of it unmarked – on which they put their own marks. James Barber (originally Hampston and Prince) in York increasingly during the nineteenth century obtained plate from the London firm of Emes and Barnard, both marked and unmarked.[17] The Wakelin Ledgers[18] show that George Wickes contracted work out to many small craftsmen which he retailed under his own firm's mark. Many small silversmiths, too, acquired labels made by somebody else and put their own mark on them if they were unmarked, or overstruck the original one. Labels from Hester Bateman's workshop have been recorded overstruck by Richard Evans of Shrewsbury, Thomas Oliphant of Chester District and Thomas Adcock (London). A later example, almost certainly emanating from a Bateman firm, has the mark of Louis Boudo, a silversmith in South Carolina.

Yet further indication of how the meaning of the term 'maker's mark' was changing is provided by the use of joint marks for partnerships (such as Phipps and Robinson). It is evident that the labels that bear their mark, although invariably of the same high quality, were wrought by many different hands. The mark carries the guarantee of quality, but does not indicate the actual workman. The development of die-stamping for manufacturing a series of labels of the same design shows the change of meaning even more clearly. The craftsman who created the design was not necessarily, indeed usually was not, the man who struck the die, and the label itself, with its mark, was not the sole handiwork of either of them. So, too, the appearance in makers' punches of phrases such as '& Co' or 'And Sons' shows that silversmiths were interpreting the term more as a trademark than as a signature of their personal workmanship.

It should be stressed that these practices – overstriking the original mark, putting your own mark on bought-in stock, making a run of die-stamped labels – were perfectly proper ways for silversmiths to execute the orders they received. If it is accepted that the mark a silversmith put on his label meant that he accepted responsibility for its quality and standard, even though he had not made it himself, which was now the case, then the hallmarking laws were being properly observed. It could even be that the customer might prefer to see the mark of a local firm, or a silversmith whom he knew, and whom he could hold responsible, to that of a maker unknown and distant. The interpretation could cover, too, the widow who continued to use her late husband's mark after his death, as she used up his stock.

The term 'maker's mark' continued, therefore, though decreasingly signifying the actual manufacturer, throughout the nineteenth century and for most of the twentieth century. It was not until the passing of the Hallmarking Act, which became law in 1973, that a change was made. This law abolished the compulsory use of all existing makers' marks. Henceforth it was to be called a sponsor's mark, which more accurately describes its function and legitimacy. The sponsor is the firm or individual silversmith who accepts responsibility for the quality and standard of an article. His mark can still be the one he used before the Act was passed, but it is no longer a compulsory hallmark.

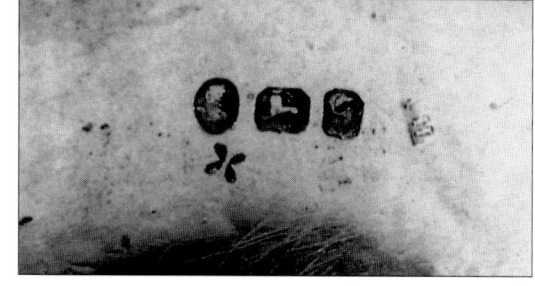

Figure 464.

Figure 465.

PART 6 – TALLY MARKS

As the major firms of silversmiths expanded during the eighteenth century, the employers took on more workmen, and needed to know who was responsible for each piece of work. Personal knowledge of an entry in a ledger might once have been enough, but if several benches were engaged on parts of a single order, a better system was needed. Furthermore, if the workmen were on piecework, the employer had to have a positive method for checking what he owed each man. Hence, each workman had his own tally mark, which he put on the article when he had finished it.

An example is to be found on a set of twelve oval labels commissioned from James Hyde between around 1786 and 1791 for the Sykes family of Sledmere. Seven of the labels have combinations of crosses and stars stamped alongside the regular hallmarks. There are four different combinations, indicating, probably, that four different workmen carried out the order. The practice has also been observed on articles made for James Barber of York by the London firm of Emes and Barnard.

Charles Hougham arranged for workman identification of his output of wine labels. A four-petalled flower device appears on two octagonal labels, one double reeded for MADEIRA dated 1792 (see fig. 464), the other one formed for LISBON with wrigglework border for 1791 (see fig. 465).[19] Charles Hougham died in January 1793. Maybe the marks helped Solomon Hougham when he joined Charles in partnership in 1790.

Tally marks are found most frequently on the Indian silver made for firms in Calcutta, Madras and elsewhere during the nineteenth century. Some of this silver is otherwise unmarked, but the employer was clearly able, nevertheless, to use the system to identify the work of his various craftsmen.

CHAPTER 5

MAKERS

PART 1 – SANDYLANDS DRINKWATER

Sandylands Drinkwater is an enigmatic figure. He was born around 1703, the son of William Drinkwater of St Clement Danes, and died in 1776. Despite his startlingly inappropriate name, he was probably the single most prolific early maker of wine labels and possibly the innovator of the standard escutcheon.

His trade card as illustrated[1] in Jane Stancliffe's book *Bottle Tickets* described him as a 'Small Worker in Gold and Silver at the Hand and Coral, in Gutter Lane, Cheapside, London'. The bulk of his output seems to have been labels, although he is also known to have made rattles, buttons and apple corers. He was apprenticed to Robert White, a smallworker,[2] and obtained his freedom in 1726, taking livery in 1737. He may have taken over from Robert White's widow, Elizabeth, at the Hand and Coral in Gutter Lane. His first smallworker's mark, S★D (see figs. 435a and 436),[3] was entered in 1735. His (presumed) second and most frequently encountered mark, S.D. in script, crown above (fig. 325),[4] is no doubt to be found in the missing smallworkers' ledger.[5] Although a smallworker he must have been successful and prosperous, rising to become Prime Warden of the Goldsmiths' Company in 1761.

The fact that he was a prominent gentleman is confirmed by his will, wherein he left a house and property including a library of books at St Albans (the city to which he had retired), together with £6,700. The will also reveals some interesting facts: he now spells his first name with an 'i' – Sandilands; his principal beneficiaries were his wife, Katherine, and his nephew, Sandilands Drinkwater, who was elected to the livery in November 1776 following his uncle's death in October 1776; and his executors were Thomas Whipham and Charles Wright, both prominent goldsmiths or former goldsmiths. Thomas Whipham was described as a 'Gentleman' of St Albans. Whipham and Wright entered their joint mark in 1757.[6]

Sandylands Drinkwater senior was active in the affairs of the Goldsmiths' Company, and the Company's minute books help to bring him alive and place him among his distinguished contemporaries. He progressed rapidly through the Company: Freeman in 1726, Liveryman in 1737, Court of Assistants in 1745, Warden in 1757 and Prime Warden in 1761. He was therefore a contemporary of illustrious figures such as Paul de Lamerie. Indeed de Lamerie, then a Warden, was a member of the committee that elected Drinkwater to the court as one of twelve Assistant Wardens. Ten members were not elected, including the great George Wickes, so it can be seen that Drinkwater was not only contemporary with the greatest silversmiths, but also on close terms with them.

Little is known about the organisation of Drinkwater's business. At the time he was working, the Wakelin Ledgers disclose that wine labels were generally retailing at about 5s.6d. each. There is no evidence from these ledgers that he supplied Wickes or Wakelin or Parker and Wakelin, whose marks are not found on wine labels, but as he was clearly one of the leading manufacturers of the period he could well have done so. One must also assume that Drinkwater supplied other retailers and no doubt sold direct to customers from his premises at the Hand and Coral in Gutter Lane. It would appear that he either retired or passed his business over to his former apprentice Richard Binley in 1760 when he was elected as the next Prime Warden – at which time Binley entered his own mark and took over the premises at the Hand and Coral, which was later to become known as 16 Gutter Lane. In 1764 Richard Binley died and the business passed to his widow, Margaret, who in turn was succeeded by Susanna Barker (already a widow).

Although the bulk of Drinkwater's work was wine labels, many of which have survived, the number of designs he produced was surprisingly small. The vast majority of his labels were 'standard' chased escutcheons, a design probably invented by Drinkwater, which are found with minor variants in the outline. An early example with pre-1739 lion passant and his first mark is shown at fig. 467 for MADEIRA. They are to be found both chased and plain (such as fig. 474 pierced for WHITE-WINE) with either engraved or pierced letters. A chased label for CLARET with his second mark is illustrated at fig. 472 and a plain label for PERRY with his second mark and lion passant of pre-1756 is shown at fig. 470. As to the marks, one finds escutcheons ranging from the first mark with the lion of pre-1739, to the second mark with the lion of both 1739-56 and post-1756. They are also to be found with the second mark and the lion of pre-1739. Looking at the face of a label it is impossible to guess its date, because the basic design of the escutcheon and its chasing went unchanged from pre-1739 to post-1756. While the majority of labels are chased with the standard pattern of vine leaves and grapes, there are at least two known labels for CYDER most attractively chased with apples. One is to be found in the Cropper Collection at the Victoria and Albert Museum (V&A), illustrated by kind permission of the Board of Trustees at fig. 478. It is not known whether a similar label for CYDER, made of Old Sheffield plate and unmarked, was copied from Drinkwater or vice versa.

The second most common label, although it is not that frequently encountered, is the 'two putti' design. This too is found with his first and second marks and exists in two sizes. Both labels are cast. The smaller label, with the first mark, is distinguished by the putti being somewhat squat and with rather coarse features. It has to be said these labels tend to be a little crude. The slightly larger version is of the very highest quality; the distinguishing feature is that the right-hand putto has elongated arms; so far it has only been found with the second mark. An example for the small label PUNCH is shown at fig. 468 and the larger is similar to the unmarked CYDER (see fig. 466).

Drinkwater also made crescents in two versions. Both tend to be large and unchased, but with bold lettering. Some have the suspension rings attached to projecting 'ears' from the horns; others have the rings fixed through holes near the end of the horns. This may be a later version of the 'eared' crescent, such as that engraved for LISBON (see fig. 473).

The most common label, and probably the latest in date, is the rather large broad rectangle with feathered edge. This is only to be found with the second mark and the lion passant of post-1756. Sometimes its top and base are incurved so that it is slightly waisted. Although the design was made and perhaps invented by Sandylands Drinkwater, it is much more commonly found with the mark of Richard Binley. Indeed this label is to Binley what escutcheons were to his master. Margaret Binley, Hester Bateman and others further modified the design. An example is illustrated at fig. 475 inscribed for CLARET. This was perhaps the inspiration for Paul Storr in producing royal labels for Buckingham Palace and Windsor (see, for example, fig. 388) of rather large, broad, rectangular shape.

Drinkwater's more rare designs are often very attractive and possibly experimental or 'one off' orders. The list below will no doubt be extended as other labels come to light.

First is a cast design for PORT embellished with vine leaves, twigs on tendrils, and grapes. It is a small cast label and is found only with the second mark and the lion passant of 1739-56. Hampston and Prince of York (c.1786), Phipps, Robinson and Phipps (1816) and others produced virtually identical labels. It could be that Drinkwater was the inventor. The label is illustrated at fig. 469.

Second is a set of particularly attractive well-chased rectangular labels with a dramatic rococo

Makers

Figures 466-476.

design of scrolls, rocaille and leaves. Only one of the set is marked – with the second mark and the lion passant of 1739-56 – and this is illustrated[7] by J. Culme and J.G. Strang in *Antique Silver and Silver Collecting*. An unmarked example for CALCAVELLA is illustrated at fig. 471.

Third is a small variant of the escutcheon, which has a gadrooned border that gives the appearance of smiling lips! This design was slightly varied later by Margaret Binley – an example survives, engraved for LISBON. The design by Drinkwater for SPANISH is a late label, marked with the lion passant of post-1756, and is shown at fig. 476.

Fourth is a set of armorial labels,[8] probably made for the Hales family, and now in the V & A. The

Makers

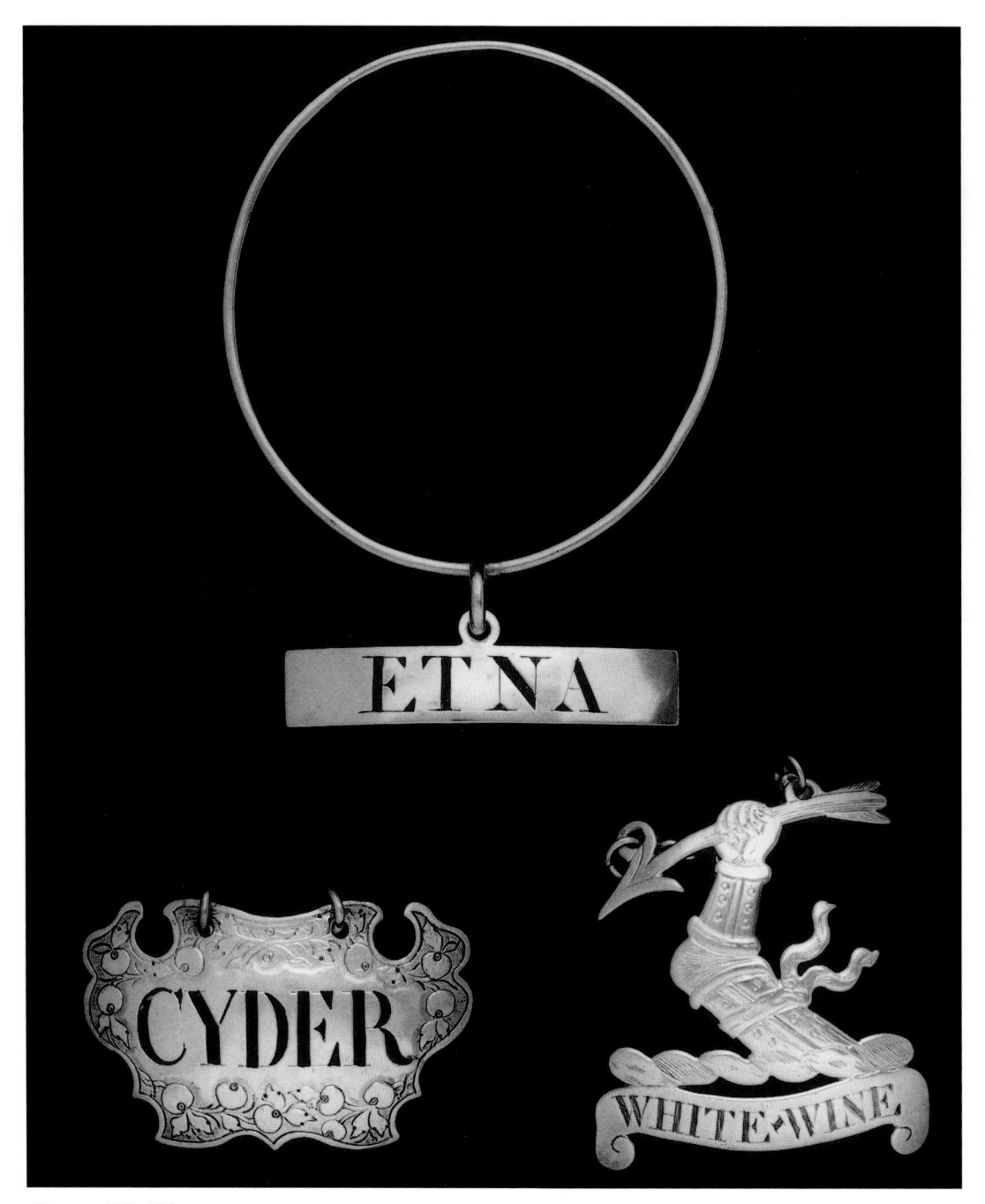

Figures 477-479.

heraldic device is 'a dexter arm, in armour, embowed, in hand an arrow'. This is illustrated at fig. 479 for WHITE WINE.

Fifth is a plain narrow rectangle on a large neck ring that bears Drinkwater's second mark. It is part of the Cropper Collection, now in the V & A, and is for the unusual title of ETNA. This is the earliest known neck ring and is shown at fig. 477.

Sixth, mention must be made of a so far unique label for BURGUNDY (see fig. 324), bearing Drinkwater's second mark and the lion passant of 1739-56 (see fig. 325), in the shape of a fat heart chased all around in the manner of escutcheons with vine leaves and grapes. It is curious that this attractive design did not catch on, as it must have been cheaper to produce than an ordinary chased escutcheon, and just as effective.[9]

Lastly, examples are known with his second mark of the early rectangles, with wavy sides and indented corners, which are discussed in Part 2 of Chapter 1, above.

Figures 480-481.

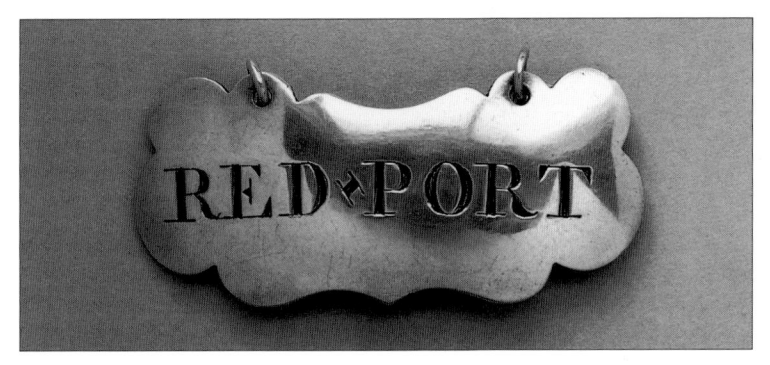

Figure 482.

PART 2 – JOHN HARVEY

John Harvey was one of the most prolific early makers of wine labels, probably second only to Sandylands Drinkwater in the period 1738-50. He made a great variety of escutcheons, both plain and chased, but his most distinctive work was cast. Besides the 'two putti' design, he made a couple of particularly fine labels that seem to have originated in his workshop: a large putto with a glass in one hand and a bottle in the other, and a quintessentially rococo concoction of vines and scrolls (see fig. 480). It is worth noting that he does not appear to have produced any rectangular or crescent shaped labels, and that his single putto design was revived in a slightly different form by Edward Farrell in the second and third decades of the nineteenth century. Likewise his vine leaves and grapes rococo design of the 1740s (fig. 481 for MADEIRA) was revived by others later.

Harvey was apprenticed around 1730 to Mathew Judkins, a silversmith who was a freeman of the Fishmongers' Company, and he was free of the Fishmongers' Company on 19 October 1737 shortly after he married Elizabeth Hazelfoot. He entered his first mark as a smallworker on 9 January 1738 at Gutter Lane (the premises known as number 33 in the later numbering). This first mark was for Britannia standard, which had ceased to be the compulsory minimum standard from 1720 and must have been extremely rarely used at this time. However, he registered a second, sterling standard mark on 7 February, again as a smallworker. He entered further marks in 1739 (18 June, in accordance with the law requiring all silversmiths to record new makers' marks), 1745, 1746, 1748 (the same mark as 1746) and 1750, all in the largeworkers' register, which suggests that he had ambitions to progress beyond smallwork. However, the evidence suggests that he was not successful in his ambitions.

Few labels can be found with the mark he registered in 1750, so it is safe to assume that the majority of his output occurred before that date. In 1746 he left his premises in Gutter Lane (which were occupied a year later by his former, and first, apprentice Thomas Hyde) and moved to Pruyean Court (or Bugeons Court), Old Bailey, a smaller and less prestigious address. In October 1748 he

Makers

moved to Fish Street, and in 1750 to Great Kirby Street. In 1753 or 1754 both his then apprentices were turned over to Thomas Hyde. Heal records him as bankrupt 1761,[10] but in February or March 1759 a mark was entered in the names of two of his children, John II and Anne, address 'Kings Bench', indicating that Harvey was then in prison for debt.[11]

Labels bearing this last mark are rarely found and they are usually plain escutcheons, although sometimes with an unusual outline. A further 'similar' mark was entered by John Harvey II alone in 1768 (see fig. 482 for RED PORT), address 'Bear Lane, near Christchurch, Surrey', and he is recorded there in the Parliamentary Report of 1773. Both John II and Anne Harvey were granted freedom of the Fishmongers' Company 'by patrimony' in 1781.

This is a short, and rather sad, account of one of the most important of the early label makers. The reasons for the decline in John Harvey's business remain obscure. He was obviously experiencing some difficulties from the second half of the 1740s. However, his fifth mark registered 12 December 1746 (re-registered 3 October 1748)[12] is found about as frequently as the third mark registered 18 June 1739, so it would appear that the final, and crucial, phase of his decline did not occur until the registration of his seventh mark in 1750.

PART 3 – THE BATEMANS

In 1761, when Hester Bateman entered her first mark, she was the widow of a chainmaker, John Bateman, whom she had married at St Botolph's, Aldersgate, on 20 May 1732 (see fig. 483). By 1790, when she retired, her firm was one of the largest manufacturers of silver in London. One of

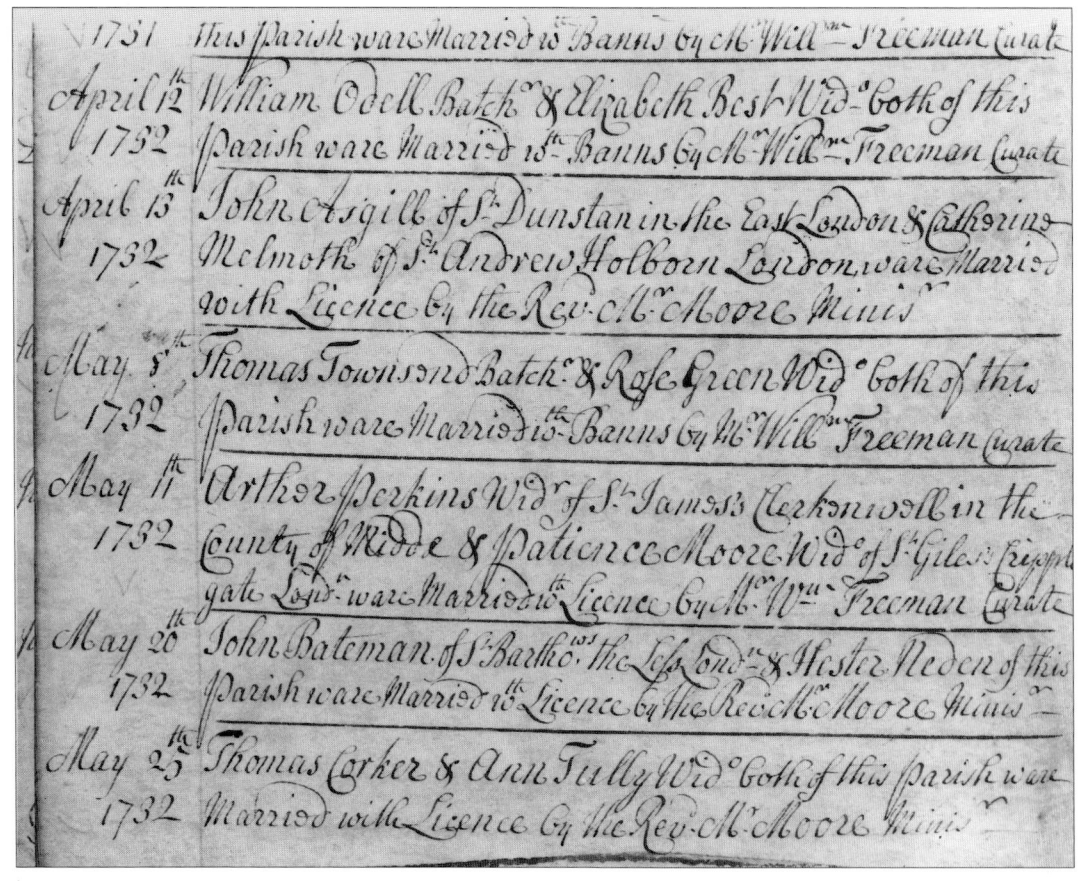

Figure 483.

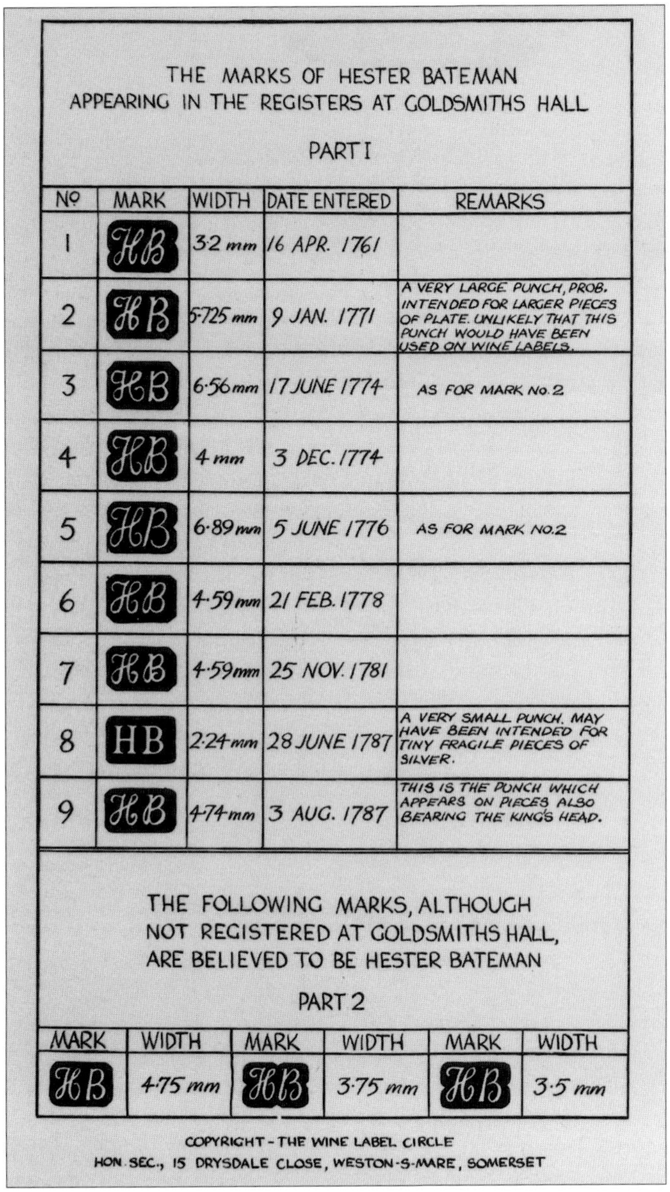

THE MARKS OF HESTER BATEMAN
APPEARING IN THE REGISTERS AT GOLDSMITHS HALL

PART I

Nº	MARK	WIDTH	DATE ENTERED	REMARKS
1	HB	3·2 mm	16 APR. 1761	
2	HB	5·725 mm	9 JAN. 1771	A VERY LARGE PUNCH, PROB. INTENDED FOR LARGER PIECES OF PLATE. UNLIKELY THAT THIS PUNCH WOULD HAVE BEEN USED ON WINE LABELS.
3	HB	6·56mm	17 JUNE 1774	AS FOR MARK No. 2
4	HB	4 mm	3 DEC. 1774	
5	HB	6·89mm	5 JUNE 1776	AS FOR MARK No. 2
6	HB	4·59mm	21 FEB. 1778	
7	HB	4·59mm	25 NOV. 1781	
8	HB	2·24mm	28 JUNE 1787	A VERY SMALL PUNCH. MAY HAVE BEEN INTENDED FOR TINY FRAGILE PIECES OF SILVER.
9	HB	4·74mm	3 AUG. 1787	THIS IS THE PUNCH WHICH APPEARS ON PIECES ALSO BEARING THE KING'S HEAD.

THE FOLLOWING MARKS, ALTHOUGH
NOT REGISTERED AT GOLDSMITHS HALL,
ARE BELIEVED TO BE HESTER BATEMAN

PART 2

MARK	WIDTH	MARK	WIDTH	MARK	WIDTH
HB	4·75 mm	HB	3·75 mm	HB	3·5 mm

COPYRIGHT - THE WINE LABEL CIRCLE
HON. SEC., 15 DRYSDALE CLOSE, WESTON-S-MARE, SOMERSET

Figure 484.

the reasons for this phenomenal success is that the Batemans were quick to exploit the rapid advances in technology that were developing at the time. Also, and perhaps no less important, they had an innate appreciation of the aesthetics of the fashionable neo-classical or Adam style.

The manufacture of metalware had been revolutionised in the third quarter of the eighteenth century by the invention of OSP, a sandwich of copper in silver, which required an improvement in the rolling of sheet metal and the employment of machine stamping to achieve embossing, piercing and applied decorative borders. The required innovations were made possible by the recent harnessing of steam power. Machines could now roll or spin metal, rather than it having to be flattened or raised by hand, and decoration could be produced with a mechanical press. The arrival of OSP, which made it possible to produce articles indistinguishable from silver at a far lower price, must have put an enormous amount of pressure on silversmiths to reduce the cost of their wares – so it is hardly surprising that they should take advantage of the new technology.

The Bateman workshop was among the first in London to install a steam engine and, from the evidence of their work, this must have taken place about 1770. The quantity of surviving pieces and the frequency of their mark found overstruck by that of another silversmith or retailer (see, for example, fig. 445) makes it obvious that they were manufacturing suppliers to the trade. Their work is almost always of light gauge and simple, if pleasing, design – as would be expected of one of the most commercially successful 'factories' of the period. The characteristic bright-cut engraving found on these pieces, attractive though it undoubtedly is, represents a far more labour efficient method of decoration than the cast, chased and finely engraved methods that preceded it.

Bateman silver, therefore, was not the best that was being produced at the time. They were catering to the middle market rather than to the royal and aristocratic clientele of the top artist craftsmen. In the field of wine labels, however, no contemporary maker can equal their record of original and superb design. Although they produced large quantities of undistinguished labels, the quality of execution of the better designs is unsurpassed. One of the more mechanical and most distinctive features of the labels bearing Hester Bateman's marks is the stamping rather than engraving of the wine title. Much as this may have been a labour saving technique, it gives such boldness and clarity to her work that it is surprising that contemporary manufacturers never copied it.

It is unlikely that Hester Bateman ever made anything with her own hands. She would not have served an apprenticeship and whatever she may have learned from nearly thirty years of marriage to a chainmaker would have been severely limited. However, her elder son Peter had completed his apprenticeship in 1761 when Hester took control of the business, and Jonathan, her younger son, completed his in 1769. It is probably these two, therefore, who were responsible for the actual making, aided by a gradually increasing staff of hired workmen, while Hester concentrated on the management.

Bateman labels fall easily into three stylistic periods: early Hester to about 1770 (see fig. 486 for WHITE-WINE), the neo-classical period to about 1795 (see cartouche type labels shown in figs. 490, 491, 492, 496, 497 and 502) and the Regency period to about 1810, after which few labels were made by this firm. Before looking at the label output more closely, however, a problem relating to makers' marks needs to be considered.

The table of Hester Bateman's marks illustrated here (see fig. 484) suggests that there was a ten year gap between the registrations of her first and second marks, and that at least three unregistered marks have been recorded on wine labels. The explanation of both these puzzles undoubtedly lies in the fact that the register of largeworkers for 1757 to 1773 has not survived. Therefore, the three marks at the bottom of the table (and there could well be more) were not 'unregistered', but were most probably entered in the missing register between 1761, when her first mark was entered in the smallworkers register, and 1773, when the lost register ended. The quick transition from smallworker to largeworker is perfectly in keeping with the rapid expansion and diversification of the workshop's production.

The early period, 1761 to about 1770, is fairly predictable as regards shapes: escutcheons (although uncommon in basic form), rectangles, crescents and scrolls were produced. Most commonly the borders are feather-edged (diagonal gadrooning), less often reeded and sometimes completely plain. The ovolo-bordered rectangle (see fig. 485 for CLARET and fig. 500 for MADEIRA) probably dates from this period. However, the range and originality of some of the shaped rectangles including cushion shapes, such as those illustrated at figs. 489, 495, 498, 501 and 506, sometimes make it hard to decide how they should be classified. There is also a highly distinctive style of floral or grape vine flat-chasing on figs. 487, 488 and 490 that can be found on many different designs. This decorative feature continues in the next period. Indeed, it should always be remembered that no analysis of the development of design should ever be dogmatic about cut-off dates because there will always be considerable overlap.

While great originality had been shown in the first decade, it was in the neo-classical period that the Bateman workshop really flowered and, in the relatively minor field of wine labels, became the leading producer of beautifully designed and superbly crafted work. Ovals, goblets and festooned drapery were added to the repertoire of shapes. Borders were bright-cut as often as gadrooned, rather rarely beaded and, most pleasing of all, sometimes pierced with entwined cables (see figs. 488, 496 and 503), zig-zags or foliate garlands (see fig. 494). An oval cartouche for the engraving of a crest or monogram was a distinctive addition at this time. It was placed above a scroll or a crescent, the latter upward or downward turned, with or without supporting swags, and almost always

Figures 485-497.

surmounted with a little bow. The most successful of the latter forms, judging from surviving examples and the number of times it was copied by other silversmiths, was the crescent whose horns curl over and join below an oval cartouche with swags either side. Although this design is commonly called the 'enclosed crescent', it looks rather like a goblet, and this brings us conveniently to a major group of related designs.

The goblet (fig. 494 for W·PORT) and the urn (fig. 492 for RED·PORT) appear to have been a Bateman family innovation.[13] Some labels produced in the neo-classical period do not fall easily into general classifications. Heraldic labels,[14] such as those shown as figs. 499 (swan) and 507 (owl) for MADEIRA and SHERRY, which were modelled on the crest of a particular family and which would have been made in a single set ordered by that family, are a case in point; but the major example shown as fig. 502 for MADEIRA, is a label that, although rare, occurs in different sizes and would probably be placed in every collector's top ten favourite designs. It consists of a banner above pierced-out grapes and vine leaves, surmounted with an oval cartouche surrounded by pierced-out laurel branches and topped with a pierced-out bow.

Makers

Figures 498-507.

Another highly successful and frequently copied design was the narrow rectangle with fretted dome above (see figs. 150 and 155 illustrating this style).

The Regency-style period of Bateman labels roughly covers the two decades from 1790 to 1810, although neo-classical designs continued to be made. These decades also saw some fairly rapid changes in the partnerships controlling the firm. Hester must have retired before 7 December 1790, when her sons Peter and Jonathan entered their mark. Jonathan died on 17 April 1791, making labels bearing the mark of Peter and Jonathan particularly rare. His widow, Ann, then took his place and the mark of Peter and Ann Bateman was used until January 1800, when William, son of Jonathan and Ann, entered the partnership. The mark of Peter, Ann and William Bateman continued in use until 8 November 1805, when Ann either died or retired. Peter and William remain in partnership until Peter retired and William registered a mark alone on 15 February 1815. Labels are less often found with William Bateman's mark, and rarely with that of his eldest son William II, which was entered in 1827, so it is safe to assume that very few were made after 1815.

Many restrained designs were made during this period, in keeping with one trend of contemporary taste, but there was a contrasting trend towards larger and more impressive forms and the best work of the later partnerships was in this style. Beside the large cherub holding a wide swag of drapery chased with fruiting vines engraved for SHRUB,[15] CHERRY or BRANDY (see fig. 289) made in 1799 by Peter, Ann and William Bateman, there is a finely engraved confection of bunched and bowed drapery engraved for BRANDY (made by Peter and William in 1807),[16] and an equally finely engraved sideways barrel.[17] By far the most characteristic, frequently made and widely copied label of the closing decades, however, was the 'Prince of Wales feathers' featuring a plume of three ostrich feathers above a bright-cut curved narrow rectangle with engraved foliate sides. This hugely successful design may have reflected a popular enthusiasm for the Prince of Wales (later George IV), whose emblem consisted of three ostrich feathers.[18]

Figure 508.

Figure 509.

PART 4 – THE BINLEYS

The careers of Richard and Margaret Binley cover an important period of wine label development – the decades from 1750 to the end of the 1770s – when rococo tastes were replaced by the neo-classical.[19] These years saw some of the first label designs, such as the escutcheon and the 'two putti', go out of fashion; the original plain rectangle develop more elaborate outlines and become the cushion in various versions; the crescent open its horns and arrival of the scroll, the oval and the kidney. Some of their designs are illustrated by figs. 508-524.

Richard Binley was apprenticed to Sandylands Drinkwater on 13 January 1732, on payment of £20. He became free on 6 December 1739. It is presumed that he then went to work in Drinkwater's workshop in Gutter Lane at the Hand and Coral (see fig. 680). The first mark we have for him, his 'R.B.', was entered twenty-one years later on 20 September 1760; a similar, but smaller, mark followed on 18 December 1760. Labels with the larger mark have been seen with the pre-1756 lion passant. It is possible that Binley was having his own work assayed from around 1745 onwards, and that his mark was entered in the missing smallworkers' register (1738-58). Alternatively, he may have thought it unnecessary to register his mark before 1760. This was the year in which Drinkwater, his employer, is believed to have retired,[20] and when Binley is thought

Makers

Figure 510.

Figure 511.

Figure 512.

to have set up on his own.

Richard Binley's output seems to have consisted mainly of wine labels, his designs for the most part being based on those of his master. He produced escutcheons, usually chased but sometimes plain, which he enlivened with the addition of a characteristic feathered border. An interesting plain example of *c*.1760, engraved for MOUNTAIN, has had DEW added below it some eighty years later, perhaps by some admirer of Sir Walter Scott, to give new life to an outmoded title when whisky began to become popular south of the Border.[21] Like Drinkwater, Binley made large, sharp-cornered rectangles with the name in large letters that fill the whole panel. He also made smaller versions, one of which has a bold double-reeded border instead of the usual feathered edge. Another innovation that he can probably be credited with is a largish rectangle with an ovolo border, which probably dates from *c*.1757 and therefore precedes similar labels by Hester Bateman and William Cafe. Drinkwater's influence can also be seen in Binley's large crescent with the tips of the horns almost touching. Examples bearing his mark can be dated to around 1760, as can similar labels by his contemporary Robert Cox. Interestingly, this is one of Binley's wine label designs that his wife, Margaret, did not continue when she took over the business.

Richard died in May 1764 and in the same month Margaret entered her two marks. They are identical to his, except that she has substituted 'M' for 'R', and like his are in two sizes (6.0mm and 5.3mm – about ¼in. and ³⁄₁₆in.; both these marks are unusually large for a smallworker). Margaret continued the business from the Gutter Lane premises until 1789, with wine labels as her principal output, though the Parker and Wakelin ledgers show that she was also supplying that firm with

Figure 513.

Figure 514.

Figure 515.

Figure 516.

Figure 517.

Figure 518.

Makers

buckles and buttons from at least 1767. There is also a revealing entry in some pages from the accounts of an unknown (perhaps London) goldsmith of the 1770s, preserved in the book known as the Kingsteignton Wallpaper Book,[22] for the sale from September to December 1772 of twenty-one labels to a Mrs Binley. If this was Margaret, it is an indication that the business was flourishing to the extent that she was contracting out some of her commissions. Margaret is believed to have died or retired by 1789, when Susanna Barker took over the premises.[23] The relationship between the two women, if any, is not known, but this succession gives rise to interesting speculation.

There is no evidence to indicate whether Margaret had any training as a silversmith or was herself a craftsman, or whether she simply ran the business with a highly trained and competent body of workmen. The firm's products were certainly of high standard and, judging by the amount that has survived, they were in great demand. She was, at first, content to continue the designs that her husband had used. There are escutcheons still to be found, and rectangles. An interesting escutcheon, which is inappropriately titled for HOCK and chased with a design of apples and apple leaves, is similar to an example of Drinkwater's that actually is for CYDER. Another takes up the feather border on a plain escutcheon that Richard had employed and yet another is a rectangle with an ovolo border. Her cushion shapes then begin to appear in a number of new versions, and one quite new shape emerges, the kidney. Her crescents become smaller and have more open horns, sometimes sharp-tipped but occasionally rounded.

Above all, Margaret introduced new styles of border decoration: variations to the standard gadroon or feathered edges; chevron, pricked and beaded edges; and, on a late crescent of *c*.1775, fine bright cutting – just as it was coming into fashion. Beecroft has noted a label of the 'two putti' design that has an unusual number of cut-out spaces around the name panel and the two boy figures, and there is a cut-out design that looks as if it was derived from a buckle, consisting of a curved name panel surrounded by flowerheads linked together by elaborately interwoven tendrils, and used at about the same date by Hester Bateman. Scrolls, another new shape of the 1770s, have been seen by Margaret Binley, both with and without a surmounting plaque. It is clear that she kept up with fashion and brought many new features into wine label production, but at the same time she continued to find customers for traditional designs and decorations. Her active days ended before the full stream of neo-classical innovation could influence her work.

Figure 519.

Figure 520.

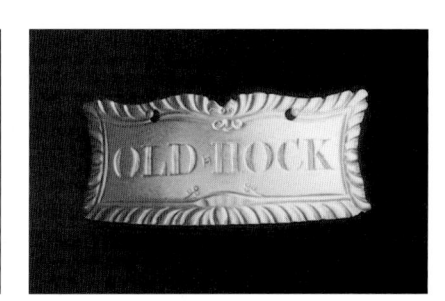

Figure 521.

Figure 522.

Figure 523.

Figure 524.

Makers

Figures 525-527.

PART 5 – THE HYDE FAMILY

Thomas Hyde was born in 1725, the son of James Hyde, a vintner. When Thomas was apprenticed to John Harvey on 25 February 1739, his father was described as 'late of Spitalfields', and so, presumably, was dead by that date. On the completion of his apprenticeship, Thomas was granted the freedom of the Fishmongers' Company 'by service' on 15 May 1747 and, in the same year, appeared in the rate books for Gutter Lane at No. 33, the premises recently vacated by his former master. He is recorded there continuously until his death in 1805 (see fig. 681). Hyde took over both of his former master's apprentices in 1753 or 1754. He took three further apprentices in 1761, 1770 and October 1784. From the evidence of wine labels, it is possible that he had retired some time before his death as no examples have been noted after 1793/94.

That he was able to set up in business so soon after he qualified, aged twenty-two, suggests that he had inherited money from his father. He must have married very soon after achieving his freedom as his eldest son, Thomas II, was born in 1748 and the younger son, James, was born in the following year. Thomas II was granted the freedom of the Fishmongers' Company on 9 February

Figures 528-538.

Figures 539-541.

1769 'by patrimony', but predeceased his father in 1789 having probably spent his whole working life in the family business, in the usual expectation of an eldest son to succeed to it on the death or retirement of his father. James achieved his freedom exactly one year after his elder brother and started his own business in 1777 for a year at No. 10 Gutter Lane and from 1778 to *c*.1794 at No. 38 Gutter Lane (see fig. 681). Around 1794 it is assumed that he moved to 6 Carey Lane and died in 1799 leaving his widow, Mary, to carry on the business until she died in 1829.

Thomas Hyde used three marks. The first, a very distinctive punch with an acorn between the initials TH and a crown above, would have been entered in 1747 in the missing register of smallworkers for 1739-57, and was in use until about 1770. The second punch was quite large at 5mm (³⁄₁₆in.) and rectangular, with a pellet between the letters T.H.[24] It was presumably entered in around 1770 in the missing register of largeworkers for 1757-73 and was in use until his third mark, a 3.7mm (⅛in.) wide, rectangular punch without pellet,[25] was entered in the smallworkers' register on 3 February 1784.

Figs. 539-544 show a group of wine labels bearing Hyde's first mark, 1747 to *c*.1770. Of these, figs. 541 for WHITE WINE and 543 for BRANDY follow designs produced by other contemporary makers, but the remaining labels exhibit elements of originality. The escutcheon (see fig. 540 for MADEIRA) is particularly elegant in its outline and very finely chased. The feather-edge, heart-shaped label for PORT (see fig. 539) was a form almost exclusive to his workshop, although examples bearing an unidentified mark, IR, are known. The armorial labels (see figs. 542 for PORT and 544 for PORT) are the most spectacular (but for Hester Bateman's version of fig. 542 see fig. 507), and are obviously related to one of Hyde's other specialities, that of badge making. He is also known to have made wine siphons, wine funnels, apple corers and silver mounts for objects such as leather tankards and coconut cups. Wine siphons appear to be exclusive to him during the middle decades of the eighteenth century, and he was possibly the earliest maker of the wine funnel incorporating a strainer.

Figs. 525-532 illustrate labels with Thomas Hyde's second mark, which was in use from *c*.1770 to 1784, whilst figs. 533-538 were produced with his third mark (1784-94). All these designs can be found by other contemporary makers with the exception of figs. 534 (SHERRY) and 537 (PACCARETTI), but their variety shows the range of his output during this period. Indeed they reflect all the basic shapes in vogue and employ every available type of border decoration: plain, reeded, beaded, feathered, bright-cut, pierced and saw-toothed. It is remarkable, however, that Hyde does not seem to have created, let alone copied, any design of exceptional quality in the neo-

Figures 542-544.

Makers

classical style. He would have been, in eighteenth-century terms, an old man when this style became fashionable, so it is quite probable that he found it difficult to enter into the spirit of changing popular taste, as is shown by the one original design (see figs. 534 and 537) of his closing years being surprisingly backward looking in form.

James Hyde, the younger son, entered his first and second marks in 1777 at 10 Gutter Lane, but moved to 38 Gutter Lane[26] the following year where he remained until transferring to 6 Carey Lane (on the corner of Gutter Lane) in 1796. He entered two more marks in 1784, at the same time that his father entered his third small 'TH' mark. He died in 1799, whereafter his business was continued by his widow, Mary, and his former apprentice and journeyman, John Reily,[27] whom she married in 1801. James was a prolific maker of wine labels, but he would appear to be a follower rather than a leader of fashion since no designs of striking originality have been discovered to date bearing any of his four marks.[28]

PART 6 – JOHN REILY AND HIS SUCCESSORS

At the beginning of the nineteenth century label production in London was dominated by three groups: the Bateman family, the Phipps family and the circle of Rundell, Bridge and Rundell including Paul Storr and Benjamin Smith. Of the minor specialists only John Rich and Elizabeth Morley showed any originality or quality. By about 1820, however, the situation had opened up considerably. The Batemans had virtually ceased to produce labels, the Phipps business was to close in 1823 with the death of Thomas, and Storr and Smith were concentrating on bigger things. Meanwhile, most of the larger firms of manufacturing silversmiths had introduced their own special lines, such as Edward Farrell with his elephants and topers, Robert Garrard with his fox and grapes, the Barnards with their five bar gates and double shells, the Angells with their cornucopias, the Hennells with their berry bordered rectangles, the Haynes with their various leopard designs and William Elliott with his distinctive shells and shell borders.

Of the new generation of smaller specialists who turned their hands to wine labels, five are particularly worthy of mention for the quality of their product and their contribution to original design: George Pearson, Daniel Hockley, William Trayes, John Reily and Charles Rawlings. The last two founded firms that were to dominate label production in London from the 1830s to the 1870s.

John Reily, son of Richard Reily of Thames Street, glazier, was apprenticed to James Hyde on 7 December 1786. He was granted the freedom of the Fishmongers' Company on 13 February 1794, after which he worked as a journeyman for his master until the latter's death in 1799. He then entered a mark in partnership with his master's widow, Mary Hyde. On marrying Mary in 1801,

Figures 545-550.

Figures 551-554.

he entered his own mark. Thus Reily acquired a business that could trace its involvement in label making back to the earliest years of their production.

In the light of this long tradition, it is surprising that his output for the first ten years (see fig. 545, OYRAS, a wine-growing district west of Lisbon at the mouth of the River Tagus; fig. 546, BRANDY, 1799; fig. 547, MADEIRA, a humped cushion shape, 1809, somewhat out of fashion at this date; fig. 548, PORT, 1804 and fig. 549, PORT, 1809) was fairly pedestrian, being mostly restricted to plain reeded designs. Only three exceptions have been noted during this period: firstly, an oval with pierced border of pales (see fig. 546 for BRANDY, one of a pair with RUM) with the rare partnership mark of Reily and Mary Hyde (lasting from November 1799 to February 1801), which could have been made by James Hyde before his death but not marked until it was sent for assay after his demise (dated 1799); secondly an armorial design of a ladder between wings,[29] which was made in 1801; and thirdly a silver-gilt bottle collar with cable borders made in 1808. This third label for MADEIRA is particularly distinctive, in that it is engraved with a description of how the wine had been sent out to China and back in order to mature.

From about 1810 Reily's work started to improve dramatically. His CLARET of 1814 (see fig. 550) varies a popular design by having small pointed ears at the corners. He introduced a distinctive border of 'reed and tie' scrolls with shells (see fig. 553 for MADEIRA, 1817), which he used for initials and for ovals on wine and sauce labels.[30] During his second decade he is also known to have produced stars and reclining Dionysus designs; but his major innovation was to produce the foliate escutcheon (see fig. 552 for COTI ROTI, 1822). While this design[31] does not always appeal to those whose taste is more in sympathy with the eighteenth century, it proved enormously popular at the time and must be one of the most commonly encountered and most often copied of nineteenth-century labels. During this period he also became a notable maker of fine snuffboxes and in 1817 he produced another armorial design depicting a lion on a chapeau. While often said to be for the Duke of Norfolk, it should be remembered that all branches of the Fitzalan-Howard family would have used this crest, as well as the Royal College of Arms, whose hereditary head is the Duke. Reily made ambassadorial plate. An example for PORT in 1823 is shown at fig. 551, the garter crest and crown being rather worn.

The last six years of his life were perhaps the most fruitful, as they saw the introduction of his distinctive triple vine leaf,[32] the oval with cast border of oak leaves and acorns, the rectangle with scroll and foliate borders and a flower on each side, which can be found with a more attractive combination of matt and burnished gilding, and a handsome large cast rectangle with an openwork border of fruiting vines (see fig. 554 for MADEIRA, date letter obliterated by piercing).

Reily took only two apprentices, both of whom went on to become significant label makers. Daniel Hockley, son of Thomas Hockley of Seven Dials, oilman, was apprenticed 25 March 1801 and free of the Fishmongers' Company 7 April 1808; George Pearson, son of John Pearson of

Makers

Figures 555-562.

Southwark, mathematical instrument maker, was apprenticed 6 December 1804 and free of the Fishmongers' Company 13 February 1812.

After John Reily died in 1826 his widow, Mary, went into partnership with their son, Charles, and a joint mark was entered (see figs. 555-557). This partnership lasted for only three years, but, besides the continuing production of John's designs, saw the introduction of the 'scroll with cupid below and cup above' design, large grapes and vine leaves bordered labels (see figs. 556 for SHERRY, 1827 and 557 for MADEIRA, 1826) and the appearance of an armorial label depicting a lion rampant on a bar within a crescent (see fig. 555 for PORT, 1826).

When Mary retired or died in 1829, Charles Reily entered into a partnership with George Storer, who served his apprenticeship as a watchmaker (see figs. 558-562). The firm's range of output expanded to include hollowware, such as tea services, claret jugs and wine coolers.[33] They also specialised in producing unusual objects, including a one-off silver-gilt Shrapnel patent mechanical corkscrew, made for the patentee to present to the royal family in the hope of obtaining the recognition that had been denied to his father, Henry, who invented a type of exploding shell. This splendid piece is now in the collection at Osborne House.

In terms of wine labels, Reily and Storer continued to produce the house designs in considerable quantities, together with copies of some of their rivals' designs such as the Rawlings' 'singing foxes' and the Barnards' 'double shell'. Only two new designs appear to have been produced by them – the handsome scroll with grapes and vine leaf below[34] and the large oval with bunches of grapes at the sides, top and bottom.[35] Illustrated are fig. 558, CURAÇAO, 1828, which the Prince Regent had been enjoying in 1819 according to I.R. Cruikshank's cartoon (see fig. 417); fig. 559, CHÂTEAU LÉOVILLE, 1836, which is interesting as just pre-dating the division of the Léoville property between Lascases and Lascombes; fig. 560, MADEIRA, 1837; fig. 561, SHERRY, 1836; and fig. 562, F. CHAMPAGNE, being this partnership's version of Emes and Barnard's 'five-barred gate' design, which is also utilised for sauce labels.

The firm seems to have ceased production a little after 1850. John Culme, the unchallenged historian of Victorian silversmiths, has been unable to discover why or what happened to their business.

PART 7 – CHARLES RAWLINGS AND WILLIAM SUMMERS

Charles Rawlings served his apprenticeship under Edward Coleman, a watch finisher, but on its completion he entered his mark as a plateworker. His first address, 12 Well Street, had been the premises of James Atkins, and later his widow Theodosia, since 1791. While this gives Rawlings a connection with an established label maker, it must be said that the Atkins' production was restricted to plain reeded labels, which were the absolute antithesis of Rawlings' work. In 1819 Rawlings moved to 9 Brook Street, the former premises of the bankrupt Daniel Hockley, a rather more distinguished label maker. There is no evidence, however, that Rawlings ever produced any of Hockley's distinctive designs, such as the elephant and 'boy on a barrel', so that it is probable that Rawlings acquired only the premises and not the stock and dies from Hockley's liquidator and cannot, therefore, be said to have continued the business. Daniel Hockley emigrated to South Africa where he again set up as a silversmith.

From the outset, Charles Rawlings was an outstanding box maker, working in both gold and silver-gilt as well as in silver. As befits such a manufacturer, his labels are distinguished by the fineness of their cast detail. His most original design, in terms of uniqueness, is the so-called 'Lady Bountiful' which he probably first made in 1821 and was still being continued by his successor, William Summers, in 1878 (see figs. 282/564 for CLARET.[36] However, it is still a rare design, as is the 'singing foxes', which he introduced about the same time. On a more popular note, his most successful innovation must have been the vine leaf (see figs. 339/563 for INDIA MADEIRA by Rawlings and Summers). While he may have not been the first to use the idea, he was certainly the first to make it a commercial success. His cast designs incorporating fruiting vines are also particularly noteworthy, such as the triangular design with central scroll tablet and the openwork design with central crescent tablet. Unlike John Reily, he also copied other makers' popular designs, such as Benjamin Smith's large cherub's head and Barnards' so-called 'five-barred gate' (see fig. 562 for Reily and Storer's version

Figure 563.   *Figure 564.*   *Figure 565.*

Makers

Figure 566.

Figure 567.

Figure 568.

entitled F. CHAMPAGNE). The quality of his reproductions was at least equal to the originals and sometimes surpassed them. He even made the button or disc shape (see figs. 273/565).

In 1829 Rawlings went into partnership with William Summers who had gained his freedom in 1826 by patrimony as a goldsmith and jeweller. Summers' influence soon became apparent as the firm expanded their production into *bijouterie* and *objets de luxe* as well as glass mounts. In terms of labels, this influence is best shown in the introduction of enamelling, which was used on 'cut-out letters' and on the three and five ring designs introduced in the 1850s. They may also have produced 'cut-out letters' in gold in around 1855.

The rich variety of 'cut-out letter' designs (see figs. 49/569 by Rawlings and Summers and figs. 48/571 by William Summers) is one of the chief characteristics of the partnership's work in labels, of which the most noteworthy incorporates the figures of Punch and Toby. Another unmistakable characteristic was the reproduction of eighteenth- and early nineteenth-century designs including escutcheons and Hester Bateman designs. From the evidence of surviving sets of eighteenth-century labels, which include Rawlings and Summers additions, it seems likely that the firm specialised in extending old sets or in replacing lost and damaged constituents. The very fine MADEIRA (see figs. 320/570) has, besides the crown, an expensive slip chain so that it can be used on a handled decanter.

Besides the continuation of house designs, the partnership is also noted for producing armorial (ostrich, sitting fox and hound – see figs. 367/567, 361/568 and 359/566) and regimental (the oak leaf – see fig. 351) labels. It was also responsible, together with Garrards, for the 'fretwork' designs of the 1850s onwards.

Charles Rawlings died in 1863 and William Summers continued to run the business until his death in 1890. The firm carried on under his son, Henry, until 1897 when it ceased trading and the stock was sold for £4,000 in a sale that lasted three days. From the catalogue of this sale it is obvious that the firm was a substantial manufacturer of jewellery. No labels have been noted bearing William Summers' mark after about 1884, so production presumably ceased well before the business was closed. However, William Summers kept up the tradition of innovation by introducing in the early 1870s two

Figure 569.

Figure 570.

Figure 571.

versions of a bottle collar with a pierced border of pales. The smaller of the two is particularly intriguing in that it is open at the back for about a fifth of its circumference and yet seems to be so narrow that it could only fit the neck of a bottle rather than a decanter. The puzzle lies in the fact that by this date all bottles had to be paper-labelled by law and, even stranger, the pierced names on these collars are often for the more expensive and esoteric wines such as La Rose, Margaux and Lafitte.[37]

PART 8 – PAUL STORR

Paul Storr was a member of the London branch of a Yorkshire family of three brothers, all Quakers, all of whom had suffered imprisonment for their faith. Early in life his father, Thomas, had decided to take up silver chasing, but he was not that successful and became a victualler. Thomas was apprenticed in 1757. His apprenticeship entry is in the records of the Vintners' Company.[38] So Paul grew up with the sounds of the silver workshop. After his own apprenticeship to William Rock of the Vintners' Company and after partnering William Frisbee, he installed himself at 20 Air Street, Piccadilly, in the autumn of 1796. It was from here that in 1801 he married Elizabeth Beyer whom he had first met at the age of fourteen when he went to Soho to be apprenticed. It was here, too, that he made a name for himself as one of London's leading manufacturing goldsmiths. His own twenty-six apprentices were also taken through the Vintners' Company. He made magnificent silver for the great houses, working from the designs of sculptors and painters. These artists knew little about silver and Storr's skill lay partly in the adaptation of their designs. His good workmanship was recognised and Storr was soon receiving orders for cups, vases, kettles, wine coolers, dishes and plates. One of his most famous commissions of this period was the gold font that he produced in 1797 for the christening of William Henry Cavendish-Bentinck, Marquis of Titchfield and heir to the Duke of Portland. Paul Storr's 'leopard's pelt' of 1818, based on a detail from the Warwick Vase (see below, Part 9, The Leopard's Pelt), is shown at figs. 31/573 for CHAMPAIGNE. It is similar to the 1810 edition with added armorial rose shown at fig. 572, marked on its face, the title for MADEIRA being in raised lettering.

In the early nineteenth century Storr was approached by Philip Rundell, who wanted him to work exclusively for Rundell, Bridge and Rundell. Storr agreed to execute any orders that Rundell might give him, but insisted on maintaining an independent company – Storr and Co. – at 53 Dean Street, Soho. In 1807 Storr had become a partner in Rundell, Bridge and Rundell, and it seems likely that the firm's orders took up most of his time. It supplied most of the new plate for the Prince Regent; the Egyptian Service; a service given by the Jamaica Assembly to the Duke of Clarence; and, beginning in 1803, the Grand Service. Various presentations were made to the Duke of Wellington, who was also issued with a service jointly made by many famous firms. Paul Storr contributed 102 items to this service, weighing 50kg (1,770 oz). The sheer bulk of these Regency orders, and their intricate designs and superb craftsmanship, are staggering.

Although Paul Storr is famous for massive works of art, he made small as well as large items for a dinner service. The Royal Collection, for example, comprised every possible item required by a royal household. Storr produced thousands of pieces for this collection, including an enormous wine cooler that weighed 227kg (8,000oz.) and cost £8,500, some sixteen candelabra (£4,374), the Warwick Vase ice-pails (£3,470), fish slices, sauce boats and ladles, salt spoons, and wine and sauce labels. These final two categories are always large cast labels of handsome design – often gilded and oval in shape, with shell and floral decoration. Good heavy labels with thick chains to suit large decanters, they are unmistakably the work of the master.

Trade continued to boom at Rundell, Bridge and Rundell, and Storr found that he had less and less time to produce his own work. Also, mechanical production methods were being introduced at the expense of individual craftsmanship. So, despite the financial implications – he had a wife and ten children to support – Storr decided to set up once again on his own. Early in 1819 he installed his workshop at 18 Harrison Street, off Gray's Inn Lane. As a 'shop window' he acquired 13 New Bond Street with a goldsmith and jeweller named William Gray. Gray's principal assistant, John

Makers

Figure 572.

Mortimer, was to manage the retail side of the business, while Storr ran the manufacturing side. However, in 1826 it became clear that Mortimer had heavily overbought. Fortunately John Samuel Hunt, the son of Storr's sister-in-law, came in as a third partner producing £5,000 capital, and the business continued successfully until 1838, when the showroom moved to 136 New Bond Street, a better site at the corner of Grafton Street. Storr and Co. also moved to 26 Harrison Street, and in 1838 the firm was described in the new Directory as 'Storr and Mortimer, Goldsmiths and Jewellers to Her Majesty, 156 New Bond Street, and Silversmiths and Goldsmiths to Her Majesty, 26 Harrison Street, Gray's Inn Road'.

The relationship between Storr and Mortimer was never an easy one, and eventually in 1838 there was an action in Chancery concerning the partnership, which was finally settled out of court. Storr was now sixty-eight and decided to retire, arranging for John Hunt (the son of John Samuel Hunt) to come in as junior partner, the firm being called 'Mortimer and Hunt'. Storr and his wife retired to Tooting, where she died in November 1843 and he the following March. His estate amounted to only £3,000, but it is likely that he had already distributed much of his earnings to his family. No silver was mentioned under his personal effects. His trade tools and draw-bench remained in his workshop together with many of his papers, but everything has been destroyed by enemy action in wartime.

Paul Storr is remembered mostly for his innovation (even if worked by others in the Rundell,

Figures 573-578.

Bridge and Rundell family, see figs. 573, 575-578) and for the perfection and quality of his work. It is impossible to find fault with his craftsmanship. As N.M. Penzer wrote: 'We may not approve of the design, we may dislike the proportions, we may criticize unnecessary elaboration of detail, we may consider a piece more suited to marble or bronze than to silver – but bad workmanship: never!' A visual appreciation however may sometimes mislead. Fig. 574, unmarked and later pierced for PORT, did not start off life as a wine label!

PART 9 – RUNDELL, BRIDGE and RUNDELL

The history of the firm of Rundell, Bridge and Rundell, celebrated for supplying plate and jewellery to royalty and nobility during the early nineteenth century, has been traced back to the middle of the previous century and begins with Henry Hurt. He traded under the sign of The Golden Salmon, later to be used as the shop name by the various Rundell firms. Hurt had an assistant, William Theed, who became a partner in the firm and later took on, as a goldsmith and jeweller, William Pickett, who had married into the Theed family. The firm became known as Theed and Pickett.

After Theed's death Philip Rundell, originally employed by Pickett as a shopman, was taken as a partner and the firm's name changed to Pickett and Rundell. This period in the firm's history is rather complicated, but is well documented by Penzer.[39] Penzer also tells us that Rundell aspired to gain full control of the firm and that, in 1785, he achieved this ambition by buying out Pickett.

Somewhat earlier, in 1777, John Bridge, having served his apprenticeship, had been taken on by Pickett and Rundell as a shopman. Bridge, like Rundell, took a great deal of interest in all the workings of the firm and, after Rundell had bought out Pickett's share of the business, was able to buy his own share in the firm by virtue of a convenient family connection. His cousin, also named John, was a wealthy and respected farmer who had gained the confidence of George III. It was from his cousin that Bridge obtained the money to buy his partnership and, even more importantly, it was from his cousin's association with royalty that the newly created firm of Rundell and Bridge gained their most important commissions.

Several other people became partners in the firm in the early nineteenth century. These included Thomas Bigge, another of Philip Rundell's nephews, John Bridge's nephew John Gawler Bridge and, importantly, William Theed, R.A. (no relation to the Theed mentioned earlier), the artist and sculptor who guided the design of much of the firm's commissioned work during this period.

Rundell, Bridge and Rundell became famous for their plate, produced by such firms as Digby Scott and Benjamin Smith and Storr and Co. (see figs. 573, 575-578) and latterly William Bateman junior and John Tapley and Co. William Theed, R.A. died in 1817 and was replaced by John Flaxman, who became the firm's artistic adviser but who, unlike his predecessor, never became a partner in the firm. Flaxman designed one of the firm's most celebrated works, 'The Shield of Achilles', bronze copies of which are in the Fitzwilliam and Ashmolean Museums.

After Philip Rundell's retirement in 1823 and the death of John Bridge senior in 1834, the name of the firm was changed to Rundell, Bridge and Co. However, the firm did not survive. Various speculative and financially disastrous investments forced Rundell, Bridge and Co. to close for business in 1843 and the partnership was finally dissolved in 1845.

Of course, Rundell, Bridge and Rundell were not without their competitors. In the earlier years these included Wakelin and Garrard, Braithwaite and Fisher, Edward Barnard and Co. (who formed a working relationship with Benjamin Smith II after he left Rundell, Bridge and Rundell), and Kensington Lewis (who employed Edward Farrell and attracted the valuable patronage of the Duke of York). From the 1840s onwards, the most important manufacturers of large-scale plate were Storr and Co., Garrards, Elkington and Co. and C.F. Hancock and Co.

Particulars of some of the silversmiths concerned are as follows:

Philip Rundell
He added in the year 1821 to Paul Storr's set of forty-six heads of Jupiter Ammon (see above, Chapter 2, Part 21) in the Royal Collection.

John Bridge I
He made for George IV in 1827 a set of thirteen heads of a Bacchante in festooned drapery slightly modifying Paul Storr's design (see above, Chapter 2, Part 21).

Benjamin Smith II
Benjamin Smith II was born in December 1764. Twice married, he had eight children of whom the eldest son, also Benjamin, entered a mark with him in January 1814. The mark was replaced in June 1818 with one for Benjamin II alone. The rapid changes of mark, also evident in Benjamin II's earlier career, give an indication of a man who was apparently 'of a difficult and irascible nature'.[40]

Benjamin Smith II was introduced to Matthew Boulton as an 'ingenious chaser' of silver in 1790. The firm of Boulton and Smith was established in Birmingham by 1792, but, following disagreements, Smith moved to London. His first mark was entered in partnership with Digby Scott in October 1802, followed by a second, also in partnership with Scott, in March 1803. This partnership lasted until May 1807 (see fig. 416), when Benjamin Smith II entered his first solo mark, which appears on the sixteen large scallop shells in the Royal Collections (see above, Chapter 2, Part 21). In total there are nine marks known for Benjamin Smith II, alone or in partnerships, the last being that entered alone in June 1818.

It appears that the various Benjamin Smith II firms in London manufactured almost exclusively for Rundell and Bridge. The most famous of the pieces created was the Jamaica Service of 1803, now in the Royal Collection, which includes silver gilt work. The designs for this service closely resemble those produced by Paul Storr, suggesting a very careful central control of the manufacture of quality products by the firm of Rundell and Bridge for their very exclusive clients.

Digby Scott
It is assumed that Digby Scott started working with Benjamin Smith II in Birmingham, but there are no records to confirm this association. Interestingly, Benjamin Smith's third son was named 'Digby': he is thought to have been Digby Scott's godson.

Digby Scott entered his two marks, both in partnership with Benjamin Smith II as described above, in 1802 and 1803 (for examples of his work see fig. 416). Little is known about the history of Digby Scott following the dissolution of the partnership in 1807, but Grimwade records an unregistered triple mark, in conjunction with Benjamin II and James Smith III (see below), in 1811.[41]

James Smith III
James Smith III, brother of Benjamin Smith II, also started his career with Matthew Boulton in Birmingham. It is believed that he left Birmingham and moved to London after his brother. The date is uncertain, but he entered a mark with Benjamin II in February 1809. The triple mark with Benjamin II and Digby Scott (see above) does not appear in the Goldsmiths' Hall *Register of Marks* for the period.

William Bateman I
He added two, presumably extra rather than replacement, labels to Paul Storr's 1812-14 set of heads of a Bacchante (see above, Chapter 2, Part 21) in 1813 for the Royal Collection.

William Bateman II
William Bateman II was the great-grandson of Hester Bateman, grandson of Jonathan and Ann Bateman and son of their second child, William I. The manufacture of Rundell's silver was transferred to his workshops, and also to those of John Tapley (see below), after the death of John Bridge in 1834. William II was apprenticed to his father and entered his first mark as a plateworker in February 1827. A second mark was entered in 1830. In 1831 he made a replacement head of a Bacchante in the Royal Collection (see above, Chapter 2, Part 21).

William II entered into partnership with Daniel Ball (first joint mark entered 31 December 1839) and items manufactured for Rundell, Bridge and Co. are recorded bearing both William's mark alone and that of the Bateman and Ball partnership, including wine labels.

John Tapley
John Tapley entered his first mark in December 1833 and three others during the period 1834-40, some in different sizes. He traded as John Tapley and Co., with his two sons, and at one time occupied premises adjacent to Rundell, Bridge and Co. in Ludgate Hill. His working life as a silversmith is known to have continued until about 1857, but no wine labels have been recorded.

The most notable piece of silver made for Rundell, Bridge and Co. and bearing John Tapley's mark is a silver-gilt model of Eton College Chapel, dated 1834. It was made on the instructions of William IV, who presented it to the college.

Makers

Paul Storr
See Chapter 5, Part 8 and Chapter 2, Part 21.

One of the secrets of success for Rundell, Bridge and Rundell was the tight hold that they maintained on the design of their plate. They employed, as did their competitors, the best artists and sculptors whose design drawings were executed by the firm's various associated craftsmen. The strong architectural design of the display plate of the early nineteenth century had its origins in Charles Heathcote Tatham's book *Designs for Ornamental Plate*, published in 1806. The desire for the grandiose was continued for Rundell, Bridge and Rundell by academic artists/designers such as Thomas Stothard, John Flaxman, William Theed and Edward Hodges Bailey. Labels like fig. 572 for MADEIRA (leopard's pelt) and fig. 575 for PORT (festooned drapery) are certainly striking.

It may never be known who actually designed some of the classic wine labels of the period, but several noteworthy examples, all heavy, cast labels and frequently gilded, are described below.

The Leopard's Pelt
This label (see figs. 31/573 and 572) is one of the classics of the period and derives from an element of the Warwick Vase (see Chapter 1, Part 6). Large sets were made with a wide variety of wine names. Paul Storr manufactured the earliest examples in 1809, but later examples, including copies by other goldsmiths, are documented. The label was produced in at least two sizes and examples are known in the form of slot labels.

Cartouche Labels
An apparent variation of the leopard's pelt, in the form of a cartouche with gadrooned edging, is illustrated in Penzer, plate 25, for CLARET. Within the cartouche is the leopard's mask and pelt, draped to each side leaving the central space for the wine name.

Another cartouche design is illustrated in Penzer's book on Paul Storr.[42] The wine name, similarly applied in raised letters on a matted background, appears in an oval segment with gadrooned edge below a palmette and trailing acanthus leaf motif. CLARET, shown in fig. 578, also comes within this category.

The Four-leaf Clover or Quatrefoil
Appearing about 1807 from the workshops of Digby Scott and Benjamin Scott II, examples of the four-leaf clover label bearing the marks of Benjamin Smith II alone and by Paul Storr (see fig. 576 for CLARET) are also known. The label was also made in a small size for sauce labels.

The Festooned Drapery Label
One of the most ostentatious labels of the period was also first produced by Benjamin Smith II in about 1807. A central, fringed drape bearing the wine name normally in cut-out letters is surrounded by a bold festoon of fruiting vines surmounted by a ribbon bow, sometimes used as the chain eyelets. Other suppliers to Rundell, Bridge and Rundell, such as Story and Elliott, occasionally produced this design (see fig. 575) and it was often recast.

The Shell
The desire for impressive pieces led to the design of a heavy, cast scallop shell (see Chapter 2, Part 19). These were produced by Benjamin Smith II from c.1807 onwards and represent probably the best shell label design.

Dionysus and Putti
This magnificent design has been fully described in Chapter 2, Part 10, along with various other Bacchic revellers.

PART 10 – THE PHIPPS FAMILY AND THEIR PARTNERSHIPS

The importance of James Phipps I as a leading figure in the developing field of wine labels during the 1760s to 1780s was first revealed by the researches of Sir Eric (then Mr Justice) Sachs in 1956-7; he was a prolific writer and researcher on the Phipps family.[43] Before that little attention had been paid to this maker and labels now acknowledged to be his were being attributed to several other silversmiths with the initials 'IP', though the work of his son, Thomas, in partnership with Edward Robinson was well recognised.

James Phipps I was the son of William Phipps, a silk thrower, who apprenticed him in 1741 to a goldsmith named William Pinnell, described by Sachs as an established member of the Goldsmiths' Company, but not listed in Jackson or having a registered mark. Later he was turned over to Robert Collier, a smallworker and clockmaker at the Blackamoor's Head in Gutter Lane, and became free of the Goldsmiths' Company in 1749. Where he spent the next five years is not known, but in 1754 he went into partnership with William Bond, a largeworker with an address in Foster Lane (see fig. 580 – copy entry at Goldsmiths' Hall), where Heal records them until 1765. Articles with their joint mark (Grimwade 3049) have been noted, but no wine labels. In 1765 Jackson records a John Phipps, probably a misreading for James, on his own, as though the partnership with Bond had ended, but gives no mark for him. Two years later, in May 1767, James Phipps recorded his first mark ('IP' without a pellet, Grimwade reference 1583, not shown by Sir Charles Jackson) as a smallworker in Gutter Lane (see fig. 579 – copy entry at Goldsmiths' Hall). Another mark was recorded in 1772 (see fig. 581).

These were years when neo-classical designs were sweeping away the old rococo styles. Crescents, scrolls and ovals were succeeding escutcheons in popular fashion, while smaller and more elegantly proportioned rectangles were replacing the rather larger sizes of earlier years. Phipps emerges as an immediate master of these new designs (see figs. 586 and 587, James Phipps' first mark 1767-1773), to which he added distinctive and original borders and edges, invariably of extremely fine workmanship (see figs. 585-589). In particular, he developed bright-cutting techniques for his borders with a success that is hard to find equalled by any other contemporary silversmith (see figs.

Figure 579.

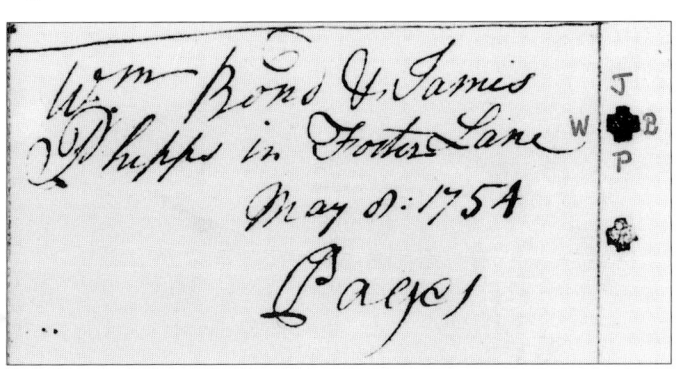

Figure 580.

Figure 581.

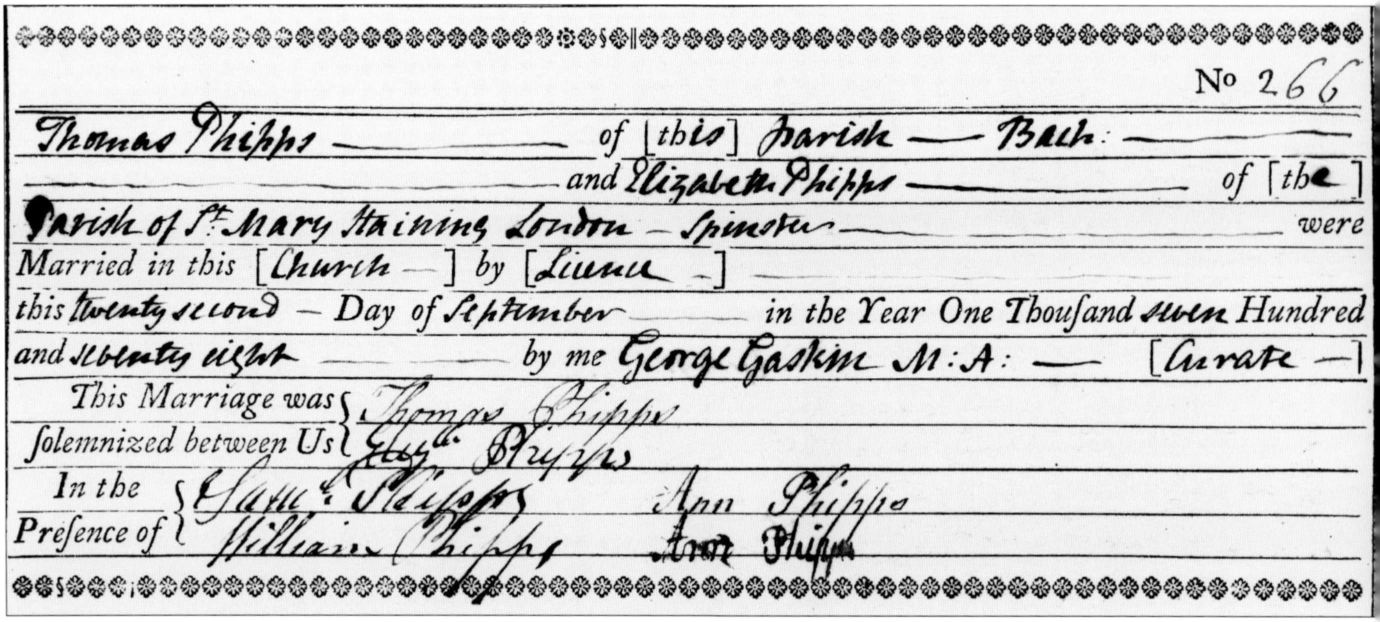

Makers

> No 266
>
> Thomas Phipps — of [this] Parish — Bach —
> and Elizabeth Phipps — of [the] Parish of St Mary Staining London — Spinster — were Married in this [Church] by [Licence] this twenty second Day of September in the Year One Thousand seven Hundred and seventy eight by me George Gaskin M:A: — [Curate]
>
> This Marriage was solemnized between Us { Thomas Phipps / Eliz. Phipps
>
> In the Presence of { Jam.s Phipps, Ann Phipps / William Phipps, Ann Phipps

Figure 582.

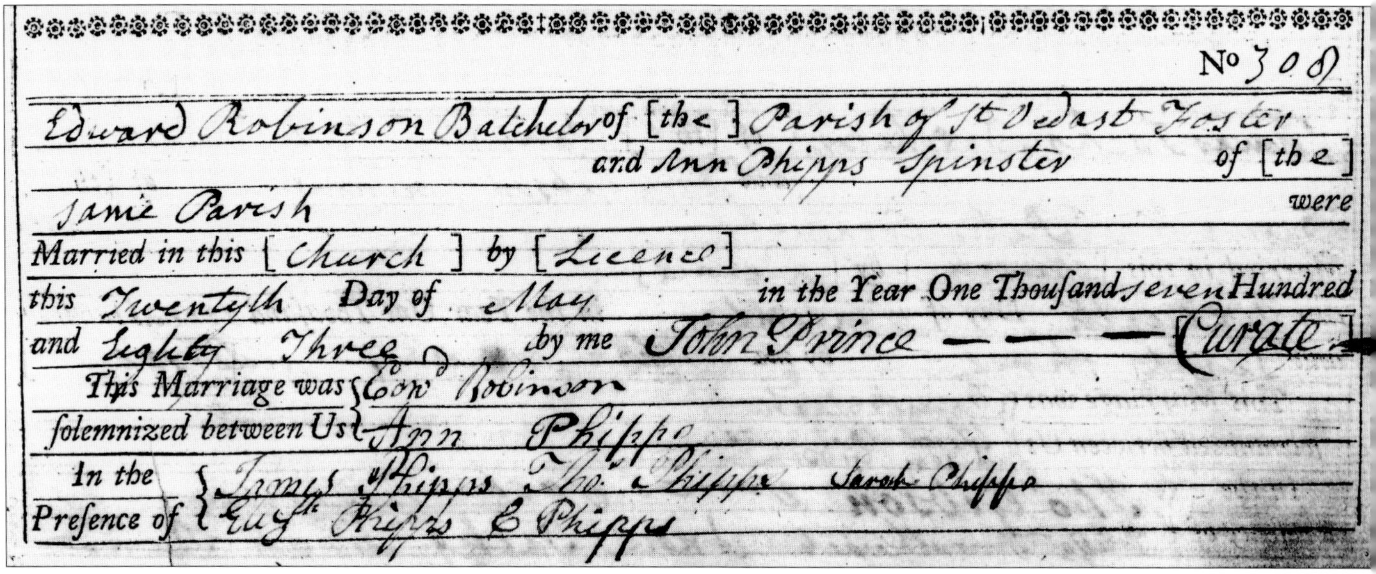

> No 308
>
> Edward Robinson Batchelor of [the] Parish of St Vedast Foster and Ann Phipps Spinster of [the] Same Parish were Married in this [Church] by [Licence] this Twentyth Day of May in the Year One Thousand seven Hundred and Eighty Three by me John Prince — [Curate]
>
> This Marriage was solemnized between Us { Edw. Robinson / Ann Phipps
>
> In the Presence of { James Phipps, Tho.s Phipps, Sarah Phipps / Eliz. Phipps, E Phipps

Figure 583.

586, 587 and 589). Phipps entered a second mark ('I.P', with a pellet between the letters – see fig. 581) in 1772, which appears on figs. 585, 588 and 589, by which time his son, Thomas, was apprenticed to him, as was one Edward Robinson. These two became free in 1777 and 1780 respectively, and presumably worked in James Phipps' establishment for a few years before entering a joint mark in July 1783 at an address further along Gutter Lane (see fig. 584 – copy of entry at Goldsmiths' Hall). New marks were added in 1789 (see fig. 584).

It seems likely that James Phipps retired at this time (Heal records him until 1783), and certainly no piece with his mark has been seen with the plate duty mark imposed on 1 December 1784. Before leaving him, a characteristic feature of the way he marked his labels should be mentioned. They are often found with the maker's mark 'I.P' struck twice, once fully and once partially. No reason for this can be suggested. Phipps lived on in retirement and eventually died in around 1795. A curious entry by Heal records a partnership between James and Thomas Phipps that was dissolved in 1783. No mark was registered for it, and no example of it has been seen, so it may have been a short-lived affair towards the close of James Phipps' career, before his son and Edward Robinson took over.

Figure 584.

Figures 585-594.

Between becoming free and registering their first mark, both Thomas Phipps and Edward Robinson were married in their parish church of St Vedast, Foster Lane, in the street parallel to Gutter Lane (see fig. 681) – and both their wives were Phipps too. Thomas Phipps was married on 22 September 1778 to Elizabeth Phipps from the parish of St Mary Staining, further east in the City of London (see fig. 582). Edward Robinson was married on 20 May 1783 to Ann Phipps, also of the parish of St Vedast; and with James, Thomas and Elizabeth Phipps among the witnesses, suggesting a very close relationship between Edward Robinson's wife and his business partner (see fig. 583). While we cannot be certain of the exact relationship between these various Phipps, the supposition is that business and family life were closely entwined.[44]

The earliest labels bearing the mark of Thomas Phipps and Edward Robinson have the mark on its own, with no lion passant or duty mark (see figs. 590 and 592, *c.*1783). They can therefore reasonably be dated to between July 1783 and December 1784. After the imposition of duty they were punctilious in applying the king's head mark (even though there was still some doubt as to whether it was necessary[45]), and they usually put the lion on too. The lion passant hardly ever accompanies the maker's

Makers

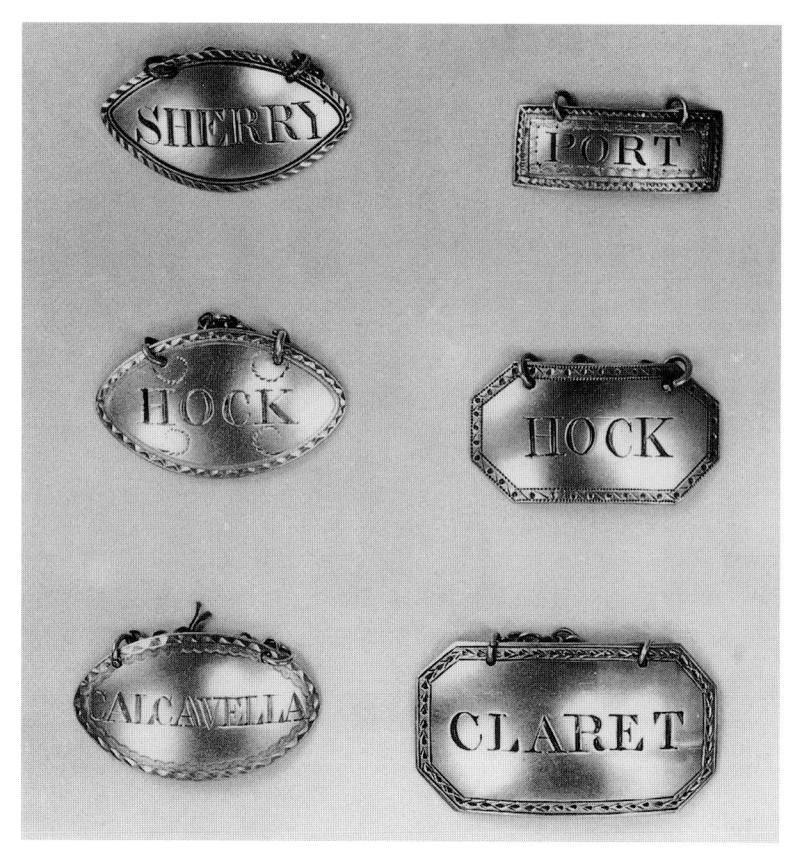

Figures 595-600.

mark on their pre-duty labels, but after December 1784 it appears more regularly. By way of contrast, it is worth noting that some of James Phipps' labels were marked, apparently at random, with the lion.

At first the Phipps and Robinson partnership used similar designs to the elder Phipps. Soon, however, they began to introduce characteristic features of their own and to apply them with as much skill as their predecessor. The high quality of their workmanship and their range of innovative designs clearly brought them a far-reaching and well-deserved reputation (see fig. 591, PORT, *c.*1788; fig. 593, CARCAVELLA, 1793 - contrast this with fig. 599 for CALCAVELLA; fig. 595, SHERRY, 1791; figs. 594/596, PORT, 1800; fig. 597, HOCK, 1792 and fig. 600, CLARET, 1803). They were one of the best-known firms in London for their labels, as the number to be found with the crests and armorials of the nobility amply demonstrates. In addition to their labels, they were famed for items of domestic silver for the dining room and the dressing table.

During their partnership, which lasted until 1811, they registered three marks (see fig. 584), one in 1783 and two in 1789.[46] The marks varied in size, but used a similar shaped punch. The final mark was possibly a prelude to the Act of 1790, which brought in compulsory hallmarking for labels and with which they were strict to comply from 1790 onwards. They also had a fourth, apparently unregistered, mark of the same shape as the others, but with no pellets between the letters. It has been seen on its own and accompanied by the duty mark and the lion passant, but not with a date letter. It has not been possible to assign a precise period of use. A rectangular TP/ER mark attributed to this partnership by Jackson[47] has been shown by Sachs to be incorrect.

Thomas Phipps' son James II was apprenticed to his father in 1800 and became free in 1807. He joined the family firm and the mark TP above ER above IP appears from 1811/12. There is a curious feature about the entry of this mark in the register, in that the space for the names and addresses of the makers is blank and the entry undated. There is an unwitnessed signature of James Phipps II which resembles his of 1816, five years later, when he and his father entered their partnership mark. From its place in the register, however, and from the fact that it first appears with the date letter for 1811/12 (while the latest appearance of the TP/ER mark is in the previous year), it seems clear that this triple mark was entered soon after May 1811.

The partnership lasted until 1816, when Edward Robinson died. The labels the family team produced continued in the vein of the previous partnership – labels of consistently high standard – but no new designs emerged. This led Sachs to propound that it was Robinson who was the real innovator in the Phipps and Robinson partnership, but there is no firm evidence to support his theory. Indeed it may be simply that, after thirty active years, Thomas was losing some of his energy.

The fourth and final Phipps family partnership, that of Thomas and James II, began immediately after Robinson's death, their joint TP/IP mark being registered in January 1816.[48] Sachs judged their work to be coarser than that of their predecessors, but examples that were not available to him do not altogether bear out this criticism. Certainly some very fine pieces bear their mark, particularly some cast designs that can claim to be firmly in the best family tradition. Sachs wondered, too, whether the young James had the same commitment to the business as his father and grandfather. Certainly output fell sharply after about 1820, and came to a sudden end when Thomas died in October 1823. No label with a date letter after 1823/24 has been seen, and the Goldsmiths' Company have recorded no articles associated with James II after Thomas' death. They evidently ceased production in that year and James, the last survivor, fades from the picture. A sad final note was that two of his children, Richard and Sarah, were petitioners for relief from the Goldsmiths' Company in March 1888, which suggests perhaps that James II had not prospered.[49]

PART 11 – SUSANNA BARKER

Successful businesswomen are not a twentieth-century phenomenon. Women of competence, determination and appropriate business skills have been essential to economic life as far back as the first written records. For centuries in the City of London, as elsewhere, women administered properties and ran businesses during their widowhood. It was often after the death of her husband that a woman came into her own and assumed a new identity.

In *The Making of the English Middle Class* by Peter Earle[50] it is recorded that one third of all women of property ran a business. In London, unmarried women lived by their own work and made up more than ten per cent of those women taking out insurance policies on business premises. Many of the women engaged in business in the seventeenth, eighteenth and nineteenth centuries were involved in the silver trade. It is against this background that the work of Susanna Barker, a London goldsmith, should be reviewed.

The history leading to the correct attribution of the SB mark to Susanna Barker is well documented. In the early editions of Jackson, such as the second edition of 1921, the only references to the SB mark are to Samuel Bradley (1783/4?) and to Name not Traced (1804/5). In 1947 Penzer, in his *The Book of the Wine Label*,[51] only gave references to Samuel Bradley – none to Susanna Barker. By 1966, when Eric Whitworth published *Wine Labels*,[52] both Samuel Bradley and Susanna Barker were included in the list of wine label makers. It was not until 1971, however, that John Beecroft brilliantly resolved the previously confused situation and as a result of his work the name of Samuel Bradley was to disappear forever to be correctly replaced by that of Susanna Barker.[53]

Considering the superb quality of her workmanship, the number of her wine labels and the very great variations in her wine label designs, surprisingly little is known about Susanna Barker. She entered her first mark on 25 June 1778 as a smallworker at 16 Gutter Lane, where she stayed until she succeeded Margaret Binley (1764-89) at 29 Gutter Lane (see fig. 681). Susanna was described in the rate books as 'widow'. She entered three further marks in 1789, probably timed to coincide with taking over the Binleys' business. There is no record of her apprenticeship or freedom.

Heal records her as a goldsmith working at 29 Gutter Lane from 1790 to 1793. Heal also suggests that she died in 1793 as that was the year in which Robert Barker entered his mark from the same address. No record of a wine label dated after 1793 and bearing the SB mark has been noted.

The locations of many of the London goldsmiths have been identified.[54] From a map of the relevant area of London, as it was in the 1770s, the relative positions of both her workshops can be seen: No. 16 where Susanna worked from 1778 until 1789 and No. 29 where she worked from 1789

Makers

Figure 601.

Figure 602.

and from where Robert Barker in 1793 was to continue production until at least 1815 (see fig. 681).

In order to ascertain some indications as to the incidence of labels manufactured in the Susanna Barker workshops, information was obtained from members of the Wine Label Circle, the Pratt Collection at Harvey's in Bristol, the Marshall Collection at the Ashmolean Museum in Oxford and from the Vintners' Hall Collection in London. In all details were obtained of 3,198 labels of which 138 were by Susanna Barker. This gave an incidence of 4.3 per cent which, when further broken down showed an incidence of 3.9 per cent for wine labels and 4.5 per cent for sauce labels.[55]

Grimwade[56] records the first mark, No. 2479, of Susanna Barker as being entered on 25 June 1778. This mark (see fig. 602) is from a very small punch of 3 x 1.25mm and is SB without a dot between the letters. In the original paper on the marks of Susanna Barker by John Beecroft in the *Wine Label Journal* of June 1971 (vol. 5, no. 1) he records the fact that the first mark had not been observed. In a review article of the labels of Susanna Barker in June 1995 (vol. 9, no. 9), in the preparation for which all the available labels of this maker had been reviewed, no examples of her work stamped with the elusive first mark were recorded. Later, whilst disturbing the tranquillity of a well-displayed stand at an Olympia antiques fair in the year 2000, the first mark was 'found' on a pair of crescent labels engraved for CLARET (see fig. 601) and PORT. These labels are of the usual thick gauge

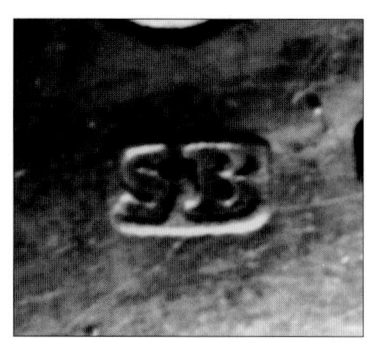

Figure 603.

Figure 604.

170

Makers

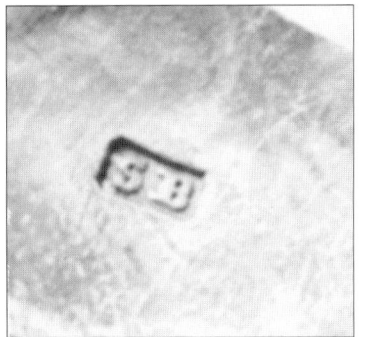

Figure 605.

Figure 606.

Figure 607.

Figure 608.

Figure 609.

Figure 610.

Figure 611.

Figure 612.

Makers

Figures 613-627.

silver and are typical of the workmanship of Susanna Barker. On the back of the label the SB mark has been punched twice, which is again typical of the date of this mark. This mark has never been seen on a wine or sauce label. No reason is apparent as to why this mark, having been entered, was then not used on labels.

Her second mark (see fig. 604), shown on LISBON (see fig. 603), was entered on 12 August 1789 and the size of this punch was 5 x 2.75mm. It is again a simple SB without a dot between the letters.[57] In his article[58] of 1971 John Beecroft reported on his examination, at Goldsmiths' Hall, of the relevant register and metal plate that related to this second mark. These metal plates were first introduced on

Figures 628-641.

30 May 1774. The mark struck showed several distinctive features but the major observation was that there was a 'flattening' to the lower front of the letter 'S' which produced a point at its base (see fig. 612), shown on the star MADEIRA (see fig. 611) compared with the punch in crisp condition (see fig. 610) shown on MADEIRA (see fig. 609). This loss of clarity of the letter 'S' clearly indicates that the punch was well worn when the mark was entered in 1789. This punch was therefore in use for some time before then, and was probably only registered later so that Susanna could regularise her position prior to the introduction of the Silver Marking Plate Act of 1790.

The second mark is by far the most common punch that Susanna used and from an analysis of

Makers

Figures 642-658.

138 of her labels ninety-nine have this mark. It has not yet been recorded in conjunction with a date letter. It is of interest to record that six of the ninety-nine labels with this mark, or six per cent of the production were armorial in design. This mark is believed to have been discontinued in 1789 with the introduction of Susanna's fourth mark.

Her third mark (see fig. 606), shown on HOCK (see fig. 605), is very similar to but much smaller than the second mark. This mark was entered on the same day as her second mark, namely 12 August 1789, the size of this punch being 3.75 x 1.5mm. This is by far the rarest of Susanna Barker's marks and from the analysis of previously mentioned 138 labels only four are recorded with this mark: two crescent designs with names pierced; one crescent design with the name in black; and one simple eye shape. This suggests an incidence of three per cent of her label production.

The fourth mark (see fig. 608), shown on SHERRY (see fig. 607), is recorded as having been entered on 26 August 1789. This is the S.B Mark and the size of this punch is 3.5 x 1.75mm. As regards the frequency of this mark, from the analysis of the original 138 labels, it would appear to have been used on thirty-five labels giving an incidence of twenty-five per cent.[59] In sixty per cent of cases this fourth mark occurs in conjunction with a date letter. The date letter 'r' for 1792 was the most commonly observed and the next most common was 'q' for 1791. The latest date letter observed was 's' for 1793.

Susanna Barker is particularly recognised for her eye shaped label designs (see figs. 603, 613, 615, 616, 618, 619, 620, 627, 636, 640, 655, 656 and 658), whether they are of the single or double reed or beaded designs or whether they are of the open work variety. There is hardly a design that Susanna has not copied and then altered it to put her most original of styles. Crescents (see figs. 601, 605, 639, 643, 648, 653 and 657), barrels (see fig. 631), urns (see figs. 609, 617 and 649), scrolls (see figs. 617, 623, 625, 641 and 651), stars (see figs. 611 and 652) and banners (see fig. 620) have all been subjected to what can only be described as the 'Susanna Barker Magical Touch' (see fig. 607 for what she could do with a rectangle). This is, of course, in addition to those designs that are totally original and thus unique to this maker (see fig. 634).

The labels are always manufactured from a thick gauge of silver plate and, prior to publication in 1993 of the article on the Silver Gilt Beckford Cruet and Sauce Labels,[60] it was believed that Susanna worked solely in silver. In that article John Salter reviews the background of William Beckford, a notable silver collector who, having inherited a vast fortune from his father, proceeded to use his resources to acquire the ultimate in silver and silver gilt pieces that money could buy.

Susanna Barker was given the accolade of being the finest label maker of that time – namely May to June 1784. She was commissioned to produce four heavy silver gilt labels with feathered edges and pierced letters for ELDER, TARRAGON, LEMON and SOY. These labels were made for the Beckford Cruet of 1784, which had been manufactured by John Scofield.[61]

Having reviewed the information on what is known about the life and work of Susanna Barker, the conclusion is reached that Susanna has been shown to be a goldsmith of outstanding skill who manufactured wine labels of exquisite designs and quality, as can be seen from examples of her work shown at figs. 613-658.[62]

PART 12 – JOHN RICH

John Rich was not recognised as a manufacturer of wine labels until researches by members of the Wine Label Circle in the 1950s aimed to discover the identity of a maker whose mark, a 'JR' script in a rectangular frame, they were finding on labels of exceedingly high quality dating from the last quarter of the eighteenth century. Mr B.W. Robinson, Curator of Metalwork at the Victoria and Albert Museum, confirmed from the registers in Goldsmiths' Hall that it was the mark of John Rich, which he had entered as a bucklemaker in August 1780, at the same time as another mark that had similar, but not identical, letters in a frame that followed the outline of the letters.[63]

Neither Heal nor Jackson were aware of John Rich, though the latter illustrates the 1780 rectangular mark, attributing it as possibly to John Robins, which Grimwade repeats. Grimwade, however, does show an earlier mark for Rich, which he entered as a bucklemaker in June 1765 in the smallworkers' register. The letters are the same as those of the later mark, but the shape of the frame is different. It and the outline mark described above have been seen on buckles, but not on other items. The rectangular 1780 mark has only been seen on wine labels.[64]

A number of other silversmiths used script 'JR' initials for their mark during the second half of the eighteenth century, but they can all be distinguished from Rich's, either by the shape of the letters, by the size and shape of the frame, by emblems accompanying the letters, or by having a

Makers

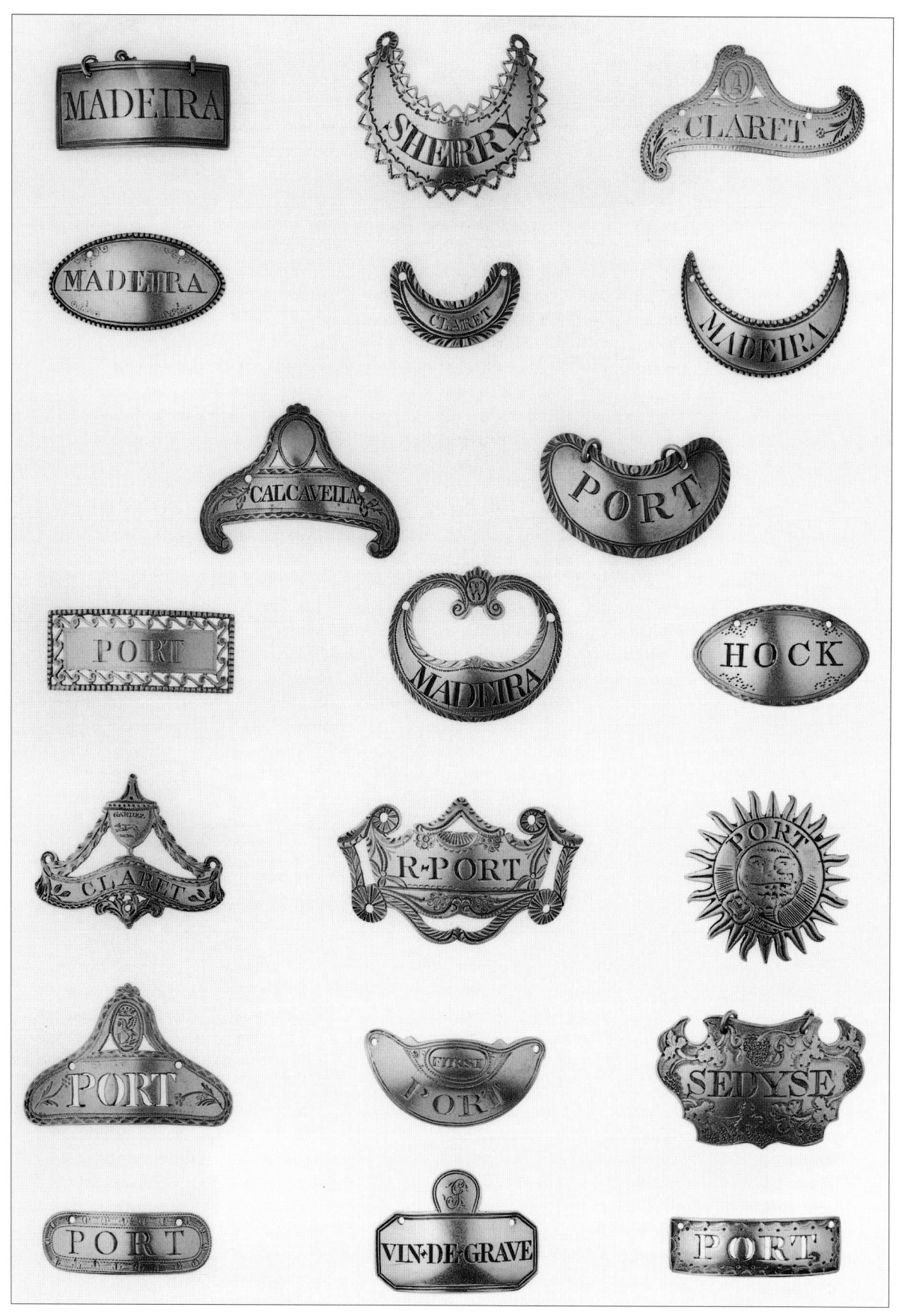

Figures 659-678.

pellet between the letters. Doubt, however, begins to be raised about his use of the mark when the dates of the labels on which it appears are considered.

Rich seems to have been punctilious in complying with the hallmarking laws. Before 1784 his labels have the lion passant, and from 1784 the appropriate duty mark. After 1791 there is a date letter. Only one example is known of a label with the maker's mark alone (see fig. 660, SHERRY). Some of these labels can realistically be dated at least ten years earlier than 1780, so the question therefore arises as to when he started to use it. It may well be that he found the need to diversify from buckles soon after he first set up business and introduced a separate mark for his new line of wine labels during the 1770s, not registering it because it was not very different from his existing one. But it is then not clear why he should decide to register it in 1780, ten years or more later. It did not coincide with a change of address. By then he was established at 14 Tottenham Court Road, where he had moved from his first address 'at the back of the Whitfield Chapel off Tottenham Court Road' before 1773. He appears in the Parliamentary List of 1773, but strangely Heal does not list him, although the list was one of his main sources of information. Perhaps he was not the householder at either place.

Whatever his circumstances, Rich's work clearly became well known; his labels are adorned with crests of the nobility and he evidently enjoyed royal patronage. Perhaps it was simply the growth in his label business that caused him to regularise the mark he was putting on them. In an article on the wine labels at Buckingham Palace and at Windsor Castle, Dr Penzer records five labels from George III's Coronation Service, plain reeded rectangles, three with rounded ends, by John Rich, dated 1794.[65] He also notes that two of a set of six silver-gilt rectangular labels for KINGS CUP are by him, the remainder being by T. Phipps and E. Robinson, all dated 1794. These labels are particularly interesting, because no other silver-gilt examples by Rich are known.

The majority of Rich's labels are the standard designs of the period – rectangles, ovals and crescents – but he also made more elaborate items, some of them quite original (see figs. 674 for FIRST PORT and 671 for R. PORT). It would seem that he followed a common practice of the time by buying in from another firm labels for which he had an order (one or two of his ovals, for instance, are indistinguishable from James Hyde's), or it may be that he operated principally as a supplier himself. T. Phipps and E. Robinson presumably had the order for the set of KINGS CUP labels mentioned above, but contracted out two to Rich. The R. PORT (see fig. 671, 1792), which has a pair for MADEIRA, is a label of high quality and a design not known by any other maker. The Sun in Splendour label for PORT (see fig. 239/672) is one of a set of four made for the Blount family, whose crest it is (see above, Chapter 2, Part 7).

High though the quality of Rich's work is, it does not equal that of the leading label manufacturers of the period, Hester Bateman, Susanna Barker, James Hyde or the Phipps family, from all of whom Rich borrowed designs. The shape of the saw-tooth crescent (see fig. 660), for instance, is not so delicate as Hester Bateman's version, and the saw-tooth border is rougher. His CLARET (see fig. 661, c.1780) appears to be based on a similar design of Susanna Barker's, which has tidier proportions. Nevertheless, whether he was copying another design or being really innovative, it can be said that his labels invariably show a characteristic individuality, and there can be no doubt that they were much sought after.

It is a pity that we do not know more about John Rich. There is no record of his apprenticeship and he was never elected to the livery of the Goldsmiths' Company. His place of work was some distance from the area around Goldsmiths' Hall where the better-known goldsmiths had their businesses. The St Pancras Parish Records show the marriage of John and Elizabeth Rich in 1755. It is the only entry for that surname for many years during that period, so it is quite likely to refer to our man. Subsequent entries record the births of five children, some deaths and some further marriages. His death is recorded in 1807. Labels bearing his mark have been noted up to 1809/10, which is consistent with the suggestion that his widow continued the business for a few years after his death, as many other women did, fulfilling outstanding orders and using up his stock. Examples of his work are shown in figs. 659-678.

PART 13 – WOMEN SILVERSMITHS

There were two outstanding women silversmiths manufacturing wine labels during the last quarter of the eighteenth century – Hester Bateman just outside the City of London and Susanna Barker near Goldsmiths' Hall (see fig. 679). Both women entered the business in their own right; nothing is known of their husbands as regards working in silver or gold. Both were innovators, introducing several new designs, and excellent craftsmen, with some reservations about how Hester Bateman stamped and engraved her letters. But both undoubtedly rank with the Phipps family as leaders in the field of wine labels during this period.

A number of other women entered marks, which are found on labels from 1760 onwards. Very often they were the widows of silversmiths continuing their late husband's business, sometimes in partnership with sons or relations, sometimes remarrying and sometimes remaining on their own, registering their own mark. Some of them continued to use their husband's mark for years after his death. On the whole they did not introduce much in the way of new features, but continued with the designs and models that their husbands had used, with minor adaptations for contemporary fashion. Margaret Binley, for instance, made considerable improvements on the designs that her husband, Richard, employed during his working life. Likewise, the name Rebecca Emes (in partnership with various Barnards) appears on labels that did more than just move with the times, though it is not clear to what extent she or her new partners should be credited with the development.

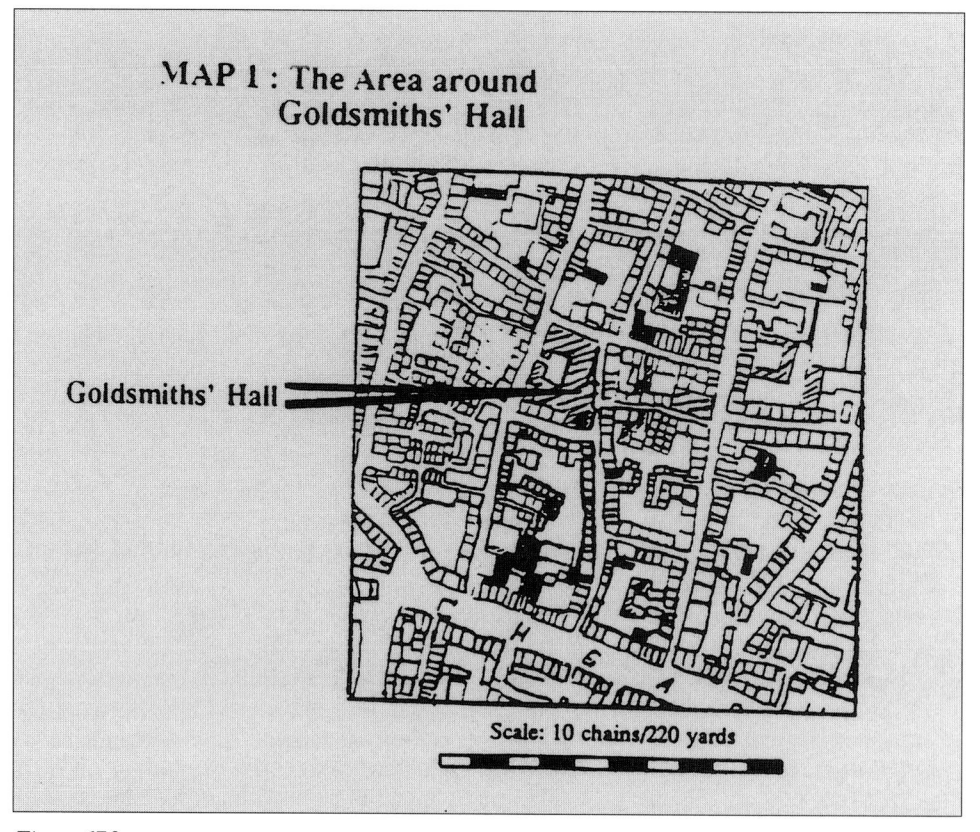

Figure 679.

The following list shows women whose marks, as indicated in Grimwade, are found on labels, either on their own, or in partnerships, and the dates when they were active.

Silversmith	Dates active	Comments
ENGLAND		
LONDON		
Anne Harvey	1759-c.1768	Probably daughter of John Harvey I. Entered mark with John Harvey II in 1759, at which time Harvey senior was in prison for debt. J. Harvey II registered an almost identical mark in 1768 when twenty-three years old.
Hester Bateman	1761-1790	Widow of John Bateman, chainmaker (1732-1761).
Margaret Binley	1764-1778	Widow of Richard Binley (1745-1764).
Elizabeth Cooke	From 1764	Widow of Thomas Cooke II (1721-1761). (A label by T. Cooke & R. Gurney is recorded.)
Jane Dorrell	1766-1771	Widow of William Dorrell (1763 to 1766). In partnership with Richard May, who also entered marks of his own (1764 and 1778).
Susanna Barker	c.1778- c.1793	Described in the Rate Books as 'widow'.
Ann Bateman	1791-1805	Widow of Jonathan Bateman (1790-1791). In partnership with brother-in-law Peter Bateman until 1800 and then with nephew William added.
Elizabeth Morley	1794-c.1815	Widow of Thomas Morley (1775-1793).
Mary Hyde	c.1794-1829	Widow of James Hyde, using his mark 1794 to 1799. In partnership with John Reily; joint mark 1799-1801. Under mark of J. Reily to 1826. In partnership with son Charles Reily (1826-1829).
Alice Burrows	1801-1819	Widow of George Burrows I (1769-1801). In partnership with George Burrows II.
Rebecca Emes	1808-1829	Widow of John Emes (1769-1808). In partnership with W. Emes (1808) and then with Edward Barnard.
Theodosia Ann Atkins	1801-1815	Widow of James Atkins (1791-1801) a bucklemaker.
Sarah Snatt	1817-c.1830	Widow of Josiah Snatt (1798-1817).
Mahala Jago	1830- ?	Widow of Jacob (1783-1828) or John Jago (1828-1830).
Mary Chawner	1834- ?	Widow of William Chawner II (1808-1834).
CHESTER		
Mary Huntingdon	1815-1827	Sent silver for assay, from 1815-1827, from premises at 38 Bridge Street Row.
EXETER		
Ann Adams	1806-1835	Widow of John Adams (1780-1806).
NEWCASTLE		
Ann Robertson	1801-1811	Widow of John Robertson I (1778-1801).
Dorothy Langlands	1804-1814	Widow of John Langlands II (1795-1804).
IRELAND		
CORK		
Jane Williams	1806-1821	Widow of John Williams (apprentice and, later, partner of Carden Terry) who died in 1806. The only woman silversmith of Cork. Worked in partnership with her father, Carden Terry, from 1806 until he died in 1821.

PART 14 – MAKERS' LOCATIONS

Some 250 years ago, many goldsmiths occupied premises in the streets around Goldsmiths' Hall (see fig. 679). The Hall occupied most of an island site, bounded by Foster Lane on the west and Gutter Lane on the east (see fig. 680). It is in these two streets, and the ones close by, that most of the early wine label makers worked – very close together given that Foster and Gutter Lanes are each only about two hundred yards long. William Abdy I was just to the north in Noble Street and James Atkins a little further in Wells Street. William Barrett was in Wood Street, Samuel Bellingham in St

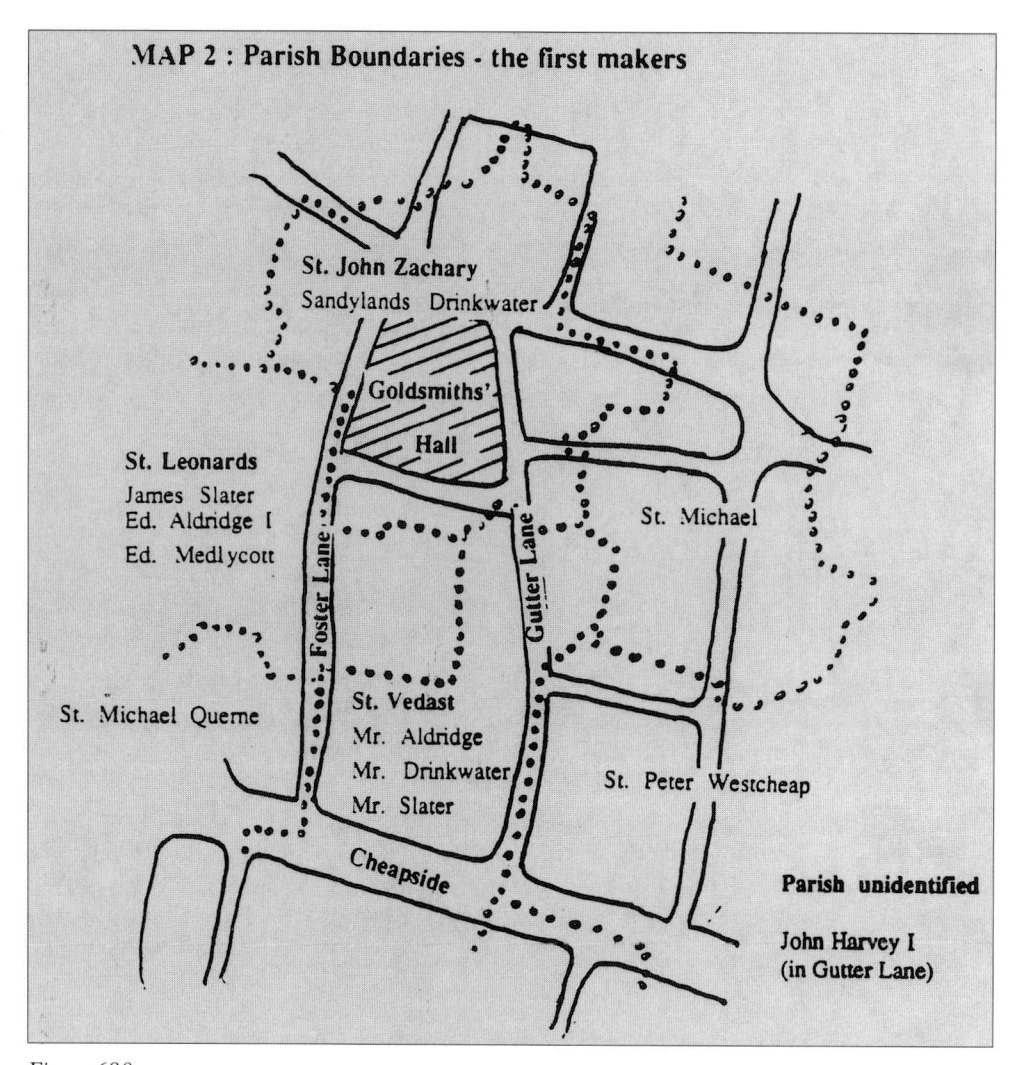

Figure 680.

Martins Le Grand, the Barnards in Paternoster Row, and Josiah Snatt, John Robins, Elizabeth Morley and the Knights in Aldersgate Street.

In evaluating just how contiguous the makers were, it should be noted that street numbering did not start until the second half of the eighteenth century. Before then, craftsmen had signs outside their premises. Sandylands Drinkwater, for instance, was to be found at the Hand and Coral in Gutter Lane, Edmund Medlycott at the Golden Ball in Foster Lane and Thomas Daniell at the Silver Lion in Foster Lane.

Before numbering of streets became common, some indication of the location of premises in the street can be divined from rate collectors' books. Assuming that the collector proceeded steadily down a street, the order of entries in the rate book should show who lived next to whom; and comparison of rate collectors' books with subsequent street numbers tends to confirm this. Unfortunately, rate collectors' books for those streets around Goldsmiths' Hall have not survived for this period.

In 1767 an Act of Parliament authorised the general numbering of premises and the removal of the projecting street signs in the City. From the 1770s it is then possible to locate the exact position of each maker in a street, using these newly introduced street numbers – though inevitably there is confusion about some makers. In the comments that follow, the street number of each maker is taken from Grimwade, which in turn shows the addresses registered at the Hall. The maps shown are based on Richard Horwood's map of London, first printed at the end of the eighteenth century and revised in the early nineteenth century. It is a little later than the period under consideration, but is the first map to show comprehensively the individual properties and house numbers; and the layout of streets around Goldsmiths' Hall had not changed in any significant way. In the maps shown here, Map 1 (see fig. 679) shows the full detail, indicating each building and how tightly packed the area was; Maps 2 (see fig. 680) and 3 (see fig. 681) exclude some of this detail, to allow the points made to come across more clearly.

Many of the earliest makers of wine labels – those working in the 1730s and 1740s – had premises in Foster and Gutter Lanes. The presence of two is well known. Sandylands Drinkwater was to be found at the Hand and Coral in Gutter Lane; he entered his first mark there in 1735, but Heal records him at that address from 1731. Sandylands Drinkwater appears in the parish records of St John Zachary[66] and was Upper Churchwarden of the parish in 1743. If his premises were within the parish, they must have been situated opposite Goldsmiths' Hall – the Hall itself faced directly on to Gutter Lane. This approximate location is shown in Map 2, which indicates the parish boundaries. Incidentally, Sandylands Drinkwater's signature, as it appears in these records, has the same script S and D as appear in his mark.

John Harvey I also had premises in Gutter Lane, at the Queen's Head. His parish was not identified, but probably was St Vedast. He entered his first mark there in 1738 and remained there for about ten years, when he moved to Fish Street Hill.

A third important early maker was also working in the area, namely James Slater. He entered his first mark in the 1720s in Great Trinity Lane, south of Cheapside, and Heal records him there in 1732. In fact, a contemporary document shows that he moved in 1730 to St Leonard's parish, which included part of the west side of Foster Lane. The document, in the Guildhall Library,[67] is the Constable's Book for Aldersgate Ward, St Leonard's Precinct. This book is described on the front as follows: 'The Names of the Present Inhabitants of St. Leonards Precinct in the Ward of Aldersgate'. Later on, this description is amplified as follows: 'This book is Called ye Constables book, by reason the Constable has it in his Keeping During ye year, in Order to Set down the Names of Each New Corner, with Y Time of ye year They Came into the Precinct'.

The book shows that James Slater, Goldsmith, moved into the precinct in midsummer 1730; and he himself served as Constable in 1742 and Collector of the Lamps in 1747. So all three of these important early makers – Drinkwater, Harvey and Slater – had premises very close together.

The Constable's Book also records a number of other goldsmiths, including several makers of wine labels. Edward Aldridge I first registered a mark in 1724, at St Leonard's Court, Foster Lane. His second mark, in 1739, found him in Lilley Pot Lane, just to the north, but he returned to Foster Lane, in 1743 according to Heal, though the Constable's Book mentions him as commencing inhabitation in the parish in midsummer 1751, as Collector of the Lamps in 1755 and as unsuccessful in the election for Scavenger in 1761.

Edmund Medlycott entered his mark in 1748 at the Golden Ball, Foster Lane. The Constable's Book, spelling his name variously Edmond and Edmund Medlicott, records that he had moved into St Leonard's parish by Christmas 1748, became Collector of the Lamps in 1752 (defeating in the election Walter Brind, another goldsmith), a position to which he was re-elected in 1753; and he was elected Constable in 1753, as well as being Scavenger and Younger of the Inquest in that year. In 1756, however, he failed to be elected Collector of the Lamps.

Another contemporary document, the Vestry Minutes of the parish of St Vedast,[68] mentions several other silversmiths, although the absence usually of Christian names in this document does not assist precise identification. Richard Binley is mentioned in 1745 and Thomas Hyde in 1755 (see Parts 4 and 5). Rather confusing in this document is the mention of a Mr Aldridge in 1734, a Mr Drinkwater in Gutter Lane in 1740 and a Mr Slater in 1745. It is uncertain whether these were the same Edward Aldridge and James Slater mentioned in St Leonard's parish and Sandylands Drinkwater in the St John Zachary parish; it seems likely, but then raises the question of why they were mentioned in two adjoining parishes. Maybe they had premises in both parishes; whatever the reason, it does not alter the fact of their location in this very small area.

It should be mentioned that there were a number of early label makers who worked outside the Gutter Lane/Foster Lane area. Such makers included Robert Cox, in Fetter Lane from 1752; William Dorrell in Grub Street from 1736; John Robinson II in the West End from the late 1730s; and Louis Hamon in Soho.

Makers

Foster Lane
18 Samuel Meriton II
20 Thomas Daniell
16 (estimated site) Robert Hennell I

Goldsmiths' Hall
Carey Lane

Gutter Lane
29 Susanna Barker (1790 on)
16 Susanna Barker (1778-1789)
33 Thomas Hyde
11 James Phipps I
10 James Hyde
38 James Hyde
40 T. Phipps & E. Robinson
47 William Plummer

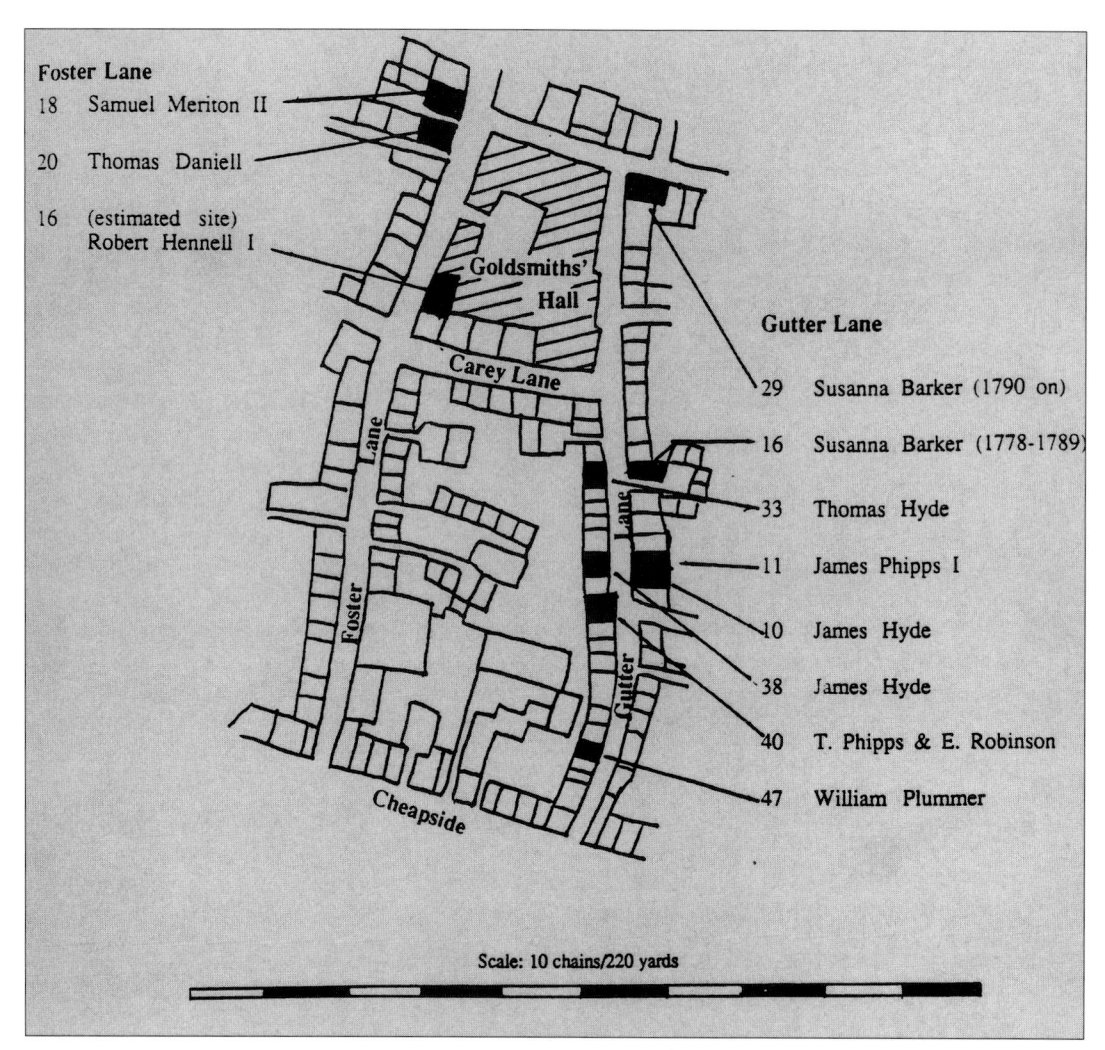

Scale: 10 chains/220 yards

Figure 681.

Moving on to the 1760s, Gutter Lane continued to be a favoured street for makers of labels. Richard Binley had taken over Sandylands Drinkwater's premises at the Hand and Coral, to be succeeded by his widow, Margaret, and then by Susanna Barker as described earlier. Thomas and James Hyde's separate premises in Gutter Lane have already been discussed. James Phipps had also moved here from Foster Lane, where he was recorded (with William Bond) in 1754. In Foster Lane, there was Edmund Medlycott until at least 1755, and Edward Aldridge until the 1760s.

Outside the area are rather more makers, including Benjamin Bickerton in Jewin Street, Aldersgate from 1761; John Humphris off the Strand in 1762, at Newington Butts in 1763; John Rich in Tottenham Court Road in 1765; John Robinson II in Bond Street from the 1740s; and William Alldridge in Fetter Lane in 1751 (Heal) and in Brook Street in 1768 (Grimwade).

Following the 1767 Act of Parliament, street numbering spread throughout the city. At the same time, wine labels were becoming more common and there were an increasing number of makers in the Foster Lane/Gutter Lane area.

Map 3 (see fig. 681) shows the location of some of the later makers.

Gutter Lane

10 James Hyde. Registered his first mark, at the address, in 1777; but moved to No. 38 (q.v.) in 1778, directly opposite No. 10.

11 James Phipps I. Originally worked with William Bond in Foster Lane, but entered his second mark in 1767 in Gutter Lane, and his third at 11 Gutter Lane in 1772.

16 Susanna Barker. First mark registered in 1778, at 16 Gutter Lane, as was her second in 1789. Moved to No. 29 in 1789.

29 Sandylands Drinkwater, followed by Richard Binley and then (1764-89) by Margaret Binley, then Susanna Barker from 1789, and Robert Barker from 1793. It is not clear from Horwood's map where No. 29 was, as there is a gap in his numbering between 26 and 30, but it was at the north end, probably on the corner with Maiden Lane, the presumed location of the Hand and Coral.

33 Thomas Hyde I. Took over these premises from his former master, John Harvey I, in 1747 and continued here until his death in 1805, together with Thomas Hyde II.

38 James Hyde. Registered his second mark here in 1778, and subsequent marks in 1786.

40 Thomas Phipps and Edward Robinson. Did not enter their first mark until 1783, but noted in view of their importance as label makers. Used also by Phipps, Robinson and Phipps until 1816 and by Thomas and James Phipps until 1823.

43 William Plummer I. Heal records him at this address from 1790-1793.[69]

47 William Plummer I. Entered his second mark in 1774 and his third in 1789 from this address, though originally worked in Foster Lane (1755-63). He is recorded as a sauce label maker.

Foster Lane

11 Robert, David and Samuel Hennell were here from 1795-1811.

16 Robert Hennell I. Registered a mark here in 1773, though later in the century moved to No.11.

18 Samuel Meriton II. First mark registered here in 1775, second in 1781. Heal says he was here until 1796. The St John Zachary Vestry Minutes (L91 MS 591/2) record a Samuel Meriton in the parish in 1764.

20 Thomas Daniell moved here in 1781 from Carey Lane. Here he established the London Silver Plate Manufactory, otherwise known as The Silver Lion, which appears to have been in part a factory and in part a retail outlet. In 1784 he stated in a handbill that he always had on hand 'Twenty Thousand Ounces of every species of Silver Goods … finished in the highest elegance of patterns and peculiarly excellent workmanship, and embellishments from the best and latest designs'.[70]

21 Robert Piercy, the soy frame maker, was here from 1760-1780.

?   James Phipps and William Bond were in Foster Lane from c.1754-1769.

Carey Lane

6   Was almost on the corner of Carey Lane and Gutter Lane. James Hyde was here from 1794. Mary Hyde, widow of James, entered a joint mark with John Reily here. John Reily was followed by the Mary and Charles Reily partnership (1826-29) and the Reily and Storer partnership (1829-50).

10 Thomas Daniell was here from 1771 until his move to Foster Lane in 1781. It is not clear from Horwood's map exactly where No. 10 was situated.

It should be emphasised that by no means all of the early label makers lived in the area highlighted here, around Goldsmiths' Hall, However, there does appear to have been a particular concentration in this area and especially in Gutter Lane, with many of the most prominent early makers working very close together. Unfortunately, only the street layout in this area now remains. Apart from St Vedast's Church and Goldsmiths' Hall, rebuilt in the first part of the nineteenth century, virtually all the buildings in these streets today are modern. Fortunately, some of the goods made and sold here have survived to our times.

CHAPTER 6

NAMES

PART 1 – UNUSUAL WINE LABEL NAMES

> The spirit of individuality and originality, and occasionally of eccentricity, permeated the whole social structure and wine did not escape. In the days of wine labels, wine merchants were individualists, proud to offer their customers wines they had discovered and which could not be bought from any other wine merchant.
>
> André Simon
> *WLCJ*, vol. I, Apr. 1953

Penzer[1] devoted many pages to the names of wines found on wine labels, and to notes on lesser-known wines. His list contained nearly 900 names. Over fifty years later, although the length of the wine list has not altered much, there are now 2,875 recorded label titles that the Wine Label Circle has compiled.[2] Some eighty per cent of them (2,300) are wines, spirits and liquors; the remainder are sauces, toilet waters and medicinal products. Some 500 different sauce titles are known.[3] A large number are variations or deviations from a basic primary name in the spelling or through some identifiable allusion, others are geographical descriptions, but that still leaves many for which it is hard to find an explanation at all. Some broad categories can be defined.

Spelling Variations and Misspellings
By far the commonest variation that occurs is in the way a name, often quite a well-known one, is spelled or misspelled. These should not really be called mistakes as neither the silversmith nor his client had firm standards to guide them. Until the mid-eighteenth century, spelling was still to a large extent an arbitrary affair. Dr Johnson did not publish his dictionary until 1755. There were, of course, atlases by then, so that some regularity existed for the names of countries and the larger cities, but for smaller places and wine-making districts the rules were far from clear, and they remained so well into the nineteenth century. It is worth remembering that bottles, whether bought abroad or delivered in a case from a wine merchant at home, would not in early days have had a paper or any other distinguishing label on them. Exporters might put a name on the barrel in their own tongue, which the English importer could take as he found or translate himself. Travellers discovering a new wine on their journeys as often as not had to rely on the name as they heard it, and perhaps did not write it down until much later. No wonder, then, that the names of even quite common wines often suffered a sea-change before they appeared engraved on a bottle-ticket. To

Figure 682.

give just one example, MADEIRA has been recorded in a dozen different spellings, ranging from MEDEARY to MEDIRA, in addition to the numerous compound titles described below, which indicated what sort of Madeira it was.

Compound Titles
In early days PORT and LISBON were adequate descriptions, but discriminating drinkers soon wished to differentiate their OLD and SWEET PORTS from their LIGHT and DINNER, their SWEET LISBON from their WHITE LISBON. There are many other such additions to a basic name over the whole range of generic wines, BURGUNDY (BURGANDER, WHITE), CLARET (DINNER, AFTER DINNER, CLAIRETTE, ENGLISH, FRENCH), HOCK (OLD, RED, DINNER), and so on. Some sixteen prefixes have been noted for MADEIRA (both RED and TINTO, CAPE, INDIA, SPANISH), as well as all five grape varieties from which Madeira can be made: BUAL (BOAL), MALMSEY (MALMSLAY), SERCIAL (CERCIAL), VERDELHO (VERDEILHA) and TERRANTEZ. SHERRY can be SCHERREY or more pedantically XERES, as well as having over forty other extra titles – COOKING, DRY, PALE, for instance – besides distinguishing between MORILES and GOLDEN, and apart from its several styles, such as OLOROSO and AMONTILLADO (MONTE LEADO).

Regional Names
Later it was no longer enough to show broadly where the wine came from: more specific details were called for as the range of wines that wine merchants were able to provide grew (as André Simon says, above). From Spain came CALCAVELLA, which is found in twenty-five different forms (such as CACAVELLOW and CARCAVELLO); MOUNTAIN (MOUNTIN), a predecessor of sherry; and PAXARETTE, clearly a difficult one for English speakers to get their tongues around as there have been twenty-five different ways of spelling it. From Portugal there was BUCELAS in fifteen guises. From France countless districts were sending their wines to England and, instead of generic WHITE, titles such as CHABLEY, FRONTIGNARY, MONTRACHET

and SOTURN, or however the client chose to spell them, were appearing. It is noticeable, however, that from earliest days, CHAMPAGNE, with eight spellings and nine variants, always seems to have merited a label of its own. From the Atlantic Isles came CANARY (CANARIAS), TENERIGGE (TINERIFFE), and VIDONIA (VYDONIA, WYDONIA). By the beginning of the nineteenth century wines were arriving from all over Europe: ESPERAN from Esparon and RIVESATTE from Rivesalte, both villages in the Rousillon district; TERRA FORTE from the slopes of Mount Etna; ASSMANNSHAUSER, a red wine from the Rhine; CYPRUS and SMYRNA and DALMATIA. From further afield, CAPE is found from the middle of the eighteenth century as a generic name for South African wines; later it becomes more specifically CONSTANTIA, and later still quite small districts have their labels, such as the Drakensburg, which appears as DRAAGENSTEIN. In this category, too, can be placed BRITISH WINE and ENGLISH WINE, though what these wines were is not known. Sometimes there can be confusion. ORANGE is a town on the Rhône, the centre of the district where Châteauneuf du Pape comes from, though that wine name itself has not been recorded. ORANGE, therefore, is a term for wine from the Rhône, but both it and LEMON are also known as sauce labels. Nearby is the village of CHUSCLAN, where a sweet dessert wine is made.

Varietals and Vineyards

As well as denoting the region or district from which a wine came, labels were sometimes required to given even more detailed information, the vineyard of the grower, and the variety of grape from which the wine was made. German wine-growing districts on the Rhone and Moselle became HOCKHEIM, JOHANNISBURGER, RUDESHEIM, MARCOBRUNNER, instead of simply RHENISH, though hock could still be SPARKLING or STILL, even RED or OLD. The last-named reveals an interesting change in taste. By 'OLD' they meant hocks that had been up to thirty or forty years in bottle, an age that even the ripest of Ausleses rarely achieves today. But that was apparently how they enjoyed even their ordinary German wines then. French châteaux names began to find their way on to labels in the nineteenth century, LAFITE, LEOVILLE, MARGAUX, for example, some years before the Classification of 1855 was made. From the Southern Hemisphere an interesting set of labels by H. Steiner of Adelaide dating from 1865 contains SHIRAZ and CARBENET (for Cabernet). These grapes were introduced to Australia in the 1820s.

Cordials and other Liquors

Fruits, flowers, roots, nuts and the leaves of shrubs have been used for brewing cordials through the ages. A list of them would read like the pages of a botanist's herbal. Just a few names from the comprehensive list of liquors in Appendix I will serve as examples of what MADE WINE and HOME MADE WINE were. CURRANT and RAISIN occur quite frequently, while COWSLIP, ELDER, GOOSEBERRY and BUDOCK (from Burdock) would be found on many still room shelves. It was a matter of course for wines to be made and beer to be brewed in country houses throughout the land, and the confection of home-made cordials was as much part of everyday life as the practice of embroidery. SPRUCE was brewed from the leaves and twigs of the tree and bottled as beer. Liquors that were imported from the Continent included CAPILLAIRE (an infusion of the Maidenhair Fern) and RASPAIL (a yellow tonic wine first made by a French pharmacist, Monsieur Vincent Raspail, in 1847).[4] GARUS was a cordial useful for stomach disorders, named after a seventeenth-century Dutch physician. MORAT was a mulberry cordial flavoured with honey, or also a wine from a vineyard on the shores of Lake Morat in Switzerland.

Foreign Names

When the names of wines and spirits on labels from countries outside the British Isles are straightforward translations from the country of origin into another language, or are simply common local names – such as the Swedish labels for BRANNVIN or CONIACH – it seems unnecessary to refer to them in this section. If they are unusual variations they are discussed in the chapters on those countries where they occur. It would, for instance, merit comment if (say) a Swedish mark, or the anglicised version of (say) a French wine, were to be found on a French label in France.

It must be remembered, moreover, that many enamel labels of the eighteenth and nineteenth centuries were certainly made for export by English factories, and they have their titles in the appropriate language (CAP BLANC, CAPO BUONO SPERANZA BIANCO, CAP ROUGE), while the French firm of Samson manufactured enamels specifically for the English market, with titles in the English language.

Spirits

The ingenuity of man for making strong liquor out of any material that can be distilled has known no bounds. Usually the spirit has been drunk at once and has not merited a label, but the more reputable kinds have appeared on labels for almost as long as wines. Brandy and rum were the traditional spirits of the eighteenth century. Their spelling does not vary. RUM was usually drunk straight, except for RUM SHRUB, but BRANDY is found with a wide range of accompanying substances – APPLE, APRICOT, BLACKBERRY, CHERRY, RASPBERRY, STRAWBERRY, TANGERINE – as well as LIQUEUR and in more mundane form as COOKING, and a rather enigmatic RY BRANDY, which might be linked in some way with a Swedish label for JERVSVEGBRANNVIN (Railway Spirits). COGNAC (COHNIACH) is known, as is COGNAC BRANDY, but strangely there is no ARMAGNAC until quite recently.

When gin became acceptable in polite society, at the end of the eighteenth century, it was at first usually styled according to its place of origin, HOLLANDS or SCHIEDAM (in several spellings) the town in Holland where much of the spirit was distilled, or GENEVA (GENEVER), not the Swiss town but because of its juniper flavouring. It is found DRY, SWEETENED and UNSWEETEN'D, as well as by a whole host of mysterious descriptions and slang terms that are discussed below.

Whisky, likewise, has many alternative spellings, and a vast number of alternative titles. It is written as WHISKEY in Ireland and as WHISKY in Scotland. It has been seen as WHISKIE on a label from Aberdeen, and as WISKIE on one from London. C. WHISKY was probably cherry whisky, usually known as GEEN WHISKY (a *gean* is a wild cherry). There is SCOTCH, IRISH, AMERICAN and WELSH WHISKY, but versions relating to other countries have not been noted. There is a collar by James Le Bass (Dublin, 1825) for SCOTCH WHISKEY that is as curious a case of cross-pollination as one could hope to meet. Other terms for this most ubiquitous of drinks are examined below. The most common developments of the whisky theme are names of particular brands: BALFOUR'S LIQUEUR WHISKEY, for example, or of distilleries, often long vanished, such as ENNISHOWEN (Irish) or CAMBUS (see fig. 73, a distillery in Clackmannanshire founded in 1806) and BURNTISLAND (Scottish), or single malts such as GLENLIVET.

In the East, ARRACK is a popular spirit that has been seen on an English nineteenth-century label, as has PISCO, a type of Brandy liquor from South America. More recently, as VODKA has gained in favour, modern labels for this title have appeared.

Slang, Jokes and Colloquialisms

As labels became accepted accessories of the dining room and sideboard, so the descriptions they bore could be expanded, or extra messages added. Upmarket, a literary allusion could be made or a Latin tag inscribed (SEMPER ALIQUID AMARI – Always Something Bitter – around the neck of your Angostura Bitters bottle). Downmarket, the contents of the decanter could be disguised with a humorous phrase or obscure words. In Georgian times and for much of Victoria's reign, gin was not a polite drink, so the contents of decanters were concealed. Expressions such as OLD TOM, MOTHER'S RUIN and CREAM OF THE VALLEY were all terms widely used for gin and all have been seen on nineteenth-century labels. The most notorious of these acronyms is NIG, found both as an original title and re-engraved over an older name. It was once reckoned to be GIN

Names

Figure 683.

Figure 684.

spelled backwards to deceive inquisitive servants, but this patronising explanation is now rightly discarded, and it is now reckoned more likely to have been just a joke. THISTLE JUICE must surely be whiskey in much the same vein. One can only speculate about a wine labelled CONVENT, or what was in THE ABBOT'S BOTTLE, or in 'A BLAMIRE BOTTLE 144 YEARS OLD' (on a label of 1865). A single vine leaf label has the letters 'MT' on it. Was this some in-house joke? Dr Johnson called PUNCH 'cant' meaning a slang word. The *Oxford English Dictionary* says that its origin is unknown. David Garrick (1717-79), the actor friend of Johnson, was an excellent mimic. He took off Johnson's Staffordshire accent and made a joke about it by squeezing a lemon into a punchbowl whilst at the same time making uncouth gesticulations and calling out 'whose for poonsh?'

Miscellaneous
Whilst categories can be found for many of the genuine names that occur on labels, some are left that fit nowhere. Parts of this group are clearly not properly labels at all, even though they may have come from a label manufacturer's workshop. There is a rectangular label inscribed 'Nolumus leges Cornubiae mutari' – 'We do not want the laws of Cornwall to be changed'. It could well have hung on a decanter and sparked off an after-dinner conversation, but it certainly is not a wine label, whereas the Irish Harp labels (see Chapter 2, Part 16) with their political message engraved on the reverse side – 'Tis new strung and WILL be heard' – presumably had the wine name as their main function.

There is an indolent Dionysus reclining in his chariot being waited on by an attendant putto. It is adapted from a well-known label design (see Chapter 2, Part 10) and was awarded by the Caledonian Horticultural Society for 'best Currant Wine', a purpose for which it is entirely suitable, but it is not really a wine label. Nor can the rectangular label inscribed with Latin hexameters of the five good reasons for having a drink be so classed, although it is certainly an appropriate exhortation to see on a decanter.

A number of curious labels are known which have simply a person's name on them: MR ALLSOPP, MR HENDRIE (see fig. 682 by R. Gainsford, Sheffield, 1812), MR TARRATT (see fig. 683), MR SNODGRASS (see fig. 684) and MRS TRAVERS. When Mr Tarratt was first recorded, it was suggested that he was the butler, in which case could one dare to suppose that Mrs Travers was the housekeeper? Probably not, but were they wholesalers, retailers, people with personal decanters in some club or tavern, presents, jokes? Who were CAPT MASTER R.M., and CAPTN SYKES R.N.? Their names were surely not perpetuated for a wine they made (such as Monsier Raspail, see above), or even for what they drank, but for who they were. There was a famous Moselle innkeeper named Peter Nicolay, and a label has been recorded for NICHOLAY, but it is moot whether there is any link and it is unlikely ever to be known.

Some Lessons from Sets
Two sets of labels that belonged to the 3rd Earl of Ilchester shed an interesting light on the tastes of one Georgian aristocratic household. There were made by T. Phipps and E. Robinson in 1810 and comprised BARSAC, CAPE, LUGON, RED MADEIRA, MALMSEY MADEIRA, RED MAJORCA, WHITE MAJORCA, MALAGA, MOSELLE, RHENISH, ROTA, SAUTERNS, M SCHIRAZ, STEIN-WEIN and SYRACUSE. He also had labels for DE-LA-COTE, COLARES,

> In the year 1789, when the French Revolution was commemorated at the Maid's Head, toasts were drunk to "The Revolution Societies in England," "The Rights of Man" and "The Philosophers of France." It is quite possible these toasts were honoured with "John Haig." Even at that time it was known as the whisky that had stood the test of more than a century and a half. Since then its reputation has been growing, and its popularity extending, among those who know and want the best.
>
> ## Dye Ken
> # John Haig?
> THE ORIGINAL
> ### The Clubman's Whisky since 1627
> ISSUED BY JOHN HAIG & CO., LTD., DISTILLERS, MARKINCH, FIFE, AND KINNAIRD HOUSE, PALL MALL EAST, S.W.1

Figure 685.

JOHANNESBURG, MONTRACHET, RUDESHEIM, SITGES and SPANISH MADEIRA. The majority of these names are noticeably unusual, and many of the commoner titles, such as claret, champagne and burgundy, are absent. Did he have a different set for everyday use, and why did he commission such an extensive collection for wines that were rarely encountered? He would hardly have had more than a few of them in his cellar at one time, and the list of wines in vogue (see Part 3, below) does not clarify the picture. Could one conclude that the Earl was the nineteenth-century predecessor of the wine buff, and wanted to be sure that he had a bottle-ticket ready for whatever he acquired? A third set from a different owner comprised an equally eclectic collection – ARTIMINA, CALCALLEA, CLARET, CYDER, CYPRUS, FRONTINIAC, LISBON, MADEIRA, MULTIPULEHANO and WHITE PORT.

Terms for Whisky

John Haig, advertising in *The Sphere* for 1923, claim to have produced the original 'Clubman's Whisky' since 1627 (see fig. 685). They told an interesting little story about the Maid's Head hostelry in Norwich (see fig. 687). In the second quarter of the nineteenth century a number of labels appeared with the title USQEBEATH, or some similar variant. This is actually a combination of two Gaelic words meaning 'water' and 'life', whose significance is obvious. The Perth silversmiths R. and R. Keay made several of these labels in the 1820s and 1830s. They are very large, long, convex rectangles, entirely plain and copiously hallmarked. Considerably earlier a label for AQUA VITAE, with the same meaning, has been noted by W. Davie of Edinburgh in around 1786.

Another term that had been in vogue at one time was MOUNTAIN DEW. The phrase seems to have been coined by Sir Walter Scott in *Tales of My Landlord*, but he may well have picked it up from an older source. It should be remembered that before 1823 whisky production was not properly legalised, so, although labels of earlier date inscribed for WHISKY are known, it was only then that it began to be generally found in respectable households. The majority of MOUNTAIN DEW labels are found, on inspection, to be MOUNTAIN labels to which DEW has been added at a later date.

Marsala and Bronte

The family of Woodhouse started to revive Sicily's wine industry in the 1770s and introduced Marsala to this country in 1773, but no labels with the name are known before the end of the century. The popularity that it then gained undoubtedly owed much to Admiral Lord Nelson. He had large quantities bought for the Fleet and it found fame in England as a consequence. In 1799

Nelson was created Duke of Bronte by the King of Naples in recognition of his delivery of Sicily from Napoleon. Bronte was adopted by the Woodhouse firm as a name for their Marsala wine and used to market it for the first half of the nineteenth century. It should be noted, however, that Bronte was also the name of a wine from a vineyard on the slopes of Mount Etna (compare TERRA FORTE), though whether it ever reached England is open to doubt. Certainly at the time when Nelson was England's Hero, following the Battle of the Nile, BRONTE begins to appear on labels, and undoubtedly it refers to the fortified wines from Marsala. The word is sometimes spelled with an 'e' and sometimes with an 'i'. MARSALA, on the other hand, has many variants – MARCELLA, MARSEILLA, and so on. Penzer considers these more likely to be variants of Marsala than to refer to some local wine from the Marseilles area, as was once suggested.

Methuen

The fame of METHUEN as a wine label rests on an example bearing John Harvey's fifth mark, which he entered in 1746 and used until 1750. It is a cast label of rococo design in production by him between *c.*1738 and *c.*1750.[5] For a long time this label was reckoned to be the only example with this name and it was also considered possible that it had been commissioned as part of a set by the 2nd Earl of Warrington for his seat at Dunham Massey in about 1750. The Earl's inventory of his silver does list a set of labels that includes one for METHUEN, but there are arguments against this being it, and that theory has been abandoned. Nevertheless, it is a high-class label that must have been made to special order for someone of importance. Why it should appear on a label more than forty years after the signing of the Treaty with Portugal that gave rise to the name as a term for red wines from that country, and generally thought of as an acronym for Port, is a question that deserves examination.

The Methuen Treaty was signed in 1703. It was intended to favour the country's trade with Portugal by lowering the duty on Portuguese wines and to disadvantage the French by raising the duty on theirs. It did, indeed, have that effect for a while, weakening the French wine trade, though smuggling across the English Channel increased in consequence and, while the imports of port rose, so did the consumption of gin, which was cheaper. As André Simon relates, 'At no time in human history did the masses respond so enthusiastically to the call of patriotism as when they were urged to be patriotically drunk'. Red wines from the Douro had been known in England since the previous century. They were then young, harsh and dry, described by Swift as a 'coarse drink whose only merit lay in its power to produce stupefaction'. It was often fortified with brandy not, as later, to check fermentation, but to try to keep it in reasonable condition until it reached these shores. In a trade journal of 1739, 'humble Port' is mentioned, an indication, perhaps, of its quality at that time.

The earliest reference in a dictionary to Methuen as a wine is in 1753, when it is described as referring jocularly to wines from Portugal, as if to infer that it was never a serious commercial description. This also happens to be within a few years of the date of our METHUEN label. The purpose of the label is therefore slightly obscure. It would seem that Methuen had never been a serious term for port, which by then was an established drink in its own right, following the improvement in standards after English families arrived in Oporto and founded their port houses there, and as the frequency of its occurrence on labels clearly demonstrates. Indeed, the name seems to have become more attached to the inferior wines from Portugal. Furthermore, allusion to a Treaty signed more than forty years earlier would surely have lost much of its meaning by then. However, taking the Dunham Massey inventory mentioned above as an example, it will be seen that the wine labels there included RED PORT and WHITE PORT as well as METHUEN. The Earl was parsimonious, proud and humourless, so he was unlikely to have had a label that he was not going to use, or denoted a wine of poor quality, still less one that was an affectation or a joke. The label must have identified a recognisable wine of some sort.

More recently further examples of the name have come to light on labels, but some of them show signs of being later 'improvements' to earlier labels. For instance, a plain unmarked escutcheon has FRONTIGNA[c] on the convex obverse side and METHUIN *(sic)* in large letters on the concave reverse. Frontignac was certainly known in England during the eighteenth century, so the label could date from around 1775, but it was not widely favoured until later. During the Napoleonic Wars, English expatriates in France were constrained by the Emperor in Frontignac, where they acquired a taste for the district's wines, a taste that continued when they eventually returned home. One has to ask what demand there could have been for a label for METHUEN, however spelled, by then, and whether FRONTIGNA^C has not had the rarer name added later. The same doubt must apply, too, to a small reeded rectangular label by T. Phipps and E. Robinson, engraved for METHUEN and dated 1796, though the title certainly appears to be the original one.

Single Letters
Single letters are discussed in Chapter 2, Section 9. In their simplest form they presumably stand for staple drinks – 'B' for Brandy, 'C' for Claret, and so on, but it is hard to imagine what some letters, such as 'I' or 'J', or even 'A', were for. Double combinations can be even more difficult. 'FV' and 'IV' were presumably for French and Italian Vermouth, and 'CB' could be Cherry Brandy, but what could 'CA' or 'CE' have been? 'R' in combination with WINE means red, but with SHRUB it means rum. 'MCW' and 'MRM' remain mysteries, as does 'MT', or was the latter just a reminder that the empty decanter needed refilling?

Beer and Cyder
CYDER, sometimes CIDER, is one of the earliest names recorded on labels, usually escutcheons, dating from the 1740s to the 1760s. It also occurs on early Staffordshire and Battersea enamels, and on OSP 'Copperbacks'.[6] ALE has been noted on early enamels and on a small rectangular label bearing Hester Bateman's first mark of 1761. BEER has been recorded on labels from the mid-1760s. This raises the question about the types of container in which these bulky drinks came to the table with labels hung around them. As we find such labels today, they usually have chains of only average length, suitable for a decanter or a bottle, but not for jugs or large vessels. In some cases, of course, the chains may not be the originals, but some certainly seem to be. However, early label decanters engraved for all these three titles are known, so the precedent for detachable silver or enamel tickets is there. Furthermore, many eighteenth-century ale glasses are of quite small capacity, so it is reasonable that a decanter would have served for refilling them. BEER as a title is a little harder to explain, as it would usually have been brought out in jugs, on which a label would not sit. But most eighteenth-century households would have brewed their own beer and made their own cider too. This might then have been bottled to await consumption, and bottle-tickets would have been required to indicate the contents.

Labels for the Blind
Intriguing narrow rectangular labels exist with eyelets above and coded tassels below, presumably for fingering by blind persons (see fig. 686). Perhaps the blind could distinguish easily between sweet and dry sherry using this method. They bear Thomas Heming's unregistered mark (Grimwade 3828) in use from *c.*1760 to *c.*1782.

Figure 686.

PART 2 – REVERSIBLE WINE LABELS (PALIMPSESTS)

One definition of a palimpsest is a monumental brass turned over and re-engraved on the reverse side. It would therefore seem to be a permissible extension of this definition to apply it to a wine label that has been engraved with a title on both sides. Such labels were obviously made for reasons of economy, but suffered certain restrictions in terms of their design and shape. In the first place, if such a label is to hang tidily on a decanter, whichever way round it goes, it has to be fairly flat. A two-sided label is not, therefore, suitable for use on a round decanter with marked curvature. Secondly, the designer has less scope for intricate decoration. Chasing is not possible, nor is relief-work, which would be hard to achieve satisfactorily on both sides of such a thin piece of metal. Embossed or pierced letters are likewise impracticable. Consequently the majority of 'palimpsest' labels are plain or have only the simplest of borders. The names are engraved, usually a wine such as would be served during a meal on one side, and a spirit or 'after dinner' wine on the other.

The earliest noted examples are two unmarked, entirely flat, plain escutcheons, rather roughly executed. The style of engraving of the titles – W: WINE with MADEIRA, and CLARET with R: PORT – together with a single reeded border placed very close to the edge, suggests a Chester origin and a date of $c.$1750 or even earlier.[7] Another early label is also an unmarked plain escutcheon of the early style usually found before $c.$1755.[8] It is engraved for FRONTIGN^C, and on the concave reverse side is METHUIN, which is such a rare name that its occurrence elsewhere calls for careful scrutiny.[9] The name has been recorded on a label by John Harvey that can be dated with certainty to $c.$1745-9, so that its presence on a label of pre-1755 style is clearly feasible, but the engraving is by a different hand so that doubt must exist as to when the second name was put there.

A label from the end of the eighteenth century is a curiously shaped open crescent with cut-out portions, a design not known apart from this example, which has CURRANT on its slightly convex face and CALCAVELLA, in a different style of engraving, on its concave reverse side.[10] This is strange as it might be expected that calcavella, the wine for the meal, would have been on the front of the label, and currant, for consumption on some other occasion, on the back. The label is unmarked.

Other examples are of Indian workmanship and were made in the third and forth quarters of the nineteenth century. One pair consists of tigers' claws held together by gilded straps that contain name panels coupling MADEIRA with BRANDY and CLARET with WHISKEY.

A set of five labels was made also towards the end of the eighteenth century by two Sheffield makers: three were by Luke Proctor and Co. in 1790 and 1793, and two were by George Eadon and Co. in 1803.[11] They are convex crescents that have the space between the horns filled by seven drapery panels drawn together in a peak. The names on the faces of the labels are MADEIRA, RUM (re-engraved over PORT), R. SHRUB, BUCELLA and RAISIN. On the reverse (concave) side are single letters, deeply engraved, 'B', 'G', 'W', 'R' and 'S', signifying presumably brandy, gin, whisky, rum and sherry. There is some mystery here about the choice of names and conjunction with the single letters. The explanation suggested above, that 'dinner' wines were coupled with 'after dinner' drinks, does not seem to apply. Nor can it be easily explained why the owner needed to replace his PORT title with RUM when there was already an 'R'. Perhaps the single letters were all later additions, with 'R' included to keep the set uniform. Still, as can be seen from an extract from *The Sphere* for November 1923 (see fig. 687) concerning frolics at The Maid's Head in Norwich, there can be various explanations in wine related matters, in this case as to how the church gate got into the river.

The John Haig Famous Hostelry Series

When the Churchwardens Paid the Piper

The Maid's Head Norwich.

AMONG the many fantastic processions witnessed by guests at the Maid's Head during the five centuries in which it has figured as a hostelry, the Guild processions of the seventeenth century were probably the most picturesque. The quaint mummeries of the clowns, the antics of the gaudily-dressed "whifflers," were outdone by Snap-dragon, the terror of the children, who snatched the boys' caps and exacted a penny or twopence for their return.

That these wild wags and frolickers were a source of some anxiety to the City Fathers we gather from an item in the churchwardens' reckoning for 1776-7, which reads: "Paid for taking the church gate out of the river, 1s."

As far back as 1472 the inn had a reputation for providing good entertainment, and we may well suppose that the noted sheriff of Norwich, John Curat, often partook of refreshment here. The old house he built during the latter part of the fifteenth century was distinguished by elaborate oak carvings, panels and ceilings, many of which are still preserved behind the business-like front of Backs, Ltd., in the Haymarket.

Figure 687.

PART 3 – DRINKS IN VOGUE AT DIFFERENT PERIODS

In 1964 T.W. Frost published a survey of almost 2,000 silver labels from all the sources then available in order to establish when the more frequently encountered titles enjoyed their greatest popularity.[12] The resultant chart is reproduced as fig. 688. His accompanying commentary is now completely revised to reflect more recent knowledge of the development of the wine trade. Throughout this study, however, it must be remembered that it is based on silver labels only, so that it represents the drinking habits of the wealthier strata of society, reflects the waxing and waning in the use of silver labels generally, and does not differentiate between original and re-engraved titles.

There are five principal factors influencing the consumption of the various alcoholic beverages covered: wars and their effect on international trade; changes in import and excise duties; improvement or deterioration in quality of wines; the effect and distribution of disease and pestilence in vineyards; and changes in fashion, both in taste and in the names used. Each of these factors will be discussed in turn.

Britain was at war with France from 1744-1748, 1756-1763, 1778-1783 and 1793-1815. The first three of these wars do not seem to have materially affected the ability of the British upper classes to maintain their supplies of claret, no doubt aided by widespread smuggling, but they must have presented some difficulties to the importation of all French wines. The Revolutionary and Napoleonic Wars of 1793-1815, however, were the first to be pursued on a purposely economic front, and they had a devastating effect on international trade.

France was inaccessible to British merchants except for short periods in 1802-05 and 1814-15, as was Spain and much of Portugal between 1808 and 1812, and the wine producing areas of Germany throughout virtually the whole period. On the other hand, Britain quickly established superiority at sea and took control of the Atlantic islands and the Cape of Good Hope, so that alternative supplies of wine from the Canary Islands, Madeira and South Africa could be exploited to make up for the shortfall in imports from Continental Europe.

The conquest of Sicily in 1806 must have provided a significant boost to the consumption of Marsala although, as we shall see below, it had already achieved an excellent reputation.

The effect of changes in import and export duties was strongly felt following the Methuen Treaty of 1703, which greatly increased the duties on French wine in order to favour the consumption of Portuguese wines. It most certainly achieved this result in the middle to lowest price ranges, but was much more limited in its effect on the upper ranges as the quality of Portuguese wines did not begin to challenge their finer French rivals until the closing decades of the century. A major reduction in duties on French wine in 1786 led to an immediate increase in imports, but this was soon reversed by the outbreak of war in 1793.

The introduction of strongly preferential duties on Cape (South African) wines in 1814 produced an instant, but short-lived, boom in their importation. Imports peaked in 1817 and quickly declined thereafter, suggesting that the quality of the bulk of the wine produced was insufficient to sustain demand despite its advantage in price. As noted above, Cape wines also benefited from the effects of the global wars of 1793-1815, but the finer wines of Constantia enjoyed a following some time before this – it was served at Stationers' Hall on St George's Day, 1778.[13]

The fact that the quality of Port during the first half of the eighteenth century was very poor is one reason why imports of it did not increase after the Methuen Treaty as much as might have been expected. The chart shows how the number of labels began to increase in the 1770s. It was in 1775 that a very fine vintage occurred. At this time the Royal Wine Company made great efforts to sell more port in England. The improvement in quality, combined with their efforts, effected a marked increase and annual sales nearly doubled in the next twenty years, as the chart shows.

The consumption of Marsala in Britain also commenced with an improvement in quality. Wine was being made in the Marsala district twenty-five centuries ago, but for hundreds of years the vignerons, impoverished in turn by the Normans and Spaniards, had neglected the roads and vineyards. However, as related in Part 2, above, it was the Englishman John Woodhouse who

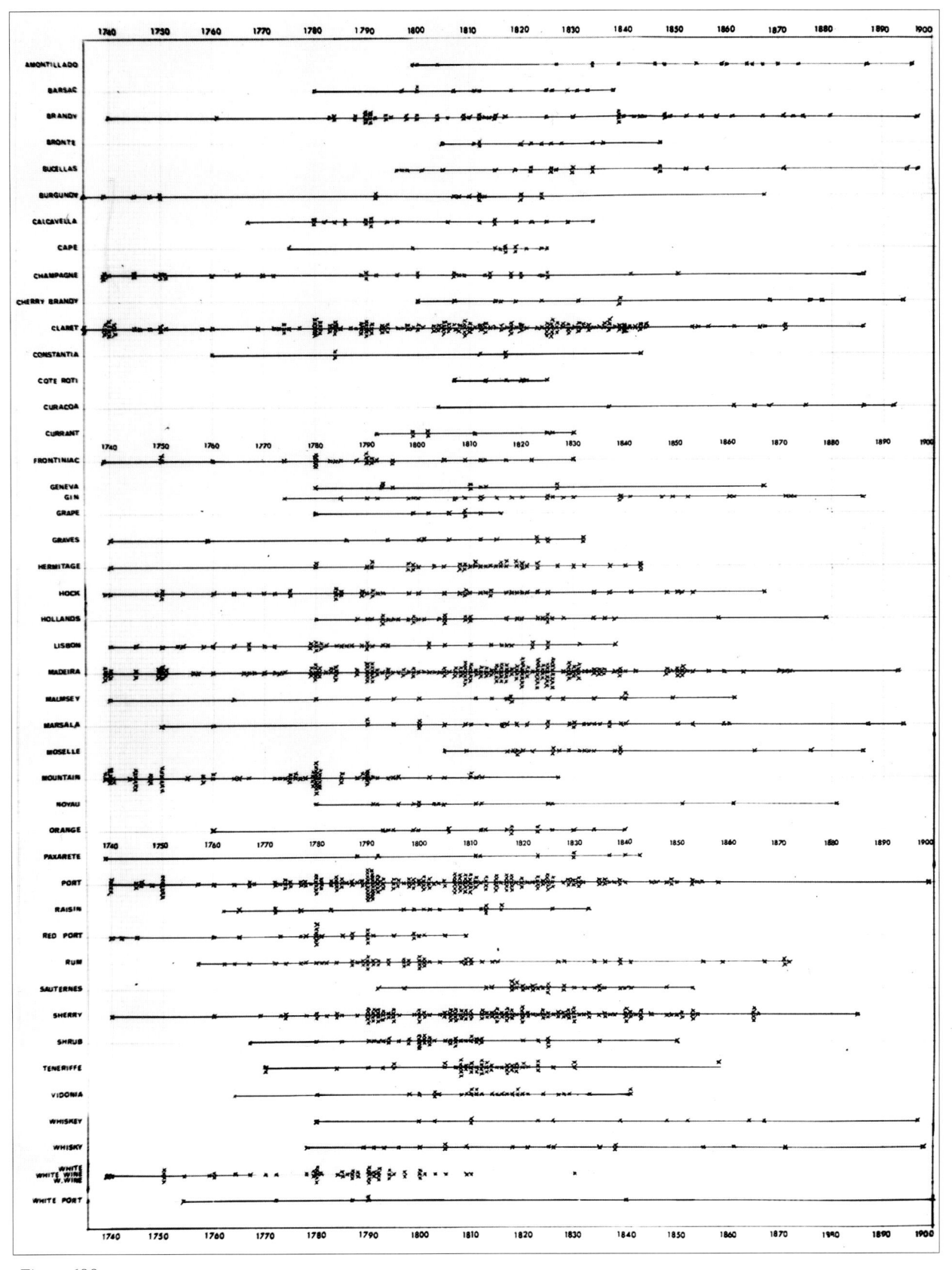

Figure 688.

developed Marsala when he established the house of Woodhouse in 1773 and the popularity of Marsala grew. The chart shows a steady incidence from *c.*1790. The earlier recorded examples of *c.*1750 and *c.*1760 might be errors in dating or, possibly, labels later re-engraved.

The marked replacement of Mountain (Malaga) by Sherry around 1790, shown by the chart, was undoubtedly due to the improvement in the quality and rapidly increased production from these more southerly Spanish vineyards following their development by British merchants from that date.

The quality and quantity of wine that a vineyard produces can be drastically altered by disease. In 1852 the mildew known as *Oidium tuckeri* spread rapidly over Europe. Vineyards that were hit badly by it produced no crop and any wine that did result was poor and did not keep. A cure, which consisted of dusting the vines with powdered sulphur, was found just in time to save the vines from destruction, but not before the disease had virtually wiped out the crop of 1852 in the Canaries and Madeira to which islands it had spread. This marked the end of large-scale consumption of Madeira for many years and of Canary wines for ever in England. In the 1840s Madeira had been imported at a rate of two million gallons per year, but after 1852 the vignerons of Madeira planted sugar cane and pumpkins. The chart shows how MADEIRA and MALMSEY labels peter out after 1851,[14] while the Canary[15] labels of TENERIFFE and VIDONIA had already gone by the 1830s. Some replanting of the vines took place a little later, but other wines had by then become fashionable in England. In any case the new vines were almost immediately knocked out by a further pest – phylloxera.

The phylloxera scourge arrived rather late in Europe but by the late 1860s and early 1870s it was widespread. By this time the use of labels had decreased anyway. Phylloxera reached Portugal in 1868, and Beaujolais and the Rhône Valley by 1870. By 1878 the Burgundy vines were badly attacked and by 1884 practically all France was severely affected. 1887 saw its arrival in South Africa. Champagne was reached by 1891 when at last a remedy was found, the grafting of European stock on to American vines.

Perhaps the most important factor in considering the popularity of drinks at particular times was fashion. The taste for the mixture of Rum and fruit juice known as Shrub is shown well by label dates to have been fairly concentrated between the years 1791 and 1812. There are a few labels with earlier or later dates but this was the period when it was fashionable to have a decanter marked SHRUB on the sideboard.

Penzer[16] gives us a full and interesting account of how the name Bronte Marsala became used by Messrs Woodhouse for their Marsala in 1799. Our earliest BRONTE label is dated 1805, which seems about right as explained above in Part 2. Penzer tells us that Woodhouse's had to revert to the name Marsala in 1868, which makes Frost's last date of 1847 somewhat of a mystery. Perhaps a later date may turn up – or did all Bronte drinkers use plated labels at this time?

There was an increasing sophistication in the appreciation of wine from the closing decades of the eighteenth century. General titles such as WHITE fell out of use as they were superseded by more specific designations such as BARSAC and SAUTERNES, while LISBON gave way to BUCELLAS and CALCAVELLA.

Table wines generally, as opposed to fortified wines, spirits and liqueurs, became increasingly less common after 1840, and the trend can be seen to have started about ten to fifteen years earlier. This might suggest that it became more usual to serve table wines from the bottle rather than a decanter, or that they were only drunk during meals when they would be dispensed by servants and that they would not be kept in decanters for use at other times. However, both these explanations are open to question. Lord Cardigan charged an officer with misconduct for having a bottle at table during a regimental dinner in 1840 (although contemporary press coverage of 'the black bottle scandal' suggested that Cardigan's attitude was already somewhat out of date) and the retailing of bottles of wine with printed paper labels seems unlikely to have become normal until much later in the century. The replenishing of diners' glasses from a sideboard, whence and whither they were carried by a servant on a small tray known as a 'waiter', was also established practice well before 1800 – indeed it would have been the custom in fashionable circles from the time when labels were first produced.

Perhaps the answer lies in the very distinction between table wines and fortified wines. During the eighteenth century all wines that had to sustain a prolonged period of passage were fortified with spirit and sugar to enable them to survive the time and the variation of temperature involved. As connoisseurship, storage and bottling improved, so did the appreciation and enjoyment of unadulterated fine wines and only then, about 1815, did the division occur between wines that would only be served with food and those that would be drunk at other times.

Spirits were obviously not much drunk in polite society until late in the eighteenth century, although brandy and rum prove earlier occasional exceptions. GIN, GENEVA or HOLLANDS appear frequently after about 1790 together with SHRUB, BRANDY and RUM in sets intended for three and four bottle decanter stands. Whisky does not seem to have become socially acceptable until after 1820.[17] This may have been because the punitive taxation on whisky from 1784 to 1823 led to most whisky being distilled illegally to avoid the duty; people prominent in society may not have wanted to proclaim by using wine labels that they were drinking an illegal spirit. Therefore, any label for this spirit that purports to be of earlier manufacture should be approached with great caution and an extremely careful examination as it is most likely to have been later re-engraved. Liqueurs such as cherry brandy were mostly a nineteenth-century fashion, although noyau, a liqueur based on nuts or fruit stones, would seem to have enjoyed an earlier popularity.

Although not included in Frost's chart, labels for ALE, BEER and CYDER can be found from around 1740 to 1770 and, very occasionally, the later decades of the eighteenth century, reflecting the fact that these beverages were served at breakfast in the houses of the landed gentry until they were replaced by tea and coffee around the turn of the century.

SHORT NOTES ON NAMES

AMONTILLADO 1799-1896
See SHERRY.

BARSAC 1780-1894
A neighbour of SAUTERNES. Regional and district appellations began to replace the generic term WHITE WINE in the last quarter of the eighteenth century.

BRANDY 1740-1897
Only two labels prior to 1783. It was not until the 1780s that the quality of cognac brandy was improved and the demand greatly increased.

BRONTE 1805-47
A fashionable name for MARSALA.

BUCELLAS 1796-1897
A district near Lisbon that produced a popular white wine. See LISBON.

BURGUNDY 1735-1867
BURGUNDY was not as popular as CLARET, partly because transport difficulties made it more expensive.

CALCAVELLA 1767-1834
A district in the south-west of Portugal that produced white wine. See LISBON.

CAPE 1775-1825
See CONSTANTIA.

Names

CHAMPAGNE 1739-1886
Although it has frequently been stated that such labels must have been for still wines, mainly red, they would also have been intended for sparkling wines that were decanted until relatively recent times.[18] However, RED CHAMPAGNE is known in the nineteenth century, as are DRY CHAMPAGNE and SWEET CHAMPAGNE. It was always the most expensive wine imported into Britain during the eighteenth century, but plated labels bear its name from the earliest date of their manufacture.

CHERRY BRANDY 1800-94
There is a lack of information in reference books about the introduction of this liqueur. The dates given therefore give a useful indication that it was not seen until the nineteenth century.

CLARET 1735-1886
One of the earliest and most common titles found on labels; a general term for French red wines from the BORDEAUX area.

CONSTANTIA 1760-1843, CAPE 1775-1825
South African wines.[19]

COTE ROTI 1807-25
Only five labels recorded, and all confined within the short period, but there are records of this fine red wine being drunk quite early in the eighteenth century. See HERMITAGE below.

CURACOA 1804-92
An orange based liqueur that may have come into vogue slightly before 1800.

CURRANT 1792-1830
Presumably a home-made wine.

FRONTINIAC 1739-1830
A high quality sweet white wine from the South of France.

GIN 1774-1886, GENEVA 1780-1867, HOLLANDS 1780-1879
There was no particular fashion or order in these types of gin except that GENEVA was not so much used as the other two and HOLLANDS tends to fade out in the 1830s. The scarcity of eighteenth-century GIN labels is interesting even though in the first half of the century huge quantities were being drunk. It was very crude and would not have been drunk by the kind of people who used wine labels or, if they did drink it, they would be loath to advertise the fact.

GRAPE 1780-1816
It is not clear to what this may refer, but it is likely to have indicated a home-made wine.

GRAVES 1740-1832
A sweet white wine from the Bordeaux region like BARSAC (see above) and SAUTERNES. Examples on labels before around 1790 are probably re-engraved.

HERMITAGE 1740-1843
Early in the eighteenth century it ranked with the great CLARETS and BURGUNDIES and it never ceased to be a wine of the first quality. Although always uncommon, it appears consistently throughout the years c.1740-1840.

HOCK 1740-1867
Shows a fairly steady popularity. As RHENISH, it was very popular in the first quarter of the eighteenth century and a few early RHENISH labels exist. Transport difficulties account for the fact that fewer German wines have been seen than French. OLD HOCK appears on early labels in both silver and Sheffield Plate reflecting the taste of the time for well-matured white wines.

HOLLANDS 1780-1879
See GIN.

LISBON 1740-1838
A title that originally simply meant a white wine exported from Lisbon. See BUCELLAS and CALCAVELLA.

LUNEL 1739-1830
A high quality sweet white wine from the South of France not mentioned in Frost's chart.

MADEIRA 1739-1893, MALMSEY 1740-1861
Another early wine label title, and one most commonly found, owing its popularity partly to its availability and its long decanter life. There were spelling variants and compound titles. Of the individual varieties, MADEIRA MALMSEY and MALMSEY MADEIRA are uncommon, BUAL and SERCIAL (various spellings) are rare. TERRANTEZ is only known from one example and VERDELHO is unrecorded on silver labels before 1900.[20]

MARSALA 1750-1894
A Sicilian wine – see BRONTE above.

MOSELLE 1805-86
The late appearance of MOSELLE on labels is surprising. It was definitely drunk during the eighteenth century, but transport difficulties and high cost probably kept down its consumption.

MOUNTAIN 1739-1827
See SHERRY.

NOYAU 1780-1881
A nut- or kernel-based liqueur, popular from the late eighteenth century.

ORANGE 1760-1840
It seems likely that this refers to Rhône wines made near Orange in France. See HERMITAGE.

PAXARETE 1739-1844
See SHERRY.

PORT 1740-1899
Another of the earliest names found on labels and popular throughout the period of label production. The apparent dearth of examples after 1858 in Frost's chart is misleading. Originally it meant any wine exported from Oporto.

RAISIN 1762-1833
Presumably a home-made wine.

RED PORT 1740-1809, WHITE PORT 1754-1840
As port developed in quality, name styles began to differ.

RIVE SALTES 1739-1830
A high quality sweet white wine from the South of France not mentioned in Frost's chart.

RUM 1757-1873
Rum was popular throughout the eighteenth century, but bonding of rum was not made legal until 1742. This allowed the spirit to be matured in casks and made for better quality and so to its appearance in decanters.

SAUTERNES 1792-1853
See BARSAC.

SHERRY 1740-1885, AMONTILLADO 1799-1896, PAXARETE 1739-1844
SHERRY started to supersede MOUNTAIN in the third quarter of the eighteenth century. The PAXARETE of 1739 is probably a re-engraved label, which would leave around 1790 as a much more believable earliest date. The date of 1799 for AMONTILLADO is also earlier than one would expect and it too is likely to have been a re-engraved label. This name is likely to be Victorian, as are MONTILLA, MANZANILLA, FINO, OLOROSO, BROWN SHERRY and PALE SHERRY.

SHRUB 1767-1850
See earlier discussion on page 196.

TENERIFFE 1770-1858, VIDONIA 1762-1841
Canary Islands wines were imported into Britain from the seventeenth century as evidenced by references to 'Canary Sack' in Shakespeare, but they had fallen out of favour until the wars of 1793-1815.[21] The earlier examples recorded in Frost's chart must be open to doubt but are not impossible.

WHISKEY 1780-1897, WHISKY 1778-1898
Whisky did not become fashionable among the wealthier classes until about 1820.[22] Any occurrence before 1795 is doubtful. The difference in spelling had no relevance until relatively modern times. IRISH WHISK(E)Y and SCOTCH WHISKY can be found after 1890.

WHITE 1680-1740, WHITE WINE 1739-1830
'Whit' appears on Lambeth wine jugs in the seventeenth century showing that white wine from France required no more than a general description during Stuart times and indeed until the later years of the eighteenth century, when names such as 'BARSAC' and 'SAUTERNES' tended to replace it.

WHITE PORT 1754-1840
See RED PORT.

Figure 689.

CHAPTER 7

THE PROVINCES

PART 1 – CHESTER AND DISTRICT

There has been an assay office in Chester since the Middle Ages and, after the re-opening of the provincial offices in 1701, Chester became the centre for assay for goldsmiths from many parts of the north-west of England, as well as serving the city itself. Indeed, by the later eighteenth century there were as many craftsmen from the rising industrial towns of Liverpool, Manchester and Salford using the office as there were local ones. Birmingham and Sheffield silversmiths, such as Matthew Boulton, also used Chester until their own offices opened in 1773.

In the late 1730s, as wine labels started to appear, the leading silversmiths in Chester were the Richardsons, a family from Worcester. A profile of Richard Richardson originally painted by G. Batenham around 1775 is illustrated (see fig. 689). The mark of Richard Richardson II (see fig. 711 for PORT), who was in charge of the firm from 1732, is the earliest to be found on Chester wine labels (see fig. 691, CYDER, *c.*1745-50 and fig. 704, R: PORT, *c.*1745-50). He used a succession of 'RR' marks, which on labels are unaccompanied by either a lion passant or a town mark, so that accurate dating is not possible. However, by comparing the labels with other plate by him that has fuller marks, a date of around 1745/50 can be suggested. Examples of his labels, which were in an exhibition of Chester silver mounted in 1984,[1] do not reveal great originality of design, but one of them, a rectangular label, has a chevron border of some distinction. His escutcheons have a markedly flat upper edge, and often a single reed border, which is particularly noticeable on plain examples (see fig. 691 for CYDER). Another feature, found on titles with compound names, is a characteristic double dot (:), as between, for example, 'R' and 'PORT' (see figs. 702 and 704) and 'W' and 'WINE' (see fig. 690).

The volume of silver assayed at the Chester assay office had substantially diminished by the late 1760s with only 824oz (23.35kg) being assayed in 1767 and only 161oz (4.56kg) in 1768-69.[2] The Richardson family sponsored virtually all the silver assayed at Chester for the thirty years preceding

The Provinces - Chester

Figures 690-703.

1769. The first Richard Richardson came to Chester from Worcester in the seventeenth century and the family was well established there by the mid-1730s, with Richard II in charge. He was Mayor of Chester in 1758 and 1759 and Assay Master from 1761 to 1769. He used at least eight types of 'RR' mark in different shapes of punch, four of which have been recorded on labels. He died in 1769 and a cousin Richard (styled as Richard III) assumed charge of the firm as Richard II's son, another

The Provinces - Chester

Richard (later to be styled Richard IV), was only aged fourteen. Work that can be dated between 1769 and around 1779, when Richard IV became free, should therefore be attributed to Richard III (see fig. 690 for W:WINE, *c*.1765-70, which can be attributed to either Richard II or Richard III, and fig. 692 for CALCAVELLA, *c*.1765-70). No labels from the Richardson workshop can be positively assigned to these years, but there are some that by style might belong to them.

Richard III was a chandler by trade. He is not known to have influenced work in the firm's workshop, but there is a mark of Richard II which appears during this minority and was evidently used by Richard III until around 1779, when Richard III's son (Richard IV) was able to take over.

Richard IV became Assay Master in 1785, but resigned in 1791 and severed connection with the Chester Company in around 1800, though remaining in charge of the firm until 1822. He entered two marks during this time that have been seen on labels, among them a curved rectangular example of 1785[3] and a Prince of Wales type label of Bateman style (see fig. 695 for PORT *c*.1788).

By then new firms were emerging, such as Walkers and Lowe, and the Richardsons were declining in importance. George Walker I was active from around 1770 and the Duty Books record that he sent bottle-tickets for assay, but his 'GW' mark has not been noted on any labels known today. His son, John Walker, also sent at least one batch of labels for assay.

In 1791 George Lowe's name appears as founder of the firm that still bears his name. For reasons undiscovered, he registered his mark first in London some months before doing so in Chester. He manufactured labels in large numbers, for the most part employing straightforward conventional designs, such as rectangles and crescents; between 1793 and 1839 he is recorded as having sponsored nearly three hundred labels. He continued to be active almost to the year of his death in 1841. Examples of his work, with his 'GL' mark, are shown at figs. 698 (MADEIRA, *c*.1788) and 701 (BUCELLAS, *c*.1800). More interesting are several sets of collars which he made between 1800 and 1810 (a MADEIRA is illustrated at fig. 697 for 1810). Several London makers were making these, as methods of showing the wine's name at this time (Phipps and Robinson for instance), but elsewhere in the country this device has only been recorded once in Newcastle, once or twice in Edinburgh, and occasionally in Dublin and Sheffield on silver labels. Lowe sent 'bottle rings' for assay on three occasions, some forty in all.

George Lowe's son, styled George II, worked in Gloucester until his father died, apparently using the same 'GL' marks as him. It is generally assumed that labels dating from after the mid-1830s can be attributed to the son. Two other brothers, John and Thomas, were also involved with the firm, and their marks are found on labels from around 1830. Labels with Lowe marks continued through the nineteenth century and into the twentieth century. In 1962, when the assay office finally closed, Margaret Lowe and John Lowe sent a pair of gold labels to be assayed to mark the occasion.[4]

As Manchester and Liverpool rose in prosperity, so did the demands of their citizens for appropriate silverware expand too, and consequently the number of silversmiths in those towns grew to satisfy their requirements. Robert Jones (see fig. 706), Nicholas Cunliffe (see fig. 694), Joseph Hewitt (see fig. 700) and Joseph Walley (see fig. 707) from Liverpool, and James France (see fig. 705) from Manchester, are all recorded as having sent batches of labels for assay during the last

Figure 704.

Figure 705.

Figure 706.

Figure 707.

Figure 708.

Figure 709.

quarter of the eighteenth century. For the most part they employed conventional shapes with slight variations (see fig. 707, Joseph Walley's FRONTINIACK; fig. 705, James France's W.WINE 1784/8; fig. 700, Joseph Hewitt's MADEIRA which bears a duty mark *c.*1789; and fig. 706, Robert Jones' OLD HOCK, *c.*1775-80). Furthermore, escutcheons deserve attention for the characteristic elongated shape that they took on (see, for example, fig. 690). Nicholas Cunliffe's CLARET (see fig. 694) likewise displays some individuality.

The names of Walley and Jones are closely linked. Both men came from Tatton. The first Jones, to whom no mark is attributed, took over the business of the famous Chester silversmith Benjamin Brancker and, when he died in 1760, Joseph Walley married his widow. Her son, Robert (styled Robert Jones I) used three 'RJ' marks, all of which have been noted on labels. An example of his work is shown at fig. 706. Labels dated later than around 1826 must belong to his son, Robert II, who continued to manage the family firm until 1876. When Joseph Walley became associated with the firm in 1760 he had his own mark and this, in two forms, has been noted on labels that can be dated between the early 1770s and around 1790 (see fig. 710 showing his marks respectively on MADEIRA and on PORT).

One other name associated with Chester requires mention. Thomas Ollivant worked in Manchester, but registered a mark in London in 1789. His 'TO' mark is frequently found overstamping that of Hester Bateman on labels presumably ordered from her workshop, but it is also occasionally found without the Bateman mark underneath, and these could be his own work. Several provincial firms imported articles from London makers, such as, for instance, James Barber in York from Emes and Barnard. Compare, too, Richard Evans, a silversmith from the neighbouring town of Shrewsbury. He, too, registered a mark in London in 1779 and he, too, put it on Bateman labels, crescents and ovals. Thomas Ollivant was the son of John Ollivant, also of Manchester, whose mark, a plain 'I.O' has been noted in the 1770s and 1780s, as has another version with a large star between the letters, which may also be his.

As the nineteenth century progressed, the Regency taste for exuberant decoration influenced designs in London, but in Chester simpler styles seem to have remained popular and the firm of Lowe, which still dominated the market, continued to satisfy demand with plain shapes, rectangles, ovals and crescents. In the middle years of the century London makers turned to architectural and geometric designs, but Chester did not follow them, remaining with the old patterns until the market finally disappeared. Sampson Mordan & Co., London and Chester, always innovative, made bridge suit markers in 1907 entitled SCOTCH on spades (fig. 709), BRANDY on hearts, GIN on diamonds and IRISH on clubs, to declare trumps in a spirited way.

The surviving Chester Duty Books for 1784-1840 now lodged with the Birmingham Assay Office show that some nine hundred labels passed through the office during those years, an estimated half of which may have been produced during the previous half century. A conservative estimate of those known to exist today would be unlikely to exceed three hundred, which is barely twenty per cent of the manufactured output. It is hard to explain this low survival figure.[5]

Figure 710.

The following silversmiths are recorded as makers of wine labels who used the Chester assay office, identified by known examples and from details of entries in the Chester Duty Books 1784-1840.

(C) Chester   (L) Liverpool   (M) Manchester

R. Richardson II (C)
R. Richardson II was admitted to the freedom of the city in 1732. He was Mayor in 1758 and 1759 and Assay Master from 1761 to his death in 1769. He is the only known maker of wine labels until *c.*1770 (see figs. 691, 704 and 711).

R. Richardson III (C)
Assumed control of the family firm from 1769 to *c.*1779. He used Richardson II's 'RR' mark[6] on labels that can be placed between these two dates (see fig. 690).

R. Richardson IV (C)
Took over the family firm in 1779 when he was admitted to the Goldsmiths' Company. He used two 'RR' marks that are found on labels, but took little interest in the firm after 1791. He sent labels for assay (see fig. 695) – 1785 four labels, 1787 six labels, 1789 thirty-seven labels and 1790 fifteen labels – and one bottle label.

William Hardwick (M)
Mark noted on label that can be dated to between *c.*1773 and *c.*1780.

Joseph Walley (L)
Joseph married the widow of R. Jones, senior, in 1760 and managed the family firm of that name, succeeding that of Benjamin and John Brancker in 1752, with Robert Jones I until 1772, when both set up independently. Labels with Walley's mark can be dated from *c.*1775, or perhaps earlier (see figs. 707 and 710). He died in 1801.

The Provinces - Chester

Robert Jones I (L)
Used three 'RJ' marks recorded on wine labels between 1789 and 1797, and possibly earlier, between c.1772 (see fig. 706 for OLD HOCK, c.1775-80) and c.1784. In 1789 he sent twenty-nine bottle labels for assay; in 1794 he sent thirty-nine bottle-tickets for assay; and in 1797 he sent ten bottle-tickets for assay. He died in 1826.

Robert Jones II (L)
Joined the firm in 1823, and it is likely that labels after this date are his. Sent nine labels for assay in 1827.

Joseph Duke I (C)
Manufactured large quantities of plate from the 1780s until 1810. Marks attributed to him by Ridgway are found on labels that can be dated c.1780 to c.1785. An unusual shape for CLARET (see fig. 703) is notable.

Joseph Dixon II (C)
Active from 1814 to 1849. An 'ID' mark, which may be his or that of a later Joseph Duke, has been seen on a label of c.1820.

James France (M)
Active from c.1785 to c.1819. 1786 sent fifteen labels for assay; 1787 sent eighteen labels for assay; 1790 sent fifteen labels for assay. None recorded after this date. His domed narrow rectangular for 1784/5 engraved for W.WINE is shown at fig. 705.

T. Hills (L)
In 1789 sent sixteen labels for assay, but none is known at the present time.

Joseph Hewitt (L)
Active from c.1790 to 1793. 1791 sent forty-four labels for assay, of which thirty-two were rejected; 1792 sent thirty-two labels for assay. His 'IH' mark has also been attributed to Isaac Hadwine, who was active from c.1766 to c.1792, but Hadwine is not listed as having sent in labels. His MADEIRA is shown at fig. 700. See also John Helsby below.

G. Walker I (C)
The Walkers were prominent goldsmiths in Chester from c.1770 until 1841. George Walker I sent in twenty-six labels for assay between 1792 and 1796 and a further five in 1803 and 1805, but their whereabouts are unknown today.

Figure 711.

John Walker I (C)
Son of George Walker I, he sent four labels for assay in 1821, but their present location is also unknown.

George Lowe I (C)
Founder of the firm of that name, which was the leading goldsmith in Chester throughout the nineteenth century and was still prominent when the Chester assay office closed in 1962. In 1793 he sent eighteen bottle-tickets for assay, and thereafter 219 bottle-tickets, labels, decanter labels and wine labels, and some thirty-three bottle rings up to 1839 (see figs. 697, 698 and 701).

Robert Lowe (C)
Son of George Lowe I. Moved to Preston. Sent fifteen labels for assay in 1831.

Robert Bowers (C)
A clockmaker by training, later referred to as a silversmith. Active from 1783 to 1814, but only two entries for labels are listed: 1797 sent twenty-four labels for assay; 1802 sent thirty-six labels for assay. He was admitted to the Freedom of the City of Chester in 1782 and was Mayor of Chester in 1811. He died in 1829.

Nicholas Cunliffe (L)
Active from 1798 to c.1835. He sent lables [sic] for assay: thirteen in 1802, three in 1804, six in 1807 and two in 1808. His 1801 CLARET is shown at fig. 694.

Mary Huntingdon (C)
The circumstances under which Mary Huntingdon founded this firm at 38 Bridge Street in 1815 are not known. By 1822 it had become H.M. and S. Huntingdon, using the same 'MH' mark. She sent bottle-tickets for assay: eight in 1821, which included a rectangular label for COGNAC BRANDY,[7] eight more in 1822, and a further two in 1825.

John Coakley (L)
He produced an enormous quantity of flatware (including 2,025 teaspoons in 1829) between 1828 and 1833. He sent six cork mounts for assay in 1829 and six bottle-tickets in 1830.

John Helsby (L)
Was active from c.1816 to c.1836. In 1833 he sent twenty-five silver tickets for assay, but no labels with the mark attributed to him by Ridgway are known today. The dates given for known labels with an 'IH' mark range from 1789 to 1793 and are therefore likely to be those of Joseph Hewitt (see above).

William Twemlow (C)
Came from Great Boughton and sponsored one label in 1818 and seven labels in 1820.[8] His crescent W.WINE, c.1790, is shown at fig. 708.

John Twemlow (C)
Related to William Twemlow (see above). He had four 'bottle tickets' assayed in 1828.

PART 2 – EXETER AND DISTRICT

Goldsmiths were active in Exeter at least since the thirteenth century, but silver was not marked with an informal town mark until around 1575. With the raising of the standard of wrought silver in 1696 to the Britannia standard, all provincial silver had theoretically to be sent to London for assay. Petitions from the provincial goldsmiths resulted in the Act of 1701, which entitled the Goldsmiths' Companies in York, Exeter, Bristol, Chester and Norwich to set up assay offices. The newly-formed Exeter Goldsmiths' Company acted promptly, appointing an assayer and changing the town mark from a letter X to a triple turreted castle.

The assay office served the whole of the West Country below Bristol and towards the end of the eighteenth century was dealing with about 1,200 Troy lbs (448kg) of silver per annum. This amount had tripled by 1825 and was over 5,500lbs (2,053kg) by 1854, most of it sent at that time by James and Josiah Williams of Bristol. However, during the 1870s this firm found it more convenient to send its work to London and the business of the assay office declined until it was closed in 1883.

The date letter was changed on 7 August every year, the day when the Exeter Goldsmiths' Company's wardens were elected for the coming year. This date has been taken as the dividing line between years in the tabulations that follow. The duty paid on silver was 6d. per ounce from December 1784; 1s. from July 1797; 1s.3d. from October 1804; and 1s.6d. from September 1814, which level was held until the duty was abolished in May 1890.

The main extant sources of information are the very full records of work sent in day by day to the assay office; the books are now kept in the East Devon Record Office at Exeter. These give, from March 1794 until the closure of the office in July 1883, details of parcels of work sent in each day by the silversmiths; the work is itemised giving for each parcel its total weight, the net weight for payment of duty (five-sixths of the total weight), and the duty paid. Typical extracts from these books have been published.[9] When the work of the Exeter silversmiths became mainly flatware, the format of the books changed to a column presentation.

From these records[10] a census of wine labels can be taken. In order firstly to be able to identify makers of West Country wine labels, and secondly to determine how many labels each produced, involved the perusal of the contents of seven large volumes and a number of smaller notebooks. A picture of changing fashions emerged; for example, the virtual disappearance of silver buckles happened quite suddenly.

The first mention of wine labels in the assay books was an entry for 13 November 1783: '6 pr. Tea Tongs, 4 Bottle Lables' by Francis Trowbridge. The next mentions were for '6 bottle labels' by John Thomas of Plymouth on 26 October 1794, followed by '1 Lable for a bottle' by Richard Ferris on 3 June 1799, followed by '4 bottle lables', also by Ferris, on 12 August 1799. From 1804 onwards the references were almost always for 'Lables'; presumably the concept had by then become sufficiently familiar to the assay office clerks for the extra words of description to be omitted. The term 'bottle ticket' does not appear to have been used.

In 1826 there was a reference to '1 spirit lable' by J. Sweet, but on no other occasion is any description given as to the type of label. Perhaps they were generally sent for assay before the name was engraved. Only on a few occasions during the eighty-three year period in which wine labels were entered is the conventional spelling 'Label' encountered. This occurred in the years 1829, 1836, 1846, 1848, 1857, 1863 and 1871; presumably these were mainly clerical errors. It would be interesting to know when the present-day spelling came into general use.

The old-fashioned spelling caused what may be termed the 'Lable – Table – Ladle' syndrome when working through the assay books, which are of course handwritten, in copperplate of varying degrees of legibility. Entries for tablespoons were usually contracted to 'Tables' in the records, the copperplate T being not unlike the L. This, together with the similarity between 'Lable' and 'Ladle' when written, demanded the exercise of great care in scanning each line of the books to see whether 'Lables' were mentioned.

Even the clerks themselves were confused on occasion. In the later books, when most of the work

Figures 712-727.

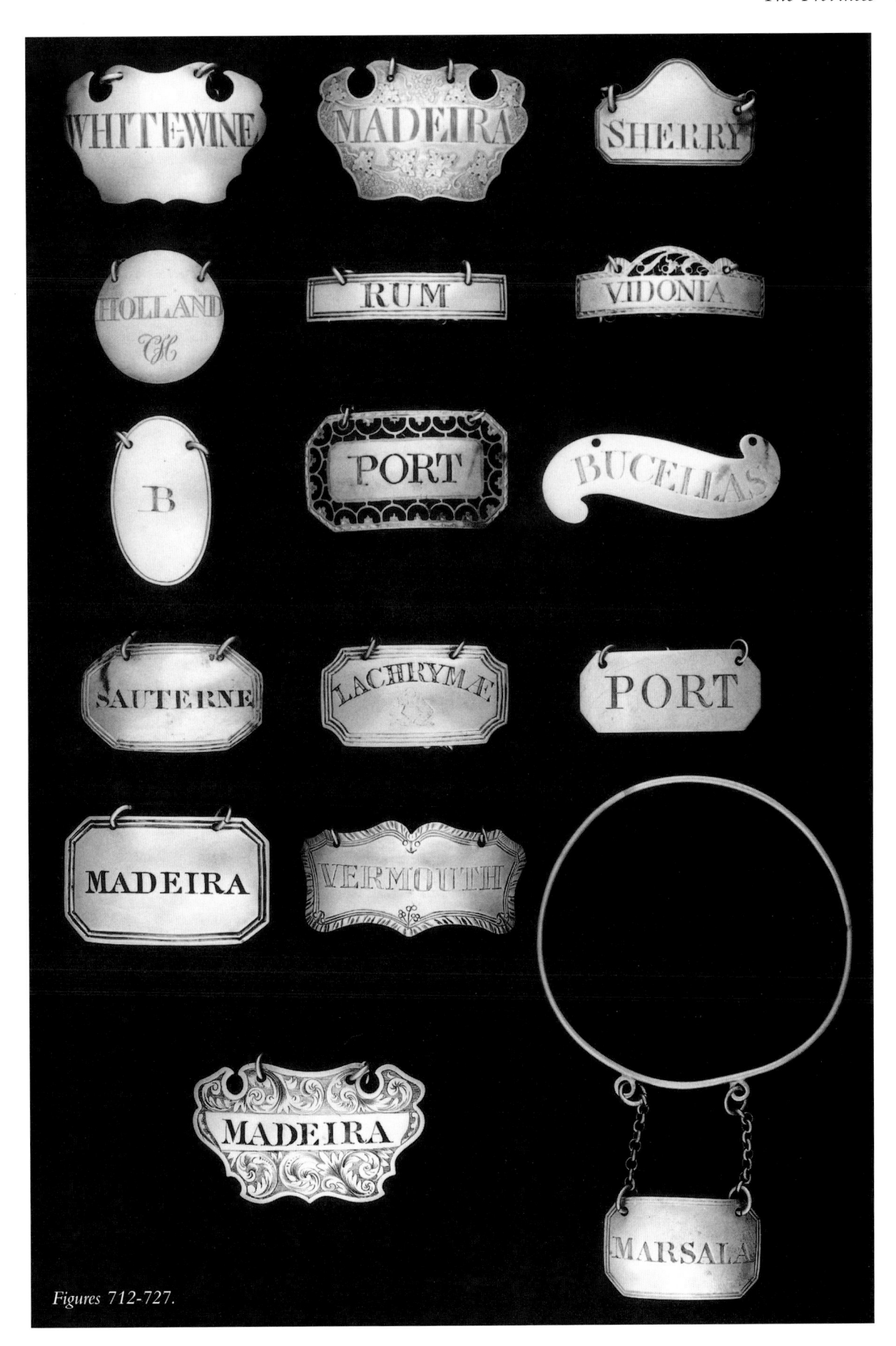

sent for assay was cutlery, the pages were ruled with columns headed 'Teas', 'Tables', 'Desserts', 'Ladles' etc. In book AS/8, the assay book for 1836-1846, the ladle column is written intermittently as 'Lables'. Again, when two records can be compared for the same period, such as the assay book AS/8 and the Goldsmiths' Company book GS/4a for the period 1836-1846, there are occasions when 'Lable' has been confused with 'Table' or 'Ladle'. For example, the entry in AS/8 for 17 March 1842 shows T. Byne as having submitted '3 Lables'; however in GS/4a for the same date, the figure 3 is entered in the 'Ladles' column.

When the two sets of records were duplicated for a period, the label entries were cross-checked, revealing the discrepancies mentioned above. It is interesting that the entry in GS/4a for 17 February 1841 of work by W.R. Sobey is '1 Lable' but in AS/8 it is entered at '1 Name' and is presumably a wine label, probably one that has already been engraved. However, it is not possible from the assay records to determine which were the most popular names. Sobey submitted thirty-six labels in 1843-44, including MARSALA (fig. 727). The evidence suggests that he may have purchased these labels in blank form from George Unite of Birmingham.

Although the first recorded entry is in 1783 there is nothing further about the production of wine labels until 1799, after which, with the exception of 1801/02, 1812/13 and 1814/15, labels were produced continuously until 1849/50. Thereafter entries are intermittent until the final label entry in September 1876. Wine label records therefore cover a period of eighty-three years, slightly less than half the life of the assay office (1701-1883).

The table below gives a summary of the variation in production with the passage of the years. The time divisions coincide with the date letter changes.

Period	No. of labels	Period	No. of labels
1783-1800	10	1830-1835	122
1800-1805	49	1835-1840	63
1805-1810	60	1840-1845	61
1810-1815	60	1845-1850	22
1815-1820	74	1850-1860	14
1820-1825	199	1860-1870	8
1825-1830	252	1870-1877	13

The total number of wine labels recorded is 1,007.

After the end of the Napoleonic Wars, the production of labels began to take off, despite the slump, perhaps coincident with a general feeling of increased security; but this period was the beginning of the golden age of vintage wine and it could therefore be argued that this would increase the demand for wine labels to identify the wine when decanted.

The peak year for the production of labels was 1820/21 with eighty-five labels, closely followed by 1825/26 with eighty-two labels. Owen Fielding of Plymouth has the most labels recorded, 228 over a sixteen-year period from 1816 to 1832. The most labels produced by one craftsman in any year was sixty by William Woodman in 1820; perhaps because he was a Bristol silversmith he saved up his production to send in a large batch due to the inconvenience of travelling. The longest standing maker of labels was Joseph Hicks who has entries recorded between 1800 and 1835, during which time he made 178 wine labels, second in output to Owen Fielding.

The distribution of label output is shown in the following table:

Production band (No. of labels)	No. of makers in that band	Total no. of labels per band	Percentage of labels in band
Over 100	2	406	40
50 to 100	3	204	20

Production band (No. of labels)	No. of makers in that band	Total no. of labels per band	Percentage of labels in band
40 to 50	1	43	4
30 to 40	4	134	13
20 to 30	1	25	3
10 to 20	9	140	14
5 to 10	6	36	4
Less than 5	7	19	2
Total	**33**	**1007**	**100**

Some sixty per cent of the West Country output was submitted by only six silversmiths (J. Hicks, R. Ferris, O. Fielding, W. Woodman, W.R. Sobey and I. Parkin). It is the work of these men that the laws of chance indicate should turn up most frequently in the market place.

There is a predominance of rectangles among Exeter wine labels. No vine leaves have been reported and only one kidney shape, one navette and one crescent. Three escutcheons are illustrated: one plain, for WHITE-WINE possibly by Edward Collier (see fig. 712), one vine leaf and tendril design for MADEIRA, also possibly by E. Collier (see fig. 713) and one of those elaborate shaped cartouches with floral and scallop borders, fairly common among London makers between 1810 and 1830, for MADEIRA by W.R. Sobey in 1836 (see fig. 726).

There are almost three hundred entries for wine labels in the records. Nearly three-quarters of the labels were sent for assay in batches of six or less. The breakdown is given in the following table:

No. of labels per parcel	Parcels No.	% of total	Labels No.	% of total	Percentage of Wakelin labels purchased
1 label	67	23	67	7	6
2 labels	70	24	140	14	7
3 labels	42	15	126	12	8
4 labels	47	16	188	18	12
5 labels	10	3	50	5	6
6 labels	28	10	168	16	15
7 labels	7	2	49	5	7
8 labels	2	1	16	2	10
9 labels	5	2	45	4	7
10 labels	0	0	0	0	9
Over 10 labels	9	3	172	17	14

Owing to a duplication of some entries in books AS/8 and GS/4a between 1836 and 1846, the total number of labels derived from this table would appear slightly larger than that shown in other tables. The discrepancy is slight, however, and the purpose of this table is to show trends.

The table shows that sets of six, four, three and two labels seem to have been quite popular as opposed to larger sets, although it should be remembered that sixes and fours could comprise smaller sets. This trend is in contrast to that found by Bruce Jones in the Wakelin ledgers.[11] The Wakelin percentages for labels purchased are shown for comparison in the table above. Some seventy-eight per cent of Exeter entries are for parcels of one to four labels, compared with sixty-four per cent of Wakelin purchases. Exeter labels in parcels of six or more comprise forty-four per cent of all labels compared with sixty-one per cent in the Wakelin ledger. It is interesting to speculate on the reasons for this. The period is of course considerably later, 1783 to 1876 compared with Wakelin 1747 to 1790, and this may have some bearing. Another reason may be the relative affluence of the Wakelin 'gentlemen' compared with their West Country cousins. The high proportion of titled Wakelin customers, thirty-seven per cent, would probably support this view.

Another interpretation of the small quantities sent for assay could be that customers commissioned labels rather than buying them from silversmiths' existing stock. This probably applied to most of their products except flatware, which was made in very large quantities. One exception to this interpretation would probably be William Woodman of Bristol who sent in a parcel of sixty labels in 1820. Residing in a large centre he could perhaps afford to make labels 'on spec' as he might have a larger turnover in the large and busy city than his competitors further west. Alternatively, he could have been submitting labels for other Bristol makers.

It was infrequent that a parcel of work contained only wine labels, but for those occasions that do occur, it is possible to determine the average weight of labels and the duty paid. Details are as follows:

Date	Maker	No. of labels	Total weight (oz. dwt)	(grams)	Average weight per label (grams)	Total duty paid s. d.
17/03/1808	Adams & Son	8	1.0	31.1	3.9	1 0
16/08/1808	A. Adams	2	0.9	14.0	7.0	7½
03/01/1809	J. Patrick	6	1.9	45.1	7.5	1 7½
19/09/1809	Adams & Son	4	0.19	29.6	7.4	10½
01/12/1809	Adams & Co.	1	0.5	7.8	7.8	4½
02/10/1810	Adams & Co.	18	2.7	73.1	4.1	2 6
03/01/1811	Adams & Co.	3	0.12	18.7	6.2	9
30/04/1814	J. Trist	4	0.19	29.6	7.4	1 3
14/11/1815	J. Sweet	4	1.6	40.4	10.1	1 9
12/02/1816	J. Trist	7	1.7	42.0	6.0	1 9
14/10/1819	J. Trist	2	0.14	21.8	10.9	1 1½
29/05/1827	J. Hicks	2	1.0	31.1	15.6	1 3
22/08/1828	J. Fowler	4	0.15	23.3	5.8	1 1½
03/09/1828	J. Fowler	2	0.15	23.3	11.7	1 1½
31/10/1829	O. Fielding	6	2.0	62.2	10.4	2 6

Thus it can be seen that for entries where the weight of wine labels is known, it varied between about 4g and 15g per label. For comparison, a normal octagonal label weighs about 8.5g, complete with chain. As expected, the size of the Exeter labels is in the same league as the 4dwt to 7dwt (6.2g to 10.9g) mentioned by Bruce Jones.

The duty paid per label varied between just over 1½d. and 4½d. prior to September 1814; thereafter the duty was increased by 3d. per ounce and a label cost between 3d. and 7½d. in duty. The duty is therefore a relatively small proportion of the final cost of approximately 6s. per label (Wakelin figures plus inflation allowance!).

It is surprising that in view of the prolific output of wine labels in the West Country, just over 1,000 in the eighty-three years, so few, relatively, turn up in the market nowadays. Wm. Bruford and Sons, antique silver specialists in Exeter, searched through their books for a period of ten to fifteen years in the 1960s and 1970s and noted only seven:

MADEIRA	by J. Hicks, 1835
BRANDY	by J. Niner, Plymouth, 1810
BRANDY	by I. Parkin, 1829
VERMOUTH	by E. Sweet, 1836 (see fig. 725)
BRANDY, GIN, RUM	by J. & J. Williams, 1870

The Exeter Museum has a BRANDY by James Niner of Plymouth (first mention in 1820, last mention in 1837), 1830/31. Mr Simon Hunt of Exeter Museum noted seven labels in the Sotheby's catalogues for 1969 and 1970:

WHITE WINE	by W. Welch (?), 1810
RUM and LACHRYMÆ	by J. Hicks, 1825 (see fig. 722)
PORT	by J. Hicks, 1828 (see fig. 723)
SOY and KETCHUP	by G. Ferris, 1822
SHERRY	by G. Ferris (?), 1827

Since E. Sweet is recorded as only having sent in one label in 1836/37, presumably the entry is for the VERMOUTH mentioned above (see fig. 725).

The following labels are among those extant:

Label	Maker	Date	Description
GINGER	Joseph Hicks (Js.H)	Late Georgian	Shell, scroll and acanthus leaves. (2 *WLCJ* 54.) Mark questionable.
W WINE	Joseph Hicks? overstamped Wm Pearse	c.1786	Bright-cut crescent with wide horns. 3 *WLCJ* 103)
CLARET/ PORT	J.N. Dunsford (JND) (Plymouth Dock)	1825	Rectangle, double thread border. (4 *WLCJ* 171)
CHAMPAGNE	J. Osment (First mark	1824	Octagon, double reeded border. (5 *WLCJ* 177)
SHERRY	O. Fielding	c.1808	Escutcheon with three marks but no date letter. (Collection)
GIN/ BRANDY/ RUM	J. Hicks	c.1800	Set of 3 broad rectangles with rounded ends. (Collection)
RUM	J. Hicks	1825	Rectangle with raised eyelets and 'hump' bearing crest and motto GANG FORWARD (probably Stirling). Fully marked. (Sotheby's 22.10.70)
BRANDY	W.R. Sobey	1832	Plain octagon, fully marked. (Sotheby's 22.10.70)
MARSALA	W.R. Sobey	1836	Reeded octagon. (Sotheby's 11.2.71)
FRONTIGNAC	O. Fielding	1824	Reeded oblong. (Sotheby's 11.2.71)
WHISKEY	W. Welch	1823	Plain octagon, fully marked. (Sotheby's 3.2.72)
R) B)	W. Welch	c.1815	Vertical oval with eyelets, single reeded border, slightly convex. (Sotheby's 9.11.72.) See fig. 718.
CLARET	J. & J. Williams & Co. (?)	1861	Shaped oblong ('architectural design') with moulded borders fully marked. (Sotheby's 15.5.75)
PORT) MADEIRA)	Owen Fielding	1828	Pair of double reeded rectangles with cut corners, fully marked. (Collection).
BRANDY	O. Lang (?) (Plymouth Dock)	1828	Plain rectangle. (Sotheby's 5.6.75)
PORT	SW below crown	Pre-1778	Large plain and heart shaped of very heavy gauge. Leopard's head crown indicates date pre-1778. (Sotheby's 29.4.71). Item questionable.
SHERRY	J. Hicks	c.1798	Domed rectangle with cut corners and double reeded border. With lion and king's head. See fig. 714.
SAUTERNE) MADEIRA)	G. Ferris	1825	Pair of rectangles with rounded ends, double reeded; fully marked. (Collection)

The Provinces - Exeter

Label	Maker	Date	Description
SAUTERNE) MADEIRA)	J. Osment (First mark)	1824	Pair of rectangles, turtle back, triple reeded, fully marked. Very broadly cut corners, almost octagonal. (See fig. 721)
GIN) BRANDY)	I. Parkin	1825	Plain, very broad rectangle with finely cut corners, fully marked. (Collections)
MARSALA	W.R. Sobey	1836	Squat plain rectangle, double reeded, suspended by chains from a neck ring; fully marked. (See fig. 727)
WHISKEY	W. Woodman (W.W in script) (Bristol)	1823	Long plain rectangle, fully marked. (Collection)
SAUTERNE	W. Woodman) (W.W in script) (Bristol)	c.1820	Small rectangle with rounded corners, triple reeded, marked with lion and king's head. (Collection)
BRANDY) RUM) HOLLAND)	Francis Parsons and Benjamin Goss	c.1797-99	Set of three button shaped labels with names engraved above a monogram. Plain, without decoration, with lion and king's head. (See fig. 715)
FRONTIGNAC	O. Fielding	1827	Small rectangle with rounded corners, fully marked. (Collection)
SHERRY	W. Pope	1810	Turtle back, cushion shaped with feathered border, fully marked. (Collection) (Shape as illustration of VERMOUTH in figure 3, 6 *WLCJ* 41)
PORT (over GIN W. WINE)	O. Lang (Plymouth Dock)	c.1825	Pair, turtle back, marked once only. (Collection)
CLARET) MADEIRA)	J. Hicks	1832	Pair of rectangles with cut corners, double reeded, fully marked, with black wax in name engraving. (Collection)
PORT) SHERRY)	J. Hicks	1831	Pair of rectangles with cut corners, double reeded, fully marked with black wax in name engraving. (Collection)
Name Unstated	J.&J. Williams	1868	Goblet and festoons similar to LUNEL in Penzer, pl. 7; fully marked. (Collection)
GIN) RUM) BRANDY)	I. Parkin	1831	Set of three rectangles with cut corners, double reeded, fully marked. (Collection)
CLARET	J. Hicks	1819	Squarish rectangle, without town mark. (Collection)
BUCELLAS	J.N. Dunsford (Plymouth Dock)	1826	(Collection)

Labels by J. Harman with the date letter for 1835/36 and by James and Josiah Williams with the date letter for 1868/69 and including both the Niner labels mentioned above are known (amongst others) to be absent from the assay records. There are three possible reasons: firstly the entries may have been overlooked; secondly, the assay office clerks may not have been completely meticulous in their entries; and thirdly, the label may have been sent in under another person's name. The other labels mentioned in the list appear to be consistent with the records.

Not all work entered in the assay book under the name of a particular maker necessarily carries the marks of that maker. Apparently it was the custom in the West Country for silver from outside Exeter to be sent in parcels of work under other people's names than those whose marks were punched. This practice is described in a letter from William Pope of Plymouth to the Exeter Assay Master on 22 March 1855 when he mentions that he makes silver for retailers who have their marks punched on it rather than his. The Parliamentary Select Committee record of 1856 also refers to the practice of retailers having their mark submitted on plate by a manufacturer.

Thus when we consider the parcel of sixty labels sent to Exeter by William Woodman of Bristol and entered on 12 October 1820 along with a large number of spoons and tongs, it may be that Woodman was a maker sending in work that carried the marks of different retailers. Similarly, some of the labels entered by Owen Fielding, who according to the assay books was the most prolific producer, almost certainly carried other marks. This would account for the fact that some of the extant labels are not apparently entered in the books (e.g. J. Harman's MADEIRA of 1835 sent from Bristol). It may be, for example, that James Niner's wine label was included in a parcel of work by Owen Fielding under the arrangements described above; hence it does not appear in the assay books. This is supported by the fact that the mark IN appears in the same cell of the assay office's copper plates punched with makers' marks as that of OF, Owen Fielding.

The search of the records revealed thirty-five different makers of wine labels. Only seventeen have been recorded on extant labels, details of which are as follows:

Maker	No. of Labels
J. Hicks	16
F. Parsons	3
G. Ferris	5
W. Welch	3
O. Fielding	5
J. Osment	3
W. Woodman	2
I. Parkin	6
W. Pope	1
W.R. Sobey	3
E. Sweet	1
J&J Williams	4
J. Niner	1
T. Mardon	2
J. Ramsey	1
J.N. Dunsford	3
O. Lang	1
Total	63

This list has examples from twelve of the thirty-five makers recorded as having entries for wine labels in the assay books, together with five makers not mentioned as having submitted labels. Niner, Dunsford and Lang, all of Plymouth, may perhaps have sent their labels in with work under Fielding's name.

Many silversmiths were producers of a wide variety of work, so that wine labels cannot be said to be the province of any particular type of worker. The craft can be broadly categorised into three classes: smallwork (such as rings, seals, medals); platework (spoons, forks and flat domestic items); and largework (mainly hollowware, such as pots, basins, cups). On this basis the wine label makers listed can be classified as follows:

Makers of smallwork, platework and largework	17
Mainly smallworkers	7
Mainly plateworkers	2
Mainly largeworkers	1
Makers mainly of smallwork and platework	2
Makers mainly of platework and largework	4

The Provinces - Exeter

As can be seen, the majority of label makers were versatile craftsmen. When they were specialists, then they tended, as would be expected, to be smallworkers.

First and last mentions in the assay books, together with the number of wine labels recorded totalling 1034, some twenty-seven more than the number of 1007 derived from scrutinising the assay books (suggesting duplication due to packages), are given below:

Maker	Town	Assay Book First mention	Last mention	Number of labels produced
Thomas Mardon	Plymouth	1775	1800	2
Francis Trowbridge	Exeter	1780	1798	4
Joseph Hicks	Exeter	1780	1835	178
Richard Ferris	Exeter	1794	1812	60
John Sweet	Exeter	1794	1829	6
John Patrick	Plymouth Dock	1794	1809	6
John Thomas	Plymouth	1794	1795	6
Richard Jenkins	Exeter	1795	1796	4
Francis Parsons	Exeter	1797	1831	5
George Ferris	Exeter	1800	1832	43
William Welch I and II	Exeter	1801	1828	37
Joseph Trist	Exeter	1801	1831	17
Emmanuel Levy	Exeter	1803	1818	14
Ann Adams	Exeter	1806	1808	2
Adams and Son	Exeter	1808	1852	35
Owen Fielding	Plymouth Dock	1808	1835	228
Simon Harris	Plymouth Dock	1811	1815	1
William Hope	Plymouth Dock	1816	1833	19
John Osment	Exeter	1818	1854	17
Simon Levy	Exeter	1818	1832	13
William Woodman	Bristol[12]	1818	1838	78
John Webb	Exeter	1818	1822	2
Isaac Parkin	Exeter	1819	1839	66
John Fowler	Exeter	1823	1829	6
Jonathan Ramsey	Devonport	1829	1836	1
William Pope	Plymouth	1830	1882	30
William Rawlings Sobey	Exeter	1835	1853	32
Edward Sweet	Exeter	1831	1857	11
Robert Williams	Bristol[12]	1832	1854	7
John Stone	Exeter	1833	1863	25
John W. Langdon	Plymouth	1833	1845	11
William Sweet	Exeter	1833	1833	4
Thomas Byne	Exeter	1835	1859	19
Henry M. Norris	Plymouth?	1835	1844	4
Joseph Fulton	Bristol[12]	1838	1860	6
John Beer	Bristol[12]	1848	1882	2
James and Josiah Williams	Bristol[12]	1854	1874	33

Biographical notes of some of the makers,[13] together with details of their products, follow. Several of the makers became Freemen of the City of Exeter but none achieved the distinction of being Mayor. Although prior to 1700 freedom conferred trading advantages, after that date it was connected with Parliamentary franchise and links with trade were largely fortuitous.

Thomas Mardon (Plymouth)

Admitted to the Freedom of Exeter in 1776 but resident of Plymouth. Listed in 1783 as a silversmith at 7 Market Place, Plymouth. Paid £5.5s.0d. in 1773-4 for 'engraving the Town's Arms', he produced small, elegant labels in the Bateman style, besides a gold Freedom box in 1785.

Francis Trowbridge Junior (Exeter)
Admitted to Goldsmiths' Company 1784. Warden in 1785, 1786, 1790, 1791 and 1794. City Freeman 2 November 1776, by succession to his father, Francis Trowbridge, also a jeweller. His apprentices were James Traies, jeweller and engraver, of Crediton and Edward Byne, silversmith of St Mary Arches, Exeter. House advertisement in *Exeter Flying Post,* 12 August 1784.

Joseph Hicks (Exeter)
Admitted to Goldsmiths' Company 1785. Warden in twenty-six years between 1786 and 1832. Died 1835. Worker in silver Fryernhay Lane 1791; New Bridge 1792; Fryernhay 1822, 1827. Mentioned in Ellis *Diaries*; supplied spoons etc. to Henry Ellis. City Freeman 11 September 1816, by order of the Mayor and Council for his work for the employment of the poor of Exeter. A versatile worker (or workshop); as well as being a prolific maker of wine labels (178), and flatware, he produced brooches, gold rings, shoe buckles, buttons, spectacles, surgeon's instruments, a feeder, padlock, compass and square, coffin plate, candlestick, teapot, trumpet, burner, chalice, funnel and toastrack. See figs. 714 (SHERRY), 722 (LACHRYMÆ) and 723 (PORT).

Richard Ferris (Exeter)
Admitted to Goldsmiths' Company 1793; Warden 1795-96, 1798-99, 1801-02, 1804-05, 1808-09, 1811; last mention in the court rolls 1811, died 1812. City Freeman 29 March 1784 as silversmith of the Close, apprentice of Thomas Eustace, jeweller. His apprentices were William Parsons of St. Kerrian (Freeman 1800), John Capron of London (Freeman 1809) and Edward Way of St. David (Freeman 1857). Mentioned as silversmith in High Street 1796. Made small work (rings, seals), flatware; hollowware (cups, basins, boatswains' calls or whistles).

John Sweet (Exeter)
Silversmith of St. Mary Arches; City Freeman 23 July 1791, by order of the Mayor and Council. Mentioned as working jeweller, Pancras Lane 1823; Fore Street Hill 1816; working silversmith, Pancras Lane 1822, 1827, 1828. Smallworker, producing medals, tops, rings, chapes, shoe and knee buckles, buttons and a silver eye glass frame.

John Thomas (Plymouth)
Listed as a 'Jeweller' in the Universal British Directory, 1798, at Market Place, Plymouth.

Thomas Welch I (Plymouth Dock)
Born in 1764, the son of William Welch I, he was probably the maker of a large plain cresent PORT label *c.*1800.

John Patrick (Plymouth Dock)
Working jeweller, Fore Street, Devonport 1814. Other work assayed included rings.

Francis Parsons (Exeter)
Working silversmith, Paul Street 1816. Worked with or for Stephen Crees and Joseph Gross. Work included flatware, cups, goblet, toastrack and buttons. 'Bottle Labels' produced in 1798.

George Ferris (Exeter)
There were two silversmiths of this name: George Ferris Senior, who was admitted to the Goldsmiths' Company in 1806, and George Ferris Junior, admitted in 1812. G. Ferris Senior was Warden in eighteen years between 1806 and 1839 and died in 1840 and G. Ferris Junior was Warden in twenty-six years between 1813 and 1859 when he died having been a member of the Guild for forty-eight years. G. Ferris Senior died in 1840. He was a jeweller in Fore Street 1816, 1822, 1827; 116 Fore Street 1828, 1831. Edward Way's apprenticeship was assigned to him from Richard Ferris. Work included flatware, small items such as buttons and medals, and large work, tureen, coffee biggin, teapot, trowel and bottle stands.

The Provinces - Exeter

William Welch I (Exeter)
Silversmith in Exeter from 1801-1827. Made the unusual vertical oval for 'B' (fig. 718) *c.*1801.

William Welch II (Exeter)
Working silversmith, Bath Yard 1822, West Street 1827. Work included flatware, gold rings, medals, boxes, cruet tops, sauceboats, cups, teapots, jugs, half pints, extinguisher, sockets for corals, nipple case, instrument case, and 'one hand for reading'.

Joshua Trist (or Joseph) (Exeter)
Silversmith and engraver, High Street 1822, 1827; Chapple's Court 1831; Waterbeer Street 1835, 1839, 1847, 1853, 1859, 1867. Trist and Son, Silversmith and Engraver 255, High Street, 1828. Mainly small work: seal, clasps, buttons, gold rings, umbrella and parasol mountings, buckles; but also spoons, spectacles and coffin plate.

Emmanuel Levy (Exeter)
Pawnbroker and silversmith, Fore Street 1807, died 1818. Succeeded by his son Simon Levy (1818-1835). Objects made by the firm included flatware, jugs, teapots, coffee pots, cups, buckles, asparagus tongs, a bird and in 1811 '24 bells' which were intended for Jewish liturgical use – they had already given a clock to the Exeter Synagogue.

Adams and Son (Exeter)
John Adams, goldsmith of Fore Street, 1791, 1796. Died after lingering illness; buried at St Stephen's, March 1806. Wife was Ann (daughter of Thomas Coffin II, goldsmith) who sent in two labels for assay in 1808 (see fig. 716 for RUM marked by Ann Adams). The business was carried on by son, Edward Hewish Adams, a prominent retailer, on corner of St Martin's Lane until about 1852. Admitted to Goldsmiths' Company 1780. Warden 1781-83, 1788-89, 1793-95. Accountant 1785, 1789, 1797 until his death in 1806. Entered mark 1787. Work included rings, buttons and belt plate. Mentioned in Grimwade's *London Goldsmiths* (first edition, 1976), page 720. See fig. 717 for VIDONIA, *c.*1800, and fig. 719 for PORT, also *c.*1800.

Owen Fielding (Plymouth Dock)
Working silversmith and gilder, Mount Street 1822. The largest submission output of wine labels (228). Work included flatware, bottle, bottletops, cork mounts, wine strainer, toys, belt plates, clasps, breastplates, pap boat, muffineer, coral socket, mounting for coconut, lions' feet, toastrack, medals, boatswains' calls, foot rules, mace, speaking trumpet, bookclasp, whistle and bells. He undoubtedly submitted parcels for assay containing the work of other goldsmiths.

Simon Harris (Plymouth Dock)
Mentioned only for a period of four years in the assay books, 1811-15 after which he returned to London. Only one wine label recorded, the smallest output of wine label makers. Most work was hollowware including basin, teapot, sauceboat, wine strainer, tumblers, rummers, tea canisters; also waiter, toastrack, snuffer stand, bottle stands and unusual items such as crowns and a set of Aaron's bells. He was Jewish and made items for local synagogues.

William Hope (Plymouth Dock)
Working goldsmith or jeweller, 29 Buckwell Street, 1850. Working silversmith, 25 Catherine Street 1823. Work was mainly flatware but included snuffer stand, bottle stand, sugar sifter, pepper (pot) and knife rests. He got into trouble for forging Exeter punches.

John Osment (Exeter)
Admitted to Goldsmiths' Company 1835, when there were only two members surviving. Warden

in 1836-37, 1841-42, 1845-46, and Accountant for several years. Died 1854. Silversmith and engraver, Mint Lane 1835; working silversmith, Mint Lane 1853. Chanter says he was more an engraver than goldsmith. Work included flatware and hollowware such as tureens, basins, egg cup; also medals, seal, gold rings and less common items such as coffin plates, padlock, dog collar, eyeglass, surgeon's instruments, square and arrow. The treble-reeded octagonal SAUTERNE (see fig. 721) seems to bear his first mark, but is dated 1824, a pair with MADEIRA. The double-reeded octagonal CHAMPAGNE is of the same date.

Simon Levy (Exeter)
Made both flatware and hollowware, including coffee pot, teapot, tureen, basins, muffineers, coffee biggin, snuff box and gun mounting (see above, Emmanuel Levy).

William Woodman (Bristol)
Third most prolific submitter of wine labels (seventy-eight); on one occasion in 1820 a parcel of sixty was sent for assay, with 250 teaspoons and other flatware. He also produced salt cellars, basins, saucepan, cups, strainer, teapot, goblets, bottle, bottletop, medals, crosses, gold rings, ink bottles; and occasional unusual items, pipe, ear trumpet, toy, race cup, trowel and gold snuff box. See fig. 739 for WHISKEY, 1823, having made another WHISKEY in 1819. His business passed to Robert Williams.

John Webb (Exeter)
Mentioned only once or twice in the assay books. With his wine label entry in 1819 are noted teaspoons and tongs.

Isaac Parkin (Exeter)
Apprenticed to John Legg in 1809. Assay Master 1849 to 1854, but mentioned in a Parliamentary report on provincial assay offices as unsuitable to hold office. Admitted to Goldsmiths' Company in 1835 and appointed Accountant. Warden of the Company in 1835-36, 1839-40, 1843-44, 1847. Died 1854. Although first assay book mention is 1819, his mark was not entered until 1825. Mentioned as working silversmith, Exe Island, 1822, 1828, 1831, 1835, 1839, where he owned an alehouse. Work showed versatility between smallwork (shoe buckles, whip mountings, shirt buttons, ink bottle tops, boatswains' calls) flatware; hollowware (coffee pot, teapot, basin, jugs, chalice, tureen, dish cover, wine strainer) to unusual items (square and compass, and 'hear trumpet'). The attractive scroll BUCELLAS bears an IP mark and has been attributed to this maker, but is dated 1806 (see fig. 720).

John Fowler (Exeter)
Mentioned as jeweller and lapidary, Bampfyle Street 1828; working jeweller, Bampfyle Street 1827.

William Blackford (Plymouth)
In assay books from late 1820s, he is the probable maker of a trio of escutcheon labels in the 'Unite Style'.

William Pope (Plymouth)
Working silversmith at 3 King Street, 1844, 1850 and 1852. A long working life with assay book entries over a period of fifty-two years. His work was varied and included smallwork (bottle mounts, horn mounts, gold rings, medals), flatware and hollowware (saucepans milk cup, sifters, teapot, basin, ewers) as well as the typical port products: boatswains' calls. He produced a model of Smeaton's Eddystone Lighthouse for use as a cruet.

William Rawlings Sobey (Exeter)
Admitted to the Goldsmiths' Company in 1835 with Isaac Parkin and John Osment, when membership had fallen to two. Warden in nine years between 1837 and 1852. He sold off his

business due to ill health in 1852 and died shortly afterwards. Described as silversmith in Ferris' Passage 1835, 218 High Street 1839, 211 High Street 1847. He was the occupier of a back dwelling and workshop owned by George Ferris (to whom he was related) at Ferris' Passage in 1838. A versatile silversmith, his work included smallwork (gold rings, medals, seals, badge); flatware including coffin plate and trowels; hollowware (tankard, basket, teacaddy, pots, bottle, flagon, saucepan, chalice, muffineer, cruets, wine funnel) and less common terms such as stirrup, bell, lap dog, six skulls, taper stands, sandwich box and breastplate. In 1841 on two occasions parcels of Sobey's spoons were spoiled by the assay office, presumably for being below sterling standard. See figs. 726 (MADEIRA, 1836) and 727 (MARSALA, 1843).

Edward Sweet (Exeter)
Varied output including tops, medals, buckle; flatware including trowel, coffin plate, tray; and hollowware (jugs, muffineers, and 'ear machine'). See fig. 725 for VERMOUTH (1836).

Robert Williams (Bristol)
Robert Williams, father of James and Josiah Williams (q.v.), took over William Woodman's business. Work included medals, gold rings; flatware (venison dish, waiter and the usual cutlery); and coffeepots, teapots, tureen, salt cellars, goblets, cups, pints, toastracks, ewers, and a cruet frame, meadle (?) and horn.

John Stone (Exeter)
Admitted to Goldsmiths' Company 1841 in place of G. Ferris Senior (deceased). Warden 1845, 1848, 1850-51, 1853-54, 1856, 1859-60, 1863-67. His son, Thomas Hart Stone, was his apprentice, admitted to the Guild in 1861. Address given as 36 High Street. Work included medals, gold rings, buttons, stickhead; flatware; cups, extinguishers, calls, bell; and less common items, including nipple bit, nosel (?), brush, shaving box, doll, square, pencil case, lip salve, trumpet, paddles, nutcracks, dagger and death's head.

John W. Langdon (Plymouth, Stonehorse)
Listed as a working jeweller of 52 Union Street, and 13 Union Street, Stonehorse (1823). Work was mainly flatware but did include small hollow items such as mustard pot and pepperbox. In 1855 William Pope wrote that 'Mr. Langdon wishes to have his name on such goods as are manufactured by me'.

William Sweet (Exeter)
Only mentioned in the assay book for 1833. Work included a buckle, cutlery and a square.

Jonathan Ramsey (Devonport)
Recorded in 1836 at 51 Fore Street, he probably submitted items via Owen Fielding.

Thomas Byne (Exeter)
Admitted to Goldsmiths' Company 1855 as one of two members in place of W.R. Sobey and J. Osment who had died. Warden in 1858. Mentioned as silversmith, Friars Walk 1835; working goldsmith, Mint Lane 1839; working silversmith, Mint Lane 1847 and 17 North Street 1853, 1859, 1860. Work included brooches, medal, cutlery, coffin plate, toastrack, dish, chalice, candlesticks, headband and nozels (nozzles?).

Henry M. Norris (Plymouth)
Mentioned as working goldsmith or jeweller, 35 Cambridge Street. Work included rings, cutlery, trowel, salver, jug, square, compass and shield.

Joseph Fulton (Bristol)[14]
Work included medals, tops, spoons, jug, teapot, soy stand and badge. His premises in Bristol were at 8 Narrow Wine Street (1839) and 8 Jerrell Street (1858).

John Beer (Bristol)[15]
Mentioned at 19 Trenchard Street in 1857. Work included ladles, mouthpiece and dram bottle.

James and Josiah Williams (Bristol)[16]
In 1856 Messrs. Williams intimated that, if they were to continue sending their plate to Exeter for assay, paying £2,500 annually in duty, it was desirable for their firm to be represented on the Guild. The Goldsmiths' Company sought counsel's opinion as to whether they were eligible for election, not being resident in Exeter. The opinion given was that they were probably not qualified, but that no legal authority would be likely to disturb the election. Anxious not to lose their share of the poundage on the duty paid by the firm, the guild admitted James Williams in 1857; he was Warden in 1861, 1862, 1865 and 1868. Josiah Williams was admitted in 1869 and was Warden in 1870, 1873 and 1880. From 1877 the work of the Exeter assay office decreased rapidly. Messrs. Williams' address is given as 14 Small Street 1857-61 and 18 St Augustine's Parade 1861-74. The Williams' work included large quantities of cutlery and occasionally special items such as a claret jug and a trowel.

PART 3 – BRISTOL AND BATH

In the early years of the eighteenth century Bristol was recognised as the second city in the kingdom, but that was for its commerce, not for its culture. In 1750 Alexander Pope described the city as a cultural desert, with no nobles or aristocrats; so, although there were rich merchants living in fine houses and despite its growing wine trade, it was an unlikely place to have much requirement for wine labels. There had been an assay office in Bristol since the fifteenth century, and it was reopened in 1701, after the closure of the provincial offices four years earlier, though hardly any use was then made of it. In the second half of the eighteenth century half a dozen silversmiths were working in the city, but they registered their marks in London. In the nineteenth century there were even fewer silversmiths and those that did exist, such as John Beer, seem to have transferred to Exeter for registration of their marks and for assay.

William Sloden, who entered a mark in 1764, made scrolls. Note that his BRANDY (see fig. 731) is in an unusual direction: left end up, right end down. He made enclosed crescents in the Bateman style, one of which has the date letter for 1791 (see fig. 728 for CLARET and fig. 730 for SHERRY). A similar crescent label has the mark of one of his apprentices, John Farr, and is of approximately the same date. Farr also made the crescent for PORT (see fig. 729), which may be rather earlier. Even earlier, possibly c.1760, may be the plain escutcheon of provincial appearance and engraving for CYDER (see fig. 733). It is stamped five times by 'GM', who just might be identified with one Miller, a jeweller whose death is recorded in 1764, when his widow, Ann Miller, registered a mark as a bucklemaker. If this is his mark it could have been in the missing smallworkers' register (1739-1758).

Bath, twenty miles away, had a different history. Famous for its waters since Roman times, it became a fashionable resort for London society in Georgian years. Naturally there were working silversmiths in Bath, but, like their Bristol colleagues, they registered their marks in London.[17] By the end of the eighteenth century Bath's popularity was beginning to fade, as the Prince Regent decided to popularise Brighthelmstone and turn it into Brighton.

At the height of Bath's fame three firms were producing silverware, including wine labels, there. An interesting saw-tooth edged crescent in the Bateman style by John Ford and John Williams can be dated to around 1780 (see fig. 738, MADEIRA, and compare with fig. 740, PORT, by T. Wigan); a large oval for PORT by Thomas Graham and Jacob Willis (see fig. 737) is some ten years later. But the man whose mark appears most frequently is Peter Merrett, who entered it in 1793. The

The Provinces - Bristol and Bath

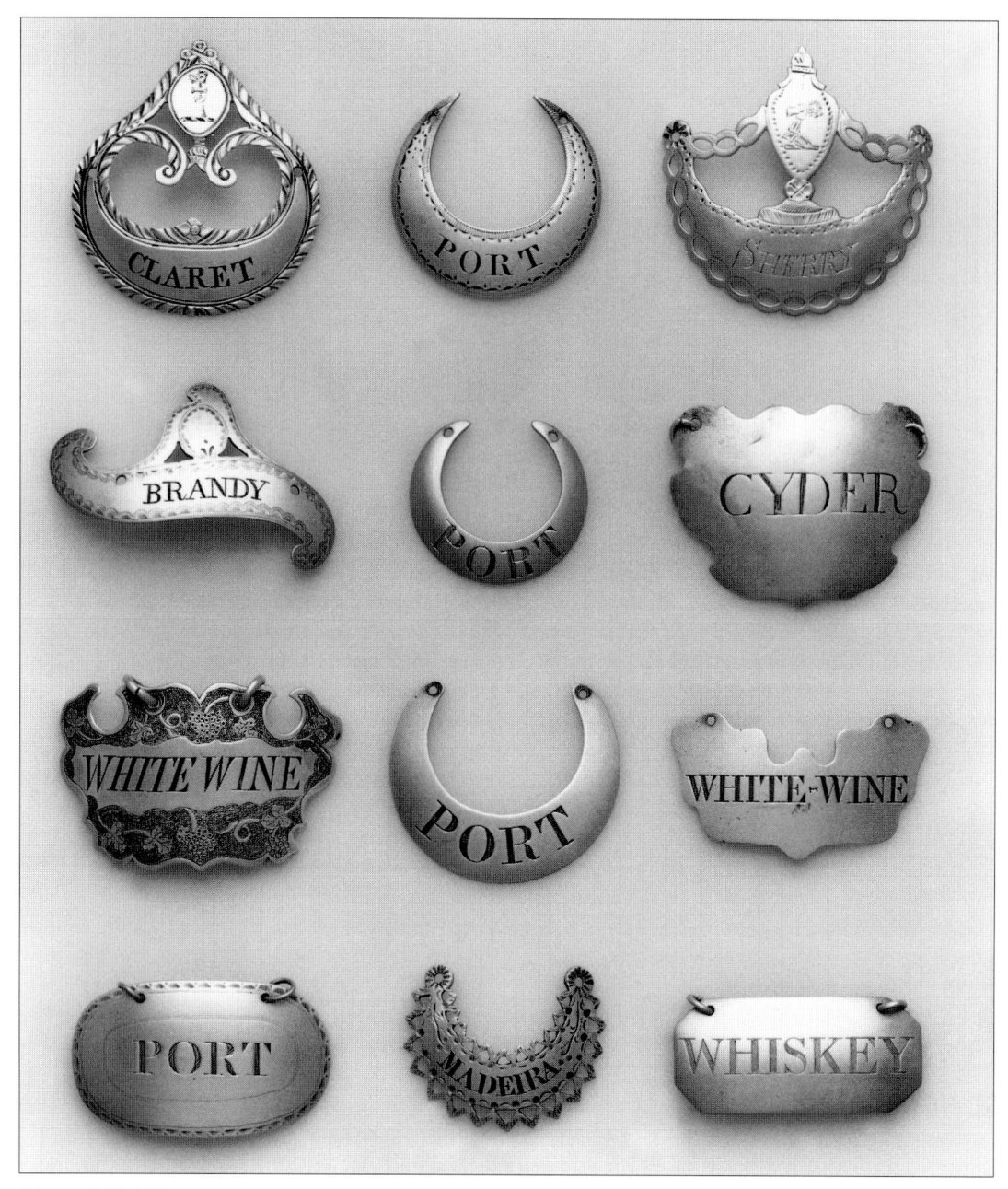

Figures 728-739.

flat-chasing on his escutcheon for WHITE WINE (see fig. 734) and the style of the engraving of the title show some individuality, though this shape of label had long passed out of fashion. He had, however, become free of his master, Thomas Rowell, in 1782, so he may have been in business for some years before this mark was registered. His curiously shaped WHITE.WINE at fig. 736 is also out of the ordinary and has not been noted by any other maker. All his recorded labels have his mark alone, which suggests that he may not have been in the habit of sending modest articles such as wine labels to London for assay, but was passing them direct to his customers. Likewise, Thomas Wigan of Bristol, with his distinctive maker's mark using cursive letters (Grimwade 3459) entered in July 1763, produced an out of the ordinary reverse scroll PORT, with zig-zag border, bearing maker's mark only (see fig. 740).

In the nineteenth century some five Bath silversmiths had marks entered for them, but only that of Peter Merrett has been seen on labels. From Bristol the only makers whose marks have been recorded on labels are William Woodman, who entered it in Exeter in 1818 (his WHISKEY label,

Figure 740.

see fig. 739, is dated 1823) and J. Harman, whose large octagonal label for MADEIRA (see fig. 724) bears Exeter marks for 1835. Joseph Fulton,[18] Robert Williams, John Beer[19] and James and Josiah Williams[20] also sent plate to Exeter for assay (see above, Part 2, especially the table of first and last mentions in the assay book).

The story would not be complete without some examination of the Bristol glass industry, to see if it could have had an effect on the use of bottle-tickets for describing the contents of its citizens' decanters. During the first half of the eighteenth century glass was one of Bristol's major industries; the city had more glasshouses than any other centre in the country. These were turning out bottles for port, cider and perry, and a big export trade was building up. In the 1750s decanters and bottles of the so-called Bristol blue glass became popular. The names of their contents were gilded on the outside; these were usually for condiments[21] and for spirits, but wine titles are also known. The extent to which they competed with plain glass decanters for which a wine label would be needed has not been thoroughly examined, but it is reasonable to suppose that there was healthy local demand for them. It must, of course, be pointed out that the manufacture of labels in London, which also had a large number of glasshouses, was certainly not so affected.[22]

PART 4 – NEWCASTLE AND DISTRICT

Whilst silver had been made in Newcastle since the twelfth century, it was not until 1702 that the Goldsmiths' Company of Newcastle-upon-Tyne was founded and the Newcastle assay office opened. The silversmiths registered their marks, which the Assay Master stamped on a copper disc prepared for the purpose. This disc is still in existence and is in the possession of the Goldsmiths' Company of the Freemen of Newcastle-upon-Tyne. An extremely important relic, it contains 296 punch marks. The disc, which is about 22cm (8½in.) in diameter, does not appear to have been used rigidly, as certain known contemporary marks are omitted. Although twelve marks remain unidentified, it is still a valuable record.[23]

When considering silver wine labels made outside London in the eighteenth and early nineteenth centuries, those made in Newcastle are unequalled, except perhaps in Dublin, both in the originality of their design and in the quality of their workmanship. Newcastle was also one of the first provincial centres to make labels, as shown in examples by Robert Makepeace that have full sets of hallmarks for 1750 and 1754.[24] This is unusual as the law did not require full hallmarking until after 1790; there are no other recorded instances of it having happened before that date and even Makepeace's contemporary local rivals, Isaac Cookson and John Kirkup, only used makers' marks. It is more than likely that labels were made in Newcastle before 1750 as all three of the smiths mentioned above were established by 1738 and it is known that Stephen Buckle of York, whose mark has been seen on early escutcheons, sent parcels of silver to be assayed in Newcastle in 1743 and 1748 (see Part 5).

The originality of Newcastle designs is evident. Virtually all escutcheons, the prevalent shape of the middle decades of the eighteenth century, have features that make them readily distinguishable, in their Newcastle form and decoration, from London versions. The most idiosyncratic type is the

The Provinces - Newcastle

Figures 741-746.

'quiffed' design (see fig. 741 CLARET by John Langlands I, *c*.1760), made by Cookson, Makepeace and the former's successor, John Langlands I. Other unusual variants are known (see fig. 742 CYDER by Isaac Cookson, *c*.1745) but, even when plain, the apparently standard form has distinct regional characteristics. The round indents at either side of the ears of the escutcheon generally tend to be enclosed circles rather than open (see fig. 743 WHITE attributed to James Lamb of Whitehaven, *c*.1750). On chased labels the fruiting vines do not follow the normal London pattern and the title is enclosed within an upward curving panel similar to that on the 'quiffed' variety (see fig. 741). The escutcheon for WHITE (see fig. 743) is particularly unusual in that it is chased with flowers rather than vines and the decoration does not have a flat-chased, ring-matted background. It has been suggested that the decorations may be Jacobite roses, the central large one for the Young Pretender and the two leafed ones for his sons. These emblems appear on Jacobite wine glasses and there were Jacobite supporters in the latter half of the eighteenth century. The label has Newcastle characteristics, and the maker's mark 'IL' closely resembles that shown by Gill for Lamb (for 1748), but, without more positive identification, the possibility that it is an early unregistered mark of J. Langlands cannot be discarded.

Mid-eighteenth-century cast designs are rare, but not unknown. Isaac Cookson made a version of the two putti design (see fig. 744 HOCK by Isaac Cookson, *c*.1745) incorporating, top centre, a crest of a phoenix in flames, 'murally gorged'. This is the crest of the Fenwick family, which had several branches in the surrounding counties of Northumberland and Durham. As with all armorial labels, these labels would have been made to a private commission and were probably in a set of six.

Very few labels seem to have been produced in Newcastle between around 1760 and 1785. The only silversmiths specialising in them who were active between 1760 and 1778 were John Kirkup and John Langlands I, but most labels bearing their marks would appear to be no later than the early 1760s (including an early version with a wire neck ring similar to that made by Sandylands Drinkwater before 1761).[25] Between 1774 and 1778 there was a considerable re-organisation among the label specialists. In 1774 Kirkup died. His business was acquired by Stalker and Mitchison and continued until they retired in 1784. In 1778 John Langlands I went into partnership with John Robertson I and the firm of Pinkney and Scott commenced. Labels bearing the mark of Stalker and Mitchison or of Pinkney and Scott (until they went their separate ways in 1790), either in partnership or individually, are extremely rare, as are those of Langlands and Robertson either without the duty mark (pre-1784) or with the incuse duty mark of 1784-85.

This gap is, however, not difficult to explain. In the last half of the 1750s silver labels came under increasing competition from the colourful enamel labels of South Staffordshire and other places[26] as

Figures 747-752.

well as from the fashion for glass decanters with engraved labels.[27] Newcastle was not only an important centre of glass manufacture, but also the home of the leading enamellers on glass of the period, William Beilby II and his young siblings. Although their enamelling of glassware was most often in beautifully executed white enamel, they could produce a stunning range of colour. This enabled them to decorate glass with the complete armorials of the owner, as is shown by the decanter in the Victoria and Albert Museum, London, which is decorated with the arms, crest and motto of the City of Newcastle together with the crest of Sir Walter Calverley Blackett (Mayor of Newcastle *c.*1764) and the decanter in the Toledo Museum, Ohio, which is decorated with the arms, crest and motto of the Royal Family together with the badge of the Prince of Wales. Signed and dated pieces from the Beilby workshop are restricted to years between 1763 and 1778, but they probably began slightly earlier. Their work, however, was certainly imitated while they were active and continued to be copied for some time after they had ceased to be directly involved.[28]

The fashion for labelled decanters had definitely waned by the late 1780s, although they continued to be popular for spirits (mostly gilt on coloured glass) well into the next century. In London the silver labels revival started with the arrival of high neo-classical style in around 1775, but in the north of Britain it seems to have suffered a delay of about ten years. Langlands and Robertson copied, in a rather provincial manner, several designs from the best London makers (see fig. 746, SHERRY by Langlands and Robertson, 1786-95)[29] with occasional moments of greater creativity (see fig. 745, SHERRY also by Langlands and Robertson, 1786-95), but after 1790 there was a glorious flowering of original design among the other specialists. Robert Scott produced some beautiful and superbly worked labels (see fig. 748, SHERRY by Robert Scott, 1790-93) as did his erstwhile partner, Robert Pinkney[30] and Ann Robertson (see figs. 747 and 749, LISBON and BRANDY by Ann Robertson, 1801-11). Fig. 749 is another rare example of a provincial armorial label. The crest, which is an integral part of the design, 'a swan, proper, dexter foot on an ogress', is restricted to the family of Clarke of County Durham. Most of the more distinctive label designs made in Newcastle around the turn of the eighteenth and nineteenth centuries tend to favour a crescent with either an openwork surmount or pierced, sometimes conjoined, horns.[31]

The Newcastle assay office did not apply a full set of hallmarks to small goods such as wine labels after 1790, as was the case in London, so labels made from 1784 until 1820 and later will normally be struck only with a maker's mark, a lion passant and a duty mark – but no town mark or date letter. While this practice presents some difficulties in attribution and precise dating, the makers' marks are accurately recorded, easily identifiable and, in this period, had a relatively short life.

Few Newcastle wine labels of truly original design were made in the Regency or late Georgian style, but there are some magnificent exceptions. The rare 'marquis's coronet' was produced by Alexander Kelty between 1803 and 1812 (see fig. 750 for PORT), many years before it was copied in London by the Edwards family. The cusped oval (see fig. 752 for CLARET) by Lewis and Wright, 1812-24, with its distinctive cast border, is also peculiar to Newcastle, but pride of place in the account of the final years of the city's contribution to label design must lie with the large escutcheons surmounted by the city's crest, 'out of a tower, a lion rampant holding a flag' (see fig. 751 for SAUTERNE 1827). These were made by Thomas Watson in 1819 and 1827 for the Corporation of the City of Newcastle and were sold among other 'effects in the Mansion House' by J. and G. Ewart on 6 January 1837. Why the City had to auction its silver and other possessions is not clear, but the catalogue in the Newcastle Museum records that thirty-five 'bottle labels' were sold to Reid and Sons, twenty-four weighing just under 1oz (28g) each and eleven weighing a little more than ¾oz (21g) each, at prices varying between 7s. and 7s.9d. per ounce. Presumably the first twenty-four were the armorial design described above and the remaining eleven of a slightly smaller form, although they would still be fairly substantial – perhaps the same design without chains.

Thanks to the published work and scholarship of Margaret Gill,[32] Newcastle is the most thoroughly researched and recorded provincial assay office in Great Britain. So it is possible to trace the development, relationships and succession of all the firms significantly engaged in label making. In the early period, c.1750 to c.1775, label production was dominated by Robert Makepeace (worked 1720-55), Isaac Cookson (worked 1728-54) and, following the latter's death, his former apprentices and journeymen John Langlands I and John Goodrich, in partnership until Goodrich's death in 1757, whereafter Langlands continued alone.

During the neo-classical period, c.1775 to c.1800, the majority of labels were made by John Langlands I, in partnership with John Robertson I from 1778, and three of his former apprentices namely Robert Scott and Robert Pinkney (in partnership between 1778 and 1790, thereafter alone until 1793 and 1797 respectively) and William Stalker (who, in partnership with John Mitchison (1774-84), had bought the long established business of the Kirkup family, though they produced few labels).

In the Regency and late Georgian periods, c.1800 to c.1830, there are three lines of succession and one newcomer. The partnerships of both Stalker and Mitchison and Pinkney and Scott dovetail into the important firm of Thomas Watson (worked 1793-1845) who had been apprenticed to Stalker in 1783 and turned over to Robert Scott on the former's retirement in 1784. The partnership of Langlands and Robertson split into two soon after Langlands' death in 1793. The Langlands side was continued by John Langlands II (worked 1795-1804) and his widow Dorothy (worked 1804-14); while the Robertson side was continued by John Robertson I until his death in 1801, his widow Ann until 1811 when it was taken over by their son John II (having been apprenticed to Thomas Watson) in partnership with John Walton until 1824 and by the latter alone until 1868. The newcomer was Alexander Kelty who came from London in 1802 and who sold his business in 1812 to George Lewis and John Wright, also from London, whose partnership ended in 1824 whereafter the business was continued by the former alone until 1845.

Few labels would appear to have been made in Newcastle after around 1830 and certainly none of any notable originality. The major makers of silver after this date were the firms of John Walton and Thomas Watson, whose origins have been described above, until their respective cessations in 1868 and 1844, together with that of Reid and Sons, which became the leading retailer in Northern England. Reid and Sons originated with Christian Ker Reid, who came from Scotland and worked for Langlands and Robertson for ten years before entering his own mark in 1791. His eldest son,

Figure 753.

William, married the eldest daughter of Edward Barnard and set up an important London workshop in 1812, and a younger son, David, married the second daughter of Barnard in 1815 and became a partner with his father in the same year. Christian and David made the scroll WHISKEY (see fig. 753) in around 1830 (no date letter or assay office mark stamped). This relationship between the Reid family of Newcastle and the Barnard family of London, one of the largest manufacturers of their day, explains much of the tailing off of locally made silver.[33]

While this survey has concentrated on those aspects of Newcastle design that are peculiar to the northern area of England, it must be stressed that plenty of labels of less obvious regional particularity were also made in the Newcastle area, especially after around 1785. The silversmiths of Carlisle, Durham and Whitehaven are necessarily included in this study of the region as the only evidence of their existence is the registration of their marks at the Newcastle assay office. As can be seen from the following table, labels are known from all three of these northern towns, but none the less they are very rare. Care is needed to avoid confusing the mark of Thomas Wheatley of Carlisle with that of Thomas Watson of Newcastle, as their dates overlap between 1826 and 1844. However, as Wheatley was not markedly active before around 1845 and Watson ceased in 1844, no real confusion should arise.[34]

There follows a list of Newcastle silversmiths showing assay entries referring to labels taken from *A Directory of Newcastle Goldsmiths*,[35] assay office records and examples recorded in the Journal of the Wine Label Circle.

Name	Date on which mark entered	Entry	Business ceased
NEWCASTLE			
BELL, James	1822	Bottle label	1841
COOKSON, Isaac	1728	Bottle label	1754
CRAWFORD, David	1768	Bottle label to Beilby & Bewick for engraving	1784
KELTY, Alexander	1803	Bottle label	1812
KIRKUP, John	1738	Bottle label	1774
LANGLANDS, Dorothy	1804	Bottle label	1814
LANGLANDS John I	1757★	Bottle label	1777
LANGLANDS, John II	1795	Bottle label	1804
LEWIS, George, and WRIGHT, John	1812	Bottle label	1824
LISTER, William	1821	–	1840
LISTER & Sons	1841	–	1884
MAKEPEACE, Robert II	1738	–	1755
MURRAY, George	1805	Bottle label	1816

Name	Date on which mark entered	Entry	Business ceased
PINKEY, Robert	1777★	–	1797
REID, Christian Ker	1783	Bottle label	1819
REID, C.K. & Sons	1819	Bottle label, soy label, spirit label, wine label	1884
ROBERTSON, Ann	1801	Bottle-ticket	1811
ROBERTSON, John I & DARLING, David	1795★	Bottle label	1801
ROBERTSON, John II & WALTON, John	1811	Bottle label	1821
SCOTT, Robert	1790★	–	1793
SEWELL, Thomas	1846	Bottle label	1884
STALKER, William & MITCHISON, John	1774	–	1784
WALTON, John	1820	Bottle label	1868
WATSON, Thomas	1793	Bottle label	1844
WRIGHT, John	1824	Bottle label	1836
CARLISLE			
HUNTINGTON, Thomas	1811	Bottle label	1822
LATIMER, Joseph	1837	Bottle label	1839
ROSS, Thomas & Michael	1839	Bottle label	1843
WHEATLEY, Thomas	1826	Bottle label	c.1860
DURHAM			
THOMPSON, Samuel	1751	–	1785
YORK			
BUCKLE, Joseph	1716	–	1761
BUCKLE, Stephen	1743	–	c.1774
LANGWITH, John	1716	–	c.1743
WHITEHAVEN			
LAMB, James	1748	–	c.1760
SOLOMON, Francis	1775	–	1786

★ Also John Langlands I in partnership with John Robertson I (1778-95), and Robert Pinkney in partnership with Robert Scott (1778-90).

In conclusion it is appropriate to discuss the Beilby and Bewick connection.[36] Thomas Bewick (1753-1828), an artist, tradesman and naturalist, occupies pride of place in the history of British wood engraving, having brought the craft to a state of near perfection, and thus ranks with the greatest illustrators. In 1767 Thomas Bewick was apprenticed to Ralph Beilby, the only engraver in Newcastle at that time. Ralph Beilby was the son of a Durham silversmith and brother of William and Mary Beilby, who are best known to collectors of English domestic glass for their enamel decorating. He was also a qualified drawing master.

In his *Memoir*,[37] Bewick describes his master's workshop as 'being filled with the coarsest kind of steel stamps, pipe moulds, bottle moulds, brass clock faces, door plates, coffin plates, bookbinder's letters, and stamps, steel, silver and gold seals and mourning rings etc. He also undertook the engraving of arms, crests and cyphers on silver and every kind of job from the silversmiths. He excelled in ornamental silver engraving and as far as I am able to judge, he was one of the best in the kingdom.'

'In due course', Bewick continues, 'I had a greater share of better and nicer work given to me to execute, such as mottoes on the inside and outside of rings and crests on silver.'

Bewick's apprenticeship expired in October 1774 when he left his master and returned home. He appears to have had plenty of work there until the summer of 1776, when he went to London. In June 1777 he returned to Newcastle where 'I set to work upon my wood cuts. This, however, was interrupted by other jobs and silversmiths also began to press their jobs upon me. I had not, however, been long at work for myself till proposals were made to me to join in partnership with my late master and this was brought about by a mutual friend John Robertson the silversmith.'

The partnership lasted for twenty years from 1777, during which period, Bewick continued, 'our main supporters in the silver engraving were John Langlands and his partner John Robertson'. In 1797 the partnership ended. Bewick carried on alone until 1812 when he took his son Robert into partnership.

It is recorded that in 1768 David Crawford sent a bottle label to Beilby and Bewick for engraving. The account books for Ralph Beilby and Thomas Bewick show that the following label makers sent them work: David Crawford, David Darling, John Kirkup, Dorothy Langlands, John Langlands I, Langlands and Robertson, John Langlands II, William Lister I, Christian K. Reid I, C.K. Reid and Sons, Ann Robertson, Robertson and Darling, Thomas Watson and John Wright. The workshop also made many of the punches used by these silversmiths.

PART 5 – YORK

The story of wine labels from York is easier to relate than that of some of the other provincial cities, because the assay office here was closed during the middle years of the eighteenth century while the label was emerging as a standard article of silverware. Earlier history need not concern us, except to remember that there was a guild of silversmiths in York as long ago as 1270, and York was one of the earliest places outside London to be granted the 'touch' in the fifteenth century. By 1698, therefore, when all the provincial offices were ordered to be closed by William III's Act of 1697, York silversmiths had a wonderful record stretching back four hundred years, and York silver had a distinction and character that were immediately recognisable. At this time a number of silversmiths were using the assay office, but when the office reopened some three years later, the fire seemed

Figures 754-759.

already to have died, because it only lasted sixteen years before lack of interest caused it to cease operating again. It reopened once more in 1776 and from then on its history is almost entirely that of one firm, Hampston and Prince, and the successive names under which it flourished, until the irregular practices of John Burrell, the Assay Master, and the death of the firm's only surviving partner, James Barber, in 1857, led to final and permanent closure in the following year.

This sequence of events should make a study of York's later silver in general, and the labels in particular, comparatively simple, but matters are complicated by the almost complete lack of records and by the increasingly unorthodox methods of the men who came to be responsible for the governance of the craft, and of the silversmiths themselves. It is fair to say, however, that, despite the lax assaying discovered by the Commission of Investigation of 1851/55, which led them to recommend that the office be closed, they could not actually point to any substandard articles. This absence of records is very frustrating. A letter from the Birmingham assay office in 1957 indicates that Jackson must have had access to many papers that have now disappeared, and it refers too to a 'small brass plate' on which hall-marks were stamped. One can only hope that one day they will come to light again.

When the office fell into disuse in about 1713, there seem to have been only two silversmiths using it – Joseph Buckle and John Langwith. These two made arrangements in 1716 to have their silver assayed in Newcastle,[38] which they must have thought an easier journey than the road across the Pennines to Chester, or the two hundred mile haul to London, with highwayman Dick Turpin lurking along the route. For sixty years no silver was marked in York and apprentices must have learnt their craft elsewhere. One case we can trace is that of Stephen Buckle, who was apprenticed by father Joseph to Isaac Cookson in Newcastle. He became free by service in 1740 and returned to York, where he became a freeman of that city too. He took over his father's business and was evidently manufacturing as well as retailing; the Newcastle registers show pieces sent by him for assay between 1743 and 1748. The WHITE-WINE label by him (see fig. 754), which is one of a pair, has his 'SB' mark on its own, as does a third more typical escutcheon with the same mark (see fig. 770 for LISBON). They all show some Newcastle influence, and ought, perhaps, to be defined as Newcastle pieces, since that is where his mark is recorded on the Newcastle copperplate. Nevertheless, Buckle worked in York, and these labels can therefore properly claim to be the earliest examples made by a York silversmith. They can be dated to around 1748, or earlier, at which time labels were still exempt from assay, so he may not have considered it necessary to include them in the parcels he sent for assay. The Buckles thus provide a slender link between the ancient Goldsmiths' Guild of York and the eighty years of activity, from the 1770s to 1858, which this part of the chapter reviews.

The link is forged more strongly by Richard Clark, who took over Stephen Buckle's business in 1774 and with John Hampston and John Prince restarted the manufacture of plate in the city. Jackson lists forty names during this closed period, but there is no evidence that any of them except Stephen Buckle were practising silversmiths, until Hampston and Prince in 1776. Clearly, however, in a city of growing prosperity there must have been quite a demand for silver, so presumably the other names are those of repairers or retailers, importing wares from London or perhaps from Newcastle. There are clear signs of both London and Newcastle influence on York silver when it began to appear again. Newcastle silversmiths, however, were a bit touchy in their relations with other places and, as the journey to London became easier, men such as John Beckwith, a leading retailer in 1765, seem to have preferred to visit the capital for their goods. A list of the articles that he brought back for his customers about that time, however, makes no mention of labels or bottle-tickets. When Beckwith died in 1770, James Hampston and John Prince, who were already in some sort of business and may have been thinking of starting a workshop, acquired his stock. But the Parliamentary Commission, which in 1773 visited York and other towns to investigate the state of the provincial silversmiths (following requests by the manufacturers of Birmingham and Sheffield to be allowed their own assay offices), reported that there was then no office in York, nor any evidence of attempts to have one.

The trade advertisements of Hampston and Prince show that they quickly started to put their plans for restarting manufacture into practice and it cannot have been long before the re-opening of the assay office became an important issue too. Together with Richard Clark, who was also

The Provinces - York

Figures 760-769.

advertising as a working silversmith, they must have seen it as a matter of civic pride that the city should have the facility for assaying its own wares, besides it being far more convenient than using Newcastle or elsewhere.

There was another factor looming too. In 1773 Parliament accepted the petition of silversmiths in Sheffield to set up their own assay office. Sheffield was growing as the centre of the metal industry. It offered advantages for the setting up of new businesses that York did not have, and it was only fifty miles away. York must act to protect its interests. Fortunately for Hampston and Prince, they had no need to promote legislation in order to reopen the office, as Matthew Boulton in Birmingham and his Sheffield colleagues had to do, because the York office had never formally closed. In 1716 people had just stopped using it. All Hampston and Prince had to do was to find suitable premises – in fact they may well have used part of their own shop at first – have the necessary punches struck and have someone appointed as Assay Master. The date when it actually re-opened is not known for certain, but Martin Gubbins[39] has shown that York's cycle of date letters must have commenced in 1776 and concludes logically that this year marks the re-start of its activities.

By then wine labels had become established dining room accessories and there was certainly a demand for them locally, as the inventories of the silver acquired by the Sykes family for their house at Sledmere, near Hull, makes clear.[40] Between 1740 and 1780 their plate, which included wine labels, came from Newcastle or London, but they then turned to Hampston and Prince, one of their first orders being for a set of escutcheon labels (see fig. 771 for CYDER, *c*.1780 with mark HP conjoined), a design that had gone out of fashion in London by then, but tastes in the province lingered on. It is worth commenting on the decoration of this label, which consisted of the standard motif of grapes, vine leaves and tendrils. This can be compared with a more appropriate apples and apple leaf motif employed by S. Drinkwater on his CYDER label, 1750, and on OSP 'copperbacks' of the same date.

The Provinces - York

Figure 770.

Figure 771.

Figure 772.

Sadly we have very little information about the early years of the industry's second incarnation as no records or assay office ledgers have survived, except for one volume between 1805 and 1821.[41] Certainly much plate exists which has dates of the last quarter of the century, and wine labels, too, can be firmly assigned to this period by their style, even though they have no date letters. Before 1791, of course, they did not have to be fully hallmarked or dated, but it is of interest that York makers did not put a date letter on their labels before the time of William IV and even then only sometimes.

When they opened their business in the 1770s, Hampston and Prince relied on London, and to an extent Newcastle, for their label designs. They made straightforward copies of escutcheons (see fig. 756 for LISBON, 1784-85 with mark H&P) and crescents (see fig. 775 for R-PORT, *c*.1780, with mark HP conjoined) that were already going out of fashion. They also produced a more contemporary domed rectangle (see fig. 776 for RUM marked H&P, similar to CLARET marked I.H/I.P in quatrefoil) and Prince of Wales feathers/crescent design (see fig. 777 for W:WINE marked I.H/I.P in octagon),[42] borrowed from the Bateman family. They used fairly heavy-gauge metal and their labels have a robustness that has characterised York silver from its earliest days. A Newcastle influence can be seen in the large initial capital letters often found in the titles (see fig. 757 for RED PORT, *c*.1787, with mark IP.IH).

It did not take them long, however, to introduce ideas of their own. The large rectangular label with humped upper edge (see fig. 758 for CLARET by J. Hampston and J. Prince, *c*.1787, following their earlier design for MADEIRA, *c*.1780, with lion passant and HP conjoined) is peculiar to York and has been noted in several variations, including one with a shield mounted above to take a crest (see fig. 759 for SHERRY by R. Cattle and J. Barber, *c*.1808). Their kidney-shaped MALMSEY MADEIRA (see fig. 760) is distinctive and makes unusual use of script lettering for the name. It has a very early 'JHP' conjoined mark that may predate the opening of the assay office in 1776. Another individual design is their CLARET in large silhouette letters, the reverse of piercing (see fig. 761), which must date from around 1796 to 1805, marked H.P.C. incuse for Hampston, Prince and Cattle. Their rectangles (see fig. 772 for FRONTINAC, *c*.1790, by Hampston and Prince) are large and solid, and after 1786/87 have noticeably broadly cut corners, another feature reminiscent of Newcastle. At the same time they persisted with sharp-cornered rectangles, usually in smaller sizes, for many years after they had been superseded in London.

In 1796 Robert and George Cattle joined Hampston and Prince and the firm's mark became 'HP&Cs'. John Hampston died in 1805 and two years later John Prince fades out of the picture. George Cattle disappears too and, left on his own, Robert Cattle took James Barber into the firm. Barber quickly came to dominate the scene and from 1814, when he became the senior partner, he was the leading personality in the silver business in York, and remained so for the next forty-three years.

Barber brought changes, not only to management but also to production. Hitherto plate had come mainly from the firm's own workshop, but Barber started to make increasing use of London manufacturers, his principal source being the leading London firm of Emes and Barnard. They sent him both unfinished and finished goods. The former, to be completed by Barber in York, and assayed there, would be commoner items, including standard designs of labels (see fig. 773 for MARSALLA by J. Barber and W. North, *c*.1840). It would not concern them that their designs were being marketed under Barber's mark, for in fact he was acting as sponsor rather than maker, and in any case Emes and Barnard were themselves employing outside manufacturers for many of the wares that went out under their own names. More elaborate labels, for which they might feel the credit should

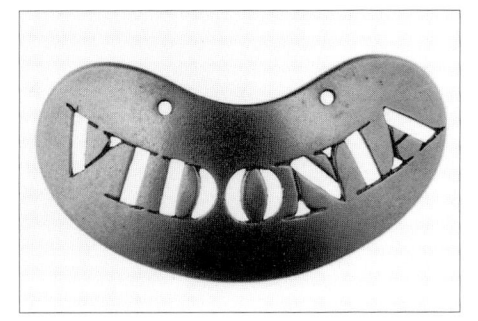

Figure 773. *Figure 774.* *Figure 775.*

remain theirs, were more likely to be sent up in a finished condition, already assayed. This might explain why a popular design such as the 'five-barred gate', a label closely tied to Emes and Barnard's name, and which Barber could well have been expected to find a market for, has not been recorded with a York mark. There are exceptions: the large cartouche (see fig. 763 for CLARET by R. Cattle and J. Barber, c.1811) with panther's head, is a handsome label usually associated with T. Wallis and J. Hayne (though it quite probably came through Emes and Barnard's hands). In this case it was apparently finished in York, and marketed under the assay of R. Cattle and J. Barber in about 1811.

A fair number of labels have survived with the marks of Barber's various partnerships between 1814 and 1847 – William Whitwell (see figs. 762 and 779), Robert Cattle (see figs. 759 and 763), George Cattle II and William North (see fig. 774 for VIDONIA, c.1825, bears the mark for Barber, Cattle and North). Until Whitwell's death in 1823, mildly innovative ideas continued to appear, such as CLARET illustrated at fig. 762. It has the mark of Barber and Whitwell's partnership between 1814 and 1823. This partnership also produced the cushion style GIN illustrated by fig. 779. After that nothing new emerges. The labels of Barber, Cattle and North are usually copies of existing designs, if made in York, or bought-in stock from London. To what extent Sheffield with its fresh designs, more cheaply produced, was supplanting the lethargic remains of the industry in York is not well documented, but there is no evidence that Barber was dealing with manufacturers in that city. After North left the partnership in 1847 Barber was on his own, but evidently doing very little business. It has to be remembered that this was a time of decline for the wool industry, which meant so much to the county's prosperity, and so general demand for silver was presumably slack anyway. So far as labels are concerned, there seems to have been hardly any demand at all.

In his remaining ten years only a couple of labels with Barber's mark are recorded, and just a couple more by the only other active silversmith, John Bell (see fig. 765, appropriately for WHISKEY, c.1850). Furthermore, the assay office had fallen into disarray. A visiting Committee of Inspection from Goldsmiths' Hall in London reported in 1851 that the tools were kept in a box in a public house; they were rusty and the Assay Master did not know how to use them. The committee recommended that the office be suppressed and so it certainly would have been if Barber had not died shortly afterwards in 1857. His son, Silburn, was a farmer and he sold the business to a retailer eighteen months after his father's death. The single letter gothic style 'H' (see fig. 764) has Barber's mark (but is probably a London label). It has the date letter 'x' for 1858/59, the last to be recorded. It is presumed that the office closed in 1858 and certainly no more silver was manufactured in York.

There remain to be mentioned some of the lesser craftsmen who were active during these eighty years. Some ten firms have been noted whose marks have been found on wine labels between c.1776 and c.1830. Pre-eminent after Hampston and Price was Richard Clark, who shares with them credit for re-establishing silver manufacture in the city. He was advertising as a 'working goldsmith' as early as 1774, after taking over the premises of Stephen Buckle (q.v.). Labels by him are known from the mid-1780s, usually rectangular, with typical broadly cut corners, but often narrower (see fig. 766 for LISBON, c.1787) than those of Hampston and Price. He borrowed a design of James Phipps, his double scroll (see fig. 769 for CLARET, c.1787), giving it a simple reeded border instead of Phipps' familiar bright-cut. This label has an interesting aberration in the hallmarking, the lion passant facing to sinister, for which no good explanation has been suggested. It was probably just a mistake: it has also been noted occasionally on Newcastle labels.

In 1795 Clark passed his business on to one of his apprentices, William Astley (who made a label for

Figure 776.

Figure 777.

BRANDY, c.1797-1810). Astley has several entries in the only surviving assay office register between 1805 and 1812 for batches of wine labels, so it is quite likely that he sent others in earlier years. None of his labels is dated, however, so we cannot be sure. He was bankrupt by 1812 and although he resumed business later nothing much is known of his later output. Another early working silversmith was William Etherington. He was one of the very few who were not connected in some way with either Richard Clark or Hampston and Prince, setting up independently in about 1785. Examples of labels made by him are an escutcheon with distinctive touches and a medium sized oval, a shape seldom noted in York (see fig. 767 for BRANDY, c.1787). He seems to have migrated to Salford ten years later, where he evidently teamed up with another obscure maker with a York connection, one Jonas Crossley. An 'IC' mark accompanied by a York style lion passant is on a curious pair of labels that can be dated to around 1800 (see fig. 768 for SHERRY), and which are part of a group of five, the others being a pair by Barber and Whitwell, of about 1814, and a later one with Barber and North's mark, of about 1835. Jonas Crossley is the only York silversmith to whom these initials can be attributed. Another maker from outside the mainstream was William Cattell, who may have come from London. His mark is found in a few undistinguished labels between around 1816 and 1825.

Only two of the sixteen apprentices taken on by Hampston and Prince are known to have become working silversmiths after completing their indentures: James Barber, whose long career we have noted earlier, and Edward Jackson. The latter sent in a few batches of labels in the early 1820s before becoming bankrupt in 1824 and moving on to other fields. Christopher Watson was an employee of Hampston and Prince until 1814, when he set up on his own. He sent small batches of labels for assay at intervals thereafter, which have certain characteristics, but are of no great merit. One of his apprentices was John Bell, whose mark has been noted on a small number of labels during the late 1840s and early 1850s, apparently of local manufacture (see fig. 765), as indicated above.

That concludes the story of the silversmiths who brought a second life to their industry in York and their successors who finally let it die of apathy eighty years later. Examples of the labels they made are illustrated,[43] and it remains to make some assessment of them as a whole. The titles that have been recorded are generally those that would be expected, but there is a satisfying wide range of unusual wines to supplement the PORTS and MADEIRAS that predominate. The labels commissioned from Hampston and Prince for Sledmere, for instance, include SMYRNA (see fig. 755, c.1780) and SYRGIS (see fig. 780, c.1780), as well as RHENISH, MOUNTAIN and PAXARETTE. Labels for spirits are less common than among London makers, WHISKEY (see fig. 765), in particular, being seldom found. Designs that may be considered peculiar to York have already been discussed, and it is fair to add that even standard designs from London, when made locally, usually display characteristics that point to York as their place of origin (for example, VIN-DE-GRAVE by Hampston and Prince, marked H&P, king's head incuse, lion passant and leopard's head crowned, c.1785). Rectangles with their broadly cut corners are the most notable examples, but York ovals and crescents can often be picked out, too. Single letters are rare. None of the early design with engraved or pierced letters has been noted,[44] and only very occasionally have cut-out letters in the style of Rawlings and Summers been seen, but see fig. 764 for a very late gothic example by John Barber in 1858-59.

Estimating the total output of York labels is made difficult by the lack of records. There is just the one Register, covering the years from 1805 to 1821, which has details of silver sent for assay. It is examined in detail below, and has the names of seven firms who were making wine labels – Prince and Cattle, which was by then the description of the original Hampston and Prince partnership, have entries for every year but one. The pattern continues when Barber takes over. Out of the total of 315 labels sent for assay, they account for 242 (seventy-seven per cent). If we extrapolate Prince and Cattle's productivity rate back from 1805 to c.1776, taking into account that the firm was expanding from scratch, that Richard Clark – Astley's predecessor – was the only other major firm active, and that this was a period of increasing interest in wine labels, it would be reasonable to suggest that the Hampston and Prince's output during these thirty years may have reached 450 labels. William Astley sent in forty-one labels up to 1812, when he went bankrupt (thirteen per cent). His output is fairly steady during these years, and one might assume that his rate of production was much the same for the years since 1795, when he started business. By the same argument, Astley and Clark may have contributed one hundred labels. If we add in the few minor makers active then we might reach a total of some six hundred labels up to 1805.

If we apply the same process to Barber's partnerships between 1821 and 1858, allowing for diminishing activity in later years, it seems doubtful that the firm made more than two hundred labels during these years, and the four minor firms perhaps another fifty. These may be generous estimates, and a reasonable figure for the whole eighty years of the assay office life is likely to be about one thousand labels. Perusal of sale catalogues and other sources indicates that the whereabouts of around two hundred of these are known today. Even if one assumes a fifty per cent loss rate, there seem to be a large number of labels still unaccounted for.

The surviving book[45] from the York assay office is entitled 'Duty paid on Manufactured Gold and Silver at the Assay Office, York, by Virtue of an Act of Parliament made in the 24th Year of His Majesty George the Third'. It covers the period from 4 January 1805 to 19 April 1821, just over sixteen years. The book came to the Minster Library more or less by accident. Someone brought it in as a scrapbook into which had been pasted some old newspaper cuttings about church organs. When the librarian examined it he found it was one of the lost assay books; the cuttings were carefully removed and are now also preserved with the book. Fortunately not many of the pages had been pasted over. The book is mentioned in *Old English Plate* by W.J. Cripps,[46] wherein it is said that the register book of the assay office from 1805 to 1821 'is now in the possession of Canon Raine'. Presumably it disappeared after that and was a scrapbook until its reappearance.

The layout of the book is similar to those at Exeter.[47] The book provided a day by day record of parcels of work entered, with details of the maker, the articles to be assayed, their gross weight, the duty, and the net duty paid after the one sixth allowance had been made.

Not many makers sent in work during the period 1805 to 1821. Only thirteen separate names are mentioned and of these three are mentioned only once. Seven entered wine labels. The first and last mentions of the makers are given below:

Name	First mention	Last mention	Wine labels	Comments
William Astley	1805	1821	Yes	Gold and silver
Prince & Cattle	1805	1807	Yes	Gold and silver
G. B. Booth	1806	1815		From Selby; made only gold rings
Goodman Gainsford	1807	1809		From Sheffield; two mentions only, for silver
Robert Cattle	1807	1807		One mention
Cattle & Barber	1807	1814	Figs. 245, 759, 763	Gold and silver
L. Creasen	1809	1809		One mention; gold rings
Messrs Roberts Cadman	1809	1809		One mention; silver
Barber & Whitwell	1814	1821	Figs. 762, 779	Gold and silver
C. Watson	1815	1821	Yes	Gold and silver
William Cattell	1816	1821	Yes	Gold and silver
G. Addinell	1817	1820		Gold worker
Edward Jackson	1817	1821	Yes	Gold and silver

The Provinces - York

Not too much significance should be attached to some of these first and last dates, owing to the relatively short time span covered by the book. Some makers were obviously at work before the book began and some continued after it finished.

At some periods Barber and Whitwell are entered as Barber and Co., for example in 1817 and 1820, sometimes in the same hand on the same page. The progression of the firms bearing the names Prince, Cattle, Barber and Whitwell is interesting. The last mention of Prince and Cattle is on 20 October 1807, while Cattle and Barber appear for the first time on 27 December 1807. Presumably two months were needed to form a new partnership. However, in the intervening period Robert Cattle has his sole entry on 4 December 1807. Did Prince die in October? At the next change of partnership in 1814 the changeover was arranged more expeditiously. On 22 June Cattle and Barber are mentioned for the last time, but Barber and Whitwell appear as soon as 4 July.

For a couple of typical years (1809 and 1819) comparisons have been made between the outputs of the leading workers, as shown below:

Year	Maker	Silver Weight (oz.)	No. of mentions	Gold Weight (oz.)	No. of mentions
1808	Astley	275	25	54	27
1808	Cattle & Barber	4874	17	65	7
1819	Astley	18	17	19	23
1819	Barber & Whitwell	6345	52	20	9
1819	Jackson	1280	53	7	5
1819	Watson	4	3	3	3

This table shows that Watson and Astley were smallworkers, which is borne out by a list of their typical products. Jackson, Cattle and Barber, and Barber and Whitwell, on the other hand, made both large and small articles.

A total of 315 labels are recorded in the book, their distribution by makers and years being shown as follows:

Year	W. Astley	Prince & Cattle	Cattle & Barber	Barber & Whitwell	C. Watson	W. Cattell	E. Jackson	Annual Total
1804-05	6	3						9
1805-06	5	1						6
1806-07		44(1)						44
1807-08	11		25					36
1808-09	9		9					18
1809-10	4		3					7
1810-11	6		19					25
1811-12			6					6
1812-13			6(2)					6
1813-14			18					18
1814-15				4				4
1815-16				4(3)	10			14
1816-17				5				5
1817-18				8				8
1818-19							3	3
1819-20				71(4)	3		6(5)	80+
1820-21				16	2	8		26
Totals	**41**	**48**	**86**	**108**	**15**	**8**	**9**	**315+**

(1) One entry is for '3 doz and 4 silver labels'.
(2) One entry includes '2 tickets; 2 labels'. This has been counted as four labels.
(3) One entry includes 'castor top and label', counted as one label.
(4) One entry is for '6 chasd labels, 30 shelld ditto'.
(5) One entry is for an unspecified number of labels, counted as at least two for this table. Another entry is for '2 caddy labels', not counted in this table.

Figure 779.   *Figure 780.*

It is assumed that the date letter changed in August, according to Martin Gubbins.[48]

There were one or two entries for 'caddy labels' *[sic]* but it may be that some of the other entries also contained 'caddy labels' if by that term is meant small silver rectangles for tacking on to wooden tea caddies, but it may well be a mis-reading or mis-spelling of 'caddy ladles' meaning caddy spoons. It is also interesting to question the difference between tickets (which appeared only once, in 1812) and labels.

The table, which may help with the dating of labels not fully marked, shows that in the sixteen year period at least 315 labels were produced with a considerable fluctuation in annual totals. The peak year with eighty or more was 1819-20, followed by 1806-07 with forty-four. The smallest annual outputs were in 1818-19 with only three labels, and 1814-15 with only four. The largest producers, who also featured most often in the book, were the partnerships bearing the names Prince/Cattle/Barber/Whitwell, who between them made seventy-seven per cent of the York labels of this period.

It is a strange coincidence that during the same period at Exeter a closely similar number of labels were recorded, 306, and there too the fluctuations were large, from eighty-five and forty-three in the peak years to zero production in 1812-13 and 1814-15. Thus the pattern of demand seems to have been fairly similar in both these provincial centres.

During the period covered by the book there were seventy-one entries mentioning labels. The spelling of the word varied from the usual 'label' to 'labell' (eight times from 1815 onwards) and 'lable' (twice, in 1809 and 1817). The labels were usually sent in fairly small numbers, as at Exeter. The details are given below:

No of labels per parcel	PARCELS No.	% of total	LABELS No.	% of total
1	17	24	17	5
2	16	23	32	10
3	9	13	27	9
4	12	17	48	15
5	2	3	10	3
6	5	7	30	10
7	2	3	14	5
8	0	0	0	0
9	1	1	9	3
10	2	3	20	6
Over 10 (2)	4	6	106	34
Total	**70**	**100**	**313 (1)**	**100**

(1) This table excludes the entry for an unspecified number of labels, counted as two in the preceding table.

(2) The largest parcels contained forty, thirty-six, eighteen and twelve labels.

As with the Exeter records, parcels of six, four and three labels seemed fairly popular after singles and pairs; seventy-seven per cent of York entries are for parcels of one to four labels (compared with Exeter seventy-eight per cent, Wakelin ledgers sixty-four per cent) and this represented thirty-nine per cent of the label production (Exeter fifty-one per cent). It does seem that the manufacturing patterns in the two towns were very similar – perhaps not altogether surprising as the type of customer must have been fairly similar. It would be interesting to know whether London, as the fashionable metropolis, differed markedly from the provinces; unfortunately we are unlikely to find out because Goldsmiths' Hall does not have this type of detailed day-to-day record.

On only seven occasions do the parcels of work contain labels only; the details are as follows:

Date	Maker	No. of labels	Gross weight (oz. dwt)	(g)	Average weight per label	Net duty paid (s.d.)
15 May 1808	W. Astley	10	1.15	54.4	5.4	1.10½
20 Oct 1815	C. Watson	2	0.19	29.5	14.8	1. 2½
5 Dec 1815	C. Watson	1	0.08	12.4	12.4	0. 6
15 Dec 1818	E. Jackson	3	0.15	23.3	7.8	0.11¾
23 Dec 1819	C. Watson	3	0.09	14.0	4.7	0. 6¾
5 Dec 1820	W. Cattell	4	1.08	43.5	10.9	1. 9
23 Jan 1821	W. Cattell	4	1.02	34.2	8.6	1. 4½

The label weight varied between about 5g and 15g, similar to Exeter, with the average being 7.8g (about ¼oz). The duty paid was only 2¼d. per label for Astley's small 1808 labels. For Watson's smaller 1819 labels the duty was also 2¼d., but the rate had increased from 1s.3d. to 1s.6d. per ounce in 1814.

York labels are found quite rarely, less frequently than Exeter labels. Yet in light of the information revealed by the assay book this is perhaps surprising for the following reason. In the period covered by the York assay book almost the same number of labels were entered in York and Exeter, about three hundred; in the case of Exeter this was thirty per cent of total recorded production. The Exeter assay office closed in 1883 while that in York closed in 1858. However between 1858 and 1883 only twenty-one labels were entered in Exeter, and prior to 1805 only thirty-two labels were entered. In other words, the great majority of Exeter labels, about 950 (ninety-five per cent), were produced between 1805 and 1858.

Since between 1805 and 1821 the pattern and quantity of output was very similar in York and Exeter, the question arises – what happened after 1821 in York, before its closure in 1858, to make it different from Exeter? Or should one be looking for another 650 York labels? It is known that irregularities, such as plate being marked without assay, occurred in later years at York, but none the less work was produced.

Perhaps this question can be answered by reference to the relative amounts produced in the two cities after 1821. Detailed figures are not to hand, but it is known (from Cripps) that, whereas in York during the five years 1843 to 1848 an average of only 2,000oz of silver was assayed, in Exeter in 1848 no less than 44,500oz was stamped – twenty-two times as much. It would be interesting to compare total amounts of silver assayed for the years for which records for both cities exist. Perhaps labels were a higher proportion of output in York than in Exeter.

One can account for some fifty to sixty labels. It is estimated that two hundred labels or less have survived. It is estimated that some 315 labels were made between 1805 and 1821; rather more were made during the previous thirty years, and possibly rather fewer in the final period. So the total number of labels made at York may have been as high as 1,000, as mentioned earlier, but more likely not so many. Apart from the principal firm active throughout the eighty years, one can be certain of only seven other makers; a label output of this size from so limited a source might seem to be stretching their capacity rather far and might also lead to unfair conclusions concerning the habits of the gentlemen of York. But even so, two hundred labels or less is still possibly only a fifth of the total, and this does seem a small proportion to have survived. Perhaps there are more yet to appear.

It cannot be claimed that the labels made by York silversmiths are outstanding for their design, but they are certainly distinctive, and even when they are simply copying London patterns they have touches of their own. York workmanship is always of high standard. This is true from the earliest labels of Hampston and Prince, and even the very late WHISKEY of John Bell (see fig. 765), which dates from about 1850, and so is among the last to be made in the city, has an unusual feature in the tick marks around the title.[49]

Brief biographical notes on York label makers are given below. Jackson (1921 and 1989) lists a number of silversmiths between around 1735 and around 1858 for whom no mark is recorded, and it is likely that they were retailers rather than working goldsmiths. The following list contains the names of those with recorded marks who are known to have manufactured wine labels:

Stephen Buckle
Son of Joseph Buckle (active from 1715). Apprenticed to Isaac Cookson in Newcastle. Free 1739 in Newcastle and 1740 in York. Assayed in Newcastle 1743 and 1748. See figs. 754 and 770.

Richard Clark
Apprenticed to J. Malton. Free 1769. Took over Buckle's business in 1774. Retired 1797. See figs. 766 and 769.

William Astley
Apprenticed to Clark. Took over his business 1797. Bankrupt 1812, but in business until c.1824.

John Hampston and John Prince
Took over business of Ambrose Beckwith in 1770. Re-opened assay office in 1776. Beckwith had been active from 1748 and Beckwith's father, Joseph, had been active from around 1690. See figs. 755-758, 760, 771-772, 775-777 and 780.

J. Hampston, J. Prince, G. Cattle I and R. Cattle
In 1796 the firm became Hampston, Prince and Cattles until 1804. See fig. 761.

Prince and Cattles
From 1804 to 1807, when G. Cattle died.

R. Cattle and J. Barber
James Barber was apprenticed to Cattle, then as a partner from 1808 to 1814. See figs. 245, 759 and 763.

J. Barber and W. Whitwell
From 1814 to 1823. See figs. 762 and 779.

J. Barber, G. Cattle II and William North
From 1824 to 1836. See fig. 774.

J. Barber and W. North
From 1836 to 1847. See fig. 773.

J. Barber
From 1847 to 1857. See fig. 764.

Edward Jackson
Apprenticed to Hampston and Prince. Free 1807. Active from 1817 to 1821.

Christopher Watson
With Hampston and Prince from c.1803. Active from 1814 to c.1844.

John Bell
Apprenticed to Watson and in partnership with him 1832 to 1844 (but no labels), then alone from 1844 to c.1864. See fig. 765.

William Cattell
Came from London *c*.1815. Active from *c*.1816 to *c*.1821.

William Etherington
Active in York from 1786 to *c*.1794, and then in Manchester and Salford alone and with Jonas Crossley until 1807, and then alone. Labels with Etherington's mark appear to be from the first York, period. See fig. 767.

Jonas Crossley
Active in Manchester and Salford from 1794 alone and with Etherington. His mark seen on labels assayed in York in *c*.1800. See fig. 768.

PART 6 – BIRMINGHAM

Although goldsmiths in Birmingham produced goods from earliest times, prior to 1773 it was necessary for them to be sent to London or Chester for assaying. This meant long journeys. There were often delays and goods were frequently returned damaged. It is possible that labels were included in these parcels from the 1730s[50] onwards, but none has been positively identified.

In 1773 Birmingham was granted a charter to establish its own assay office in Newhall Street, chiefly due to the drive, energy and vision of one man – Matthew Boulton – who revolutionised the making of silver (throughout Europe and America) in two ways.

Firstly, he introduced die-stamping machines. He did not invent the process, but he was quick to perceive how it could be used to speed up manufacture of many small articles, such as wine labels, and economise in the amount of metal used. With dies, which were cut in reverse on hardened steel, he could obtain a crisper result showing more detail and intricacy in the pattern than had been possible with cast or raised manufacture. Furthermore, dies could be used repeatedly without losing definition.[51]

Secondly, Boulton adopted new methods for selecting and training his craftsmen, a system of 'division of labour' that raised their standards and their wages. In his new Soho Factory he could now increase production, reduce manufacturing times and still keep up the quality of his wares.

1762-73
In 1762 Boulton had entered into partnership with John Fothergill and they celebrated the opening of the Birmingham assay office on 31 August 1773 by submitting a parcel of 841oz (23.84kg) of silver. There is no record that labels were included in this parcel, but in the following month of September 1773 the first entry for labels was made. It weighed 10dwt (14g) and was in a parcel of silver weighing over 101oz (2.86kg). On 12 October 1773 they sent forty-five bottle-tickets and on 21 December 1773 a further forty-seven bottle-tickets were dispatched weighing 16oz 6dwt 12grs (about 463g). In May 1774 they sent in nineteen labels weighing 10oz 3dwt (288g).

1773-79
As regards assay records, for the period 1773-79 the assay record daybook shows that Boulton and Fothergill submitted 280 bottle-tickets (ninety-two in 1773-74, seventy-eight during 1774-75, forty-six during 1775-76 and sixty-five during 1776-77). A drapery festoon design was made for CALCAVALLA and FRONTINIAC (see fig. 781) in 1774 and a cushion shape for MOUNTAIN (see fig. 782) in 1775. In the same period John Moore submitted fifty-one bottle-tickets, and James Burbridge submitted seven 'bottle labels' weighing 1oz 9dwt (13 September 1774), none of which seems to have survived.

1779-94
From 1779 to 1794 there appears to be a gap, both in the assay office records and indeed in surviving labels. From 1794 to 1839 the only record available at present is that obtained from sales

The Provinces - Birmingham

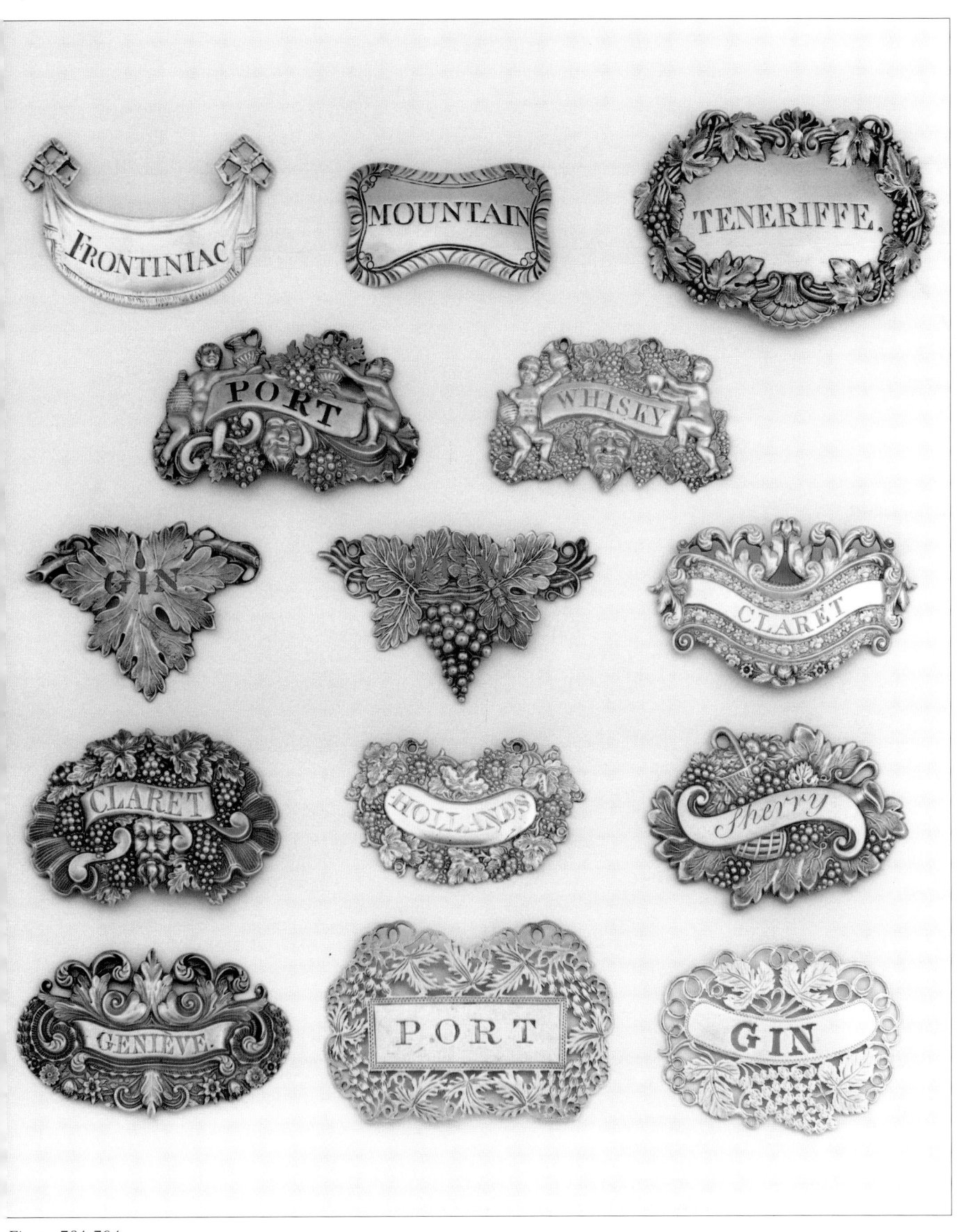

Figures 781-794.

catalogues and journals, which at least give some idea of the number of labels still known today and, although far from complete, give some guide to the silversmiths who made labels and the numbers they produced.

1794-1803
Joseph Taylor (six, including a label for RUM dated 1794), John Thornton (one, see fig. 805, HOLLANDS, 1795), R Mitchell (one), Thomas Willmore (one), W. Bennett (one, see fig. 803, PORT, 1796).

1804-17
Matthew Linwood II (thirty-eight), Joseph Willmore (twenty),[52] Spooner and Coles (one), Wardell and Kempson (one, see fig. 791, SHERRY in script and unusual design, 1814), Unknown (one).[53]

1818-28
Joseph Willmore (forty-five),[54] Joseph Taylor (thirty-eight),[55] Matthew Linwood II (nine), John Bettridge (five), Lawrence and Co. (four),[56] Matthew Boulton and Co. (three), R Mitchell (two),[57] Taylor and Perry (twelve), Sir Edward Thomason (one), Samuel Horton (one), Postans and Tye (one), Turner and Simpson (one), Unknown (one), Francis Clark (one, see fig. 806, GINGER WINE, 1826).

1829-38
Joseph Willmore (forty-six),[58] Taylor and Perry (twenty-five),[59] George Unite (nineteen), Matthew Linwood II (three), Ledsam, Vale and Wheeler (three),[60] Francis Clark (three), John Bower (see fig. 800, PORT, 1829, marked on the face of the label), John Tongue (three), Joseph Taylor (two), James Collins (two), J.C. (one), Sir Edward Thomason (one), Unite and Hilliard (one), Thomas Tyland and Son (one), Unknown (one).

1839-45
The assay office duty books that cover the period 1839 to 1849 have survived. Unfortunately all the entries are composite, for example '1 parcel, buttons, boxes, and labels 40 doz. & 3', so there is no means of knowing how many are labels.

The design of Birmingham labels generally follows those of London silversmiths, as would be expected and in common with the rest of the country, but a range of innovative designs was also introduced. One design apparently peculiar to Birmingham is a thin gauge cartouche consisting of a broad accumulation of delicate tracery or fretwork surrounding a thin scroll or rectangular name panel (see figs. 793 and 794). As examples of die-stamping producing much sharper, more distinct results than was possible with the old casting methods, the 'two putti' labels of Matthew Linwood II or his excellent die-stamper should be noted (see fig. 784). It should be remarked, however, at the same time, that careless die-stamping will result in much less satisfactory results and, unfortunately, there are plenty of these to be seen.

But if there was one design that dominated Birmingham wine label production during the middle years of the century, it was the vine leaf in its many forms – with or without bunches of grapes and tendrils, and with double and triple vine leaves. This again was no doubt because die-stamping enabled the silversmiths to produce crisply cut labels with considerable detail. Yapp and Woodward's single vine leaf for SHERRY of 1856 might have been used for an archery prize as it has a single arrow incorporated across the chain.[61]

Today Birmingham continues to produce large numbers of labels compared with other silver centres. The vast majority originate from Turner and Simpson who distribute to other firms in blank form, allowing them to add their own names, details and marks. This firm is still using some of the original plates purchased at auction by the present owner's forefathers in the last century.

Electroplate certainly had an effect on the market for silver labels.[62] Electroplating was born in Birmingham on 25 March 1840 when George and Henry Elkington patented the process.

The following is a list of some of the more prominent makers in Birmingham:

Matthew Boulton

Matthew Boulton was born in 1728. In 1759 he took over his father's button-making business and in 1762 he learnt and adopted Sheffield plating. He probably never handled a goldsmith's tool in his life, but he built new premises at Soho and had a number of aristocratic contacts. He 'borrowed' designs from James Wyatt, Robert Adam and Josiah Wedgwood. A good master, he gave regular employment with reasonable wages, insurance and sick relief. He paid his heads of department well, but kept them in the background whilst he employed agents to seek designs from abroad to copy. In 1762 he went into partnership with Fothergill, who developed the sales side. He entered his mark in 1773, when Birmingham was granted its Charter, and during the period 1773-1801 he entered a further two marks with John Fothergill. In 1780 Fothergill retired and Boulton went into partnership with James Wyatt. Boulton died in 1809. In 1810 the Matthew Boulton Plate Co. was formed and its mark registered in May 1820 appears on a label for TENERIFFE dated 1830 (see fig. 783).[63]

Two sample invoices from Matthew Boulton are reproduced[64] below:

```
Soho the 30th December 1780
Oatridge and Marindin Dr.
A Card containing 1 Doz. plated bottle labels engraved
Vin de Rhin
Vin de Chares
Vin de Bourgogne
Vin de Muselle
No. 976002 22s.6d        £1-2-6
        Dis 20pc          4-6
                         18-0


Soho the 3rd April 1781
Lord Craven Dr.
1 plated label each
Port
Madeira
Claret 2/- each          £0-6-0
Box                       3-0
                          9-0
Sent by his Lordship's order.
Directed to Mrs. Wood No. 23 Charles St.
```

Matthew Linwood

There were three members of this family with the same name. Matthew Linwood I was born in 1726. He entered two marks – an oval and a rectangular punch – in 1773, went into partnership with John Turner in 1779 and died in 1783. His eldest son, Matthew Linwood II, was born in 1754 and entered a similar rectangular mark in 1801. He was appointed a Guardian of the Assay Office in 1811, and two years later entered a second mark, 'ML' conjoined. Matthew Linwood III, the son of Matthew Linwood II, was born in 1783 and died in 1847. An oval mark similar to that of 1773 was entered for M. Linwood and Son in 1820. An 1806 label for PORT (see fig. 784) follows the well-known two cupids design. An 1807 label engraved for LISBON of irregular shape, the border ornamented with putti, vines and scrolls in relief, with a scrolled rectangular cartouche and an 1814 label inscribed PORT, oval, with an elaborate cresting engraved with a flower, with a matted border were exhibited in the Assay Office Bicentenary.[65]

The Provinces - Birmingham

Joseph Taylor

Joseph Taylor registered his first mark in Birmingham in the 1780s and later in London (as a watchmaker). He had premises off Fleet Street in London. He entered further marks in April 1813 in Birmingham and was appointed a Guardian of the Assay Office in that year. His premises were in Newhall Street. In 1820 he produced the rare and unusual urn design for LISBON.[66] On his death the business was transferred to his brother John Taylor and his brother-in-law John Perry, who entered Taylor and Perry marks in July 1829 and April 1832. Joseph was a prolific maker of wine and sauce labels (see fig. 798, BRANDY, 1820; fig. 801, BRANDY, 1814; and fig. 802, PORT, 1820). Examples of his work are in the Birmingham assay office. An oval label with double reeded border engraved with the unusual title of CONNELL was displayed at the Bicentenary Exhibition in 1973.[67] So also was a cushion shaped label with filigree style borders, being mechanically pierced to create this effect, engraved for HOLLANDS.[68] Also exhibited, but not illustrated, was a die-stamped label engraved for VESPETRO with an irregular edge decorated with vines, scrolls and rocaille work in relief.[69] Examples of Taylor and Perry's work are shown at fig. 789, CLARET, 1841; fig. 790, HOLLANDS, 1842; fig. 796, MARSALA, 1840, and fig. 804, SPIRITS, 1830.

Joseph Willmore

Joseph Willmore (born 1790) was the grandson of Thomas Willmore (Willmore and Alston). Joseph's mark was entered around 1808. He took in George Unite as an apprentice. In July 1832 he entered another mark, the punches of which continued to be used after 1834 when he went into partnership with John Yapp and John Woodward. Yapp and Woodward registered their own mark in May 1845. Joseph died in 1855. See fig. 792, GENIÈVE, 1827 and fig. 794, GIN, 1833. He produced a rather elaborate design for BUCELLAS in 1822.[70]

George Unite

After a brief partnership with John Hilliard in 1831-32 (see the partnership's WHISKY, illustrated at fig. 785), George Unite entered marks in August 1832, November 1834 and April 1838, followed by the firm that bore his name in February 1859, May 1861, August 1861, May 1864, November 1864, October 1873, November 1890, January 1901 and August 1910. He gradually built up his business during the 1840s to become the leading producer of labels, confirmation of which can be seen by the numbers still to be found in the salerooms. See fig. 786, GIN, 1843; fig. 787, RUM, 1843; fig. 795, MOSELLE, 1826; and fig. 797, WHISKEY, 1824. In 1839 he copied a Bateman scroll design for BURGUNDY.[71]

Hilliard and Thomason

This partnership entered marks in January 1847, August 1859, April 1861, August 1875 and March 1888. The firm produced some interesting labels and made a serious contribution to the trade. Sir Edward Thomason had a genius for self-advertisement. He was born in 1769, the son of a buckle manufacturer, and was apprenticed to Matthew Boulton. In 1793 he took over his father's business and expanded it, with silver plate and medallion manufacturing. He died in 1849, having taken in John Hilliard – who had been on his own since leaving George Unite in 1832 – to continue the business in 1847. He sent in labels for assay between 1818 and 1838.

The names on Birmingham labels follow the pattern of names produced at other centres.

	Percentage		Percentage		Percentage
MADEIRA	14.0	GIN	4.8	WHISKEY	1.6
PORT	10.7	CLARET	3.8	'S' (cut-out letter)	1.6
SHERRY	10.3	BUCELLAS	3.2	'C' (cut-out letter)	1.3
BRANDY	7.1	HOLLANDS	2.7	'M' (cut-out letter)	1.3
RUM	5.7	WHISKY	2.2	SAUTERNE	1.0

The percentage is of the total number of labels produced.

The Provinces - Birmingham

Figures 795-808.

It will be seen that the three fortified wines, PORT, SHERRY, MADEIRA, and four spirits (including HOLLANDS) account for sixty per cent of the total number of labels. More than ninety (including sauce labels) occur less often than one per cent each. Some of these must be 'one off' examples, commissioned to suit an individual taste, ROB ROY,[72] for instance, perhaps an in-house joke for whisky, or NIG,[73] of which the only known example with an original title is by a Birmingham maker (see fig. 808). There are other NIG labels, but they all seem to be re-engraved and later in date. Hilliard and Thomason also used enamel on silver in 1906 to produce an oval-shaped MOTHER'S RUIN.[74] Finally it should be noted that the popularity of BUCELLAS is perhaps a little surprising, almost as great as CLARET.

The Provinces - Sheffield

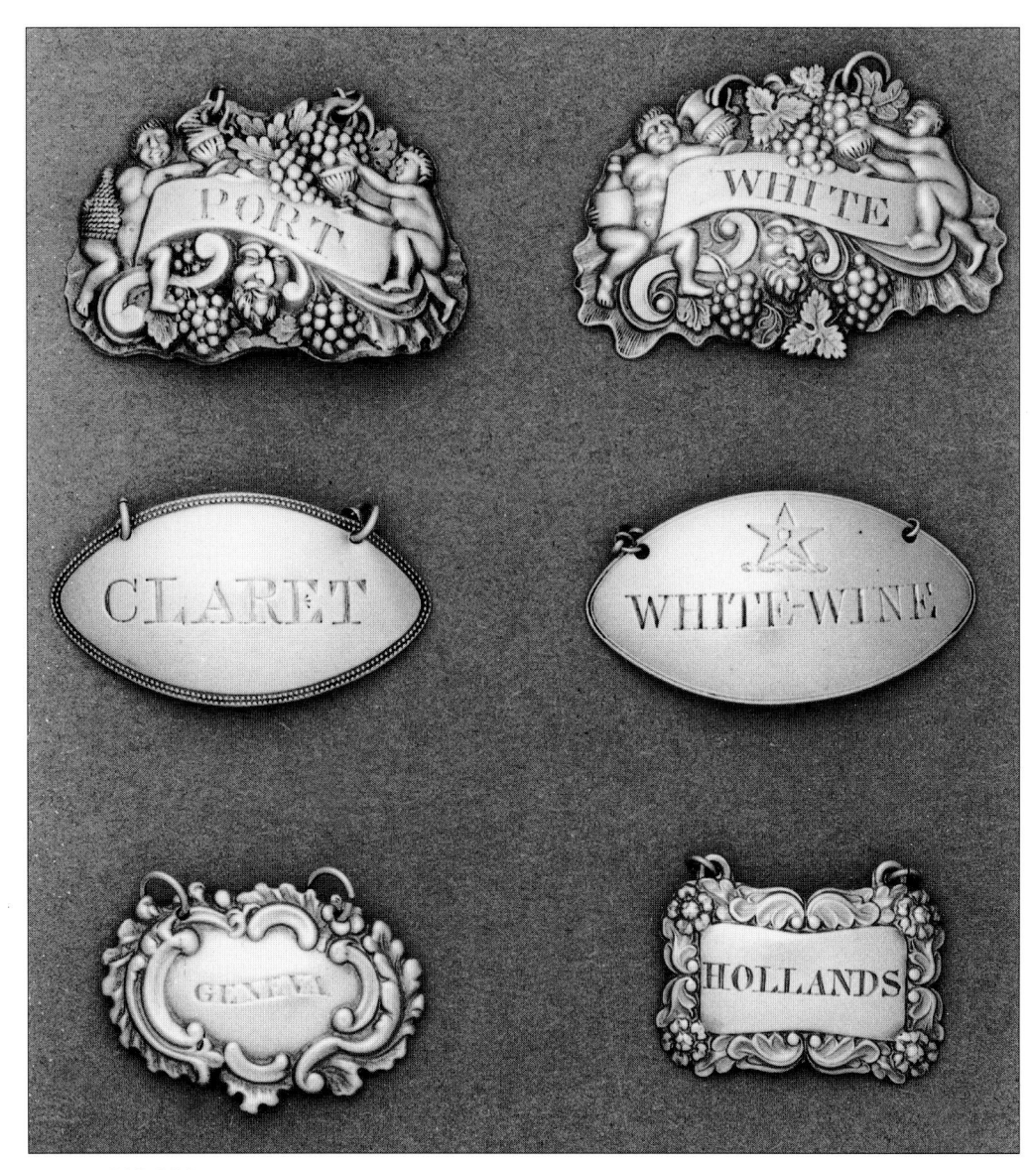

Figures 809-814.

PART 7 – SHEFFIELD

An assay office was authorised to be opened in Sheffield in July 1773, following the agitation created by silversmiths from there and Birmingham to be allowed to send their wares to be assayed close at hand and in a place more convenient than Chester or London, which they had to use up until then. Articles by Sheffield firms made before 1773 were certainly being assayed in both Chester and London, but there are no recorded instances of wine labels amongst them. However, as the hallmarking of labels was not compulsory before 1791, there may be unmarked labels by Sheffield makers that predate 1773 and are unattributed.

The assay office in Sheffield is one of four in the country that are still open. The records of its early days are still held there, but in more recent times there are sad gaps caused by the inadvertent consignment of its Registers for the years 1828-1832 and 1837-1931 to be recycled for the war effort in 1939. Nevertheless enough information exists from which to form a good picture of wine label manufacture from the early days to the present.[75] The men who founded the office in 1773 included several whose names appear on wine labels from 1773 onwards, the earliest of whom is John Winter with the date letter for that year.[76] Richard Morton sent in labels in 1775, as did Matthew Fenton, Richard Creswick and the firm of Tudor and Leader a year or so later. A feature of many of these early labels is that they have date letters, not found on London labels or those of other provincial offices before 1791.

Several other anomalies distinguish the hallmarking processes of the Sheffield office. During its early years it adopted a highly irregular method of assigning date letters, selecting them apparently at random, though perhaps choosing initials of the patrons of the office, and using only some of the alphabet. Full regular cycles did not start until 1825. Between 1780 and 1825 the crown is contained in the same punch as the date letter, above or alongside it. Between 1815 and 1825 the crown is placed upside down, perhaps to help distinguish it from the previous cycle.

The majority of the Sheffield-made labels are die-stamped, and indeed the die-stamping process was an important factor marking the city's progress as a manufacturing centre for the new age. The dies were used for articles in OSP as well as in silver, and several examples are known of labels of similar design in the two materials.[77] No cast labels have been noted, but there are a few wrought or cut from plate. Many of the usual London designs have been recorded by Sheffield makers, usually with some adaptation that marks them as more than mere copies, and identifiable as products of Sheffield.[78] Robert Gainsford's single vine leaves, for instance, have characteristic veining (see fig. 828 for SHERRY, 1833); Thomas Watson's revival in 1824 of an eighteenth-century style cushion-shaped label has an elaborate border of festoons and flowers, and another has an unnaturally narrow waist (see fig. 826 for VIDONIA). Some indication of the variety of designs on recorded silver labels is shown below.

Shapes and Designs of Recorded Silver Labels

1.	CARTOUCHE with flowers and/or fruit and/or scroll border	32
2.	CRESCENT	
	(a) Seven sided lower border	8
	(b) Plain and reeded	7
	(c) Beaded	6
	(d) With drapery	2
	(e) Other	8
3.	RECTANGULAR	
	(a) Plain	16
	(b) Cut corners (wine labels)	8
	(c) Cut corners (sauce labels)	3
4.	CUPIDS AND SATYR	15
5.	CUT OUT WORD	8
6.	NECK RINGS	9
7.	OVAL	
	(a) With scrolls, flowers	5
	(b) Without scrolls, flowers	5
8.	CUSHION	8
9.	RECTANGLE	
	(a) With dome surmount	8
	(b) With supported shield above	3
	(c) With gadrooned border	3
	(d) With rounded ends	3
10.	VINE LEAF	7
11.	SCROLL	4
12.	ESCUTCHEON	3
13.	KIDNEY	4
14.	ESCUTCHEON WITH LION'S MASK	4
15.	CANOE	2
16.	EYE	2
17.	STAR	1
18.	INITIAL	1
19.	MISCELLANEOUS OR SHAPE UNKNOWN	22

Among early makers, however, the favourite shape seems to have been the crescent; at least seven variants having been identified, in OSP and silver. The earliest versions are large and often have a

The Provinces - Sheffield

Figure 815.

Figure 816.

Figure 817.

distinctive beaded border (see fig. 820 for CALCAVELLA by John Love and Co., 1799 and fig. 819 for W. WINE by Thomas Watson and Co., 1813). Others have a reeded border (see fig. 822 for VIN DE GRAVE by Daniel Holy and Co., 1806). Later on, bright-cut borders became popular. A smaller and fatter crescent was developed, one of which by Thomas Law and Co. and dated 1797 has its set of hallmarks on the face, a practice noted on other Sheffield labels, but seldom met elsewhere (see fig. 821 for MADEIRA and for an example by Underdown, Wilkinson & Co. in 1827, see fig. 815 for BUCELLAS). A similar one for TENERIF, dating from around 1795 and considered to be Irish, is unmarked.[79] Perhaps this is another example of a Sheffield label sent elsewhere for finishing. A more elaborate design, found in OSP and silver, has the crescent supporting a festooned urn and has been seen on a Dublin marked label of the same period.[80] A crescent with drapery for RUM by Luke Proctor and Co. and dated 1790 (see fig. 817) has been made many times in OSP. A particularly distinctive crescent variant has the lower edge composed of seven sections.[81] It was made, among others, by T. Watson and Co. in 1803 (see fig. 818 for PORT). A label of the same design has the mark of William Auld, an Edinburgh silversmith (see fig. 839 for GIN), who may have copied the Sheffield prototype or even have imported it, or maybe Sheffield makers copied Auld's design. There is no doubt that Sheffield developed a considerable trade in labels, often unfinished, with other parts of the kingdom. Some Irish 'two putti' labels, for instance, have characteristics that seem to indicate a Sheffield origin. A further indication can be the suspension chain. Sheffield manufacturers developed a particular figure-of-eight link to attach the chain to the eye of the label, and when it is found in other parts of the country, it may denote a Sheffield association.

The names of fifty-four Sheffield silversmiths who submitted labels for assay between 1773 and 1981 can be ascertained from the records, though no examples for some twenty-five of these have been recorded in museums or sale catalogues. Their output has been estimated at over 6,500 labels up to the mid-1850s, a date which marks the decline of label popularity. Nevertheless, manufacture continued in Sheffield for some years after that, perhaps longer than anywhere else in the country.

The Provinces - Sheffield

The number of labels consigned and recorded survivals by makers from 1773 to 1836 and 1843 to 1854 is shown below.

	Consigned	Recorded
1. R. GAINSFORD	900	20
2. Thos. LAW & Co.	684	3
3. RICHARD MORTON & Co. (includes MORTON, HANDLEY & Co.)	539	7
4. S&C YOUNGE & Co.	382	8
5. Thos. WATSON & Co.	379	13
6. Daniel HOLY & Co.	299	
7. FENTON, CRESWICK & Co. (includes M. FENTON & Co.)	298	20
8. SMITH, KNOWLES & Co.	260	
9. T&D LEADER	232	
10. Nathaniel SMITH & Co.	222	4
11. John WATSON	213	3
12. TUDOR & LEADER	211	4
13. John YOUNGE & Co.	166	4
14. TUCKER, FENTON & Co.	136	
15. NOWILL & KIPPAX (includes ROBERT KIPPAX)	127	9
16. WALKER KNOWLES & Co.	109	2
17. KIRBY, WATERHOUSE & Co.	108	
18. ROBERTS CADMAN & Co.	90	3
19. Daniel LEADER	85	
20. JT YOUNGE & Co.	78	
21. H WILKINSON & Co.	72	5
22. Alex GOODMAN & Co.	70	
23. John LOVE & Co.	66	1
24. Luke PROCTOR & Co.	65	1
25. KIRKBY, GREGORY & Co.	64	
26. KITCHEN & WALKER	61	1
27. Samuel WALKER	60	
28. HAWKSWORTH, EYRE & Co.	51	4
29. Henry TUDOR & Co.	50	
30. Geo ASHFORTH & Co.	45	
31. DIXON & SONS	44	
32. SHORE & ROTHERHAM	42	
33. BLAGDEN HODSON & Co. (includes THOMAS BLAGDEN)	40	5
34. BATTIE, HOWARD & HAWKSWORTH	39	1
35. Thos. RODGERS	31	
36. John ROWBOTHAM	26	4
37. Joseph NOWILL	24	2
38. FURNISS, POLES & Co.	19	
39. J&T SETTLE	16	1
40. EADON, KIBBLES & Co.	12	5
41. WATERHOUSE & Co. (includes WATERHOUSE, HODSON & Co.)	12	3
42. ELLIS TUCKER & Co.	10	
43. WRIGHT & FAIRBAIRN	10	
44. Wm. ALLANSON & Co.	9	
45. John LAW	9	
46. John PARSON & Co.	8	
47. ROBERTS & HALL	7	
48. John WINTER & Co.	6	3
49. Thomas SETTLE (includes THOMAS and JONATHAN SETTLE)	5	1
50. S ROBERTS, SMITH & Co.	4	3
51. B ROOKE & SON	3	
52. James CRAWSHAW	3	
53. ROBERTS & SLATER	3	
54. John HOYLAND	2	

The firm of Roberts and Belk, founded in 1865 was making a commemorative label to mark the bi-centenary of the assay office in 1973, and another for a royal occasion in 1977.[82] The whereabouts of fewer than five hundred Sheffield labels are known today, a number that indicates, as do similar figures from the rest of the country, the vast mortality there has been in the two centuries of their existence.

Escutcheons are common in OSP but rare in silver. An example by William Damant made in 1777 shows a curved belly rather than a point.[83] The die-stamped 'Two Putti' labels have an additional vine leaf at the lower edge if made by Robert Gainsford (see fig. 682 for MR HENDRIE, the owner or butler, fig. 810 for WHITE, 1811, and fig. 827 for TENERIFFE, 1809). If made by William Tucker, the main leaf design is not of the vine but of the oak tree (see fig. 809 for PORT, 1809). An attractive ribbon above vine leaves and grapes for SHERRY was made by Creswick and Co. about 1858 (see fig. 816).

Scrolls, on the other hand, are seen less commonly in silver than OSP and as many were made to hang 'upside down' as were made to hang with the armorial plaque uppermost (see fig. 825 for W. PORT by Tudor and Leader, 1781). A 'canoe'-shaped design is probably a scroll variant. Three have been recorded, made in 1809 by Nathaniel Smith and Co.[84] In 1791, John Younge and Sons produced an oval label surmounted with a vine leaf (see fig. 824 for GIN). Eye-shaped designs have beaded borders (see fig. 831 for PORT by Richard Morton and Co., 1786), a reeded edge, a bright-cut border[85] or an unusual ovolo border.

Robert Kippax in 1796 made two sets of rectangular-shaped labels with cut corners and domed surmounts bearing crests of either a ram's head or a dove and olive branch.[86] John Watson in 1809 and Joseph Nowill in 1812 made narrow rectangles with raised eyelets (see fig. 830 for PORT) and one with raised eyelets and a flower stalk surmount is probably unique.[87] Gadrooned borders are occasionally seen[88] and the illustration of T. and J. Settle's PORT (see fig. 829, 1819) shows the name raised on a matted panel with a matted border, containing a wavy tendril from which spring florets on alternate sides.

Cartouches include a lion's mask with a border of vines and scrolls for RYE WHISKY by Martin, Hall and Co. in 1883.[89] Labels with a border of scrolls and leaves abound (see fig. 813 for GENEVA by J. Settle and H. Wilkinson, fig. 833, for MADEIRA by J. and T. Settle, 1826, and fig. 814 for HOLLANDS by S.C. Younge and Co., 1825). A larger version is surmounted by an unusual five-petalled flower (see fig. 832 for SHERRY by Walker, Knowles and Co., 1844).

Some thirteen cut-out words are recorded and all are Victorian. The Roberts and Belk examples are hand fretted and finished using heavy plate.[90] Neck rings are usually large, at around 9cm (3½in.) in diameter, and have single reeded borders top and bottom. They are of thin gauge silver with the name pierced and were made by M. Fenton and Co. in 1791 and 1794. No silver examples have been recorded of the pierced decoration seen on OSP rings. One example is recorded in heavy gauge, made by Thos. Watson in 1804, and is quite plain with name engraved and a diameter of 6cm (2½in.).

The following notes give brief biographies of the leading makers.

Richard Morton
Morton established his plating business in about 1767 and was one of the first to enter his mark when the assay office opened in 1773. His partners were John Winter, Samuel Roberts, Thomas Warriss, John Elam, Thomas Settle, John Eyre and Nathaniel Smith. All except Morton and Warriss were also partners in the Samuel Roberts firm, which registered its mark on the same day. Winters, Roberts, Eyre and Smith appear to have parted company in 1780 and Morton registered his mark again. Most of his silver output was in small articles, especially salt cellars, but fused plate formed the major part of his business. In 1796 a new partnership of Morton, Handley and Co. still included Thomas Settle. A London warehouse was maintained until 1814, but Richard Morton had retired in 1806 and died in 1812. Examples of his work are fig. 811 for CLARET, *c.*1790, and fig. 812 for WHITE-WINE, 1791. See also fig. 831 for PORT, 1786, and fig. 823 for PORT, *c.*1785.

Figures 818-827.

The Provinces - Sheffield

Robert Gainsford
Gainsford was from 1793 to 1795 a partner in Luke Proctor and Co. (Luke's RUM of 1790 is shown at fig. 817), with Luke Proctor, George Kibble, John Weaver and George Eadon. On its dissolution he joined Alexander Goodman and George Fairbairn who registered their mark in 1797 and again in 1801. This partnership was dissolved in 1808 and became Gainsford, Nicholson and Co. until 1816. The business continued with Robert Gainsford and Thomas Nicholson alone until 1828 when it became Gainsford, Fenton and Nicholson. The firm continued until 1853 with addresses in Eyre St, Sheffield, and Bouverie St, London. The last recorded label was made in 1833. He was Assay Office Guardian from 1807 to 1853, when he died. There are records of mysterious and perhaps illegal sending of goods for assay to York in 1807 and 1809. See figs. 810, 827 and 828.

Robert Kippax and Co.
This firm registered in 1774 as a 'Cuttler'. It is referred to in the daybooks as Kippax and Nowill, and had an ironmonger's shop on Sheffield High St. Usually eighteenth-century firms made either cutlery or general domestic silverware; wine labels may have been a new venture for them.

Young, Walker, Kitchen and Co.
Developed from John Hoyland and Co., this was one of the first firms to register at the Sheffield assay office. The partners were John Hoyland, John Trevor Younge, Thomas Smith and Elizabeth Middleton. When John Hoyland died in 1779, the firm continued with John Trevor Younge, Edmund Greaves and William Hoyland. However, this partnership was dissolved in 1787 and the firm continued as J.T. Younge and Co. (partners J.T. Younge, John Allanson, Henry Walker and William Crowder; mark registered 1788). By 1802 Younge's two sons, Samuel and Charles, had joined the partnership, and William Crowder had left. In 1810, a new eleven-year partnership was drawn up. The partners were Samuel and Charles Younge and George Kitchen of Sheffield and Henry Walker of London. They were in business until 1830 at Union St, Sheffield, and Beaufort Building, The Strand, London, making all kinds of domestic ware in silver and fused plate. For John Younge & Sons see fig. 824 for GIN, 1791; for S.C. Younge & Co. see fig. 814 for HOLLANDS, 1825.

Daniel Holy and Co.
Mark first registered in 1776. Daniel Holy's partner was a merchant, George Woodhead. In 1783 a new partnership – Daniel Holy, Wilkinson and Co. – was formed with Joseph Drabble, Robert Frederick Wilkinson and Robert Robinson. This was renewed for fourteen years in 1790 and continued, with various changes of partners, until 1831, when Daniel Holy died. From 1825 there was also a London branch at 106 Cheapside. The firm made a wide variety of domestic silver and fused plate wares. See fig. 822 for VIN DE GRAVE, 1806.

Thomas Law
Law was born in 1717 and became Master Cutler in 1753. He was a noted maker of fused plate snuffboxes. He died in 1775, but he entered his mark in September 1773 on the same day as those of Henry Tudor and Thomas Leader and Samuel Roberts. His son, John Law, continued the business until his death in 1819 and, after various changes of partnership, Atkin Bros emerged as successors. See figs. 230 for RUM and 821 for MADEIRA.

Henry Tudor
Tudor was born in 1738, died in 1803, and was an Assay Office Guardian. With Thomas Leader he entered his mark in September 1773, but they were prominent fused platers in the 1760s when they had the assistance of Thomas' younger brother, Daniel, who was apprenticed as a box maker in 1783. Samuel Nicholson joined the plating business. In 1797 Thomas Leader retired, a wealthy man, to his native Essex, leaving Daniel and his son Thomas Leader Junior, who entered their mark in 1798,

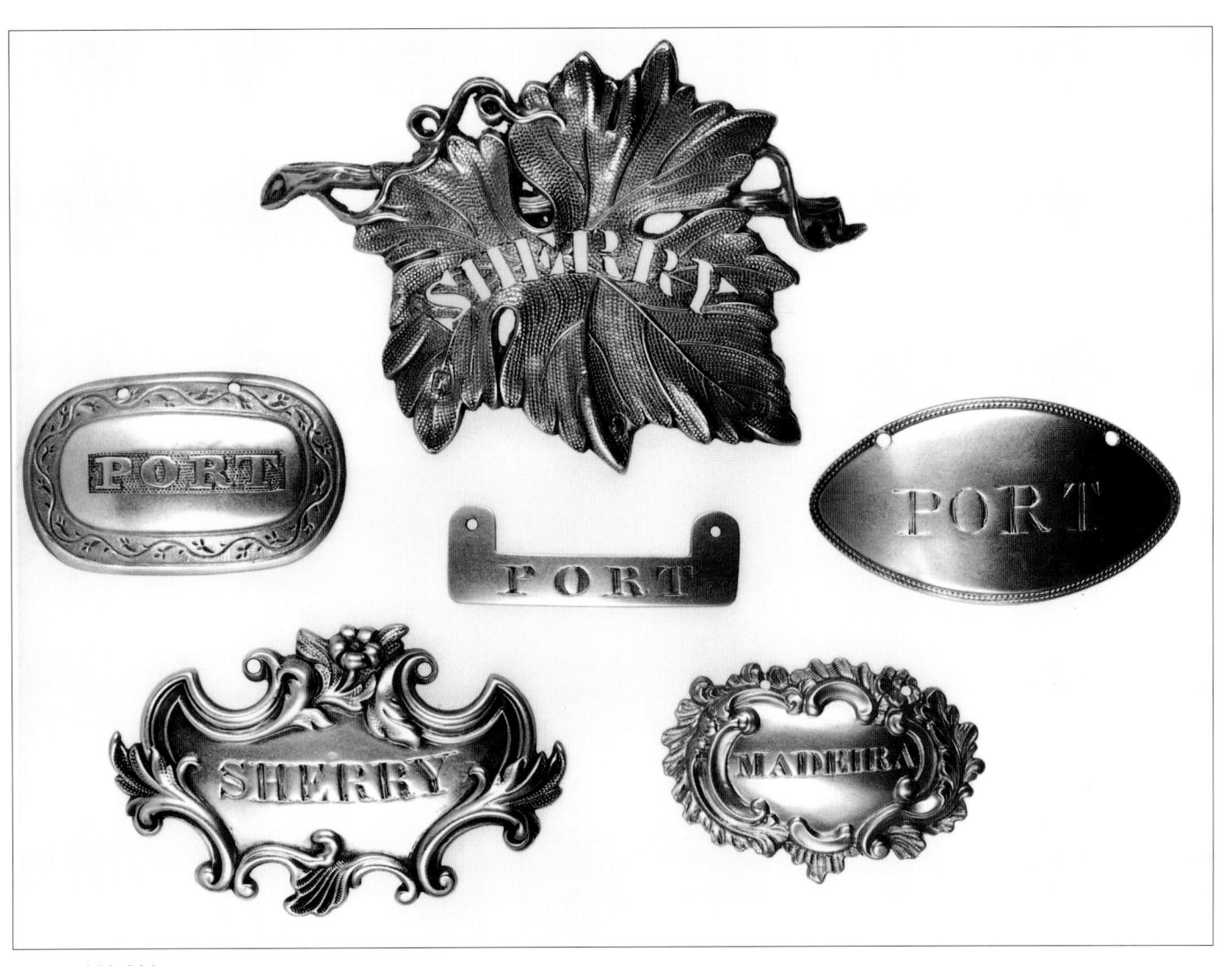

Figures 828-833.

whilst Henry Tudor and his plater partner Samuel Nicholson entered theirs in 1797. Tudor died in 1803, but T. and D. Leader continued until 1816. See fig. 825 for W. PORT by Tudor and Leader.

Matthew Fenton, Richard Creswick and William Watson
The second group of silversmiths to register their mark when the assay office opened in 1773. William Watson was probably the father or brother of Thomas Watson, but was only a financial partner. Matthew Fenton died in 1795 and the business was sold to Thomas Watson, who was joined by Thomas Bradbury. In 1825 Thomas Watson was replaced by his nephew, William Watson, and the Watson interest ended in 1832. Little is known of Richard Creswick, but he does not appear to be connected with the firm of Thomas James and Nathaniel Creswick. Thomas Watson's PORT of 1803 and W. WINE of 1813 are shown at figs. 818-819, and VIDONIA of 1824 at fig. 826.

Roberts and Belk
This firm was originally Furniss, Poles and Turner, who registered their mark in 1810. In 1841 William Briggs joined them. In 1845 the company was styled Roberts and Slater, whose mark was entered in that same year. This name was used until 1859, when the mark was entered as Roberts and Briggs. Then, in 1864, the name was changed to Roberts and Belk. After several more changes the mark R and B was revived in 1892. Samuel Roberts was probably of the same family as that in Roberts, Cadman and Co., and was born in 1800 and died in 1887. The firm still exists.[91]

PART 8 – EDINBURGH

Edinburgh was the only city in Scotland authorised to assay silver until 1819, when Glasgow opened its own office. No other royal burghs had assay offices, but some did adopt their own system of marking. If for some reason a silversmith needed to have his wares fully assayed he had to send them to Edinburgh or, after 1819 if in the relevant catchment area, to Glasgow. Domestic circumstances in most parts of Scotland outside the big cities were not conducive to a demand for the smaller dining room accessories such as wine labels before the last decades of the eighteenth century, although clearly much fine silver was being made. Two early examples can be cited of labels made by Patrick Robertson, probably c.1770 (see fig. 842 for WHITE WINE) and by William Davie, perhaps earlier, c.1765 (see fig. 838 for AQUAVITAE).

However, an analysis of the surviving assay office records show that by 1800 the demand was by no means insignificant: nearly 1,500 labels passed through the office in the course of that year, a number much greater than anywhere else outside London, and one that does not take account of production by the other burghs.

The records of the Edinburgh assay office have been used as the basis for a sample of silver wine label makers between 1800 and 1880. The lists of wares assayed were examined in detail for the period January to March at intervals of six years. The list appended gives the number of wine labels assayed and the makers during the first three months of each of the years selected.

When production of the wine labels was at its height, the numbers assayed in the three months periods are more likely to be a satisfactory guide to the rate at which they were being produced over the whole year. Where the numbers are small, however, the sample may not be as reliable. The names of all the craftsmen who made labels will not be revealed, but this is inevitably a disappointing feature of a limited analysis of this kind.

The total figures themselves are very interesting. They suggest that the demand for labels was at its greatest during the second and third decades of the century.

Number of Wine Labels Assayed at Edinburgh (January-March)

Year	Number	Year	Number
1800	168	1842	24
1805[x]	91	1848	6
1812	352	1854	95
1818	326	1860	8
1824	352	1866	2
1830	55	1872	18
1836	69	1880	5

x – 1806 records not available.

A sharp fall-away in production seems to have followed, with an unexpectedly high number assayed in 1854. One silversmith, James Mackay (sometimes spelt McKay), was responsible for more than half the number in that year. He was a quality maker of labels and departed from the plain, un-decorated and rather dour concept. His HOLLANDS for c.1820 is illustrated at fig. 841. It bears a crest with the motto 'Gang Forward'. His NOYAU is set in a Regency frame of shells and reed tie scrolls.[92] In this he was followed by George McHattie who produced rounded rectangulars for CLARET, PORT and SWEET WINE with gadrooned borders in 1822.[93] Earlier, around 1815, he provided a rectangular label in old style with the title of HOCK in large letters made bold by filling with black wax (see fig. 840). James Hay also produced a scroll and floral border with which to adorn an early nineteenth-century SHERRY label.[94]

The crescent with a seven-sided bottom may be a Sheffield design or a Scottish design produced in Edinburgh by makers such as William Auld in the 1780s (see fig. 839 for GIN), and reproduced in OSP. The Sheffield City Museum has an OSP label of this kind. It was also produced in silver in 1803 by T. Watson & Co. of Sheffield. Examples of William Auld's work have been illustrated in the *Wine Label Circle Journal*.[95] George McHattie and George Fenwick followed the design during the

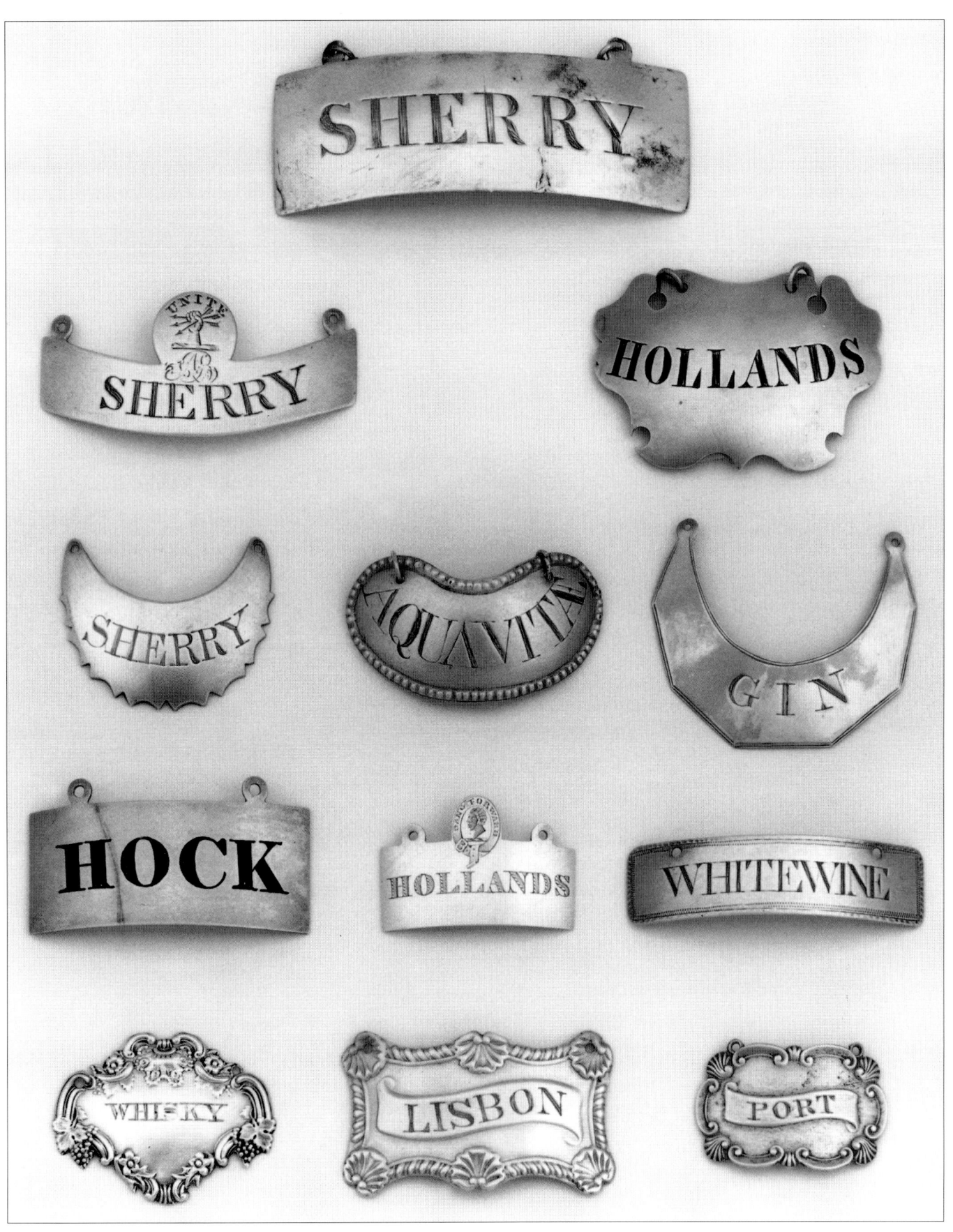

Figures 834-845.

earlier part of the nineteenth century in Edinburgh.

The silversmiths themselves belonged almost entirely to Edinburgh, although there are a few burgh craftsmen in the list – James Douglas of Dundee, Robert and William Gray of Glasgow, and Jonas Osborne of Greenock. Before 1836 burgh silversmiths[96] were under no legal obligations to send silver to Edinburgh for assay (or to Glasgow except for those in the Glasgow catchment area under the Act of 1819) although some of them sent spoons and other small wares in plenty. After 1836 the records of the assay office at Edinburgh contain many references to silversmiths from all over the country, but by that time, as can be seen from the table above, the production of silver wine labels was on the wane and there were only a few silversmiths in Edinburgh making them.

In certain years there were makers who produced wine labels in large numbers – at the rate of over four hundred a year. Robert Gray of Glasgow in 1800 is a good example. He made 108 in the first three months of that year which is almost exactly two-thirds of the total number assayed. James Mackay in 1812 was outstanding as a large-scale producer and in 1824 the lead was taken over by George McHattie with James Home close behind. Most of the craftsmen who had large thriving businesses appear to have made labels in large numbers as they made, for example, tea services, punch bowls and spoons. In some years the leading maker of tea services also produced more wine labels than anyone else. Examples include James Mackay in 1812 and Elder and Co in 1836.

Alex Ziegler's SHERRY of c.1790 (see fig. 837) has an interesting serrated edge. The HOLLANDS (see fig. 836) of John Law follows a traditional design like George McHattie's HOCK mentioned above. Plainness was admired in silver. Armorials were popular as shown by Robert Frazer's SHERRY, c.1825, calling for UNITY (see fig. 835) and James Mackay's probable club label for HOLLANDS calling for going forward (see fig. 841). Size also lent impact – see Dick and Macpherson's SHERRY (see fig. 834) of c.1815. After 1820 labels tended to have restrained decoration, as shown by fig. 843 (WHISKY by W. Cunningham, c.1825), fig. 844 (LISBON by J. McDermid, c.1820), fig. 845 (PORT by John Ziegler, c.1820) and fig. 886 (SHERRY by P. Cunningham, c.1830).

Some makers, such as William Mackenzie (1805), John Ziegler (1812), David Macdonald (1818), Thomas Speirs (1824), James Robertson (1836), William Mackay (1842), Samuel Weir (1848), Thomas McKenzie (1854) and Miss Jennie Moon (1872), concentrated on small wares. The last-named is one of the very few women who sent silver for assay at Edinburgh during the nineteenth century, another being Mrs Alexander Cunningham in 1812. It may be that some of these makers became renowned for their labels and so received a good deal of custom.

The label makers never numbered more than a third of all the silversmiths sending gold and silver for assay during the years for which records have been examined. After 1830 the number of label makers was only a very small fraction of the total.

The labels were often sent to hall in even numbers, and sometimes in dozens in the earlier years. After 1830 they often appear in odd numbers, with only one really large lot of thirty-six (in 1854). Unfortunately the lists of the assay office are very barren of detail and the labels are described merely as 'lables', 'bottle labels' and 'wine labels' with no reference at all to the design.[97] It is, however, very satisfying to be able to determine the names of some at least of the makers and their rate of production of labels.[98]

PART 9 – GLASGOW, GREENOCK AND PAISLEY

From very early times the Incorporation of Hammermen has governed the Silversmiths of Glasgow. The motto of this incorporation is 'By hammer in hand all arts do stand'. It is the premier of the fourteen trade guilds still comprised in the federation constituted by the guildry or convenery of trades of Glasgow (the 'Trades' House'). It can trace its origins to at least a royal charter granted by King Malcolm III in 1057, although formal legal recognition by the grant of a Seal of Cause to incorporations did not begin to occur until the sixteenth century. The Incorporation of Hammermen received its Seal of Cause on 11 (or possibly 14) October 1536. The hall of the Trades' House, designed by the great Robert Adam just before he died in 1792, still stands in Glassford

The Provinces - Glasgow, Greenock and Paisley

Figures 846-870.

The Provinces - Glasgow, Greenock and Paisley

Street. The hammermen are shown prominently in the frieze of the banqueting hall, woven on silk made in Belgium during the nineteenth century.

They comprise in Glasgow the goldsmiths, the silversmiths, the swordmakers, the blacksmiths, the saddlers, the belt-makers and the shipbuilders. Portraits of two deacon conveners belonging to the hammermen hang in the hall of the Trades' House; one is of Archibald Maclellan (1831-32 and 34) by Sir John Gilbert and one is of Andrew McOnie (1879-1880) by Herbert James Gunn. The arms of the incorporation are engraved on a silver shield forming part of the decoration of the deacon convener's chair. Glasgow was not a royal burgh and merchants and craftsmen formed component parts, namely, a merchant guildry and a craft guildry of the guildry established by a letter of guildry dated 1605. This letter set up a dean of guild's court with eight councillors, four of merchant rank and four of craft rank. The inclusion of craftsmen is unusual. It then set up two component councils, the dean of guild's council later known as the Merchants' House and the deacon convener's council, later known as the Trades' House.

In November 1818 some twenty-seven goldsmiths, silversmiths and platemakers living and working in Glasgow or within forty miles to the west and south of Glasgow formed themselves into the Glasgow Goldsmiths' Company and petitioned Parliament for a private Act to establish the Company as a statutory body corporate and to acquire Parliamentary authority for the setting up of an assay office. The forty-mile range (but note that this was not a radius) brought in such personalities as John Heron of Greenock and William Hannay of Paisley (both being label makers – see for example William Hannay's shell and gadrooned GIN of c.1818[99]), both of whom were signatories to the Parliamentary Petition. An enabling Act was rushed through and given Royal Assent on 19 May 1819. The reason for speed was that the Westminster Parliament wished to collect duty on articles assayed in this prosperous part of Scotland. Before 1819 the only assay office in Scotland that accounted for duty to the Inland Revenue was in Edinburgh. Whilst there were legitimate assay systems set up under the various Scottish Acts preserved after the Act of Union, the burghs did not actually have 'assay offices'. Thus, their activities, due to the wording of the Duty Act, upon a strict interpretation meant that they did not have to collect and account to the Government for duty. For this reason the burghs (except Edinburgh and after 1819 Glasgow) never marked plate with a duty paid mark.

The Glasgow assay year ran from the first Monday in July by virtue of a provision in this regard in the 1819 Act. Under that Act, no person could put to sale, exchange or sell any manufacture of silver within the stipulated area (that is to say Glasgow and forty miles to the west and forty miles to the south of Glasgow) unless it had stamped on it the maker's mark, the lion rampant to show the standard of silver at least 11 oz 2dwt fine per pound Troy, a variable date letter to indicate the year, and the mark of the Glasgow Goldsmiths' Company as prescribed by the Act (being a representation of the arms of the City of Glasgow peculiar for these purposes) – such a mark to be put on silver only by the authority of the assayer. It was also prescribed that there should be an 'additional mark' being the sovereign's head showing that duty had been paid.

The arms of the City of Glasgow reflect events in the life of St Kentigern, who was born in Fife in the earlier part of the sixth century of royal birth, was trained in the monastery of St Serf at Culross, and was generally known as St Mungo meaning St Serf's 'dear friend'. The bird was the pet robin of St Serf brought back to life by St Mungo. The bell is said to be the one given to St Mungo by the Pope. The tree represents the hazel tree branches broken off by St Mungo to create a fresh fire in the refectory. The fish with the ring in its mouth was one caught by a monk in the Clyde following St Mungo's instructions. The ring was restored to Queen Languoreth who had ill advisedly given it to a knight and been threatened by the king with death for failure to produce it.

The Glasgow assay office was closed in March 1964, but the Incorporation of Hammermen still flourishes, although largely stripped of its former powers.

Many Glasgow silversmiths when wine labels were required simply bought in a die-stamped label from Birmingham or Sheffield, presented it for marking, polished it and sold it. The die-stamping process began as early as the 1770s in Birmingham under the supervision of Boulton and Fothergill.

The Provinces - Glasgow, Greenock and Paisley

Figures 871-879.

Examples of die-stamped labels mass-produced and marked as and when required are fig. 888 marked in 1825 by David MacDonald (Glasgow), fig. 887 being an identical label marked in 1829 by Daniel Sutherland (Glasgow) and fig. 886, a third identical label without date letter, marked by Patrick Cunningham *c.*1830 (Edinburgh). These labels are modelled on a design of Story and Elliott of about 1809 when the labels were cast. For a William Elliott die-pressed example of 1828 see fig. 884, a sauce label with pierced title for SOY.

On the other hand some Scottish designs are (as are 'provincial' designs in general) highly individualistic and emanate from north of the border. In this category may fall the 'mask of Pan' design (see fig. 859 for MADEIRA). Labels of this design exist by William Russell, 'J. M. Junior' (J. Muir or J. Murray) and D. Crichton Rait all dated 1827/1828. Figs. 854, 877 and 878 certainly constitute a Scottish design. Figs. 855 for SHERRY and 856 for 'S' appear to be unique Scottish designs. Figs. 851 (1796) and 858 (the 'leaf covering the label end' design) are typically and individually Scottish, although copied by Taylor and Perry in Birmingham in 1840[100] where the leaf does not actually cover the label but extrudes from it. The design concept, illustrated by fig. 863 for RUM follows, however, a Peter and Ann Bateman design of 1791[101] (for BRANDY), Scottish examples being slightly elongated. Figs. 852, 795, 860 and 879 set a style also which is unique to Scotland. The large cut-out letters (such as fig. 861 for the letter 'P' by Alexander Mitchell II in 1836) are distinctly Scottish, and the spirit of the Victorian age is captured by the cut-out label at fig. 850 and given special Scottish treatment in terms of design impact. It is similar to labels south of the border but unique to Scotland in the actual detailed design. Figs. 870 and 881 are thought to be a Scottish design. Figs. 865, 866 and 867 were thought also to be a design of Philip Grierson of the 1820s bought in perhaps by Lawrence Aitcheson *c.*1830 (see fig. 869 for WHISKY) and by Peter Aitken in 1822 (see fig. 872 for HOLLANDS). In the event it appears that Thomas and James Phipps in 1819 and Charles Rawlings in 1822 produced very similar designs (see figs. 873 for MADEIRA and 871 for BUCELLAS respectively) and a HOLLANDS label dated 1822.[102] It may be, of course, that Phipps and Rawlings copied Grierson. Even well-known designs are given a special Scottish shape with plain treatment such as figs. 861 and 862. A familiar rectangular with cut corners has special workmanship north of the border where a particular kind of applied raised double reeding is employed with black-wax filling in between the reeds (see fig. 880 by Alexander Mitchell II for BRANDY).

The crescent with a seven-sided bottom is thought to be a Scottish design produced in Edinburgh by makers such as William Auld in the 1780s and reproduced in OSP and, as stated above (see Part 8, Edinburgh), Alexander McHattie and George Fenwick followed the design during the earlier part of the nineteenth century in Edinburgh.[103]

The simple narrow rectangular was given special topside treatment in Edinburgh and Glasgow, sometimes in a very elaborate manner as in fig. 852 for PORT, and sometimes with simple but individualistic designs. See, for example, William and Patrick Cunningham's crested rectangular of c.1800 for MADERA [sic] illustrated in the *Wine Label Circle Journal*.[104]

Details of some of the Glasgow makers are as follows:

Milne and Campbell (c.1764–c.1790)
This firm could be one of the earliest of the Glasgow label makers. It would not be unusual for their work to be assayed in Edinburgh. They may have produced a very individualistic Scottish design, represented by the label engraved for HIGHLAND referred to in 5 *WLCJ*[105] and there attributed to Mackay and Chisholm, but probably dating from around 1790. This design was followed by John Ziegler and W.C. (unidentified Jackson p. 505) in Edinburgh around 1805-10 – see Ziegler's SHERRY label referred to in 5 *WLCJ* 38 at B2 and W.C.'s PORT label illustrated in 1 *WLCJ* 155 at C5 – and copied later on by Sheffield makers (e.g. John Kay and Co in 1813, see 3 *WLCJ* 198, row 5.2). It could be that the HIGHLAND label is a late copy by Mackay and Chisholm, but if so why was it not fully marked?

Jonas Osborne (c.1765–c.1805)
He worked in and around Glasgow, mainly from Greenock, from about 1765 to about 1805. He is known as a Glasgow maker to have sent silver to Edinburgh for marking which included labels. He might well have also worked in Paisley. He is not to be confused with Osborne, the Irish maker, recorded from 1787 to 1794 (see Part 11, Ireland, below).

Robert Gray (c.1776–c.1825)
Robert Gray was very much the father figure of the Glasgow silversmiths. He was admitted about 1776 and, after his son had been admitted, he formed, in about the year 1805, the firm of Robert Gray and Son. The son referred to was probably William Gray. An entry for Robert Gray and Son, Goldsmiths, appears in each copy of the Glasgow Directory for 1810 to 1819.

Robert Gray was the chief petitioner to Parliament in 1818 for the grant of Parliamentary authority to The Glasgow Goldsmiths' Company, and to the statutory rights of assay within the prescribed area. He was proud of his work, and labels made by Robert Gray and by Robert Gray and Son are usually extremely well and boldly marked. For examples of his work see MARSALA, illustrated in 1 *WLCJ* 55, no. 7 and fig. 851 (marked in Edinburgh, 1796) for SHERRY being of curved design with 1770s type decorative borders but leaves added as a Robert Gray design inspired perhaps by the work of the Batemans (see the RUM by P and J Bateman mentioned below) and fig. 874 (marked in Edinburgh) engraved for SHRUB, being a plain peaked crescent c.1804 (blipped duty mark), again a Robert Gray design, inspired perhaps by the work of the Batemans (see the RUM by P and J Bateman illustrated in 1 *WLCJ* 74 at row 3, no. 1; also SHERRY by P and A Bateman in 1 *WLCJ* 90 at row 4, no. 6) and followed by his firm, Robert Gray and Son (see fig. 876 marked in Edinburgh in 1815, the duty mark with three blips, and engraved for SHRUB, with black wax infilling).

He was a prolific maker of wine labels. Of the 168 labels sent to Edinburgh for assay in the first quarter of 1800 Robert Gray produced 108! This can be compared with Robert Gray and Sons' production of eighteen out of ninety-one (sample 1805), sixty of 352 (sample 1812) and two out

Figures 880-888.

of 326 (sample 1818). During the period from about 1790 to 1819 it appears that Glasgow silversmiths were in the main sending work to Edinburgh for marking, as the Glasgow system had tended for some reason (yet to be ascertained), to break down and perhaps not to command respect from the discriminating purchaser, falling into disuse until revived in 1819. A similar example to the SHERRY shown at fig. 851, but engraved for PORT, is the example of *c.*1815 shown at fig. 853 and another example (unusually) with a crest on the right-hand side of the wine name, is illustrated at 7 *WLCJ* 180, no. 2. Also of Robert Gray's or his son's workmanship are the plain oval CLARET, again marked in Edinburgh about 1800, referred to in 7 *WLCJ* 26, the delightfully decorated PORT of 1818 shown at fig. 852, the Regency style SHERRY of 1830 (see fig. 855), the rope-like raised 'S' of 1828 (see fig. 856), the decorated HOLLANDS of 1825 (see fig. 860) and the decorated 'Sherry', unusually in script, of 1829 (see fig. 878).

William Gray (*c.*1800–*c.*1853)
William Gray undoubtedly made labels because of the entry in the Edinburgh records showing that he presented eight labels for marking in the first quarter of 1800. He was probably the son of Robert Gray, and reasonably senior in the Glasgow Goldsmiths' Company as he was the second petitioner to Parliament for the Act of 1819. After *c.*1805 his labels were presumably marked Robert Gray and Son.

Robert Gray and Son (*c.*1805–*c.*1853)
This firm was created around 1805, and became the leading firm of silversmiths in Glasgow actively working until about 1853. Examples of the work of the firm are mentioned under Robert Gray.

The designs of figs. 852 (PORT), 860 (HOLLANDS) and 878 (SHERRY) are special to Scotland and to this firm. The label illustrated at fig. 852 was made in 1818 but assayed in Edinburgh (as was usual at this date) and marked with date letter, duty mark, castle and thistle. It could even be one of the two labels produced by Robert Gray and Son for assay in Edinburgh during the period January to March of that year! Its pair is in fact illustrated in 5 *WLCJ* 178 at A2 being in Malcolm

Gray's collection numbered 57, and engraved for SHERRY. The Shafto family crested labels show a development of the fig. 852 design. For details of two sets made in 1819 please refer to 4 *WLCJ* Issue No. 8 and to 5 *WLCJ* 105. Another label for WHITE WINE marked in Edinburgh in 1809 has been noted bearing this crest – a salamander regardant, vert, in the midst of flames.

The fig. 851 design for SHERRY was modified by Robert Gray and Son around 1815 (see fig. 853) and followed by D.C. Rait in 1838 (see fig. 858). For other examples see 4 *WLCJ* 150 for MARSALA and 1 *WLCJ* 55, no. 7, also for MARSALA (the latter being attributed by the late Mr A.C. Cuthbert to this maker). A further example of the design being followed by Robert Gray and Son is LISBON illustrated in 1 *WLCJ* 106 at row E, no. 1. The fully marked Glasgow labels illustrated are at fig. 860 (1825), fig. 856 (1828), fig. 878 (1829) and fig. 855 (1830). Fig. 860 for HOLLANDS (1825) is a typical Robert Gray and Son design, reproduced again in 1829 (see 3 *WLCJ* 198, 199 row 6 no. 4, engraved for PORT and J2 engraved for SHERRY in calligraphic style). The letter labels, M, S and T, of 1828 (see fig. 856) are described in 7 *WLCJ* 26/28 and further illustrated in 5 *WLCJ* 259, row B3. The fig. 856 design seems to be a Scottish variant of an Emes and Barnard design of 1825 (Whitworth, page 19) and similar London designs.

Philip Grierson (1810-1823)
At one time fig. 865 for SWEET WINE (*c*.1817), fig. 866 for PORT (*c*.1817) and fig. 867 for RUM (1820) were thought to be an exclusive Grierson design. In fact it may well have been copied from London; see for comparison fig. 873 made in 1819 by Thomas and James Phipps for MADEIRA, HOLLANDS made by IH in 1821 (a cast label described in 4 *WLCJ* 169, 172 row A), BUCELLAS (see fig. 871 by Charles Rawlings in 1822) and HOLLANDS (7 *WLCJ* 226, row F5) made in 1822 also by Charles Rawlings, and fig. 872 for HOLLANDS (1822 by Peter Aitken). The Glasgow design is not quite as large or as heavy as the London labels. On the other hand London may have copied Glasgow. SWEET WINE (see fig. 865) and PORT (see fig. 866) have maker's marks only and are thus datable to 1816-1819. Fig. 847 for 'B' (1820), fig. 870 for BRANDY (1823) and fig. 881 for PORT (1824) are also by this maker, who seemed to use at least two widely differing punches, one 'P.G.' (sometimes marked three times) and one with the 'G' resembling a circuit breaker. For another example of lettering see 4 *WLCJ* 14. Philip Grierson was the seventh signatory to the 1818 Petition. The fig. 870 design for BRANDY and the fig. 881 design for PORT seem to be unique to this maker, and of particular quality, as compared with fig. 883 for SHERRY (Joseph Taylor, Birmingham, 1826) and fig. 885 for CLARET (Peter and Ann Bateman, London, 1793) and the unmarked plated examples for CHARTREUSE GREEN and MILK PUNCH illustrated in 1 *WLCJ* 100, row A1 and row E1 and for RED HOCK and TANGERINE illustrated in 1 *WLCJ* 136, row B1 and row C3. A true oval, with garland and flower border, engraved for GIN, with Philip Grierson's maker's mark and the date 1816-19, is described in lot 66 of Sotheby's sale of 29 April 1976. Philip Grierson also made a 'postage stamp design' initial label for 'B' (see fig. 847).

James Newlands and Philip Grierson (1811-1816)
James Newlands entered his first mark in 1808 and worked until some time after 1819. He was the sixth signatory to the 1818 Petition. He was in partnership with Philip Grierson (entered 1810) for the period 1811 to 1816 after which they appear to have gone their separate ways. Two labels are known by the partnership, one marked in 1811 and the other (see fig. 864) being an oil and vinegar frame label of 1813 assayed in Edinburgh, but the partnership mark overstrikes that probably of a specialist Scottish sauce label maker. The plain design of this OIL label is typically Scottish.

Luke Frazer Newlands (1816-1820)
He was admitted in Glasgow in 1816. Like Philip Grierson, he seems to have used at least two marks, in his case LN and LFN. He was the eighth signatory to the 1818 Petition. Illustrated is his RUM of 1817 (see fig. 861), marked in Edinburgh, which may be part of a set with BRANDY and SHRUB now in the Glasgow museum (see 7 *WLCJ* 26, 27). He was with James Newlands from 1820 until 1823.

Peter Aitken I (*c*.1808-*c*.1836)

His mark has been wrongly attributed to Peter Arthur. Peter Arthur was admitted in 1808 but retired or died before November 1818, as he was not a founder member of the Glasgow Goldsmiths' Company. The mark P.A. found after 1818 must belong to Peter Aitken, admitted around 1818, who was a petitioner and founder member of the Goldsmiths' Company and in fact the nineteenth signatory. His younger brother John Aitken was entered in 1822. Peter Aitken was succeeded by his son Alexander Aitken, a watchmaker and jeweller who entered his mark around 1836. John Aitken was succeeded by his son, Peter Aitken II, a jeweller in 1845. John Arthur (entered 1840) and Robert Arthur (entered 1844) are presumably the Arthurs who joined up with R.K. Muirhead to form the firm of Muirhead and Arthur. Whether these Arthurs had a family connection with Peter Arthur remains to be established.

Peter Aitken made the labels illustrated at figs. 846, 848 and 850, being a set of initial labels fully marked Glasgow 1827, and the label illustrated at fig. 872 for HOLLANDS, fully marked Glasgow 1822, in the style of figs. 865-867 (see above). It is interesting to note that the initial letters have single point suspension, are hand raised, being sawn out of a single sheet, and are of undeniable quality.

Macdonald and Reid (*c*.1818)

A single letter M of similar style to figs. 846, 848 and 850 but die-pressed, with an applied back plate to give added substance and a feel of quality, was made by M&R (believed to be David Macdonald and John Reid) of Glasgow, *c*.1818, and marked as usual in Edinburgh (see for details 5 *WLCJ* 54). John was the sixteenth and David the twentieth signatory to the 1818 Petition. The Scottish individuality of this style is apparent from the face of the label.

David Macdonald I (*c*.1812-*c*.1837)

David Macdonald I (*sic*) was the twentieth signatory to the 1818 Petition. He marked the 'D McD' die-stamped HOLLANDS (see fig. 888) which is similar to the die-stamped HOLLANDS (see fig. 887) marked by Daniel Sutherland in 1829, following a cast Story and Elliott design of 1809 (see for similar labels Whitworth page 44 and William Elliott, cast 1822, 6 *WLCJ* 7 and an example by Patrick Cunningham of Edinburgh around 1830 for SHERRY at fig. 886). Later examples can be found for SCHIEDAM (by Charles Rawlings and William Summers 1832, 7 *WLCJ* 228-9, row D3) and for CLARET, PORT, MADEIRA and SHERRY (by Robert Keay II, Perth, between 1825 and 1856, 7 *WLCJ* 29, 30). David Macdonald also made the MADEIRA label of 1825, re-engraved for WHISKY, illustrated at fig. 857, fully marked in Glasgow (see for a 1828 example 4 *WLCJ* 14), the GIN *c*.1818 illustrated in 7 *WLCJ* 226 at row G3, and the MADEIRA with the Shafto family crest 1837 (probably a replacement label – see 5 *WLCJ* 105).

John Murray I (*c*.1818-*c*.1861)

John Murray was the tenth signatory to the 1818 Petition. He was probably succeeded by his son, John Murray II, who entered his own mark in 1862. He marked fig. 854 for WHISKY in 1828, which is similar to the fig. 877 for PORT and fig. 879 SHERRY by James Mackay (1836).

Alexander Mitchell II (*c*.1822-*c*.1850)

It appears that there were two Alexander Mitchells working in Glasgow, probably father and son. The dates of Alexander Mitchell I were probably about 1797 to about 1830. He was the fourth signatory to the 1818 Petition. Two labels are illustrated by Alexander Mitchell II, one for BRANDY shown at fig. 880 (fully marked in Glasgow for 1833), with an applied double-reeded border (compare with fig. 882, an Irish label of 1785 by Joseph Gibson of Cork) and one for PORT, the single letter 'P', dated 1836 (see fig. 861) in each case fully marked in Glasgow. Dundee Art Museum has a single loop plain single letter 'S' for SHERRY also dated 1836 (probably its pair, see 7 *WLCJ* 24, 25) and a late label (1847) is described in 6 *WLCJ* 124,125. Prior to 1830 his labels were marked Mitchell and Son (see below). He also made sauce labels, such as for PIQUANT fully marked Glasgow 1833.

Mitchell and Son (c.1822-c.1834)

Alexander Mitchell was the fourth signatory to the 1818 Petition and founder (or co-founder if he was with William Mitchell, the third signatory to the Petition) of the firm. His son was Alexander (entered c.1822) who entered his individual mark in 1830 and worked on until about 1839. The father and son partnership used the mark M&S. Fig. 868 (HOLLANDS) may be an example of their productions, fully marked in Glasgow for 1823. A more correct attribution may, however, be to Marshall and Sons of Edinburgh (c.1824-c.1850).

James Law (c.1826-c.1839)

Law was apprenticed in Glasgow and entered as a silversmith there about 1826. It is believed that he then moved to the East Coast working in Dundee and Aberdeen and then in Cupar from about 1830 to about 1839. The classic plain escutcheon, one of the earliest designs – compare this, for example, with the RHENISH and the OLD-HOCK illustrated by Penzer, Plate 3 and with Richard Binley's HOCK, c.1760, illustrated at fig. 875 – is reproduced by him c.1830 for HOLLANDS (see fig. 863). It bears as marks JL and the fleur-de-lys stamped twice, similar to the marks on one of his wine labels recorded by Jackson on page 522. This design remained popular – it was even copied by John Rich in 1793 (see his MADEIRA illustrated in 6 *WLCJ* 141E, row C3) and by way of further comparison reference can be made to the PORT illustrated at 4 *WLCJ* 121, row E3 and the mid-Victorian reproductions favoured by a group of Birmingham silversmiths such as George Unite.

William Russell (c.1802-c.1855)

Russell made a wide range of silver of good quality and possibly was the originator of the mask of Pan design. An example of one of his labels dated 1827 engraved for HOLLANDS is illustrated at 1 *WLCJ* 75, row 7.1. A similar label for RUM is illustrated in 1 *WLCJ* 90, row 6.2, dated 1828 and there attributed to J. Muir Junior. The retailer in question is probably John Murray I. A third example of the mask of Pan design is marked by D.C. Rait in 1827 and is shown at fig. 859 for MADEIRA.

David Crichton Rait (c.1827-c.1846) and D.C. Rait and Son

D.C. Rait marked the MADEIRA label, fig. 859 (1827), a design referred to in 4 *WLCJ* 18 (1832) and the WHISKY label, fig. 858 (1838). When his son joined him, the firm of D.C. Rait and Son was formed c.1846 and a partnership mark was entered (see Jackson list of 1848-1903). Fig. 859 for MADEIRA is similar to the PORT illustrated by Penzer, Plate 5, A1, and to Murray's RUM of 1828 and Russell's HOLLANDS of 1827. His WHISKY (see fig. 858) follows the Robert Gray design (see fig. 851). An interesting single letter 'C' with foliate design marked DCR with gothic 'B' for 1846 was exhibited at the Wine Label Circle AGM in October 1986. It had an armorial crest engraved on the reverse side of the label.

Daniel Sutherland (c.1829-c.1831)

Daniel Sutherland in 1829 marked the HOLLANDS label shown illustrated at fig. 887, the wine name having black wax in-filling. This is the thinnest of the die-pressed labels of this style and there is a flaw in this particular die, a line of silver being observable on the right-hand side.

James Muir II (c.1828-c.1850)

Jackson attributes the mark 'J.M.J.' to J. Muir Jr. (?) (page 529). A mask of Pan RUM of 1828 marked 'J.M.J.' and illustrated in 1 *WLCJ* 90, row 6, is similar to the HOLLANDS marked by William Russell in 1827. The earliest known mask of Pan design appears to have been made either by Russell or by D.C. Rait in Glasgow in 1827. Russell's entry was also in 1827. These circumstances suggest that the mask of Pan design may have been a manufactured die-pressed design available for purchase by retailers in the usual way.

The Provinces - Glasgow, Greenock and Paisley/Scottish Provincial

Lawrence Aitcheson (*c*.1830-*c*.1865)
The WHISKY label by Lawrence Aitcheson c.1830 illustrated at fig. 869 bears the maker's mark only. Aitcheson was a reasonably prolific maker of silver of various kinds in Glasgow, particularly medals during the mid-Victorian period.

James Mackay I and II (1793-*c*.1845)
Identified from the researches of Joy Scott Whyte, it is likely that there were two makers using identical marks, probably father and son, the elder James Mackay I being entered in Edinburgh in 1793. Work with this maker's mark 'J.McK' is seen on pieces regularly from 1793 through to about 1854. Two labels made by James Mackay in 1836 are shown for PORT (see fig. 877) and SHERRY (see fig. 879) fully marked in Glasgow. These are die-pressed and the marks are clear, well spread, and individually struck. Presumably near to, or soon after, 1845 the firm of Mackay and Chisholm was created to achieve a succession.

John Mitchell (*c*.1832-*c*.1850)
The single letter 'P' for PORT illustrated at fig. 849 fully marked Glasgow 1849 has a maker's mark JM which probably stands for John Mitchell as a noted maker of labels of this period. However, there were at least four other makers using the JM mark during this period, namely James Myres, J. Muir II, J. Mark and J. Moir. A similar but plainer label was made by Rawlings and Summers in 1849, the same year, and illustrated in 5 *WLCJ* 229 at B1. A label of similar style and truly Scottish was made by the Edinburgh maker William Marshall who distinguished himself by putting a crown over his maker's initials (Jackson 507) being a single letter 'B' c.1835 and referred to in 5 *WLCJ* 54. Reference should also be made to 4 *WLCJ* 14. Another earlier maker using the JM mark was John Mann but no work of his has been recorded since 1816 and he does not appear as a Petitioner in 1818.

J. and W. Mitchell (*c*.1850)
Lot 61 in Sotheby's catalogue for 8 March 1973 refers to a label by J. and W. Mitchell, Glasgow *c*.1850.

Barclay and Goodwin (1852)
Lot 162 in Sotheby's catalogue for 21 March 1968 refers to a pair of reeded letter, S and P, by Barclay and Goodwin, 1852.

Glasgow label makers made some interesting designs of good quality and their workmanship has not been fully appreciated. No Scottish labels were exhibited in the Goldsmith and the Grape Exhibition apart from a silver mounted bottleneck label, Edinburgh, 1903. No Glasgow makers are given by Penzer at page 441. Much needs to be done to redress the balance.

PART 10 – SCOTTISH PROVINCIAL

The identification of Scottish provincial silver (i.e. other than Edinburgh and Glasgow) is somewhat elusive. Apart from the peripatetic silversmiths at one time called tinkers (who undoubtedly did make labels), the resident silversmiths in a single burgh – but not usually more than two of them working there at any one time – could have been making labels in say Ayr, Old Aberdeen, New Aberdeen, Arbroath, Banff, Canongate, Cupar, Dalkeith, Dingwall, Dumbarton, Dumfries, Dundee, Elgin, Govan, Greenock, Inverness, Kelso, Kilmarnock, Leith, Montrose, Paisley, Perth, Peterhead, St Andrews, Stirling, Tain, Thurso and Wick, to name only some.[105] The choice is wide ranging. In Part 10 we concentrate on Aberdeen, Arbroath, Banff, Canongate, Dumfries, Dundee, Elgin, Greenock, Inverness, Leith, Montrose, Paisley, Perth and Peterhead. In Part 9 we dealt with James Law of Cupar (see fig. 863) and James Osborne of Greenock.

The study of Scottish silvermakers is interesting because of the necessity of their joining an association of hammer-wielding trades. The individuality of marking by provincial silversmiths is notable in Scotland, with control by deacons instead of by assay masters, leading to the use of a variety of punches made and kept by the makers themselves. There was no assay office.

Compliance with enactments emanating from Westminster was contemplated with varying degrees of enthusiasm. The Duty Act of 1784 applied to Scotland and ordered the sovereign's head mark to be struck on all silver made and assayed from 2 December 1784. This lasted until 31 December 1786. Perhaps it was thought that if there was no assay office then there was no need for the mark to be struck! The Act of 1836,[106] which gave to the Edinburgh goldsmiths' incorporation jurisdiction over the whole of Scotland excepting the Glasgow district, was also met with little enthusiasm in provincial burghs. Articles exempt from assay (which did not officially include labels) continued to be made and marked by provincial makers.

The most informative records of an incorporation of hammermen are those relating to the Royal and Ancient Burgh of Banff. In Banff, like Elgin, there were only six incorporations; these consisted of (in approximate average order of size) hammermen, wrights, shoemakers, tailors, weavers and coopers (Banff) or glovers (Elgin). In Aberdeen there were ten branches of the incorporation, all of whom had to use metal tools in their trade. The branches of the Banff hammermen varied: included with goldsmiths and silversmiths were the trades of blacksmiths, masons, gunsmiths, bakers, glovers, fleshers, saddlers and watchmakers, and on one occasion an apothecary.

The six Banff incorporations were informally set up by contract with the town council (the provost and others and representatives of the trades being parties) in 1680. This contract gave each of the incorporations a right to choose their own deacon (the quorum being five at any election meeting) and set out privileges for the six incorporated trades as a whole, such as three votes in the election of magistrates and such as the right to have two deacons sitting on the town council. That each incorporation was informally established was settled by a case brought in the Court of Session in 1783, where it was held that the 1680 contract granted no seal of cause erecting the six trade groups into regular incorporations. Thus, the trades could not prevent other workmen from working in the burgh without paying dues to one of the incorporations. In England, £1 per annum (as of 1717) was paid by non-members of the Newcastle Company for assaying services.[107] Subsequently non-payment of such annual dues led to hostility towards visitors.[108] The Banff Town Council, however, passed byelaws and from time to time a visiting silversmith was allowed to make articles provided he paid an appropriate contribution by way of fine. Whether this was enforced against makers of flatware, brooches, labels and specially commissioned work, that is to say articles made by the so-called tinkers, remains to be established.

The deacon convener represented all the trades – all the six incorporations in the case of Banff. Each deacon represented the trades within each incorporation. He was assisted by a box master who acted as treasurer and three masters who acted as advisers. The main object of the Banff hammermen's incorporation was to raise funds by way of admission fees and quarterly payments to secure suitable provision for members who fell on hard times and to provide annuities for their widows. The deacon tried to promote his own incorporation's interest and to promote trade within the burgh. As control was by the deacon it seems likely that it was exercised by punching silver with his own mark. Such control was intermittent and was by letter punches or deaconal initial punches. A Scottish Act of 1457 had provided that both the maker and the deacon should stamp their marks on all plate. The deacon was assumed to be a wise man of good conscience. The responsibility in the case of Edinburgh was transferred from the deacon to an assay master in 1681, but provincial silversmiths do not appear to have been controlled by assay masters as such.

In view of the Commission on the Royal Burghs, reporting early in the eighteenth century, which decreed that only two silversmiths, who had to be members of a Hammermen's Association, should work in a town at one time, it would seem that provincial silversmiths were left very much to themselves as to the choice of marking both in terms of town mark punch and other punches. John Keith, for example, of Banff may well have introduced the Banff 'H' mark – probably standing for Hammermen's Incorporation. The punch was perhaps acquired a little later on by William Simpson

The Provinces - Scottish Provincial

Figures 889-899.

when he moved to Keith's premises and started marking his own silver with the 'H' mark. Certainly the members of an incorporation within a burgh were very jealous of their privileges. Thus, when in 1703 one George Leith set up on his own in Inverness, his workshop was ransacked by established silversmiths in the town. Somehow or other the travelling silversmiths made a living but work within the Royal Burghs was very much in the hands of the trades. Thus, as Margaret Holland notes, 'despite the Turnpike Act of 1751 which largely opened up the country the burgh craftsman continued along his individual way caring nothing for London and not a lot for Edinburgh'.[109]

It seems that the Banff Hammermen's Incorporation first had their quarterly meetings in a private house, usually that belonging to a deacon. Then they purchased a house adjoining St Andrew's Chapel and this was often used as a trades meeting place. They sold this later and built a new building to house the incorporation in Bridge Street in 1758 and extended this substantially in 1775. In 1818 they sold the Bridge Street property and thereafter kept their funds reasonably liquid by lending the proceeds of sale to the town council. It seems likely that after 1818 they met in the Trades' Hall, which seems to have been near the Town House.

There were close ties between the hammermen and the Church. The town council exercised fairly strict control over what fees could be charged for entrance. Before any smith could normally be admitted into the Incorporation of Hammermen as a freeman he had to make a test piece or 'sey' in the presence of a 'sey-master'. Records of admission often note the sey performed, and the fee paid upon admission. In Banff Gordon paid £3.10s.0d. (Scots) and Forbes £6 (Scots) for admission. The sey of Thomas Forbes was a gold ring, a pair of silver buckles and a ladle. Gordon's sey was a gold ring, a silver watchcase and a spoon. However, if the candidate for admission was of known standing, like William Byres, he could be admitted without sey upon payment of a composition fee (which in his case was £3 sterling).

As a general guide to allocating marks to a particular burgh it would appear to have been quite usual for silversmiths to take a device from the burgh arms as a town mark or, if this would have been similar to a device already adopted by the silversmiths of another burgh, an abbreviation of the burgh name was often used.

One must not think that the standard of the provincial silversmiths in the North East of Scotland was necessarily lower than that of Edinburgh or Glasgow – in many cases it was, in fact, quite the reverse. Many of the provincial silversmiths were apprenticed in Edinburgh and the motivation for practising in a provincial centre was perhaps family ties or environmental considerations or business opportunities. Independence from an Edinburgh master tended to afford such silversmiths an opportunity for full creativity. That is why so many provincial labels are unusual and very much individualistic in shape, design and standard of perfection. It is said that William Simpson in Banff in about 1830 employed twelve working goldsmiths and silversmiths as assistants.

Scottish provincial labels are comparatively rare and the following text is in no way intended to be exhaustive or even authoritative. It merely sets out a few comments and references for the purposes of indicating the general trend. The PORT label attributed to Hay of Leith and marked 'HAY' is quite different from the SHRUB label marked by JH in Edinburgh in 1819 and which is in the Anderson Collection.[110] This could be the work of John Heron. The CARCAVILLA label attributed to James Cornfute of Perth has also been attributed to Joseph Cullen of Dublin! The information contained in the following text must therefore be viewed with considerable caution.

Aberdeen

James Gordon was born in 1743 and worked from 1766 to his death in 1810. He was apprenticed to one of Aberdeen's famous goldsmiths, Colin(e) Allan and admitted as a goldsmith burgess on 28 August 1766.[111] He produced silver of fine artistic workmanship, such high standard being reflected in his elegant fretted and foliate in-filled crescent WHISKIE and BRANDY labels of c.1790 (see fig. 891).[112] He took no less than twelve apprentices, one of whom was William Jamieson on 1 May 1793.

James Erskine was the son of an Aberdeen vintner and apprenticed to James Smith in 1781. He was admitted as a goldsmith burgess on 27 September 1796,[113] and went on working to about 1820. His maker's mark was sometimes a Roman capital letter E and sometimes IE or JE. One punch was damaged and misses the bottom of the mark, making it look like IF.[114] It is therefore probable that he was the maker of the c.1810 plain eye-shaped label for LISBON and similarly for WHISKEY (see fig. 889).[115] Whilst his apprenticeship ended in September 1787 he was not admitted into the Incorporation of Hammermen[116] until September 1792. He was not a high-flyer. He either marked or copied the design for WHISKIE and BRANDY by James Gordon mentioned above, titled for CLARET.[117] There has been mentioned the existence of other labels, described as a 'pretty set'[118] and as 'fully marked'.[119] A shaped crescent label with embryonic Prince of Wales feathers above and extra scrolls or plumes at the ends has been noted,[120] rather like fig. 891. The plain domed rectangle (see fig. 890 for SHERRY, c.1800 was also one of his designs.

John Leslie was born in 1749 and apprenticed to James Wildgoose. He was admitted as a goldsmith burgess on 4 October 1782 and became Deacon of the Incorporation of Hammermen in 1784, 1785 and 1802, becoming in that year Deacon-Convenor. He retired around 1821 and died in 1837.[121] Around about 1785 he made a plain narrow octagonal PORT label of no particular

Figures 900-906.

significance.¹²² A number of his labels attributed to the periods 1798-1815 have been noted.

Nathaniel Gillett came from outside Aberdeen,¹²³ probably already trained, to be admitted as a goldsmith burgess on 25 September 1786. He was Deacon in 1806 and retired around the 1820s. He died *c.*1841. Around 1790 he produced a shaped rectangular label for HOME, engraved with an armorial, the label having a moulded edge.¹²⁴ He took seven apprentices between 1785 and 1809.

George Booth started off as a watchmaker, apprenticed in July 1791 to an Aberdeen clockmaker. He was admitted as a watchmaker burgess on 25 September 1801. From 1801 to 1840 he took eight watchmaker apprentices. In 1818 he took on John Allan as a foreman silversmith and took three silversmith apprentices between 1818 and 1836. He retired in 1850. His son Alexander Allan Booth worked in partnership with him from 1826 until his death in 1839.¹²⁵ George Booth's rectangular label for WHISKY has been illustrated between two trencher salts.¹²⁶ Another reeded rectangular label for SHRUB has been noted,¹²⁷ and a rectangular with rounded corners for W.WINE.¹²⁸

James Douglas began in Edinburgh where he was admitted to the incorporation in 1785. Around 1800 he worked in Dundee. From 1810 it appears he may have worked in Aberdeen.¹²⁹ However the ID mark is stylistically very different from the JD mark used in Dundee. Dr James suggests¹³⁰ that ID may have been John Davidson (who ended his training in 1748 in Aberdeen and is referred to in Aberdeen in 1780). Sotheby's¹³¹ have attributed a GIN (*c.*1810) – a plain narrow rectangular – to a J. Douglas, as have Christie's¹³² – a star design for WHISKY of the same approximate date (illustrated at fig. 894).

William Jamieson was the son of an advocate in Aberdeen, admitted as a goldsmith burgess on 27 September 1808. He had nineteen apprentices, the last being his son, George, in 1833. He retired in October 1840 and died the following year. He was a reasonably prolific maker of wine labels. Firstly, attractive cut-out letters for M¹³³ and W¹³⁴ have been observed. For PORT and SHERRY he made squarish rectangulars.¹³⁵ For spirits he made double reeded octagonals for GIN,¹³⁶ RUM¹³⁷ and BRANDY.¹³⁸ A similar style was employed for CLARET¹³⁹ and SWEET WINE.¹⁴⁰ For RAISIN and VEDONIA he employed a narrow octagonal double reeded design.¹⁴¹

George Jamieson, his son, may have retailed an escutcheon with engraved vine leaf and grape design similar to those produced in Birmingham¹⁴² around 1845 engraved for CÔTE-RÔTIE, which is in the reserve collection of the Aberdeen Art Gallery.¹⁴³ It bears only a maker's mark GJ although after 1835 in date.

William Fillan may possibly have made a plain escutcheon wine label marked WF stamped twice.¹⁴⁴ Aberdeen makers at this time (1839-1848) often stamped their maker's mark twice.

Arbroath

The Glasgow Art Gallery and Museum at Kelvingrove has an Arbroath label for WHISKY in its Victor J. Cumming Collection.¹⁴⁵ It is rectangular with concave cut corners, after Susanna Barker, in a style also adopted by John Pringle of Perth with single reeded edge, marked with AD and portcullis, by **Alexander Davidson**. A shaped oblong capital initial M within a gadrooned cast and chased border with shells at the angles by Alexander Davidson (1835-50) has been reported.[146] His BRANDY of c.1840 is illustrated (see fig. 900) to show the elegance of shaped corners and of the decorative border.

Banff
William Byres was apprenticed to James Wildgoose in Aberdeen in 1767 and became a member of the Banff Hammermen's Incorporation from 1778 to 1792, coming to it as an experienced craftsman because he was not required to produce a test piece on entry. He was recorded as 'master' in 1779 and became deacon in 1781. Around this time he made a set of four escutcheon spirit labels for RUM, GIN, WHISKY and BRANDY. He chose for them an engraved scroll decoration.[147] In 1792 he moved back to Aberdeen and died there on 9 October 1811.[148]

George Elder's GIN, a rounded narrow rectangular, is decorated with an interesting wavy double line.[149] He used the Banff vase mark sometimes (wrongly) attributed to Elgin.

William Simpson (the elder) made two labels in Banff, which were exhibited in 1946 in Edinburgh as part of the Major J. Milne-Davidson Collection. The date attributed was 1825.[150]

Canongate
Any of the eleven Canongate makers from the 1730s to 1777 could have made wine labels. Unfortunately the records are bedevilled with inaccurate attributions. The style of a small flattish crescent label engraved for HOCK (unmarked)[151] is similar to one in the Sanders Collection[152] then attributed to one David Greig said to be Canongate, now thought to be **David Gray** of Dumfries (1810-41). Labels in the collection of Major Sandeman were also attributed to Canongate.[153]

Dumfries
The marks of **David Gray** (1810-41) and **Mark Hinchsliffe** (1820-40) have been positively ascribed. Within these time frames a plain rounded rectangular PORT label[154] was made by David Gray and an octagonal BRANDY label[155] with threaded border and use of serifs for the 'B' of BRANDY was made by Mark Hinchsliffe, c.1835 (see fig. 901). David Gray also produced a pair of bevelled edge rectangular labels for CLARET and MADEIRA.[156] The attribution of labels to **Joseph Pearson** (1794-1817) must be somewhat tentative. A neck-ring label has been recorded with IP, anchor and wheatsheaf.[157] A similar label (perhaps the same) has been reviewed.[158] It is kidney shaped with flattened ends, engraved for MADEIRA. The ring is hinged somewhat unusually directly into sockets on the upper edge. The design is also recorded for the same maker but with chain suspension.[159]

Dundee
Five notable label makers of Dundee in approximate historical order were William Scott I (1774-85), Edward Livingstone (1790-1810), William Constable (1806-20), David Manson (1806-20) and Alexander Cameron (1818-47).

Scott around 1776 produced a quality feathered-edge shaped rectangular for SHRUB[160] in the style of Richard Binley and around 1780 a simple crescent for RUM with bright-cut border.[161]

Livingstone is renowned for his twelve-pointed stars. A set of six dating c.1795-1800 has survived with titles engraved at the top of the circle for BRANDY, GIN, MADEIRA, PORT, RUM and GINGER.[162] He made a toilet bottle label of a similar star design engraved for ACID.[163] Other designs employed include the plain eye for WHITE[164] and the feather-edged crescent for CLARET[165] and LISBON (see fig. 892) of c.1790.

Constable around 1810 made a plain octagonal label, engraved for CURRANT, with double bevelled edges,[166] marked pot of lilies, WC, pot of lilies. He also made a fine domed rectangular label for MADEIRA copying other examples but with individualistic wrigglework.[167]

Manson produced a narrow octagonal plain label for GINGER wine with bold lettering, the label being curved. It is, however, too big for a sauce label.[168] He also used a plain oval design for GIN[169] and SWEET WINE[170] in about 1810.

Cameron made around 1818 in narrow rectangular form a plain label for the unusual title of QUILERN.[171] He marked profusely with CAMERON, C, thistle, pot of lilies and DUNDEE on a plain curved rectangular label engraved for WHISKY.[172]

Elgin

William Stephen Ferguson (mark WF) was a busy silversmith, not only in Elgin. He came to Elgin from Edinburgh in 1828 and worked in neighbouring burghs including Peterhead. His VIOLETTE toilet preparation label is said to be the smallest label recorded.[173] His EAU DE PORTUGAL (a hair lotion) would grace any gentleman's dressing case.[174] Both are oval with single reeded borders and stamped WF ELGIN in rectangular punches, datable to c.1830. He produced his own slender cushion shaped design for PORT with heavily gadrooned borders.[175]

Thomas Stewart worked in Elgin and produced the SHRUB label shown at fig. 902 around 1815.

Greenock

The Revd. Whitworth has recorded[176] a fine armorial label with festooned drapery similar to the CLARET illustrated by Penzer on his Plate 17, middle of the left-hand side, stamped RN, and suggests that the maker could be the unidentified RN of Greenock (c.1820?). It is more likely that the maker was **Robert Naughton** of Inverness, since RN of Greenock was mainly a flatware specialist.

Inverness

Alexander Stewart worked in Inverness (1796-1812) and in nearby burghs such as Tain, Cromarty and Dingwall. His GIN label is of an uninteresting single reeded octagonal design[177] and his MILK PUNCH, a plain octagonal, is not much better.[178] For some unstated reason Mr Alexander Cuthbert attributed the unmarked MILLBURN label to Inverness.[179] It is a plain rectangular label with rounded ends and the title is in script. Alexander Stewart made some good quality silver, however, such as the Inverness Communion Cups.

Jamieson and Naughton (c.1835) made a pair of labels, one for SHERRY, of the usual plain double reeded octagonal design.[180] **Robert Naughton** around 1820 made the Hester Bateman style SHERRY (see fig. 898) and plain rounded rectangular GIN having, however, an applied border (see fig. 905).

Donald Fraser (1804-c.1829) was admitted to the Inverness Hammermen's Incorporation on 7 September 1804.[181] His advertisement of 1807 indicates that he was in the habit of making an annual visit to the principal manufacturing towns in Britain where he selected fashionable items. He certainly marked DF INS on a set of four spirit labels[182] for BRANDY, GIN, RUM and WHISKY of narrow octagonal shape with single black line border.

Leith

An octagonal double reeded PORT label stamped HAY in a rectangular punch has been ascribed[183] to **James Hay** (1810-29) of Leith c.1820. He sometimes used his surname in full (instead of his initials), which was usually accompanied by Edinburgh marks and sometimes with LEITH added. Leith did not have a separate assay office from Edinburgh. James Hay is said to have produced a scroll and floral border with which to adorn an early nineteenth century SHERRY label marked JH.[184] The mark JH may, however, be that of John Heron. From about 1818 Charles Galli and Robert Smeaton also worked in Leith.

Montrose

Two wine label makers of Montrose were William Mills (1811-30) and Peter Lambert (1833-38). **William Mills** made a plain octagonal in 1815-20, a very ordinary design.[185] He made the narrow rectangular HOLLANDS label shown at fig. 904 around 1815 with attractive engraving.

Peter Lambert seems also to have worked in Dundee and Aberdeen. A label for RUM marked PL has an unusual and interesting shaped design.[186] Lambert originally came from Berwick-on-Tweed and had a mark registered in Newcastle in 1816 and later ones in 1820 and 1844. Illustrated is his domed crescent for WHISKY (see fig. 893) of around 1835.

Paisley

The leading maker in Paisley, not far from Glasgow, was **William Hannay**. Paisley, like Greenock, was amalgamated for assay purposes with Glasgow from 1819, but still maintained its Incorporation of Hammermen (founded in 1742) mainly for charitable purposes. Illustrated (see fig. 899) is Hannay's GIN, c.1818, of oval shape, gadrooned, with four shells inserted into the border at the points of the compass. The lettering used is more artistic than bold.

Perth

One of the earliest Scottish labels was produced by **James Cornfute** (1772-96) for CARCAVILLA, crescent shaped, c.1775.[187] Reeded crescents for PORT and MADEIRA were made later on by **Robert Keay I** (1791-1825).[188] In Scotland there seemed to be a preference for octagonal plain or single reeded labels. Thus Robert Keay I produced single reeded octagonals for HOLLANDS,[189] RUM and SHERRY,[190] for VINEGAR[191] and a plain very large long narrow rectangular for UISGEBEATHA which bears five maker's marks and four town marks.[192]

Other Perth makers were David Greig (1810-55), John Pringle (1827-67), William Ritchie (1796-1814), Archie McNab (1825-35), John Sid (1808-15) and J.W. (unidentified) working around 1820. **David Greig** produced a plain shaped escutcheon for MADEIRA c.1810-20[193] and **John Pringle** rectangulars with shaped corners in the style of Susanna Barker, single thin reeded for GIN c.1830[194] and double reeded for CURRANT.[195] **William Ritchie** favoured the plain rectangular in making a PORT label,[196] but his CALCAVELLA of c.1800, with its armorial (see fig. 897), looks quite splendid. **Archie McNab's** WHISKY c.1830 is of plain octagonal form, marked three times with maker's mark only.[197] Another WHISKY by **John Sid** c.1810 is rectangular but this time with an engraved border.[198] **J.W.** made the shaped rectangular with curved ends for R. PORT with festooned shield shaped vacant cartouche above (no bow), c.1820 (see fig. 895).

Robert Keay I and Robert Keay II produced the standard octagonal double reeded WHISKY label[199] as one might expect. Robert Keay I (1791-1825 on his own) favoured the use of script titles on plain (FRONTIGNIAC[200]) or single reeded (MALAGA and NOYEAU[201]) rounded end rectangular labels. Another of Robert Keay's unusual titles is PAXARETTE, but he also managed to produce unusually decorative labels for Scottish taste such as for CALCAVELLA[202] and a single reeded oval but this time with an armorial surmount.[203]

Robert Keay was the most prolific label maker in Perth.[204] He, in partnership with his nephew (mark R & RK, 1825-39), may have the record for engraving the longest title on a gadrooned cushion shaped label which included a shell and leaf motif: 'Presented to Miss Barron Nether Balhary by the Strathmore Horticultural Society for the best GOOSEBERRY WINE Autumn 1829'.[205] The second longest may be George McHattie's CURRANT WINE of the same period.[206] The Keay partnership produced a set of escutcheons, with scroll, shell and leaf borders, for BRANDY, HOLLANDS and WHISKY.[207] **Robert Keay II**, when on his own (1839-56), made cushion-shaped, waisted rectangular labels with heavy gadrooned edges and corner scallops for CLARET, PORT,[208] MADEIRA and SHERRY,[209] and, on a shaped rectangle, a title for SHERRY surrounded by scrolling, a much lighter touch (see fig. 896), c.1840.

Peterhead

As well as working in Elgin, **William Stephen Ferguson** worked in Peterhead. Illustrated is his NOYEAU, c.1830, marked PHD and WF (see fig. 906) in long or narrow rectangular format with characteristically wide cut corners and a single reed.

The Provinces - Ireland

Figure 907.

Figure 908.

PART 11 – IRELAND

Very few Irish labels that can be attributed to dates earlier than the 1770s are known to exist. One outstanding survivor from previous years is shown at fig. 908.[210] A cast label, the design comprises vines and grapes around a central scroll bearing the name CLARET. Above the scroll is the reclining figure of Dionysus being offered a libation by a putto. Prominently struck on the scroll are the harp crowned and Hibernia hallmarks of the Dublin assay office. A date letter is absent but the finer surface details of these two marks enable them to be identified as those used in combination with the date letter of 1747 on other pieces fully stamped at the time in the Dublin Goldsmiths' Hall.[211] The maker's mark, SW, has been found on other pieces of plate additionally stamped WALSH, and consequently it is reasonably certain that Stephen Walsh made this imaginative label, one which was copied in London sixty and more years later.[212] While he is known to have moved to Dublin at a later stage in his career, Walsh is generally regarded as a Cork silversmith. Though it was not usual practice for provincially-based plateworkers to submit their wares for assay at Dublin at the time, Walsh, who was then at an early stage of his career, seems to have wanted this piece given the full stamp of approval of the law.

Another similarly inspired Bacchanalian label made by Walsh consists of a rather corpulent figure of a juvenile imbiber, described by Penzer, rather improbably, as the chubby infant Dionysus, set amidst a confection of grapes and C-scrolls, and holding a goblet in one hand and a flask in the other. A scrolling panel in front of the figure carries the name of the wine (WHITE WINE). Another is in the Victoria and Albert Museum, engraved for BOAL. They are stamped WALSH but bear no hallmarks. A mid-eighteenth century date would be tenable. The design is not unique to Walsh and was adapted in London around this time by Edmund Medlycott (shown at fig. 293, 1748-c.60) and John Harvey (1746-50).[213]

These elaborate rococo creations are not, however, the earliest labels encountered in an Irish context. In his will dated 3 May 1740, Dr Jonathan Swift, Dean of St Patrick's Cathedral, Dublin, fig. 434, bequeathed what he described as 'the enamelled Silver Plates to distinguish Bottles of Wine by, given to me by his Excellent Lady' to his friend the Earl of Orrery. Whether these were made in England or Ireland we do not know. The wealthy Lady Orrery may have brought them as a gift from London when she and her husband were visiting Swift in Dublin in August 1739 en route to her home in the North of Ireland after their year-long honeymoon.[214] A clue to the shape of these labels may be revealed from an inventory of Swift's possessions taken on 30 September 1742 which lists inter alia '…Scrolls and Chains to mark Wine'.

The scroll idea in one form or another features in other early Irish labels. Another Walsh label consists of an escutcheon of unusual multidentate outline. Here the pierced name PORT is displayed on the otherwise plain label within a banner delineated as a scroll (see fig. 907), while a mid-eighteenth century PORT by Robert Calderwood takes the form of a scroll with a small projecting flourish, a subtle rococo touch (see fig. 909).

As the eighteenth century progressed and wine labels became established as basic accessories for the sideboards of the fashionable and well to do, a broad standardisation of English and Irish styles

The Provinces - Ireland

Figure 909.

of label becomes apparent. Thus we encounter very little difference in the escutcheons of the two kingdoms in the third quarter of the century except perhaps in the proportions, Irish specimens appearing occasionally to be slightly less deep in relation to the width than the average English escutcheon and sometimes also appearing to be narrower on the bottom side. An eighteenth-century marked characteristic of later labels is their thin gauge. Subtle differences such as these encourage experts to hazard identifying an Irish label at a distance without recourse to marks. It would, however, be rash to set hard and fast rules for determining country of origin by distant sight alone.

Probably because of their provincial origin, an explicit departure from the standard trapezoid escutcheon outline has been noted on a set of three labels emanating from Cork. They follow the triangular outline often adopted for brass escutcheon plates for furniture of the mid-century. One of the three is by William Reynolds and the others, including the CLARETT illustrated (see fig. 919), by an unidentified maker I H, initials which no less than five eighteenth-century Cork silversmiths possess.[215]

With the advent of neo-classical design and bright-cut engraving in the 1770s, Irish labels really come into their own. While all the standard shapes and forms seen in London-made labels are generally to be found, it is the proportions, but more especially the way the labels are embellished with bright-cut engraving, that add distinction and distinctiveness. A few Dublin silversmiths were particularly good at expressing Bacchic and topical themes within the neo-classic framework. Exemplifying this genre is the label generally referred to as 'Boy on a barrel'.[216] Here the eye-shaped nameplate, heightened with a bright-cut border, is surmounted by a barrel supported by foliate branches on either side. Astride the barrel is a figure, usually a boy but occasionally a girl, holding a bottle or decanter in one hand and a goblet in the other. The earliest examples noted bear the maker's mark of Benjamin Taitt and the harp crowned and Hibernia of the 1773-86 cycle. Examples of a later date have been seen bearing the marks of George Nangle (see fig. 912 for SHERRY, *c.*1790), John Osborne, John Teare, Samuel Teare and William Law (see fig. 911 for CLARET, *c.*1796).

A label exhibiting a skilful fusion of a topical subject with the elements of neo-classical design is one by Benjamin Taitt, discussed above in Chapter 2, Part 13, presumably issued in the wake of the public excitement generated by the balloon ascents over Dublin in July 1785 by a Richard Crosbie, Ireland's first adult aeronaut (see fig. 312). The Belfast Volunteers had their Review in July 1785 and may well have had some connection with another extremely interesting label, again by Benjamin Taitt. This consists of a scroll surmounted by a harp and has also been discussed above in Chapter 2, Part 16. On the reverse is the inscription 'It's New Strung And WILL be Heard' (see fig. 321a).

Another label with a political charge shows the Prince of Wales' feathers emerging from an 'Irish' crown. Some bear the harp crowned and Hibernia of 1787-92, the makers being George Nangle, B. Taitt, S. Law and John Teare. It seems very likely this label had its origins in the attempt in the Irish Houses of Parliament in February 1789 to have the Prince of Wales assume the regency of Ireland. George Nangle's CLARET of *c.*1787-92 is illustrated at fig. 924 and S. Law's W.WINE of *c.*1785 is illustrated at fig. 915.

Of the more orthodox labels of this period, the eye-shaped forms exemplify the pleasing quality

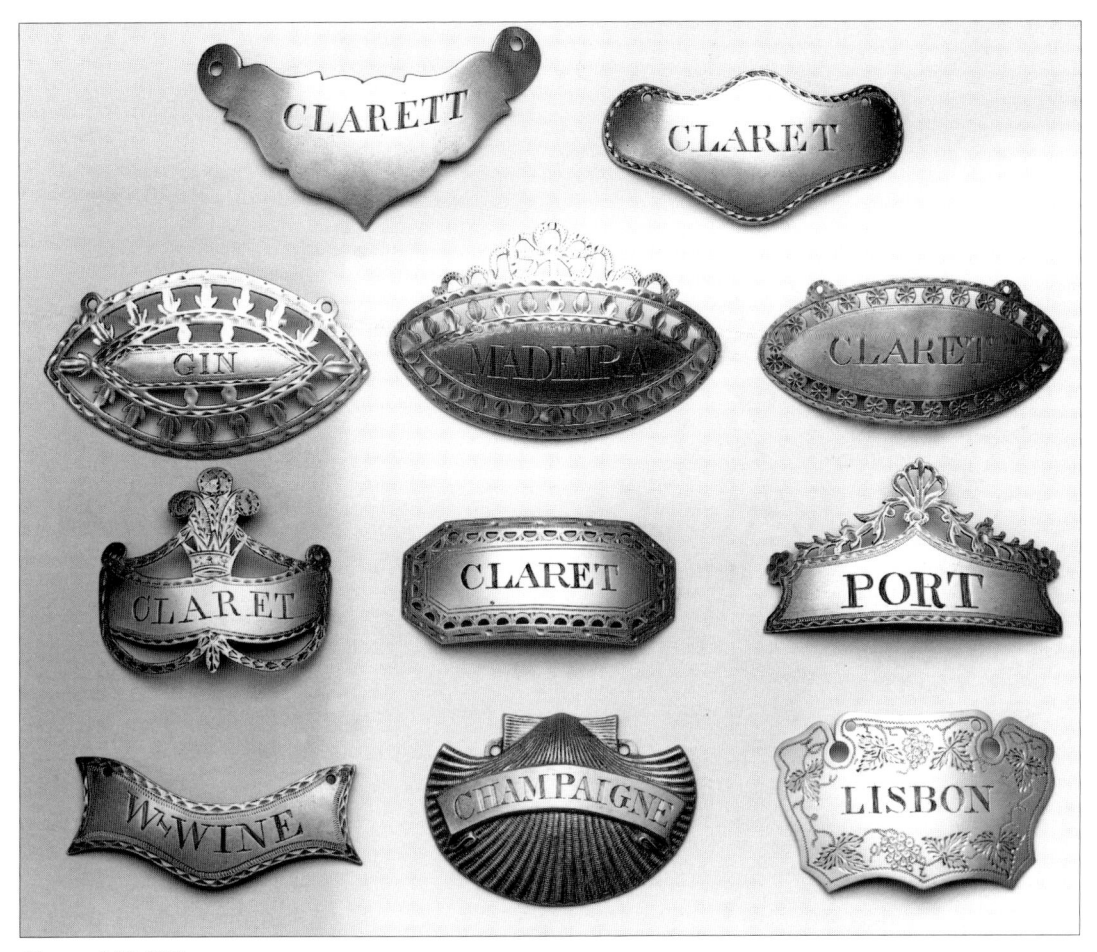

Figures 919-929.

Richard West Smith
He became a freeman in 1818 and for several years from 1821 worked in partnership with James Gamble. Smith was a warden of the Goldsmiths' Company 1834-41. Both of the marks R W S and S & G, struck with punches of various sizes, are registered against the name Smith and Gamble on a plate in the Dublin assay office.

Benjamin Taitt
Arguably the most innovative of Irish wine label makers, he was a particularly successful exponent of bright-cut engraving. Though nothing definite is known about his background, it is conceivable that he is the same Benjamin Taitt who was admitted in Edinburgh in 1763 (Jackson, 3rd ed. p. 561). The earliest piece by Benjamin Taitt that has been documented is a sugar tongs, Dublin 1775, in the collection of Trinity College, Dublin. Another Taitt sugar tongs known, though undated, bears the harp and Hibernia marks used in 1770, suggesting that Taitt's Dublin career commenced around then. He married in Dublin in 1785. The surviving assay records of 1787-1800 show that Taitt regularly submitted plate during those years. As well as the familiar marks B T in serrated-edged oblongs, Taitt also used an oblong with plain sides. This mark is found on his early work and usually appears as if struck from a damaged punch.

Henry Teare
A son of John Teare Senior, free by birth in 1814. He had plate assayed between 1815 and 1820, including some wine labels in 1818 and 1819. He succeeded his father as Weigher and Drawer in 1843, became Deputy Assay Master later that year and resigned in 1874. An earlier Henry Teare was working in Dublin in the 1760s.

The Provinces - Ireland

Figure 930.

Figure 931.

John Teare Senior
Born in 1760, a son of Samuel Teare, a goldsmith, and later apprenticed to him. He was admitted a freeman of the Dublin Goldsmiths' Company in 1797. He was appointed Weigher and Drawer in the Assay Office on 27 August 1811, a position that precluded him from working independently as a goldsmith after that. He used various maker's punches employing the mark J T in script, the crossbar of the T characteristically shaped as a scroll.[221]

John Teare Junior
A son of John Teare Senior above, he was born in 1790. He became a freeman in 1813 by service to his father. He may well have commenced working as an independent goldsmith as soon as his father took up the official position in the assay office, possibly using his father's maker's punches. He himself appears to have used a variety of maker's marks, employing both I T and J T as his initials. In 1828 he moved to London, registering a J T mark in Goldsmiths' Hall on 17 March 1828. Between then and 1 July 1847 he registered a further four versions of his J T mark at Foster Lane. Some time around 1852 he returned to Dublin, becoming junior warden almost immediately. He was elected Master of the Dublin Company in 1860. During his year of office he emigrated to New York where he died in 1874.

Samuel Teare Senior
He was admitted a freeman of the Dublin Goldsmiths' Company in 1772 by service to the then deceased Benjamin Stokes. It is not known when his apprenticeship commenced. He was working as a quarter brother in 1758 and was married in 1759. A record of his advancing £45 to the Goldsmiths' Jubilee Fund in 1811 is evidence that he was alive in that year.

Samuel Teare Junior
The Assay Master's accounts show that plate was assayed for a Samuel Teare Junior in 1796 and 1798. However, no further information about him has yet come to light. Presumably he was a son of Samuel and brother of John Senior.

Carden Terry
Born in Cork in 1742, he was advertising as a goldsmith in Cork in 1764 and again in 1770 when he announced he was setting up following his return from Dublin and London. From 1791 to 1807 he worked in partnership with his son-in-law John Williams, and on the latter's death in 1807 carried on the business with his widowed daughter Jane. He died in 1821, she in 1841. Close familiarity with Hester Bateman's work is very evident in a great deal of the output from Terry's workshop. Her well-known 'festooned goblet' label has been noted with Terry's mark as well as those of the partnerships.

Stephen Walsh
He was apprenticed to William Bennett of Cork in 1742. His mark appears on the face of the reclining Dionysus (see fig. 908) of 1747-48 and on the Powerscourt soy frame bottle mounts of 1750 (see *Sauce Labels*). By 1780 he had moved to Dublin. His application for freedom of the Dublin Goldsmiths' Company in 1781 was rejected.

PART 12 – THE CHANNEL ISLANDS

There are records of silversmiths in Jersey and Guernsey dating back to the fourteenth century and certainly they were well established by the time of the Civil War. Some of their work survives from the eighteenth century, the most characteristic pieces being the Christening mugs, of which each island had its typical form. Tankards, wine cups and beakers from this period also exist. English though they were, the islands were close to France and the threat of invasion was never far removed, a situation not conducive to a settled existence and the accumulation of much domestic silver. Furthermore, apart from the few seigniorial families, the population was poor; a middle class only began to emerge towards the end of the eighteenth century, bringing a demand for appropriate plate.

The major industries of the islands were fishing (opening up the Newfoundland Banks), cider-making and dairy cattle, but the most profitable enterprises were privateering and smuggling. None of these occupations demanded labelled decanters on the sideboard, so it is hardly surprising that only one pair of eighteenth-century wine labels is known. Two chased escutcheons for CLARET and PORT have the mark of Guillaume Henry (1720-67), one of the most illustrious of Guernsey's silversmiths (see fig. 932 for PORT, c.1760, and fig. 933 for CLARET, c.1760).[222] It has to be said, however, that they were very probably manufactured in England and imported, as was a great deal of silverware at that time. There are many instances of Jersey and Guernsey marks overstriking English ones, though in this case they are clear and original. The workmanship, however, closely resembles the early escutcheons of London makers such as Sandylands Drinkwater, and particularly Louis Hamon. Indeed it is tempting to speculate that if Henry did place an order, he went to the Huguenot Hamon. There were many Huguenots on the islands, following the French persecutions, including a Hamon family. In 1760 it would not have been necessary for the articles to be assayed by the London maker and Henry would reasonably have put his own mark on them when they arrived, to show that he assumed responsibility for them. They would also have been left blank for the required names to be engraved locally.

No other labels with eighteenth-century marks are known, but some were certainly being made in Jersey and in Guernsey from about 1820 until the middle of the century, when the fashion for them started to decline. Examples by the partnership (1831-46) of T. de Gruchy and J. de Gallais (c.1835) with the interesting names BORDEAUX and SOTERNE *(sic)* have been noted,[223] and by Charles William Quesnel (c.1840) with more usual titles such as PORT.[224]

Figure 932.

Figure 933.

Figures 934-939.

CHAPTER 8

LABELS FROM OTHER MATERIALS

PART 1 – OLD SHEFFIELD PLATE

For years prior to the mid-eighteenth century various methods of producing a silver surface on a base metal were tried and developed. These methods generally involved constructing the article in a base metal and applying the silver layer later.[1] About 1743 a method, generally attributed to Thomas Boulsover, a Sheffield cutler, was developed in which a thick sheet of silver was fused, using heat and pressure, on to an ingot of copper. It was found that the combined metals could be rolled out to a thin plate, without distortion, and worked as one sheet of metal.[2] This not only produced a surface of silver that protected the copper base metal from corrosion, but also, most importantly, it resulted in a material that could be worked in a manner similar to silver, but that cost considerably less. Old Sheffield Plate (OSP) initially had a layer of silver on only one side of the copper. Production methods were developed and it is estimated that by 1770 plate was being produced with the copper sandwiched between two thin layers of silver. It is not appropriate to go into more detail in this book, but a description of the people and processes involved can be found in *A History of Old Sheffield Plate*.[3]

Exactly when wine labels in OSP first appeared is not easy to determine. Boulsover apparently did little to exploit his discovery and almost certainly kept it secret for some years. Working away

Labels from other Materials - Old Sheffield Plate

Figure 940.

Figure 941.

Figure 942.

in his new material, without competition, he produced buttons, boxes and other similar items but left it to others to exploit the full commercial possibilities of his invention.

Before considering the designs of labels produced in OSP it is important to appreciate that, with a few possible exceptions, all were produced by the die-stamping process. It should be remembered that the early workers in Sheffield plate were cutlers. From early times dies had been essential to the cutlery trade, and their adoption by the workers in OSP followed as a matter of course. Die-stamping was an ideal method of working this new material. Principal among these early cutlers to turn to the manufacture of OSP was Joseph Hancock and it is from his workshop that the earliest wine labels may well have come. When all the evidence is considered, it seems probable that Hancock began working in OSP in about 1755.

The known exceptions to manufacture by die-stamping are neck rings and some crescents surmounted by Prince of Wales' feathers, or a bunch of grapes flanked by vine leaves (see fig. 967, LA VAUX) all of which appear to have been made entirely by hand. The latter were probably made in Birmingham, as a silver example of the former design is known from that city.

The predominant shape for wine labels in the 1750s was the escutcheon, so it was natural for the earliest OSP labels to follow this pattern. It is among the commonest designs to be found for OSP labels and they are usually of the older style of manufacture, produced from plate with silver on only one side of the copper. Labels made from this type of plate are generally termed 'copper backs'.[4] Such examples may be dated as early as 1755.

The design roughly follows that of its silver counterparts: examples for VIDONIA, MOUNTAIN, RED,PORT [the comma is present], RAISIN and LISBON are shown at figs. 934-939, and for PORT, MADEIRA, MOUNTAIN, LISBON, CYDER (with apples), W.WINE and RHENISH at figs. 940-946, whilst one for BRANDY is shown at fig. 947 and one for MADERA at fig. 978. In these early escutcheons the name is also stamped and, whilst it is still a matter for discussion, there is a view that the title formed part of the main die. Apart from the practical problems of stamping the title at a later time, this view is supported by the fact that each name has its own particular surround, although some of the more popular names had more than one die. The designs included not only vines and tendrils, as illustrated, but also, appropriately, cornucopia, apples and foliage for a label stamped for CYDER (see fig. 944) and hops and barley in different variations for ALE and BEER. To add to this discussion, fig. 978 shows a 'copper back' escutcheon stamped

Figure 943.

Figure 944.

283

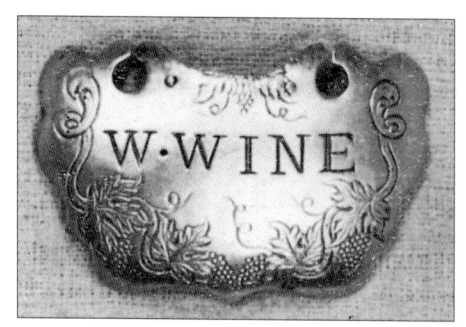

Figure 945.

Figure 946.

for MADERA. The doubt must exist as to whether a main die, including the title, would have been used with this apparent error. The question as to whether labels were stamped complete with their decoration and title or left blank for the name to be die-stamped later is a matter on which more research is needed before it can be completely resolved.

This method of manufacture, where both the surface design and name are an integral part of the die, occurs on another early OSP label. It is the large feather gadroon edged rectangular label similar to its silver counterparts of about 1765, but markedly more convex. A 'copper back' example stamped for MADEIRA is shown at fig. 949.

Although OSP labels often follow designs of contemporary silversmiths,[5] on some occasions completely new designs and variations occur. This is the case with the escutcheon shaped label engraved for LISBON shown at fig. 951. This interesting variation of the usual escutcheon shape is known only on 'copper backs' and is judged to be of about 1760. This label, with its distinctive outline, floral motif above the title and fruiting vine below with C scrolls on either side, corresponds so closely to enamel labels made around Birmingham between the 1750s and 1770s that it seems very likely that it was manufactured there during the same period.

It is believed that 'copper back' labels were still being made in the early nineteenth century, probably for reasons of economy of material costs. A small, enclosed crescent for W.PORT with stamped flower design border is shown at fig. 950. The date is difficult to establish, but from the overall shape and size is probably around 1790.

Labels of basically crescent shape design were made from plate with silver on both sides. An example is illustrated at fig. 953. They are all typical OSP designs and include reeded and corded borders. Pseudo bright cutting and beaded borders are also known. Some labels have Sheffield hallmarked contemporary counterparts in silver dating from the late eighteenth century. The label entitled CLARET (see fig. 954) occurs with a number of variations in detail in the OSP examples; this has a corded border, which is unusual.[6] A plain button holds the drapery above the crescent. Another variation, marked for RUM, is shown with a much more elaborate means of holding the drapery (see fig. 966).

Apart from the neo-classical examples described below, crescent based designs particular to OSP also include infill above with grapes and vine leaves (see figs. 965 and 967) and Prince of Wales' feathers, previously mentioned above.[7] Two rare varieties of the crescent are illustrated in figs. 969 and 972. The LISBON label (see fig. 969) has unusual drape infill and the scripted White or perhaps Red Wine (see fig. 972) is a very rare design.

Neo-classical or Adam-style labels with a 'goblet and festoons' on a crescent are shown at figs. 956 and 958. They are similar in design to contemporary silver labels of about 1780, but adapted to production by die-stamping, and were made in at least five different versions.

Labels in OSP made in the early part of the nineteenth century incorporate such features as acanthus leaves, vines and tendrils well suited to die-stamping production. Figs. 957 and 959-961 show typical examples. Labels identical to fig. 961, the so-called cushion shape engraved for CLARET, were produced in silver and hallmarked in Sheffield in the early 1820s.

Some variety of labels is shown by the pattern books. An example is shown at fig. 980. Research over the last few years shows that more than seventy different designs of wine label were made in OSP, many not having a silver hallmarked known counterpart. One explanation of this is that the

Labels from other Materials - Old Sheffield Plate

Figures 947-964.

manufacturers of Sheffield and Birmingham did not slavishly follow the design of the London makers. Silver labels of both centres are rare before 1800 and frequently, if a label does not have a London silversmith's base for its design, the OSP version of a label is more common than silver. Matthew Boulton was particularly responsible for the manufacture of OSP labels of innovative design. He was, by far, the most important early Birmingham manufacturer of OSP at his famous Soho factory, and his pattern book of around 1780 shows various elaborate label designs of which OSP examples are known to exist.[8]

Rather surprisingly two designs do not appear to have been made in OSP; these are shells and the grape and satyr label. Nearly all other designs expected were copied in some form. Of these and not previously mentioned, the star, oval and rectangle are of particular note. Three variations of the oval with various borders are illustrated including fig. 963 marked for MILK PUNCH, fig. 968 for HOLLANDS and fig. 970 for MADEIRA.

A narrow rectangular label with dome above, named for BRANDY, is shown in fig. 952. Seven other labels based on the rectangle are illustrated in figs. 948, 962, 964, 973, 974, 976 and 979. Two of the designs, fig. 964, named for ORANGE, and fig. 974, named for RUM, are not produced in silver, and others illustrated include the unusual names of STRAWBERRY, LACHRYMÆ and CAPE.

There are several important characteristics of OSP labels that can be summarised to help in their appreciation and identification when compared with electroplated items.

1. With the possible exception of neck rings[9] and those mentioned above, all labels were produced by the die-stamping method. In early examples of 'copper back' escutcheons and large feather gadroon edge rectangular labels, the name was also die-stamped. This can best be ascertained by inspection of the reverse of the label.
2. Turned back edges on labels occurred from about 1780 onwards. Because of the nature of OSP, the copper core is visible on a cut edge. Early labels did not try to overcome this but from about 1780 manufacturers developed their die-stamping so that the label edge was bent back concealing the copper from the front. This also helped produce a more rigid label as thinner gauge plate was introduced in the latter years of the century. From the second decade of the nineteenth century the bare, turned back edges were often tinned, giving a dull, matt finish. Much more rarely the edges were cut obliquely and folded back.[10] In 1830 ways were found both to interpose a layer of nickel alloy between the copper and the silver and to fuse silver directly on to nickel alloy.[11] Wine labels were probably made by both these processes, but they will be difficult to distinguish from early electroplate unless, in the former case, they are very worn.
3. The edges of OSP labels will usually reveal the copper core of the plate. Sometimes slight shrinkage of the silver away from the copper may be noted. This is particularly evident on early examples and in crescents with turned back edges.
4. The colour of OSP is that of sterling silver (925 parts per 1000), which has a mellow warm colour compared with the brittle white colour of the pure silver on electroplated items.
5. Being a laminated material, the thickness of the silver layer is much greater than that deposited by electroplating.
6. As mentioned above, early labels had the name included as a die-stamping process. On some later examples the name has been formed using letter punches, but more common is hand scratched engraving. In this case the lettering is boldly incised right into the copper and the resulting letters are then filled with black wax. Examples still exist with this intact, but where it has been lost scrutiny will reveal that the letters have never borne silver whereas, on worn electro-plated items, the recesses of the letters will be the last places where the silver shows wear. Pierced lettering has not been recorded on OSP wine labels whereas on electroplated items it is very common.
7. The original chains used on OSP labels were formed from fine-drawn wire. They were formed from a series of figure-of-eight shaped double links in which the two loops of each 'eight' were twisted to be at right angles to each other. This type of chain occurs in silver on contemporary Sheffield hallmarked labels but not on later electroplated examples.

Labels from other Materials - Old Sheffield Plate

Figures 965-979.

Labels from other Materials - Old Sheffield Plate / Other Metals

8. The name of the wine may also be a useful test when it is known that the wine ceased to be drunk before the introduction of electroplating.
9. Finally, in comparing OSP and electroplate, the chemical acid test commonly available[12] is a method of differentiating between the pure silver deposited by electroplating and the varying silver alloys used generally for OSP (see Part 6, below).

It is extremely rare for OSP labels to have a marker's mark.[13] These labels were cheap to manufacture and makers probably did not consider it worthwhile marking their name on them, nor was it legally necessary. One exception was Holy D., Wilkinson and Co. whose mark has been noted on a number of octagonal and reeded rectangular labels, one of which is shown at fig. 948, for R-PORT.

Although termed Old Sheffield Plate due to its origin, the plate soon came to be extensively produced in Birmingham and to a far lesser extent in London. Both Birmingham and Sheffield had manufacturers well established in die-stamping from the 1760s onwards and would have been capable of making OSP labels from the time of their introduction. A study of the history of makers' marks on OSP in general produces the interesting fact that between 1784 and 1835 the makers of OSP in Birmingham outnumbered those in Sheffield by seventy-six to fifty-one.

The introduction of electroplating a base metal with silver by the Birmingham manufacturer Elkington and Co. in around 1840 led to the end of OSP manufacture. Intricate goods, including wine labels, could be produced at far lower cost in electroplate (see Part 6, below).[14]

PART 2 – OTHER METALS

Gold

Until 1798 the only permitted standard for gold manufacturers in Britain was 22 carats (91.67 per cent pure). In 1798 the 18 carat standard (75 per cent pure) was permitted, and in 1854 further standards of 15 carats (62.5 per cent), 12 carats (50 per cent) and 9 carats (37.5 per cent) were introduced. New hallmarks were also then introduced to indicate the relevant standard, but it should be remembered that, up to 1815, 22 carat gold was struck with exactly the same marks as were used for sterling silver. An article made in 22 carat gold would cost more than twelve times the equivalent

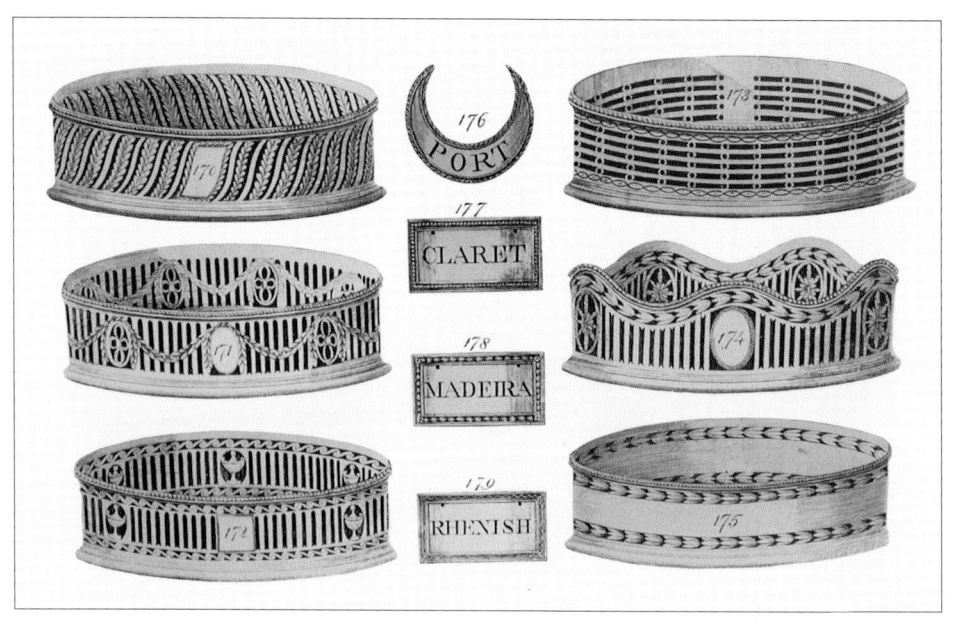

Figure 980.

Labels from other Materials - Other Metals

Figures 981-982.

in silver and even the modest 9 carat standard would be more than five times as expensive. Unsurprisingly, therefore, gold wine labels are extremely rare.

The exhibition of wine labels shown at the 1984 Chelsea Antiques Fair included a pair, CLARET and PORT (see figs. 981-982), from a set of six by Daniel Fitch, London 1792. Of light gauge, modest proportion and restrained decoration, they are crescent-shaped with relatively straight tops, almost semi-circular in outline. They have bright-cut borders and both the chains and the support rings are also made in gold. Why such unassuming objects were made in so expensive a material is a question that has no obvious answer. Large cut-out letters in gold by Rawlings and Summers, *c.*1845, have been reported but their existence has never been confirmed. Chapter 9, Part 6 illustrates an ivory label with gold mounts, and it would not be surprising if the Indian tusk and claw labels discussed in the same chapter were found with gold mounts since jewellery and vinaigrettes were certainly thus fashioned.

In 1962, when the Chester assay office was closed, a pair of 22 carat gold rectangular labels was sent for assay by Margaret and John Lowe, of the famous Chester firm of that name, to mark the occasion.

Gilt Metal other than Silver-gilt

In the mid-eighteenth century escutcheons, flat-chased with fruiting vines similar to contemporary silver labels, were made in gilded brass (see fig. 983 for CLARET, made in London, 5.6cm (2¼in.) wide). They all appear to have been made in the same workshop and some are struck with the maker's mark CP in incuse capitals, possibly for Christopher Pinchbeck the younger of London

289

(1710-83), whose father, Christopher Pinchbeck I (died 1732) invented a recipe for brass (an alloy of copper and zinc which, by varying the proportions of the components, can produce shades ranging from grey, through yellow and orange, to dark red) of a particularly golden hue to which he gave his name. Christopher Pinchbeck II described himself as a 'toyman and mechanician' and became one of the leading clockmakers of his day.

In terms of wine labels, gilding generally seems to have fallen from favour during the neo-classical period, but came back into fashion during the Regency and late Georgian periods. Some of the cast 'grape and vine' designs popular at this time can occasionally be found in gilded brass (see fig. 984 for MADEIRA, made in London, cast, *c*.1820) and were, almost certainly, made in London. Also at this time, die-stamped labels produced in Sheffield can, equally rarely, be encountered in gilded copper (see fig. 988 for SHERRY, die-stamped, made in Sheffield, *c*.1820). These, like the brass labels, would have been fire-gilded as it was not possible to produce gilded copper by fusing and rolling ingots in the manner of OSP and electro-gilding had yet to be invented.

One of the most intriguing gilt metal labels is in the Marshall Collection at the Ashmolean Museum. Of cut-corner, rectangular shape, it has openwork lettering for MADEIRA and the border is set with 'jewels' of coloured paste.

Pewter
Although it has been stated elsewhere that pewter was not used in the manufacture of wine labels, at least one label apparently made of this metal has been recorded. It is of oval shape (5.8 x 4cm, 2¼ x 1½in.), mounted in a beaded and reeded gilt-metal frame. The title for RUM is scratch-engraved in thin letters. The chain is composed of copper links and the date is probably mid-nineteenth century. Other examples of this design are believed to exist.

Silvered Brass
Before the invention of OSP silver plating was achieved by burnishing silver leaf in progressive layers on to brass. Such wares were known as 'French Plate' and their makers called themselves 'French Plate Workers', probably because Huguenot refugees brought the skill to Britain in the late seventeenth century. An important private American collection of what Americans refer to as 'English silver-form brass' contains a set of three plain escutcheons, all with traces of silvering to the fronts only, for ALMADE, CHAMPAGNE (see fig. 986, made in London, *c*.1750) and SETUVAL. The last is obviously a corruption of Setubal, a town south of the Tagus near Lisbon that still produces a rich, white dessert wine. ALMADE, however, is a bit of a mystery and this is the only recorded instance of the name. There was an old Portuguese wine measure spelt 'almude' so it might relate to another wine of Portuguese origin.

Brass
While we have seen above that brass was used for labels that were to be plated either in gold or silver, it does not appear to have ever been employed in its pure state. A cast design in the Art Nouveau style was made in heavily patinated brass (although it might be bronze, an alloy of copper and tin) with an enamelled central tablet for SHERRY (see fig. 987). It is stamped on the back 'Made in England' and probably dates from the early years of the twentieth century.

Tin
Tin, painted and then lacquered with one or more coats of fired varnish was a highly popular material for decorative domestic wares from about 1730 to the middle decades of the nineteenth century. It is usually now referred to as 'Toleware' or 'Tole' after the French *tole peinte* (literally painted sheet metal). Among the antiques trade it was also commonly called 'Pontypool ware' after the leading centre of production, although it was made equally extensively in Usk and Birmingham – not to mention Continental Europe and the USA. In the eighteenth century, however, it was called 'Japanned ware' or simply 'Japan' as all types of painted and lacquered decoration were known as japanning.

Labels from other Materials - Other Metals

Figures 983-988.

That labels were made in this material from a relatively early date is evidenced from the trade card of Thomas Bingham 'Ironmonger, Brasier and Toyman in Middle Row, Holborn, London'[15] which lists 'Bottle tickets' among the 'very great Variety of curious Japans' that he has in stock. Bingham is listed in London street directories at this address continuously from 1767 until 1818. However, the trade card also states that he is the 'son and successor of Mr. Abel Bingham' who last appears in the directories in 1765, so we can assume that it was printed towards the beginning of his tenure. The presence of 'French Plate' among the goods listed would certainly support this assumption.

The dearth of surviving examples in this medium, there being none in the major institutional collections, is explained by the friable nature of the metal and the ease with which the decoration could be chipped. Once damaged, the article had no intrinsic value and would simply be thrown away. The collection of the late Dr Bernard Watney included a plain escutcheon with gilt letters for MOUNTAIN on a red ground. Dating from the mid-eighteenth century, its state of preservation confirmed the failure of toleware to withstand the test of time. Fig. 985 illustrates a much later toleware example for SHERRY, *c.*1840, painted with red roses and green foliage on a light brown ground (possibly originally white), like the related label depicted in the Wine Label Circle's *Journal*.[16]

Tin Alloys
Pewter, an alloy of tin and lead with some copper and antimony, was employed for centuries in the manufacture of domestic metalwares, but it appears to have been only very rarely employed in the making of wine labels. Britannia metal, an alloy similar to pewter but without any lead, was a popular base for plating with silver after the invention of electroplating in 1840 and some early EP labels may have been so manufactured, but nickel alloys were much more commonly used.

Nickel Alloys
Alloys of nickel, copper and zinc produce a hard metal very similar in colour to silver. Before the 1820s, when Europeans mastered the technology of refining nickel, this alloy was imported from the Far East and was quite expensive. Now known, and much sought after, as 'paktong', it was usually called 'tutenag' in the eighteenth century and no labels in this material have ever been recorded.

Labels from other Materials – Other Metals/Battersea Enamels

Figure 989a.

Figure 989b.

Figure 989c.

After about 1825 nickel alloyed with copper and zinc was known by a variety of names including 'German Silver'[17] (the process of refining nickel was discovered in Germany) and 'Argentan', but the title 'Nickel Silver' (as in EPNS – Electro-Plated Nickel Silver) soon became the norm and the most popular base for silver plating. It also played a little discussed part in the closing stages of the OSP industry.

In 1830 Samuel Roberts of Sheffield took out a patent (No. 5963) for the fusing of a layer of nickel alloy between the silver and copper of OSP. In the same year Thomas Nicholson and Robert Gainsford, also of Sheffield, succeeded in fusing silver to nickel alloy.[18] Both these methods went into production and it is quite likely that labels were made by these processes. Unfortunately, evidence of the former could only be seen if all three layers have been worn through (which would probably ensure that the article has not survived) and the latter would be extraordinarily difficult to distinguish from electroplate.

Aluminium

Another metal that needs to be mentioned in the context of wine labels is aluminium, from which an unmarked example incised MARSALA was fashioned during the First World War and engraved with an inscription recording that it had been made from a part of the first 'Zeppelin brought down in England. ...1st April 1916' (see figs. 989b and 989c).[19] Two other labels are known for BRANDY and GIN (see fig. 989a) with heavy large-linked chains. The original inscription is defaced on GIN and overstamped ORIGINAL PRODUCT, for reasons that are not known.

Platinum

Michael Druitt and Co. made a limited number of labels in platinum to mark the institution of a hallmark for that metal in 1975. The design is a peacock's head, couped, for the Arbuthnot family, which was originally produced by Peter and Anne Bateman in 1796 (see fig. 76 for PORT). It is stamped with Druitt's characteristic 'MWD' initials in a bottle-shaped frame, the new platinum mark and the date letter 'a' for 1975, the first year of the new cycle.

PART 3 – BATTERSEA ENAMELS

The story of Battersea enamels begins in Paris in 1706 with the birth of Simon Francis Ravenet. Ravenet's early life and antecedents are obscure. He is known to have worked as an engraver for the Paris publisher Louis Surugue. In 1724 he contributed four engraved plates from designs by Le Bas and other French artists to Surugue's edition of *Don Quixote*. These plates are a notable performance for a young man then only eighteen years of age and testify to his exceptional skill as an engraver. Thereafter he worked for twenty years in association with Le Bas (some of whose designs he later used at Battersea) and for other leading French engravers, and was the author of many fine plates, both portraits and book illustrations.

Ravenet appears to have come to London in 1744, in response to an invitation from Hogarth. Hogarth's purpose was to find a better engraver for prints of his pictures, notably the well-known series of paintings *Marriage à la Mode*, by publishing engraved prints of them, as the leading French artists were then doing. The scheme, however, came to nothing, mainly because of Hogarth's quarrelsome and domineering character. Ravenet remained in London, working for a time for the engraver and publisher Richard Dalton.

In 1753 he began his connection with the Battersea enamel works, established in the autumn of that year at York House, Battersea, by the firm of Janssen, Delamain and Brooks to exploit Brooks' recent discovery of a process for transferring engraved designs on to enamel surfaces. The Battersea factory was unfortunate from its inception. The venture finally collapsed in 1756, and there are good reasons for thinking that it may have come to an end in July 1755. During its short life the factory produced transfer-printed enamel trinkets and 'toys', snuff boxes and portrait and other plaques of unsurpassed quality. The products of the York House factory were manufactured to appeal to the cultivated classical taste of the eighteenth century, and it is perhaps not surprising that they seem to have failed to make any popular appeal, at least in Britain.

After the failure of the York House factory, Ravenet continued to work in England, becoming one of the first Engraver Associates of the Royal Academy. He died in 1774, and is buried at St Pancras.

As the firm's principal engraver, Ravenet played a leading part in the achievement of the factory at York House. His work is usually in monochrome, in delicate shades of red, puce, brown or mauve, and less commonly in black. Sometimes the transferred impression is painted over in natural colours, so that the lines of the engraving are not easy to distinguish. For many years no piece was known marked either with the name of the firm or of the artist. Two portrait plaques of William Augustus, Duke of Cumberland, marked with Ravenet's name (appropriately signed 'Ravenet Etfor fecit' or 'made by'), have recently come to light, thus confirming in a striking fashion the attribution made by Mr Rackham in 1924 in his celebrated catalogue of the Schreiber Collection, but it has been suggested that this signature looks as if it might have been added to the plate by another hand! Attribution to Ravenet must, therefore, rest largely upon comparison with known examples of the artist's engraved work, and the field for error is consequently wide.[20] Some pieces are appropriately signed 'S. Rav, fecit' and this may be his genuine mark.

The enamelled wine labels probably designed by James Gwin, the Irish artist, are generally attributed to Ravenet. Where the engraving can be seen through the colour, or where, more rarely, the label is uncoloured, the engraving has all the characteristics of Ravenet's work.

The exciting discovery that the Irishman John Brooks started transfer-printing at Birmingham in 1751[21] before he took charge of operations at the Battersea Factory (1753-56), under Alderman Stephen Theodore Janssen, leads one to search for the pre-Battersea enamels of Brooks' Birmingham period (see fig. 1008 for a possible considerate). It is now known that Brooks in fact filed three unsuccessful petitions for patents concerning transfer-printing: the first, dated 10 September 1751, when he was in Birmingham and the other two from York Place, Battersea, on 25 January 1754 and in April 1755. The Birmingham entry is the 'humble petition of John Brooks of Birmingham in the county of Warwick, engraver, sheweth that the petitioner has by great study application and expense found out a method of printing, impressing and reversing upon enamel and china from engraved, etched and mezzotinto plates, and from cuttings on wood and mettle, impressions of History, Portraits, Landskips, Foliages, Coats of Arms, Cyphers, Decorations and other devices. That the said art and method is entirely new and of his own invention and for as much as it will be for the service of the public…'. The first York Place petition of 1754 adds glass wares to those Brooks can print upon and makes special mention of transfer-printing on stone and earthenware. The final petition adds Delftwares to the list.

The first direct mention of wine labels occurs somewhat later in an advertisement in the *Daily Advertiser* of 28 February 1756 announcing the sale of Janssen's belongings following his bankruptcy. Here amongst 'a Quantity of beautiful Enamels, colour'd and uncolour'd, of the new Manufactory carried on at York House at Battersea, and never yet exhibited to public View' are mentioned 'Bottle Tickets with Chains for all sorts of Liquor, and of different Subjects…'.

The fact that a further sale advertisement of 31 May 1756 concerning the contents of York House lists enamel blanks and copper plates 'beautifully engraved by the best Hands' is a fair warning that

Labels from other Materials - Battersea Enamels

Figures 990-995.

one may not always be correct in one's attributions to Battersea. Certainly one should be wary of accepting as Battersea substandard transfers taken from worn copper plates, or prints on poor quality enamel; for even the backing enamel on Battersea examples is a fine milky-white and this is not always the case from elsewhere.

The group of printed wine labels classed as Battersea is of very high quality, being beautifully engraved by Ravenet whose magic touch gave an almost three-dimensional effect to the sensitive designs of James Gwin. No printed wine labels have yet been discovered that could be classed as pre-Battersea and contemporary with the earliest copper based painted enamel wine labels from Birmingham (*c.*1748-*c.*1753). These latter painted escutcheon labels are decorated with finely painted scrolls, grapes and flower sprays that parallel the decoration on early Birmingham painted snuff boxes and could be compared with the style of flower painting, of similar dates, seen on raised-

Labels from other Materials - Battersea Enamels

Figure 996.

Figure 997.

anchor Chelsea porcelain (1749-52). The two painted escutcheon enamel labels, CREME DE MENTHE and RUM, from the Weed Collection,[22] seem rather to belong to the not uncommon group that dates from the 1760s or even later, a counterpart, if one is stretching a point, of gold-anchor Chelsea flower painting (1758-69).

The enamel labels printed at Battersea only reveal their full quality when there has been no over-painting. This bears out Brooks' recommendation 'that his work may not be spoiled by Committing it into the Hands of unskilful Daubers'.[23] However, coloured enamels were certainly part of the stock at Battersea and it may be that some of the finest over-painted examples were done there. These contrast with a few others, which may only have a faint outline print or none at all. For example, the Venus and Cupid/Satyr design is sometimes so crudely painted that it leads one to suspect that these labels are post-Battersea. Certainly, some of the wine label designs were re-engraved and used subsequently at Birmingham and possibly elsewhere. Some post-Battersea period productions from Birmingham incorporated Ravenet transfer printed material originating from Battersea. A few large escutcheon wine labels exist (see fig. 1007 for RUM) with rather heavy, black-printed Battersea designs, long recognised as later than Battersea.[24]

The fact that Brooks started printing enamels at Birmingham, where there was a multitude of different specialised manufacturers, adds new weight to Cyril Cook's far-seeing remarks,[25] 'It is becoming increasingly clear that Janssen must have obtained his materials – blank enamels, mounts, frames, tiles and chains – from [a] manufacturer who specialised in such work'. He continues, 'There are thus excellent reasons for thinking that the Battersea enamel works were set up with the primary object of exploiting John Brooks's invention for applying printed decorations to enamels and tiles and that the hand-painted subjects, like the painted decorations, which were frequently superimposed on a printed base may have been added elsewhere'.

Figure 998.

Figure 999.

295

Labels from other Materials - Battersea Enamels

Figure 1000.

Figure 1001.

Herbert C. Dent[26] lists and describes twelve labels in his collection with eleven different titles and eleven different designs. He also mentioned three other titles and one design known to him elsewhere making a total of fourteen titles and twelve designs. Dent illustrated two of his labels. However, Penzer[27] did not illustrate any examples, although he compiled a most careful list of twenty-four different names on Battersea wine labels with descriptions of eighteen or nineteen different designs. The two enamel labels he did illustrate, however, with Battersea-type escutcheons are unattractive fakes and the other enamel labels surrounding these two on Plate 1 of his book are for the most part from Emile Samson's factory in Paris and comparatively modern (c.1890-1910).

Cyril Cook[28] followed on in the Penzer tradition and expanded the latter's list to include a total of thirty titles, although one of these, JURANSON, is known only from a brief description in 1862, and another, SAUTERNE, a label illustrated by Penzer, has nothing to do with Battersea. Amongst the twenty-eight or twenty-nine titles remaining are twenty or twenty-one different designs. However, he omitted two title variants that are mentioned by Penzer: CHAMPAIN and MADERE. Cook also mentioned a number of titles, some of them in a later note in *The Connoisseur*, which have been inscribed on labels that are usually associated with other names – for example, MADEIRA on a BURGUNDY and W. WINE label design (design number 1 in the list that follows).

More than forty titles are mentioned in the following list, with seventeen different designs. An example of ESPAGNE, mentioned by Penzer and Cook, survives, but the only other recorded example, from the Ionides Collection, was destroyed by fire. The great rarity of Battersea wine labels is not always appreciated, possibly because of their variety both in subject and design, which may well give the impression that a greater number exists than is actually the case. For example, nearly all the labels listed below are unique as far as is known.

An example for W. WINE exists that has not been coloured. This label is printed in monochrome in

Figure 1002.

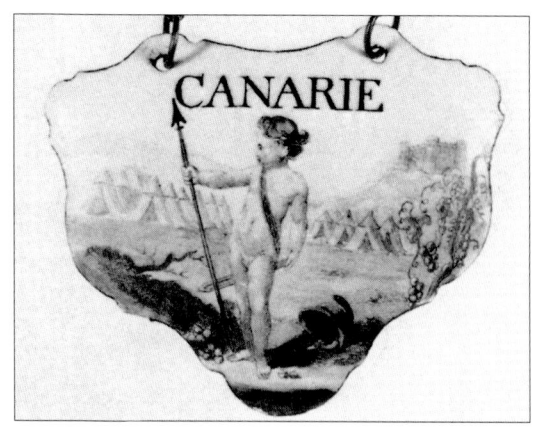

Figure 1003.

Labels from other Materials - Battersea Enamels

Figure 1004. *Figure 1005.* *Figure 1006.*

a delicate shade of red, and the lines of the engraved print are clearly visible. Two versions of MADEIRA are known. The engraving is the same in each case, but there are substantial differences in the colour (see figs. 994 and 995). BURGUNDY is a design (see fig. 990) used by the York House factory in somewhat different taste. Cupid draws aside the veil, revealing Venus. This design appears on a snuff box, which was certainly not of Battersea origin; but that does not necessarily discredit a Ravenet attribution. CHAMPAIN illustrated at fig. 1006 is often regarded as the highest achievement of Battersea wine label production. The design is certainly intricate, and so is the colouring. In this label the colour has rendered almost completely invisible the lines of the engraved print. A box lid is illustrated at fig. 1002 with a design showing Cupid protecting a lamb from a leopard or a tiger. This design is used for the FRONTINIAC wine label of which there is an example in the Ionides Gift at South Kensington. Cyril Cook illustrates it.[29] This box lid is a good example of Ravenet's engraved work. It is printed in deep red and not coloured, as is the 'FRONTINIAC' label.

CAPE (see fig. 1005), transfer printed in red and overpainted with a blackamoor embracing a leopard, and BEER (see fig. 1004), transfer printed in sepia and overpainted with two putti or cherubs harvesting barley, were both in the Bernard Watney Collection.[30]

List of seventeen designs for alleged Battersea wine labels[31]

Figs.		Design	
990	1	BURGUNDY	Design is also used for BURGOGNE[32], MADEIRA, MULSEAU[33] and W. WINE[34]
–	2	HUILE DE VENUS[35]	Design is also used for MUSCAT
1001	3	RHENISH	Design also used for LUNEL[36] and MALVOISIE
993	4	MOUNTAIN	Design also used for MALAGA[37] and HONGRIE
1002	5		Design used for MARASQUIN[38] and for FRONTINIAC
–	6	MORACHE	Design also used for RUM and MOSELLS
996	7	PALME[39]	Design also used for SHERRY and ESPAGNE
–	8	PUNCH	An individual design showing a Punch Bowl[40]
997	9	RANCIE[41]	Design also used for CHAMPAGNE,[42] CURRANT and ALE
999	9	St EMËLION	Ibidem
1006	9	CHAMPAIN	Ibidem
998	10	RHEIN	Design also used for HOCK,[43] ALE and RHIN (the up-ended barrel)
1000	11	TOQUAY	Design also used for LISBON,[44] QUETSCHE and PONTAC (the long-ways barrel)
994	12	MADEIRA	Design also used for another MADEIRA (the end barrel)[45]
995	12	MADEIRA	
992	13	W. WINE[47]	Design also used for ROTA[46] and W. PORT
1003	14	CANARIE	An individual design[48]
991	15	CLARET	An individual design[49]
1004	16	BEER	An individual design[50]
1005	17	CAPE	An individual design[51]

297

Labels from other Materials - Non-Battersea Enamels

Figures 1007-1010.

PART 4 – NON-BATTERSEA ENAMELS

It has previously been assumed that, if any enamel wine labels were produced before the Battersea specimens, none has survived. This may not be the case. Enamellers were working in Bilston, Wednesbury, and other places in South Staffordshire, in Birmingham, Dudley, Liverpool and London in the 1740s, and it would have been possible for them to make enamel labels to match the silver labels that were beginning to become popular. Transfer printing began in Birmingham as early as 1751. Saddler and Green of Liverpool were also active in this field.

The RUM label illustrated (see fig. 1007) is probably related to the Battersea specimens. Possibly some of the copper plates engraved by Ravenet were acquired at the Battersea sale by a Staffordshire factory, and were then used to produce such labels as this. The gilt scroll border is typical of the decoration of the Midlands enamellers. Some say that the Battersea artists never added a border to their transfer prints, but the word 'never' is always a risky one to use. However, failing any definite evidence that this is a Battersea Ravenet, it should be considered a probable 'Staffordshire Ravenet' or 'Birmingham Ravenet'– a sort of second cousin. The label is 5 x 5cm (2 x 2in.), of smooth white enamel, and the scene is delicately coloured.

Labels were prepared for painting, or transfer-printing. Briefly and simply a thick layer of opaque white glass was fused on to a thin sheet of copper (of the required shape) at bright red heat. After the decoration was applied to the resulting enamel, firing would again take place.

The large label illustrated, BRANDY (see fig. 1008), was probably made either in London or Birmingham, and is of the Battersea period, or earlier. The label, which is milk-white in colour with enamel of even quality on both sides, measures 5 x 5cm (2 x 2in.). The scroll decoration is a golden brown colour; the floral decoration at the top appears to be a rose, while grapes are featured at the base. The eyelet holes are encircled with a blue ring. This feature is usually an indication that a label was made during the eighteenth century or, at the latest, very early in the nineteenth century. A set of six of these labels is illustrated at figs. 1040-1045. Similar labels have been noted, one without the blue ring, for PORT and LIQUOR. Smaller versions exist in the same style (see fig. 1035) for

Labels from other Materials - Non-Battersea Enamels

Figures 1011-1015.

MALAGA and fig. 1031 for COGNAC). Also milk-white in colour on both sides are, of the same outline but completely different pattern, MOUNTAIN (not illustrated), and of a different outline and pattern of the same size, MADEIRA (not illustrated), and of a smaller size, PACARET (not illustrated). Still following the bottom grapes and golden brown scroll design, labels were made in a small size (for ANISETTE and CLARET, not illustrated) and miniature size (for BRANDY, PORT and SHERRY, not illustrated), all with a creamy white paste. A wine label size escutcheon has been noted for FLORENCE M in black on a plain white background. A plain white escutcheon for ALE in black letters is in the collection of the museum of the Thomas Coram Foundation for Children in Bloomsbury, London. In 1739 Thomas Coram, a retired sea captain, set up a Foundling Hospital. Mothers, who left their children in care, were required to leave a token, in this case a wine label, which they could use at a later date to help identify a child should their financial situation improve.

The two labels, CLARET and PORT (see figs. 1011 and 1012) present a slight problem. They are quite rare examples and the style and colouring of the decoration are so alike that one would expect a similar date of manufacture. The problem is that the rectangular label follows a design common in silver in around 1780 (by makers such as Margaret Binley), while the escutcheon shape is akin to the silver version that appeared early in the nineteenth century (for examples see the work of John Reily). Did the enamellers copy the silversmiths, or vice versa? The close similarity of the style and colouring of the decoration inclines one to hold the second view, and to date them both to the last quarter of the eighteenth century. The CLARET label (see fig. 1011) is 6.3 x 2.5cm (2½ x 1in.); the PORT (see fig. 1012) is 6 x 3.5cm (2⅜ x 1⅜in.), the decoration being yellowish-brown scrolls, roses and small blue flowers. Both are probably Bilston- or Wednesbury-made.

The two escutcheon labels BRANDY and CLARET (see figs. 1009 and 1010) are both 5.7cm (2¼in.) wide, but the narrower one is 3.5cm (1⅜in.) in depth and the other 3.8 cm (1½in.). The BRANDY is a very rich glossy enamel, with bright floral decoration, very pale reddish scrolls on

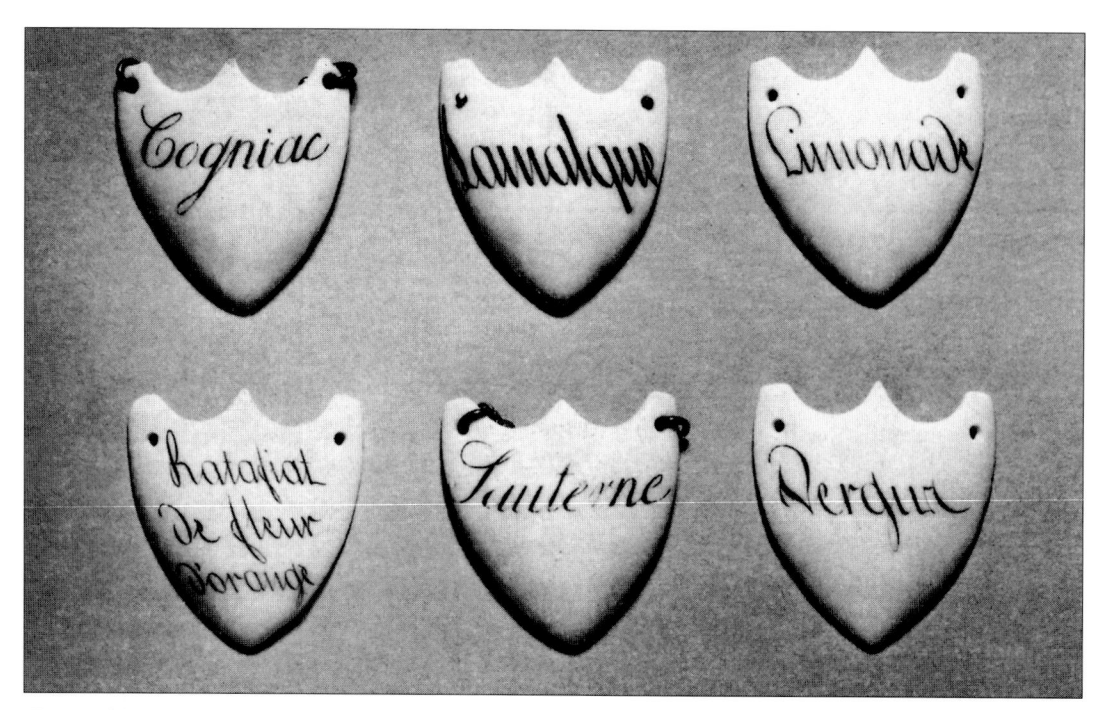

Labels from other Materials - Non-Battersea Enamels

Figures 1016-1021.

the outside edges and blue eyelets. It probably dates from the last quarter of the eighteenth century. The CLARET label has a very white enamel of slightly inferior quality. The decoration is somewhat dull, and the outside scrolls of a greenish colour. It is probably late eighteenth century. Both labels are likely to be of Staffordshire origin.

The escutcheon, EAU DE COLOGNE (see fig. 1015), is an example of the deterioration in quality of enamel labels by the late nineteenth century – the colouring is dull, the decoration is crowded and the enamel slightly muddy.

Enamels later than those shown in figs. 1040-1045 show some sophistication in style. They precede the introduction of the domed escutcheon. COGNAC (see fig. 1031) is simply a smaller version of the design. MALAGA (see fig. 1035) copies the design but is of poorer quality. CLARET (see fig. 1037) and HOCK (see fig. 1039), as well as W.PORT (not illustrated) date to about 1770 and have attractive pink colouring with flower eyelets (note that figs. 1037 and 1039 are shown reduced in size). CLARET (see fig. 1034), PORT (see fig. 1036) and LISBON (see fig. 1038) date to some ten years later, around 1780, and have delicate multi-colouring. R.PORT (see fig. 1030) and W.PORT (see fig.1032) are a more modern pair to decorate twin port decanters. Of late Victorian times, the small CORDIAL (see fig. 1025) and GRAND MARNIER (see fig. 1027) go with BENEDICTINE (not illustrated) as liqueur labels. They have brass chains and browny-grey mottled backs.

The French firm Dreyfous copied English labels. Sometimes their labels are signed on the back, as in the case of ANISETTE on a two-handled vase of flowers (not illustrated). They can be identified by the use of serifs on the capital letters 'C' and 'S' as in CURACAO and CHARTREUSE (not illustrated). The backs are green stained mottled creamy white. The copper tends to show through all along the edges. Dreyfous had a London outlet (see Chapter 9, Part 8, France, below) that distributed small toiletry labels such as for VERVEINE (verbena) and JASMIN.

Another French firm, Delvaux, of 18 rue Royale, Paris, produced 'stove-back' enamels, so-called because of the reverse side being mottled black in colour. A small kidney-shaped label for KIRSCH is signed by this firm. Another stove-back label has semi-precious stones inset as part of the border, the title being for BRANDY. Labels with identical styles of labelling and colouring, for EAU-DE-VIE in kidney shape and for CHARTREUSE in shaped narrow escutcheon format, have different compositions. The first and earlier label is of white paste. CHARTREUSE is a stove back and of a newer generation. Both are decorated with a single pinky-brown rose in a floral spray. Other stove backs have been noted of unique design in an escutcheon shape for PORTO, MARC, CALVADOS and KIRSH.

Labels from other Materials - Non-Battersea Enamels

Figures 1022-1049.

French nineteenth-century enamels certainly have some interesting names, such as ROUSSILLON, FOUGERE, FRAISETTE and others mentioned below in Chapter 9, Part 8, France.

The attractive WHITE LILAC (see fig. 1014), with top ribbon decoration, probably comes from France.[52] These were imported during the late eighteenth and early nineteenth centuries. The chains on all enamel labels appear to be steel, with large rings through the eyelets. Also from the Continent is MOSEL (see fig. 1026), probably from Austria or Germany, and CURAÇAO (see fig. 1022), probably from France and reminiscent of CASSES (see fig. 1228) electroplated on copper.

301

Labels from other Materials - Non-Battersea Enamels

Figures 1050-1060

The domed escutcheon, BRANDY (see fig. 1013) is the most common of the enamel labels. Such labels were probably made in the Midlands or in France between 1850 and 1930. The general colour can be red, green or blue. Many labels of this design poured in from France. These, which are sometimes marked 'France', are usually deeper in colour than the home product, and this is perhaps a quick way of differentiating between them, but other tests can be made.

Emile Samson's factory in Paris specialised in making replica enamels of a bygone age. They copied between 1870 and 1930 domed crescent English Staffordshire style labels in wholesale quantities. The remnants of Samson's enamelling department were fortunately purchased by a London based antiques dealer in 1975.

Small size Samson labels are shown in figs. 1023 and 1050-1060. They usually measure 26 x 36mm (1 x 1½in.). This in fact is the size of the blank originally used by Samson in Paris now held by the Victoria and Albert Museum, London. They are consistent in style. Three labels for KUMMEL (see fig. 1057 and two not illustrated) are of this size and all have an umlaut over the 'U'. The height of the lettering for titles is consistent. Small size Staffordshire labels are shown in figs. 1061-1068. Some indeed are marked 'England' on the back. They all measure 28 x 39mm (1⅛ x 1½in.). There is a variety of decorative styles. This variety indicates production by a number of different factories in the area. Thus fig. 1063 may come from Factory 1, figs. 1065 and 1068 from Factory 2 and figs. 1061 and 1064 from Factory 3 mentioned below. Some, unlike Samson labels, fluoresce, pointing to different sources of copper being used.

Normal size Samson labels are shown as a group (see figs. 1069-1080) identified as having approximately the same size of 40 x 51mm (1½ x 2in.) and hence the same copper template. It should be noted that once again the design is similar both above and below the title. Regular size selected English labels (some are marked 'England' on the back) are shown all coming from one factory (Factory 1) in figs. 1081-1088. They measure 38 x 49 mm (1½ x 2in.). In these English titles Kummel does not have an umlaut. The capital letter 'I' has a dot above it in GIN (see fig. 1086) and in WHISKEY (see figs. 1049 and 1088). The floral arrangements beneath the title are less centralised and organised than in the French version. Serifs are used on the capital letter 'C' in fig. 1047 (HOCK), fig. 1081 (CURACAO) and fig. 1083 (CHARTREUSE). And of course KUMMEL (fig. 1082) does not have an umlaut.

Another English factory (Factory 2) produced labels having a leaf either side of the flower stalk immediately above the title. Such titles include BOURBON, INDIAN and SAUTERNE. These clearly identifiable labels are almost identical in size to Samson labels, measuring 40 x 51mm (1½ x 2in.).

Another English factory (Factory 3) produced labels measuring 38 x 51 mm, having a crowded floral arrangement in the cartouche. Once again the capital letter 'I' in titles is dotted as in CASSIS,

Figures 1061-1068

Figures 1069-1080

FINE CHAMPAGNE, MALVOISIE, WHISKEY and BENEDECTINE.

Fig. 1089 shows a features comparison of cartouche, bottom spray and edge decoration for Samson, Factory 1, Factory 2 and Factory 3 respectively. With regard to the chain test, fig. 1090 shows two types of chain found on (above) small Samson labels and on (below) normal size Samson labels. In each case the upper chain type is similar to chains on French marked objects. Fig. 1091 shows two types of chain found on English Factory 1 and Factory 2 labels. The slimline chain used here is quite distinctive. The larger chain is of a type almost universally found on hallmarked English silver wine labels during the period 1770-1850. With regard to the fluorescence test, none of the Samson labels fluoresces, unlike, for example, VERMOUTH (see fig. 1061), ELDER FLOWER (see fig. 1063) and BRANDY (see fig. 1064) and all of figs. 1081-1088. Finally, with regard to the spelling test, none of the Samson labels contains miswritten 'A's or 'N's, whereas there are a number of examples amongst the English labels. The miswritten 'A' has the thick stroke on the left-hand side of the 'A' instead of on the right-hand side. The miswritten 'N' has a thin bar between two thick uprights instead of a thick bar between two thin uprights.

Finally, mention should be made of shield or plaque type labels. A number of these exist as

Labels from other Materials - Non-Battersea Enamels

Figures 1081-1088

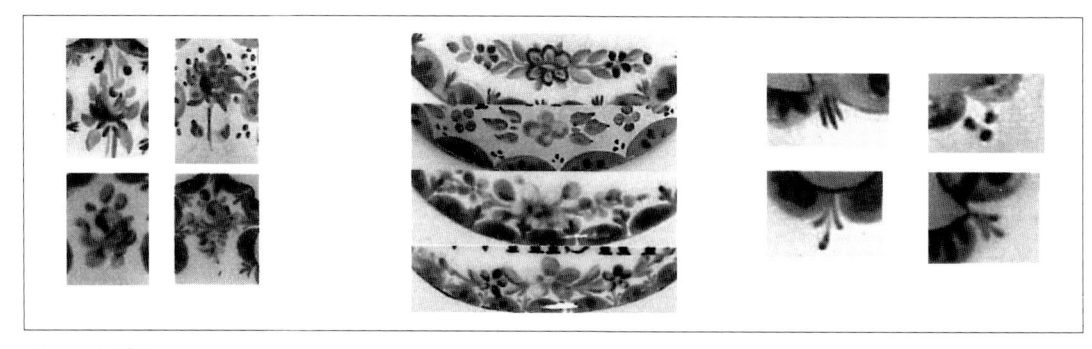

Figure 1089

Figure 1090   *Figure 1091*

illustrated by figs. 1016-1021. Some have freehand script titles in the French language. Factory 3 produced the rare if not unique shield shape design for RUM (not illustrated) having Factory 3 style of floral decoration above the title and a bunch of grapes below the title. The edge decoration and colouring on RUM is identical to that used on Factory 3 labels mentioned above, such as CASSIS or FINE CHAMPAGNE, which incidentally also have COGNAC, RUM, CHARTREUSE, SHERRY and BRANDY in the same or a similar set.

PART 5 – BIN AND BARREL LABELS

Wine bin labels are the lowly but elder relations of decanter labels and, as Penzer notes,[53] they had a different purpose. Their origins date back to the mid-seventeenth century, when the binning of wines first became important. They then served a utilitarian purpose identifying unmarked bottles lying in the depths of gentlemen's cellars. It took a few years before the nomenclature of the bin label ascended to grace the decanter on the table. At least 183 differently inscribed bin labels have been recorded.[54] Two of the eighteenth century, for No 3 PORT and No 12 PORT, are shown at figs. 1182 and 1183 with interesting decoration and shapes.

Bin labels are in the main made from pottery, including Delftware and creamware. They are therefore highly susceptible to damage and destruction and there are naturally far fewer bin labels than decanter labels in existence. However, there is a most interesting collection at Knole in Sevenoaks, made from lead. They were probably not a commercial production but were 'homemade' on the estate.

Most bin labels are approximately 9cm deep by 13cm wide (3½in. by 5in.), but there are many variations and some miniature labels are approximately 4 x 6cm (1½ x 2½in.). Except for the blue glaze of Delftware labels, the oldest of all (see figs. 1115, 1126, 1129 and 1132), most bin labels are white or cream coloured with black lettering, although some have brown lettering (see fig. 1119). The hole from which the label was hung varies from round to rectangular (see fig. 1106 for SILLERY CHAMPAGNE and fig. 1119 for RUM) and bell shaped (see figs. 1139 and 1140 for CAPE and MOSELLE, fig. 1114 for HOLLANDS, fig. 1122 for ORANGE and figs. 1124 and 1125 for ALE and MADEIRA). Small rectangular bin labels from France (see MADÈRE vieux, fig. 1155, for example) have twin round holes for hanging.

The typography varies from the almost primitive to some fine lettering, generally below but sometimes above the glaze. The lettering nearly always consists of upper case characters, but occasionally lower case has been used. Some have titles painted in manganese purple.

Many bin labels are impressed on the reverse with the potter's mark. Spode,[55] Wedgwood and Minton are the most frequently seen. A few of the marks provide evidence of the exact date of manufacture. Delftware bin labels have some unusual names such as NECKAR and NICE. Some bin labels helpfully give a date such as 1822 PULSFORDS PORT (see fig. 1092), 1819 WALTER'S PORT (see fig. 1095), 1819 E.I. VINA TINTA (see fig. 1099), 1815 RAISIN (see fig. 1105), 1818 E.I. SERCIAL, 1815 E.I. MALMSEY and PREIGNAC 1818 (E.I. standing for East India).

Many labels, particularly by Wedgwood and Minton, are partly unglazed on the face and completely unglazed on the back. Circular labels are often completely unglazed with no lettering so that the owner can inscribe with a pencil his own information, bin number, source, vintage and other particulars. The round labels inscribed with numbers seem mostly to date from the late nineteenth century.[56]

The major producers or suppliers of bin labels are as follows.[57]

Copeland
CHABLIS is illustrated at fig. 1130.

Copeland and Garrett
CLARET and NO.1 PORT are illustrated in 7 *WLCJ* 45, GOOSBERRY at fig. 1137 and CHAMPAIGNE (*c.*1833, being made of new faience) at fig. 1100.

Delft
Wine name painted, usually in aubergine; glazed only on the front. One central eyelet hole. In shape they are wider than the Wedgwood labels. About 16.5cm (6½in.) wide. For possible Bristol Delftware see figs. 1126, 1129 and 1132. For possible Lambeth Delftware see fig. 1115.

Labels from other Materials - Bin and Barrel Labels

Figures 1092-1112.

Labels from other Materials - Bin and Barrel Labels

Wedgwood
Bearing an impressed mark WEDGWOOD, usually with a four point star below; only the lower half of the label is glazed. In shape these labels are about 14.6cm (5¾in.) wide and up to 8.3 cm (3¼in.) high at the centre. The sides slope, from the central eyelet hole to within 3.8cm (1½in.) of the base, in a straight line. Labels appear in Josiah Wedgwood's first pattern book of 1770. A label of this era for BARSAC has been noted with all the letters of the title having serifs. See figs. 1098, 1118, 1121, 1123, 1124, 1131, 1134, 1147 and 1150.

Spode
These bear an impressed SPODE and a number; the whole label is glazed. In size they are rather narrower and taller than the Wedgwood labels and the shoulders have a double ogee curve from the top of the central eyelet hole to the lower outside edge. It is perhaps interesting to record that the only Spode examples noted have the wine name in transfer, not printed. See figs. 1092, 1095, 1099, 1101, 1105, 1109, 1111, 1113-1114, 1116-1117, 1122, 1124-1125, 1127, 1135-1136, 1138-1141, 1144-1146, 1149 and 1153.

Minton
Again with an impressed mark, MINTON, and very similar in shape to the Spode labels. The only difference is that they are a little wider. See figs. 1112, 1142 and 1152. Re-usable blank labels were made in 1843 (bearing ciphers for that date).

Davenport
These have an impressed mark DAVENPORT, an anchor and a number. Smaller in size, 10cm (4in.) wide and 7.6 cm (3in.) high, but with deeply cut-away sides and rounded shoulders.

Maw
Maw and Co. of Benthall Works in Broseley produced their re-usable bin labels. One has been noted for '1846 Sherry' from Walker and Thompson.

Barthes-Roberts, suppliers
This firm supplied bin labels.

W. and J. Burrow, London and Malvern, suppliers
These are the smallest labels measuring about 7.6cm (3in.) wide by 5cm (2in.) high. The sides slope to within 2.5 cm (1in.) of the base.

L. Lumley and Co. Ltd, suppliers
This firm supplied bin labels.

Macord and Arch, suppliers
See their unusual COOKING PORT, fig. 1093.

Charles Farrow and Farrow and Jackson, London and Paris, suppliers
This impressed mark is found on two unglazed circular plaques. The wine name is written on the rough biscuit. These are the only two circular examples recorded and may not originally have been intended as bin labels. They have a single eyelet hole like all the other pottery labels, 7.6cm (3in.) in diameter. They were advertised in Farrow and Jackson's catalogue for sale at 2s. per dozen, described as bisque porcelain 'to write on in pencil',[58] under the heading of 'Bin Labels'. Farrow and Jackson were 'Manufacturers of Machines, tools and utensils for the wine and spirit trade'. It is thought that the bin labels they sold were in fact made by Wedgwood.[59] See fig. 1143 for SPARKLING MOSELLE and fig. 1103 for CHAMPAGNE, Thomas Rathbone and Co, suppliers. A distinctive label from the Portobello district of Edinburgh, Scotland, has attractive lower-case lettering (see fig. 1128 for Madeira).

Labels from other Materials - Bin and Barrel Labels

Figures 1113-1133.

Labels from other Materials - Bin and Barrel Labels

Figures 1134-1154.

Labels from other Materials - Bin and Barrel Labels

Details of the labels illustrated are as follows:

Fig.	Name	Size	Comments
1092	1822 PULSFORDS PORT	3⅜ x 5¼in.	Spode. Pulsford the owner (?)
1093	COOKING PORT	3 x 5in.	Impressed: Macord & Arch, 47 Great Tower St, London
1094	OLD HOCK	3 x 4¾in.	
1095	1819 WALTER'S PORT	3⅜ x 5½in.	Spode. Walter the owner (?)
1096	TENT	3¼ x 5½in.	Early Wedgwood
1097	BRANDY	3¼ x 5½in.	Early Wedgwood – A pair of B 2 above
1098	PORT	2⅞ x 3¾in.	Wedgwood
1099	1819 E. I. VINA TINTA	3½ x 5¼in.	Spode E. I. (East India)
1100	CHAMPAIGNE	3½ x 5⅜in.	Impressed: Copeland & Garrett New Fayence (*c.*1833)
1101	VERY OLD. PORT.	3⅜ x 5in.	Impressed Spode (*c.*1790)
1102	TINTO	3 x 4¾in.	
1103	CHAMPAGNE	3 x 5⅜in.	Impressed: Farrow & Jackson, London & Paris Upper part unglazed
1104	PORT A	3 x 4¾in.	
1105	1815 RAISIN	3⅜ x 5⅝in.	Spode
1106	SILLERY CHAMPAGNE	3 x 4⅝in.	Note hole shape
1107	PORT B	3 x 4¾in.	
1108	BURGUNDY	2⅞ x 4⅛in.	Wedgwood – Fine lettering
1109	CHAMPAIGN	3¾ x 5½in.	Spode
1110	OLD PORT	2⅞ x 4⅞in.	Early creamware
1111	HOCK	3 x 4¾in.	Spode
1112	CLARET	3¼ x 5⅜in.	Impressed: (Minton 1868) Upper part unglazed
1113	BUCELLAS	3⅜ x 5¼in.	Impressed: Spode 30 (*c.*1790)
1114	HOLLANDS	3¾ x 5⅜in.	Spode
1115	CALCAVELLA	3 x 4⅞in.	Delftware (Lambeth?)
1116	BUCELLA	3⅜ x 5¼in.	Spode
1117	WHITE WINE	3¾ x 5⅜in.	Spode
1118	SHERRY	3¼ x 5½in.	Wedgwood
1119	RUM	3⅛ x 5in.	Note hole shape – Brown lettering
1120	GIN	3⅛ x 5in.	Impressed: X (early Wedgwood cream ware)
1121	PALE SHERRY	2⅞ x 4¾in.	Wedgwood
1122	ORANGE	3¾ x 5¼in.	Spode
1123	WHISKEY	3 x 5½in.	Impressed: Wedgwood (*c.*1830)
1124	ALE	5⅛ x 3⅜in.	Spode
1125	MADERIA	3½ x 5⅛in.	Spode
1126	LISBON	3 x 5¼in.	Delftware (Bristol?)
1127	MUSCATEL	3⅜ x 5¼in.	Impressed: Spode 30 (*c.*1790)

Labels from other Materials - Bin and Barrel labels

Figure 1155.

Fig.	Name	Size	Comments
1128	Madeira	3⅝ x 5⅝in.	Impressed: TR & Co. (Thomas Rathbone & Co. Portobello Scotland 1810-). Unusual and attractive lower-case lettering.
1129	PORTER	3⅛ x 5¼in.	Delftware (Bristol?)
1130	CHABLIS	3⅝ x 5½in.	Impressed: Copeland
1131	CURRANT	3¼ x 5½in.	Impressed: Wedgwood (c.1830) Upper part unglazed
1132	RUM	3 x 5¼in.	Delftware (Bristol?)
1133	BROWN STOUT		
1134	GOOSEBERRY	3⅛ x 5½in.	Impressed: Wedgwood (c.1830). Upper part unglazed
1135	1818 E.I. SERCIAL	3⅝ x 5¼in.	Spode
1136	CONSTANTIA	3⅝ x 5⅛in.	Spode
1137	GOOSBERRY	3⅝ x 5⅝in.	Impressed: Copeland & Garrett Late Spode 20 (1833-1846)
1138	1815 E.I MALMSEY	3⅝ x 5¼in.	Spode
1139	CAPE	3¾ x 5¼in.	Spode
1140	MOSELLE	3¾ x 5¼in.	Spode
1141	ELDER FLOWER	3½ x 5⅛in.	Impressed: 19 – (Spode)
1142	DANTZIC	3¼ x 5½in.	Minton
1143	SPARKLING MOSELLE	3 x 5½in.	Impressed: Farrow & Jackson London Upper part unglazed
1144	PREIGNAC 1818	3½ x 5⅛in.	Impressed: 19 – (Spode)
1145	MOUNTAIN	3⅝ x 5⅛in.	Impressed: Spode (c.1770)
1146	SHRUB	3½ x 5⅛in.	Impressed: E– (Spode)
1147	MARSALA	3 x 5⅝in.	Impressed: PQF Wedgwood (c.1860) Upper part unglazed
1148	VIDONIA	4⅜ x 5¼in.	An unusual shape
1149	ORANGE SHRUB	3⅝ x 5¼in.	Spode
1150	MARSALLA	3 x 5½in.	Impressed: Wedgwood (c.1860) Upper part unglazed
1151	ST. PERAY	3 x 5½in.	Impressed: Wedgwood (c.1830)
1152	PERRY	3 x 5⅝in.	Minton. Upper part unglazed. Unfortunately a broken top ring.
1153	MARCELLA	3⅝ x 5⅛in.	Spode
1154	TENERIFFE	3 x 5½in.	Impressed: Wedgwood (c.1830)

Labels from other Materials - Bin and Barrel Labels

Figure 1156.

Figure 1157.

Figure 1158.

Figure 1159.

Figure 1182.

Figure 1183.

Bin labels seem frequently to attract unusual names such as MONHYLIANA, REDRO DI CHINNES, PORT URQUHART and ST. MAMSEY. A range of shapes and materials were in fact used to make them,[60] including the use of the oval for No. 3 PORT (see fig. 1182) and for BURTON. ALE. (see fig. 1158). Mid- and late Victorian bin labels tend to give much more detail than merely the name of the wine, such as the vintage, shipper and bin date (see figs. 1160-1181). In 1863/4 Wedgwood made circular numbered bin labels distributed by Farrow and Jackson to identify shelves mentioned in the cellar book. Finally, brief mention should be made of the flexible barrel labels, such as for SHERRY, IRISH and HELDERBERG, which were nailed or screwed onto the cask – these are dealt with under the heading of 'Celluloid' (below, Part 8), of which they were made – and of bin shelf labels, such as for CALVADOS, TARRAGONE and MALAGA – these are dealt with below in Chapter 9, Part 8, under the heading of France.

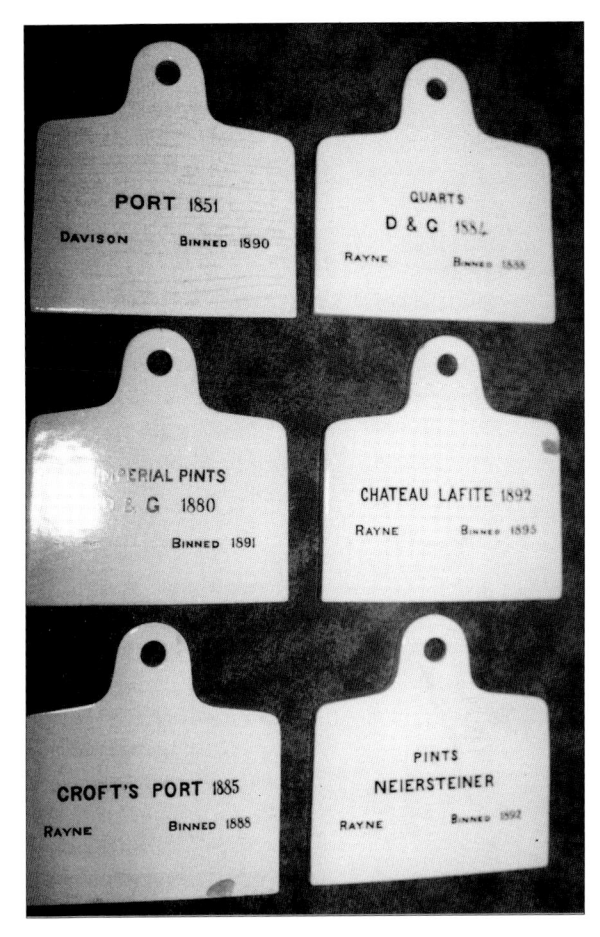

Labels from other Materials - Bin and Barrel Labels

Figures 1160-1181.

313

PART 6 – ELECTROPLATE

The silver wine label had not long appeared before it was joined by a counterpart in fused ('Old Sheffield') plate. For most of a century, the two types advanced thereafter side by side, competing at the margin, no doubt, but both able on the whole to prosper by serving different segments of a growing market – solid silver for the big house and the formal entertainment, plated for the humbler home, the family supper, the servants' hall. Albeit with some recognisable particularities, especially of decoration, patterns of silver and fused plate labels remained much alike. What distinguished one group from the other was not so much design as cost and price.

To contemporary observers, the appearance of electroplated wine labels in the 1840s must have promised a broadly similar outcome. Derided at first by makers of the 'old plate', but proclaimed by others as a technical miracle, electroplating offered to replace the thermal fusing of silver on to copper. But it did not seem to follow that it would challenge the established partition of the wine label market between solid and plated products. In the event, however, it did just that.

Instead of merely supplanting fused plate as the poor but respectable relation of sterling silver, the electroplated wine label advanced during the nineteenth century into new territory, not only replacing fused plate but also broadening the entire market. On the one hand, cheaply produced representatives of the type even penetrated catering, supplying anything from the PORT label in a restaurant to a GIN label (see fig. 1184) in plated pewter for the saloon bar. On the other hand, well-designed and well-made electroplate became the accepted alternative to silver for the wine labels on the middle class sideboard, notably with that most Victorian of artefacts, the tantalus. In the process, moreover, electroplaters contrived by exploiting their material's special character to add a steady trickle of new entries to the catalogue of wine label patterns while swimming with the shifting current of fashion.

Commercial success followed naturally. Wine label statistics are inevitably scarce, few relevant records survive, and many labels have been destroyed. It can be seen, however, that the output of solid silver wine labels clearly declined steadily from the mid-nineteenth century, whereas that of electroplated labels expanded, overtaking and even dwarfing the production of silver – something that fused plate had never done.

It has been suggested that the silver wine label in Britain fell victim to the 1860 Act of Parliament. The success of plated labels argues otherwise. The fact is that silver electroplate was a Victorian success story in which wine labels were caught up, because it offered what were initially novel and eventually affordable pledges of the period's love affair with technical progress, but even more because its practical utility and stylistic accessibility were so much in harmony with the century's themes of social change in an age of reform. Judged by how few sterling and how many electroplated labels survive from the years after 1850, the former came to represent an increasingly beleaguered anachronism while the latter stood for extension of the silver-owning franchise.

This is not the place to unravel the remarkable – and remarkably complex – history of nineteenth-century electrometallurgy. Suffice it to say that electroplating was invented neither by any one person nor at any one time. Its development was gradual and at many hands, from the moment when Volta identified the basic principle of a liquid electrolyte in 1799. As a truly commercial method for making such things as wine labels, however, electroplating was born in Birmingham on 25 March 1840, when George Richards Elkington and his cousin Henry Elkington patented after long experiment their electrical process for 'coating, covering, or plating certain metals' with silver.[61]

Many in 1840 doubted the Elkingtons. Many others – above all the fused plate makers – feared and, as they could, denigrated them. At least in their apprehension, the latter proved right. Within ten years, although a handful of traditionalists held on, electroplating had effectively wiped out the 'Old Sheffield' plate industry. (Of all the significant firms making fused plate in Sheffield itself, for instance, two thirds were reported to have closed between 1840 and 1850.) Within twenty years, despite the

Labels from other Materials - Electroplate

Figures 1184-1201.

scramble to follow the Elkingtons' example in Sheffield and Birmingham and as far afield as London and Paris, Elkington and Co. had established a pre-eminence which they retained for the next half-century. Before the end of the 1840s they had acquired by one means or another patents crucial to every major part of the electroplating process, granted selected rights on advantageous terms to the leading London firms of Barnards (1842) and Garrards (1843), made a broadly similar agreement with Charles Christofle and Cie in Paris after winning a legal battle (1842) and, above all, built up a body of scientific acumen. Two of their company chemists, James Napier and Charles Glassford, contributed to the Chemical Society during those years a series of papers on the cyanides – key to electroplating – ranked by the modern historians of the matter, Robert Bud and Gerrylynn Roberts, as 'the most sustained effort at applied chemistry to be found in the Proceedings'.[62]

It is not known how many electroplated wine labels, if any, were made by Elkington and Co. under any of their changing company titles. Few plated labels were ever marked by their Victorian manufacturers. What was important, in any case, was not whether Elkington made wine labels, but that the quality and quantity of their silver electroplate in general, demonstrated to public acclaim in the Great Exhibitions of 1851 and 1862, made the material itself familiar and fashionable. Those who did manufacture and sell electroplated labels were by the 1850s appealing to a market that was already converted.

The secret of successful electroplating lay not only in the method of depositing a precious metal, but also in the choice of a base metal substrate. Thus it ranks as one of the more notable gifts of chance that at the critical time the best possible solution first became generally available in Europe. Nickel had been used as an alloy component in Asia for centuries. In Europe, however, it was not isolated chemically until 1751. Thereafter, it was adequately characterised only in the 1770s, purified in commercial quantities in 1804, and alloyed with zinc and copper in a form fitted to accept electrodeposition in the mid-1820s in Germany, whence it reached Britain in that form in 1830 as 'German silver' (or 'nickel silver') – though it included no silver at all.[63]

The potential value of this new 'German silver' for plating – and not only electroplating – was quickly understood in Sheffield and Birmingham. Those interested in improving the established fused plate process found the fusible copper content of an alloy with greater structural strength than copper alone immediately attractive. Those beginning to experiment with electrodeposition found that the new alloy was also a more efficient electrical conductor than copper. All also learned that 'nickel silver' could be safely die-stamped and was easier than copper to cast, especially after the appearance of a less brittle 'argentan' alloy in 1836. However, it was the colour of 'German silver' that most commended it to both the schools. Pure nickel has much the colour of pure silver. Alloyed with zinc and copper in a ratio of 1:1:2, its colour remained dominant enough to disguise – as copper did not – any deficiency or abrasion in a plated covering of silver, whether fused or electrolysed (an advantage sometimes sacrificed later in the century by those whose cost-cutting increased the copper proportion to sixty per cent or more).

Makers of fused plate divided over the best way to exploit the new material. Samuel Roberts senior, one of the Sheffield community's leaders, chose to interpose thinner layers of nickel alloy between the copper and silver to be fused and rolled into his firm's plate – a silver-saving method patented in July 1830, but in the event not widely adopted. Others preferred to substitute nickel alloy for the whole of the copper ingot formerly used, producing a type of plate marketed as 'British' – an alternative pioneered by Thomas Nicholson and Robert Gainsford in Sheffield in about 1835 and demonstrated by another leading Sheffield firm, Padley Parkin and Co., at the 1851 Great Exhibition. Briefly it seemed that 'British Plate' might revive all their fortunes. In the end, however, it was the upstart electroplaters who gained the greatest advantage, simply by adopting nickel alloy as the base for the preponderance of all that they made.

The potential size of that advantage was not at all obvious in the 1840s. Compared to fused plate, electroplated ware had the short-term commercial merit of embodying the apparently almost magical properties of a new science, as well as the technical merit of being able to reproduce finer detail in relief while better concealing minor blemishes. At first, however, it was far from being able to compete on price. The base metal alloy needed was reckoned in 1840 to cost two-and-a-half times as much as the copper in a comparable quantity of fused plate, while the total cost of plating and polishing, including materials and labour, was almost twice as much. The gap widened further, moreover, as the demand accelerated for Saxony nickel, the refined price of which in Britain rose from 4s. a pound to 13s. in 1849, before falling back to 4s.6d. after the discovery of New Caledonian nickel in 1863. Until at least 1847, when a major improvement in the chemistry of electroplating greatly reduced the amount of subsequent polishing needed, Elkingtons were reportedly running their new business at a loss. Only from 1850 did the new plating method begin to forge ahead of its fused predecessor in economic terms, adding to the lead it had by then opened up as a function of novelty, fashion and utility.

So much electroplated ware has been based on a nickel/zinc/copper alloy since 1840 that 'EPNS' (Electro-Plated Nickel Silver) is often presented as a sufficiently accurate name for all of it. If the characteristic tint of nickel alloy shows through a worn silver coating, it is taken as a proof of electroplating, just as a gleam of copper beneath a silver exterior is widely thought to identify fused plate. The truth, however, is more complicated. Most electroplated labels do have 'nickel silver', albeit of varying assay, as a base, but there has always been, and still is, a minority of labels electroplated on to copper or brass. Indeed, the Paris firm of Christofle, to which Elkingtons licensed their plating method, continued to use copper for that purpose long after most others abandoned it. Meanwhile, one of Elkingtons' technicians, Thomas Fearn, had succeeded in 1846 in solving the difficult problem of electroplating silver successfully on to the increasingly popular tin-based alloy known as Britannia metal, in which a few wine labels (and innumerable tea and coffee sets) were thereafter produced, particularly in Sheffield.

Conversely, but by the same token, while the great majority of fused plate wine labels are of silver fused to copper, there exist a few labels of 'British Plate' where the silver is fused instead to a nickel alloy. Nor is the quality of the silver used for plating a simple guide. Electroplating necessarily produces a surface of pure 100 per cent silver. However, many modern authors notwithstanding, fused plate was sometimes also clad in pure or nearly pure silver, rather than sterling. Contemporary recipes for the 'Old Sheffield' process, recorded by senior members of firms that used it, prescribe plating metals with a silver content ranging from the sterling standard of 92.5 per cent[64] to 97 per cent[65] and even 98-100 per cent.[66] Nevertheless, the darker tinge of even a small admixture of copper is often the best visual guide to fused plate in general. Wine labels, however, or at least those with engraved or pierced titles, offer another recourse. In the case of fused plate (including 'British Plate'), every such title had necessarily to be cut after plating, revealing the underlying base metal. With those labels, therefore, copper or any other base exposed in the title lettering or concealed beneath a black filling may provide an additional clue, although not a conclusive proof. Conversely, almost all British electroplated labels with engraved titles were titled before being plated, so that the incised ground within engraved lettering can usually be expected to show a coating of silver.

The material of most electroplated wine labels was different from that of all other labels, as were, in important respects, the manufacturing methods employed in producing them. What did not differ, at least in the earlier years, was the relation of electroplated labels to the styles and fashions generally prevalent in their host society. Albeit within rather narrow limits, makers of fused plate labels had developed a number of design features that are rarely if ever found in silver. Initially, electroplaters were less ambitious. During the 1840s and 1850s, designs for electroplated labels remained generally faithful to their silver and fused plate antecedents. One or two of the patterns thus copied had actually originated in fused plate: an almost rectangular trellis of stamped vines and grapes on a lined ground surrounding a reserved title block, for instance (see fig. 1185), or a small kidney shape surmounted by a bracket of converging grape bunches (see fig. 1186). However, most had served, and many still served, for both silver and fused plate, including not only 'run-of-the-mill' rectangles, octagons, crescents and ovals but also such conceits as an extravagantly hirsute and saturnine mask among even more grape bunches (see fig. 1187): a pattern previously made in silver by William Eley and others and commonly attributed in its 'Old Sheffield' form to Matthew Boulton.

Sometimes the appropriation of an existing silver or fused plate design involved stamping with an identical die – or perhaps even the same die. A case in point is an EPNS PORT label (see fig. 1188) in the form of the silver rococo escutcheons or cartouches widely produced in and after the 1820s. Another is an even earlier BRANDY label (see fig. 1189), electroplated on copper, probably in the 1840s, which is exactly similar to silver labels made by Henry Manton in Birmingham in the 1830s. On other occasions, the die used was evidently inspired by one made earlier to stamp in silver, but did not slavishly copy it. One such is an elegantly simple cartouche for MARSALLA [sic], whose curvilinear profile and convex stamped border are much in the spirit of so-called 'architectural' labels made in London in the early 1840s, especially by Charles Rawlings and William Summers (see fig. 1190), while another more elaborate example (see fig. 1191), titled for BRANDY and bordered with stamped C-scrolls and yet more grapes, was probably made in about 1850 but is reminiscent of a silver pattern used fifteen years earlier, particularly by Scottish makers.

Even when linked to an established pattern, die-stamped labels such as these are in most cases more difficult to date with confidence than their silver predecessors, not only because they rarely bear indicative marks of any kind but also because the dies used were not infrequently ones that had been put into store when their patterns first went out of fashion, only to be resurrected when fashion's wheel had come full circle. Another stamped pattern shown here, for example, titled I(rish) WHISKEY (see fig. 1192), was modelled on silver predecessors of the 1820s and 1830s, but survived, or perhaps resurfaced, to appear in a catalogue produced by the firm of Silber and Fleming as late as 1883. Even at the very end of the nineteenth century, one large manufacturer of electroplated articles, Walter Sissons, could write of the satisfaction he and his business partner felt

> to know that even if fashion changed many times their predecessors did not sell their dies as useless and done with, but carefully stored them, and now as fashion has returned to the original and beautiful patterns which characterised The Old Sheffield Plate, they are able to reproduce all these fine examples of an early age under the present-day process.[67]

In the face of such durability as that, dating an individual electroplated label can clearly become a matter of instinct or mere conjecture.

Not only old stamping dies survived to be adapted or applied to electroplated labels; so did traditional handworking techniques, despite the growing role of machinery. The hand skills needed to produce the most basic patterns, such as the plain octagon for BRANDY (fig. 1193) or rectangle, were hardly rare or remarkable, although some of the individual labels concerned were remarkable for other reasons. A quaintly titled EAU DE NUIT (see fig. 1194), for instance, probably French, is notable as an unusually early example of machine engraving, while a crudely formed and lettered GIN (see fig. 1195), plated on copper, displays on its reverse (shown by fig. 1231) the most blatant of attempts to imitate on electroplate the marks for sterling silver, including both a crowned leopard's head and a lion passant – even if the latter faces the wrong way and more nearly resembles a poodle. The fact remains that most unadorned rectangles, octagons, crescents and ovals could be stamped out, titled and electroplated by relatively unskilled hands, even in the early years of the process. Other cases of handworking in electroplate, however, deserve greater respect. Electroplated labels came into being at a time – the 1840s – when there was a revival in the vogue for silver wine labels in the form of single initial letters. Makers of electroplate naturally exploited the opportunity by launching what became a very long series of stamped or cut-out and engraved initials. Even in the earlier years many were rather cheaply made, initiating a sequence that, by the last years of the century, culminated in some of the least appealing of all the patterns used for wine labels, in which a cut-out initial had the remainder of a wine or spirit name cut, stamped or engraved across its face. In parallel, however, the perennial fashion for initials had also produced a range of excellent electroplated labels, sawn by hand from the nickel alloy sheet and meticulously hand-engraved in patterns to match prevailing silver styles: a cusped M for Madeira (see fig. 1196), for example, which exactly reproduces the style and embellishment of 1840s silver labels by such London smiths as Rawlings and Summers. More imaginatively, electroplaters also took advantage of the fact that nickel alloys were much stiffer than silver to produce a smaller number of hand-sawn script initials, here exemplified by a B for BRANDY (see fig. 1197), whose delicacy and apparent fragility hark back to rare silver examples of the late eighteenth century. A nickel alloy base made such fine lines possible – and usable – where copper could not.

Much less frequently, electroplaters faced the complementary difficulty of having to fight against the harder and stiffer nickel alloy in order to reproduce an older silver design, as witnessed by a crescent-shaped WHISKEY label in the Georgian mould (see fig. 1198) on which the graduated lettering is hand-engraved and then outlined, again by hand, with not only a band of wrigglework but also a border of beautifully executed bright-cutting. Accurate bright-cutting in nickel is something of a feat. The result, even in the more obdurate metal, would not have disgraced the silver workshops of the Batemans or Phipps and Robinson.

Labels such as that last crescent were frank reproductions, possibly made in electroplate to match an older set in silver. In most cases, however, electroplated labels were made to suit the fashion of the day, and thus to resemble silver labels of the present rather than the past. In the 1840s, as we have seen, that could still imply an important element of restraint, or even severity: simple shapes, clear outlines, smoothly curved borders, all in tune with the mood of recaptured modesty that followed briefly upon the passing of Regency and post-Regency exuberance. Within only a few years, however, such simplicity was giving way to another kind of exuberance: not the febrile indulgence or the hothouse orientalism of past fashion, but something proclaimed instead as a fresh and blameless regard for the richness of nature itself. As the new vogue for displays of 'arts and sciences' gathered pace, through the Paris Exposition of 1834, the Manchester Exhibition of 1845 and the Birmingham Exhibition of 1849, and as preparations thereafter began for the Great Exhibition of 1851 in London, that new naturalism was springing up in every kind of applied art, scattering leaves, flowers and fruit in all directions. A due share of the largesse landed upon silver and plate designs, including those for wine labels. In their case, however, the main emphasis was on a particular segment of the natural world. Sea-shells, flower heads and leaves of acanthus or oak, complete with acorns, are indeed found. One or two distinctly successful but still restrained interpretations of that material are the saw-pierced and hand-engraved arrangement of stylised leaves and tendrils in a WHISKEY label, probably of about 1850 (see fig. 1199), whose treatment of the theme even recalls pierced silver work by Susanna Barker in the 1780s. Above all, however, naturalism in mid-century wine label designs meant a festival of the vine and its harvest of grapes.

Ostensibly, the vine motif was now offered in praise of botanical nature, but the means used to that end hardly differed from those employed no less enthusiastically thirty years earlier when offering the wine label's tribute to Bacchus. In the case of electroplated labels, whose range of patterns was often more eclectic than that in solid silver, the inherent ambiguity encouraged a more than ordinary assortment of leaves and fruit as several design strands converged. As we have seen, there was first the relatively restrained use of vines and grapes as peripheral decoration, especially with other motifs such as C-scrolls, in the borders of die-stamped labels. Examples from that group of patterns might trace their genesis back even to the vines chased on wine labels in the middle of the previous century. Next there was the newer but hardly more ebullient use of a single vine leaf or a group of two or three leaves, with or without a few branches, grapes and tendrils, as a label in itself, to be further embellished only by a pierced or engraved title (see figs. 1200-1202 for RUM, BRANDY and BUCELLAS), a category revived in the 1840s for electroplate, but already familiar from work in both silver and fused plate twenty years earlier. And finally, at least for the years to 1851, there was the use of a stamped or cast vine branch or branches to frame or surmount a visually distinct titled label, usually in the form of a drapery or ribbon.

Most of those last were modest enough in scale, naturalistic in spirit, and apparently designed in the vernacular of the mid-century as labels only in electroplate (see fig. 1203 for SHERRY). A few, however, were conscious references back to the far more ostentatious use of the vine in sumptuously cast silver during the century's earlier years and through those of the Regency thereafter. Of those, the most remarkable, represented here by a label for SHERRY (see fig. 1204), were actually cast in nickel alloy directly from earlier silver originals, in this case from a label made by Digby Scott and the elder Benjamin Smith for the royal goldsmiths, Rundell Bridge and Rundell, in 1807 (fig. 416) – the cast so faithful that the gouge marks where cast-in reproductions of the original silver marks had to be removed before electroplating can still be distinguished. Whatever the aesthetic significance, the choice of technique in this case served incidentally to underline the superiority of nickel alloy over its older rival, since fused plate could not be cast at all. It remains only to remark that the silver original used in this case was one designed by Benjamin Smith senior, a major author of patterns for Rundell Bridge and Rundell, that his son was the younger Benjamin Smith who became in 1840 the London agent for Elkington and Co.'s electroplate, and that it was the younger Benjamin's daughter, Emma Smith, who thereupon married George Richards Elkington's son, Apsley Elkington. It does seem possible that the rebirth in electroplate of this 1805 hymn to the vine was not unconnected to those other events. At least Elkington and Co. properly marked their plate. A splendid cruet stand of 1843 has four marks in punched outlines, E and Co. under a crown, ELEC, TRO and PLATE.

The Victorian passion for naturalism, although never extinguished, grew a little less ardent after 1851. At least in the shorter term, the label-makers' passion for vines did not. What did happen in the 1850s and 1860s, however, was a subtle change in their treatment of electroplated vine leaves. Instead of punching or piercing a title through the leaf, or more rarely engraving a title directly on to its surface, they began in the second half of the century to provide a ribbon set across the face of the leaf, on which the title was thereafter engraved. The effect was sometimes quite successful, as here with a label for BURDEOS, the Spanish for Bordeaux (see fig. 1205), or another for RUM (see fig. 1206). At its worst, however, the result risked converting the vine from a symbol of the naturalistic philosophy into the mere backdrop to an implausibly stiff scroll (see fig. 1207 for WHISKEY). Less objectionable from that point of view is the scroll for PORT attached to another hand-pierced view of the vine's product: an ample cask (see fig. 1208). Such cask labels were still being made in electroplate at the end of the nineteenth century. Here, however, the handling of the theme points to a date forty to fifty years earlier (see Chapter 2, Part 11, Barrels, above).

As naturalism began slowly to give way during the years leading up to the International Exhibition of 1862, there stepped into its place a new enthusiasm for historicism: a taste for supposedly antique decorative features drawn from any period and none – Greek classical, French gothic, Italian Renaissance, English Elizabethan, even Moorish arabesque, and sometimes all on the same object. Wine labels were small enough to escape for the time being the worst excesses of the trend. In any case, the continuing availability of the vine as an 'appropriate' motif was still there to protect them. There did, however, appear in electroplate at least one pattern that owed its existence to the historicist imagination. In a style sometimes advertised for no good reason as 'François Premier', it merely involved an oval surmounted or surrounded by simulated scrolls and strapwork (see fig. 1209 for BURGUNDY in the so-called architectural style, and also fig. 1372 for CITROEN in alpaca, an electroplated nickel silver, described below in Chapter 9, Part 13, The Netherlands). The result was neat and practical, without being exciting. It was also evidently popular, since the pattern continued in production for at least the next twenty-five years. So did another wine label motif in electroplate drawn from the historicist repertoire: the heavily beaded border. Differing from Georgian beading (pearling) of the late eighteenth century both in scale and in its frequent association with subsidiary details of 'rococo revival' origin – scrolled edges or decorated chain brackets, for example – this Victorian beaded border was evidently meant as another tribute to the Renaissance. By the end of the nineteenth century, labels paying that tribute, often as ovals stamped in thin metal, less generously beaded and mechanically titled in one action of the press, had an almost gimcrack appearance (see fig. 1210 for BRANDY), an impression highlighting the underestimated part played in determining the merit of Victorian label designs by the style and execution of lettering. During the third quarter of the century, however, well-proportioned and skilfully engraved labels with beaded borders were among the most elegant ever made in electroplate (see figs. 1211 and 1212, both for CLARET).

Labels from other Materials - Electroplate

Figures 1202-1216.

Labels from other Materials - Electroplate

Something similar was true of the rococo scrolls used to border so many plated wine labels. At its worst – clumsy, overblown and heavily stamped – the effect could be disastrous. At its best, used with restraint to define rather than overwhelm a surrounded field, it also produced some of the Victorian period's most quietly satisfying designs, whether in the middle of the century (see fig. 1213 for GIN) or in its final quarter (see fig. 1214 for BRANDY). As in the case of beading, proportion was everything.

Clumsy or adroit, late nineteenth century attempts to recall in electroplated wine labels the sixteenth-century Renaissance or the eighteenth-century rococo had one thing in common. With only rare exceptions, the labels were all die-stamped, by now with steam-powered presses. The physical nature of 'nickel silver' had always lent itself to stamping. Rolled thin, the metal could reproduce very fine relief detail while staying more rigid in the sheet than either silver or copper of similar gauge: a characteristic reflected in low material and processing costs. The same alloy had another merit, however, noted earlier in the case of initial labels. Rolled to a much thicker gauge, often well over a millimetre, the hardness and tenacity of nickel alloy allowed it to be cut into surprisingly narrow strips and surprisingly sharp curves and angles without becoming dangerously fragile. This allowed wine label makers much greater liberty to use piercing, sometimes with machine punches but especially with hand saws, and in doing so to produce finer tracery than they could have attempted in silver – just as thirty years earlier it had encouraged them to cut finer initial letters – without the risk of a label fracturing or distorting in normal use. Materials and labour both cost more than for stamping, but the higher prices obtainable for such a better quality of product were justification enough.

During the last quarter of the nineteenth century, as the aesthetic dust settled after the age of the great international exhibitions and harsh commercial considerations loomed larger, those two characteristics of 'nickel silver' – the ability when thinly rolled to reproduce fine detail at a low cost, and the ability when thick in the sheet to tolerate extensive piercing, albeit at a premium – became the key technical factors in dividing the wine label market between two plated styles, each with roots in the 1850s but each now appearing in a new guise.

On one side, and at one level, stood a new generation of stampings, embodying design elements which might be characterised summarily as High Victorian: high relief, heavy mouldings, aggressively angular or curved outlines, all stamped in thin 'nickel silver', together with a rich crop of sometimes incongruously related details, including a little strapwork, some rococo shells and scrolls, a few lilies of the valley and a lot of beads and leaves. Samples illustrate the range (see figs. 1215 for RUM, 1216 for WHISKEY, 1217 and 1218 for PORT and 1219 for IRISH WHISKEY). Occasionally, a large stamping of the period achieved greater effect with less effort, as with a CLARET label (see fig. 1220) whose naturalistic laurel wreath and unusual Imperial Crown cresting might even have been intended to mark Queen Victoria's 1887 Golden Jubilee. In most cases, however, stampings in this group rank as evidence against manufacturers who believed that nothing succeeds like excess.

On the other side of the late Victorian wine label divide appeared the 'cut-outs': labels cut from substantial sheet and intricately saw-pierced by hand, with cut-out titles themselves often providing the dominant motif. They were not, as we have seen, the only labels to exploit the robust character of nickel alloy. In addition to the single initials of the 1850s and after, there were short-lived efforts in the 1880s and 1890s to popularise unpierced electroplated labels decorated with engine-turned borders: a form of decoration common on silver boxes but unknown on silver wine labels. Most were in the form of strong convex discs, associated with the Birmingham firm of Evans and Matthews, but some favoured instead a more expansive oval (see fig. 1221 for CYDER). Engine-turning by machine proved no more than an ephemeral distraction, however, from the business of piercing labels by hand. The 'cut-outs' brushed them aside.

London makers of the mid-century such as Rawlings and Summers, and even more Birmingham makers from Nathaniel Mills in the 1820s to Alfred Taylor in the 1850s, had produced notable saw-pierced silver labels in which intricate openwork borders surrounded conventionally engraved titles.

Labels from other Materials - Electroplate

Figures 1217-1230.

A few electroplated labels followed suit while developing their own design details, as in a POTASH label (see fig. 1222), written in Puginesque style with Gothic script, probably of the late 1860s, whose border is saw-pierced in graceful curves. (It should perhaps be pointed out that the potash concerned was not a fertiliser but a briefly fashionable alternative to soda water, based on potassium bicarbonate.) So did one or two later Victorian specimens: a MARSALA label for instance (see fig. 1223 with script title), in which the superbly sawn border is a genuine *tour de force*. However, by the late nineteenth century most cut-out labels built their whole design around a cut-out title. At the bottom of the range numerous electroplated labels consisted of nothing more than a row of crudely carved block letters strung together by a meanly represented cord. But there are also more distinguished designs to consider, such as a delicately executed RUM (see fig. 1224), an imaginative GIN with an almost heraldic air (see fig. 1225), a second RUM, solid but dignified and showing the influence of William Morris (see fig. 1226), and a WHISKEY whose S-scrolls and engraved panels capture exactly the spirit of late Victorian furnishing (see fig. 1227). Some are better designed or better made than others. Most by modern standards are over-ornate. Yet, taken together, compared with the confused design and insubstantial structure of late nineteenth century machine stamping, and bearing in mind the effective disappearance by then of silver competitors, the best of these handmade cut-outs rank as the last aristocracy among nineteenth century wine labels. Not for another half century – and perhaps not even then – did anything original emerge in British wine label design to succeed or to match them.

The insertion of 'British' into that last sentence is important. Serious interest in wine labels, particularly including plated labels, has been pursued pre-eminently in Britain and with a focus on styles and products native to the British Isles. We know that labels were electroplated in at least eight other countries and in at least three continents – and probably in twice as many countries as that – but we have almost no systematic knowledge of them. Yet each of the three non-British electroplated labels shown here has something of interest about it, as well as something puzzling.

The most striking of the three (see fig. 1229), if only by virtue of its size – more than 9.5cm (3¾in.) wide – is a Swedish escutcheon, probably from the second half of the nineteenth century. It is plated on to a particularly white nickel alloy, surmounted by a separately stamped crown, and hand engraved to identify an akvavit. The title, DISTILERADT BRANVIN AF E. SATHENSTENS TILLVERKNING, means 'Distilled brandy of E. Sathersten's Production'. Quite apart from all the questions prompted by the title, what is the history in Sweden of such a high-grade alloy or of such a design, recalling in its outline British patterns of a century earlier?

Despite the eccentric spelling, the next, an oval label for CASSES (see fig. 1228, probably meant for CASSIS), comes from a group apparently of French origin and, although presumably of the late nineteenth century, is still electroplated on copper. We know that the great Paris firm of Christofle was still using copper for the same purpose until late in the nineteenth century, instead of the nickel alloy which was both more durable and a better conductor. Was this general among French electroplaters who made wine labels? If so, why?

The remaining oval label of about 1875-80 for BRANDY (see fig. 1230), this time on nickel silver, is interesting for its unusually intricate border of tangled vines and its title stamped with a single die at a time when that practice was still new in Britain, but it is interesting most of all because the male section of the double die used to form it has stamped on to the back of the label the mark of Thomas Stokes of Melbourne, a die sinker and medallist by original trade, who migrated from England in about 1854 and, turning his hand to silverware nearly twenty years later, founded the family firm which became Stokes (Australasia) Ltd. On the evidence of this label, he made good dies and was willing and able to develop his own designs. How many other electroplated patterns did he produce? How many competitors did he have? (See further below, Chapter 9, Part 1, Australia.)

No one should seriously propose comparing British electroplated wine labels of the nineteenth century with their silver forebears, or even their silver contemporaries. Indeed, their importance depends exactly upon the fact that they are not thus comparable – which is by no means to minimise the achievement of their makers. Those who made electroplated goods, led by the remarkable Elkingtons in Birmingham, understood that they were competing initially with fused plate, and did not consider that their wine labels, for example, were competing also with sterling silver. Yet the production and sale of silver labels dwindled steadily from the late 1840s onwards, judged at least by those surviving, while the output of electroplated labels grew and flourished for another fifty years.

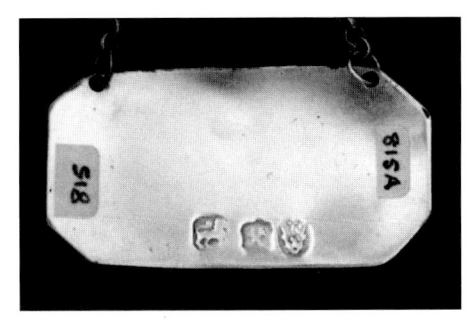

Figure 1231.

The latter began in the second quarter of the century as products of a speculative and essentially imitative enterprise, but ended it as the dominant force both in wine label design and in the marketplace. If that tells us anything, it is that the electroplated label was in tune with its times.

How that came about and what it meant has more to do with changes in an economy and a society than with aesthetics or individual skills. The emergence and rise to predominance of electroplating for labels was a small but symptomatic part of larger processes. At the beginning of Queen Victoria's reign wine labels were made in workshops. By its end they were made in factories. At the beginning those in charge of their manufacture were artists and handworkers. Only twenty years later they were chemists, engineers and machine minders. In other words, label-making, with much else, began the period as a craft and ended it as an industry. In the process, its geographical centre of gravity, as that of so much other productive activity, shifted in Britain from London and the South to Sheffield in the North and, above all, Birmingham in the Midlands.

Meanwhile, the market for wine labels also shifted, or rather expanded. Silverware, although never only the rich man's indulgence, was for a small and reasonably well-endowed minority. By the last quarter of the nineteenth century, the cheaper sorts of electroplated labels were within the reach of perhaps a third, or even a half, of all the households in the country. All that denoted enormous changes in technology, manufacturing and social structure. But labels pointed also to a remarkable change in the social habits of their owners. Looking, albeit unscientifically, through various lists and descriptions of stocks or collections of silver labels from the years up to 1825 suggests that more than eighty per cent were for wines (including roughly fifty per cent for fortified wines) and less than fifteen per cent for spirits. A random selection of one hundred British electroplated labels made between 1840 and 1900 reveals a very different picture, with twenty-three for fortified wines, nine for unfortified wines and a remarkable sixty-four for spirits. Not only the label-making industry had changed.

Traditionally, most curators, collectors and dealers have looked upon electroplated labels as trivia, stereotyped in design and inferior in material and construction. The editor of the Victoria and Albert Museum's 1958 booklet on *Bottle-Tickets* dismissed them in a single phrase, as 'specimens stamped out of base metal and obviously intended for use in the gin-parlour or wine-lounge'. To hold that view, however, is to close one small but strategically placed window on to the whole of the Victorian age. Precedents counsel against doing so. Little more than half a century ago, and excepting the wise judgement of only one or two individuals, fused plate labels were regarded as disposable junk and many Georgian silver labels as scrap fit to be melted. Some twenty years before that dealers would buy antique labels only to remove the silver chains to make bracelets. The truth is that electroplated labels, in both design and substance, cover the whole spectrum of quality and evidential interest. Some are worthless. Many are not. A few are beautiful.

One of the most interesting contemporary accounts of the decline of fused plate and rise of electroplate is that cited earlier, by William Ryland of the Birmingham silver and plate makers Waterhouse and Ryland, published in 1866. He concluded it in Solomonic terms:

> Having now described the leading features of manufacture, in both the old and new trade, I cannot conclude without expressing my firm conviction, that a well-made and a well-plated article, manufactured by the electro-process, is a far better production than those made by the old method of plating. On the other hand, I am as much convinced that a poor electro article is far inferior to the worst class of work manufactured under the old system.

That, it is submitted, is a reasonable summing-up.[68]

Labels from other Materials - Mounted Corks

PART 7 – MOUNTED CORKS

It is difficult to say when the first mounted cork stopper was made. The Parker and Wakelin ledgers record the sale of a set of six to a customer in January and a further six in February 1766, but these were presumably not labelled. For the period 1766-74 the ledgers record twenty-eight orders for cork stoppers, some of which had labels. Charges varied widely, for example, 'four cork stoppers with labels £1-4s.'; 'four very strong cork stoppers labelled £1-19-8'. If the stoppers had chains and labels the cost was higher; 'six gilt labelled stoppers for carafe £2-11s.'. From about 1772 they were usually listed as 'decanter corks'.

Stoppers were often sent in for repairs and the fitting of new corks. The Wakelin ledgers record the sale of two stoppers with steel 'worms' (screws) in 1781.

The Plate Offences Act of 1738, clause 6, exempted from hallmarking certain small articles of silver; amongst these exemptions were mounts, screws and stoppers to stone and glass bottles. It is speculation to decide whether these glass bottles included wine bottles, but Penzer thought they did not,[69] so there was some confusion as regards whether under the Act it was obligatory for silver-mounted cork stoppers to be marked before the law was changed in 1790 and even then the law does not seem to have been enforced until about 1821.

One of the earliest stoppers with a name that can be dated is one with a plain capping surmounted by a finger ring with a label above engraved on one side for LISBON (see fig. 1247). This bears the lion passant (and therefore was sent to assay) and the mark of William Stephenson, which was entered in 1781 and superseded by a new mark in 1787, thus giving a rough date of 1781-84.[70]

It is unfortunate that none of the pattern books available, and very few seem to have survived, shows designs for cork stoppers, except for one for Sheffield Plate, dated 1792 by John Green of Sheffield.[71] This shows a design (No. 1227) for a stopper with a finger ring and a label over incised for PORT, priced at 9s. per dozen. Thus one is led to think that the unmarked stoppers with finger rings and labels over are likely to date to the last quarter of the eighteenth century.

Another style of stopper has a flat top with the name incised upon it (see list below, items 12 and 13). Apart from the absence of the label and finger ring these are identical to the MOSELLE and CHAMPAGNE (list items 10 and 11) and would appear to belong to the same period.

A further early style has a decorative finial above the capping with the name incised around the rim of the capping. Examples of this are the unmarked SAUTERNE and SHERRY and the slightly smaller SHRUB, which have a finial of grapes, vine leaves and a cherub's head on either side and, from the style of the lettering and other features, are thought to date to around 1780.

Yet another style was armorial as exemplified by an unmarked pair engraved on both sides for MADEIRA and FRONTINIAC, accompanied by a crest depicting an ibis above a mantling, probably dating from the late eighteenth century.

Most silver mounted stoppers had a pin soldered on to the underside of the capping which passed through the cork and screwed on to the footing so that the cork was firmly held but could easily be replaced. With some, as in the case of the MADEIRA and FRONTINIAC, the footing was riveted on to a disc and in the case of plated examples this was the usual practice.

Stopper labels were made of graduated cork of excellent quality on top of which was a metal cover. In some cases this was flat topped with the name engraved on the top (style 1 – name on top). Another style consisted of a finger hold surmounted by a label on which the name was engraved (style 2 – name on ring). A third style had a decorative finial with the name of the wine engraved round the rim of the capping (style 3 – name on rim). The positioning of hallmarks varied. A Scottish example is marked on the footing, underneath the bottom of the cork. With the exception of one that seems to have the maker's mark of William Sutton, which was entered in 1784, and a lion passant, none of those so far known in the first two categories is marked.

There are various types of capping; some are flat with the top of the cork, some have overlapping

Labels from other Materials - Mounted Corks

Figures 1232-1241.

Labels from other Materials - Mounted Corks

rims that are reeded or plain and some have gadrooned borders. There are also various types of footing: some are inset underneath the cork, some are co-extensive with the bottom of the cork, as in the case of the George Pearson PORT and CLARET of 1820, and some overlap the cork with plain or reeded rims.[72]

Another type of bottle-cork is plated and shaped like a horse's head. In this case the liquid in the bottle can be poured out through the head, rather as in the case of a cow-creamer the cream can be poured out through the cow's mouth.[73]

Apart from silver mounted stoppers there were plated examples, where the top of the finger ring was beaten out and flattened to receive the name. In another plated type the label was kidney shaped and made of bone, ivory or mother-of-pearl. This was secured by a metal band, whose ends passed down through the capping, and was riveted to a metal disc at the footing. These were often used for coloured glass bottles and appear to date from the second quarter of the nineteenth century.

An early fully marked mount must be the unnamed silver bottle cork consisting of a cork secured by a silver ring with the top of the mounting decorated by vine leaves and grapes. This was made by J.W. Story and William Elliott and hallmarked for 1812.

It is fair to conclude that named silver-mounted bottle-corks appear to be uncommon.[74]

There follow some details of silver mounted cork stoppers.[75]

1.	1764	A bottle or flask neck mount, the hinges secured by detachable pins, with chains connected to a stopper or cork mount, the cork missing; unnamed, by John (I) and George Foster of London, in partnership between 11 July and 27 October 1764.[76]
2.	1766	Two sets of six cork stoppers presumably silver and unnamed, supplied by Parker and Wakelin in January and February to Mr Clutton.
3.	*c.*1780	SAUTERNE – unmarked; cast silver cherub's head with face on either side flanked by fruiting vines; name incised on rim of mounting (see fig. 1233).[77]
4.	*c.*1780	SHERRY – pair with SAUTERNE.
5.	*c.*1780	SHRUB – same as Nos 3 and 4, but slightly smaller.
6.	1781-87	LISBON – mark of William Stephenson – entered 1781; new mark entered 1787 – and a lion passant. Name on one side of label above a finger ring and a plain capping (see fig. 1247). Datable to between 1781 and 1787 because Stephenson entered a new mark in 1787.
7.	*c.*1790	MADEIRA and FRONTINIAC – unmarked; names on both faces; good patina; the finial a crest showing an ibis about a mantling on the mount.
8.	1792	PORT – a design for a Sheffield plate stopper with the label about a finger ring and a shaped capping by John Green of Sheffield. The illustration is a tracing taken from John Green's Pattern Book (at the V & A), Design No. 1227.
9.	1775-90	MACON – a heraldic lion rampant, one paw raised, one resting on shield with engraved device, no mantling and mounted foot.[78] Two heraldic birds modelled on the flamingo have been noted of this period in silver for MADEIRA and FRONTINIAC.
10.	*c.*1775-1800	MOSELLE – unmarked; rounded ends to label over finger ring; plain capping with five reeds on rim; full footing with reeding on rim (see fig. 1232). Labels of this kind were made for one of the Inns of Court: an example for CHAMPAGNE with Inner Temple on the reverse and the winged horse on the shoulder has been noted.
11.	*c.*1775-1800	CHAMPAGNE – unmarked; three reeds to mounting; otherwise similar to No. 10 (see fig. 1234).
12	*c.*1775-1800	RUM – unmarked; plain cap mounting on which title engraved; otherwise similar to No. 10 (see fig. 1237).
13	*c.*1775-1800	BRANDY – unmarked; pair to No. 12 (see fig. 1236).
14	*c.*1775-1800	PORT – unmarked; flat top cap; variegated frame to label similar to that employed by George Pearson in 1820.
15	*c.*1790	SHERRY – unmarked; finger ring handle surmounted by title, name incised (see fig. 1246).[79]
16	*c.*1790	RUM – unmarked; pair with No. 15 (see fig. 1248).
17	*c.*1790	BEER – unmarked; finger ring handle surmounted by title label; incised name.[80]
18	*c.*1795	PORT – John Constable (Maker's mark IC) of Dundee (1795-1809 marked on

Labels from other Materials - Mounted Corks

Figures 1242-1248.

Labels from other Materials - Mounted Corks

		footing, the pot of lilies with the thistle contained within an oblong punch).
19	c.1800	CHAMPAGNE – marked on surface of mounting; finger ring handle with title above, engraved, with black wax filling; example of corkscrew style having no footing.[81]
20	1820	PORT – title black wax filled in fretwork frame above a shell with the cap of the mounting gadrooned. Full width footing. Maker George Pearson, London.
21	1820	CLARET – a stunning label. Three or four other examples are known including one of magnum-size (see fig. 1240).
22	1822	BARSAC – also by George Pearson. Same as CLARET, above, though much smaller.
23	1829	HERMITAGE – Ledsam, Vale and Wheeler, Birmingham. Raised foliate scroll border and knop top with ring handle; swinging crescent label incised on both sides (see fig. 1239).
24	1829	CLARET – see fig. 1235, part of the set with HERMITAGE (see fig. 1239).
25	1829	MADEIRA – see fig. 1238, part of the set with HERMITAGE (see fig. 1239).
26	1829	SHERRY – see fig. 1241, part of the set with HERMITAGE (see fig. 1239).
27	1829	HOCK – part of the set with HERMITAGE.[82]
28	c.1830	BRANDY – John Settle and Henry Wilkinson of Sheffield. Name in script incised on kidney shaped ivory set in silver, on leaf base, with triple reeded footing.[83]
29	1832	RUM – Henry Wilkinson & Co., Sheffield; similar to No. 27 listed above for HOCK.[84]
30	1841	CLARET – 34 identical examples in electroplate by John Gilbert of the Electro Works, Ryland Street, Birmingham, with full platers' marks ('JG', 'AI', 'r' and an inverted triangle surmounted by a cross, resembling hallmarks, well struck. Good quality and probably survivors from a set of three dozen belonging to a City Livery Company. The label is semi-circular integrated into the pull ring attached to the mounting. A screw is soldered into the cap.
31	1833	BRANDY – T. Simpson & Son of Birmingham but assayed in London; title within shell and foliate scroll ring handles set upon a fruiting vine base.[85]
32	1833	WHISKEY – pair to BRANDY (listed as No. 31 above).
33	1844	MADEIRA – Messrs Barnard; curved scroll, surmounted by a Chinese Dragon, placed on fruiting vines; pin and cork missing; mounted on a circular wooden stand. Applied with oval badge engraved with the insignia of the 38th Grenadiers.[86]
34	1844	MADEIRA – C. Rawlings & W. Summers; tapered cork in two unequal sections. Bottom plate marked with lion passant held to cork by nut on threaded pin.
35	c.1850	PORT – unmarked (see fig. 1245).
36	1868	WHISKEY – maker 'A.M.' for Alexander Macrae, assayed in London. Bottom plate welded to pin.
37	1869	BRANDY – Robert Hennell; shell and foliate ring handle set upon a heavy fruiting vine base: title engraved on label applied around rim, possibly added later (see fig. 1243).
38	1869	WHISKEY – see fig. 1242, in set with BRANDY (see fig. 1243).
39	1869	GIN – see fig. 1244, in set with BRANDY (see fig. 1243)
40/41		MARRASQUI and ROSA – possibly Portuguese; no other details available.
42	c.1870	BRANDY – incised in black in Gothic style lettering on ivory in an electroplated holder.
43	c.1930	A BURDON SHERRY – incised in black in unusual capitals on a ceramic base set in an electroplated holder marked 'FOREIGN'.

Labels from other Materials - China, Pottery, Glass and Celluloid

PART 8 – CHINA, POTTERY, GLASS AND CELLULOID

Wedgwood was using bone china for a range of domestic wares in the nineteenth century. At some time they began to retail some of their wares through T. Goode and Sons, among them wine labels in the form of vine leaves, coloured as in their well-known green vine leaf plates, but only 2.5cm (1in.) wide.

Coalport (established 1750) made escutcheons in bone china with good quality chains fitted with slip rings, for example for WHISKY.

Crown Staffordshire (established 1801) produced fine bone china domed escutcheons (for example for PORT) retailed through T. Goode and Co. Ltd of London in 1900-1910 and reissued in the 1950s in harder colours and slightly less fancy lettering (for example for CLARET). They also produced smaller labels between 1892 and 1900, again retailed by T. Goode and Co. of South Audley Street, London, with the pattern number A6796 for WHISKEY, GLYCERINE, BORACIC LOTION, LIQUID POWDER, BATH POWDER, EAU DE COLOGNE and EAU DE ROSE. In the 1920s Hammersley produced, in creamy white fine bone china, an escutcheon for

Figures 1249-1257.

Labels from other Materials - China, Pottery, Glass and Celluloid

WHISKEY in gold titling with gold scrolling borders. Aynsley had already produced, c.1895, a similar pair for SHERRY and BRANDY using the elongated escutcheon format and an attractive bumpy face with smooth back and silver chains.

There is no record of other ceramic firms in England executing labels in this material until very recently. In 1986 a set of nine labels from Royal Grafton appeared for sale with coloured designs illustrating themes connected with hunting and the chase, the military, sport and love. They are signed or initialled by Eric Elliot and are basically of escutcheon shape, but more heart-shaped (in five cases) or rectangular (in four cases). Their precise date has not yet been ascertained (see figs. 1249-1257). Champagne (see fig. 1251) is singled out for having a title in script.

In France, a factory was established at Bayeux in 1810 in the grounds of a Benedictine convent to manufacture porcelain wares. From 1849 the proprietor was Mr M.F. Gosse. In the 1860s he made small porcelain heart-shaped wine labels in large numbers, inscribed with gilt or black titles. Two, for CORNAS and CHYPRE, are on display in the Bayeux Museum. The majority of the names are for regional wines, seldom encountered outside France, and the spellings are sometimes idiosyncratic. LAMALQUE, for example (see fig. 1017), probably refers to a wine from La Malegue in Provence, near Toulon.[87] Other titles include COGNIAC, LIMONADE, RATAFIAT DE FLEUR D'ORANGE, SAUTERNE and VERGUS or VERGUN (see figs. 1016 and 1018-1021),[88] and those mentioned in Chapter 9, Part 8, France.

Also of this period are attractive crescents with script titles for 'Champagne.' (two), 'Grave.', 'Frontignan.' and 'Hermitage.'. In the Aynsley style and of the same period but in kidney shape with script titles are Château Latour, Curino, Volney and Saint-Estèphe. These are probably French porcelain labels and rare. Two unmarked French faience labels have been noted (see below, Chapter 9, Part 8, France) for VOLNAY and MULSEAUX.

With regard to glass, reproduction labels on Bristol blue glass decanters are quite common both for wines and sauces (see pages 170-171 in *Sauce Labels*). Less common are reproduction rectangular shaped labels with decorative borders engraved on white glass faceted decanters, for example in a stand of 1809 made by Rebecca Emes and Edward Barnard for HOLLANDS, RUM and BRANDY. Similar labels are found on soy frames (see figs. 112 and 116 in *Sauce Labels*).

Celluloid is the registered trademark for a thermoplastic made from nitrocellulose, camphor and alcohol that is elastic and very strong. It was an ideal substance to use for labels being attached by nails to a wooden barrel (42 imperial gallons of wine or 36 of ale), tun (252 imperial gallons of wine or 216 of ale) or cask (various sizes) to mark its contents. Early in the twentieth century the wine estate on the slopes of the mountain known as Helderberg in the Cape District of South Africa near Stellenbosch called its produce after the mountain and marked its barrels with a cream coloured celluloid label with deep set black lettering for HELDERBERG (see fig. 1258). Similar labels have been noted for SHERRY and IRISH.[89]

Figure 1258.

Labels from other Materials - Mother-of-Pearl

Figures 1259-1267.

PART 9 – MOTHER-OF-PEARL

The fourth most commonly used material for making labels (after silver, silver-plate and enamel) and perhaps the most intrinsically beautiful, mother-of-pearl, is taken from the inner lining of the shells of several varieties of mollusc. The slow accumulation of this lining involves a succession of prismatic folds that act like tiny mirrors to produce the iridescent qualities for which it has been prized since ancient times.

Mother-of-pearl labels are relatively easy to date by reference to silver designs, but it is not always so easy to say where they were made. The earliest examples are undoubtedly those of escutcheon shape (one of the earliest must be an escutcheon W. WINE and fig. 1268 for CHAMPAGNE; see also fig. 1260 for CALCAVELLA and fig. 425 for CLARET) and, as the majority of these follow

333

Labels from other Materials - Mother-of-Pearl

so closely, both in outline (see fig. 1266 for TENT and in similar style PAXARETTE, not illustrated) and, when decorated, in their motifs, the enamel labels produced in the Midlands during the third quarter of the eighteenth century they must be attributed to the Birmingham area which was then the centre of the pearl-shell industry in England. The crudely engraved fruiting vines often seen on these escutcheons can also be found on crescents with a jagged lower edge, a design exclusive to this material (see fig. 1259 for CLARET and fig. 1261 for PORT and note a similar design for W PORT not illustrated). Large 'horseshoe' crescents, silver examples of which tend to date from the 1760s and 1770s, are sometimes encountered with a stylised foliate engraving that has also been noted on the jagged edge crescents (see fig. 1263 and compare with fig. 1259), so both of these designs can also be attributed to Birmingham. Smaller crescents, often with a narrow engraved border of groups of three lines as noted for MADEIRA (not illustrated) and illustrated by figs. 424 for W.WINE, 426 for HOLLANDS and 431 for PORT, are the most commonly found eighteenth-century labels in this material (see also figs. 1265 for BRANDY and 1267 for GRAPE). Their production probably continued into the early decades of the next century and it is highly likely that they were made in the Birmingham area. Other designs of eighteenth-century style but uncertain attribution are the two varieties of kidney (see fig. 1262 for LISBON and fig. 1264 for CLARET, a pair with CALCAVALLA). Perhaps these come from Sheffield as a Boulton and Fothergill style mother-of-pearl label for SHERRY has been noted with a different style chain. A highly decorated example is shown for BRANDY in fig. 430.

Some time around the turn of the eighteenth century the disc (see fig. 1269) and the bottle collar make their appearance (see fig. 1270), although both are rare in this material and the collar is unusual in that it has been cut from a spiro-form shell, a section of abalone, a shellfish of the Haliotis family, found in California; it is incised for SHERRY, a pair with GIN, and the disc is incised for SILLERY. Presumably it is also in this period that ordinary rectangles appear. The most common form is a narrow rectangle (as shown by fig. 419 for LISBON) with a shallow border of triangular cuts (see fig. 1275 for BRANDY). A little later, in around 1825, labels were made with extraordinarily delicately pierced and engraved borders of fruiting vines in two designs that so closely resemble silver examples made in Birmingham that they must also have been made in that city (see fig. 1271 for SHRUB). The large rectangular version of this work can be found in mother-of-pearl in Stancliffe[90] and in silver by Richard Morton, Birmingham 1823 in *Birmingham Gold and Silver 1773-1973*.[91] Next, in terms of English work, comes a group of carved labels that are strongly related to mother-of-pearl caddy spoons dated to the early Victorian period and that have no counterparts in silver design but bear some similarity to the 'animal' designs found in electroplate. The most striking of these feature alternatively a fox (see fig. 1272 for WHISKY) and an eagle (see fig. 1273 for GIN) within a foliate surround, but foliate arrangements are interesting (see fig. 1274 for BRANDY and fig. 432 for GINGER). Towards the mid-nineteenth century labels were made

Figure 1268.

Labels from other Materials - Mother-of-Pearl

Figures 1269-1276.

335

Labels from other Materials - Mother-of-Pearl

Figure 1277.

Figures 1278-1285.

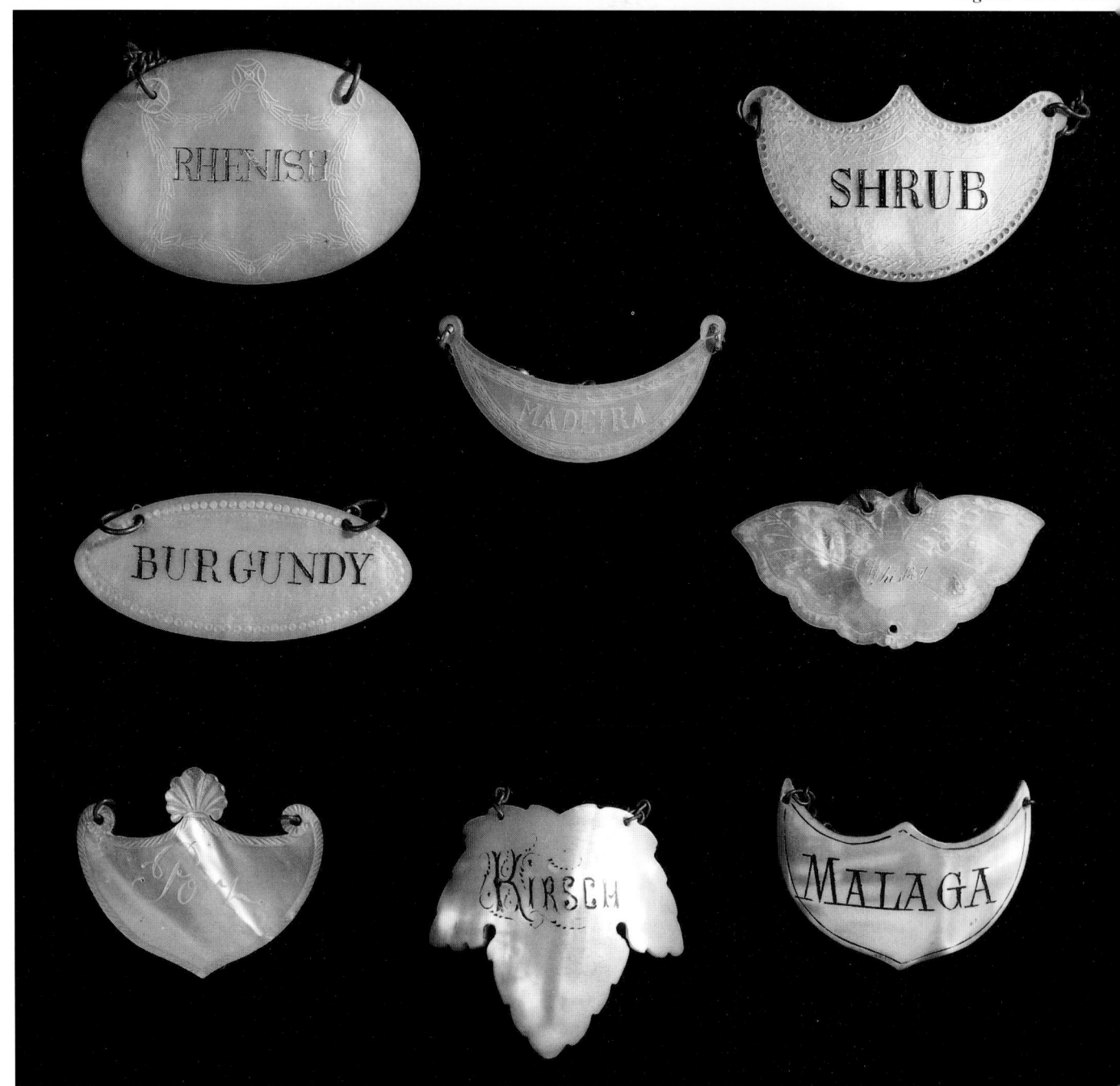

Labels from other Materials - Mother-of-Pearl/Other Organic Materials

in the form of cut-out letters such as P for port and the Marshall Collection in the Ashmolean Museum, Oxford has a set of these in mother-of-pearl. An example of the 'postage stamp' type of initial, where the letter is pierced from a rectangle, has also been seen. The principal use of this material in England during the latter part of the century and beyond was on corks, where the wine name is engraved on a mother-of-pearl panel held within a metal mounting, usually silver-plate. Occasionally, this later type can also be found as a label with suspension chain. In Victorian times rectangular labels were made with cut corners and Gothic lettering for WHISKEY, PORT and RUM (for RUM see fig. 1276).

In the English context it must be remembered that London also had a significant colony of pearl-workers by the end of the eighteenth century, although it is probable that its principal production was buttons and no other work can be attributed with any certainty. A far more important centre of mother-of-pearl production was China, where fans, boxes and gaming counters were made in significant quantities for the European market. It is highly likely, therefore, that wine labels were also made in China. An obvious clue to such an origin would be the inclusion of specifically Chinese scenes or motifs, but these only occur on a particularly rare type of butterfly-shaped label (see fig. 1277 for Sherry in lower case lettering, enlarged to show an engraved Chinese village scene, and fig. 1282 for Whiskey). Another approach, however, is to study the engraving on known Chinese work such as gaming counters and fan panels which are similar in scale to wine labels; and several characteristics quickly emerge. The most general is the lightness and shallowness of the engraving, which has sometimes been referred to as 'scratch engraving'. Certain motifs, such as reverse beading (that is concave rather than convex), harebell garlands and a variety of geometric sequences also become easily recognisable. The group illustrated (see figs. 1278-1282) show several combinations of these characteristics, and it is interesting to note that beside the butterfly (see fig. 1282 for Whiskey), crescents, especially cusped (see fig. 1281 for MADEIRA and fig. 1279 for the cusped SHRUB) and ovals predominate (see fig. 1278 for RHENISH and fig. 1280 for BURGUNDY). From the evidence of the titles and the shapes it seems probable that the production of Chinese mother-of-pearl labels fell mostly within the period 1780 to 1840.

Beside England and China, mother-of-pearl labels were also made in Europe, almost certainly in France. A completely different variety of shell appears to have been employed so examples can easily be identified, although the spelling of the titles can sometimes also be of help. Notably darker in hue, the iridescence is also more vibrant with strong mauve and green tones. As well as the peaked and cusped crescent so popular in Continental label design, the only known example of a mother-of-pearl vine leaf (see fig. 1284 for KIRSCH) occurs in this group, most of which appear to date from the middle quarters of the nineteenth century (see figs. 1283-1285 for PORT, KIRSCH and MALAGA, and for a list of unusual titles employed see below, Chapter 9, Part 8, France).

PART 10 – OTHER ORGANIC MATERIALS

Wine labels made from organic materials other than mother-of-pearl range from those using animal parts in pure form such as claws and teeth, through animal products that have been worked such as ivory, to processed and plant materials such as fabrics – and our survey continues in this order.

1. Claws and Teeth
The practice of mounting claws and teeth with silver to serve as wine labels, as well as vinaigrettes and jewellery, undoubtedly started in India in the mid-nineteenth century. By far the most common examples are tigers' claws, mounted doubly or singly (see fig. 1286 for BRANDY) and boars' tusks (see fig. 1287 for SHERRY – and also CLARET and MADEIRA). Presumably this fashion originated in the habit of using heads and skins as trophies to commemorate a successful hunt but, judging from the numbers produced, the use of tigers' claws and boars' teeth for wine labels quickly achieved commercial proportions. Although usually unmarked, occasionally examples can be found with the marks of Hamilton and Co. of Calcutta and Orr and Co. of Madras or with full English

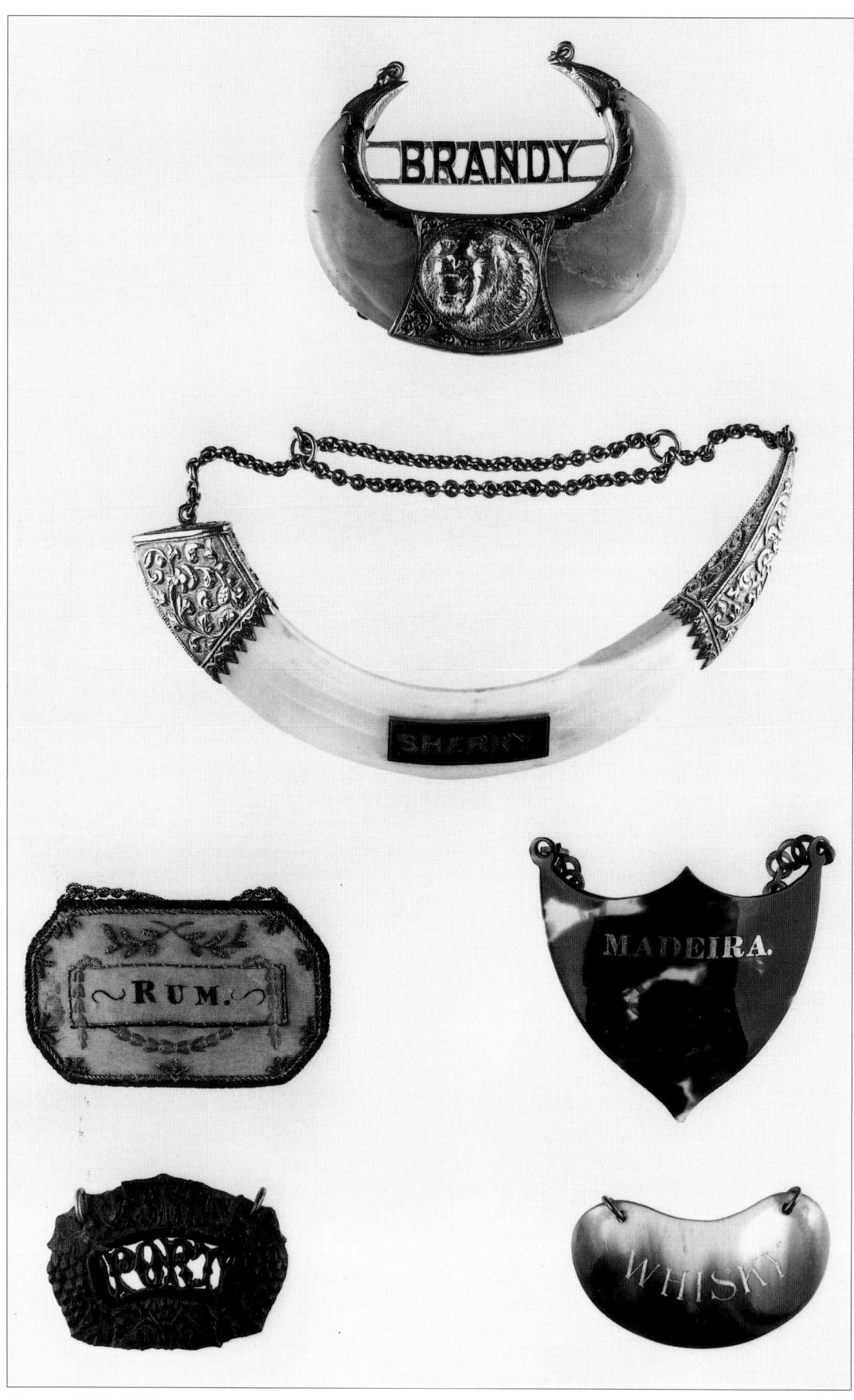

Labels from other Materials - Other Organic Materials

Figures 1286-1291.

Labels from other Materials - Other Organic Materials

Figures 1292-1301.

Labels from other Materials - Other Organic Materials

hallmarks from about 1875 through to the 1930s. Much less common are labels made from the deep-rooted canine teeth of the larger felines,[92] and rarer still are sharks' teeth (see fig. 1455).

2. Tortoiseshell
The material universally called tortoiseshell is neither tortoise nor, strictly speaking, shell. It is made from the carapace of several species of sea turtle and its composition is more closely related to that of horn or hooves. Given the extensive use of this material through the centuries, both for entire objects and for embellishment, it is surprising that it was so rarely used for wine labels. The first example illustrated is a large shield shape for MADEIRA (see fig. 1289), of which the chain is also made from tortoiseshell, and comes from a set of six that would appear to date from the first half of the nineteenth century. All have English titles, which were printed or painted in gilt letters on a strip of translucent material applied to the face.[93] The second example illustrated is for WHISKY (see fig. 1291), of kidney shape with the letters painted in white, and probably dates from the second half of the nineteenth century. So also does a set of three octagonal labels for PORT, WHISKY and BRANDY with gilt letters and border (not illustrated).

3. Ivory and Bone
The difficulty of laying down hard and fast rules for distinguishing between these two materials in small portions makes it wiser to treat them together.

Ivory is most commonly encountered in the form of bottle collars, which were cut concentrically from a tapering tusk so that they vary in diameter and pitch. They are, however, usually flatter than their counterparts in silver and OSP, which suggests that they may have been intended more often to sit on the shoulders of a wine bottle rather than the sloping sides of a decanter. There being no obvious reason to believe that ivory collars were not contemporary with metal collars, it can be assumed that the majority were made in the period 1790-1830 (see fig. 1297 for GIN).

Very few ivory labels can be dated confidently to the eighteenth century. An escutcheon shaped example exists (see fig. 1293 for GIN), but it is probably an 1840s revival. A tap handle for PINE/APPLE RUM (see fig. 1300), inlaid in brass and coloured ivory, is undoubtedly of late eighteenth-century date, and the tiny crescent for PORT (see fig. 1295) could also be as early, but these, together with bottle collars with distinctly eighteenth-century titles, are rare. It would appear, therefore, that labels in ivory and bone were mostly a nineteenth-century phenomenon. Some, by their titles such as ST PERAY or VIDONIA, or by their shapes such as collars (see fig. 1297 for GIN) and discs (see fig. 1296 for PORT No. 9), can be ascribed to the early decades. Others, by the dates included in the title such as the gold-mounted cut-corner rectangle for BRANDY 1841 (see fig. 1301) or the 1856 inscribed on the reverse of the BRANDY label decorated with vines (see fig. 1299), can be ascribed to the middle decades – as can the cut-out letter A with ivory chain in the Cropper Collection at the Victoria and Albert Museum.[94] The BROWN BRANDY cauldron-shaped label (see fig. 1292), which is definitely made from bone rather than ivory, probably dates from the closing decades of the nineteenth century. So also does a pair of small octagonal labels for Moselle and Hock in lower-case Gothic script with silver chains.

Some designs in ivory and bone, such as the BROWN BRANDY (see fig. 1292), VIDONIA (see fig. 1294) and BRANDY (see fig. 1299) do not have exact counterparts in other materials, while sauce labels in any organic medium are extremely rare (see fig. 1298 for VINEGAR). Ivory labels have been reported for CURAÇAO and VANILLE (see below, Chapter 9, Part 8, France).

4. Coconut
In terms of primary materials, the only remaining substance that requires discussion is the coconut, from whose shell wine labels were occasionally carved (see fig. 1290 for PORT). They are decidedly rare and the ornately incised fruiting vine decoration suggests that they were made in the third quarter of the nineteenth century.

Labels from other Materials - Other Organic Materials

Figures 1302-1305.

5. Leather and Silver

A set of four canted neck rings made from leather dyed a deep crimson (known in the eighteenth century as Russian Leather) measuring 4.5cm (1¾in.) in diameter (top) and 6.2cm (2½in.) bottom and 1.5cm (½in.) deep are shown in figs. 1302-1305.[95] They have plain silver cut corner rectangular panels attached to the leather by studs and fashioned to fit the curve of the leather. The black-wax filled titles are for PORT, SHERRY, SHRUB and VIDONIA, which seems to indicate a date towards the end of the eighteenth century or beginning of the nineteenth century. This was also the time when Russian Leather was most popular and when neck rings were beginning to be manufactured.

Jane Stancliffe in *Bottle Tickets* mentions leather as a material from which labels have been made, but does not give examples.[96]

6. Woven Fabrics

Labels made from processed organic substances, that is woven fabrics such as cotton, silk and wool, are not frequently encountered. The large, cut-corner rectangle for RUM (see fig. 1288), however, comprises a veritable symphony of different fabrics and yarns. Dating from the late eighteenth or early nineteenth centuries, the sheet metal core has been covered in dark green silk on the back and cream silk on the front with a border of silver brocade and dark green velvet. On the face, the decorative detail has been embroidered in silver brocade, gold thread and wool of mid green, light green and yellow, while the title has been picked out in black cotton and the chain made from gold brocade. Much later, in Edwardian times, some home-made labels were produced on pierced card with title and decoration stitched in cotton thread and the 'chain' fashioned from silk ribbon.

CHAPTER 9

LABELS FROM OUTSIDE THE BRITISH ISLES AND IRELAND

PART 1 – AUSTRALIA

The settlements in Australia remained small until the goldrushes of the 1850s and 1860s. Nevertheless, silversmiths were active there from the 1820s (the First Fleet arrived in 1823) and, as in other colonies, the practitioners in silver usually combined their craft with others such as jewellery, clock-, watch- and instrument-making as well as general engraving and casting. Wine labels would not be expected to have formed a significant portion of the output required by these early communities, but some were made.

There are six labels known by Alexander Dick of Sydney c.1835, four in the collection of Goldsmiths' Hall, London[1] and two in the Ashmolean Museum, Oxford; all are simple rectangles with cast, applied, foliate and floral borders and are engraved BRANDY, MADEIRA, PORT, RUM, BROWN SHERRY and PALE SHERRY respectively. Dick was born in Scotland in around 1800 and arrived in Sydney as a free settler in 1824. By 1826 he was advertising in the *Sydney Gazette* as a 'Gold and Silver Plate Manufacturer, Brass founder and Plater'. In 1829 he was sentenced to seven years on Norfolk Island for receiving stolen property, but was granted a free pardon in 1833, whereafter he continued his business until his death in 1843.

We have to wait another thirty odd years until there is any further evidence of Australian labels – a set of six by Henry Steiner of Adelaide during the 1860s. Large, broad crescents with a border of wrigglework reeding and suspended from a highly unusual chain formed from articulated, tubular links, they were engraved for BURGUNDY, CLARET, MADEIRA, CARBENET (see fig. 1306), RIESLING and SHIRAZ. The last three titles of grape varieties are particularly interesting in that they are undoubtedly for locally made wines, which were then still in the early days of their development. While 'CARBENET' might, at first sight, appear to be a misspelling of Cabernet, it was spelt thus in the first book on wine and viticulture to be published in Australia (1833)[2] and it was still the normal Australian pronunciation of Cabernet in 1974.[3] This set[4] may have been the set of six Australian silver labels shown by W. Verner at the Sydney Exhibition of 1861.[5]

Labels from outside The British Isles and Ireland - Australia

Figure 1306.

Steiner was a German silversmith from Bremen who probably arrived in Adelaide in 1858. He does not appear in local directories until 1864, but is believed to have been working on his own account from 1860. He was a prolific and, in his later years, a flamboyantly Australian manufacturer. He is thought to have returned to Germany after the death of his immediate family in 1883. A few other labels are known by him – a deep, fat crescent (like a horse's hoof) dated around 1870 with single reeded border for MARSALA (see fig. 1307),[6] a fat crescent with single reeded border for MADEIRA,[7] a cut-corner rectangle with foliate eyelets for HOCK,[8] and a rectangle for IRISH WHISKEY that has a matching SCOTCH WHISKEY by Jochim Matthias Wendt, also of Adelaide and dated around 1865.[9]

From about 1874 Thomas Stokes of Melbourne was producing electroplated nickel silver labels. An example for BRANDY (with further commentary) will be found above in Chapter 8, Part 6, Electroplate, see fig. 1230.

Figure 1307.

Labels from outside The British Isles and Ireland - Belgium

Figure 1308.

PART 2 – BELGIUM

Measuring 6.35cm (2½in.) wide, a gourmet at his table slot label is die-stamped in fairly thin metal in order to take up the extremely fine detail of the die. It depicts a gentleman behind a table covered by a cloth decorated with flowers beneath which his ecstatically splayed feet can be seen. He is tucking into a large fish on an oval plate while, waiting for him on the right are two goblets, a pig's head and a chicken. In front of his plate are a condiment pot, a piece of bread, a bottle and a beaker. On the left, a rack of meat, a jelly and another bottle await his pleasure. The table is flanked by two baskets brimming with fruit to round off this image of overwhelmingly self-indulgent gourmandise (see fig. 1308, on a scale times two).

This label, which was one of a pair, is struck on the face, on the lower border of the slot window, with the Belgian guarantee mark for small silver objects in use between 1814 and 1831, when Belgium formed part of the Kingdom of Holland. It was also made in silver plate, however, in the same technique as Old Sheffield Plate (OSP). Harvey's Wine Museum has an example in OSP and the design is illustrated in Bradbury's *History of Old Sheffield Plate*.[10] Should any reader think that this type of plating was only made in England, it must be remembered that the technology had been mastered, and patented, in France as early as 1770.[11]

Slot labels were particularly popular in Continental Europe. Besides this rare example from Belgium, slot labels were made in Austria, Germany, Holland, Malta and Poland, as well as France where it was by far the most common form in both silver and silver plate. The outline of a fat, cusped crescent with figural flanks (horses, swans and foliate scrolls) is also typical of French design. Much as it may be tempting, therefore, to speculate that this label might have been made in France, the evidence of the marks must take precedence; and it would hardly be surprising if French-speaking Belgian silversmiths followed the French fashion. Moreover, this is not the only evidence which has been seen of Belgian label-making. A rounded rectangular with reeded border engraved for COGNAC with the same assay mark has been noted.

Illustrated is a crescent shaped label for SHERRY (see fig. 1309). At first sight this label seems

Labels from outside The British Isles and Ireland - Belgium

typical of the 1760s and 1770s, with its feathered edge, popular when this shape started to appear. Fig. 216 shows Margaret Binley's CLARET and figs. 588 and 590 James Phipps' inspired RUM and RED.PORT. It is a bit early for SHERRY, perhaps, but earlier examples are known. A closer look, however, raises doubts. The title is not engraved as one of that date should be, but has cross-hatched letters that did not come in until the next century. Turn it over and one will find the maker's mark of a leading Belgian silversmith, J.G. Datalis, whose workshop was in Brussels, and the Control Mark ordained in Netherlands Law of 1814 for smallwork of Belgian origin. It should be remembered that Belgium, as we call that country today, did not exist separately from The Netherlands until 1830. There were, of course, Flemish silversmiths with a great tradition, dating back much earlier, but this is not the place to discuss them. They developed their own identities, depending on which part of the Low Countries they lived in. The label shows no sign of having been re-engraved, or traces of an older (English) mark, and one therefore has to conclude that it was indeed a product of the Datalis shop in Brussels from the second decade of the nineteenth century. Indeed, if one proceeds on that assumption, one can notice aspects of its workmanship and appearance that support the theory that it is not as old as its design suggests.

Well, if it was made in Belgium at some time after 1810, then why? The date 1815 springs to mind, a date as familiar to every English schoolchild as 1066 and all that. The military campaign that culminated at Waterloo in that year brought many English regiments to the Low Countries and, of course, they brought their regimental mess silver with them. There were, too, many English palatial households established in Brussels, with a significant social life, as Byron has it:

> There was a sound of revelry by night
> And Belgium's capital had gather'd there
> Her beauty and her chivalry…
> But hush, hark, a deep sound strikes like a raising knell…
> Arm, Arm, it is, it is, the cannon's opening roar.

There was the proper domestic plate in army officers' messes, and in 'Brunswick's lofty hall', and if joy was so unconfin'd that one of the wine labels went missing, the sensible remedy was to go to the local silversmith for a replacement, to make a copy of it. That, at any rate, seems a logical reason for finding a replica of an essentially English device, in a style that had disappeared half a century earlier, in a country with practically no other examples of manufacturing such items.

Figure 1309.

Labels from outside The British Isles and Ireland - Burma

Figure 1310.

Figure 1311.

PART 3 – BURMA

The late nineteenth- or early twentieth-century 'Burmese Dancer' labels in the Cropper Collection at the Victoria and Albert Museum are well known and are illustrated and discussed in Penzer.[12] A pair of dancers arranged symmetrically supporting a curved nameplate pierced for SHERRY is shown at fig. 1310.

They are not, however, the only designs attributed to Burma. Fig. 1311 also illustrates a triangular shield pierced for PORT on a ground of pierced, scrolling foliage and flanked by lions or mythological beasts. Comparison with the three single figures in Penzer's plate 24 reveals similarities of design and chasing. The piercing of the wine titles is similar.

The labels illustrated in figs 1310 and 1311 are, however, half as large again as Penzer's and together weigh 2oz 9dwt (76g) including chains.

The repoussé work is unusually deep – 9mm or nearly ½in. – and enhances the two-dimensional effect well shown in fig. 1311, which is slightly less than full size, the width across the base of the lions being 9cm (3½in.).[13]

A different design is illustrated by figs 1312 and 1313. These shaped ovals, a pair for PORT and SHERRY with cut-out letters on a ground of pierced, scrolling foliage, are flanked by mythological beasts in high relief and have been raised, embossed and cut from a single piece of sheet – evidence of an extraordinary degree of technical skill. They can all be attributed to the second half of the nineteenth century.

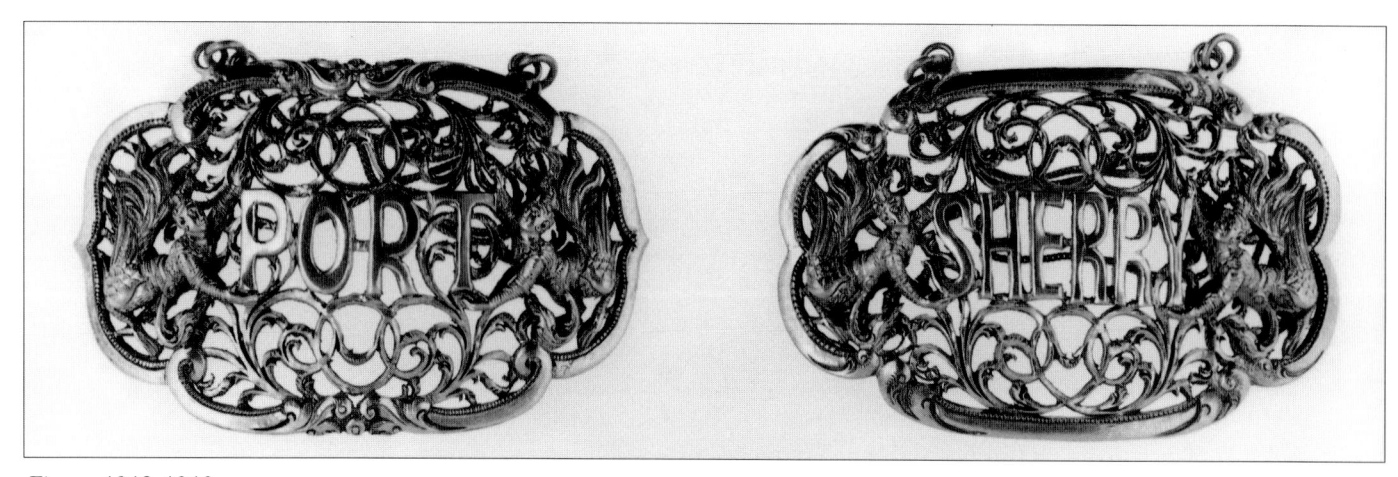

Figures 1312-1313.

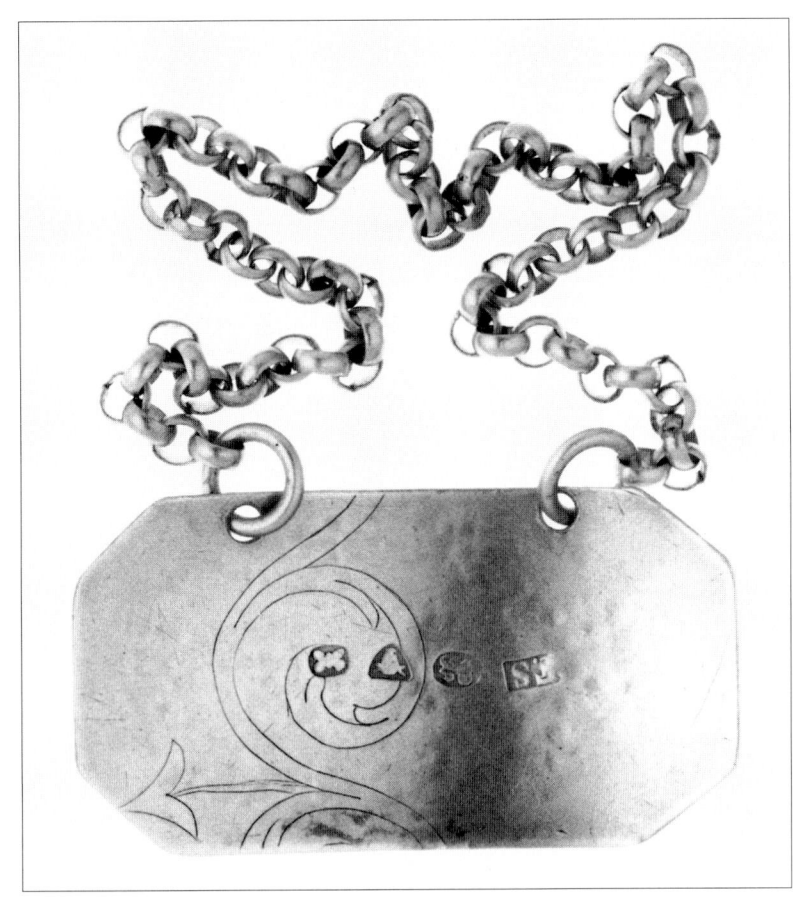

Figure 1314.

PART 4 – CANADA

Canada had no meaningful Anglo-Saxon population until the influx of loyalist emigrants occasioned by the American Revolution of the mid-1770s – and many of these returned to the USA after peace had been established; so it was not until after 1800 that a sufficiently large market of British origin began to reach the proportions that would engender the production of silver labels. As would be expected, silversmiths of British origin made most of the labels, which are of simple design and hand-raised.

The only examples that have been documented previously[14] are a set of three cut-out letters for P, M and S by James Langford of Halifax, Nova Scotia (worked 1815-47).[15] However, a private enquiry by a Wine Label Circle member in 1988 to all Canadian Museums resulted in a single reply from the National Gallery, Ottawa revealing that they had nine labels by Montreal makers, one by Peter Arnoldi (worked 1792-1808) and eight by Nelson Walker (worked 1831-55), without giving any information on the shape or title. A survey of private collections by the writer of this section uncovered a further eight Canadian labels: a reeded crescent for PORT and a small, reeded cut-corner rectangle for RUM, both struck with a tiny punch; IT in a serrated oblong, similar to that attributed by Langdon to Joseph Thompson of Montreal (worked from around 1810 onwards); a pair of cut-corner reeded rectangles for PORT and MADEIRA by Adam Ross of Halifax (worked 1813-43); a rounded-end rectangle for SHERRY by Peter Nordbeck of Halifax (worked 1819-61); a cut-corner reeded rectangle for MADEIRA (the reverse of which is illustrated in fig. 1314) by François Sasseville of Quebec (worked c.1820-64);[16] an oval with gadroon border for SHERRY by Robert Hendery of Montreal (worked 1837-97); and a reeded, shaped rectangle for CHERRY BRANDY by Thomas Page of Pugwash (worked 1823-65). No doubt there are more to be discovered.

In addition to a maker's mark some labels have 'pseudo hallmarks', such as a king's head and the lion passant that purchasers of silver expected to see (see fig. 1314).

Labels from outside The British Isles and Ireland - China

Figure 1315.

Figure 1316.

Figure 1317.

PART 5 – CHINA

Silver in Western forms began to be made in Canton from about 1785. Initially wares were produced to the order of visiting merchants and ships' officers for their own use or to private commissions obtained from their home ports. After about 1815, however, they began to be exported to British settlements in other parts of Asia – especially Bombay – and Australia. Until about 1845 the forms were strictly occidental in style and are usually struck with pseudo English hallmarks. This early period is now commonly referred to as 'China Trade' and wine labels made during these years are extremely rare. A strong caveat is necessary at this point as some of the earlier British and later American manufacturers of electroplated silver used pseudo hallmarks that might be confused with China Trade or Colonial silver. These wares, however, are always machine made, whereas all China Trade wine labels are made entirely by hand. ENGLISH CLARET (see fig. 1315) is a delightful and unusually sophisticated example of a China Trade wine label. Struck with the mark of Lin Chang of Canton, it is a faithful copy of a rare design by Robert Morton of Birmingham *c.*1825,[17] except for the lettering, which looks as though it was taken from a child's primer – reflecting the Chinese workman's total unfamiliarity with the Roman alphabet.

The years between around 1845 and 1885 are now usually referred to as 'late China Trade'. During this period the former British colony of Hong Kong was founded with an ever-growing population of Westerners and, after 1860, Shanghai also developed a significant Western populace. The silver starts to become increasingly Chinese in its decoration and pseudo hallmarks become much less frequent, with Chinese character marks becoming more normal, although makers' marks in Roman capitals remain the most usual. Wine labels from this period are infrequently encountered. Cut-out letters, unmarked and flat-chased on both sides with Chinese scenes, undoubtedly date from these years, as do initial labels with the letter applied to a heart shaped, enamel bordered design with a ring matted ground and raised oriental motifs.

After about 1885 the 'post-China Trade' period begins, when silverware took on an uncompromisingly, even exuberant, Chinese appearance and, in accordance with the then fashion for all things Oriental, was widely exported to Western markets in Europe and America as well as to European communities in the Eastern hemisphere. Wine labels were produced in prodigious quantities, most commonly rectangles and crescents surmounted by a dragon or Chinese characters and large, variously shaped designs embossed with similar motifs. Makers' marks in Roman capitals remain the norm but are often accompanied by standard marks such as '90'. All these labels, however, are entirely hand raised and worked. The most prolific manufacturer of this relatively modern era was Wang Hing of 10 Queen's Road, Hong Kong (Mr Wang's maker's mark was HW in Western style – see fig. 1316) whose output was exported throughout the globe and retailed by such major emporia as Tiffany's in New York. His late nineteenth-century label for JEREZ is illustrated (see fig. 1317).

One of the most spectacular and desirable of Asian labels is the bat with wings spread and displaying the letters of the wine title.[18] It is difficult to date precisely, although it is most probably *c.*1880, and comes in at least three different sizes. The smallest, and least distinguished, variant often bears a maker's mark, which is difficult to read, while the larger versions are always unmarked. In the larger forms it is entirely hand made and has particularly finely chased detail. Dr Bernard

Watney, when discussing this label in *Christies' Wine Companion,*[19] revealed that a similar design had been registered by the London silversmith James Barclay Hennell in 1883 and that the mammal section of the British Museum thought that it could be a stylised depiction of the Indian dog-faced fruit bat, *Cynopterus sphinx*; but the workmanship definitely suggests a Chinese manufacture and it must be significant that the bat is a potent symbol of happiness in Chinese iconography while it would appear not to feature in Indian symbolism.

China was also a centre of mother-of-pearl production (see above, Chapter 8, Part 9, and in particular fig. 1277 for SHERRY with its engraved Chinese village scene).

PART 6 – DENMARK

Wine labels did not appear in Denmark before about 1820, according to Bo Bransom in his *Dictionary of Silver Collectors*. He explains that Norway, which was in union with Denmark until 1814, had a monopoly for glass production until they separated in that year, and it was not until 1825 that the first Danish glassworks was founded. The earliest Danish decanters date from around 1831, and the labels to hang on them are unlikely to be much earlier. Danish wine labels are difficult to date accurately as small articles of silver were not required to have the Copenhagen town mark, which has a date below it, but only a maker's mark. The King Hong hotel in Copenhagen boasts a Jensen made mobile decanter set (see fig. 1318) located beneath an oil painting of King Frederick

Figure 1318.

Labels from outside The British Isles and Ireland - Denmark

Figures 1319-1337.

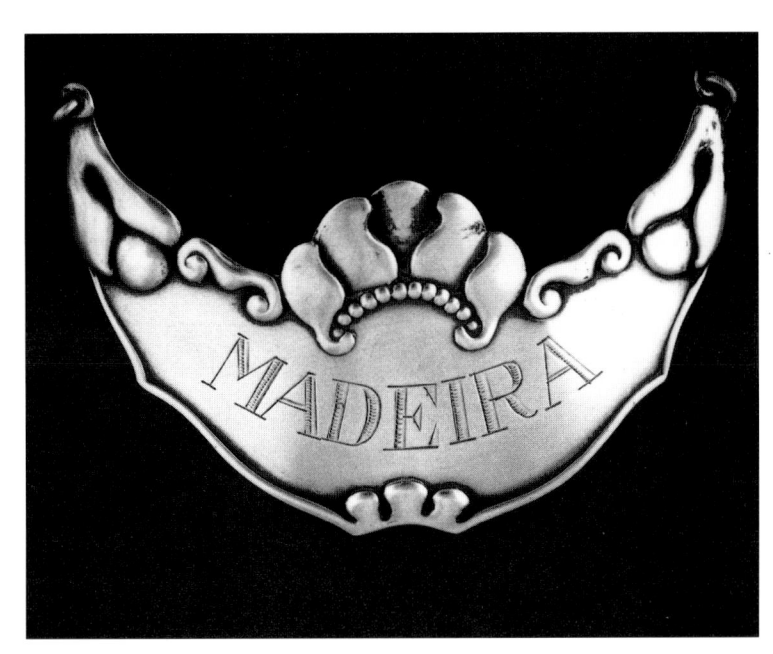

Figure 1338.

II (1559-88). It consists of seven labelled decanters, a central ice pail and two further decanters. It was wheeled around the dining room to serve guests with VODKA, GENEVA, JUBILES, SKÅNE, SWART-VINBÅR, LYS HOLMER, AALBORG, and similar delights.

It was probably Nicolai Christensen, goldsmith to King Frederick VI and active from 1797 to 1832, who started label production: several labels made by him have been noted. Other silversmiths from whose workshops labels of these years have been seen include Nicolai Carstens, Peter Kyhl (1822-47) and Samuel Prahl (1825-53) from Copenhagen, Peter Hiort (1842-93) and Jeremiah Schmidt (1852-79) from Horsens, and Christian Albrecht Jorgensen (1826-59) and Julius Hogrefe (1841-66) from Vejle in Jutland. There are others who have not been identified.

The commonest design for Danish labels is a style of domed crescent (see fig. 1338). The dome is often decorated by a sun shining down on the name of the wine (see figs. 1319-1334), linking it to the overall design, and perhaps symbolising the sunnier south of the country where the grapes were grown. It may be noted that the motif of a radiant sun is found in Danish glassmaking and other decorative arts of the seventeenth century, but it is doubtful whether Danish silversmiths two hundred years later would have been much influenced by this. It is more likely that it was peculiar to Danish silver, and perhaps only to wine labels. Another design used by Danish wine label makers was a type of banner, comparable to Penzer's Type 7, possibly taken by P.L. Kyhl from a Danish topographical work *Den Danske Atlas*[20] where it is used in many variations as a frame around the name of a building. Nicolai Christensen has a twelve-pointed star-shaped label that differs from English stars in having oak branches as a motif on the face instead of palm leaves, and the name engraved on a curve, which improves its appearance. The chain is attached to two eyes on the back of the label.

Most of the names on Danish wine labels (see figs 1319-37)[21] are commonplace. RØD WIIN (see figs 1322-24) is simply red wine (at that time, claret) and G: ROM (see fig. 1320) is old rum. BISKOP (bishop, see figs 1325-26) requires some explanation. It is a hot drink, or punch, in Denmark and in England, based on claret.[22] It became popular in the clubs of Copenhagen in the first half of the eighteenth century, when the manager of the first Danish faience factory, founded in 1723, learnt to drink it in his club, 'The Pope Society'.[23] This enterprising gentleman is also credited with inventing a new shape of punch bowl, shaped as a bishop's mitre, and called in Danish 'a bishop's bowl' or 'bishop's cap'. Punch is also said to be the national drink of Sweden.[24] In 1845[25] a Swedish firm, J. Cederlund, started to bottle it and to export it to Denmark, where it was mixed in a bowl and served hot, to be replaced later in the meal by a cold punch served as a liqueur with the coffee. The Danish word is spelled 'punch'; the Swedish version is punsch' (compare Kyhl's banner-shaped label for PUNSCH, mentioned above, which could mean that the label was intended for Swedish import, or perhaps for export to Sweden, or just a misspelling).

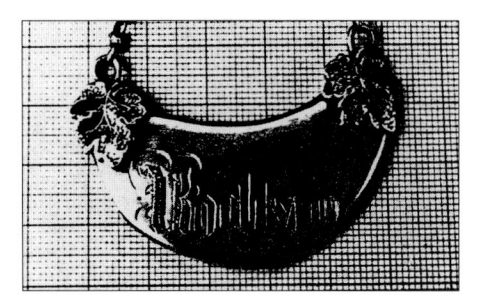

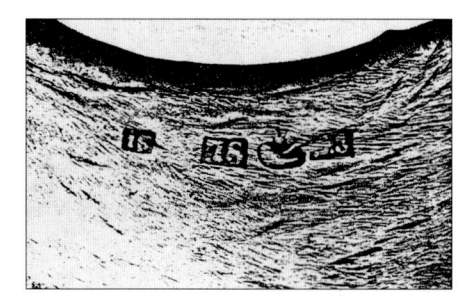

Labels from outside The British Isles and Ireland - Finland/France

Figure 1339.

Figure 1340.

PART 7 – FINLAND

Only an extremely small number of Finnish wine labels have been produced. A kidney shaped label (see fig. 1339) embellished with vine leaves at the points engraved in a kind of Gothic script for RÖDTVIN apparently bears Finnish marks which appear to read IS (maker's mark, identity unknown), 78 (for 78 zolotniks, the standard of fineness being .8125), the city device for Helsinki,[26] and D3 (the Finnish Date Letter for 1861).[27] It measures 5.6cm (2¼in.) in width and the marks are illustrated at fig. 1340.[28]

RÖDTVIN is Swedish with an old spelling. It means in English 'red wine'. The Swedish language has been and is still used in certain parts of Finland. Until 1809, when Finland was separated from Sweden, Finland had the same marking system as Sweden – a system that dates from 1759. The post-1809 Finnish system is reminiscent of the Swedish system.

PART 8 – FRANCE

The French developed the slot-in wine label (see figs 1341-44 and 1346) in preference to the more conventional incised labels used elsewhere. Dating them is extremely difficult, because all French silver after 1838 bears exactly the same hallmark, the head of Minerva in an octagonal frame (see fig. 1345). Although letter codes distinguish nineteenth-century silver from that of the twentieth century, these are so small as to be unreadable when stamped on small objects such as wine labels. Hallmarks are placed on 'decanter labels' under the French system of marking on the top near the edge and also on the chain. The mark on the chain has to be at every 10cm (4in.).[29] The slots shown at figs 1342 and 1343 have the Minerva mark. Fig. 1343 is thought to be a representation of fig. 1342. It is included to show how inaccuracies can arise and complicate historical research. Fig. 1344 has no marks; the slot is open at the back. Fig. 1346 has no marks and is made of silver plated on copper.

Christofle, the well-known Parisian firm, made a pair of labels engraved for PAJARETE and JINEVRA.[30] This firm also made slot labels. One marked Christofle, Paris, has been illustrated in the *Journal*.[31] The French slot label is sophisticated. A set of silver-gilt name tablets for SAUTERNE, CAPE, HERMITAGE and GRAVE fit into the silver-gilt holder illustrated with GRAVE (see fig. 1341).[32]

Figure 1341.

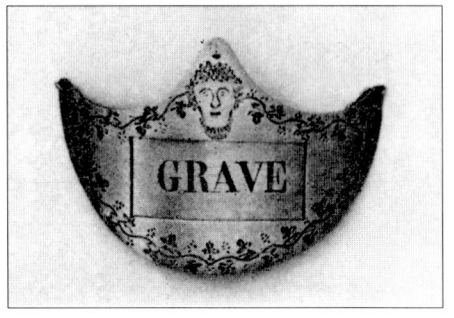

Figure 1342.

Figure 1343.

352

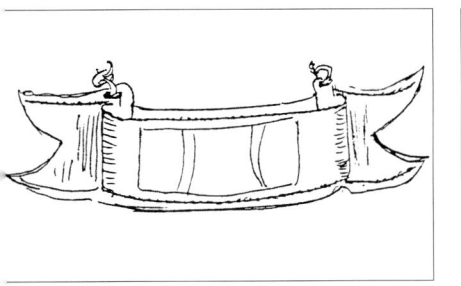

Labels from outside The British Isles and Ireland - France

Figure 1344.

Figure 1345.

Figure 1346.

Two unmarked faience labels, 6.5 x 8.5cm (2½ x 3⅜in.), for VOLNAY and MULSEAUX have also been illustrated in the *Journal*,[33] as have seven nineteenth-century enamels for EAU D'ORANGE, ROUSSILLON, ANISETTE (2), BEAUNE, FOUGÈRE and FRAISETTE.[34] Porcelain labels for VERZENAY (2), CANARY and CHIPRE have also been reported as well as the titles mentioned above in Chapter 8, Part 8,[35] as have ivory labels for CURAÇAO and VANILLE,[36] and plated broad kidneys for BENEDICTINE, CHARTREUSE, COGNAC, CURAÇAO, GRAND MARNIER and MENTHE.[37] A set of eight silver-gilt labels said to be from Alsace and of eighteenth-century date have been recorded in the *Journal* for CHAMPAGNE, BOURDEAUX, BOURGOGNE, TOKAY, CÔTE ROTÍE and three HOUSE WHITES. Jean-Baptiste-Lazare Clérin made a pair of silver gilt domed fat crescent or shield shaped labels, with slot labels in panel format that slid into the slot, raised for DRY CHAMPAGNE, SWEAT CHAMPAGNE [*sic*], TOKE and HERMITAGE. The labels date to 1793 or 1794 and are engraved with a Bacchus mask and trailing vines.[38]

All the wine labels illustrated are nineteenth-century in style, with the possible exception of the mystery PORT SECCO label discussed below. There are two fundamental types, one with an open or backed slot for slipping in a paper label, and the other with an ivory inset that one can write on and erase. On a more permanent basis, a set of silver labels would allow for changes but is not as flexible. By British standards, the labels are very elaborately worked, with relief, hatching, and extremely rich designs. Some are very small by British standards too, with the exception of the banner (see fig. 1344). And, again except the first, they are light, being die-stamped.

The smaller labels were probably used for tiny decanters, holding spirits or liqueurs rather than wines. They probably were part of sets of decanters and glasses in intricate wooden boxes. These French tantalus-type *caves à vin* are too tiny in most cases to hold any drink other than liqueurs. They are a popular collectors' item, although few of them still have their labels.

One clue to what may have been written on their paper or ivory tablets comes from another set of wine labels of similar size, also clearly mid- to late nineteenth century in feeling, made of mother-of-pearl. These seem to have been variations on the silver slot models, and the following have been recorded: BYRRH, CHARTREUSE, CURAÇAO, KIRSCH, MIRABELLE, QUETSCHE, FRAMBOISE and COGNAC (see also above, Chapter 8, Part 9, Mother-of-Pearl).

Another much cruder label type has been discovered in Rouen, where, according to the dealer, or *brocanteur*, they had come from a derelict shop. They seem to have been nailed to the shelf on which a bottle or a keg may have stood and include CALVADOS, TARRAGONE and MALAGA. These labels are made of enamelled metal, with a black border and black lettering. Also known are six domed rectangular white enamel bin labels for BEAUJOLAIS ROUGE, CIDRE ORDINAIRE, FINE LUNEL, SAINT-CHRISTOL, VAR and VIN POUR VINAIGRE; and four plain rectangular pottery bin labels, with two holes, for MADÈRE VIEUX, MUSCAT LUNEL, TINTOT and VIN D'ESPAGNE; also a pottery domed rectangular bin label for COGNAC CARTE BLANCHE.

Among silver labels, four have been found that had been made outside France and overstamped with the French hallmark for imported silver, a crab in a lozenge. One is mysterious since it bears no foreign hallmark at all, only a monogram, and since it reads PORTO SECCO, which, if it is Portuguese, is misspelt. This 'classic' design (by French standards) is similar to British wine labels in

Labels from outside The British Isles and Ireland - France

Figures 1347-1349.

style, size, weight and how it was made (the back is not hollow). But misspelling is not confined to Portuguese exports. A set of three Birmingham-hallmarked labels of 1880 was overstamped with the French crab, so that the mark is visible on the front of the labels. These read: ANNISETTE, CHARTREUSE and COGNAC.[39]

A matching porcelain set of three for FINE CHAMPAGNE, MALAGA and MADÈRE and an enamel on copper label for VERVEINE have been noted.[40] The three porcelain labels are all unmarked. The VERVEINE label is quite an unusual name and the spelling is perhaps unique. It is enamel on copper and bears the name 'Dreyfous' on the back. The name VERVEINE is French for Verbena; it is thus a toilet water label,[41] or perhaps a medicinal label.[42] Another enamel label for JASMIN, for a toilet water, of different design and style,[43] has on the reverse the inscription 'Dreyfous 99 Mount St W' for their London outlet.

Three crescents with pricked borders and wavy tops and a dome surmounted by a bunch of three leaves are for ANISETTE (see fig. 1347), CURAÇAO (see fig. 1348) and EAU-DE-VIE (see fig. 1349). All are marked with the post-1838 Minerva (see fig. 1345) for 0.950 silver. The last two are a pair with the name in script and are also marked with PB on either side of a pelican within a lozenge, the maker's mark. ANISETTE has the name in capital letters and the maker's mark is AD on either side of a bird, probably a stork. The names are hand engraved on all three labels. Stylistically they look to be mid- to late nineteenth century, but could be earlier.

Labels from outside The British Isles and Ireland - Germany

Figure 1350.

Figure 1351.

PART 9 – GERMANY

Not many labels have been recorded from Germany. One is a fairly massive slot label, *c*.1895 (see fig. 1350), long, basically rectangular, with a heavy cast border of fronds surmounted by two putti lying facing one another clinking wine beakers. The slot background has been engraved, probably after manufacture, with COLOGNE in script and underlined (the label was found in a perfume shop). The back is marked with 800, the Reich's mark of crown and moon used from 1888, and two other badly worn marks, one of which is a crown surmounting two indecipherable letters. Another German art nouveau large slot label is shown at fig. 1352.

Another label (see fig. 1351) of thin gauge silver, is triangular with wavy edges. It is hand chased with grapes, vine leaves and branches. The name, engraved in italics, is for PORTWEIN, which points to a German provenance. Stylistically the label would seem to date from about 1850.

A third label of an elongated heart shape (see fig. 1391) with double domes, also for PORTWEIN but in capital letters, points to a German provenance but was made in Russia (fig. 1392 shows the marks).

Figure 1352.

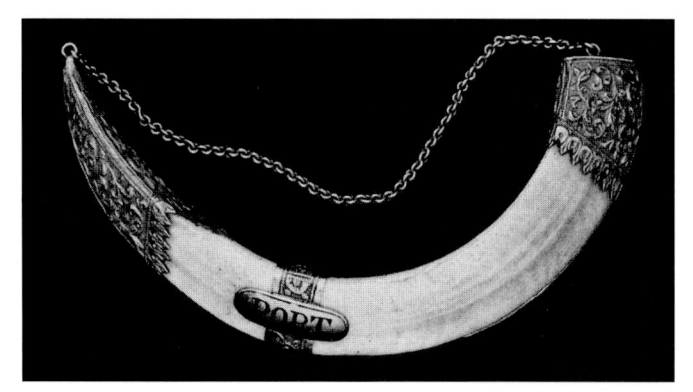

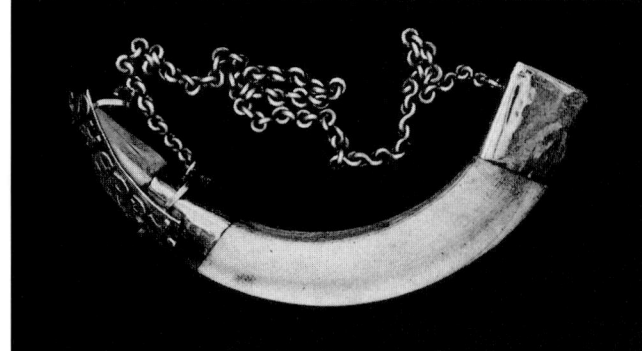

Labels from outside The British Isles and Ireland - India

Figure 1353.

Figure 1354.

Figure 1355.

PART 10 – INDIA

Although there were British (usually Scottish) silversmiths supplying the local British populations, both civil and military, before 1800, wine labels do not appear to have been made much before about 1820 and they remain uncommon until about 1850. Plain crescents and cut-corner rectangles are known by Hamilton and Co and W.H. Twentyman (who also produced mounted corks), both of Calcutta, and by George Gordon of Madras, while large cast vine leaves were made from about 1830 by Pittar and Co. of Calcutta (e.g. for CLARET, see fig. 1356; the firm also made hand-raised and engraved vine leaves) and by Hamilton and Co. (e.g. for SHERRY, see fig. 1357). A die-stamped leaf by George Gordon and Co, however, was possibly imported from England.

During the second half of the nineteenth century simple labels continued to be made by Hamilton and Co and by Orr and Co of Madras, but the speciality of this region became the mounted boars' tusks and tigers' claws (already described in Chapter 8, Part 10, Section 1). Unmarked designs including military motifs, such as cannons and kukris,[44] probably also originate from the Indian sub-continent and were made for regimental use. Illustrated are a boar's tusk for PORT (a pair with SHERRY) picked out in black (see fig. 1353), a boar's tusk for SHERRY (a pair with PORT) with cut-out letters soldered on to a backplate (see fig. 1354) and one of a set of four unmarked silver filigree labels for MARSALA (see fig. 1355), SHERRY, PORT, and BRANDY.[45]

Figures 1356-57.

Labels from outside The British Isles and Ireland - Malaysia and Singapore/Malta

PART 11 – MALAYSIA AND SINGAPORE

Silver wine labels were almost certainly made in Malaysia and Singapore from the later decades of the nineteenth century well into the 1920s and 1930s. Pierced designs flanked by exotic birds and hand-raised bamboo leaf designs can probably be ascribed to this area. An example of the bamboo leaf design is illustrated for BROWN SHERRY (see fig. 1358). It has an Oriental feeling about it and is unique.

Figure 1358.

PART 12 – MALTA

While the bottle-ticket was evolving in England during the eighteenth century it remained unknown and unneeded in the rest of Europe. In Malta, ruled by the Knights of the Order of St John, it was not surprisingly also unknown. The Knights were recruited mainly from the noble families of Spain, Italy, France and Bavaria, and it was those countries' customs that prevailed in the Auberges where they lived. The Maltese nobility, proud and independent, descending from Aragon and Sicilian ancestry, were influenced by their neighbours in the southern Italian peninsular. There was no English presence in the island, and certainly no wine labels.

The Knights lived in style; as many as ten different wines were served at dinner, one visitor reported. But they lived aloof in their Auberges. Their role as defenders of Christendom against the Turks had ceased and by the end of the century they had become ineffective and effete. In 1798 Napoleon, on his way to Egypt, had to make sure of the Mediterranean. He seized Malta, threw the Order out, and stole their plate, and the Church's too, to melt it down and pay his troops. Unfortunately for him, he reckoned without the Maltese people. Disgusted by the excesses of the Revolutionary Republican army, they rebelled, and called on England, who was leading the fight against the French tyrant, and whose maritime exploits were plain for all to see, to come to their aid. Nelson sealed the fate of the Egyptian Expedition at the Battle of the Nile, and sent Captain Alexander Ball in the seventy-four-gun *Alexander* to deal with the situation. The French surrendered, but the Knights of St John were not allowed to return. Instead Malta willingly became part of the British Empire and there began a century and a half of British rule and influence. The navy made Valetta its main base in the Mediterranean. An army garrison arrived, trade followed, and Malta was soon a thriving entrepôt for goods to Europe. Social life, however, was slow to establish itself. Not until Napoleon was finally banished to St Helena in 1815 did conditions become stable enough for administrators, merchants and service personnel to consider bringing their families out.

Figure 1359.

Figure 1360.

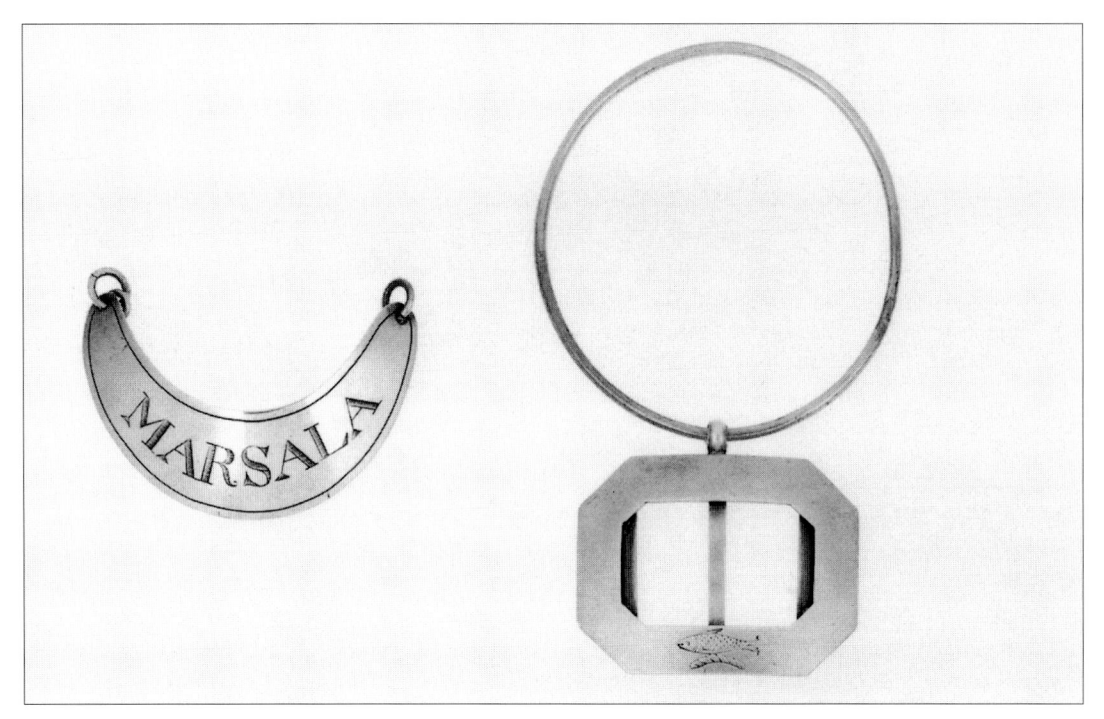

Labels from outside The British Isles and Ireland - Malta

Figures 1361-1362.

There was a health factor too. Outbreaks of plague occurred regularly in the islands. There was a particularly serious one in 1813, when thousands of the population died. Byron, on his way to Greece, was held in quarantine in the Lazaretto, and carved his name on its sandstone walls. For the first two decades of the century there was not likely to have been much of a social round, or introduction of English dining and drinking customs, limiting the context for wine labels.

When the English newcomers did begin to require silver there were plenty of local craftsmen to supply their needs. Silversmiths have a long tradition in Malta.[46] They were there when the Knights of St John arrived in 1530 and from the seventeenth century they had their Guild, the Confraternity of St Helen. This lady, usually St Helena, was the saintly mother of Constantine the Great, but it is not clear why the silversmiths of Malta adopted her as their patron. Most European countries have gone to St Eloi (St Eligius) to protect them; apart from the Maltese, only the English, looking to their native St Dunstan, turned elsewhere. Victor Denaro records[47] the marks of some 150 silversmiths registered during the first half of the nineteenth century, which seems more than could have earned a living among the limited patronage of the time. However, many of these may have been only retailers, and certainly fewer than half a dozen of their marks have been seen on wine labels.

The earliest labels recorded are in a group with hallmarks that suggest a date between 1802 and 1809. They are large open crescents bearing the maker's mark of Gioacchino Lebrun, together with an open hand sinister and the letter 'M' in a shield (see fig. 1361 for MARSALA, 1802-09). Examples are also known for CLARET, MADEIRA and PORT. Lebrun was Master of the Mint from 1787 (that is to say, head of the Confraternity, and virtually in control of the silversmiths' craft) and he seems to have been a worthy disciple of the Vicar of Bray. Having taken office under de Rohan, last but one of the Grandmasters, he kept his position under French rule and indeed helped to compile the inventory of the plate looted by the French, and then managed to continue under Admiral Ball. The labels are wrought from thin gauge silver and have shallowly engraved titles. The letter 'M' features as an assay mark on Maltese silver from early days. Later, the letters 'F' and 'R' are also found, and they then denote three standards of silver: French, the highest, approximating to sterling, then Roman and then Maltese. During the struggle against the French, a clenched fist was used as an assay mark, and when normality returned and Ball was appointed Civil Commissioner, it was replaced by the open hand. The story goes that it was derived from the badge of the Baronetcy, to which Ball had just been admitted, an open hand sinister. It is interesting to note that Jackson mistakenly attributed[48] the mark to Belfast, associating it with the Red Hand of Ulster, and

Figures 1363-1365.

compounded the mistake by confusing the stag's head, which is sometimes found with the standard 'F', 'R' and 'M' letters, with the rather similar stag of Canongate.

After these crescent labels there comes a gap until the 1820s, when single vine leaf labels start to appear. This design is recorded in England from 1820 or 1821, first as a rather large label and, later, die-stamped and cast, in various sizes. In Malta the labels are usually small and stamped with characteristic tooling of the veins on the leaves. They are hard to date accurately, except to say that they start to occur quite soon after their first appearance in England (see fig. 1364 for CANELLA and fig. 1365 for MADEIRA). The MADEIRA was made by Guiseppe Bonello around 1826 and bears the letter 'F' and a crown. In about 1825 to 1830 Emilio Critien made an unusual version, with the leaf placed horizontally along the tendril bearing his 'EC' mark only (see fig. 1363) for SHERRY. It has a pair for PORT, and an unmarked BRONTE has been added to the set, possibly later. BRONTE is the name by which the Sicilian wine MARSALA is sometimes called. Critien also made the barrel label for TERRANTEZ (see fig. 1359), which is probably unique. Terrantez is the rarest of the Madeira grapes and makes the most prized wines. It was always scarce, but it is recorded that an English traveller in Funchal in 1720 obtained two pipes in exchange for two used suits and three second-hand wigs. There is a Portuguese verse that says that the Terrantez grapes should not be eaten or given away, as God made them for making wine. The label has the letter 'F', denoting French (the highest) standard of silver, and the date stamp for 1825. Sir Thomas Maitland, who was appointed governor in 1820, instituted the practice of dating. Critien also made the substantial SHERRY label in a shells and vines design, dating from around 1820, which is shown at fig. 1360. CANELLA is unmarked and dates to 1830-40. Its workmanship, tooling and engraving are very similar to that of comparable labels by G. Lebrun and G. Bonello. Although small, it is not in this instance a sauce label (*Canelle* is French for cinnamon) being in a set with AMINTA and MARASHINO. It is thus a tonic based on bark from the cinnamon tree.

Two other designs have been noted with Maltese marks. One is the rectangular slot label shown at fig. 1362, suspended on a solidly formed wire ring.[49] It bears the letter 'F' surmounted by the stag's head, which was in use between 1810 and 1820, together with the lion rampant and an unidentified crest showing a salmon naiant proper. It was possibly made by Francesco Fenech in about 1820 and at first glance it might be suspected of having originally been a buckle. However, it is considered that the outline is not quite right, and the edges too sharp for that to be the case. Furthermore, several other examples of the design are recorded. There are no signs of the attachments that a buckle would have had. Another design, known by a single label, is a cartouche with scallops and scrolls, used by J. Emes and W. Barnard in the 1820s, so probably here up to ten years later.[50]

It would seem, then, that except for the one set of early crescents, labels were only being manufactured locally for a short period during the 1820s and 1830s. No labels have been found dating from later than the middle of the century, even though the English population continued to rise. It would have been only they who had a requirement for these articles. There would have been no demand from the Maltese, so it seems likely that they were only made to order and not kept as stock. This would account for their scarcity. It would be fascinating to know for whom those early crescents were made.[51]

Labels from outside The British Isles and Ireland - The Netherlands

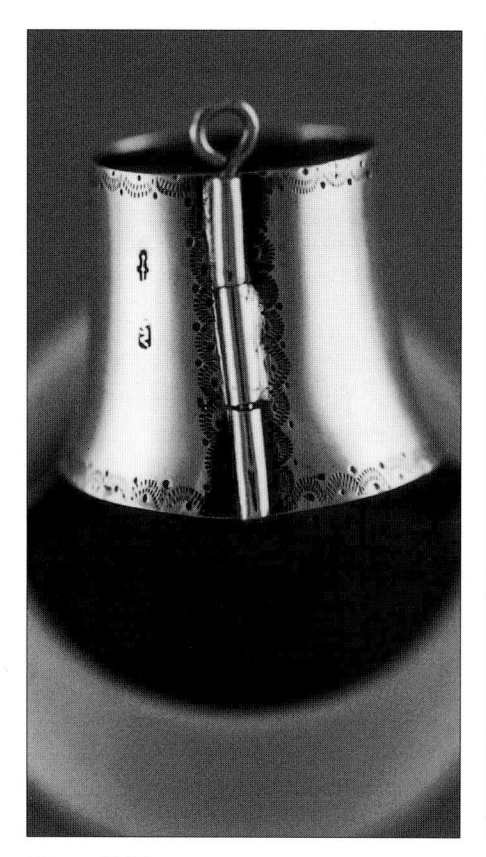

Figure 1366.

Figure 1367.

PART 13 – THE NETHERLANDS

Although the Empire style in Dutch silver appears to be influenced more by the earlier English Adam style than the French Empire from which it derived its name, the then prevailing South Westerly winds apparently failed to bring the decanter label to the Low Countries. An octagonal label for GIN, silver, marked for Hoorn 1810, maker unidentified, must be considered a very rare and early bird.[52] Two shield shape labels for ANISETTE and CURACAU, made by Harmanus Lintveld of Amsterdam, date to the period 1817-33.

The earliest known remaining Dutch silver wine siphons date from the early 1780s,[53] so to assume a certain need for decanter labels at that time does seem logical. However, as far as is known, none of these labels has survived, if indeed they ever existed in the late eighteenth-century Netherlands. Very much the same applies to the earlier bottle-ticket. Dutch examples are believed to be totally non-existent. Even Wittewaal, lifetime collector and author of the excellent and unique book on Dutch small silverware from the seventeenth century onwards, only records one Dutch COGNAC label dating from about 1860.[54] It has an engraved title in large letters with horizontal lines hatching and a scrolling border of an escutcheon type. However it has a large 'blip' at the bottom and a peaked top with unusual decoration. Wittewaal's observation supports the earlier statement that Dutch labels from the first half of the nineteenth century are indeed very rare.

Most Dutch labels appear to have been made in the second half of the nineteenth century. Exact dating is almost impossible as there was no need for full marking which was obligatory only for largework. The labels normally carry a small size maker's mark,[55] in the worst case consisting of an unreadable combination of letters, digits and devices. They also carry 'a little sword' – a small device mark introduced for use on smallwork from 14 January 1814 (model slightly changed in 1906 and 1953) to indicate the fineness in compliance with at least the lower standard of 0.833. As there was no separate mark for smallwork of the higher standard, which was laid down at 0.934, one may assume that smallwork was generally made to the lower standard and that the difference in silver content and value of these small objects was of no significance.

Labels from outside The British Isles and Ireland - The Netherlands

Figure 1368.

Figure 1369.

Unfortunately, one will not find assay office marks and/or date letters to assist in identification and dating. Intended in the first place to indicate the responsible assay master, they now allow collectors to identify the towns and dates of origin of their labels. These two marks also provide a possibility to double-check on the maker's mark found. Does the information on the maker concur with the information given by the other marks? The absolute absence of these two assay marks might be the reason why Dutch labels do not appear to have been collected other than for actual use on one's decanters. When it is possible to read the maker's mark correctly, rough dating can be achieved by reference to the working period of the silversmith concerned or, even better, by the period in respect of which a specific maker's mark was registered to be in use. Silversmiths in the nineteenth century often had more than one mark registered, differing in design or outline.

Dating on stylistic grounds will prove to be very difficult as all previous styles were revived in the second half of the nineteenth century and continued to be used well into the twentieth century, alongside labels made with Art Nouveau (see fig. 1371 for PORT, silver cast, lettering incuse punched, by Johannes Albertus Adolf Gerritsen .833, Amsterdam/Zeist, 1906-19) and later Art Deco features. Unfortunately there are no large collections known of Dutch labels that could act as a source of reference. Dutch nineteenth-century silver in general was not seriously collected, as there was enough eighteenth-century silver to go for (this statement of course excluding the presumably non-existent eighteenth-century Dutch wine label as said before). The disapproving attitude towards the nineteenth-century revival style did not change until fairly recently.[56]

Judging only from too small a quantity of extant Dutch labels one could perhaps say that the

Figure 1370.

Figure 1371.

Figure 1372.

Labels from outside The British Isles and Ireland - The Netherlands

Figure 1373.

Figure 1374.

Figure 1375.

decorative styles (see fig. 1373 for PORT A PORT, silver, hammered, engraved, in rococo revived style by Willem and Cornelis Baksteen and Johannes Middendorp, .833, Rotterdam, 1861-89)[57] were in favour for the real wines and the classical styles (see fig. 1372 for CITROEN in electroplated nickel silver, trade name alpaca, die-stamped, c.1900 by John Gilbert of Birmingham, an English export of the so-called architectural style)[58] were popular for the more straightforward spirits. This observation has a lot going for it, but may not be proven when more Dutch labels come to light.

Although the range of the Dutch label appears to be limited as far as age is concerned, unusual names (see figs 1375-76 for Kaapsche Sherry and Kaapsche Pontac, silver, hammered, engraved by Petrus Franciscus van Maarseveen, .833, Amsterdam, 1883-92)[59] and deviating shapes, sizes and constructions (see fig. 1367 for COGNAC in the form of a silver rococo revival collar – the rear pin fixing and maker's mark are shown by fig. 1366 – by Manicus Verhoef, .833, Arnhem, c.1880) can be found. A MADERA label was made in Breda between 1840 and 1900 by Antonius Henricus Besier in .833 silver in an unusual revival rococo format. Straightforward puzzles (see fig. 1368)[60] may happen to make the Dutch wine and spirit label an interesting item to study. The barrel is a commemorative design in cast silver .833 standard by J.F. Kikkert of Amsterdam issued between 1906 and 1923. Even sauce labels,[61] rare as they are, can be very puzzling.

Close friendship over the centuries, sometimes debouching into serious war between Britain and the Netherlands,[62] in the end presumably smoothed the path for the 'all-English wine label' to get accepted in the Netherlands.[63] This may be why wine labels are not often found in adjacent countries such as Belgium and Germany, and why the name of the national drink (GENEVER) of the Netherlands (see fig. 1377) is often found on English labels as HOLLANDS (see figs 1369 and 1374, the latter by Joseph Price, Grimwade reference 1840, London, 1839, similar to a label by George Pearson of the same year) and on labels made in other 'English' speaking countries (see fig. 1370 by Tiffany and Co., New York, c.1920, for SCHIEDAM). One should not forget, of course, that most British of drinks, PUNCH, engraved on an unmistakably Dutch label (see fig. 1378 for PUNSCH) by Antonius Alphonsus Kalberg, Den Bosch, 1877-1908. Called by whatever the prefix – Rum, Rack or Toddy – the welcome given to PUNCH should be just the same according to a rhyme in praise of it!

Figure 1376.

Figure 1377.

Figure 1378.

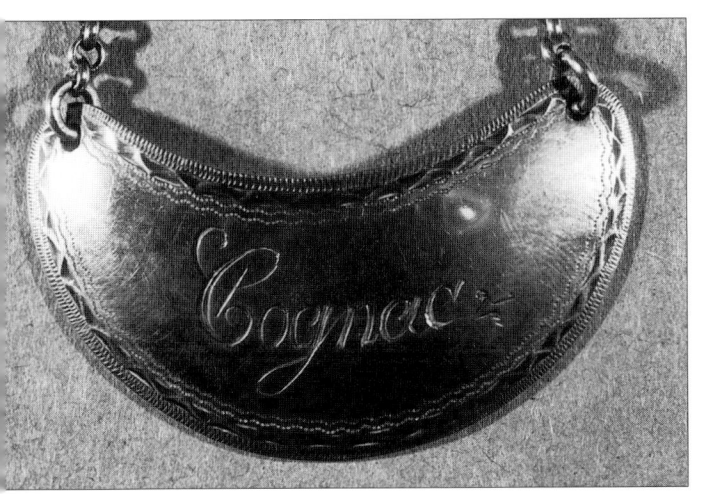

Labels from outside The British Isles and Ireland - Norway

Figure 1379.

Figure 1381.

Figure 1380.

PART 14 – NORWAY

Until 1814 Norway was joined to Denmark. Its small, widely scattered population and poor economy at that time did not make for conditions conducive to the use of wine labels, nor did the very strict laws that were introduced to control the consumption of alcohol. It is therefore surprising to find two such sophisticated labels as those by Wisting dated as early as 1810.

These are a pair of good quality kidney-shaped labels with bright-cut wrigglework borders engraved for Cognac (see fig. 1379) and Rom (see fig. 1381 – Rum) marked HPW (see fig. 1380) in a rectangle for Hans Petter Wisting, LV in an oval for the town mark of Larvik in Norway and 1810 in a rectangle for the year of self 'assay', Larvik having no assay office.[64] Wisting was a silversmith working from around 1782, who came originally from Germany,[65] worked in the small Swedish town of Amal from 1799 to 1800 as a guldsmedmester and became a master silversmith in Kristiania in 1802.[66]

In 1804 he moved to Larvik situated on the west coast of Oslo Fjord some seventy miles south of Oslo. He bought an estate there in 1806, went bankrupt in 1807,[67] recovered, and died in 1826. Wisting's labels are similar to the MALMSEY label[68] illustrated by Butler and Walkling in plate 167 of their book, decorated by bright cutting. The label measures 5 x 2.2cm (2 x ⅞in.) and the chains measure 13cm (5in.).

A pewter Norwegian label for MADEIRA is known to exist,[69] presumably from the twentieth century, and three Art Nouveau labels (after 1893) have been recorded for VERMOUTH, MADEIRA and GIN.[70] The first two are crescents with a bulbous fruit and leaf decoration along the top edge and are marked on the back with 830S and a symbol of unclear shape. The GIN is triangular with similar ornamentation but no marks. The S beside the purity mark was used in both Denmark and Norway. However, from 1893 the minimum purity in Denmark was 826/1000 whilst from 1891 the minimum purity in Norway was 830/1000. Hence these labels are Norwegian and not Danish.

363

Labels from outside The British Isles and Ireland - Poland/Portugal

Figure 1382.

Figure 1383.

PART 15 – POLAND

A slot label, unfortunately without the paper or ivory slip-in wine title, has been illustrated in the *Journal*.[71] It measures some 5cm (2in.) in width. It appears to be marked in an oval punch (see fig. 1383) Norblin and Co., Warszawa, with the letters OALW in the centre of the oval. It also bears the impressed figures 1325 spaced somewhat randomly.

The design (see fig. 1382) includes a shell like device at the top, a bunch of grapes at the bottom, with wine related scrolling borders. It is probably die-pressed. The mark appears on the back of the slot compartment, but not on the body of the label.

PART 16 – PORTUGAL

A label engraved with NIEPOORT'S PORT (see fig. 1384) measuring 5cm (2in.) in width x 4.5 cm (1¾in.) in height bears the Oporto silver mark.[72] Vine tendrils and grapes border the title. An escutcheon engraved for BRANDY also bears the Oporto silver mark.[73] It appears to have scrolling foliate borders.

Two small rectangular labels of late nineteenth- or early twentieth-century date with Portuguese marks have been noted for VERDELHO and PORTO.

Figure 1384.

Labels from outside The British Isles and Ireland - Russia

Figures 1385-1390.

PART 17 – RUSSIA

A rectangular heart shaped label, with double peaked top, titled in plaque format for PORTWEIN (i.e. Port in the German language) with delicate tracery decoration, is shown at fig. 1391. It was purchased in Stockholm.[74] The maker's mark H GRUNBAUM (see fig. 1392) suggests that the maker could have been a German silversmith living and working in Russia when the label was made. It is marked 84, which it is suggested stands not for the year but for the standard of 84 zolothniques (that is 87.5 per cent silver). Above the 84 is another mark, probably the place of origin.

Figs 1385-90 illustrate some Russian wine labels, 5cm (2in.) in width, with matted background. The cutting out produces a striking effect, somewhat reminiscent of those onion-shaped cathedral towers with spiky surmounts. Three labels (fig. 1386 for HOCK, fig. 1387 for CLARET and fig. 1390 for SHERRY) have English capital letters. Three labels (see fig. 1385 for XERES, fig. 1388 for COGNAC and fig. 1389 for PORT WINE) have titles in Cyrillic letters.

Figure 1391.

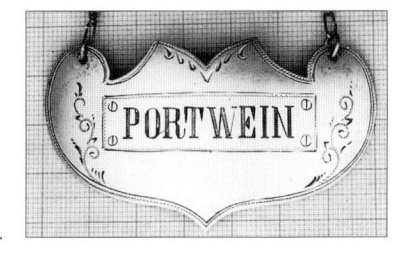

Figure 1392.

365

PART 18 – SOUTH AFRICA

Vines are not indigenous to South Africa; they were introduced to the Cape Town area by Dutch settlers in the seventeenth century and the soil and the climate suited them so well that the Dutch leader Jan van Riebeck was able to write triumphantly in 1659, 'Today, praise be to God, wine was pressed for the first time from Cape grapes'. The first plantings had taken place in 1655. It was probably a Muscat grape and the wine soon acquired a high reputation in England and on the Continent. It was known as CAPE (see fig. 1394) or CONSTANTIA and labels bearing these names were being made by English silversmiths for their clients from the mid-eighteenth century. There was no market for wine labels among the predominantly Dutch population in the rough conditions prevailing at that time, so the labels were clearly intended for English clients. Enamels, too, were being manufactured both at Battersea and in Staffordshire, some of the latter having titles in French and Spanish, presumably intended for the Continental market. There are references to Cape wines in English literature of the period, and in trade registers – 'The ship *De Hoot* returning to the Netherlands from the Cape with a Cape-produced Pontac' (see fig. 1393) 'onboard'. This was in 1772. PONTAC is near Drakensburg in Cape Province; it was settled by Huguenots in 1688 and named after the village south of Bordeaux that produces a white Graves. The name has been noted on a wine label bearing the mark of Lawrence Twentyman and is discussed below.

English interest in Cape Town as a strategic port on the sea-route to India and the Far East started in about 1795, but it was not until 1803 (when Cape Province came firmly under British rule) that English settlers started to arrive and to colonise the coastal areas, and some years later before conditions became stable enough for trades such as silversmiths to establish themselves and a demand for domestic silver to emerge.

Cape-made labels are rare and are usually of plain, manual construction. Stefan Weiz illustrates[75] a set of three cut-corner rectangles for BUCELLAS, MALMSEY and SHERRY by Lawrence Twentyman (worked 1818-32) in the Afrikaaner Museum and says that the few other examples that he has seen were all made by silversmiths who had come from England, as is confirmed by the narrow octagonal (see fig. 1395 for MADEIRA, a pair with CLARET, *c*.1820-25, marked TT above, IT in a squarish punch with pseudo king's head and pseudo lion passant) by John and Thomas Townsend (worked 1815-49) that appeared at Phillips, London in the 1980s. Lawrence Twentyman, for instance, migrated to Cape Town in 1818 from Calcutta, where the firm of Twentyman and Co. had been in business since 1810.[76]

Thomas and John Townsend, who were active from 1815 to 1849, may have come straight from England. Labels have been recorded by both these firms. The South African Cultural History Museum in Cape Town possesses a very fine, apparently unique, crescent label with an impressive diamond shaped cusp for MADEIRA, marked for Thomas Townsend, from the Heller Collection. A similar label, marked for Thomas Townsend, with pseudo king's head, also for MADEIRA (see fig. 1397) comes from the Mullane Collection in the National Cultural History Museum in Pretoria.

Daniel Hockley, who served his apprenticeship with John Reily, was another émigré from England, arriving in Cape Town in 1819 after working in London from 1810. Labels were certainly included in his output whilst in London, but there is no record of any made by him after he emigrated. He practised in the Cape as a silversmith until his death in 1835.

The kidney-shaped label for PONTAC (see fig. 1393) is similar to CAPE (see fig. 1394), though the engraving of the two names differs slightly. They both have a maker's mark that may be a 'T', which has been ascribed to Lawrence Twentyman, *c*.1825, accompanied by pseudo lion and pseudo king's head. Three other labels of this design with very similar reeded border have the same marks, and are for MADEIRA, BARSAC and SAUTERNE. This assemblage of names is a curious combination of local and French wines. PONTAC, on a South African label, ought to refer to the wine from the Drakensburg region. Two or three English labels for DRAKENSBURG or a variant spelling are recorded. However, doubt begins to mount when one finds BARSAC and

Labels from outside The British Isles and Ireland - South Africa

Figure 1393.

Figure 1394.

Figure 1395.

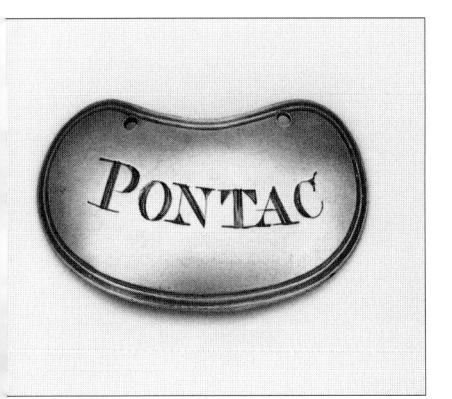

SAUTERNE in the same set, since these names can only refer to French wines from the Graves, where PONTAC also lies. The fifth label is for MADEIRA, which was being made in Cape Province from about 1815, and by the mid-1820s was popular enough for the addition of CAPE to the title to denote its origin to have become unnecessary. The label could refer to either the local or the Island wine.

A reeded oval for PORT (see fig. 1398) makes an interesting exception to English expatriate silversmiths in that it was made by Oltman Ahlers (worked 1810-27) a Cape born and, presumably, trained silversmith of German and Bengali parentage. It originally formed part of a set of nine, three each for CLARET, PORT and MADEIRA.

The mark 'IC' in an oval punch, which has been seen on a medium-sized crescent label for CLARET, c.1830, may be that of Johannes Combrick Senior, who worked in Cape Town from 1810 to 1853 (see fig. 1396).

The demand for wine labels was apparently never very great. All those that have been recorded can be dated from the early 1820s to about 1840.[77] The style of living for which wine labels were produced only began in South Africa in the second decade of the century and, as in England, labels began to fall out of use by the middle of it. The collapse of the wine trade with England, due to the abolition of preferential duty on imported wine in 1861, affected production, while the arrival of *phylloxera* in the country in 1885 destroyed most of the Cape's wine lands and brought the industry to its knees.[78] Presumably consumption during this period was satisfied by wines from abroad, but there was no demand for labels to identify them. No labels of South African origin dating later than the middle of the century have been found, except for barrel labels for SHERRY, IRISH and HELDERBERG (a wine estate on the slopes of the mountain of that name in the Cape District near Stellenbosch) made out of celluloid (see fig. 1258).

Figure 1396.

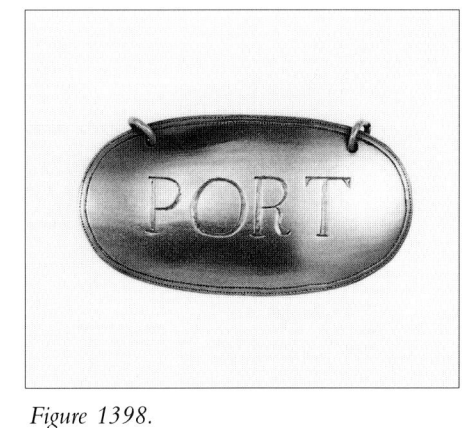

Figure 1397.

Figure 1398.

367

Labels from outside The British Isles and Ireland - Spain/Sweden

Figure 1399.

PART 19 – SPAIN

Two similar style octagonal labels are engraved for JEREZ (Sherry) and OPORTO (Port). The 'r' of JEREZ is engraved differently from the 'r' of OPORTO. The JEREZ label is marked on the face at bottom right, whereas the OPORTO label (see fig. 1399) is marked on the face by breaking the single reeded frame at the top.

These are eighteenth-century labels bearing the mark of a lion for Madrid,[79] not to be confused with the marks of Cordoba where the lion is clearly statant. Next is the quality mark, a five pointed star for the second standard (*Plata de segunda*) of 0.750 fineness used for articles weighing less than 30g.[80] The third mark is a rubbed shield, being the maker's mark.

PART 20 – SWEDEN

Wine labels were quite popular in Sweden,[81] but first the context of drinking habits in Sweden during the eighteenth and nineteenth centuries should be described. Though it is known that Sweden has imported wine since prehistoric times, consumption during the eighteenth and nineteenth centuries was generally limited to the upper classes. As Sweden in those days had a population of less than two million people, it is quite natural that marked silver wine labels are very rare. People commonly drank beer and 'braennvin'. Braennvin is generally an unflavoured spirit, for consumption, with an alcoholic strength of 45-50 per cent, in those days almost a national beverage. It was sold as pure rectified spirit or as flavoured aquavit with spices of many kinds. One of the oldest known Swedish aquavit recipes is from 1589. This was made of wine distillate and angelica root and was meant to be used against the plague. People also distilled it at home for their own consumption. The total number of stills in the country in 1756 was estimated to about 180,000, that is one still per ten inhabitants![82]

Pre-1900 marked wine labels are very rare. Two made in Gothenburg in 1861 for PORTVIN and COGNAC (see fig. 1436) were by Carl Tengstedt. One made in Borås, a little town and a centre of textile fabrication near Gothenburg, and engraved in script for PORTVIN (see fig. 1427), was made by Peter Eduard Lönberg (worked 1834-42). Two more very remarkable examples from Borås, made by Hans Lyberg (worked 1806-48), are engraved in script for CONJACH (see figs 1411 and 1426) and ROMM (see fig. 1413). Other nineteenth-century makers were Diedrich Schvart, Johan Malmstedt, Hans Lyberg, Hans Tellander, Gustaf Möllenborg and Peter Lönberg. This concentration in the western part of Sweden may depend on the easier connections with England in those days compared with other parts of Sweden.

The majority of extant labels are plated or metal without any mark and were probably all meant for use on decanters.

The wine names follow the English pattern, with titles such as MADEIRA, PORT, SHERRY, MARSALA, WHISKEY and VERMOUTH, but national variations occur such as PORTVIN or PORTWIN (see figs 1408, 1412, 1418, 1422, 1423, 1427 and 1430), FAHLU (see fig. 1407), SAMO (see fig. 1419) and RHUM, as well as CONJACH (see figs 1411 and 1426), ROMM (see fig. 1413), as mentioned above, and, of course, BRAENNVIN.

A substantial number of labels have names of braennvin in different forms. There is a proverb in Sweden that says: 'A dear child has got many names'. The Swedish braennvin is perhaps such a dear

Labels from outside The British Isles and Ireland - Sweden

figures 1400-1401.

child! The most common form of braennvin is RENADT (see fig. 1402), which means 'rectified'. KUMMIN (see fig. 1405) and POMERANS (see figs 1406 and 1421) are also common. FALU or FAHLU (from a small town in the middle of Sweden, see fig. 1407), FINT (fine) BRÄNVIN, DANSKI (Danish, see fig. 1402, in the same set as SÄDES and GAUFFIN), SÄDES (distilled from corn, see fig. 1404), GAUFFIN (a chemist from the eighteenth century with a famous recipe, see fig. 1403) and HALLON (which means raspberry, see fig. 1420) are examples of other interesting titles. One label even exists for JERNVEGSBRÄNNVIN, which means railway braennvin![83]

Many labels are of the vine leaves and grapes design. They may have been die-stamped in Sweden or imported and their names applied in Sweden.

One label for MARSALA exists in the form of a bat. This is an important label. It is supposed that this and other bat labels are influenced by the possibility that bats live and fly around in wine cellars.[84]

Single letter wine labels for P (portvin, see fig. 1400) and S (sherry, see fig. 1401) set amongst vine leaves and grapes, were made by W.A. Bolin in 1919 in Stockholm.[85] The labels are impressive and indeed heavy, weighing 43g each. Hans Bolin, the present owner of the firm, could not give any explanation as to why the chains for the two wine labels were different.

The W.A. Bolin jewellery shop is in the centre of Stockholm. The name of the firm is 'W.A. Bolin Hovjuvelerare', which means that it has been granted the appointment to His Majesty the King of Sweden to take care of the crown jewels of Sweden and of jewels belonging to the Royal Family. W.A. Bolin had first of all worked in Russia as a jeweller by appointment to the Tsar. He came to Sweden in 1916, took over an existing firm, and gave it his own name. W.A. Bolin made sketches and drawings for the silversmiths undertaking the detailed work. He had learnt in Russia that when

Labels from outside The British Isles and Ireland - Sweden

Figures 1402-1422.

Labels from outside The British Isles and Ireland - Sweden

Figures 1423-1438.

making silver, or indeed any artistic work, it was not appropriate to have regard to the economic costs of the work to be done. This non-commercial approach did not work in Sweden and when an economic crisis occurred in the 1920s the Bolin firm of silversmiths went bankrupt.

Centres of label manufacture included Borås, Carlscrona, Gothenburg, Jönköping, Stockholm and Uddevalla. At least seventeen different silversmiths have been identified.[86] Examples of some of their productions are shown in figs 1400-38[87] and between 1800 and 1850 in fig. 1423 for Portvin by Diedrich Schvart of Carlscrona in 1806, in fig. 1424 for PORT by Johan Malmstedt of Gothenburg in 1806 – along with MADERA (see fig. 1425), 1807, CLARET, 1810, CHERRY, *c.*1810 and SHERRY, 1816 – in fig. 1428 for MADEIRA by Gustaf Magnus Sjöblom of Stockholm in 1841, in fig. 1429 for COGNAC by Gustaf Folcker of Stockholm in 1846 and in fig. 1430 for PORTVIN by Gustaf Theodor Folcker of Stockholm in 1850, a pair with SHERRY.

Labels from outside The British Isles and Ireland - Sweden/United States of America

Figure 1439.

Plated labels were also produced, such as for RUSTER AUSBRUCH,[88] an escutcheon with cable border for a wine from Rust in Burgenland in Austria.

Some labels from 1850 are illustrated. The work of William Lyon of Gothenburg (1834-70) is represented by figs 1431 and 1432, both for COGNAC and dating to or around 1851. A SHERRY (see fig. 1433) is by Pehr Fredrik Palmgren of Stockholm and is also dated 1851. Gustaf Möllenborg from that city made the PORT shown at fig. 1434 in 1855 and the SHERRY shown at fig. 1435 (a pair with PORT) in 1859. Christian Hammer, another Stockholm maker, produced the SHERRY shown at fig. 1437 in 1866 along with (not illustrated) MADERA and COGNAC in 1855 and PORTVIN in 1856. Mention has already been made of Carl Tengstedt's COGNAC and PORTVIN of 1861. Finally, the work of Carl Frederik Jonssén from Uddevalla is shown at fig. 1438 for RÖDVIN, a pair with SHERRY, dated 1867.

PART 21 – UNITED STATES OF AMERICA

That labels were in use in British North America from a relatively early date is clearly documented in the papers of George Washington. In November 1762 he acquired '4 fash. labels for wine bottles viz for: Claret Port Madeira Lisbon', and in April of the following year he paid Richard Weale, cutlery merchant, 4s. for '4 enamelled bottle tickets'. In 1784 he noted that among the plated wares available from Birmingham and Sheffield were bottle labels at 12s. per dozen, while the 1797 inventory of his household furniture included eight silver labels valued at £5.8s. (13s.6d. each) 'furnished by the United States' and two silver labels valued at £1.10s. 'purchased by George Washington' – the latter, at 15s. each must both have weighed more than 2oz (62.2g) a piece and been particularly magnificent.[89]

Despite this unquestionable evidence of their use, the entire body of literature on both wine labels and on American silver does not record a single instance of an eighteenth-century label bearing the mark of an American silversmith; so it must be assumed that the demand was wholly met by imports from Britain.

This suggests that a relatively simple object could be made in Britain at a price so much lower than an American silversmith could achieve that the considerable costs of shipping and insurance could be absorbed and still result in a lower price than the local product. If such a disparity is difficult to believe, the absence of American made labels in the eighteenth century is rendered yet harder to understand when account is taken of the several long periods during which war would have put a virtual stop to imports and meant that clients would be forced to rely on domestic makers. It might be possible that American silversmiths were not then in the habit of placing their marks on such small wares and, therefore, American labels of the period were all unmarked, but a fairly strong case could be made to refute this suggestion. The answer lies more probably in the pattern of demand, that is to say that the use of labels was restricted to the English gentry strata of American society who furnished their houses exclusively with fashionable metropolitan goods, and that they were not used by the merchant classes who patronised local manufacturers.

The dearth of American labels continues, however, throughout the first half of the next century, but it ceases to be a total absence. The account books of Joseph Richardson of Philadelphia for 1796-1801 contain a few references to his having made 'an engraved label for a decanter'.[90] The Winterthur Museum has an oval label with an undulating wriggle-work border engraved for LEMON by Nathaniel Vernon who was working in Charleston, South Carolina between 1802 and 1820.[91] The Metropolitan Museum of Art, New York has a 'Prince of Wales feathers' engraved for MADEIRA by Louis Boudo (1786-1827) who also worked in Charleston, South Carolina, but from 1810 to 1827 (see fig. 1439).[92] There is a bright-cut crescent for MADEIRA by Frederick Marquand who operated in Savannah, Georgia 1820-25 and in New York 1826-39, and a plain, cut-

Labels from outside The British Isles and Ireland - United States of America

Figures 1440-1454.

corner rectangle for WHISKY attributed to William Moulton IV who worked in Newburyport, Mass., was born in 1772 and died in 1861, both in private collections.

There are also some unidentified silversmiths who made labels during this period who could well be American. The most prolific of these employed a very small maker's mark consisting of the letters SS in an oval, usually struck two or three times. He made several different designs, but the most commonly encountered is a round-ended crescent with a wriggle-work border similar to the border on the label by Nathaniel Vernon in the Winterthur Museum. Most of this maker's labels are fairly plain with the exception of a domed rectangle, a design that has also been found with a mark

Labels from outside The British Isles and Ireland - United States of America/Other Colonial Territories

Figure 1455.

Figure 1456.

WA conjoined, similar to but differing from that of William Astley of York. The SS mark has previously been attributed to a Silas Sawin of Boston, but current authorities on New England silver have found no evidence of the existence of such a person.[93] A final candidate is the maker whose mark was IM in a small, unclear oblong punch which has been found on 'Prince of Wales' feathers' labels with similar provincial feel as the label mentioned above by Louis Boudo.[94]

American labels become increasingly less difficult to find after about 1860 and a representative group made between 1869 and the 1920s is illustrated at figs 1440-54.[95] A Tiffany and Co. label for SCHIEDAM has been shown above at fig. 1370, indicating the work of a New York firm in the 1920s for export (see above, Part 13, The Netherlands).

PART 22 – OTHER COLONIAL TERRITORIES

There were silversmiths active throughout the eighteenth and early nineteenth centuries in the Caribbean, an area then equal in economic importance to the Gulf Oil States in our own era. To a much more modest extent this was also true of Bermuda and, in the period from the Napoleonic Wars until about 1840, to certain major naval bases or trade stop-overs such as Gibraltar and St Helena. No wine labels have yet been positively attributed to any of these places, but there are some unascribed examples that might have originated from them. A serrated silver-mounted shark's tooth for WHISKEY is unmarked (see fig. 1455) but suggests a provenance from tropical or southern climes. A gadrooned, up-curved rectangle for SHERRY (see fig. 1456) is struck with the marks HG (possibly for Hugh Gordon) or HC and a key, both in oblong punches. There are several variants of these marks on objects including other labels, all of which suggest possibly a Scottish but more likely a British colonial origin.[96] H.C, key, C with a right pointing key and key, HC, key appear on tablespoons as does HC conjoined, key, HC conjoined, key and HC with a foliate device between, key and C.[97] HC appears on the spring wire neck ring label engraved for HOCK illustrated at fig. 243, similar to the unmarked VIN DE GRAVE (see fig. 241) which is reminiscent of the work attributed to Hugh Gordon of Fortrose in Scotland. Upside down left pointing key, HC, key again appears on flatware, as does HC conjoined, left pointing key, HC conjoined, left pointing key. IC, CC, CC, IC, right pointing key appears on a bottom-marked tablespoon and right pointing key, HC, MC, MC on a Hanoverian pattern crested tablespoon.[98] JC, CC, JC, upside down right pointing key appears on teaspoons.[99] The Scottish key stamped along with HG[100] and HLG (the H and L being conjoined)[101] are quite different. HLG appears on a pair of Old English pattern tablespoons and on another tablespoon with a Scottish crest.[102] HG appears on sauce labels for VINEGAR, CORACK and KETCHUP which is attributed to Hugh Gordon of Fortrose.[103] The single key is that of St Benedict, taken from the Burgh Arms of Fortrose. It has been suggested that the mark J right pointing key belongs to John Mair of Calcutta, perhaps another emigrant from Scotland like Hamilton. It has also been suggested that, since the arms of Gibraltar incorporate a key, some of these examples might come from there.

CHAPTER 10

PATTERNS OF OWNERSHIP

PART 1 – EARLY COLLECTIONS

This chapter records the beginning of interest in wine labels as a field for the collector, together with an account of some of the men and women who formed the first collections and their contacts with each other. It concludes with the impetus that led to the formation of the Wine Label Circle (WLC) by Edward Pratt in 1952.

In order to be desirable to a collector – and an object worth making into a collection – an article has to have some significance as an antique and intrinsic merit in its style and design. It should have features that point to its usage and there must be enough of the articles to make the formation of a collection worth while.

We know that silver wine labels generally began to fall out of common use in the last quarter of the nineteenth century, so it would be reasonable to expect interest in them as antiques to develop then or shortly afterwards, and this is indeed the case. Certainly by the beginning of the present century they were appearing in salerooms, dealers had them in their stock and collectors of antiques had them in their collections. Furthermore, their function was clear and enough were appearing to justify making a collection of them.

The earliest certain collector was J.H. Fitzhenry who lent nine labels to the Victoria and Albert Museum in 1902 and a few years later presented another fifty-five, just one part of a vast array of artefacts that he had in his collection. Miss M.V. Brown, whose collection is now in the London Museum and the Holbourne Museum in Bath, must have started to collect at about the same time, but the best known of this first generation of collectors was Major Herbert Dent, whose interests covered a wide field to which he seems to have added wine labels in about 1910. He was the first person to write a book devoted to the subject of wine labels, publishing it in 1933.[1]

Clearly interest was growing, but the First World War (1914-18) must have halted the pursuit of antiques, wine labels amongst them. After the war active collecting resumed and by 1921 both Percy Cropper and Mrs Marshall had begun their collections. A few years later (1925), Raphael Weed enters the field, possibly the first United States citizen to discover labels. We do not know when George Panter started to collect, but when his collection was sold in New York in 1929 it contained five hundred labels, which must have been the fruit of many years' labour. Herbert Hollebone, F.J. Anderson and W. Sandeman all began to make their collections during these early post-First World War years. It would be interesting to discover what set in motion this simultaneous surge of interest by so many people. No publication can be traced to account for it, though Percy Cropper had written an article about his collection for *The Connoisseur* in 1921, and in it he refers to an article on wine and spirit labels in *The Wine and Spirit Trade Record* of the previous year. This may well have been seen by F.J. Anderson, W. Sandeman and Ormond Blyth, all of whom were engaged in the wine business. It is clear, too, that these early enthusiasts were soon in touch with each other, Mrs Marshall being a leading light in promoting correspondence between them, while the dealers likewise played a part in bringing kindred spirits together.

The Second World War (1939-45), like its predecessor, inhibited collecting, but interest was aroused by articles on wine labels in 1941 and 1942 by Lady Ruggles-Brise.[23] This was reinforced in 1947 by the publication of Dr Norman Penzer's *The Book of The Wine Label*, an exhaustive piece of research, five years in gestation, and for the last half-century the definitive work on the subject. It certainly introduced Edward Pratt to the field of labels and to his gathering together twenty fellow enthusiasts to found the WLC in 1952. Within a few years membership had grown to more than fifty; by early 1999 it stood at 150, whilst in its Golden Jubilee year a membership number of four hundred was issued, a remarkable measure of the wine label's rise in popularity in less than a century of collecting history.

Joseph Henry Fitzhenry

The story starts with one of the more unusual characters. Joseph Henry Fitzhenry was born in 1836. In the latter part of the nineteenth century he gave or lent thousands of items to what was then the Art Museum, South Kensington. The name was changed to the Victoria and Albert Museum (V&A) when Queen Victoria laid the foundation stone to a new building in 1899. Items of bronze, porcelain, silver, clocks and even wrought iron gates were presented to the museum, many delivered direct from the dealer or saleroom.[2]

Nothing is known of Fitzhenry's early life and it appears that he had no family, for *The Times* when he died stated that it believed that the residue of his estate was to go to charity. His obituary went on to say that he was a figure familiar in the art world of London, and to a lesser extent in Paris, for many years.[3]

Having lent nine wine labels to the V&A in 1902, he presented the fifty-five wine and sauce labels in two batches in 1903 and 1905. His collection is often forgotten because it came to be dwarfed by the much larger Cropper Collection (see below), but, for some forty years, up to 1944, his were the museum's only silver wine labels. They seem to have been acquired in a somewhat random fashion and Fitzhenry seems to have never described or catalogued them. At the time of his death the curator had schedules prepared of the items that had been lent and department heads were requested to indicate items that they considered important for the museum to retain. An agreement was made with the executors for an accepted valuation of a number of these chosen items and arrangements were made for payment to be made the following financial year when sufficient funds would be available! None of the nine lent wine labels was included.[4]

Miss M.V. Brown

Very little information has come to light concerning this lady and the date when she started to collect, in 1905 or earlier, is only an estimate. She may have been inspired by seeing Fitzhenry's labels in the V&A.

Miss Brown made two donations of labels to museums. The first of approximately 340 labels was made to the London Museum in 1915. (The London Museum combined with the Guildhall Museum to form the Museum of London in 1975.) The second of about fifty labels was to the museum in Bath, now the Holbourne, in 1931.[5] Whether this was a second collection or labels retained from the earlier gift is not known.

In discussing reasons for the gift to the London Museum, Mrs Wendy Evans, at the Museum, says that with the accession of King George V and Queen Mary in 1910 and their Coronation the following year, the London Museum was being established and nationwide support was being sought by national figures for acquisitions. A large number of loans and donations were made as a result. It could well be that Miss Brown was encouraged to donate her labels in support of this cause.

Although at the time of her death in 1931 Miss Brown was living at Milford-on-Sea, Hampshire, it is possible that she had retired there from the Bath area or had family connections with that town. Research has revealed nothing positive, and no other information about her has been uncovered.

George W. Panter
Panter was a general collector, a patron of the arts and in particular a patron of the Royal Irish Academy. He attended Trinity College, Dublin, and was a resident of that city at the time of his death in 1928. His collection of over five hundred wine labels was sold at Sotheby's in 1929.

His collecting taste, like most early collectors, was omnivorous and, although an academic, he appears not to have published any papers on the subject of wine labels.[6]

Percy J. Cropper
Cropper was one of the first collectors known to have written articles on wine labels and thereby helped to publicise this field for collectors. He himself was prompted to collect by a publication. In April 1921, Cropper wrote an article for *The Connoisseur* headed 'Collecting Bottle Labels as a Hobby'.[7] In it he refers to having read an article on old wine labels some twelve months earlier and goes on to say 'with this in mind, passing through a street market shortly afterwards attention arrested on two fine specimens lying on a barrow – the price (9d each) was paid and the collection started'. The article to which Cropper refers could have been 'Wine and Spirit Decanter Labels, the M.V. Brown Collection' by A.G. Le Reek printed in the *Wine and Spirit Trade Record* on 13 September 1920.[8]

It is not known what profession or training Cropper had, but he was certainly writing articles very soon after the date by which it is judged he commenced his collection. He is considered by some to have been something of a dealer or agent. He certainly purchased labels at the Panter sale and a number of these found their way into the Weed Collection. In the 1930s he was in communication with a number of other collectors,[9] but no record has been found of him writing to or meeting Dr Penzer. At the time of his death in 1943 he had a London address, but his executor refers to him as 'a native of Nottingham'. It was to the museum of Nottingham that he first offered his labels, but they were declined because the museum was unable to display such a large collection. In 1944, therefore, as his will directed, the collection of 1,625 labels, was given to the Victoria and Albert Museum.

Raphael Weed
Articles in the *Wine Label Circle Journal* by Mrs Josephine Bethel and Leslie Forrow, together with the Sotheby's sale catalogue mentioned below, help to give a picture of this collector.

Raphael Weed comes over as a man full of enthusiasm and energy who amassed his collection of 551 wine labels in six years.[10] He studied art and was an authority on the theatre. Mrs Bethel comments on the labels that he was attracted to, the beauty of their appearance and their association rather than their period or maker, a natural outcome of his background. With such a man, interested in both the arts and theatre, it is natural to consider what decided him to collect wine labels in particular. In July 1929 Weed published an article in the New-York *Historical Bulletin*[11] describing his labels, styles and makers. He says: 'When it was decided six years' ago to start the present collection, we went to such wealthy old centres of social life as Boston … two years elapsed before … [we were] rewarded.' Whilst his first purchase was not made until 1925, he indicates that the decision to collect was made in 1923.

Cropper's first paper, published in the *Connoisseur* in 1921, was reprinted in the American journal *Antiques* in Boston in 1923. It seems likely that a man such as Raphael Weed could well have included this journal in his reading and that this was the article that inspired his collecting instinct.

He made numerous visits to Britain and acquired many of his labels here. He made copious notes of the purchases, many recorded on the notepaper of the hotels in which he stayed or the liners on which he travelled.

He was a fellow of the New York Historical Society and of the Royal Society, London. He exhibited his labels at the former in 1920 and it was to this Society, on his death in November 1931 aged fifty-eight, that his labels were donated. The gift was known as the 'Raphael A. and Gertrude Weed Collection'. The New York Historical Society sold the collection through Sotheby's, New York, on 12 April 1995.

Major Herbert Dent, MBE

Born about 1859, Major Dent is one of the few collectors and authors about whom considerable information[12] has been found. He trained as a medical doctor and served in the army for many years. In the 1930s he lived in Cromer. He had several collecting interests and published articles on subjects other than wine labels. The start date of 1910 for his label collection is not known accurately, but it is known that he bought and sold many labels; he mentions that at one time his collection had over 1,000 items.

Letters[13] from him to Herbert W. Hollebone between the years 1932 and 1938 help to give a picture of collecting at this time and the personalities involved. In December 1932 Major Dent says: '[I] just bought 500 labels from a doctor friend of Cromer ... [I] sent all duplicates to Sotheby's'. At this sale on 1 December 1932, Hollebone apparently purchased a number of lots and Dent goes on to say that he was delighted that they were bought by a collector – not the trade, and expresses his feeling 'that the charming souvenirs of the 18th and 19th centuries will shortly come into their own, I feel assured'.

A further insight of Major Dent comes when he purchased eight labels from a local dealer. He offered four to Hollebone at half of his purchase price, that is one guinea, wishing to make no profit. He writes that the London silversmiths would charge 6s. to 10s. each for the items. In all his letters Dent comes over as a quiet English gentleman.

An interesting anecdote comes out of this correspondence. In his letter of 22 September 1935, Dent refers to the purchase of two labels from a local pawnbroker. He goes on to describe that when he was 'attached to the Battalion [3rd Battalion of the Rifle Brigade] in India 50 years ago (as MO-in-Charge) I drank out of decanters adorned by two weighty and attractive labels. How I acquired them from a Norwich pawnbroker 30 years later is, as Kipling says, another story too long to relate.' These two labels are illustrated in Plate III of Dent's book, *Wine, Spirit and Sauce Labels of the 18th and 19th Centuries*, which he published privately in 1933, the first publication to be devoted to the subject, other than magazine articles.

In 1935 Dent sold his labels, then numbering about 525, to Hollebone for £250 to help his daughter 'send her two bairns to public school'.

Herbert W. Hollebone

Despite Hollebone's fame as a collector of wine labels, little is actually known about him as a person. He was certainly collecting labels by the late 1920s and on his death his collection was sold by his widow through Sotheby's on 1 December 1955. The sale of 1,800 labels was the first auction wholly devoted to wine labels.

In the 1930s he was living in London and during this period he purchased the collection of a Miss Beattie. From a letter Penzer wrote to Mrs Marshall,[14] it is known that Penzer was trying to contact him in 1943 and apparently succeeded as Hollebone's help is acknowledged in the preface to his book.

It is an interesting aside to mention that in correspondence in 1933, Dent and Hollebone discussed the tarnishing effect of London's atmosphere on Hollebone's labels. Dent advises against the use of lacquer, but in the *Wine Label Circle Journal* Sir Eric Sachs in 1962 commented, 'Incidentally, a high proportion of those that were lacquered or varnished had come from the Hollebone collection'.[15]

Miss Beattie

Very little is known about this collector except from two items of correspondence[16] when Cropper is responding to her letters concerning the origins of wine names and makers in 1933 and 1934. At that time she had an address in Woodbridge. As mentioned above, her collection was sold to Hollebone.

Mrs H.R. Marshall

Mrs Monica Marshall and her husband collected porcelain, glass and wine labels. It would appear that the first two collections were the province of her husband. She commenced collecting in 1921, but the birth of her son, William, in the early 1920s meant that it was not until the 1930s that she again became active in this collecting field.

Although interested in the makers of wine labels, her special attraction was in the origins of unusual names. She had correspondence particularly with André Simon on this subject, and also communicated with Dent, Lady Ruggles-Brise, Sotheby's and Penzer. Penzer received details of Mrs Marshall's collection within a short period of correspondence in 1943. She wrote at least one paper on wine labels in February 1949 for the *Journal of the Circle of Glass Collectors* of which Lady Ruggles-Brise was also a member.

Although living for most of her collecting life in Hampstead, her latter days were spent at Kidlington, near Oxford, both her husband and son having studied at Trinity College.

In 1957 her collection of wine labels was given to the Ashmolean Museum, Oxford, together with the comprehensive card index she had developed and two boxes of correspondence.[17] The collection included 671 wine and sauce labels and thirty-four bin labels. It was given in memory of her son, who was killed in action in Holland in 1944.

Although she remained interested in labels, was still collecting them in 1952 and certainly knew both Penzer and André Simon, she took no action to join the WLC when it was founded in that year.

The boxes of correspondence referred to above include letters written to Hollebone and it is interesting to record how they survived through having been passed by his wife with his collection of labels to Sotheby's in 1955. Mrs Marshall had helped Sotheby's with the cataloguing of Hollebone's collection, and in a letter of 30 September 1955[18] Sotheby's thank her for her help and promise that the letters will be sent to her after the sale. Two letters which Cropper wrote to Miss Beattie in 1933 and 1934 passed with Miss Beattie's collection to Hollebone and thus also found their way to the Ashmolean archive.

André Simon

As the acknowledged leading authority on all aspects of wine and author of many books on the subject, André Simon was one of two eminent persons elected as honorary members of the WLC on its foundation.

He had a collection of wine labels. This is confirmed in a letter which Penzer wrote to Mrs Marshall dated 12 December 1943 when he said, 'I had an interesting day with André Simon who has a very good collection of labels and library'.[19] It is probably more correct that André Simon was a collector of items associated with wine rather than a specific collector of wine labels. Mrs Marshall, as previously commented, received much assistance in the mid-1930s from André Simon with the origin of wine names. André Simon wrote the foreword to Penzer's *The Book of the Wine Label* and Penzer acknowledges in detail help received from him. André Simon died in 1970 at the age of ninety-three; his labels were dispersed some years later.

Frederic Joseph Anderson and F. St J. Kevin Anderson

In the collection of Frederic Joseph Anderson we may perhaps have the inspiration that set Cropper and other collectors of the early 1920s on their paths. He evidently began to collect labels before 1921, as his collection, which then already contained 250 examples, formed the basis for the article on labels in the *Wine and Spirit Trade Record* of that year, to which Cropper makes reference (q.v.).[20]

His business was in the wine trade and he certainly knew Major Dent, writing to him in March

1933 with an account of his labels – which had by then risen to 600 in number – and adding that he intended to exhibit the best pieces at the Vintners' Hall in June of that year. The labels did indeed appear as part of an exhibition, mainly of drinking vessels, entitled *The History of the Wine Trade in England*.

At his death in 1938, Frederic Joseph left his collection of 619 labels to his son, F. St J. Kevin Anderson, to hold until he died or left the wine trade, when they were to pass to the Vintners' Company, of which, surprisingly, Frederic himself was not a member.[21] His son, however, was a member and Master of the Company in 1961.[22] He was also a founder member of the WLC, active in its affairs, though he did not add to the collection. The Steward of the Vintners' Company recalls the labels coming into their possession in 1972, when Anderson retired. Since then they have been on display in Vintners' Hall.

Lady Ruggles-Brise

Lady Ruggles-Brise was an important influence in spreading interest in the collecting of wine labels, particularly following articles she wrote in 1942 and 1943 in *Country Life* magazine.[23] Several early members of the WLC have mentioned these articles when recalling how they were introduced to wine labels and their collection. She knew Mrs Marshall and was responsible for introducing her to Penzer in 1943.[24]

It is not known when Lady Ruggles-Brise commenced collecting labels, but it was probably in the late 1930s. She died in 1953 and her collection of 170 labels was sold at Sotheby's on 28 January 1954.[25]

Dr Norman Penzer

Because of his research into the origins of wine labels, and his pioneer book on the subject, Penzer is probably the best-known name in the field, though apparently he had no collection himself. Mr Pratt acknowledged his help and advice when he founded the WLC in 1952, and he was elected an honorary member of the circle in that year. He was president in 1957-58.

Dr Penzer was educated at Marlborough College and was there at the same time as Mr Marshall (husband of Mrs Monica Marshall). Later he attended Corpus Christi College, Cambridge.

From his obituary[26] it appears that he did not become interested in antique silver until about 1936. His approach to collecting wine labels was that of an academic. This is illustrated in correspondence he had with Mrs Marshall in 1943[27] when he was deciding how to categorise labels into different styles and was interested in listing different makers and the wine names on labels, factors that are apparent in his book. Even before publication of the book, he was a catalyst for the flow of information and for making connections between collectors.

It is interesting to recall an item of correspondence with Mrs Marshall in 1943 when he was describing his proposals for three articles on wine labels. In a reference to his meeting with André Simon he writes, 'he read through the first 40 pages of my article and had decided … [that it was] much too large to publish in his magazine … he will issue in book form immediately after the war'.

It was in fact not until 1947 that *The Book of the Wine Label* was published, with acknowledgement of André Simon's help. He died on 27 November 1960.

Dr Greville Tait

Although not a founder member, Dr Tait was the WLC's first President in December 1952. He recounts[28] starting to collect in 1933 as a result of interest aroused by reading Dent's book. He built a collection of five hundred labels which was dispersed in 1963 on his death.[29]

Ormond Blyth

The origin of this collection has always been a puzzle, as Edward Pratt related in 1953.[30] In December of that year, referring to the Ormond Blyth collection, Penzer wrote, 'this collection now exhibited in 3 glass-fronted wall cases in the board room of Messrs W and A Gilbey, at Gilbey

House, Oval Road, Regent's Park, is notable more for the wide variety of the types of label presented than for the actual number of specimens, which totals 134.'

By 1990 the exhibition had dwindled to one hundred labels in two cases. At the WLC annual meeting in November of that year, held in the Company's office, members were told that the Company archive had been stolen and the early history of the collection lost (W. and A. Gilbey are now part of International Distillers and Vintners).

The name of Blyth had been associated with W. and A. Gilbey since 1858, only one year after the Company's foundation.[31] Enquiries at Companies House[32] produced many annual reports, but the crucial ones for 1935-55 are missing. From 1914 to 1935 the Register of Shareholders included the name 'Ormond Alfred Blyth'. He had various London addresses in the Regent's Park locality and his occupation was described as a Merchant, but he was not a director of the Company during those years.

Sandeman Family

This family collection involved three generations and four members of the family associated with the wine company of George G. Sandeman and Sons. The collection was started by Ernest S. Sandeman and had reached eighty items when he died in 1926 and the collection was passed to his brother, the father of Major Patrick Sandeman.[33]

Major Patrick Sandeman inherited this still small collection in the late 1930s/1940 and it is really with Major Patrick that the story takes off when the collection expanded rapidly after World War II. Patrick Sandeman was a founder member of the WLC and by 1955 the collection had reached about 260 labels.[34] Two years later it had reached 609 and by 1958 was described as more than seven hundred.[35] Major Patrick was an active member of the Circle and died in 1959 when his collection passed to his son, Tim Sandeman.

The enthusiasm of his father was echoed in Tim Sandeman, who frequently arranged meetings for fellow collectors at his office. He arranged for the collection to be illustrated in the WLC's Journals. Many WLC members will recall when, in 1984 at the AGM at Vintner's Company, Tim Sandeman brought eleven large boxes containing trays of labels for members to inspect and enjoy. When he died in 1994 the collection was split between his three children. Sadly, large sections of it were stolen a few years later and have not been recovered.

Mrs Jean Rhodes

A founder member of the WLC, Mrs Rhodes was Honorary Editor of the *Journal* until 1959. She was the wife of a doctor, practising in Leamington Spa, who was also a member of the WLC at its foundation and President during 1953-54. She started collecting before 1939 and from a description of her collection in 1954 it was extensive.[36] It was gradually dispersed around 1960.

Alexander Cuthbert

Alexander Cuthbert was the founder of another family collection. He lived in Edinburgh and was a chartered accountant. He started collecting in 1941 having been, as he wrote in an early *Journal*, 'introduced to Wine Labels by Lady Ruggles-Brise's article'.[37] He informed the readership that his first purchases were in Edinburgh, London and East Anglia. He corresponded with Lady Ruggles-Brise and Dr Penzer.[38]

Alexander Cuthbert was a Founder member of the WLC and Honorary Auditor from its founding to 1965. He gave a fine selection of fifty-five labels covering every aspect of his collection of six hundred pieces to the Royal Scottish Museum, Edinburgh, in about 1965. Labels by Scottish craftsmen were strongly represented. The museum had not previously been in possession of wine labels.

He was still collecting and an active member of the WLC when he died in 1974. His collection passed to his nephew, John Cuthbert, who shared it with his two sons.

Edward Pratt

Edward Pratt is deservedly acknowledged as the most influential figure in current wine label collecting because of his activity in the formation of the WLC, which he founded in 1952. He was its first secretary from 1952 to 1960, and president from 1962 to 1964.

He has written[39] that he was inspired to start collecting in 1948 by Penzer's book. By profession Edward Pratt was a civil servant and lived in the Taunton and Weston-Super-Mare area.

By April of 1955 he had built his collection to 565 labels of which he presented a selection in 1960 to Messrs Harvey's of Bristol. They were admirably displayed in the company's museum situated in the old wine vaults of their property at 12 Denmark Street, Bristol until 2003 when the museum was closed and the contents sold by Messrs. Bonhams on 1 and 2 October 2003.[40] The labels he retained became the basis of a second collection which was dispersed after his death in 1969.

PART 2 – NOTABLE EIGHTEENTH-CENTURY FAMILIES

In Chapter 1, Part 1, dealing with early references to wine labels, mention was made of the inventories of plate kept by eighteenth-century families as likely to be fruitful sources of information about the early days. Every person of importance felt it incumbent on him to have imposing displays of contemporary plate and so, as bottle-tickets came into fashion, they were added to the display and entered into the inventory. In this chapter an example is given of one about which something is known in the first half of the eighteenth century and some conjectures are made about the wine labels included in it. Another example shows a family's acquisitions during the second half of the century.

Dunham Massey

One of the most detailed inventories to survive was compiled by George Booth, 2nd Earl of Warrington, for his principal seat at Dunham Massey in Cheshire.[41] In 1702 he married Mary Oldbury, daughter of a rich merchant, and she brought with her a dowry of £40,000. The marriage was not a success, and for the next fifty years they lived separately in the same house without speaking to each other. He was clearly a difficult person, careful with money to the extent of parsimony, 'the stiffest of all stiff things', according to one acquaintance,[42] and she not much easier. But she did bring him money and this enabled him to pay off his considerable debts and go on to amass an outstanding collection of silver, which he recorded carefully in an inventory written in his own hand. He was deeply religious, as the quantity of plate commissioned for the chapel shows, a staunch Protestant and a strong Huguenot supporter. He patronised Huguenot silversmiths, though usually, in line with his parsimonious habits, not the most expensive ones. Those whom he did go to included Philip Rollos, Isaac Liger, Peter Archambo and, after 1739, David Willaume II, James Shruder, Daniel Piers and Magdalen Feline, none of whom, it should be noted, is known to be a label maker. Nevertheless, wine labels feature in the inventory, where they are referred to as 'bottle tickets'.

The inventory is entitled 'Particulars of my Plate in February (deleted) October 1752'. It lists all the pieces, over 1,000, weighing more than 25,000 oz., that he had when he began it in April 1750, and he kept it amended up to August 1754. It gives the weight of every piece, including the wine labels, and this was incised on each piece as well. Unfortunately, it does not give descriptions or the names of makers, or dates of purchase. The labels are listed as follows:

Bottle tickets	oz	dwt
CHAMPAGNE	0	16½
BURGUNDY	0	16½
CLARET	0	15
FRENCH WHITE	0	15
RED PORT	0	16½
WHITE PORT	0	15

METHUEN	0	16
MADEIRA	0	15½
MILD ALE	0	15½
STRONG BEER	0	14½
TOTAL NUMBER	**10**	
AVERAGE WEIGHT		**15½**

These weights offer no clue to the designs of the labels. The variations might suggest that there was more than one, but the differences are small and, taking wear into account, they are in fact within the range of a single style. John Salter points out that they may date from before 1750 when the inventory starts.[43] At that time three designs of label predominated: the wrought escutcheon, the cast two putti, and the cast plumed rococo cartouche.[44] The earl's taste was for heavy silver, which might suggest that the labels were plain, or perhaps chased, heavy escutcheons. A typical escutcheon weighs around 10-12dwt, even with the chain. The other two designs, besides being more ornate, are heavier, but usually not more than 15dwt. The earl's penchant for weight brings them within the range of possibility.

The names on the labels are those that might be expected for the age, with the exception of METHUEN. This unusual name is discussed in more detail in Chapter 6. In the context of this set it needs to be remembered that this red wine from Portugal was, in the middle years of the eighteenth century, more than thirty years after the signing of the treaty from which it got its name, not reckoned to be a wine of particularly high quality, so it is rather surprising to find it here. In general, the choice of wines indicates, as might be expected, a conservative taste: four French wines, despite the treaty that was supposed to make them less attractive in price than those from Portugal; MADEIRA, of course; and three from Portugal. Lisbon, the Portuguese white wine so popular throughout the eighteenth century, is conspicuous by its absence. The labels for MILD ALE and STRONG BEER stand out from the remainder and may, perhaps, have been of different design.

Unfortunately, the labels are no longer at Dunham Massey. It is known that ten labels were sent by the 5th Earl of Warrington and Stamford to Garrards to be repaired in 1820. It is also known that they were removed to Enville in Staffordshire, another of the earl's estates, during the lifetime of the 7th and last earl in 1848, but since then all trace of them has been lost.[45] At one time they were identified with some plumed rococo cartouches by John Harvey, illustrated by H.C. Dent,[46] on the strength of one of them being engraved for METHUEN. The label is certainly of the right date (c.1746-50), but the names on the others in Dent's set differ from those in the inventory.

Sledmere
Information about the plate at Sledmere,[47] twenty miles north of Hull, comes from a different source. There undoubtedly was an inventory, but the best descriptions are in the sales catalogue of the silver's disposal in 1979.[48] Sir Richard Sykes, an important shipowner in Hull, went to live there in 1748, inheriting it from his mother, whose family home it had been for several generations. It then contained silver dating back to the previous century by London, Newcastle and York silversmiths. Sykes and his successors added more, including a number of wine and sauce labels.

The earliest marked labels are a pair of escutcheons by John Harvey, one with his mark of 1739/45, and the other with that of 1745/46. They are for LISBON and RED PORT, and may well have been in the house when he went to live there, or he may have brought them with him from wherever he was living before 1748, to join two unmarked plain triangular escutcheons of early shape and provincial workmanship for PORT and MADEIRA.[49] It would be tempting to speculate that they might have been manufactured in Hull, but there is no evidence for this, nor indeed does it seem that there were any working silversmiths in the city at that time. A quantity of plate dates from the years immediately after Sykes took up residence, made by silversmiths in Newcastle between 1750 and 1760, including three wine labels by J. Langlands I, and at the same time he was commissioning plate from London, amongst his acquisitions being four chased escutcheons by Robert Cox, up-to-date contemporary pieces by a silversmith who only entered his mark in 1752. This was the year in which Richard Sykes was High Sheriff for the county.

When Richard died in 1761, his brother, the Reverend Mark, went to live at Sledmere. During his twenty-two years in residence he added a little to the plate and a few wine labels, bought as pairs or single items, and to no recognisable pattern. There was a pair of feather-edged cushion-shaped labels for PORT and WHITE by Richard Binley, made between 1760 and 1764, a feather-edged crescent for MADEIRA made by John Rich, *c.*1765 to *c.*1771, another MADEIRA, a chased escutcheon by Joseph Steward II of *c.*1770, and an unmarked plain escutcheon for CALCAVELLA, probably dating from a few years later, as that sweet Spanish white wine began to become popular.

It cannot be certain, however, whether it was Mark or his son, Christopher, who acquired some of these. Christopher married into the Egerton family of Tatton Park near Manchester in 1770, and must have kept an establishment for which he would have required adequate silver before succeeding to Sledmere on Mark's death in 1783. He was a man of more ambitious tastes than his father and a keen collector. One of the most interesting groups of labels was acquired, probably by Christopher, between 1776 and 1780: four escutcheon labels by the York firm of Hampston and Prince, who had just been responsible for reopening the assay office in that city after its sixty-year closure.[50] He would undoubtedly have been eager to extend patronage to this newly established and prominent county firm. The labels include an early example for SHERRY, which was beginning to supplant mountain in popularity, one for SMYRNA, the Turkish port to which the family's ships had been trading, and a third for SYRGIS, probably a corruption of Sitges, a wine-growing district south of Barcelona and another port of call for Sykes' ships. A fourth label in the group, of different design, is for CYDER, an unusual title to be found in that part of the country.

When he arrived at Sledmere Christopher extended the range of wines in the cellars and commissioned more labels to go with them – two sets of oval or navette-shaped labels from James Hyde, one of five and one of twelve, only a few years apart. The earlier set can be dated with certainty to the years 1784-1786 as they have the incuse duty mark. The larger, later set has marks that suggest a date between 1787 and 1790. There is a curious repetition of titles in these last sets. SMYRNA, which is an uncommon name in itself, occurs in the York labels of around 1776-1780 and in both the Hyde sets, as does CYDER, while SYRGIS appears in the York trio and in Hyde's labels of 1784-86. CALCAVELLA also appears three times, on the unmarked escutcheon of *c.*1775 and then on the Hyde labels.

Between 1800 and 1810 Sir Mark Masterman-Sykes acquired twelve sauce labels.

In 1911 Sir Tatton Sykes acquired five plain rectangular labels from Sheffield, names unknown.

Hyde's PORT of 1787-90 brings up to date the PORT cushion that Binley had made in 1760-64, and his MADEIRA replaced the older examples, a crescent and four escutcheons. Every successive owner seems to have felt it necessary to have a new label for this wine. MOUNTAIN and CHAMPAGNE in the 1787-90 set take over from Robert Cox's labels of 1752, though it is not really clear why Christopher needed a new MOUNTAIN label when he already had a label for the more fashionable SHERRY from the York escutcheons. There are six new titles in the final Hyde set: three white wines from France, Spain and the Canary Islands, BURGUNDY for the first time and, also for the first time, two spirit labels for GIN and RUM. The year 1787 is early for gin, while it is very noticeable that throughout the whole succession of labels, French red wine labels only appear once each, CLARET in the 1760s, some fifteen years after the family first went to live at Sledmere, and BURGUNDY another twenty years later.

This set of Hyde's was in fact the last of the wine label acquisitions to be made. When Christopher died in 1801 he was succeeded by Sir Mark, the famous bibliophile whose vast collection of books passed to the British Museum in 1823. He acquired several important pieces of Regency silver and six sauce labels, including three from York makers R. Cattle and J. Barber, but for wine labels for his decanters he was seemingly content with those left to him by his brother, Christopher. It remained so for the final 160 years of the family's tenure of the house, until the disposal of its silver in 1979.

APPENDIX 1

ALPHABETICAL LIST OF NAMES OF WINES, SPIRITS, LIQUEURS AND ALCOHOLIC CORDIALS ON BOTTLE TICKETS AND BIN LABELS AS AT JUNE 2003

INTRODUCTORY NOTES

1. Names are listed alphabetically without distinction between letters with and without accent marks, or between initials with and without periods after them.
2. Numbers are ordered between the letters as if spelled, e.g 2 is positioned as Two but dates are in numerical order under letter E (Eighteen).
3. Names on more than one line are indicated by / between lines.
4. Every capital letter, A to Z, has been reported as a single letter label for Section 1.
5. Lower case variants are not listed unless first reported as script or lower case, and shown therefore by script or lower case lettering.
6. Names with superscript letters are regarded as variants.
7. Names with words in letters of different font size from others are regarded as variants.
8. Names with different punctuation marks are regarded as variants, e.g . • – – : ★ + are all variants.
9. Some letter and symbol configurations cannot be reproduced in type; these are described beside the name.
10. Because the above strict criteria were not observed in all earlier lists from 1975 onwards, this list probably contains some errors.
11. Different spellings shown in parentheses have occurred in the earlier cross-referenced lists and it is not known, at the time of compilation of this purely alphabetical list, which is correct.
12. There are some names for which positions of periods or letters are not exactly reproduceable in word-processed typescript. In these cases the name is represented as closely as possible and the accurate version is described alongside it.
13. Names engraved in lower case or in a script form or with non-Latin lettering are reproduced, where known, as closely as possible. Variations in font type have not been fully recorded in earlier lists.
14. **[B]** indicates that the name has also been noted on a bin label. **[B1]** indicates that the name has only been noted on a bin label. Because this distinction has not been made previously, some names categorised as **[B]** may actually be **[B1]**.
15. This list does not include names of 1) sauces, flavourings, essences, condiments, herbs, spices, extracts, pastes, fruits, jams, seasonings, dressings, oils, vinegars, catsups, pickles, for which see *Sauce Labels* and updates in *Wine Label Circle Journal,* or 2) non-alcoholic cordials, spa waters, lotions, medicines, perfumes, salves, toilet waters, and miscellaneous or unclassifiable names.
16. It would be helpful if corrections of all types and additions of new names or variants are reported to the Wine Label Circle via the email address at the web site: www.winelabelcircle.org.

Appendix 1 - Names

A
A. BRANDY
A / BURDON / SHERRY
A. SHERRY
AALBORG
ABRICOTINA
ABRICOTINE
ABSINTH
ABSINTHE
ACQUA D'ORO
ACQUAVITE
ADEGA
ADVOCAAT
AFTER DINNER CLARET
AGUARDENTE
ALBA
ALBA FLORA
ALBAFLOR
ALBAFLORA
ALCHERMES
ALCOHOL
ALE [B]
ALE HODGSON
ALICANT
ALICANTE
ALICANTI
ALIZE
ALLCATICO
ALMADE
ALMEIDA
ALOQUE
AMARGAS
AMERICAN WHISKEY
AMESTROSS
AMINTA
AMONTILADO [B]
AMONTILHADO
AMONTILLADO
AMONTILLEDO
AMONTILLIADO
AMOROSO
ANDAYE
ANGELICA CHATEAU Y'QUEM
ANGELIQUE
ANGOSTURA
ANGOSTURA BITTERS
ANISEED
ANISETTE
ANJOU
ANNICETTE
ANNISCETTE
ANNISEED
ANNISETTE
APITIV
APPLE BRANDY
APRICOT
AQUAVIT
AQUAVITAE
AQUAVITE
ARAC
ARBAFLOR

ARBOIS
ARGOSTOLA
ARINTA
ARINTO
ARMAGNAC
ARMONTILLARDO [B]
ARRAC
ARRACK
ARTHUR
ARTIMINA
ASMUSS
ASSMANSHANSER [B]
ASSMANSHÄNSER VENTAGE [B1]
ASSMANSHAUSER
ASTI
ATHALIE
AULD KIRK
AUSTRALIAN CLARET
AUSTRALIAN HOCK / SYDNEY BINNED 1894 [B1]
AUSTRALIAN SHERRY
AVALON
AVIGNON
AY [B]
AY MOUSSEU

B
B. ALE
B. BRANDY [B]
B. CREAM
B. CURRANT
B. MADEIRA
B. PORT
B. SHERRY
BAGAÇO
BAKANO
BALFOUR'S LIQUEUR BRANDY
BALM [B]
BANANES LIQUEUR
BANYULS
BAROLA
BAROLO
BAROSSA
BARSAC
BARSACK
BAUME HUMAIN
BEASAC
BÈASAC
BEAUCELLAS
BEAUJOLAIS [B]
BEAUJOLAIS / ROUGE [B]
BEAUME
BEAUNE
BEER
BEER MUG
BEESWING
BEESWING PORT
BÉNÉ
BENE DICTINE

BENEDICT
BENEDICTIN
BENEDICTINE
BÉNÉDICTINE
BENEDIKTINER
BENICARLO
BENRIG
BERNE
BERNIS
BERSAC
BEST CLARET
BEST SHERRY
BIRRA D'INGILTERRA
BIRTHDAY PORT
BISCHOFF
BISKOP
BITTER SHERRY
BITTERS
BLACK
BLACK CURRANT
BLACKADDER
BLACKBERRY
BLACKBERRY BRANDY
BLACKBURN
BLACKCURRANT GIN
"BLAMIRE BOTTLE 144 YEARS OLD" / T DONALD ESQ: T JAMES 1865
BN CURRANT
BOAL
BOÁL (Accent above A may be a dot or a comma; photo unclear)
BOCHET
BONECAMP
BORCELLAS
BORDEAUX
BORDEAUX BLANC
BORDEAUX ROUGE
BORDEAUX ROUGE / LA MAGDELAINE
BORDEAUX, PREMIER
BORDEOS
BORDO
BORGOGNA
BORGOÑA
BORGONA
BOTTOMS
BOUNCE
BOURBON
BOURDEAUX
BOURGOGNE
BOURGOGNE BLANC
BOURGOGNE MULSEAUX
BOURGOGNE VOLNAY
BOURGONE
BOURGUILLE
BOUSFIELD
BRAENDEVIN
BRAENNVIN
BRANDEWYN
BRANDY [B]

Appendix 1 - Names

BRANDY 13	C	CAPO BUONA SPERANZA
BRANDY 1841	C. A.	BIANCO
BRANDY SHRUB	C. B.	CAPRI
BRANVIN	C. BRANDY	CAPT. MASTER R. M.
BRESCIA	C. CHAMPAGNE	CAPTAIN WHITE'S
BRISTOL CREAM	C DE M	Captn Sykes R.N.
BRITISH	C. DE. ROSE	CARBENET
BRITISH WINE	C. E.	CARCAVALLA
BRITTEN	C. MADEIRA	CARCAVELLA
BRONTE	C. SHRUB	CARCAVELLAS
BRONTÉ	C. WHISKEY	CARCAVELLO
BRONTE MADEIRA [B]	C.YQUEM	CARCAVELLOS
BRONTI	CACAO	CARCAVILLA
BRONTI MADIERA	CACAVELLA	CARCOVELLO
BROWN BANG	CACAVELLO	CARCOVELLOS
BROWN BRANDY [B]	CACAVELOS	CARLO WITZ
BROWN INDIA SHERRY	CAHORS	CARLOWITZ [B]
BROWN SHERRY [B]	CALABRE	CARLOWITZ 1
BROWN SHERRY 1862 /	CALAMITY WATER	CARLOWITZ 2
RAYNE BINNED 1892 [B1]	CALCAR-VILLA	CARTON
BROWN STOUT	CALCAUILLA	CASSES
BROWN.STOUT [B1]	CALCAVALHA	CASSIS
BUAL	CALCAVALLA	CASSIS BLANC
BUCALAS	CALCAVELA	CATALAN
BUCALLAS	CALCAVELEA	CAVEZA
BUCCELLAS	CALCAVELLA [B]	CAVO
BUCELAS	CALCAVELLE	CB
BUCELLA [B]	CALCAVELLO	CEDRA
BUCELLAS [B]	CALCAVILLA	CELIA
BUCELLASE	CALCAVLLA	CENEVER
BUCELLES	CALEAVELLA	CENTURIN
BUCELLIS	CALEDONIA	CERCIAL
BUCELLOS	CALKAVELLA	CERCIAL M[A]
BUCELLUS	CALLISTE	CERCIAL MADEIRA [B]
BUCHANANS ROYAL	CALVADOS	Ceres (in Gothic lettering)
HOUSEHOLD	CAMBUS	CERISES
BUCILLAS	CAMPARI	CÉRONS
BUDA	CANADIAN	CETTE
BUDOCK	CANADIAN CLUB WHISKEY	Ch. BRANDY
BUGUNDER	CANARIA	CH. LAFUE
BUGUNDY	CANARIAS	CHABLEY
BUOL	CANARIAS SECO	Chabley [B]
BURBON	CANARIE	CHABLIS [B]
BURCELLAS	CANARY	CHABLIS MOUSSEUX [B1]
BURCELLOS	CANARY SACH	CHABLY
BURDEOS	CANDIA W	CHAGNY BLANC
BURGANDER	CANNELLA	CHAMBERRY
BURGANDY	CAORE	CHAMBERTIN [B]
BURGONDY	CAP	CHAMBERY
BURGUNDY [B]	CAP BLANC	CHAMBÉRY [B]
BURGUND[Y]	CAP BRETON ROUGE	CHAMBLIS GRAVES
BURGUN[Y]	CAP DE BONNE ESPÈRANCE	CHAMBOLLE
BURG[Y]	BLANC	CHAMPAGN
BURNETT	CAP ROUGE	CHAMPAGNE [B]
BURNTISLAND	CAPE [B]	CHAMPAGNE BLANC
BURTON. ALE	CAPE Berkeley Square [B1]	CHAMPAGNE CIDER
BURTON. ALE. [B1]	CAPE MADEIRA [B]	CHAMPAGNE CREMANT
BUSELLAS [B]	CAPE WINE	CHAMPAGNE D'AY
BUSHBY	CAPEWYN	CHAMPAGNE IN ICE
BUSHMILLS	CAPILARE	CHAMPAGNE MOUSSEU
BYRRH	CAPILLAIRE	CHAMPAGNE MOUSSEUX

Appendix 1 - Names

CHAMPAGNE MOUSSEX	CHERRY GIN	COLTSFOOT
CHAMPAGNE R.	CHERRY MADEIRA	COMBER
CHAMPAGNE ROUGE	CHERRY RATIFIA	COMMANDARIA
CHAMPAGNE SILLERY	CHERRY WHISKEY	COMMANDER
CHAMPAGNE SWEET [B1]	CHIANTI	COMO
CHAMPAGNER	CHICHES	COÑAC
CHAMPAIGN [B]	CHINA	CONDRIEUX
CHAMPAIGNE [B]	CHIPRE	CONIAC
CHAMPAIGNE MOUSSEUX	CHRISTI	CONJACH
CHAMPAIN	CHT. LAFITTE	Conjach
CHAMPAINE	CHUSCLAN	CONNELL
CHAMPAÑA	CHUZELAN	CONSTANCE
CHAMPAYNE	CHYPRE	CONSTANCIA
CHAMPERTIN	CIDER [B]	CONSTANIA
CHAMP^N	CIDRE / ORDINAIRE [B]	CONSTANTIA [B]
CHANBOLLE	CIERCEAL	CONVENT
CHARECK	CINZANO	COOKING BRANDY
CHARKEUSE	CIPRO	COOKING PORT [B1]
CHARTREUSE	CISCOURS 1865 [B1]	COOKING SHERRY [B]
CHARTREUSE GREEN	CITROEN	COOK^{NG} SHERRY
CHARTREUSE JAUNE	CLAIRRET	COPENHAGEN CHERRY BRANDY
CHARTREUSE VERTE	CLARET [B]	
CHARTREUSE YELLOW	CLARET.	CORACAO
CHASSAGNE	CLARET BEST	CORDIAL GIN
CHATEAU	Claret Cape [B1]	CORDIAL MEDOC
CHATEAU BRAUAIRE 1877 / RAYNE BINNED 1895 [B1]	CLARET LIGHT	CORIN
	CLARET NO 1	CORK
CHATEAU GRILLÉE	CLARET NO 2	CORNAS
CHATEAU LAFITE 1847	CLARET 66	CORRASH
CHATEAU LAFITE 1848	CLARET 2	CORREMILLA
CHATEAU LAFITE 1892 / RAYNE BINNED 1895 [B1]	CLARETE	CORRENILLA
	CLARETT	CORTON
CHATEAU LAFITTE	CLARETTE	COS D'ESTOURNAI [B1]
CHATEAU LAGRANGE	CLARRET	COS D'ESTOURNEL
CHATEAU LANGOA 1875	CLART	COSSINS PORT
CHATEAU LAROSE [B]	CLARY	CÔTE RÔTE
CHATEAU LATOUR [B1]	CLÔS DONGEAU (script)	COTE ROTI
CHATEAU LATOUR 1851	CLOS VEUGEOT	COTE ROTIE
CHATEAU LÉOVILLE	CLYNELISH	CÔTE ROTIE
CHATEAU LÉOVILLE 1870 / BARTLETT & JONES BINNED 1889 [B1]	COCKAGEE	COTE-ROTE
	COCKBURN'S PORT 1878 / RAYNE BINNED 1892 [B1]	COTEROTI
		CÔTE-RÔTIE
CHATEAU MARGAUX [B]	COCKTAIL	COTI-ROTI
CHÂTEAU MARGAUX	COCNAC	COTILLION
CHATEAU MARGO	COGNAC	COULAISSE
CHATEAU MARGOT	COGNAC / Carte Blanche / + / 8f [B1]	COULANGE
CHATEAU MEURSAULT 1878 [B1]		COULANGES
	COGNAC 1840	COUNTRY
CHATEAU-LATOUR	COGNAC.	Courvoisier / 97 (script)
CHATEAU Y'QUEM	Cognac. (in Cyrillic lettering)	COWSLIP [B]
CHATEAUN	COGNAC BRANDY	CREAM OF THE VALLEY
CHATREUSE	COGNAC VIEUX	CREAMING CHAMPAGNE
CHERAC	COGNAK	CREMA DI VINO
CHERES	COGNIAC	CRÈMA DIVINO
CHERESSE	COINTREAU	CREME D'ALLASCH
CHERRY	COLARES	CRÈME D'AMANDE
CHERRY B	COLDINGHAME	CREME DE BARBADE
CHERRY BOUNCE	COLDRINGHAM	CREME DE CAÇAO
CHERRY BRANDY	COLENSO	CREME DE CAFÉ
CHERRY BRANDY B. L.	COLERAINE	CREME DE CASSIS
CHERRY B^Y	COLLARES	CRÈME DE FLEURS D'ORANGE

Appendix 1 - Names

CRÊME DE MÊNTHE
Creme De Menthe
CRÈME DE MOKKA
CRÊME DE NOYAU
CREME DE NOYEAU ROUGE
CRÈME DE PORTUGAL
CRÈME DE THÉ
CREME DE VIOLETTES
CREMEDEROSE
CREOLE
CROFT'S PORT 1885/
    RAYNE BINNED 1888 **[B1]**
CUIRASSAUS (or with single S?)
CUIRASSEAU
CUMIERE
CURA,COA
CURAC,OA
CURACAO **[B1]**
CURAÇAO
CURACAO BLANC
CURACAS
CURACAU
CURACOA
CURAÇOA
CURACOA MARNIER
CURAFLO
CURASCOA
CURASÇOA (unusual shape of
    cedilla)
CUROCOA
CURRANT **[B]**
CURRANT WINE
CURRENT
CURINO
CURROSOS
CURR.T WHISKEY
CUR.T WINE
CY. BRANDY
CYDER **[B]**
CYLIN
CYPRESS
CYPRUS **[B]**
CYPRUS DOVER STREET **[B1]**
CYSER

D
D & G 1880
D & G 1884
D CHAMPAIGNE
D.E.V.
D. O. M.
D'ARBOISE
D'ERBOIS
D'GRAVE
D'MADRAS
D'OEIL DE PERDRIX
D'ORANGE
D'ORGEAT
DACTILUS
DALMATIA
DAMASCENE

DAMSON
DAMSON GIN
DANSKI
Danskt (Letters in an unidentifiable
    script)
DANTZIC **[B]**
DAVIDSON
DE CAPE BLANC
DE CAPE ROUGE
DE CASSIS
DE CASTRO
DE COTE ROTIE
DE LANGUEDOC
De Rhin
DE TOKAY
DE. LA. CÔTE
DEIDES HELMER
DERDESHEIMER
DESMERAIL **[B1]**
DESSERT SHERRY
DINNER CLARET **[B]**
DINNER HOCK
DINNER PORT
DINNER SHERRY **[B]**
DINNER WINE **[B1]**
Distileradt Brånvin af E. Såtherstans
    tillverkning
DOM
DONALD
DRAAGENSTEIN
DRAKENSBURG
DRY
DRY CHAMPAGNE
DRY / CHAMPAIGNE
DRY CHAMPAYNE
DRY FLY SHERRY
DRY GINGER
DRY MALAGA
DRY ORANGE CURACAO
DRY PACARETTE
DRY PAXARETE
DRY.PAXARETE
DRY PORT **[B]**
DRY SHERRY **[B]**
DUBLIN
DUBONNET
DUBOUNET
DUCHY OF BRONTE
DUKE **[B]**
DUNKEMSPEHLS BROWN
    SHERRY
DUNKEN SPEHLS BROWN
    SHERRY **[B1]**
DUNRENSPHEILHL'S /
    BROWN SHERRY (or
    DUNRENSPHEIHL'S?)
DUNVILLE
DURHIN

E
E. CLARET
E. I. SHERRY
E IND TENERIFFE 1824 **[B1]**
EAST INDIA
EAST INDIA MADEIRA
EAST INDIA SHERRY
EAU, D'ANDAILLE
EAU D'ORANGE
EAU DE DANZIC
EAU DE LUBIN
EAU DE NOYAUX
EAU DE NUIT
EAU DE VIE
EAU-DE-VIE
Eau-de-vie (in Gothic lettering)
EAU DE VIE D'ANDAYE
EAU DE VIE DE CIDRE
EAU DE VIE DE COGNAC
EAU DE VIE FROM FRANCE
ECKAU
EDINBURGH ALE
EI / MADEIRA
1802 VINTAGE
1814 GREEK WINE
1815 / E. I. / MALMSEY **[B1]**
1815 PORT BIN.D JUNE 1822
    [B1]
1815 RAISIN **[B1]**
1818 / E.I / SERCIAL **[B1]**
1818 SHERRY A. 1.
1819 / E.I. / VINA TINTA **[B1]**
1819 / WALTER'S / PORT
1820 AMONTILLADO
1822 MADEIRA **[B1]**
1822 PULSFORDS PORT **[B1]**
1825 BURGUNDY **[B1]**
1833 SAVOCA **[B1]**
1838 STEIN WINE
1842 MUSCATEL
1845 BROWN SHERRY L.D
    BELHAVEN **[B1]**
ELDER
ELDER FLOWER **[B]**
ELDER FLOWER WINE
ELDER WINE **[B]**
ELDERBERRY WINE
ELIE
ENGLISH
ENGLISH CLARET
English CLARET
ENGLISH GIN
ENGLISH WINE
ENNISHOWEN
ERLAURE
ESCUBACY
ESCUBANCY
ESPAGNE
ESPANAU
ESPARAN
ESPAVAN

Appendix 1 - Names

ESPINOSA
ESPIRITU SANTO
ESSENCE
EST-EST
EST-EST-EST
ESTE-ESTE
ETNA
EXTRA RESERVE
EXTRA RESERVE X X X X
EXTRAIT D'ABSINTHE

F
F. CHAMPAGNE
F. CLARET (or F. CLART?)
F. C. SHERRY
F.V.
F.W. WINE
FACEL
FAHLU
FALERNIAN
FALERNO
FALERNUM
FALU
FARINGTOSH
FARO
FERNET BRANCA
FIN CHAMPAGNE
FINE
FINE / LUNEL [B]
FINE CHAMPAGNE
FINE OLD IRISH
FINO
FINO FINISSIMO
FINT BRÄNVIN
FIRST PORT
FISCHERS
FLORA
FLORANCE
FLORE
FLORENCE
FLORENCE M.
FONTANIAC
FONTENAY
FONTENOY
FONTINIAC
FONTONIAC
FOUGÈRE
FOUNTANYOCK
FOUNTINIAC
484 MADEIRA
FOYOLLE [B]
Foyolle. [B1]
FR. VERMOUTH
FR. VIIN
FR:WHITE
FR. WINE
FR. W-WINE
FRAISETTE
FRAMBOISE
FRENCH
FRENCH CLARET

FRENCH VERMOUTH
FRENCH W. WINE
FRENCH WHITE
FRENCH WHITE-WINE
FROM HOLLAND (or it may be SCHEIDAM GENEVA / FROM HOLLAND)
FRONTAGNON
FRONTANIAC
FRONTENAC
FRONTIGNAC [B]
FRONTIGNAN
FRONTIGN^C
FRONTIGNIA
FRONTIGNIAC
FRONTIGNON
FRONTIGUAN
FRONTINAC [B]
FRONTINEAC
FRONTINIAC [B]
FRONTINIACK
FRONTINIAK
FRUIT
FRUITY PORT

G
G. BEER
G. BRANDY
G. MARNIER
G: ROM
G. WHISKEY
GAMELROM
Gammalt Sädes:B$^{\underline{v}}$ (Unidentifiable joined up script. Underlined v is superscript)
GARACHICO
GARUS
Gauffin. (Letters in an unidentifiable script; dot at end of word)
GEAN
GEENSHRUB
GEEN BRANDY
GEEN WHISKY
GELDER CHARTREUSE
GENEBRA
GENEIVER
GENEROIDE VECCHIO
GENEROIDE VIEUX
GENEVA
GENEVER
GENEVER FROM HOLLAND
GENEVRE
GENIEVE
GENIÈVE
GENIEVRE
GI ROM
GILKA
GI. ROM.
GIN [B]
GIN SWEETENED

GIN SYRUP
GINEVA
GINGER [B]
GINGER BRANDY
GINGER CORDIAL
GINGER SHRUB
GINGER RUM [B1]
GINGER WINE
GINGERETTE
GINGERHAM
GISCOURS
GL:ROM
GLEN
GLEN DRONACH
GLENDRONACH
GLENLIVET
GLENRONACH
GLORIA MUNDI
GOLD SHERRY [B]
GOLD WATER
GOLDEN SHERRY
GOOSBERRY [B]
GOOSBERY
GOOSEBERRIE
GOOSEBERRIES
GOOSEBERRY [B]
GOOSEBERRY WINE
GOOSEBERY
GOOSERERRY
GOSEBERRY
GOUTTES DE MALTHES
GRAIN
GRANACHA
GRANACHE
GRAND MARNIER
GRANDE MAISON
GRANDE MANIER
GRANDE MARNIER
GRAPE [B]
GRAPE FRUIT
GRAPILLON
GRAPPA
GRAPPE CURE
GRAU
GRAVE
GRAVES
GRAYES WINE
GREEK WINE [B]
GREEN
GREEN CHARTREUSE
GREEN CURAÇOA
GREEN GOOSBERRY
GREEN GRAPE
GREEN WHISKY
GREENGAGE
GRENACHE
GRENATCH
GROENDRUIF
GUBSCHABBES
GUJAVA
GUYNE

Appendix 1 - Names

H
H. GENEVA
H, GIN
H, GIN
H. WHISKEY
HALLON
HALLOW'EEN
HAMMICKS MOLITES NO 7
HAMMICKS MORILES NO 5
HAMMICKS MORILES NO 7
HARMITAGE
HARVEY'S BANK
HAU BRION
HAY
HEAVY WHISKY
HELDERBERG
HELPYERSEL
HERMITAGE [B]
HEYWARD
HIGHLAND
HIGHLAND LIQUEUR
HIGHLAND WHISKY
HINOJO
HIPPOCRAS
HOCHEIMER
HOCHHEIMER
HOCK [B]
HOCK.
HOCKHEIM
HOLLAND
HOLLANDS [B]
HOLL^{DS} GINN
HOME
HOME-MADE
HONEY [B]
HONGRIE
HUNGARY
HUNGARIAN
HUNGARIAN TAKAY or ST GEORGE
HYPOCRAS

I [B]
I Champaign. [B1]
I.V.
I.VERMOUTH
I.W.
I.WHISKEY [B]
I WHISKY
IDEAL
IMPERIAL
IMPERIAL PINTS / D & G 1880 / RAYNE BINNED 1891 [B1]
IMPERIAL PINTS / D & G 1884 / RAYNE BINNED 1892 [B1]
IMPERIAL PINTS / JULES MUMM 1884/85 / RAYNE BINNED 1892 [B1]
INA MADEIRA
INA SHERRY
IN^A SHERRY

INDIA
INDIA MADEIRA
INDIAN
INDIAN MADEIRA
INDIAN SHERRY
INGEFAER
INNISHOWEN
INTERNATIONAL
IONIA
IRISH
IRISH SETTER
IRISH W
IRISH WHISKEY
IRISH WHISKY
ISCHIA
ISLAY
ISLAY MALT WHISKY
IT
IT VERMOUTH
It.VERMOUTH
ITALIAN
ITALIAN VERMOUTH

J
J S BONTEIN
J. W. DENNISTOUN
JAMAICA
JEREZ
Jernvägs:B^V (Unidentifiable joined up script)
JERNVEGSBRÄNNVIN
JINEVRA
JOHANESBERG
JOHANNESBURG [B]
JOHANNISBERG [B]
JOHANNISBURG
JRISH WHISKEY
JUBILES
JULES MUMM 1884/85
JUNIPER
JURANCON
JURANSON
JURANSON BLANC

K
Kaapsche Pontac (script)
Kaapsche Sherrij (script)
KEFFESIA
KERES
KERVASER
KHOOSH
KIMEL
KIMMEL
KINGS CUP
KINGS PORT
KIRCCH WASSER
KIRCHENWASER
KIRCHEVASSER
KIROCHWASSER
KIRSCH [B]
KIRSCH A WASSER

KIRSCH 1850
KIRSCH WASSER
KIRSCH-WASSER
KIRSCHENWASER
KIRSCHENWASSER
KIRSCHWASSER
KIRSEBAER
KIRSIIWASSER
KITCHEN BRANDY [B]
KOHNSTAMM [B1]
KUEMMELL
KUHMEL
KÜMEL
KUMMEL
KÜMMEL
KUMMEL P. B.
KUMMELL
KUMMIN
KUMMIN.
KURAMEL
KUYPER HOLLANDS [B1]

L
L. BRANDY
L. CHRISTIE
L. PORT
L. SHRUB
L'HERMITAGE
LA COMENDERIE
LA COTE
LA CÔTE
LA FILLE
LA FITTE
LA MALGUE
LA ROSE
LA VAUX
LACHRIMA CHRISTI
LACHRYM AE CHRISTI
LACHRYMA
LACHRYMAE
LACHRYMAE CHRISTI
LACKRYMA
LACRIMA
LACRIMA CHRISTI
LACRIME CRISTE
LAFFITTE
LAFITE
LAFITTE
LAGAVULIN
LAGRANGE
LAGRIMA CHRISTI
LAMALGUE
LAMALQUE
LAMBRUSCO
LANALQUE
LANGON
LANGUEDOC ROUGE
LANQUEDOC ROUGE
LAROSE [B]
LATOUR
LAVRADIO

391

Appendix 1 - Names

LE DE NON	MADEIRA **[B]**	MALVASIA DE SITGES
LE VIN CLAIRET	Madeira **[B1]**	MALVASIA DI MADERA
LEAGUS	MADEIRA (in Greek lettering)	MALVEZIE
LENTOLACCIO	MADEIRA & LIQUEUR	MALVOISE MADEIRA **[B1]**
LEOVILLA	MADEIRA / ATHENÆUM	MALVOISEE
LEOVILLE **[B]**	MADEIRA C	MALVOISIE
LEOVITTA	MADEIRA 1818 / FROM THE ISLAND **[B1]**	MALVOISIE de MADERE
LICQUER		MANDARINETTE
LIDENON	MADEIRA 1820 **[B1]**	MANEATER
LIEBFRAUENMILCH **[B]**	MADEIRA 1860 / FROM THE ISLAND **[B1]**	MANHATTAN
LIGHT CLARET		MANSANILLA
LIGHT PORT	MADEIRA 1862 / FROM THE ISLAND **[B1]**	MANZANILLA
LIGHT WINE		MANZANILLA DRY
LILLET	MADEIRA PRESIDENT USA / COSSART GORDON BINNED 1896 **[B1]**	MANZANILLO
LIQUER		MANZILLA
LIQUER BRANDY		MARACHINO
LIQUERE	MADEIRA SERCIAL	MARAS^C
LIQUEUR	MADEIRY	MARASCHINI
LIQUEURS **[B1]**	MADERA	MARASCHINO
LIQUEUR BRANDY	MADERAWIJN	MARASQUE
LIQUEUR BRANDY / RAYNE BINNED 1892 **[B1]**	MADERE	MARASQUIN
	MADÈRE	MARASQUINA
LIQUEUR D'OR	MÁDERE	MARASQUINO
LIQUEUR de BIRSE	MADERE VIEUX **[B1]**	Marasquino.
LIQUEUR DES-ISLES	MADÈRE / Vieux	MARAVELLA
LIQUEURS	MADERIA **[B]**	MARC
LIQUOR	MADEWINE	MARC VIEUX
LIQUOR BRANDY 1801. **[B1]**	MADIERA	MARCALLA
LISBON **[B]**	MAGNUMS / CHATEAU LANGOA 1875 / BUCKLER BINNED 1896 **[B1]**	MARCEILLES
LISBON COLLARES		MARCELAS **[B1]**
LISSA		MARCELLA **[B]**
LISSA PORT **[B1]**	MAHON	MARCELLAS
LITTLE MOUSE	MAHONEY BOY	MARCELLA'^S
LOCHLOMOND	MAILLY	MARCELLE
LOIRE **[B]**	MAJORCA	MARCLLA
LOMBOCK	MAL. MADEIRA	MARCO BRUNNER **[B1]**
LONDON	MALAGA **[B]**	MARCOBRUNNER
LORD BENTINCK	MALAGA D'AMSTERDAM	MARESCHINO
LORD ROUSSILLON	MALAGA ROUGE	MARGAUX
Lt. CLARET	MALEGO	MARGAUX 1861 **[B1]**
LUNEILLE	MALLAGA	MARGRAVIAT
LUNEL **[B]**	MALLAGA SECT	MARIE BRIZARD ANISETTE
LUNELL	MALMSAY **[B1]**	MARIE-BRIZARD
LUNELLE **[B]**	MALMSAY, MADEIRA **[B1]**	MARQUIS OF TITCHFIELD
LUTOMER	MALMSEY **[B]**	MARRASQUI
LYSHOLMER	MALMSEY / RAYNE BINNED 1895 **[B1]**	MARRAVELLA
		MARSAILES
M	MALMSEY DRY	MARSALA **[B]**
M. C. W.	MALMSEY MADEIRA	MARSALA.
M. MADEIRA	MALMSEY RICH	MARSALLA **[B]**
M. P. M.	MALMSLAY	MARSEILLA
M. PUNCH	MALMSLY	MARSEILLES
M:PUNCH	MALMSY	MARSELA
M / T	MALMSY MADEIRA	MARSELLA
M WINE	MALMSY RICH	MARSELLAS
M,WINE	MALSMEY	MARSELLIA
MACABER	MALT	MARSELLIS
MACABOR	MALT WINE	MARSOLA
MACON	MALUS: MADEIRA	MARTINI
MADAIRA	MALVAGIA DE MADERE	MASALA
MADE WINE	MALVASIA	MASDEN **[B1]**

MASDEU
MASDIEU
MASDU
MASDUE
MASSALA **[B]**
MASSELA
MAUMSELL MADEIRA
MAZZARA
MEAD
MEAD COCKTAIL
MEADERA
MEDEARY
MEDEIRA
MEDERE, PAGLIARINO
MEDERIA
MEDFORD
MEDINA
MEDIRA
MEDOC **[B]**
MELNIEK
MELOMEL
MENA
MENDIA
MENTHE
MERICA
MERIFICA **[B1]**
MERISICA
MESSINA
METHEGLIN
METHUEN
METHUIN
MILDALE
MILK PUNCH
MILLBURN
MINT
MINTE
MIRABELLE
MIRABOLANTE
Mirobolanty
MISCHANZA
MISCHIANZA
MKI
MKII
Mk PUNCH
MOESEL
MOET & CHANDON 1884
MOKA
MOLESCOT
MONALTA
MONHYLIANA **[B1]**
MONROSE
MONT RACHE
MONT RACHET
MONTAGNE
MONTALLAS **[B1]**
MONTBLAIRY
MONTE CATINI
MONTE CATTINI
MONTE LEADO
MONTE PULCIANO
MONTESQUIEUE

MONTFERRATO
MONTI PULEHANO
MONTILLA
MONTILLA SHERRY
MONTILLADO
MONTILLIO
MONTILLO
MONTIS **[B1]**
MONTPELIER
MONTPILLIAR **[B1]**
MONTRACHET
MORACHE
MORACHEE
MORACHET
MORACHEZ
MORASCHINO
MORAT
MORILES SHERRY
MÖRK COGNAC
MOSC^O DI CIPRO
MOSCATO DI CIPRO
MOSEL
MOSELL **[B]**
MOSELLA
MOSELLE **[B]**
MOSELLE, BRAUNEBERG.
MOSELLE, OBEREMMEL. **[B1]**
MOSELLS
MOSELWEIN
MOSSEL
MOSSELLE
MOTHERS RUIN
MOUNT
MOUNT ÆTNA CREMO
    DI, VINO.
MOUNT ÆTNA RED TOKAY.
MOUNTAIN **[B]**
MOUNTAIN DEW
MOUNTAIN Frisby **[B1]**
MOUNTIN
MOUNT^N
MOURACHE
MOURACHE ROUGE
MOYEAU
MOZELLE
MR. ALLSOPP
MR. HENDRIE
MR. SNODGRASS
M^r. Snodgrass (script)
MR. TARRATT
MR. TARRATTE
MRS. M. WHYLOCK / HOME
    MADE WINE
MRS. TRAVERS
M^S.
MT
MULSAUT
MULSEAU
MULSEAUX
MUNK
MUNK LIKOR

MURACHE
MURATORE
MURON
MURSEAULT BLANC
MUSCADELL
MUSCADINA
MUSCAT
MUSCAT / LUNEL
MUSCAT LUNEL **[B]**
MUSCAT LUNELL **[B1]**
MUSCAT BLANC
MUSCAT DE FRONTIGNAN
MUSCAT DE FRONTIGNE
MUSCAT DE LUNEL
MUSCAT DE PERALTO
MUSCATEL **[B]**
MUSCATELLA
MUSCATELLE
MUSGAT DE FRONTIGUAU
MUSIGNY
MUSKADELLA
MUSKAT
MUSKATEL
MUSKATVIN

N
N. PUNCH
NATIVE
NECKAR **[B]**
NECTARINE
NECTOR
NEECE
NEICE
NEIERSTEINER / RAYNE
    BINNED 1892 **[B1]**
NELSON
NEUCHATEL
New:Madaira.
NEWTONIA
NICE **[B]**
NICE WINE
NICHOLAY
NIEPOORT'S / PORT
NIERSTEIN REISLING 1884
NIERSTEINER **[B]**
NIERSTEINER / RAYNE BINNED
    1892 **[B1]**
NIG
NIZZA
N^O 1
NO 1 CLARET
NO 1 MADEIRA
N^O 1 PORT **[B1]**
NO.1 SHERRY
NO 2 CLARET
NO 2 GIN
NO 2 MADEIRA
NO. 2 SHERRY
No. 3. BURTON. ALE.
N^O 3 PORT **[B1]**
No. 3 Madeira 159 **[B1]**

Appendix 1 - Names

No.4.SHERRY.
No. 5 Claret 283 **[B1]**
No. 7 Packaretta 147 **[B1]**
No. 11 PORT **[B1]**
No. 11 Sherry 317 **[B1]**
N⁰. 12 PORT **[B1]**
No. 15 Hermitage 32 **[B1]**
No. 16 Chabley 21 **[B1]**
No. 17 Pontac 34 **[B1]**
No. 19 HOCK 19 **[B1]**
No. 20 Pontac 152 **[B1]**
1 .... 122 (All these numerals occur as individual bin labels) **[B1]**
NOIEAU
NOISET
NORFOLK
NORFOLK 1799
NOUSSA
NOYAU
NOYEA
NOYEAN
NOYEAU
NOYEO
NOYEU
NUIS
NUIT
NUITS **[B]**

O
O. BRANDY
O. D.V.
O. D.V. DE DANZIC
O,O,PORT
O. PORT
O=SHRUB
O.W.
O. WHISKY
OBERMMEL
OBRION
OBRYON
ODÅKRA
OEIL DE, / PERDUX,CHAMPAGNE. **[B1]**
OFNER
O^GE GIN
Old Brown Cognac
OLD BROWN SHERRY / RAYNE BINNED 1892 **[B1]**
OLD CLARET
OLD HOCK **[B]**
OLD-HOCK
OLD. HOCK
OLD J.
OLD MOUNTAIN
Old Pale Cognac
OLD PALE SHERRY
OLD PAXARETE
OLD PORT **[B]**
OLD RUM **[B]**
OLD SHERRY **[B]**

OLD SNEED COCKTAIL
OLD TOM
OLD WHISKEY
OLLIVER RILY
OLO ROSO
OLOROSO
OMNIUM
OPORT
OPORTO
ORANGE **[B]**
ORANGE BITTERS
ORANGE BRANDY
ORANGE CURACAO
ORANGE GIN
ORANGE LIQUEUR
ORANGE SHRUB **[B]**
ORANGE SIRUP
ORANGE WHISKEY
ORANGE WINE
ORANGESHRUB
ORRINGE
ORIS
OUISETTE D'ORANGE
OVILE
OYRAS

P
P. CHAMPAGNE
P. SHERRY
PACARET
PACAROTTI **[B]**
PACARSSTI
PACCARET
PACCARETT
PACCAROTTI **[B1]**
PACCARROTTI
PACCHEROITE
PACHARETTA **[B1]**
PACHERETTI
PACKERETTA
PACKERETTE
PAGARÈS
PAID
PAJARETE
PAJARETTE
PAKARET
PAKE
PALATINATE
PALE BRANDY
PALE SHERRY **[B]**
PALIARATTA
PALME
PALMELLA
PALMER, CHT
PALMY DAYS
PANDO
PAPE CLÉMENT **[B]**
PAQUARET
PAQUARETE
PARFAIT AMOUR
PARFAITE AMOUR

PARSNIP
PARTNERS
PASS THE BOTTLE
PASTO
PATRAS
PAUILLAC **[B1]**
PAXARETE
PAXARETTA
PAXARETTE
PAXARETTI
PAXARITE
PAXARITTA
PAXAROTTA
PAXERETTE
PAXERITTA
PEACH
PEACH BITTERS
PEACH BRANDY
PEARL OF RHINE **[B1]**
PEAU D'ESPAGNE
PEDRO JIMENEZ
PEDRO XIMENEZ
PEDRO XIMINEZ
PEDRO-DI-CHINNES
PEDRO•DI•CHINNES **[B1]**
PEI XIMELES
PEPPER WINE
PEPPERMINT
PERALTA
PERALTE
PÉRE KERMAN
PERIGNAC
PERPIGNAN
PERRY **[B]**
PERSICO
PERSICOA
PICARDON
PICCOLIT DE L'ANNÉE
PICO
PICOLITO **[B]**
PIERRY
PIMMS NO. 1
PINE APPLE RUM
PINEAPPLE RUM
PINTS / D & G 1880 / RAYNE BINNED 1890 **[B1]**
PINTS / MOET & CHANDON 1884 / RAYNE BINNED 1892 **[B1]**
PINTS / NEIERSTEINER / RAYNE BINNED 1892 **[B1]**
PISCO
PLAIN SHERRY
PLONK
PLUM RUM
PLUMB BRANDY
PLYMOUTH
PLYMOUTH GIN
POMAR
POMARD
POMERANS
POMERANZ

Appendix 1 - Names

POMINO
POMMERANS
POMMERANZ
POMONE
PONG WONG
PONTAC
PONTAC 2,^(DE) QUALITE'
PONTAC P,^(RE) QUALITE'
PONTE
PONTET CANET
POPT
POR
PORNIAC [B1]
PORT [B]
PORT A [B1]
PORT À PORT
PORT A. L.
PORT B [B1]
PORT COCKBURN / 1812
PORT COCKBURN 1912 [B1]
PORT 1812
PORT 1840
PORT 1847 [B1]
PORT 1851 / DAVISON BINNED 1890 [B1]
PORT NO. 1
PORT NO. 9
PORT SECCO
PORT URQUHART [B1]
PORT VEIN
PORT VIIN
PORT VIN
PORT WEIN
PORT-WIN
PORT WINE
Portwine. (in Cyrillic lettering)
PORT=VIIN
PORTAPORT
PORTER
PORTER. [B1]
PORTIVEIN
PORTO
PORTO PAXARETE [B1]
Porto / Paxarete
PORTO ROUGE
PORTO SEABRA
PORTO SECCO
PORTUGAL
PORTVIIN
PORTVIN
PORTVIN.
PORTWEIN
PORT-WIJN
PORTWIN
PORT-WIN
PORTWYN
POTIEN
POTTEEN
POTURON
POUILLAC [B1]
Pouillac

PREGNAC
PREIGNAC
PREIGNAC 1818 [B1]
PREIGNACK
PREIGNAT
PREMIER CLARET
PREMIER HOCK
PRENIAC
PRIEST
PRIGNAC
PRIGNAE
PRIGNIAC
PRINIAC [B]
PRINIACK
PRIOSATO
PRUNELLE
PRUNES
PRUNIAC
PRYNILL
PTISSANE ROYALE
PUCURET
PULSFORDS PORT 1812 [B1]
PUNCH
PUNSCH
PYMENT

Q
QUARTS / D & G 1884 / RAYNE BINNED 1888 [B1]
QUEENS HOCK
QUEENS PORT
QUESTCHE
QUETSCH
QUETSCHE
QUILERN
QUINCE
QUINQUINA
QUINTA DE PONTE
QUINTA. DE. PONTE
QUINTA DE PORTO
QUUETCHÉ

R
R. BRANDY
R. CAPE [B1]
R. CHAMPAGNE
R. CHAMPAIGN
R. CONSTANTIA
R. CURRANT
R. HERMITAGE
R. HERM^T
R. NOIOU
R. PORT
R+PORT
R★PORT
R-PORT
R. S.
R. SHRUB
R=SHRUB
RACK
RAISEN

RAISIN [B]
RAISIN W.
RAISIN WINE [B]
RAISON
RAKI
RALPH JAMES & ROBERT
RÅNÄS
RANCIAUX
RANCIE
RANCIO
RANCIOT
RANSFORD
Rare-FANK-Old
RARE OLD FANK
RASBERRY
RASIN
RASIN WINE
RASP BRANDY
RASPAIL
RASPBERRY
RASPBERRY BRANDY
RASPBERRY WHISKEY
RASPBRANDY
RAT
RATAFIA
RATAFIA DE CERISES
RATAFIA DE DANTZIC
RATAFIA DE DANZIG
RATAFIA DE FLEUR / D'ORANGE
RATAFIE
RATIFEE
RATIFIA
RATIFIE
RATIFIE. [B1]
RATTAFIER
RATTFIA
RATZERSDORF
RAUZAN
Rd. CONSTANTIA
R^D PORT
REASIN
RED
RED BURGUNDY
RED CAPE
RED CHAMPAGNE
RED CHAMPAIGNE [B1]
RED CHAMPA^N
RED CONSTANTIA
RED CONSTANTIAN [B1]
RED COTE ROTIE [B1]
RED CURRANT [B]
RED HERMITAGE
RED HOCK
RED MADEIRA
RED MAJORCA
RED NEICE
RED NOYAU
RED PORT
RED◆PORT
RED⁻PORT

395

Appendix 1 - Names

RED WINE
REDEMPTINE
REDRO DI CHINNES **[B1]**
REFOSCO DEL ANNÉE
REGENT
REIGNAC
REIN
REINA
RENADT
RENAT
RENISH
RENISH WINE **[B1]**
RENNO
RENO
RENSWIN
RERES
REVESALTI
RHEIN
RHEINISH
RHEINWEIN
RHENISH **[B]**
RHIN
RHINSKIVIIN
RHONE
RHUBARB **[B]**
RHUM
RHUM BACARDI **[B]**
RICELING
RIESLING
RIN
RIN WINE
RIO TORTO 1820
RIOJA CLARET
RIVERHEAD
RIVESALTE
RIVESATTE
ROB ROY
ROBERTSON'S PORT
ROCAMADORA
RØD
ROD WIIN
RODEGO
RÖDT
RÖDTVIN
RÖDVIN
ROMANEE
ROMANEE CONTI **[B1]**
Romanée Conti
ROMM
Romm (script)
ROMMSINT
ROQUEMAURE
ROSA
ROSTER
ROTA
ROTA ROUGE
ROTA TENT
ROTTA
ROUBLON
ROUSILLON
ROUSSILLION

ROUSSILLON **[B]**
ROYAL
RÜDESHEIM
RUDESHEIMER **[B]**
RUIN
RUM
Rum **[B1]**
RUM. **[B1]**
RUM SHRUB
RUSTER AUSBRUCH
Ry. BRANDY
RYALL SPECIAL
RYE
RYE GIN
RYE WH.
RYE WHISKY

S
S. BEER
S / CHAMPAGNE
S. CHAMPAGNE
S. EMELION
S. GIN
S W
S.W
S / WHISKEY
S. WHISKEY **[B]**
S-WINE
SACK **[B]**
SACK Lord March **[B1]**
SACK MEAD
SACK METHEGLIN
SACKE
Sädes (letters in an unidentifiable script)
SAINT-ESTÈPHE
SAINT GEORGE
SAINT PERE
SAINT-CHRISTOL **[B]**
SAMO
SAMOS
SAMUR
SAN LORANO
SANCTA
SANDEMAN'S PORT
SANDIMAN'S PORT / RAYNE BINNED 1892 **[B1]**
SANTA
SANTENAY
SANTO
SANTO VIN
SANTO-BIANCO
SANTO-NERO
SANTORIA
SANTORIN
SANTORNEI
SARCEAL
SARÇEAL
SATUERNE
SATURN
SAUMAR

SAUMUR
SAUTERINE
SAUTERN
SAUTERNE **[B]**
SAUTERNES
SAUTRNE
SAUTURN
SAVOCA **[B]**
SAYES
SCHARSHOPBURG **[B1]**
SCHEEDAM GENEVA
SCHEIDAM
SCHEIDAM GENEVA (or maybe SCHEIDAM GENEVA / FROM HOLLAND)
SCHERRY
SCHERRY.
SCHIEDAM
SCHIRAZ
SCHUSELAN
SCHUSELANE
SCICELY
SCOPOLI
SCOTCH
SCOTCH ALE **[B1]**
SCOTCH W.
SCOTCH WHISKEY
SCOTCH WHISKY
SCUBAC
SCYES
SECK
SECOND PORT
SEDYSE
SEGES **[B]**
SEGUS
SEITGES
SELLERY
SENTENAY
SERCHALL
SERCHIALL
SERCIAL
SERCIAL MADEIRA
SETGES **[B]**
SETJUS
SETUBAL
SETUBAL DE PORTUGAL
SETUVAL
SÉVÉ
SEVILLIA
SEYES
SHARRY
SHERREY
SHERRIJ
SHERRY **[B]**
SHERRY / ATHENÆUM
SHERRY.
SHERRY BRANDY
SHERRY 1833 **[B1]**
SHERRY 1834 **[B1]**
SHERRY MORO
SHERRY SACK

Appendix 1 - Names

SHERRY / 2
Sherry 239 **[B1]**
SHERRY VENTAGE **[B1]**
SHIRAZ
SHRUB **[B]**
SIAGES
SICHES
SICILE
Sicilian.
SICILLY
SICILY
SIEGES
SIETGES
SILERY
SILLERY
SILLERY CHAMPAGNE **[B]**
SILS
SILY
SILY CHAMPAGNE
SILy CHAMPe
SIRCEAL
SITGES
SITZES
SKÅNE
SKYDAM
SLOE
SLOE GIN **[B]**
SLOE WINE
SMYRNA
SMYRNA WINE
SOLERA
SOLFERINO
SOMA
Somme.
SOTERN
SOTERNE
SOUMUR
SOUTERN
SOUTERNE
SOUTHERN
SPANISH
SPANISH MADEIRA
SPANISH WINE
SPARKLING CHAMPAGNE
SPARKLING HERMITAGE
SPARKLING HOCK **[B]**
SPARKLING HOCK VENTAGE **[B1]**
SPARKLING MOSELLE **[B]**
SPIRITS
SPOONER SHERRY **[B]**
SPRUCE
ST. ELIE (or ST ELIE?)
ST. EMËLION
ST EMILION **[B]**
ST ESTEPHE **[B1]**
ST. ESTEPHE
ST. GEORGE
S,T GEORGE
St. GEORGE
ST. GEORGES

ST. JOSEPH
ST JULIEN **[B1]**
ST. JULIEN
S,T LAURENT
St LORENT DU REIN (period is exactly below superscript t)
ST. MAMSEY **[B1]**
ST. PERAIS
ST PERAY **[B1]**
St. PERAY
St. PERAZ
ST. PEREST
ST. PERET
ST. PEREY
ST PEREZ
S.t PEREZ
St. PEROY
St. PERRET
ST. PERRET
S. T. PERRY
STARBOARD LIGHT
STEEN
STEIN
STEINBERG
STEINBERG CABINET **[B]**
STEINE
STEIN-WEIN
STEINWEIN
STIKELSBAERVIN
STILL HOCK
STISTED
STOUT
STRABOS WINE
STRAWBERRY
STRAWBERRY BRANDY
STRONG BEER
STRONG WHITE WINE
STUBAC
STYER
STYNE
SULTANA
SV. BANCO
SWARD-VINBÅR
SWEAT / CHAMPAIGNE
SWEET
SWEET CHAMPAGNE
SWEET DRAM
SWEET LISBON
SWEET MALAGA **[B1]**
SWEET PORT
SWEET W
SWEET WINE
SWEET-WINE
SWEETWINE
SWT. CHAMPAGNE
SYDER
SYRACUSE **[B]**
SYRGIS

T
T. SACK **[B]**
T. STEVENS
TAFIA
TAITSING
TANAZON
TANGERINA
TANGERINE
TANGERINE GIN
TARRAGONA
TAVEL
TAWNY PORT
TENEDOS
TENERIEFE
TENERIEFF
TENERIFE
TENERIFF
TENERIFFE **[B]**
TENIRIEFE
TENNERIFFE
TENT **[B]**
TENT Berkeley Square **[B1]**
TENTILLA
TERMEAU
TERMO
TERRANTEZ
TESSY
THE ABBOTS BOTTLE
THE ANTIQUARY
THE DUKE 1812
THE OLD
THE OLD KIRK
THE USUAL
THERA
THISTLE JUICE
THOMPSON'S GRAND / HIGHLAND LIQUEUR
THOMPSONS GRAND HIGHLAND LIQUEUR
THORNES KILTY WHISKY
TINDA
TINE
TINERIFFE
TINTA
TINTA MADEIRA
TINTIGLIA DE ROTTA
TINTILLA
TINTILLA DE ROTA
TINTO **[B]**
TINTO DE ROTA
TINTO MADEIRA
TINTOT **[B]**
TIO PEPE
TISANNE DE CHAMPAGNE
TOAST
TODDY
TOKAY **[B]**
TOKE
TOKEY **[B]**
TOM GIN
TONNERE

397

Appendix 1 - Names

Tonnerre
TONNERT
TOQUAY
TORINO
TORRIN
TOUR [B1]
TOURIGA
TOURNEAU
TOURS
TRAPPISTINE
TRIA JUNCTO IN UNO
TRIPLE SEC
TURANFON BLANC
TURIN
TURMEAU
TUSCANY
TWELFTH NIGHT
27 MAGNUMS [B1]
2 BEER [B1]
2 PORT

U
UISG NABA
UISGEBEATHA
UNSD. GIN (or UNS. GIN)
UNSP$^{D.}$ GIN
USQUEBAUGH

V [B]
V. DE-GRAVE
VAL DE PENAS
VAL DE PINHAS
VALEDPÉNAS
VALLENAY
VALMUR
VALPOLICELLA
VAN DE PURLL
VAN DER HORN
VANDEGRAVE
VANDUHUN
VAR [B]
VARGES [B1]
VEDONIA
VELHEDRO
VERDAGLIO
VERDEILHA
VERDELHO
VERES
VERGUN
VERGUS
VERJUICE
VERMOUTH [B]
VERMOUTH / FRENCH
VERMOUTH / ITALIAN
VERMOUTH DRY
VERMOUTH FRANCAIS
VERMOUTH / FRANÇAIS
VERMOUTH IT
VERMOUTH SEC
VERMUTE
VERSENET

VERY OLD PORT [B1]
VERY / OLD. PORT.
VERZENAY
VESPETRO
VHISKEY
V^{HO} ROMANO
VICTORY
VIDONA
VIDONIA [B]
VIEILLE CURE
VIELLE-CURE
VIENNE VERGUS
VIEUX COGNAC
VIEUX MARC
VIN
VIN / POUR / VINAIGRE
VIN D'ALOQUE
VIN d'ECOSSE
VIN D'ESPAGNE [B1]
VIN DE BEAUNE ROUGE
VIN DE BORDEAUX PONT
 CARRÉ
VIN DE BOURGOGNE
VIN DE BURGOGNE
VIN DE CAP
VIN DE CHAMBERTIN
VIN DE CHAMPAGNE
VIN DE CHAMPAGNE ROSSET
VIN DE CHAMPAGNE ROUGE
VIN DE CHARES
VIN DE CHERES
VIN DE CLOS VOUGEOT
 ROUGE
VIN DE GRAIR
VIN DE GRAVE [B]
VIN·DE·GRAVE
VIN DE GRAVES
VIN DE GREVE
VIN DE GREVO
VIN,DE,LA BLONDE
VIN DE LA COTE [B1]
VIN DE LAGRIMAS
VIN DE L'HERMITAGE
VIN DE LUNELLE
VIN DE MADERE SEC
VIN DE MALAGA
VIN DE MALVOISIE DE
 MADERE
VIN DE MEDOC
VIN DE MOESELLE
VIN DE MOSELLE
VIN DE MUSCADE
VIN DE MUSCAT DE MALAGA
VIN DE MUSCAT GREC
VIN DE NUIS
VIN DE PAILE [B1]
VIN DE PALLAS [B1]
VIN DE PERNIS [B1]
VIN DE PASTO
VIN DE PAYS
VIN DE PIRCARET

VIN DE PROVINCE
VIN DE PURLL
VIN DE RHIN
VIN DE SCOPOLO
VIN DE ST VALLERY
VIN DE TAVEL
VIN,DE,TAVEL
VIN DE TOKAI
VIN DE VERGE [B1]
VIN DE VERMONT
VIN DE VERSÈNE
VIN DE VIERGE
VIN DI GRAVE
VIN DI PASTO
VIN DU PAYS
VIN-DU-PAYS
VIN DU RHIN
VIN DU RHYN
VIN ORDINAIRE [B]
VIN POUR VINAIGRE [B1]
VIN VIERGE
VINAM
VINDEGRAVE
VINE DE GRAVE
VINO CLARETE
VINO DE PASTO
VINO DE XERES SECO
VINO DELLA BOYSSONADE
VINO DI BELLAGIO
VINS DE LOQRIMAS
VINTAGE
VINTAGE 1834
VINTAGE PORT
VIRGINIA
VIRMOUTH
VODKA
VOLLENAY
VOLNAY
VOLUAIJ
VOSNE
VYDONIA

W
W. C. SHRUB
W. CONSTANTIA
W. CONSTANTINE
W. CURRANT
W. HERMITAGE
W. HERM^{T}
W. I. MADEIRA [B]
W. NOIOU
W. NOYEAU
W PORT
W. PORT
W. SHRUB
W. WINE
WALPORZEIM
W^{E} PORT
WEBBER
WEISSENWEIN
WELSH WHISKEY

398

WEYR-MOUTH
WH. HERMITAGE
WH. WINE
WH^E WINE
WHI: WINE
WHISKEY **[B]**
WHISKEY 1846
WHISKY **[B]**
Whisky
WHITE
WHITE BORDEAUX
WHITE BRANDY **[B1]**
WHITE BURGONDY
WHITE BURGUNDY
White Burgundy **[B1]**
WHITE CAPE
WHITE CHAMPAGNE
WHITE CLARET
WHITE CONSTANTIA
WHITE CURACOA
WHITE CURRANT **[B]**
WHITE HERMITAGE **[B]**
WHITE-HERMITAGE
WHITE LISBON
WHITE MAJORCA

WHITE PORT **[B]**
WHITE PORT WINE
WHITE PORTVINE
WHITE SATIN
WHITE WHISKEY
WHITE WIN
WHITE WIN (with ^{E} above the I of second word)
WHITE WINE **[B]**
WHITExWINE (note cross instead of period)
WHITE◆WINE
WHKSE
WHYSKY
WIDONIA
WIGHT
WIJN
WILLIAMS & HUMBERT / SHERRY
WINDSOR
WINE
WISKEY
WISKIE
WITARNA
WT. BURGUNDY

Wt. CONSTANTIA
W^T PORT

X
XALOQUE
XERES
XERÈS
XÉRÈS
XERES ZEKA
XEREZ
Xeres. (in Cyrillic lettering)

Y **[B]**
YAP
YGNEM **[B]**
YQUEM
YVOINE **[B]**
YVORNE

Z
ZANTE
ZANTERA
ZELTINGEN
ZERRY
"Zq"

TOTAL NUMBER OF NAMES INCLUDING SINGLE LETTERS: 2353
BIN LABELS: 305

APPENDIX 2

MAKERS OF WINE LABELS

Makers whose marks have been recorded on wine labels, with the dates during which they were active, or the recorded date of the label. All dates given are approximate. The use of circa indicates a likelihood of imprecision. Thus this list is only a general guide.

The list includes makers whose marks overstamp those of the original manufacturer, or are found on labels manufactured by another hand, but it does not include labels for assay, or from other sources as having manufactured them, but for whom no examples are known at the present time. Nor does it generally include makers to whom attribution of a mark is doubtful or uncertain.

Maker	Town	Recorded Dates		Died	Illustration
		First	Last		Fig. No.
Begg, James	Aberdeen	1837	1844	1844	
Booth, G. & Booth, A.A.	Aberdeen	1826	1850		
Booth, George	Aberdeen	1801	1826		
Byres, William	Aberdeen (and Banff)	1792	1811	1811	
Douglas, James	Aberdeen (and Edinburgh, Dundee)	1810	1811		
Erskine, James	Aberdeen	1796	c.1820		889, 890
Ewen, John	Aberdeen	c.1770	c.1820	1821	
Fillan, William	Aberdeen	1839	1845		
Fray, J.	Aberdeen	c.1780	c.1790		
Garden, John	Aberdeen	1825	1840	1841	
Gillett, Nathaniel	Aberdeen	1786	1824	c.1841	
Gordon, James (I)	Aberdeen	1766	1810	1810	891
Jamieson, George	Aberdeen	1840	1845		
Jamieson, William	Aberdeen	1806	1840	1841	
Leslie, John	Aberdeen (and Montrose)	1774	1821	1837	
Rettie, James	Aberdeen	1845	1847	1896	
Rettie, M. & Son	Aberdeen	1824	1847		
Rettie, M. & Sons	Aberdeen	1847	1892		
Steiner, Henry	Adelaide	1860	1870		1306, 1307
Wendt, Jochim Matthias	Adelaide	1860	1870		
Gerritsen, Johannes A.A.	Amsterdam (Zeist)	1906	1919		1371
Kikkert, J.F.	Amsterdam	1906	1923		1368
Lintveld, Harmanus	Amsterdam	1817	1833		
Van Maarseveen, Petrus F.	Amsterdam	1883	1892		1375, 1376
Davidson, Alexander	Arbroath	1835	1858		900
Verhoef, Manicus	Arnhem	1880	1890		1366, 1367
Argo, J.	Banff	c.1771	c.1795		
Byres, William	Banff (and Aberdeen)	1778	1792		
Elder, George	Banff	1819	1852		
Keith, John	Banff	c.1789	1825	1823	
MacQueen, John	Banff	c.1816	1839		
Simpson, William (I)	Banff	1825	1855		254
Ford, J. & Williams, J.	Bath	1767	c.1785		738
Graham, T. & Willis, J.	Bath	1789	1792		737
Merrett, Peter	Bath	1793	c.1819		734, 736
Alder & Sons	Birmingham	1859			
Aston & Son	Birmingham	1857	1867		
Bartleet, T.	Birmingham	1812	1830		
Bennett, William	Birmingham	1796			803
Bettridge, John	Birmingham	c.1817			
Boulton & Fothergill	Birmingham	1765	1780		781, 782
Boulton, Matthew	Birmingham	1762	1809	1809	
Boulton, Matthew Plate Co.	Birmingham	1810	1830		783
Bower, John	Birmingham	1829			800
Brown & Clark	Birmingham	1851			

Appendix 2 - Makers

Maker	Town	Recorded Dates First	Recorded Dates Last	Died	Illustration Fig. No.
Brown, Joseph	Birmingham	1823	c.1839		
Burbridge, James	Birmingham	1773	1801		
Cheshire, C.H.	Birmingham	1865	1927		
Clark, Francis	Birmingham	1826			806
Cocks & Bettridge	Birmingham	1773	1801		
Cronin & Wheeler	Birmingham	1846			
Deakin & Francis	Birmingham	1892			
Elkington & Co.	Birmingham	1807	1910		36
Evans, S.F. & Co.	Birmingham	1894			
Foxall & Co.	Birmingham	1850			
Freeman, Thomas	Birmingham	1822			
Gilbert, John	Birmingham	1876	1900		45, 1372
Harwood, T. & Son	Birmingham	1864			
Hilliard, J. & Thomason, J.	Birmingham	1847	1888		50, 51, 54
Hukin & Heath	Birmingham	1909			
Lawrence, J. & Co.	Birmingham	1813			
Ledsam & Vale	Birmingham	1818			
Ledsam, Vale, Wheeler	Birmingham	1825			
Linwood, Matthew (I)	Birmingham	1773	1783	1783	
Linwood, Matthew (II)	Birmingham	1783	1821		182, 332, 333, 334, 784
Linwood, Matthew (III)	Birmingham	1821	1847	1847	
Manton, H. & Son	Birmingham	1832			
Mills, Nathaniel	Birmingham	1825	1831		354
Moore, John	Birmingham	1773		1801	
Owen, J. & Boon, W.H.	Birmingham	1856			
Pemberton, Samuel & Son	Birmingham	1821			
Richards, T.	Birmingham	1773	1800		
Robinson, Edkins & Aston	Birmingham	1834			
Spooner, William	Birmingham	1815			
Taylor, A.	Birmingham	1851	c.1865		
Taylor, Joseph	Birmingham (and London)	1773	1829	1829	327, 798, 801, 802, 883
Taylor & Perry	Birmingham	1829	1842		34, 789, 790, 796, 804
Thomason, Edward	Birmingham	1803	1830		
Thornton, John	Birmingham	1795			805
Thropp, J.	Birmingham	1814			
Tongue, John	Birmingham	1831	c.1863		
Turner and Simpson	Birmingham	1933	1960		63, 71, 72
Unite, G. and Hilliard, J.	Birmingham	1831	1832		785
Unite, George	Birmingham	1832	1861		40, 314, 346, 786, 787, 795, 797
Vale, Jabez	Birmingham	1813	1828		
Walton, G.E. & Co.	Birmingham	1890			
Wardell & Kempson	Birmingham	1814			791
Wheeler, Gervase	Birmingham	1831			
Wilkinson, T. & Co.	Birmingham	1835			
Willmore, Joseph	Birmingham	c.1807	1845	1855	276, 279, 288, 345, 792, 794
Willmore, Thomas	Birmingham	1773	1804		
Yapp & Woodward	Birmingham	1845	1874		
Lönberg, Peter Eduard	Borås	1834	1842		1427
Lyberg, Hans	Borås	1806	1848		1411, 1413, 1426

Appendix 2 - Makers

Maker	Town	Recorded Dates First	Recorded Dates Last	Died	Illustration Fig. No.
Sawin, Simon	Boston	c.1870	c.1890		
Farr, John	Bristol	c.1784	c.1795		729
Miller, G.	Bristol	c.1750	1764	1764	733
Sloden, William	Bristol	1764	c.1795		181, 728, 730, 731
Wigan, Thomas	Bristol	1763	c.1780		740
Williams, James & Josiah	Bristol	1854	c.1874		
Williams, Robert	Bristol	1832	1854		
Datalis, J.G.	Brussels	1820			1309
Hamilton & Co.	Calcutta	c.1830			355, 1357
Pittar & Co.	Calcutta	1830			1356
Twentyman, W.H., & Co.	Calcutta	1810	1830		
Lin, Chang	Canton	1845	1885		1315
Ahlers, Oltman	Cape Town	1810	1827		1398
Combrick, Johannes (I)	Cape Town	1810	1853		1396
Hockley, Daniel	Cape Town	1819	1835	1835	
Townsend, John and Thomas	Cape Town	1815	1830		1395
Townsend, Thomas	Cape Town	1830	1849		1397
Twentyman, Lawrence	Cape Town	1818	1832		1393, 1394
Huntington, Thomas	Carlisle	1811	1822		
Latimer, Joseph	Carlisle	1837	1839		
Ross, Thomas and Michael	Carlisle	1839	1843		
Wheatley, Thomas	Carlisle	1826	c.1860		
Schvart, Diedrich	Carlscrona	1806			1423
Boudo, Louis	Charleston	1786	1827		1439
Vernon, Nathaniel	Charleston	1802	1820		
Boulger, Robert	Chester	1791	1792		
Bowers, Robert	Chester	1782	1829	1829	
Coakley, John	Chester (Liverpool)	1828	1833		
Cunliffe, Nicholas	Chester (Liverpool)	c.1792	c.1835		694
Dixon, Joseph (II)	Chester	1814	1849		
Duke, Joseph (I) & (II)	Chester	c.1764	c.1810		703
France, James	Chester (Manchester)	1784	c.1819		705
Hardwick, William	Chester (Manchester)	c.1772	c.1781		
Hewitt, Joseph	Chester (Liverpool)	1789	c.1795		700
Hills, T.	Chester (Liverpool)	1789	1789		
Huntingdon, Mary	Chester	1815	1827		
Jones, Robert (I)	Chester (Liverpool)	1772	1826	1826	706
Jones, Robert (II)	Chester (Liverpool)	1826	1876		
Lowe, Edward	Chester	1800	1810		
Lowe, George (I)	Chester	1791	c.1840	1841	697, 698, 701
Lowe, George (II)	Chester	1827	c.1835		
Lowe, John and Thomas	Chester	c.1830	c.1840		
Lowe, Margaret and John	Chester	1962	1962		
Lowe, Robert	Chester	1831	1831		
Mordan, Sampson & Co.	Chester (and London)	1822	1941		709
Richardson, Richard (II), (III), (IV)	Chester	1732	c.1835		689-92, 695, 702, 704
Twemlow, John	Chester	1828	1828		
Twemlow, William	Chester	1787	1823		708
Walker, George (I)	Chester	1770	c.1806		
Walker, John (I)	Chester	1821	1821		
Walley, Joseph	Chester (Liverpool)	1760	1801	1801	707, 710
Carstens, Nicolai	Copenhagen	c.1820	c.1850		
Christensen, Nicolai	Copenhagen	1797	1832		
Kyhl, Peter	Copenhagen	1822	1847		
Prahl, Samuel	Copenhagen	1825	1853		
Gibson, Joseph	Cork	1784		1820	882, 918

Appendix 2 - Makers

Maker	Town	Recorded Dates First	Recorded Dates Last	Died	Illustration Fig. No.
Hillery, John	Cork	1756		1780	
Mahony Kean	Cork	1779	c.1824		
Martin, William	Cork	1716		1739	
Nicholson, John	Cork	1756	1805		
Nicholson, John & Nicholas	Cork	1807	c.1820		
Reynolds, William	Cork	1758	1790		114
Seymour, John	Cork	1809	1827		
Terry, Carden	Cork	1764	1807	1821	
Terry, Carden and Williams, Jane	Cork	1806	1821		
Teulon, William	Cork	1791	1844		
Tolekien, John	Cork	1795	1836		917
Walsh, Stephen	Cork	1747	1785		907, 908
Warner, James	Cork	1799	1830		
Warner, John	Cork	1775	1810		
Kalberg, Antonius A.	Den Bosch	1877	1908		1378
Innes, William	Dingwall	c.1804	c.1870		
Adams, Thomas	Dublin	1765	1812		
Beergin	Dublin	1824			
Calderwood, Robert	Dublin	1765			909
Cummins (Cumyng)	Dublin	1817			
Daffron, Joseph	Dublin	1784	1819		925
Eades, Christopher	Dublin	1818			
Egan, W. & Co.	Dublin	1973			402
Egar, John	Dublin	1804	c.1830		
Flavelle, Henry	Dublin	1821	1850		931
Fray, James	Dublin	1813	1842	1843	
Garde, R.	Dublin (Cork)	1809	1828		
Godfrey, Peter	Dublin	1816	1827		186
Goodwin, Andrew	Dublin	1730	1787		
Graham, John	Dublin	1765			180
Green, T.	Dublin	c.1790			
Haines, Christopher	Dublin	1788			
Ham(e)y, William	Dublin	1802	1809		
Hamy, W. & Le Bass, J.	Dublin	1812	1825		
Harris, Charles	Dublin	1809	1811		
Henfrey, Benjamin	Dublin	1784			
Hunt, Thomas	Dublin	1764	1812		
Jackson, Joseph	Dublin	1775	1809	1810	
Kavanagh, John	Dublin	1784	1807		
Keating, J.	Dublin				
Kehoe, Darby	Dublin	1765	c.1787	1800	
Law, S.	Dublin	1785			915
Law, William	Dublin	1774	c.1810	1820	911
Le Bass, James	Dublin	1795	1825	1845	928
Moulang, D. & Gibson, W.	Dublin	1830	1831		
Nangle, George	Dublin	1770	1816		912, 924
Nowlan, Lawrence	Dublin	1813	1840		
Nowlan, William	Dublin	1814	1845		
Osborne, John	Dublin	1787	1809		
Osborne, Thomas	Dublin	1820	1820		
Rice, T.	Dublin	1787	c.1795		
Sherwin, John	Dublin	c.1784	c.1805	c.1819	26, 214, 922, 923
Smith & Gamble	Dublin	1819	1835		272, 319, 910, 913
Smith, Richard West	Dublin	1818	c.1842		929
Stewart, Charles	Dublin	1803			

Appendix 2 - Makers

Maker	Town	Recorded Dates First	Recorded Dates Last	Died	Illustration Fig. No.
Taitt, Benjamin	Dublin	1763	1791		24, 215, 312, 322, 914, 916, 921, 927
Teare, Henry	Dublin	1814	1843		
Teare, John (I)	Dublin	c.1784	1811		920
Teare, John (II)	Dublin	1813	1860	1874	330
Teare, Samuel (I)	Dublin	1758	1811	1812	926, 930
Teare, Samuel (II)	Dublin	1796	1798		
Ticknell, Alex.	Dublin	1784	1788		
Townsend, Charles	Dublin	1770	1784		
Townsend, John	Dublin	1802	1855		
Townsend, Thomas	Dublin	1787	1812		
Tudor, Thomas	Dublin	1797	c.1821		
Tweedie, John	Dublin	1875			
Weathered, Joshua	Dublin	1823	c.1840		
West, George	Dublin	1792		1828	
West, John	Dublin	1762		1806	
Whitford, Richard	Dublin	1816			
Gray, David	Dumfries	1810	1841		
Hinchsliffe, M.	Dumfries	1820	1840		901
Pearson, Joseph	Dumfries	1794	1817		247
Austin, John	Dundee	c.1824			
Cameron, Alexander	Dundee	1818	1847		
Constable, William	Dundee	1806	1820		
Douglas, James	Dundee (and Edinburgh, Aberdeen)	1795			894
Elder, George	Dundee	1819	c.1843		
Kermath (or Kennoth), W.	Dundee	c.1830			
Lambert, Peter	Dundee, (and Montrose, Aberdeen)	1804	1816		893
Livingstone, Edward	Dundee	1790	1810		892
Manson, David	Dundee	1806	1820		
Scott, William (I)	Dundee	1774	1785		
Thompson, Samuel	Durham	1751	1785		
Auld, William	Edinburgh	1788	c.1800		219, 839
Aytoun, William	Edinburgh	1797			
Caw, J.B.	Edinburgh	1820			
Crichton, Walker	Edinburgh	c.1854			
Cunningham & Simpson	Edinburgh	1807			
Cunningham W. & P.	Edinburgh	1778	1803		
Cunningham, P. & Sons	Edinburgh	1808	c.1830		886
Cunningham, William	Edinburgh	1811	c.1825		843
Dalgleish, Charles	Edinburgh	1816			
Davie, William	Edinburgh	1740	c.1785		838
Dick & Macpherson	Edinburgh (and Kelso)	1807			834
Duke & Robinson	Edinburgh	c.1800			
Edmondson, Alexander	Edinburgh	1779	c.1820		
Elder, Adam	Edinburgh	1822	c.1840		
Fenwick, George	Edinburgh (and Tobago)	1807	c.1825		
Forrests, F.	Edinburgh	1821			
Frazer, Robert	Edinburgh	1824			835
Grierson, Robert	Edinburgh	1805			881
Hamilton & Inches	Edinburgh	1879	1910		
Hay, John	Edinburgh (Leith)	1810	c.1820		
Henderson, Alex.	Edinburgh	1812			
Heron, John	Edinburgh	1800			
Home, James	Edinburgh	1817	c.1830		

Appendix 2 - Makers

Maker	Town	Recorded Dates First	Recorded Dates Last	Died	Illustration Fig. No.
Howden, Francis	Edinburgh	1781			
Howden, William	Edinburgh	1824			
Johnston, James	Edinburgh	1840	1873		
Law, John	Edinburgh	1824	1824		836
Macdonald, David	Edinburgh	1818	1818		
Mackay, William	Edinburgh	1842	1842		
Mackay & Chisholm	Edinburgh	1845	1887		184
Mackay, James (I)	Edinburgh	1793	1804		
Mackay, James (II)	Edinburgh	1804	c.1845		185, 841
Mackenzie, William	Edinburgh	1783	c.1810		
Marshall & Sons	Edinburgh	c.1824	c.1865		
Marshall, J.S. & W.M.	Edinburgh	c.1817	c.1823		47, 277
Marshall, William	Edinburgh	1863	1900		
McDermid, J.	Edinburgh	c.1810	c.1830		844
McDonald, John	Edinburgh	1799	c.1820		
McHattie & Fenwick	Edinburgh	1800	1806		
McHattie, George	Edinburgh	1806	1835		344, 840
McKenzie, James	Edinburgh	1806			
McKenzie, John	Edinburgh (and Inverness)	1835	1845		
McKenzie, Thomas	Edinburgh	c.1854			
Meade, J.M.	Edinburgh	1860			
Millidge, Jonathan	Edinburgh	1818			
Mitchell & Russell	Edinburgh	1813			
Moon, Jennie	Edinburgh	c.1872			
Naismyth, J.	Edinburgh	c.1870			
Paton, George	Edinburgh	1820			
Robb & Son	Edinburgh	c.1860			
Robb & Wittett	Edinburgh	1848			
Robertson, James	Edinburgh	1800	c.1840		
Robertson, Patrick	Edinburgh	1751	1770		842
Robertson, William	Edinburgh	1789	1800		
Ronald, Thomas	Edinburgh	1816			
Speirs, Thomas	Edinburgh	c.1824			
Stewart, James	Edinburgh	1806			
Weir, Samuel	Edinburgh	c.1848			
Wighton, A.G.	Edinburgh	c.1842			
Wilkie, Alexander	Edinburgh	c.1795	c.1825		
Zeigler, S.	Edinburgh	1811			
Ziegler, Alexander	Edinburgh	1782	1795		837
Ziegler, John	Edinburgh	1798	1820		845
Ferguson, William Stephen	Elgin (and Peterhead)	1828	c.1835		906
Fowler, William	Elgin	1820			
Stewart, Thomas	Elgin	1815	1815		902
Adams, Ann	Exeter	1806	1808		716
Adams, Ann & Son (Edward)	Exeter	1808	1835		
Adams, John	Exeter	1780	1806	1806	717, 719
Beer, John	Exeter (Bristol)	1848	1882		
Bennett, John & Goss, Joseph	Exeter	c.1805	1815		
Blackford, William	Exeter (Plymouth)	1820	1830		
Byne, Thomas	Exeter	1825	1860		
Collier, Edward	Exeter	c.1760			712, 713
Dunsford, J.N.	Exeter (Plymouth Dock)	c.1823			
Farr, John	Exeter (Bristol)	c.1775			729
Ferris, George Snr.	Exeter	1799	1840	1840	
Ferris, Richard	Exeter	1784	1812	1812	
Fielding, Owen	Exeter (Plymouth Dock)	1808	1835		
Ford, J. & Williams, J.	Exeter	c.1780			738

Appendix 2 - Makers

Maker	Town	Recorded Dates First	Last	Died	Illustration Fig. No.
Fowler, John	Exeter	1823	1829		
Fulton, Joseph	Exeter (Bristol)	1838	1860		
Graham, T. & Willis, J.	Exeter	c.1790			737
Harman, J.	Exeter (Bristol)	1835	1835		724
Harris, Simon	Exeter (Plymouth Dock)	1811	1815		
Hicks, Joseph	Exeter	1785	1835	1835	714, 722, 723
Hope, William	Exeter (Plymouth Dock)	1816	1833		
Jenkins, Richard	Exeter	1764	1807	1807	
Lang, Oliver	Exeter (Plymouth Dock)	1799	1828		
Langdon, John	Exeter (Plymouth)	1823	1855		
Levy, Emmanuel	Exeter	1803	1818	1818	
Levy, Simon	Exeter	1818	1835		
Mardon, Thomas	Exeter (Plymouth)	1776	1785		
Merrett, P.	Exeter	c.1793			734, 736
Miller, G.	Exeter	c.1760	1764	1764	733
Norris, Henry M.	Exeter (Plymouth)	1835	1844		
Osment, John	Exeter	1818	1854	1854	721
Parkin, Isaac	Exeter	1818	1854	1854	720
Parsons & Goss	Exeter	1797	1799		715
Parsons, Francis	Exeter	1797	1831		
Patrick, John	Exeter (Plymouth Dock)	1794	1809		
Pearse, William	Exeter	c.1786	c.1786		
Pope, William	Exeter (Plymouth)	1830	1882		
Ramsey, Jonathan	Exeter (Devonport)	1829	1836		
Skinner, Matthew	Exeter	1757	1775		
Sloden, William	Exeter				728, 730, 731
Sobey, William Rawlings	Exeter	1835	1852	1852	726, 727
Stone, John	Exeter	1825	1867		
Sweet, Edward	Exeter	1831	1857		725
Sweet, William	Exeter	1833	1833		
Sweet, John	Exeter	1791	1829	1830	
Symons, Roger Berryman	Exeter (Plymouth)	1755	1773	1773	
Thomas, John	Exeter (Plymouth)	1794	1798		
Trehane, Sampson	Exeter	1805	1833		
Trist, Joseph (Joshua)	Exeter	1801	1831		
Trowbridge, Francis Jnr.	Exeter	1776	1815		
Webb, John	Exeter	1818	1822		
Welch, Thomas (I)	Exeter (Plymouth Dock)	1787	1800		
Welch, William (I)	Exeter	1801	1827		718
Welch, William (II)	Exeter	1822	1827		
Welshman, James	Exeter	1813	1830		
Wigan, Thomas	Exeter (Bristol)	1763	1770		740
Williams, James and Josiah	Exeter (Bristol)	1854	1880		
Williams, Robert	Exeter (Bristol)	1832	1854		
Woodman, William	Exeter (Bristol)	1818	1838		739
Gordon, Hugh	Fortrose	1790			1456
Aitcheson, Lawrence	Glasgow	c.1830	c.1865		869
Aitken, Peter (I)	Glasgow	c.1808	c.1836		270, 846, 848, 850, 872
Barclay & Goodwin	Glasgow	1852	1852		
Graham & Maclean	Glasgow	c.1810			
Graham, Adam	Glasgow	1763	c.1784		
Graham, Adam	Glasgow	1784			180
Gray, Robert	Glasgow (and Edinburgh)	c.1776	c.1825		851
Gray, Robert & Son	Glasgow (and Edinburgh)	1810	c.1840		263, 458,

Appendix 2 - Makers

Maker	Town	Recorded Dates First	Last	Died	Illustration Fig. No.
					852-53, 855, 856, 860, 874, 876, 878
Gray, William	Glasgow (and Edinburgh)	c.1800	1805		
Grierson, Philip	Glasgow	1810	1823		847, 865, 866, 867, 870, 881
Law, James	Glasgow (Cupar)	c.1826	c.1839		836, 863
Macdonald & Reid	Glasgow	1818			
Macdonald, David (I)	Glasgow	c.1812	c.1837		857, 888
Mackay, James (I), (II)	Glasgow	1793	c.1845		877, 879
McDonald, Donald	Glasgow	c.1793	c.1845		
Milne & Campbell	Glasgow	c.1764	c.1790		
Mitchell & Son	Glasgow	c.1822	c.1834		868
Mitchell, Alexander & Son	Glasgow	1822	1830		
Mitchell, Alexander (II)	Glasgow	c.1822	c.1850		862, 880
Mitchell, J. & W.	Glasgow (and Edinburgh)	c.1850	c.1851		
Mitchell, John	Glasgow	c.1832	c.1850		849
Muir, James (II)	Glasgow	c.1828	c.1850		
Murray, John (I)	Glasgow	c.1818	c.1861		854
Myres, J.	Glasgow	c.1848			
Newlands, James & Grierson, Philip	Glasgow	1811	1816		864
Newlands, L.F.	Glasgow	1816	1820		861
Osburn, Jas.	Glasgow	1765	1805		
Rait, D.C.	Glasgow	c.1827	c.1846		858, 859
Russell, William	Glasgow	c.1802	c.1855		
Sutherland, Daniel	Glasgow	c.1829	c.1831		368, 887
Malmstedt, John	Gothenburg	1783	1831		1424, 1425
Tengstedt, Carl	Gothenburg	1861	1821		1417, 1436
Lyon (Leijon), William	Gothenburg	1834	1870		1431, 1432
Osborne, Jonas	Greenock	c.1765	c.1805		
Taylor, John	Greenock	1775			
de Gruchy, T. and de Gallais, J.	Guernsey	1831	1846		
Henry, Guillaume	Guernsey	1720	1767	1767	932, 933
Quesnel, Charles William	Guernsey	c.1835	c.1845		
Langford, James	Halifax	1815	1847		
Nordbeck, Peter	Halifax	1819	1861		
Ross, Adam	Halifax	1813	1843		
Wang, Hing	Hong Kong	1890			1316, 1317
Hiort, Peter	Horsens	1842	1893		
Schmidt, Jeremiah	Horsens	1852	1879		
Fraser, Donald	Inverness	1804	c.1829		
Jamieson & Naughton	Inverness	1833	c.1845		
McLeod, A.	Inverness	1827			
Naughton, Robert	Inverness	c.1810	1833		898, 905
Stewart, Alexander	Inverness (and other towns)	1796	1812		
Quesnel, C.W.	Jersey	1800			
Wisting, Hans Petter	Larvik	1788	1810	1826	1379, 1381
Hay, James	Leith	1810	1829		
Abdy, William (I)	London	1765	1790	1790	111, 197, 232
Abdy, William (II)	London	1784	1823		
Adams, Stephen (I)	London	1760	c.1790	1802	
Adams, Stephen (II)	London	1792	1840	1840	
Adcock, Thomas	London	c.1772	c.1790		
Alderhead, John G.	London	1750	1794		
Alldridge, William	London	1768	1773		

Appendix 2 - Makers

| Maker | Town | Recorded Dates | | Died | Illustration |
		First	Last		Fig. No.
Angell, George	London	c.1857			
Angell, John	London	1815	1837		
Angell, Joseph	London	1811	c.1831	c.1851	
Angell, Joseph & John	London	1831	c.1850		
Ansill, James & Gilbert, Stephen	London	1766	1772		
Arnell, John	London	1773	1793		
Ash, Joseph (I)	London	1801	1818		373
Atkins, James	London	1792	1815		453
Atkins, Theodosia Ann	London	1815	1818		
Austin, John (I)	London	1804	1814		
Balliston, Thomas	London	1812			
Barker, Robert	London	1793	1814		371
Barker, Susanna	London	1778	1793		173, 196, 201, 231, 298, 601-58
Barnard, Edward & Sons	London	1829	1910		41, 56, 58, 364
Barrett, William (I)	London	1771	c.1793		172, 202
Barrett, William (II)	London	1812	c.1828		
Bateman, Hester	London	1761	1790	1794	171, 174, 175, 177, 225, 226, 227, 326, 328, 329, 484-507
Bateman, Peter & Ann	London	1791	1799		25, 223, 228, 381, 885
Bateman, P. & A. & W.	London	1800	1805		217, 274, 449
Bateman, Peter & Jonathan	London	1790	1791		
Bateman, William (I)	London	1815	c.1825	c.1840	
Bateman, William (II)	London	1827	1839	c.1874	
Bateman, William (II) & Ball, Daniel	London	1840	1843		
Bayley, Henry	London	1750			
Bayley, William	London	1759	1770		
Beebe, James	London	1811	1837		
Bellchambers, W.	London	1827			
Bickerton, Benjamin	London	1762	1796	1808	
Bickerton, Henry	London	1762	1796		107
Binley, Margaret	London	1764	1778		113, 178, 216, 508-24
Binley, Richard	London	1745	1764		104, 875
Boyton, C.	London	1937			92
Brasier, George	London	1780	1793		
Bridge, John	London	1823	1827	1849	389
Brind, Walter	London	1749		c.1795	
Brown, William	London	1823			
Burrows, Alice & George	London	1807	1818		
Burton, F. & Johnson, T.	London	1793	1795		
Burton, Robert	London	1758			
Cafe, William	London	1757	c.1802		125
Camper & Rutland	London	1827	1836		
Capper, Edward	London	1792	c.1820		
Carter, Peter	London	1783			
Cattell, William	London	c.1771			
Chawner, Henry	London	1786	1796		199
Chawner, Mary	London	1834			
Chawner, Thomas	London	c.1773	c.1802		200
Chawner, William (II)	London	1808	1834		

Appendix 2 - Makers

Maker	Town	Recorded Dates First	Recorded Dates Last	Died	Illustration Fig. No.
Clark, Alexander	London	1891	1898		
Comyns & Son	London	1885	1953		
Comyns, William	London	1898			258
Cooke, Elizabeth	London	1764			
Cooke, T. & Gurney, R.	London	1727	1761		
Cowie, George & John	London	1822			
Cox, Robin Albin	London	1752		1826	
Cradock J. & Reid, W.K.	London	1812	1825		340
Crespel, Sebastian (II)	London	1820	1836		
Creswick, J. & N.	London	1853	1855		
Crichton, L.A.	London	1953			84
Cripps, William	London	1743	1767		
Cruikshank, Robert	London	c.1773	c.1782		
Crump, Francis	London	1746	c.1775		
Daniell, Thomas	London	c.1775	c.1792		
Darouitts, James	London	1787	c.1800		
Davenport, Samuel	London	1786	1794		
Davenport, William	London	1902			82
Death, Thomas	London	1812	c.1828		
Dee, H.W.	London	1864	1867		259
Dee, H., W. & L.	London	1867	1880		
Devlin, Stuart	London	c.1950	1987		64, 87
Dick, Lexi	London	1983			69
Dixon, J.	London	?			
Dominey, Allen	London	1789			
Donald, J.A.	London	1967			83, 86
Dorrell, Jane	London	1766	1771		
Dorrell, William	London	1736		1766	
Drinkwater, Sandylands	London	1735	c.1761	1776	168, 278, 324, 325, 435, 436, 467-70, 472-79
Driver, J.M.	London	1971			70
					297
Druitt, Michael	London	1945	2003		62, 67, 76, 297
Durbin, Leslie	London	c.1945	1953		78
Eaton, Elizabeth	London	1847	1850		
Eaton, John	London	1760			
Eaton, William	London	1813	1834		
Edington, J.C.	London	1828	c.1858		350
Edwards, Edward (II)	London	1828	1831		318
Edwards, Thomas	London	1816	1830		317
Edwards, W.	London	1809	c.1840		
Eley, William (I)	London	1777		1824	
Eley, William (II)	London	1824	1841		
Ellerby, William	London	1802			
Elliott, William	London	1795	1830		212, 454, 884
Elliott, William & Story, J.W.	London	1809	1815	c.1854	
Elson, Anthony	London	1977			97, 99, 100, 101
Emes, John	London	1796	1808		
Emes, Rebecca & Barnard, Edward	London	1808	1829		336
Emmanuel	London	1915			91
Evans, Richard	London (and Shrewsbury)	1779	c.1795		193
Farrell, Edward	London	1813	c.1840		291
Ferris, Matthew	London	1759			

409

Appendix 2 - Makers

Maker	Town	Recorded Dates First	Last	Died	Illustration Fig. No.
Field, Alexander	London	c.1780	c.1802		208
Fitch, Daniel	London	1792			981, 982
Fitzpatrick, Mark	London	1992			60
Flitton, J.	London	c.1975	1977		74
Fogelberg, A. & Gilbert, S.	London	1780			
Foster, Joseph	London	1797			
Fountain, William & Pontifex, Daniel	London	1791			
Fox, Charles	London	1804	1841		
Fox, Charles, James & Co.	London	1884	c.1916		
Fox, Charles, Thomas & George	London	1841	c.1929		
Fuller, Brian	London	1937	1985		61, 96
Fuller, Crispin	London	1792	c.1833		
Garrard & Co.	London	1903	1981		75, 89
Garrard, Robert (I)	London	1792	1818		
Garrard, Robert (II) (Garrard & Brothers)	London	1818	1900		261, 296, 369, 378, 380
Garrard, Sebastian	London	c.1900	1909		376
Gibson & Langman	London (and Sheffield)	c.1881	1897		410
Gibson, Charles	London	1828			
Giles, George	London	1762			
Glanville, Richard	London	1768			
Glenny, George	London	1815			
Godbehere, S., Wigan, E & Bult, Jas.	London	1800	1818		
Godbehere, Samuel & Wigan, Edward	London	1786	1800		
Goldsmiths' & Silversmiths' Co.	London	1898	1911		90
Green, Henry	London	1773		c.1818	
Halford, Thomas	London	1807			
Hamon, Louis	London	1736	1753		218
Harris, C.S.	London	1852	1897		406, 407
Harris, John	London	1818	1831		
Harrod's Stores Ltd.	London	c.1905			
Hart, Napthali	London	1812	1834		
Harvey, Anne and John (II)	London	1759	c.1773		
Harvey, J. & Son	London	1961			
Harvey, John (I)	London	1738	c.1760		108, 480, 481
Harvey, John (II)	London	c.1761	c.1775		482
Hayne, Jonathan	London	1808	1810		
Hayne, Samuel & Carter, D.	London	1836	c.1842		
Hayter, Thomas	London	1805	1816		
Heming, Thomas	London	1745	1791		21, 248, 686
Hennell, David (I)	London	1736	1763		
Hennell, David (I) & Robert	London	1763	1773		
Hennell, R.G.	London	c.1844			
Hennell, Robert & David (II)	London	1795	1802		
Hennell, Robert (I) & David (I)	London	1763	1789		
Hennell, Robert (I) & Samuel	London	1802			
Hennell, Robert (II)	London	1834	1869		
Hennell, Robert (III)	London	1834		1868	
Hennell, Robert with Henry Nutting	London	1808	1809		

Appendix 2 - Makers

Maker	Town	Recorded Dates First	Recorded Dates Last	Died	Illustration Fig. No.
Hennell, Robert, David (II) & Samuel	London	1802			
Hennell, Samuel	London	1811	1843		
Hennell, Samuel with John Terry	London	1814	1816		
Hewitt, William	London	1829			
Higgins, Francis	London	1817			
Hills, John	London	1773	c.1790		
Hockley, Daniel	London	1810	1819		
Hockley, Daniel & Bosworth, Thomas	London	1815			
Holland, Henry	London	1838	1864		
Holland, John (II)	London	1739	1779		
Holland, Thomas (II)	London	1798			
Hougham, Charles	London	1769	1792		464, 465
Hougham, Solomon	London	1793	1805		210
How, William	London	c.1771	c.1784		
Humphris, John	London	1760	c.1770		
Hunt and Roskell	London	1843	1897		39, 262
Hussey, Richard	London	c.1737	c.1750		
Hyams, Hyam	London	1821	c.1845		
Hyde, James	London	1774	1799		22, 169, 191, 192, 198, 204, 220
Hyde, Mary & Reily, John	London	1799	1801		546
Hyde, Thomas (I)	London	1747			112, 539-544
Hyde, Thomas (II)	London		1804		525-32
Hyde, Thomas (III)	London				533-38
Jackson, J.	London	1819			233
Jackson, Orlando	London	1759			
Jackson, Samuel	London	1829			
Jackson, W. & Deere, P.	London	1887	c.1900		
Jacob, John (?Jacobs)	London	1734	c.1773		103
Jago, Mahala	London	1830	c.1842		
James, Thomas	London	c.1804			
Jenkinson, Thomas	London	1807	1827		
Johnson, Thomas (see also Purton, Frances)	London	1826	1851		365
Jones, Sarah	London	1985	1987		77, 403, 404
Kay, Charles	London	1815			
Key, William	London	1783	c.1800		
King, Abstainando	London	1791	1821		213
King, Jeremiah	London	1723	c.1750		
Knight, George	London	1816	1825		408
Knight, Samuel	London	1810	1827		195
Knight, William (II)	London	1816	1846		
Lambe, John	London	c.1770	c.1796		
Lambert, George	London	1868			
Langlands, J. & Goodrich, J.	London	1754	1757		
Le Jeune, Joshua	London	1773			
Lias & Sons	London	1848	1871		
Lias, Henry and John	London	1837	1848		375
Lias, John, Henry & Charles	London	1823	1837		
Linnit, J. & Atkinson, W.	London	1809	1815		
Lucas, R.	London	1740			105
Lucas, Robert	London	1727	c.1750		
Mappin & Webb	London	1859	1898		93

Appendix 2 - Makers

Maker	Town	Recorded Dates First	Recorded Dates Last	Died	Illustration Fig. No.
Mappin & Webb Ltd	London	1898	2004		
Marshall, Wendy	London	2002			59
Medlycott, Edmund	London	1748	c.1773		110, 167, 293
Meriton, Samuel (II)	London	1775	1796		
Meriton, Thomas	London	1791	c.1815		
Moody, William	London	1756	c.1770		
Mordan, Sampson & Co.	London (and Chester)	1822	1941		33, 284, 400, 709
Morley, Elizabeth	London	1794	1814		23, 384, 452
Mortimer, John & Hunt, John Samuel	London	1839	1843		
Mott, William	London	1802			
Mowden, David	London	1758	c.1775		
Ollivant, John	London (and Manchester)	c.1765	c.1785		
Ollivant, Thomas	London (and Manchester)	c.1785	c.1795		
Paul, John	London	1811			
Pearce, Richard & Burrows, George (II)	London	1826	1835		
Pearson, George	London	1812	1821		209, 287
Peppin, Susannah	London	1835			
Pertt (or Perth), Robert	London	1738	c.1753		
Phipps, James (I)	London	1754	1783		170, 321, 585-89
Phipps, T. & Phipps, J.	London	1816	c.1823		264, 374, 399, 873
Phipps, T. & Robinson, E.	London	1783	1811		179, 194, 203, 206, 207, 224, 229, 235, 242, 244, 246, 255, 267, 268, 269, 308, 335, 383, 450, 456, 457, 590-600
Phipps, T., Robinson, E. & Phipps, J.	London	1811	1816		251, 256, 280, 455
Pickering, Charles	London	1738	c.1750		
Pinnell, G.F.	London	1830	1852		
Powell, F. & Coates, P.	London	1818			
Powell, Francis	London	1818			
Price, Joseph	London	1833			1374
Priest (or Preist), W. & J.	London	1764	1802		
Prime, T.	London		1870		46
Purton, Frances	London	1783	1800		
Ramsden, Omar	London	1917			65
Rawlings, Charles	London	1817	1829		253, 273, 565, 871
Rawlings, Charles & Summers, Wm.	London	1829	1863		249, 265, 266, 320, 339, 351, 359, 361, 367, 372, 382, 398, 409, 563, 564, 566-70
Reece-Goldsworthy	London	1983			95
Reid, Edward K.	London	1844	c.1860		
Reid, George	London	1811	c.1850		
Reid, William Ker	London	1825	c.1851	1868	
Reily, C. & Storer, G.	London	1829	1855		35, 38, 234,

Appendix 2 - Makers

Maker	Town	Recorded Dates		Died	Illustration
		First	Last		Fig. No.
Reily, John	London	1800	1826		275, 343, 347, 348, 353, 558-62 188, 379, 411-14, 448, 545, 547-54
Reily, Mary & Charles	London	1826	1829		341, 360, 555-57
Renou, Timothy	London	1792	1816		
Rich, John	London	1765	1810		176, 239, 659-78
Richards, Alison	London	1973			309-11
Roberts & Briggs	London	1858			
Robins, John	London	1774	1801	1831	
Robins, Thomas	London	1801	1816		
Robinson, John (II)	London	1738			
Robinson, Thomas (II) & Harding, S.	London	1810			
Rowe, John	London	1823			
Rundell, Bridge & Rundell	London	1828			
Rundell, Philip	London	1819			
Rush, Thomas	London	1724	1733		
Sanders, J.	London	1800			
Savory, Jos. & Albert	London	1833			
Schofield, John	London	1776			
Schurman, Albertus	London	1756			
Scott, Digby & Smith, Benjamin (II)	London	1802	1807		283, 416
Seaman, William	London	1804	1827		
Shapland, S.C. & T.L.	London	1919			
Sheen, William (or Skeen)	London	1755			
Sibley, Richard	London	1836			
Simpson, Benjamin	London	1802			
Slater, James	London	1725	c.1750		435
Smiley, W.	London	1855	1887		42, 44
Smith, Benjamin (II)	London	1802	c.1818		331, 337, 338
Smith, Benjamin (II) & James (III)	London	1807	1812		
Smith, Benjamin (III)	London	1818	c.1842	1850	37, 342
Smith, George & Hayter, Thomas	London	1792	1805		205
Smith, George (II)	London	c.1758	1792		
Smith, George (III)	London	1774	1786		
Smith, S.	London	1875			352
Smith, Stephen & Nicholson, William	London	1851	1864		
Smith, William (I)	London	1758	c.1781		
Snatt, Josiah	London	1798	1817		
Snatt, Sarah	London	1817	1830		
Stamp, James	London	1764			
Stephenson, Benjamin	London	1775			
Steward, Joseph (II)	London	1753	c.1785		
Storr, Paul	London	1793	1838		31, 271, 386-88, 390, 392-97, 572-78
Story, J. & Elliott, W.	London	1809	1815		

Appendix 2 - Makers

Maker	Town	Recorded Dates First	Recorded Dates Last	Died	Illustration Fig. No.
Streetin, Thos.	London	1794			
Sudell, W.	London	c.1767	c.1785		
Summers, William (see C. Rawlings)	London	1863	1884	1890	48, 260, 282, 571
Sumner, William (II)	London	1787			
Sutton, J. & Bult, J.	London	1782			
Sutton, James	London	1780			
Symons	London				
Tayleur, John	London	1775	1801		
Terrey, L.F.T.	London	1816	1848		
Thompson, John	London	1785			
Trayes, William	London	1822			
Troby, John	London	1787	1804		
Troby, William Bamforth	London	1804	1824		292
Troika	London	1986			66
Turner, George & Biddell, Thomas	London	1820			
Turton, W., Wallbanks, W.	London	1784			
Turton, William	London	c.1770	c.1784		
Tweedie, Walter	London	1768	1786		
Twemlow, John	London	1814	1833		
Urquhart, D. & Hart, N.	London	1791	1805		
Vander, C.J.	London	c.1886			60, 68
Vonder, Richard	London	1961	1992		
Wakelin, Edward	London	1748	1760		
Wallis, J. & Haynes, J.	London	1810	1821		211
Wallis, Thomas	London	1773	1806		187, 315
Walther, Herman John	London	1770			
Watson, Thomas	London	1784	c.1796		
Weir, Thomas	London	1987			80, 405
Weley & Wheeler	London	1909			
Wellby, D. & J.	London	1863	1905		
Whitford, S. & G.	London	1802	1807		
Whitford, Samuel	London	1801	1852		
Whittingham, John	London	1788	1820		
Wickes, George	London	1748	1760		
Wimbush, Thomas	London	1828			
Wintle, James	London	1812	c.1840		
Wintle, Samuel	London	1778			
Witham, Edward	London	1813			
Wren, John	London	1777			
Wright, W.T. & Davies, F.	London	1864	1866		
Gordon, George & Co.	Madras	1830			
Orr & Co.	Madras	1850			
Bonello, Guiseppe	Malta	1806	c.1830		1365
Critien, Emilio	Malta	1818	c.1835		299, 1359, 1360, 1363
Fenech, Francesco (I)	Malta	1776	1821		252, 1362
Lebrun, Gioacchino	Malta	1775	1815		1361
Crossley & Etherington	Manchester (and Salford)	1797	1807		
Crossley, Jonas	Manchester (and Salford)	1794	1796		
Etherington, William	Manchester (and Salford)	1794	1808		
Ollivant, Thomas	Manchester	1789	1830		
Stokes, Thomas	Melbourne	1870	1880		
Arnoldi, Peter	Montreal	1792	1808		
Hendery, Robert	Montreal	1837	1897		
Thompson, Joseph	Montreal	1810	c.1840		
Walker, Nelson	Montreal	1831	1855		

Appendix 2 - Makers

Maker	Town	Recorded Dates First	Recorded Dates Last	Died	Illustration Fig. No.
Lambert, Peter	Montrose (and Aberdeen, Dundee)	1833	1838		
Leslie, John	Montrose (and Aberdeen)	c.1810	1821	1837	
Mills, William	Montrose	1811	1830		904
Bolin, W.A.	Moscow	c.1900	1916		1400, 1401
Grunbaum, H.	Moscow	c.1800	c.1800		1391, 1392
Marquand, Frederick	New York	1826	1839		
Tiffany & Co.	New York	c.1910	c.1925		1370
Moulton, William IV	Newburyport	c.1800	c.1850		
Bell, James	Newcastle	1822	1841		
Buckle, Joseph	Newcastle (York)	1716	1761		
Buckle, Stephen	Newcastle (York)	1743	c.1774		
Cookson, Isaac	Newcastle	1728	1754	1754	742, 744
Crawford, David	Newcastle	1768	1784		
Huntington, Thomas	Newcastle (Carlisle)	1811	1822		
Kelty, Alex.	Newcastle	1803	1812		316, 750
Kirkup, John	Newcastle	1738	1774	1774	
Lamb, J.	Newcastle	c.1750			743
Lamb, John	Newcastle (Whitehaven)	c.1738	c.1774		
Langlands & Goodrich	Newcastle	1754	1757		
Langlands & Robertson	Newcastle	1778	1795		221, 745, 746
Langlands, Dorothy	Newcastle	1804	1814		
Langlands, John (I)	Newcastle	1757	1777	1793	250, 741
Langlands, John (II)	Newcastle	1795	1804		
Langwith, John	Newcastle (York)	1716	c.1723		
Latimer, Joseph	Newcastle (Carlisle)	1837	1839		
Laws, G. & Walker, J.	Newcastle	1794			
Lewis, George & Wright, John	Newcastle	1812	1824		752
Lister, William.	Newcastle	1821	1840		
Lister & Sons	Newcastle	1841	1884		
Makepeace, Robert (II)	Newcastle	1738	1755		
Murray, George	Newcastle	1805	1816		
Pinkney & Scott	Newcastle	1778	1790		
Pinkney, Robert (I)	Newcastle	1777	1797		
Reid & Sons	Newcastle	1833	1884		
Reid, C. & D. (Reid & Sons)	Newcastle	1819	1833		
Reid, C.K.	Newcastle	1791	1819	1834	
Reid, Christian & David	Newcastle	1830			753
Robertson, Ann	Newcastle	1801	1811		747, 749
Robertson, John (I) & Darling, David	Newcastle	1795	1801		
Robertson, John (II) & Walton, John	Newcastle	1811	1824		
Ross, Thomas & Michael	Newcastle (Carlisle)	1839	1843		
Scott, Robert	Newcastle	1790	1793		748
Sewell, Thomas	Newcastle	1846	1884		
Solomon, Francis	Newcastle	1775	1786		
Stalker, W. & Mitchison, J.	Newcastle (Whitehaven)	1774	1784		
Walton, John	Newcastle	1820	1868		
Watson, Thomas	Newcastle	1793	1844	1845	401, 751
Wheatley, Thomas	Newcastle (Carlisle)	1823	c.1860		
Wright, John	Newcastle	1824	1836		
Hannay, William	Paisley	c.1818	c.1819		899
Christofle	Paris	1850			1341
Clérin, Jean-Baptiste-Lazare	Paris	1793	1794		
Cornfute, James	Perth	1772	1796		
Greig, David	Perth	1810	1855		

415

Appendix 2 - Makers

Maker	Town	Recorded Dates First	Recorded Dates Last	Died	Illustration Fig. No.
Keay, R. & R.	Perth	1825	1839		
Keay, Robert (I)	Perth	1792	1825		
Keay, Robert (II)	Perth	1839	1856		896
McNab, Archie	Perth	1825	1835		
Pringle, John	Perth	1827	1867		
Ritchie, William	Perth	1796	1814		897
Sid, John	Perth	1808	1815		
W., J.	Perth	c.1820	c.1820		895
Ferguson, William Stephen	Peterhead (and Elgin)	c.1825			906
Richardson, Joseph	Philadelphia	1796	1801		
Page, Thomas	Pugwash	1823	1865		
Sasseville, François	Quebec	1820	1864		1314
Baksteen, W. & C., & Middendorp, J.	Rotterdam	1861	1889		1373
Crossley & Etherington	Salford (and Manchester)	1797	1807		
Crossley, Jonas	Salford (and Manchester)	1794	1796		
Etherington, William	Salford (and Manchester)	1794	1808		
Marquand, Frederick	Savannah	1820	1825		
Alsopp, G. and McConachie, G.	Sheffield	1989			
Archer, Machin & Marsh	Sheffield	1900			
Atkin Bros	Sheffield	1899	c.1922		
Battie, Howard & Hawksworth	Sheffield	1815	c.1825		
Blagden Thomas	Sheffield	1798	1817		
Bradbury Thos. & Sons	Sheffield	1892	1924		
Creswick & Co.	Sheffield	1858	c.1858		816
Creswick, T.J & N.	Sheffield	1819	1853		
Creswick, Thomas & James	Sheffield	1810	1812		
Damant, William	Sheffield	1775	1777		
Dixon, James & Sons	Sheffield	1829	1863		94
Fenton, Creswick & Co.	Sheffield	1773	1812		
Fenton, Matthew & Co.	Sheffield	1773	1794		
Furniss, Poles & Turner	Sheffield	1810	1845		
Gainsford, Robert	Sheffield	1808	1853	1853	682, 810, 827, 828
Gibson & Langman	Sheffield (and London)	c.1881	1897		410
Goodman, Alexander & Co.	Sheffield	1797	1808		
Goodman, Gainsford & Co.	Sheffield	1798	c.1807		
Gregory, R. & Co.	Sheffield	1797			
Harrison, John	Sheffield	1833	1866		
Harrison, John & Co.	Sheffield	1833			
Harrison, T. & Co.	Sheffield	1866	c.1890		
Harwood, Wm. & Co.	Sheffield	1801	1826		
Harwood, Samuel	Sheffield	1835	1839		
Harwood, T. & Sons	Sheffield	1865	c.1879		183
Hawksworth, Eyre & Co.	Sheffield	1833			
Holy, Daniel & Co.	Sheffield	1776	1831	1831	822
Hutton, William Carr	Sheffield	1857	1896		
Jewesson, Robert	Sheffield	1800			
Kay, John	Sheffield	1804	1815		
Kippax, Robert	Sheffield	1774	1796		
Kirkby, Gregory & Co.	Sheffield	1822			
Kirkby, S.	Sheffield	1812			
Kirkby, Waterhouse & Co.	Sheffield	1793	c.1820		
Kitchen and Walker	Sheffield	1835			
Law, John	Sheffield	1790	c.1820		

Appendix 2 - Makers

Maker	Town	Recorded Dates First	Recorded Dates Last	Died	Illustration Fig. No.
Law, Thomas	Sheffield	1740	1795		
Law, Thomas & Co.	Sheffield	1773	1819		230, 821
Lea & Wigfull	Sheffield	1905			
Leader, Daniel	Sheffield	1797	1798		
Leader, Thomas (II) & Daniel	Sheffield	1798	1816		
Love, John & Co.	Sheffield	1783	c.1805		820
Martin Hall & Co.	Sheffield	1854	1891		
Morton, Handley & Co.	Sheffield	1796	c.1810		
Morton, Richard & Co.	Sheffield	1773	1796		811, 812, 823, 831
Nowill, Joseph	Sheffield	1812			830
Padley, Staniforth & Co.	Sheffield	1857			
Proctor, Luke & Co.	Sheffield	1785	1796		817
Rhodes, J.A. & Barber	Sheffield	1882			
Rhodes, Jehoida A	Sheffield	1870			
Rhodes, J.R.	Sheffield	1875			52
Richardson, Richard	Sheffield	c.1913			711
Roberts Cadman & Co.	Sheffield	1818		1877	
Roberts & Belk	Sheffield	1865			85
Roberts & Slater	Sheffield	1845	1864		
Roberts, Samuel (II)	Sheffield	1773	1834		
Roberts, Smith & Co.	Sheffield	1826	c.1845		
Rodgers, Joseph	Sheffield	1812			
Rowbotham, John & Co.	Sheffield	1773			
Settle J. & T.	Sheffield	1815	1826		829, 833
Settle, John & Wilkinson, Henry	Sheffield	1829			813
Smith, Nathaniel & Co.	Sheffield	1780	c.1800		
Staniforth, J. & Co.	Sheffield	1783	c.1815		
Tucker, Fenton & Machin	Sheffield	1801	1812		
Tucker, William	Sheffield	1808	1809		809
Tudor, Henry & Leader, Thomas	Sheffield	1773	1797		825
Underdown, Wilkinson & Co.	Sheffield	1826	1827		815
Walker and Hall	Sheffield	1862			
Walker Samuel & Co.	Sheffield	1836			
Walker, Knowles & Co.	Sheffield	1840	1844		832
Waterhouse, Hodson & Co.	Sheffield	1822	c.1835		
Watson, Fenton & Bradbury	Sheffield	1795	1827		
Watson, John	Sheffield	1795	1817		
Watson, John & Co.	Sheffield	1822			
Watson, Thomas & Co.	Sheffield	1801	1824		818, 819, 826
Watson, William and Bradbury	Sheffield	1827			
White & Sons	Sheffield	1879			
Wilkinson, H & Co.	Sheffield	1831			
Wilkinson, John	Sheffield	1812			
Winter, John & Co.	Sheffield	1773			
Younge, John & Co.	Sheffield	1787	1791		
Younge, John & Sons	Sheffield	1791	1802		824
Younge, S & C. & Co.	Sheffield	1802	1830		814
Evans, Richard	Shrewsbury (and London and Birmingham)	1773	c.1801		
Bolin, W.A.	Stockholm	1919			1400, 1401
Folcker, Gustaf	Stockholm	1846			1429
Folcker, Gustaf Theodor	Stockholm	1850			1430
Hammer, Christian	Stockholm	1866			1437

Appendix 2 - Makers

Maker	Town	Recorded Dates		Died	Illustration
		First	Last		Fig. No.
Möllenborg, Gustaf	Stockholm	1833			1434, 1435
Palmgren, Pehr Fredrik	Stockholm	1851			1433
Sjöblom, Gustaf Magnus	Stockholm	1841			1428
Dick, Alexander	Sydney	c.1830	c.1850		
Innes, William	Tain	c.1804	c.1870		
Jonssén, Carl Frederik	Uddevalla	1867			1438
Norblin & Co.	Warsaw	c.1890			1382, 1383
Lamb, James	Whitehaven	1748	c.1760		
Solomon, Francis	Whitehaven	1775	1786		
Astley, William	York	1797	c.1824	1833	
Barber, J., Cattle, G. (II) & North, W.	York	1824	1836		774
Barber, J. Cattle, R. & North, W.	York	1824	1836		774
Barber, J. & North, W.	York	1836	1847		773
Barber, J. & Whitwell, W.	York	1814	1823		762, 779
Barber, James	York	1847	1857	1857	764
Bell, John	York	1844	c.1864		765
Buckle, Joseph	York	1716	1761		
Buckle, Stephen	York	1740	1774		754, 770
Cattell, William	York	1816	1821		
Cattle & Barber	York	1808	1814		245, 759, 763
Cattle, Robert	York	1807	1807	1842	
Clark, Richard	York	1769	1797	1797	766, 769
Crossley, Jonas	York	1794	c.1806		768
Etherington, William	York	1786	c.1794		767
Hampston J. & Prince J.	York	1776	1796		755-58, 760, 771, 772, 775-77, 780
Hampston, Prince & Cattles	York	1796	1804		761
Jackson, Edward	York	1817	1821	1859	
Langwith, John	York	1716	c.1743		
Prince & Cattles	York	1804	1807		
Watson, Christopher	York	1814	c.1844	1848	
Whitwell, William & Barber, James	York	1814	1823		

APPENDIX 3

GLOSSARY

The terms and definitions given are those commonly applicable to wine labels and not necessarily to silver ware in general.

Architectural A style of label which has architectural features included in its main design.

Baroque A style characterised by rich decoration using foliage, rounded contours and heavy symmetrical curves.

Beading Decoration, usually on the border of an item, giving the effect of one or two rows of closely placed small round beads. They can be formed by either handworking, casting or die stamping.

Bright Cutting Surface decoration where the silver is cut or gouged away to produce designs with clean cut facets to reflect the light.

Cabled Decoration similar to a corded border.

Cameo The effect produced in a hallmark where the punch leaves the design proud in the surrounding frame that has been struck down.

Cartouche Term used to describe a framed panel, formed either by engraving or fretwork, to take an armorial, crest or initials.

Cast/Casting Method of production where molten silver is poured into a mould commonly made of metal or plaster.

Chased/Chasing Surface relief decoration formed by the use of punches without the removal of any silver. Work is carried out from the front surface of the silver plate and has a visible effect on the back.

Copper-back OSP label with copper visible on reverse, i.e. silver on face side only. See Chapter 8, Part 1, Old Sheffield Plate.

Corded/Cording Decoration usually to the border of an item where the silver is worked to simulate the twisted strands of a cord or rope.

Die Stamping Mechanical production method where an item or an area of design is formed in relief and/or pierced by a steel die being pressed into a thin sheet of silver.

Dionysus God of Wine, whose representation in whole or part is used as decoration.

Double Reeded Border see Reeded/Reeding.

Dwt see Pennyweight.

Embossed/Embossing Forming of a relief decoration on a thin plate of silver by the use of flat punches working from the back surface.

Engraving Surface decoration where sharp pointed tools are used to incise a design or pattern by producing lines of various depths and widths.

Feathered Edge Border decoration resembling the undulating edge of a feather; it can be likened to diagonal gadrooning.

Festoon A descriptive term relating to delicate looping of fruit, flowers and drapery - often pierced and/or cut-out. It is associated with neo-classical design.

Foliate Garland Similar to festooned flowers.

Flat Chasing Low relief chasing common in the period 1730-1750 - see Chased/Chasing.

Gadrooned Decoration consisting of a row of adjacent moulded lobes, usually to form a border.

Gilding see Silver Gilt.

Incuse or **Intaglio** The effect produced when the punch impresses the image more deeply into the silver than the surrounding frame (usually with reference to the King's Head Duty Mark of 1784/85, or to some makers' marks incised into the silver).

Intaglio see Incuse.

Appendix 3 - Glossary

Mask Head, human or other, male or female, used as decorative motif.

Mantling Plumes, foliage or drapery used as ornament about a coat of arms.

Neo-classical Mid-18th century to the style of the Graeco-Roman era, as epitomised by Adam design in reaction to the excesses of the rococo.

Niello This is a term used for a black material used for filling engraving on silver and other metals in order to highlight the work. Technically, niello consists of an alloy of sulphur with silver, lead or copper. In the case of infilling of engraved names on wine labels, niello is the term often incorrectly used where the material actually used was black wax, as applied to engraved clock faces.

OSP Old Sheffield Plate.

Ounce Troy A unit used in a system of weights for precious metals and gems equal to one twelfth of a pound troy. One ounce troy is equal to 31.10 grams.

Ovolo Surface decoration consisting of a row of raised ovals within a border.

Pales A series of vertical bars with slits between them.

Pennyweight (abbreviation dwt) A unit of weight one twentieth of an ounce troy equal to 1.555 grams. (See Ounce Troy.)

Pierced/Piercing Relates to decoration or marking of the wine name where areas of silver are cut away to form the design or letters of the name.

Pressed/Pressing A term sometimes used for die stamping.

Pricking Decorative engraving of small dots, usually numerous and close together, made with a needle point to form part or the whole of a surface design.

Putto A figure of a small chubby infant boy, cherub or cupid, generally naked, used as decoration.

Reeded/Reeding Border decoration consisting of one or more incised lines running parallel to the edge, i.e. single, double or triple reeded.

Rocaille Ornamentation based on rocks and the seabed, including stylised scrolls, shells, seaweed and rock forms. Rocaille was a forerunner of the Rococo style.

Rococo Asymmetrical design incorporating scrolls, sometimes also including shells and stylised rocks. See also Rocaille.

Repoussé Refinement of embossed decoration. Once the basic shape has been achieved, work with flat punches from the front is carried out to add to or to detail the design.

Rope Border see Corded.

Saw Tooth Elaborate border decoration where the edge is cut to abutting 'V' shapes which are themselves engraved and often pierced.

Silver Gilt Descriptive of a silver surface on which a thin layer of gold has been deposited. An amalgam of gold and mercury is applied to the silver surface and heated, resulting in the mercury vaporising, leaving the layer of gold. This is then burnished. Because of the toxic nature of mercury vapour this process has been replaced by electro-gilding.

Stamping A term used for Die Stamping.

Sterling Term applied to British Hallmarked Silver which indicates a standard of purity of 92.5 parts of pure silver alloyed with 7.5 parts of copper to make it harder. When the word 'Sterling' is found stamped on foreign silver, particularly American, it should indicate a similar standard.

Swags Term associated with Neo-classical decoration using festoons and bows. Often applies to adornment hanging from one point.

Trefoil Decoration consisting of three leaves or lobes spreading from one point. Can be engraved or cut-out.

Troy Ounce see Ounce Troy.

Vitruvian Scroll Border decoration of conjoined angular stylised waves.

Wrigglework Surface decoration consisting of a wavy or zig-zag band of serrated incisions. Frequently used on border decoration.

APPENDIX 4

BIBLIOGRAPHY

1. Books and Journals Entirely About Wine Labels
Dent, Herbert C., *Wine, Spirit & Sauce Labels of the 18th & 19th Centuries* (Norwich, H.W. Hunt, 1933).
Penzer, N.M., *The Book of the Wine Label* (London, Home & Van Thal, 1947).
Rhodes, Jean, 1952-56; Pratt, E.J., 1957-1959; Beecroft, J. and M., 1959-2001; Barrington, Celia and Jones, Bruce, 2002 to date (eds); *The Wine Label Circle Journal*. Vol. 1, No. 1, April 1952. Published twice yearly by the Wine Label Circle. Each volume comprises 10 to 15 issues (206 to 287 pages).
Stancliffe, Jane, *Bottle Tickets* (London, Victoria & Albert Museum, 1987).
Victoria and Albert Museum, *Bottle-Tickets. Small Picture Book 44. 1958* (London, HMSO, 1964).
Whitworth, E.W., *Wine Labels. Collectors' Pieces 8* (London, Cassell, 1966).

2. Books with Some Material on Wine Labels
Bannister, Judith, 'Silver Wine Labels' in John Hadfield (ed.), *The Saturday Book*, 33rd edn (London, Hutchinson & Co., 1973), pp.67-73.
Barr, Elaine, *George Wickes Royal Goldsmith 1698-1761* (London, Studio Vista / Christies, 1980), p.172.
Bennet, Douglas, *Irish Georgian Silver* (London, Cassell, 1972), pp.114 and 116.
—-, *Collecting Irish Silver* (London, Souvenir Press, 1984), p.27.
Bradbury, Frederick, *History of Old Sheffield Plate* (Sheffield 1912 and 1968), pp.197, 253, 303 and 399.
Butler, Robin and William Walkling, *The Book of Wine Antiques* (Woodbridge, Suffolk, Antique Collectors' Club, 1986), pp.160-73.
Clayton, Michael, *The Collector's Dictionary of the Silver and Gold of Great Britain and North America*, 2nd edn (Woodbridge, Suffolk, Antique Collectors' Club, 1985), p.469.
Culme, John and John G. Strang, *Antique Silver and Silver Collecting* (London, Hamlyn, 1973), pp.45, 50 and 56-57.
De Castres, Elizabeth, *A Guide to Collecting Silver* (London, Queen Anne Press in association with J. Goddard and Sons Ltd, 1980), pp.119-20.
—-, *The Observer's Book of Silver* (London, Frederick Warne, 1980), pp.140-43.
Delieb, Eric, *The Great Silver Manufactory: Matthew Boulton and the Birmingham Silversmiths 1760-1790* (London, November Books, 1971), pp.88.
—-, *Investing in Silver* (London, Barrie & Rockliff, 1967 and Transworld, 1970), pp.127-52.
Finlay, Ian, *Scottish Gold and Silverwork* (Stevenage, Strong Oak Press, revised by Fothringham, H.S., 1991), p.165.
Frost, Tom, *Price Guide to Old Sheffield Plate* (Woodbridge, Suffolk, Antique Collectors Club, 1971), pp.375-82.
Gill, Margaret, *Directory of Newcastle Goldsmiths* (Newcastle on Tyne, 1980).
—-, *Handbook of Newcastle Silver* (Newcastle, F. Graham, 1978), p.61.
Glanville, Philippa, *Silver in England* (New York, Holmes & Meier, 1987; London, Sydney, Unwin Hyman), pp.88-89.
Glanville, Philippa and Jennifer Faulds Goldsborough, *Women Silversmiths 1685-1845: Works from the Collection of the National Museum of Women in the Arts* (Washington D.C., USA, National Museum of Women in the Arts and Thames and Hudson, 1990), pp.43, 44.
Hawkins, J.B., *19th Century Australian Silver* (Woodbridge, Suffolk, Antique Collectors Club, 1990), Vol. 2, pp.158, 270, 274 and marks pp.238-39).
—-, *Australian Silver 1800-1900* (National Trust of Australia, 1973).
Holland, Margaret, *Old Country Silver: An Account of English Provincial Silver, with Sections on Ireland, Scotland and Wales* (Newton Abbot, David & Charles, 1971), pp.165-67, 194, 207 and 224.
Hughes, G. Bernard, *Small Antique Silverware* (London, Batsford, 1957), pp.133-44.
—-, *Antique Sheffield Plate* (London, Batsford, 1970), pp.127-32.
—-, *Phaidon Guide to Silver* (Oxford, Phaidon Press, 1978; Englewood Cliffs, NJ, Prentice-Hall, 1983), pp.231-34.
James, I.E., *Goldsmiths of Aberdeen* (Aberdeen, Bieldside Books, 1981), pp. 104, 121.

Appendix 4 - Bibliography

Jones, Kenneth Crisp, *The Silversmiths of Birmingham and Their Marks 1750-1980* (London, NAG Press, 1981), pp. 61, 78, 104.
Luddington, John, *Antique Silver: A Guide for Would-Be Connoisseurs* (London, Pelham Books, 1971) pp.67-68, 75, 94 and Plate 2.
—-, *Starting to Collect Silver* (Woodbridge, Suffolk, Antique Collectors' Club, 1984), pp.74-78 and 178.
Mackay, Donald C., *Silversmiths and Related Craftsmen of the Atlantic Provinces* (Halifax, Petheric Press, 1973), p.8, plate 28b.
Mayne, R.H., *Channel Islands Silver* (Phillimore, 1985), p.48.
Oman, C.C., *English Domestic Silver*, 5th edn (London, A & C Black, 1962), p.141.
Penzer, N.M., *Paul Storr 1771-1884: Silversmith and Goldsmith* (London, Hamlyn, 1971), pp.150 (plate 36) and 194 (plate 58).
Ridgeway, M.H., *Chester Silver 1727-1837* (York, Ebor Press, 1983), pp. 57, 68, 74, 90, 93, 111-12, 171, 182, 184, 195 and 227.
—-, *Chester Silver 1837-1862* (Denbigh, Gee & Son, 1996), pp. 77, 79, 80, 82, 85-88, 90-93, 96 and 99-102.
Salter, John R., *Sauce Labels 1750-1950* (Woodbridge, Suffolk, Antique Collectors' Club in association with Wine Label Circle, 2002).
Simon, André L., *Bottlescrew Days, Wine Drinking in England during the Eighteenth Century* (London, Duckworth, 1926), pp.243-52.
Waldron, Peter, *The Price Guide to Antique Silver*, 2nd edn (Woodbridge, Suffolk, Antique Collectors' Club, 1988), pp.348-50.
—- (comp.), *The Price Guide to Antique Silver Price Revision List* (Woodbridge, Suffolk, Antique Collectors' Club, annual).
Welz, Stefan, *Cape Silver* (Cape Town, 1976), p.115.
Williamson, G.C., *Everybody's Book on Collecting* (London, Jenkins, 1924), pp.216-23.
Wittewaall, B., *Nederlands Kline Zilver* (Abloude, 1994), pp. 167-68.

3. Magazine and Newspaper Articles about Wine Labels

Anon., 'Additions to the Weed Collection of Wine Labels', *The New York Historical Society Quarterly Journal* (Oct. 1929), p.116.
Anon., *Exeter Silver,* pamphlet, Exeter Museums publication no. 83.
Anon., 'Old Silver Bottle Labels', *The Wine and Spirit Trade Record* (14 June 1933), p.746.
Anon., 'Old Wine Labels', *Country Life* (12 Sep. 1941), pp.469-70.
Anon., 'Report on Acquisition of the First Pratt Collection of Wine Labels', *Vintage. House Magazine of J. Harvey and Sons*, Vol. 1, No. 1 (1960).
Bannister, Judith, 'Silver Bottle Tickets', *The Antique Dealer and Collectors' Guide* (Dec. 1958), pp.39-41.
—-, 'A Wealth of Bottle Tickets', *Antique Collector* (July 1975), 36-41.
—-, 'The Emes and Barnard Ledgers', *Proceedings of the Silver Society*, 2.9/10 (1976).
—-, 'Wine and Spirit Labels in Harvey's Wine Museum', *Magazine Antiques* (formerly *Antiques*) (Aug. 1977), pp.278-81.
—-, 'The Not-So-Humble Bottle Ticket: A Collectors' Subject Deserving of Proper Scrutiny', *The Antique Dealer and Collectors' Guide* (Sep. 1986), pp.82-83.
Barlow, T.E., 'A President's Badge and a Wine Label for the Wine Label Circle', *The Silver Society Journal*, Vol. 4 (1993).
Beecroft, John, 'A Collector's Comment [On "Wine Labels at Buckingham Palace and Windsor"]', *Connoisseur* (June 1962), p.104.
—-, 'Wine Labels', *Proceedings of the Silver Society*, 2.2 (1963).
—-, 'On Collecting Wine Labels', *Proceedings of the Society of Silver Collectors*, Vol. 11, No. 2 (Spring 1971), pp.34-36.
Chanter, Rev. J.F., 'The Exeter Goldsmiths Guild', *Transactions of the Devon Association* (July 1912).
Clark, J.W., 'The Copper Plate of the Goldsmiths Company of Newcastle on Tyne', *Archaeological Aeliana; Journal of the Society of Antiquaries of Newcastle on Tyne*, 4th ser. 47 (1969).
Cook, Cyril, 'The Art and Artists of the Battersea Enamel Wine-Label', *The Connoisseur, with Which is Incorporated International Studio* (Dec. 1952), pp.177-80.
—-, 'The Art and Artists of the Battersea Enamel Wine-Label', *The Connoisseur, with Which is Incorporated International Studio* (Mar. 1959), p.101.
Cropper, P.J., 'Collecting Bottle-Labels', *The Bazaar* (1, 8 and 15 Apr. 1921).
—-, 'Collecting Bottle Labels as a Hobby', *The Connoisseur: A Magazine for Collectors* (Apr. 1921).
—-, 'Antique Decanter Labels', *The Connoisseur: A Magazine for Collectors* (Oct. 1922), pp.88-96, 117.
—-, 'The Ticket Collector', *Antiques* (Part I, March 1923), pp.124-27; (Part II, April 1923), pp.166-69.
Culme, John, 'Beauty and the Beast. The Growth of Mechanisation', *Proceedings of the Silver Society*, 2.9/10 (1975).
Davis, Frank, 'Bottle Labels', *The Illustrated London News* (4 Oct. 1958), p.570.

Appendix 4 - Bibliography

Druitt, Michael, 'The Fascination of Decanter Labels', *Wine Magazine* (May-June 1962), pp.122-24.
Drury, W.D., 'Problems Which Old Decanter-Labels Present', *The Bazaar* (14 July 1921).
Du Cann, C.G.L., 'The Tags They Put on Drinks', *The Antique Dealer and Collectors Guide* (Mar. 1963), pp.46-48.
Edelstein, Fran, 'The Choice Depends on the Palate', *Ontario Showcase* (16 Mar. 1981), pp.20-21.
Ford, Patricia M., 'Variety in Wine Labels', *The Antique Dealer and Collectors' Guide* (Jan. 1965), pp.35-37.
Forster, Michael, 'The Puzzle of "Wine Labels"', *The Tatler and Bystander* (23 Feb. 1953), p.324.
Gray, M.C., 'Collecting Decanter Labels', *The Antique Dealer and Collectors' Guide* (Dec. 1974), pp.103-9.
Hansen, Ann Natalie, 'The Social History of the Wine Label', *Silver* (July-Aug. 1988), pp.28-32.
Holland, Margaret, 'Silver Made in Birmingham', *Magazine Antiques* (formerly *Antiques*), (Apr. 1976), pp.760-65.
Hughes, G. Bernard, 'Old English Decanters and Their Labels', *Old Furniture* (Apr. 1929), pp.227-33.
—-, 'Old English Decanters and Their Labels', *Antiques* (Boston), (Jun. 1929), pp.475-80.
—-, 'Silver Wine-Labels', *Country Life Annual* (1955), pp.78-81.
—-, 'The Labelling of the Wine', *Country Life* (18 May 1972), pp.1263-64.
Jones, E. Alfred, 'Wine and Wine Labels', *Country Life* (19 Sep. 1941), letters' page.
Keeler, G.A., 'More About Decanter Labels', *The Wine and Spirit Trade Record* (12 May 1921), pp.1-6.
Landau, E. O., 'A Few Words About Wine Labels', *Silver* (Nov.-Dec. 1987), pp.36-40.
Le Reek, A.G. [Anagram of G.A. Keeler], 'Wine and Spirit Decanter Labels: The M.V. Brown Collection', *The Wine and Spirit Trade Record* (13 Sep. 1920).
Loyd, Don, 'Antique Wine Labels', *Wine Tidings* (Sep. 1986), pp.7-9.
Metcalfe, George, 'Artistry in Decanter Labels', *Country Quest: The Magazine for Wales, the Border & Midlands* (Dec. 1976), pp.15-17.
Newton, Pauline, 'Lure of the Wine Label', *The Antique Dealer and Collectors' Guide* (Feb. 1957), pp.35-37.
Parry, C.J., 'The Burdett-Coutts Decanter-Labels', *The Bazaar* (9 June 1922).
—-, 'Bottle-Labels', *The Bazaar* (8, 15 and 22 Apr. 1924).
Paul, C.M., 'Wine Bin Labels', *Sussex Life* (1968), pp.39-40.
Penzer, N.M., 'The Bin-Label', *The Antique Collector* (Dec. 1960), pp.221-26.
—-, 'Wine Labels at Buckingham Palace and Windsor', *Connoisseur* (June 1962), pp.101-4.
Pickford, Ian, 'Wine Labels', *Antique Collecting* (Apr. 1977), pp.31-33.
Price, Pamela Vandyke, 'Forgotten Wine Labels', *The Antique Collector* (Dec. 1986), pp.62-63.
Rhodes, Jean, 'Silver Wine Labels', *Apollo* (May 1951), pp.129-32.
Robinson, B.W., 'Bottle Tickets in the Collection of the Hon. Sir Eric Sachs', *Connoisseur* (June 1958), pp.24-26.
Rocyn Jones, John, 'The Heyday of the Ancient Silversmiths', *Hobby Doctor*, Vol. 4, No. 9.
Rowe, Margery and T.M. Jackson, *Exeter Freeman 1266-1967* (Devon and Cornwall Record Society, December 1973).
Ruggles-Brise, S., 'Wines and Wine-Labels', paper no. 19, read before the Circle of Glass Collectors (8 Sep. 1941).
—-, 'Wines and Wine Labels', paper no. 21, read before the Circle of Glass Collectors (22 Oct. 1941).
—-, 'Wines and Wine-Labels', *Country Life* (8 Aug. 1941), pp.244-45.
—-, 'Wines and Wine-Labels - II', *Country Life* (23 Jan. 1942), pp.164-65.
—-, 'Sauces and Sauce-Labels', *Country Life* (19 June 1942), pp.186-87.
—-, 'The Fred J. Anderson Collection of Wine Labels', *Ridley's Wine & Spirit Trade Circular* (16 Nov. 1946), pp.760-66.
Ryall, R.B.C., 'On Collecting Wine Labels', *The Antique Collector* (Apr. 1968), pp.78-84.
Salter, John, 'Discovering Silver Condiment Labels', *Country Life* (30 Sep. 1976), pp.896-98.
—-, 'Sauce Labels - How to Impress your Guests at Dinner', *Antique Collecting* (Feb. 2003), pp. 26-31.
Simon, André, 'Wine-Labels', *Wine and Food*, no. 49 (Spring 1946).
Smith, Eric J.G., 'The Smith Family of Silversmiths. Part 1: Benjamin Smith', *The Antique Dealer and Collectors' Guide* (Sep. 1977), pp.94-99.
Soules, Ann, 'Collectors Toast Silver Wine and Liquor Labels', *American Collector* (Mar. 1980), p.28.
Sturt, John, 'Dating Silver Wine-Labels', *The Connoisseur, with Which is Incorporated International Studio* (May 1952), pp.83-85.
Townshend, Francis, 'Wine Labels of Irish Silver', *Country Life* (15 June 1967), pp.1539-40.
Udy, D., 'The Influence of C.H. Tatham (Examples of Paul Storr Wine Labels)', *Proceedings of the Silver Society*, 2.5/6 (1972).
Vivian, Val., 'Wine and Wine Labels', *Country Life* (19 Sep. 1941), letters' page.
Watney, Bernard M., 'Wine Labels', *Christie's Wine Review* (1975), pp.22-31.
Weed, Raphael A., 'Silver Wine Labels', *The New York Historical Society Quarterly Bulletin* (July 1929), pp.47-67.
Whitworth, E.W., 'Pounds, Shillings, Pence of Wine Labels', *Antique Collecting* (Jan. 1967), pp.18-22 (unnumbered).
—-, 'Eighteenth Century Wine Labels', *Antique Collecting* (Nov. 1968), pp.5-7.
—-, 'Enamel Wine Labels', *Antique Collecting* (Apr. 1970), pp.21-23.
Wilkinson, Wynyard R.T., 'China Trade Silver from Canton', *The Connoisseur* (Jan. 1975), pp.46-53.
Williamson, G.C., 'Labels of Delight', *The Weekly Dispatch* (5 Nov. 1922), p.6.

Appendix 4 - Bibliography

4. Catalogues of Collections, Exhibitions, Etc.
Anon, *[Wine Trade] Loan Exhibition of Drinking Vessels, Books, Documents, Etc., Etc., Etc., Held at Vintners' Hall, London, June-July, 1933* (London, Parry & Co., c.1933), p.53.
Anon., *Birmingham Gold and Silver 1773-1973* (Birmingham, City Museum and Art Gallery, 1973), pp.272-91.
Anon., *Catalogue of Exeter Silver* (Exeter Museum and Art Gallery, undated, c.1975), p.43.
Anon., *Chester Silver* (Sotheby's in conjunction with the Grosvenor Museum, Chester, 1984), pp. 10, 65, 67, 77-79, 85, 91.
Anon., *The International Silver & Jewellery Fair & Seminar* (London, The Dorchester, 1985), p.33.
Anon., *Wine Label Circle's Decanter Label Exhibition,* Olympia, 2003.
Barlow, T.E., *Wine Label Circle's Loan Exhibit* (London, 58th Chelsea Antiques Fair, 1984).
Beecroft, J. and Sanders, G.S., *The Second Pratt Collection. A Collection of 128 Silver Labels* (WLC, 1964), from p.93.
Beet, Brian and Jeanette Hayhurst, *Champagne Antiques* (Catalogue raisonné of an antiques exhibition, 3B Burlington Gardens, London, W1X 1LE, 1985).
Blair, C., *The Goldsmith & the Grape: Silver in the Service of Wine* (London, A Goldsmiths' Company exhibition, 1983), pp.34-35.
Bonhams, *The Contents of Harveys Wine Museum,* New Bond Street, 1 October 2003.
Bonhams, *The Sandeman Collection,* New Bond Street, 29 November and 26 March 2004.
Christie's, *The Hadad Collection of Wine Labels,* South Kensington, 5 December 2000.
Duerden, Marilyn, *Sheffield Silver 1773-1973* (Sheffield City Museum, 1973).
Hipkiss, Edwin J., *The Philip Leffingwell Spalding Collection of Early American Silver* (Cambridge, Mass., Harvard UP, 1943), pp.79.
Pratt, Edward J. and John Beecroft (comp.), *A Collection of Bottle Tickets Formed by Gerald S. Sanders* (Weston-Super-Mare: Typescript, 1963).
Sandeman, Major P.W., *A Collection of Silver Wine Labels* [a catalogue without illustrations, in two parts], *The Wine Label Circle Journal,* Vol 7, p.97.
Woolley and Wallis, *The Silver Reference Library of Brand Inglis* and wine labels, Salisbury, 28 January 2004.
Woolley and Wallis, *The Remaining Stock of Brian Beet* and other labels, Salisbury, 24 October 2003.

5. Books on the Wine Trade and Drinking Habits
Allen, H. Warner, *History of Wine* (London, Faber and Faber, 1961).
Croft-Cooke, Rupert, *Madeira* (London, 1961).
Francis, Alan D., *The Wine Trade* (London, 1972).
Jeffes, Julian, *Sherry* (London, 1861).
Johnson, Hugh, *Wine* (London, 1974).
—-, *The Story of Wine* (London, Mitchell Beazley, 1989).
Lord, Tony, *The World Guide to Spirits, Liqueurs, Aperitifs and Cocktails* (London, Macdonald and Jones, 1979).
Redding, Cyrus, *History of Modern Wines*, 3rd edn (London, 1860).
Robinson, Jancis, *The Oxford Companion to Wine* (Oxford, Oxford University Press, 1994).
—-, *Vines, Grapes and Wines* (London, Mitchell Beazley, 1986).
Simon, André, *Dictionary of Wines, Spirits and Liqueurs,* 2nd edn, revised by Lynne McFarland (London, Hutchinson, 1983).
—-, *Wines of the World,* 2nd edn, revised by Serena Sutcliffe (London, Macdonald Futura, 1981).
Vandyke Price, Pamela, Dictionary of Wines and Spirits (London, Peerage Books, 1986).

6. Books and Articles About Silver Marks and Makers
Belden, Louise, *Marks of American Silversmiths* (Charlottesville, University Press of Virginia, 1980).
Bradbury, Frederick (comp.), *Bradbury's Book of Hallmarks: A Guide to Marks of Origin on British and Irish Silver, Gold and Platinum and on Foreign Imported Silver and Gold Plate 1544 to 1987 and Old Sheffield Plate Maker's Marks 1743-1860* (Sheffield, J.W. Northend, 1927+. Updated regularly).
Brett, Vanessa, *The Sotheby's Directory of Silver 1600-1940* (London, Sotheby's, 1971).
Bunt, Cyril G.E. (ed.), *Chaffer's Handbook to Hall Marks on Gold and Silver Plate*, 7th edn (London, Victoria and Albert Museum, 1949).
Cripps, W., *Old French Silver*, Illustrated edn (Christchurch, Dolphin Press, 1972).
Culme, John, *The Directory of Gold and Silversmiths Jewellers and Allied Traders 1838-1914: From the London Assay Office Registers,* 2 vols. (Woodbridge, Suffolk, Antique Collectors' Club, 1987).
Cumming, W.O., *History of Elgin Silver: Elgin Silver Marks* (Saltburn, Cleveland, 1985).
Denaro, V., *Goldsmiths of Malta and Their Marks* (Florence, L. Olschki, 1972).
Divis, Jan, *Silver Marks of the World* (London, Hamyln, 1976).
Dobie, Kirkpatrick H., *Dumfries Silversmiths* (Dumfries, private publication, 1986).

Drillis, Catherine, 'The Unseen Hand: The Maker's Mark Versus the Sponsor's Mark', *Antique Collecting* (Sep. 1990), 41-45.
Ensko, Stephen, *American Silversmiths and their Marks IV* (Boston, 1989).
Fallon, J.P., *Marks of London Goldsmiths and Silversmiths. 1697-1837* (Newton Abbot, David and Charles, 1972).
Forbes, H.A. Crosby, John Devereux Kernan and Ruth S. Wilkins, *Chinese Export Silver 1785 to 1885* (Milton, Massachusetts, Museum of the American China Trade, 1975).
Gill, M.A.V., *Marks of the Newcastle Goldsmiths 1702-1884*, offprint from Archaeologia Aeliana, 5th series, Vol. 2 (Newcastle Society of Antiquaries of Newcastle upon Tyne, 1974).
Grimwade, Arthur G., *London Goldsmiths 1697-1837 Their Marks and Lives from the Original Registers at Goldsmiths' Hall and Other Sources*, 3rd edn (London, Faber and Faber, 1990).
Gubbins, Martin, *The Assay Office and Silversmiths of York 1776-1858* (York, William Sessions, 1983).
Heal, Ambrose, *London Goldsmiths 1700-1800* (Cambridge, Cambridge University Press, 1935; Newton Abbot, David and Charles, 1972).
Kovel, Ralph M. and Terry H. Kovel, *A Directory of American Silver, Pewter and Silver Plate* (New York, Crown, 1961).
Langdon, John E., *Guide to Marks on Early Canadian Silver: 18th and 19th Centuries* (Toronto, Ryerson Press, 1968).
MacDougall, Margaret, *Inverness Silversmiths* (Inverness Museum, undated).
Pickford, Ian (ed.), *Jackson's Silver & Gold Marks of England, Scotland & Ireland*, 3rd rev. & enlarged edn. (Woodbridge, Suffolk, Antique Collectors' Club, 1989).
Rainwater, Dorothy T., *Encyclopaedia of American Silver Manufacturers* (New York, Crown, 1975).
Salter, John, 'Hospitallers' Riches – The Silver of the Knights of St. John (*Country Life,* 27 Jan. 1983), on Maltese marks.
Schroder, Timothy, *The National Trust Book of English Domestic Silver 1500-1900* (London, Penguin, 1988).
Sheffield Assay Office, *The Sheffield Assay Office Register* (Sheffield Assay Office, 1911).
Tardy (comp.), *International Hallmarks on Silver Collected by Tardy* (Paris, Tardy, 1981).
Traquair, Ramsay, *The Old Silver of Quebec* (Toronto, Macmillan, 1940).
Wilkinson, W.T., *Makers of Indian Colonial Silver* (London, Chameleon Press, 1987).
Wyler, Seymour B., *The Book of Old Silver: English, American, Foreign, with All Available Hallmarks Including Sheffield Plate Marks* (New York, Crown, 1937).

7. Books and Articles about Caring for and Cleaning Silver
Author not recorded, *I.I.C. News* (Victoria and Albert Museum), Vol. 6, Winter 1966.
Author not recorded, 'The Silver Solution', *Antique Collector*, (Jan. 1987).
Butler, Robin, 'Notes on Cleaning Silver', *Newsletter* (Jan. 1999).
Glanville, Philippa (ed.), *Silver, History and Design*, Victoria and Albert Museum, London, 1996.
Pickford, Ian, 'Care, Cleaning and Conservation of Silver', *Antique Collector* (March 1992).
Sachs, Sir Eric S., 'To varnish or not to varnish', *The Wine Label Circle Journal,* Vol 3, No. 4 (Dec. 1962), p.93.
Tubbs, Cecil B., 'A Recipe for Cleaning Silver Labels', *The Wine Label Circle Journal*, Vol 2, No. 3 (Dec. 1957), p.43.

NOTES

Page references in 1 and 2 *WLCJ* are to the original edition (not to the reprinted A4 edition)

Chapter 1

1. Droper Hill (ed.), *The Satirical Etchings of James Gillray*, Dover Publications, New York, 1976.
2. *O.E.D.* vol. I, letters A and B, published 1888; vol. X, part 2, letter W, published 1927.
3. Jane Stancliffe, *Bottle Tickets*, p.5.
4. 8 *WLCJ* 224. Information from Mr B. Parker.
5. Benjamin Mildmay, 12th Baron Fitzwalter, was created Earl Fitzwalter by George II on 16 May 1735; he was appointed Treasurer to the Household in 1737. It is tempting to speculate that the labels that needed mending in 1737 had been commissioned to mark his elevation to an earldom. He died in 1756 without issue, and the earldom became extinct.
6. N.M. Penzer, *The Book of the Wine Label*, p.33.
7. Stancliffe, p.14.
8. 9 *WLCJ* p.13.
9. Stancliffe, p.5.
10. See I. Pickford (ed.) *Jackson's Silver and Gold Marks of England, Scotland and Ireland* (1989), A.G. Grimwade, *London Goldsmiths 1697-1837: Their Marks and Lives* (1982) and J.S. Forbes, *Hallmark*, Unicorn Press. 1999.
11. See Chapter 7, Part 11: Ireland.
12. The painting is reproduced on page 5 of Jane Stancliffe's *Bottle Tickets*. One early shape is the rounded rectangular with top and bottom dome.
13. In the Sir John Soane Museum, London.
14. Sold Christie's, 25 Feb. 1955, Lot 141, illus. in catalogue at p.162. The painting is also illus. in *The Dictionary of 18th-Century Painters in Oils and Crayons* by Ellis Waterhouse (Antique Collectors' Club, 1981).
15. Both paintings were also hung in the Tate Gallery's 1996 exhibition *The Grand Tour: The Lure of Italy in the 18th Century*. Full-page colour reproductions of the paintings were published in both exhibition catalogues.
16. Labelled bottles are shown on the table in a plate in *Town and Country Magazine*, vol. II (July 1770), p.361, illus. p.4 of Jane Stancliffe's *Bottle Tickets*. See also 8 *WLCJ* 118 where the escutcheon shape is detailed.
17. Kenneth Baker Collection. Illus. fig. 38, in *Sauce Labels*.
18. Published 30 Mar. 1793 by H. Humphrey of 18 Old Bond Street.
19. *Port and Good Company*, published by H. Humphrey of 37 New Bond Street.
20. Published 4 Feb. 1797 by H. Humphrey of New Bond Street.
21. Published 7 May 1803 by H. Humphrey of St James's Street.
22. *The Queen's Matrimonial Ladder*, published by William Hone.
23. Reproduced in the *Guardian* for Tuesday 22 Dec. 1992.
24. The *Independent on Sunday*, 11 Oct. 1992.
25. *The Spectator*, 1992.
26. Further details of bottle-tickets in the Wakelin Ledgers are given by B.W. Robinson in 3 *WLCJ* 45-49, 76-80, 117-23 and 136-40. See also Arthur Grimwade's paper read before the Silver Society on 10 Apr. 1961 on 'The Garrard Ledgers'.
27. A. Grimwade, *London Goldsmiths 1697-1837*, p.3650.
28. See further below, Chapter 7, Part 3.
29. See further below, Chapter 8, Part 6: Electroplate.
30. See *Sauce Labels*, p.140, para 7.48, style 38, fretwork.
31. A plated oval with leaf and ribbon top edge and Art Nouveau decoration along the lower edge, possibly Danish, marked I/O or O/I depending upon the way it is viewed, is illus. in 7 *WLCJ* 241.
32. By S. Garrard, 1902, with Crown and Garter cipher, probably ambassadorial but possibly another escapee from the Royal Service No. 1193.
33. By Goldsmiths and Silversmiths Company, 1911, die-stamped with leaves, flowers and at the base a scallop shell.
34. By L. Emmanuel, 1915, in Birmingham, a late example of the cut-out letters design.
35. See the PORT, WHISKEY and GIN illus. in 7 *WLCJ* 208.
36. Birmingham, 1933, silver with black, white and silver-grey enamel. A set of four in similar style of the same year for BRANDY, RUM, WHISKY AND SHERRY were auctioned by Christie's in Edinburgh on 18 Nov. 1993, lot 638 and are illus. in 9 *WLCJ* 151. PORT is illus. pl.2, B3, 7 *WLCJ* 201.
37. OPORTO is a pair with JEREZ. The reverse is stamped 'Made in England'. The design is illus. in James Dixon and Sons' catalogue of 1925.
38. 1937, a completely plain triangle with the name but lightly engraved. The label is not signed, unlike other commemorative pieces made by Charles Boyton who ranks perhaps with Omar Ramsden.
39. Maker's mark PandW, 1969. On the reverse of the Courage Breweries trademark cockerel are the words 'TAKE COURAGE'. Illus. pl.1, B1, 7 *WLCJ* 198.
40. C.J. Vander, 1961, for BRISTOL CREAM with the sponsor's mark of John Harvey and Sons registered in 1960 (see 7 *WLCJ* 197). Vanders produced a similar set but surmounted by the crest of the City of Bristol with a Naval Crown for presentation to HMS *Bristol* in 1973 (see 5 *WLCJ* 180 and illus. at 5 *WLCJ* 181). The design was reproduced by John B. Chatterley and Sons Ltd of Birmingham for OLD TOM to celebrate the bicentenary of the Birmingham Assay Office in 1973.
41. By Elkington and Co, Birmingham, 1915. The white horse is enamelled on a black ground. Illus. pl.1, B3, 7 *WLCJ* 198.
42. The design is illus. in 7 *WLCJ* 208, fig.9.
43. The Dixon labels are illus. in 7 *WLCJ* 208, fig.10.
44. BRANDY, a cast label of 1977 in the original numbered edn. of 2,500 for the Queen's Silver Jubilee, and GIN, a cast label of 1977 in a second design also with a limited edn. of 2,500, are illus. pl.1 at D1 and D3 respectively in 7 *WLCJ* 198.
45. VERMOUTH by SJR of Birmingham, 1977 for the Queen's Silver Jubilee. Illus. pl.1 at E3 in 7 *WLCJ* 198.
46. Not illus.
47. Produced in 1967, in a limited edn. of 112 to commemorate the Circle's achievement of its 100th member, in Britannia silver with oxidised finish to a heavy cast label; see 7 *WLCJ* 199 and 7 *WLCJ* 97.
48. Made by Garrard and Co. Ltd in 1981 to commemorate the wedding of Prince Charles to Lady Diana Spencer. A pair with PRINCESS OF WALES SHERRY.
49. Made by William Egan and Co. of Cork, Dublin, 1973. It commemorates the entry of Ireland into the European Community in 1973 and carries the special hallmark for that year, the Glenisheen Collar, of which the label is a representation. Limited edn. of 104. MALMSEY is shown on pl.1 at C3 in 7 *WLCJ* 198.
50. The cast PORT label by Leslie Durbin, 1953, bears the Coronation mark and was sponsored by Saccone and Speed Ltd, the London wine merchants (see fig.78). WHISKY in the same series is illus. pl.1, A1, in 7 *WLCJ* 198.
51. ANJOU by L.A. Crichton, 1953, bears the Coronation mark and was produced in a limited edn. of 56 for Circle members - see 1 *WLCJ* 53.
52. MEAD was designed by John Flitton for the Queen's Silver Jubilee, but with the date letter for 1978. HM The Queen was 'delighted to accept this charming gift' - see 7 *WLCJ* 199.
53. A SHERRY by John Flitton is shown in 7 *WLCJ* 204, fig.3 and in 7 *WLCJ* 241 (DURRANTS SHERRY).
54. This is a striking and original label by Robert Goldsworthy and Stanley Reece made in 1983. The hatched polygons around the edge are gilded and the centre ground stippled. A set was displayed in the *Goldsmith and the Grape* exhibition.
55. The designer and maker of the snake label for CLARET, which is illus. in 7 *WLCJ* 204, fig.1.
56. Made in 1977 with the Queen's Silver Jubilee mark. Brian Fuller often uses the glis-glis, a type of mouse, which is soldered on to the heavy gauge plate, as a signature.
57. Made in 1980 with two flowers characteristic of her style, WHITE is illus. pl.2 at E2 in 7 *WLCJ* 201.
58. The swan SHERRY, made by Sarah Jones, has garnet beads in the chain and is a design based on swan-upping, illus. in 7 *WLCJ* 206, fig.5.
59. Cast label dated 1977 with the Queen's Silver Jubilee mark. His lion tower labels for WHISKY, BRANDY and WHISKY are illus. in 7 *WLCJ* 204, fig.2. The work of other modern makers is also illus.: Elizabeth Hill (fig.4), Walter Lowndes (fig.6), Ian Rodger (fig.7) and Troika Designs (fig.8). The work of Michael Bolton is reviewed in 7 *WLCJ* 240.
60. Described in 4 *WLCJ* 10.
61. Described in 5 *WLCJ* 6.
62. Made in 1971. The wavy pattern reflected strongly the maker's style at the time.
63. Made by Hennells. Note the elaborate arrangement of chains for affixing the labels to the decanters.
64. In preparing this contribution the author is indebted to Sir Thomas Barlow, John Beecroft and Norman Krestin for providing information and lending labels for the illus.; to several currently practising silversmiths - Anthony Elson, John Flitton, Brian Fuller, Robert Goldsworthy, Elizabeth Hill, Sarah Jones and Alison Richards - who kindly responded to requests for information and illus.; and to David Beasley, Assistant Librarian at Goldsmiths' Hall, who helped to trace silversmiths. Labels not described in the text but featured in 7 *WLCJ* 197-203 are pl.1, C1, WHISKY by W and W 1934; Plate 1, E2, CLARET, Cosmacs Ltd, 1959; pl.2, A1 and A2, PORT and SHERRY in gold, Lowe, Chester 1962 on the closure of the assay office; pl.2, C1, WHISKEY, Elkington, 1905; and pl.2, C3, PORT, a green and yellow vine leaf in Wedgwood China. Also featured in 7 *WLCJ* 203 and following pages are notes on silversmiths making labels between 1970 and 1985.

Chapter 2

1. A.G. Grimwade, *London Goldsmiths 1697-1837: Their Marks and Lives*, mark 3650, p.260.
2. See also Chapter 2, Part 2: Rectangles. Attribution has been made to Thomas Rush, c.1739-55, see 4 *WLCJ* 120 (WHITE.WINE).
3. For CHAMPAGNE with John Harvey's first mark, c.1738, see 3 *WLCJ* 126; for CLARET with James Slater's mark entered 1725/28 with lion of 1729-1739 see 4 *WLCJ* 120-21; for CLARET with

Notes

Sandylands Drinkwater's mark entered 1735 with lion of 1729-1739 see 4 *WLCJ* 120-21.
4. Sandylands Drinkwater made a MADEIRA of this kind, c.1735-39.
5. A label for MADEIRA by Benjamin Bickerton is illus. in 4 *WLCJ* 121 at E1.
6. See 8 *WLCJ* 128 for details and illus.
7. See the Newcastle section for an illus. of this label, Chapter 7, Part 3, below.
8. Ashmolean Museum.
9. See below, Chapter 7, Part 4.
10. Labels attributed to Samuel Teare, John Graham and Richard Tudor are illus. in 4 *WLCJ* 121 at E1-3, which show clearly the small lettering.
11. See 9 *WLCJ* 59.
12. See below, Chapter 8, Parts 3 and 4.
13. See below, Chapter 8, Part 1.
14. For details see 5 *WLCJ* 61 and 8 *WLCJ* 8 where the nineteen titles are listed. Seven labels are illus. in 5 *WLCJ* 63.
15. For further details of domed rectangles see 6 *WLCJ* 96 and 8 *WLCJ* 9.
16. See, for example, the complex label for HOLLANDS illus. at 8 *WLCJ* 163, which has a row of inverted triangular piercing.
17. The label was originally for CALCAVELLA and was re-engraved, perhaps only a few years later, to reflect the owner's taste for the new wine coming into favour.
18. The label is unmarked, but its companion, for CALCAVELLA, is fully marked.
19. *Encyclopedia Britannica*, 11th edn. Articles on CAPITAL and ORDER.
20. See 1 *WLCJ* 142.
21. See further 8 *WLCJ* 112, especially for range of decorative borders.
22. See further 8 *WLCJ* 170.
23. Illus. in 8 *WLCJ* 171.
24. Illus. in 8 *WLCJ* 5.
25. Illus. in J. Stancliffe, *Bottle Tickets*, p.36.
26. On 26 Apr.1757 Wakelin made six 'half-moon bottle tickets' out of 2 ounces of silver (at a cost of 6s.) for George Wickes and Samuel Netherton - see 3 *WLCJ* 48. Three more were made on 9 Jan. 1758, and nine more in 1760.
27. An example of flamboyant style is the 'Gentleman at Table' design, for Madeira (in script) c.1800, illus. by Michael Druitt in 'The Fascination of Decanter Labels', 3 *WLCJ* 83.
28. The set of three labels and one marked label for 1792 were sold by Phillips 19 Feb. 1988 (lot 55) and were subsequently dispersed.
29. Note that the Blount crest as shown in Debrett has a sun with sixteen rays.
30. See 9 *WLCJ* 199.
31. See below, Chapter 6, Part 1, and Fig.477 for ETNA.
32. See 9 *WLCJ* 202.
33. See 3 *WLCJ* 48. Two more were made on 28 Apr. 1759 and again on 12 Dec. 1759 (3 *WLCJ* 49).
34. See 5 *WLCJ* 173.
35. Penzer, p.78, type 14.
36. Penzer, p.78, type 15.
37. See further, *Sauce Labels*.
38. See above, Part 1.
39. By J.F. Pidgeon in 4 *WLCJ* 141 and 4 *WLCJ* 174.
40. See below, Chapter 8, Part 8.
41. See 'Reclining Dionysus Still Reclining', 10 *WLCJ* 17.
42. Engraved BOAL, in the Victoria and Albert Museum, stamped WALSH; see below, Chapter 8, Part 8; see Penzer, pl.5.
43. See Penzer, pl.5.
44. See Penzer, pl.9.
45. See above, Chapter 2, Part 9: Single Letters.
46. See below, Chapter 8, Part 8.
47. The Descriptive Inventory was prepared by Messrs Garrard and Co.

48. N.M. Penzer, 'Wine Labels at Buckingham Palace and Windsor', *The Connoisseur*, June 1962.
49. Penzer in his *Paul Storr* at pp.150-51 describes and illus. part of the Belmore Collection of similar labels, eight of which now belong to the Goldsmiths' Company. See further 8 *WLCJ* 4-6.
50. Illus. as D4 in 5 *WLCJ* 170.
51. The electroplated sideways barrel is illus. by Penzer pl.26.
52. Taken from 1 *WLCJ* 222.
53. See 4 *WLCJ* 70 for the CLARET by John Osborne of Dublin.
54. See below, Chapter 8, Part 8, Ireland; see 1 *WLCJ* 25, 26 for SHERRY.
55. See 3 *WLCJ* 138 and 144-5 and Chapter 1, Part 3.
56. See 8 *WLCJ* 3.
57. See 5 *WLCJ* 155.
58. See below, Chapter 8, Part 8, Ireland and 10 *WLCJ* 240-245 for further details.
59. See above, Part 4 for the oval shape.
60. See 4 *WLCJ* 95 (1968).
61. For a set of four similar labels for CLARET, PORT, SHERRY and MARSALA see 8 *WLCJ* 3 and 5.
62. MADEIRA: see Eric Delieb, *Investing in Silver*, 1967, p.142. The suggested association with the end of the Crimean War in 1856 cannot be sustained. PORT: see 8 *WLCJ* 3 and 5. WHISKEY: see the Cropper Collection, Victoria and Albert Museum, London.
63. See H. Chesshyre, 'Identification of Coats of Arms on British Silver', *Antique Collecting* (Dec. 1977/Feb. 1978).
64. LISBON, said to be in the form of a 'ducal coronet', by Edward Edwards in London (1831) is illus. in 2 *WLCJ* 29, and PORT in 2 *WLCJ* 67. See also 1 *WLCJ* 122.
65. See 4 *WLCJ* 207 and 1 *WLCJ* 41, number 3.
66. See Chapter 7, Part 8, Ireland and 6 *WLCJ* 193 (1979).
67. See 3 *WLCJ* 209 (1965).
68. See 8 *WLCJ* 101 (1987).
69. See 3 *WLCJ* 64 (1962).
70. See below, Chapter 6, Part 3
71. Sotheby's, New York, Catalogue 6686; 12 Apr. 1995, Lot 6.
72. See 3 *WLCJ* 195.
73. Penzer, pl.14.
74. The set was illus. in *Country Life*, 2 Dec. 1976, in an advertisement for W.H. Wilson Ltd.
75. See Chapter 5, Part 1, Drinkwater.
76. See below and Chapter 5, Part 3, The Batemans.
77. See Chapter 9, Part 9, India.
78. See Chapter 7, Part 11, Malta.
79. See 10 *WLCJ*, 184.
80. See Chapter 2, Part 3, Scrolls.
81. See above and Chapter 5, Part 3, The Batemans.
82. This label could be recorded as a form of vine leaf.
83. See Chapter 5, Part 1 and Stancliffe, *Bottle Tickets*, V and A. Probably arms of Hales, but six other families have this crest.
84. See Chapter 5, Part 10. Arms of Colston.
85. See 9 *WLCJ* 272. An owl is displayed, probably for Nicholas or Snell. T Hyde, c.1760.
86. See 1 *WLCJ* 174 and 9 *WLCJ* 34.
87. See 4 *WLCJ* 59.
88. See Chapter 5, Part 8.
89. See Chapter 8, Part 3.
90. See Chapter 1, Part 8.
91. See Chapter 9, Part 4.
92. See Chapter 9, Part 10.
93. See Chapter 8, Part 10.
94. See 3 *WLCJ*.
95. See Chapter 5, Part 3 and Chapter 2, Part 2.
96. See Chapter 7, Part 11.
97. See Chapter 5, Parts 8 and 9.
98. Lot 333 (with photograph of crest), Bonham's sale, 21.3.03.

99. Lot 311, Bonham's *ibidem*.
100. Lot 355, Bonham's *ibidem*.
101. An example for SHERRY has been noted.
102. See Chapter 2, Part 13.
103. See Chapter 2, Part 16.
104. See Chapter 2, Part 2 and Chapter 5, Part 3.
105. See Chapter 7, Part 11.
106. See 10 *WLCJ* 164.
107. See 9 *WLCJ* 35.
108. See 8 *WLCJ* 208.
109. Roger Perkins, *Military and Naval Silver*, 1999.
110. See 8 *WLCJ* 108.

Chapter 3

1. The scimitar label, mentioned in Chapter 2, Part 20, is unmarked.
2. By Sandylands Drinkwater prior to 1739.
3. To make that easier, both master and sand surface may have been dusted in advance with a 'parting' powder.

Chapter 4

1. See Chapter 1, Part 1 and Chapter 7, Part 11.
2. J.S. Forbes, *Hallmark*, 1998.
3. See Chapter 1, Parts 1 and 3.
4. Jackson.
5. Penzer.
6. Paper receipts in writing for duty paid were given prior to 1758, including in Scotland.
7. Scottish Acts authorising this method of marking were preserved under the Act of Union and thus remained in force. Apart from Edinburgh the only other 'assay' office in Scotland was at Glasgow, established under an Act of 1819, which specifically provided for a duty mark for this reason.
8. 30 Geo III c31. The provisions of this Act are thoroughly explained in Penzer, Chapter 2.
9. These are examined further in Chapter 7, Part 11: Ireland.
10. Birmingham examples with unusual shattered punches exist - see the unusual 1837 (no lion passant but two anchors!) and 1840 examples illus. in 10 *WLCJ* 95.
11. For the full story see Susan Hare, 'Heads You Win', the *Goldsmith's Review* 1984/85, p18.
12. These can be seen from the Company's mark plates.
13. Four of the five dies concerned are reproduced in fig. 460 showing proof impressions (five times enlarged) of a large and small duty head and of leopard's head and lion passant punches for hallmarking silver, prepared by William Wyon RA in 1839 for submission to a Court Meeting of the Worshipful Company of Goldsmiths on 20 Nov. and used in 1840/41, struck on silver discs each one 11mm (⅖in.) in diameter. The fifth disc shows another size of duty head and is in the collection at Goldsmiths' Hall.
14. See below, Part 4, The Britannia Marks.
15. J.S. Forbes, *Hallmark*, 1998.
16. The 'Touchstone for Gold and Silver Wares', 1677. Jackson 1921/64.
17. See Chapter 7, Part 5.
18. See Chapter 1, Part 3.
19. See Ralph Hoyle's note in 9 *WLCJ* 37.

Chapter 5

1. See Stancliffe, p.44.
2. See further Grimwade, pp.494 and 699.
3. Grimwade, p.2499.
4. Grimwade, p.3792.
5. See Chapter 1, Part 1.
6. Grimwade, p.2976.
7. At page 45(a).
8. See further, Chapter 2, Part 21.

Notes

9. See Chapter 2, Part 17.
10. Ambrose Heal, *The London Goldsmiths 1200-1800*, Cambridge: Cambridge University Press, 1935; David and Charles, 1972.
11. Grimwade p.539.
12. See photographs of the register in Grimwade between pages 413 and 417 (in 3rd edn. between pages 422 and 423).
13. See above, Chapter 2, Part 18.
14. See further above, Chapter 2, Part 21, on animal heraldic labels.
15. Illus. in Stancliffe, pl.64, p.45.
16. Illus. *idem* at pl.53, p.38.
17. Illus. in 5 *WLCJ* 170; see above, Chapter 2, Part 11.
18. For further reading see 1 *WLCJ* 51 and 2 *WLCJ* 199.
19. Beecroft, 7 *WLCJ* 135 and Gilmour, WLC AGM 1999
20. See Chapter 5, Part 1.
21. In *Tales of my Landlord* (4th Series), 1829, Sir Walter Scott uses the phrase to describe whisky.
22. See 6 *WLCJ* 156.
23. See Chapter 5, Part 11 and 5 *WLCJ* 2.
24. These marks are not recorded in Grimwade or Jackson. For full details of the Hyde family, their lives, work and marks, see *Silver Society Journal*, vol. 10, pp.16-19, 9 *WLCJ* 260-72 and 10 *WLCJ* 48-50.
25. Grimwade p.199, 1st edn., ref. no. 2784. Grimwade attributes this mark to Thomas Hyde II because he would not have been aware of the details of Thomas Hyde I described above, nor Thomas II's death in 1789. See further, note 24 above.
26. Heal records James and Thomas Hyde together at '? 33 or 38' assuming wrongly that there had been some confusion between these numbers. They were, however, two separate addresses for two distinctly separate businesses. See further, note 24 above.
27. See below, Chapter 5, Part 6.
28. For photographs of all four marks (Grimwade illus. only two) and eighteen different labels with these marks see 6 *WLCJ* 241-248. See further, note 24 above.
29. In the Forrow collection.
30. Stancliffe, pl.51, p.37, BURGUNDY, wrongly attributed to John Robert.
31. Penzer, pl.11, bottom right, TINTA; Stancliffe, pl.51, p.37, TINTA.
32. Penzer, pl.14, GIN; Stancliffe, pl.58, p.41, CHAMPAGNE; 11 *WLCJ* 63-65.
33. Sold at Sotheby's in 1996, marked on opposing figural handles: Vanessa Brett, *Sotheby's Directory of Silver 1600-1940*, London, 1986, pp.289-90.
34. Stancliffe, pl.28, p.23.
35. Penzer, pl.5, lower left.
36. See Chapter 2, Part 10.
37. For a fully illus. account of Rawlings and Summers' output see 5 *WLCJ* 221, and for illus. of labels by these makers see 5 *WLCJ* 259 and 262.
38. See 8 *WLCJ* 1.
39. N.M. Penzer, *Paul Storr 1771-1844, Silversmith and Goldsmith*, 1971 edn..
40. This comment is made by Grimwade (3rd edn., 1990, p.662) having studied the Boulton papers in the Birmingham Assay Office and Family information.
41. Grimwade, 3rd edn., 1990, p.250, no.3522.
42. See pl.LVIII of N.M. Penzer, *Paul Storr 1771-1844, Silversmith and Goldsmith*, 1971 edn.
43. Sir Eric Sachs (then Mr Justice Sachs) carried out extensive researches into the lives of three generations of the Phipps family and their partnerships and their work, publishing his results in the *Wine Label Circle Journal* from 1956 up to his death in 1979. He was President of the Wine Label Circle from 1959 to 1961. The articles that he wrote were: 1 *WLCJ* (Dec 1956), 'The Phipps Family and Edward Robinson, Part 1'; 2 *WLCJ* (Apr 1957), 'The Phipps Family and Edward Robinson, Part 2'; 2 *WLCJ* (Aug 1958), 'Bottle Tickets in the Collection of Sir Eric Sachs'; 2 *WLCJ* (Apr 1959), 'The Phipps Family - Further Sidelights'; 2 *WLCJ* (Dec 1959), 'The Perils of Secondary Evidence'; 4 *WLCJ* (Jun 1967), 'A Trio by T. Phipps and E. Robinson'; 5 *WLCJ* (Dec 1973), 'Finding the Phipps Family'; 5 *WLCJ* (Dec 1975), 'The TP/ER/IP Mark - 1'; 6 *WLCJ* (Jun 1976), 'The TP/ER/IP Mark - 2'; 6 *WLCJ* (Jun 1978), 'In the Phipps Constellation a Star is Found'; 6 *WLCJ* (Dec 1979).
44. The marriage certificates researched by Bruce Jones are from the St Vedast, Foster Lane, parish registers, kept on microfilm at the Guildhall Library, London. Many of the records of St Vedast were destroyed in the Second Word War, and these microfilms are, it is understood, of bishop's transcripts (copies the parish had to provide for the bishop). Because of this, one wonders whether the signatures would be originals or copies, but the variations in the signatures suggest that they were signed personally by those involved. Indeed, in the certificate following that of Thomas Phipps, both bride and groom make a mark rather than a signature. Both Thomas Phipps and Edward Robinson were married by licence rather than after the calling of banns. Details of the certificates are as follows:

THOMAS PHIPPS
This certificate is dated 22 Sept. 1778. Thomas Phipps married another Phipps, Elizabeth, from the parish of St Mary Staining. If this is 'our' Thomas Phipps, we might have expected his father, James Phipps, to have been a witness, another reason for further checking. The certificate, the central one on the next page and numbered 266, reads 'Thomas Phipps of this Parish, Bach, and Elizabeth Phipps of the parish of St Mary Staining London Spinster were Married in this Church by Licence this twenty second Day of September in the year One Thousand seven Hundred and seventy eight by me George Gaskin M.A. Curate. This Marriage was Solemnized between Us Thomas Phipps, Eliz Phipps In the Prefence of Saml Phipps, Ann Phipps, William Phipps, Ann Phipps'.

EDWARD ROBINSON
This certificate is dated 20 May 1783, with Edward Robinson of St Vedast parish marrying Ann Phipps from the same parish. The signature of Ann Phipps looks similar to the Ann Phipps who was a witness at Thomas Phipps' marriage. As for witnesses, these include James Phipps and Thomas Phipps. The certificate, number 300, reads 'Edward Robinson, Batchelor of the Parish of St Vedast Foster and Ann Phipps Spinster of the same Parish were Married in this Church by Licence this Twentyth Day of May in the Year One Thoufand and seven Hundred and Eighty Three by me John Prince Curate This Marriage was Solemnized between Us Edwd Robinson Ann Phipps in the Prefence of James Phipps, Tho Phipps, Sarah Phipps, Elizth Phipps, E Phipps'.

45. See Chapter 4, Part 3.
46. Recorded by Grimwade ref. no. 2891.
47. Jackson, p.224, 1989 edn..
48. Strangely, it is not recorded by Jackson (1921 edn.).
49. Information kindly provided by David Beasley of the Goldsmiths' Company.
50. Peter Earle, *The Making of the English Middle Class: Business, Society and Family Life in London, 1660-1730* (London: Methuen, 1989).
51. N.M. Penzer, *The Book of the Wine Label* (London: Home and Van Thal, 1947).
52. E.W. Whitworth, *Wine Labels* (Collectors' Pieces 8. London: Cassell, 1966), p.37.
53. See 5 *WLCJ* 2 and the illus. on pp.7 and 10.
54. See Chapter 5, Part 14.
55. See for further details *Sauce Labels 1750-1950*.
56. In 'London Goldsmiths 1697-1837, their Marks and Lives'.
57. Examples are shown in 9 *WLCJ* 230 and 233.
58. See 5 *WLCJ* 2.
59. Examples are illus. in 9 *WLCJ* 236.
60. See 9 *WLCJ* 109.
61. See for further details *Sauce Labels 1750-1950*.
62. Examples are illus. in 9 *WLCJ* 231, 234 and 237; also in 5 *WLCJ* 7 and 10.
63. See 2 *WLCJ* 48.
64. All three marks are illus. in *The Marks of London Goldsmiths and Silversmiths* by J.F. Fallon, 1972. The dimensions of the mark found on labels correspond with those of the mark illus. by Jackson and Grimwade, but Fallon's representation has a squarer frame.
65. See 3 *WLCJ* 81; *The Connoisseur,* June 1962, pp.100-104.
66. Guildhall Library L91, M5 591/2.
67. Ibid., L91, M 2057.
68. Ibid., L91, MS 779/1.
69. Number 159 in Chapters 5 and 6 of *Sauce Labels 1750-1950*.
70. See *Antique Collector*, Feb. 1987.

Chapter 6

1. Penzer, *The Book of the Wine Label*, 1947.
2. See Appendix 1.
3. Salter, *Sauce Labels 1750-1950*, pp.35-38.
4. *WLCJ*, 2 Dec 1961.
5. A label of this design for PORT has been noted, made by Sandylands Drinkwater, c.1739-56.
6. See Chapter 8, Parts 1, 3 and 4.
7. See Chapter 7, Part 1.
8. See Chapter 2, Part 1.
9. See Chapter 10, Part 2:
10. See 9 *WLCJ* 162.
11. Information from M. Hichon, 9 *WLCJ* 154.
12. See 3 *WLCJ* 161-73.
13. André Simon, *Bottlescrew Days*, p.78.
14. For a detailed account of the production and consumption of Madeira wines see 9 *WLCJ* 117-21.
15. For a similar account of Canary Island wines see 7 *WLCJ* 12-13.
16. Penzer, *The Book of the Wine Label*, p.107.
17. See 8 *WLCJ* 162 and 173-6.
18. See Beet and Hayhurst, *Champagne Antiques*, London, 1985 (p.2 and pp.10-12).
19. For a fuller discussion of Cape wines see 7 *WLCJ* 142-44.
20. See 9 *WLCJ* 117-21.
21. See 7 *WLCJ* 12-13.
22. See 8 *WLCJ* 173-76 and 211.

Chapter 7

1. The Grosvenor Museum Catalogue, 1984, p.67.
2. Cripps, 1926, p.147
3. Illus. in Ridgway, *Chester Silver 1727-1837*, pl.37.
4. These appeared in a 1984 loan exhibition, exhibit 164.
5. Reference has been made by the authors of this part to *The Great Silver Manufactory*, E. Delieb, 1971; *Chester Silver, 1727-1837*, M.H. Ridgway, 1985; *Chester Silver, 1837-1962*, M.H. Ridgway, 1966; and *York Assay Office and Silversmiths*, M. Gubbins, 1983.
6. Ridgway Type 6.
7. This appeared in a 1984 loan exhibition, exhibit 146.
8. Ridgway, vol. 3, p.100.
9. In 6 *WLCJ* 31, fig. 1.
10. Documents are in the care of the East Devon Area Record Office, whose staff were very helpful in directing the author of this part to the material and

Notes

in providing photocopies. Thanks also to Tim Kent for reviewing the text.
11. 5 *WLCJ* 236, table 6.
12. See Chapter 7, Part 3.
13. The biographical notes were mainly provided by Simon Hunt and revised by Tim Kent.
14. See Chapter 7, Part 3.
15. Idem.
16. Idem.
17. Grimwade lists fifteen Bath silversmiths who registered their marks in London.
18. See Chapter 7, Part 2 and note 14.
19. See Chapter 7, Part 2 and note 15.
20. See Chapter 7, Part 2 and note 16.
21. See *Sauce Labels 1750-1950* for details. A fine example for Ketchup, Kyan, Vinegar and Lemon on a silver stand is in Cheltenham Spa Museum reference 1948.7.
22. For the position in Newcastle see Part 4.
23. *The Copper Plate of the Goldsmiths Company of Newcastle-Upon-Tyne* by J.W. Clark, I.D.S., R.C.S. Offprint from *Archaeological Aeliana*, 4th series, vol. xviii, published by The Society of Antiquaries of Newcastle-upon-Tyne 1969. These two introductory paragraphs were contributed by Keith Thacker.
24. For the earliest example see 4 *WLCJ* 1 and for the latest see the Marshall Collection at the Ashmolean Museum, Oxford.
25. 9 *WLCJ* 202-3, pl.61.
26. Christie's *Wine Companion 2*, London, 1983, pp.110-13
27. Thorpe, W.A, *A History of English Glass and Irish Glass*, London, 1929, pp.319-20.
28. For a brief history of the Beilby glasshouse illus. of the two decanters mentioned and further reading see Simon Cottle, *Apollo*, June 1989, pp.393-8 and 445.
29. This is a copy of a Phipps and Robinson design of c.1785 (see 2 *WLCJ* 36-37). For copies of Hester Bateman designs see Gill 1978, pl.23, p.61 and 6 *WLCJ* 107-8. There are other, different, imitations of Bateman and Phipps and Robinson productions known.
30. For a superlative example of Pinkney's work, exhibited in 1997 at the refurbished silver galleries of the Victoria and Albert Museum, London, see Stancliffe, pl.45, p.35.
31. For another example of this type, by Robert Scott, see 6 *WLCJ* 143-44.
32. See Gill, Margaret *A Handbook of Newcastle Silver*, Newcastle, 1978 and *A Directory of Newcastle Gold-smiths*, privately printed, 1980.
33. See Chapter 7, Part 1 and Part 5 for increasing purchases by silversmiths from Chester and York of silver from the Barnard family, both assayed and unassayed.
34. Deep felt gratitude for assistance must be recorded to Nicholas Dolan Esq., of the Laing Gallery, Newcastle, who provided indispensable help in the research on the attribution of the Fenwick crest and the fate of the Newcastle Corporation armorial labels by Thomas Watson.
35. A *Directory of Newcastle Goldsmiths* by Margaret A.V. Gill published by the Goldsmiths' Company, Foster Lane, London, EC2. See further *The Marks of the Newcastle Goldsmiths 1702 to 1884*, offprint from *Archaeological Aeliana*, fifth series, vol, II, by M.A.V. Gill B.A., Ph.D., published by The Society of Antiquaries of Newcastle-Upon-Tyne, 1974.
36. This conclusion has been contributed by Keith Thacker. See also 'John Langlands I, Goldsmith of Newcastle' by Ian Pickford, *Antique Collecting*, vol. 38, no. 7, pp.4-9.
37. Thomas Bewick, *A Memoir*.
38. See Chapter 7, Part 4.
39. In *York Assay Office and Silversmiths 1776-1858* (1983).

40. 6 *WLCJ* 165 (1979).
41. See further 9 *WLCJ* 61.
42. See Chapter 5, Part 3, on the Batemans.
43. For a description of the labels illus. and not referred to in the text see 6 *WLCJ* 149 (figs 514-27), 6 *WLCJ* 153 (figs 528-41) and 9 *WLCJ* 64 (figs 542-54).
44. See Chapter 2, Part 9.
45. York Minster Library, ref. MS Add 134/1.
46. John Murray, 1886.
47. See Chapter 7, Part 2.
48. M. Gubbins, *York Assay Office and Silversmiths*, 1983, p.42.
49. Sir Thomas Barlow has re-examined the wine labels of York, see 9 *WLCJ* 44,61. The authors of Part 5 have been greatly helped in compiling notes by the advice of Mr Martin Gubbins, whose extensive knowledge of York makers' marks has been invaluable, and who willingly answered questions. They are also extremely grateful to Miss Margaret Gill, Curator of Tunbridge Wells Museum, for allowing them to quote from her excellent paper 'The Latter Days of the York Assay Office' (*Yorkshire Archaeological Journal*, vol. 49, 1977).
50. Sketchley lists the names and addresses of fifty-seven so-called 'Toymen', makers of small articles of silver including wine labels, with additional lists of more specialised manufacturers such as buckle makers, snuffer makers and watch chain makers, in his *Birmingham, Wolverhampton and Wallsall Directory* of 1767.
51. See Chapter 3.
52. Willmore's crescent MOUNTAIN of 1810 was exhibited, see *Birmingham Gold and Silver 1773-1973*, published by City Museum and Art Gallery Birmingham, no. B275.
53. This could refer to Cox and Bettridge's PORT of 1812, a rounded rectangular, no. B276, or to John Lawrence's MADEIRA of 1817, an unusual crescent shape with pendant triangle, the sides and triangle being engraved with vines, illus. as no. B278.
54. Willmore's octagonal double-headed illus. ROB ROY of 1826 and rectangular MADEIRA with stamped and pierced repoussé decorated border of vines of 1827 could fall with this category (nos. B282 and B283).
55. Taylor's VESPETRO of 1824, a die-stamped label with irregular edge, with vines, scrolls and rocaille work in relief, was exhibited as no. B280.
56. Lawrence and Co's plain and inscribed STRAWBERRY of 1825 was exhibited as no. B281.
57. A rectangular label by R. Mitchell, 1823, engraved for BUCELLAS, with a border pierced and engraved with vines, was exhibited as no. B279.
58. Willmore's NIG was exhibited (no. B285) - a rounded rectangular with reeded border. See also 3 *WLCJ* 53 for an 1836 label and 10 *WLCJ* 95 for an 1837 label with curious hallmarking (two makers marks, two anchors, date letter but no lion passant).
59. Taylor and Perry in 1831 produced a letter M with scrolled serifs and acanthus leaf ornament, illus. no. B284.
60. For assay master's notes see 3 *WLCJ* 53. Gervase Wheeler produced in 1833 a three vine leaf and tendril design for CLARET illus. in Ryall, p.80, fig. 5.
61. Illus. in Ryall, p.80, fig. 5.
62. See below, Chapter 8, Part 6 on electroplating.
63. For further reading see *Birmingham Gold and Silver 1773-1973*, Section A, and the bibliography cited therein. Boulton's MADEIRA 1830 is illus. in Ryall, p.80, fig. 5.
64. By courtesy of Birmingham Public Library Records Office.
65. 1807 label was exhibit no. B273 and the 1814 label was exhibit no. B277.
66. Illus. in Ryall, p.80, fig. 5. See above, Chapter 2,

Part 18, Goblets.
67. Illus. in Birmingham City Museum Gallery catalogue no. B272 (Birmingham Public Library Records Office).
68. Illus. *idem*, no. B274.
69. Idem, no. B280.
70. Illus. in Ryall, p.80, fig. 5.
71. Idem.
72. Joseph Willmore, 1826, exhibit no. B282.
73. Joseph Willmore, 1831, exhibit no. B285. There is also a small NIG sauce label.
74. See below, Chapter 8, Part 6 on electroplating.
75. The Rough Books from 1843 to 1854 have been preserved. The Plate Books indicate the number of labels (sometimes spelled 'lables' in the early registers) that were sent for assay by named manufacturers. The Wine Label Circle has tables showing (i) the yearly production of labels, (ii) the makers with the number of labels submitted by each, (iii) sixty-three makers with their date of entry and date of their first recorded label, (iv) twenty makers who submitted labels for assay, though no examples have yet been recorded, and (v) 272 labels dating from 1773 (John Winter and Co.) to 1981 (Roberts and Belk). The assay office also recorded goods that did not reach the required silver content and these were broken before being returned to the makers. Four examples of parcels containing labels have been noted. In Oct. 1800, Thos. Law and Co. submitted a lot of '30 tops and 5 lables' weighing 6oz 11dwts and were charged 3s.3½d. for the privilege of having their goods broken and returned because they were '12 dwts worse'. W. Hutton and Sons suffered the same fate twice in 1864 and 1870 (two labels in each parcel) and in 1875 Roberts and Belk's parcel, which included thirty-six labels and a napkin ring, cost them 6s. to no avail because they were '1oz 3 dwts worse'.
76. 8 *WLCJ* 24, row 7.
77. See Chapter 8, Part 6.
78. Four single letter labels are all Victorian. The letters are 'B', 'W', 'S' and the earliest 'R' was made by Jas. Dixon and Co. in 1863. Illus. in *Bottle tickets in the Victoria and Albert Museum*, 1948 edn., 16f. Two stars are known. One has 'petal shaped' rays and is the only example from any assay office that does not have sharp points with straight rays (7 *WLCJ* 74). A second, by John Younge and Co., 1786, for GIN, is of the more common shape. One stylised pecten shell has been reported dating from the first quarter of the nineteenth century, but it is possible that some of the die-stamped Irish versions were made in Sheffield.
79. 7 *WLCJ* 60.
80. 4 *WLCJ* 205, G2.
81. See also Part 8 below on Edinburgh.
82. 7 *WLCJ* 199, ref. D3.
83. Illustrated in *WLCJ*.
84. 7 *WLCJ* 125.
85. See J.T. Younge and Sons' BRANDY of 1791, illus. in Ryall's article in *Antique Collector* for 1968, p.80, fig.4.
86. 8 *WLCJ* 24, row 3.
87. 7 *WLCJ* 179.
88. Robert Gainsford produced a HOCK in 1828.
89. 1 *WLCJ* 182.
90. 1 *WLCJ* 90 for GIN, 1872. James Dixon and Sons' single letter 'R' of 1863 is shown in the 1958 edn. of 'Bottle Tickets in the V & A Museum' at 16f.
91. The assistance of the Assay Master and especially his librarian, Mrs Richardson, for allowing use of the library and particularly of the old plate books, is gratefully acknowledged.
92. Illus. in 7 *WLCJ* 27, no. 23, bearing three marks: JMc, King's head and Edinburgh thistle.
93. Illus. in 7 *WLCJ* 27, no. 20, bearing five marks: GMH, king's head, castle, Edinburgh thistle and date letter q.

94. See 7 *WLCJ* 26, marked with JH, king's head and castle.
95. See 7 *WLCJ* 226, row BS and 7 *WLCJ* 61, row C2. See also Part 7, above, on Sheffield.
96. Namely, those outside the Edinburgh and Glasgow statutory catchments.
97. See 4 *WLCJ* 67 for Extract from Assay Office Records, Edinburgh Makers of Wine Labels (Jan.-Mar.) 1800-1880.
98. See for details of makers 2 *WLCJ* 91, 145; 3 *WLCJ* 143; 8 *WLCJ* 176.
99. Illus. in 7 *WLCJ* 226, row G1.
100. See the SHERRY illus. in 1 *WLCJ* 75, row 6.
101. Illus. in 1 *WLCJ* 90, row 5, no. 2.
102. Illus. in 7 *WLCJ* 226, row F5.
103. See 7 *WLCJ* 226, row B5 and 7 *WLCJ* 61, row C2.
104. See 7 *WLCJ* 180, no. 1.
105. A list of provincial silversmiths registered at Glasgow's assay office is given in Jackson's *Silver and Gold Marks*, 3rd edn., 1989, at p.579.
106. 6 and 7 William IV Cap. 69.
107. Minutes of the Goldsmiths' Company of Newcastle for 31 July 1717.
108. M.A.V. Gill, 'The Latter Days of the York Assay Office', *Yorkshire Archaeological Journal*, vol. 49 (1977) p.115.
109. In 'Old Country Silver' (1971) p.218.
110. Reference W III.
111. For full and further details see James, p.76.
112. Illus. in 5 *WLCJ* 178. Sold at Sotheby's 11 Feb. 1971, lot 29 (illus.).
113. For full and further details see James, p.87.
114. Illus. by James on p.87, fig. 11, using the gothic A.
115. Illus. in 5 *WLCJ* 259 at C1.
116. For details see James, p.4.
117. See 2 *WLCJ* 37.
118. 1 *WLCJ* 165.
119. 1 *WLCJ* 173.
120. See 10 *WLCJ* 107.
121. See further James, pp.83-5.
122. Sold Sotheby's 3 Feb. 1972, lot 108 (illus.).
123. William Walker, *The Banks of Bon-Accord, 1375-1860*, p.357.
124. Sold Sotheby's 8 Mar. 1973, lot 60 (illus.).
125. For further details see James, p.105.
126. James, p.104, pl.15.
127. By Jackson, p.535 and in Phillips' sale for 12 Apr. 1978, lot 227.
128. Illus. in 7 *WLCJ* 22.
129. The Edinburgh records from 1811 to 1850 contain no mention of his sending in plate for assay, whereas when he was in Dundee the book for 1800-1805 is full of items sent.
130. On p.109.
131. Sale dated 8 Mar. 1973, lot 54 (illus.).
132. Sale dated 26 July 1972, lot 283.
133. Phillips sale 6 Dec. 1977, lot 257.
134. Illus. in James, pl.16, p.121.
135. Illus. in 7 *WLCJ* 27, with WJ struck twice.
136. 7 *WLCJ* 26.
137. Illus. at 4 *WLCJ* 7, with marks. Possibly in Phillips' sale 16 Oct. 1981, lot 57. Illus. at 7 *WLCJ* 22 is an example in the Art Gallery, Schoolhill, Aberdeen.
138. Referred to in footnote in 4 *WLCJ* 6.
139. Illus. at A5 in 2 *WLCJ* 148 (2nd edn.).
140. Illus. at C5 in 2 *WLCJ* 148 (2nd edn.).
141. Illus. in 7 *WLCJ* 27.
142. See PORT and SHERRY by J.T. 1845, illus. in 7 *WLCJ* 22.
143. Illus. in 7 *WLCJ* 22; maker's mark GJ shown at 7 *WLCJ* 23.
144. 8 *WLCJ* 178.
145. See 2 *WLCJ* 146 and 7 *WLCJ* 26, 27.
146. See 10 *WLCJ* 107.
147. Sold by Phillips on 21 May 1982, lot 117.
148. His mark appears on an Aberdeen cream ladle, James, fig. 18, p.92.
149. Illus. in 5 *WLCJ* 31; see also 4 *WLCJ* 7.
150. See 2 *WLCJ* 146 (2nd edn.).
151. See 9 *WLCJ* 16.
152. See 9 *WLCJ* 17.
153. In 2 *WLCJ* 40 (2nd edn.).
154. Sold at Sotheby's 11 Feb. 1971, lot 331.
155. Sold at Phillips 16 Oct. 1981, lot 104.
156. Illus. in 6 *WLCJ* 125.
157. See 2 *WLCJ* 113, 121.
158. 9 *WLCJ* 200.
159. 9 *WLCJ* 199.
160. 1 *WLCJ* 77 (2nd edn.) illus.
161. 9 *WLCJ* 152.
162. Sold at Christie's 26 July 1972, lot 282. BRANDY was reviewed in 9 *WLCJ* 194 and illus. in 5 *WLCJ* 178; RUM was sketched in 7 *WLCJ*.
163. 7 *WLCJ* 111.
164. See 5 *WLCJ* 182.
165. See Ryall (illus.).
166. Illus. in 7 *WLCJ* 25, fig. 10. In Central Museum and Art Gallery, Dundee.
167. He copied designs shown on plates in 6 *WLCJ* 104 and 107 by Hester Bateman at B2, S. Teare at A1, J. Keating at A2, and J. Langlands II at C3. His label is shown in row D.
168. Illus. in 2 *WLCJ* 148 (2nd edn.), said to be dated 1809 (2 *WLCJ* 150). The marks (DM and pot of lilies) are illus. at 2 *WLCJ* 149, fig. 7 (Alex Cuthbert Collection).
169. Sold Sotheby's 11 Feb. 1971, lot 30. Illus.
170. See Ryall (illus.).
171. See Dent.
172. See 7 *WLCJ* 25 for illus.
173. In 5 *WLCJ* 77. VIOLETTE measures 17.5 x 9.5 mm (¾ x ⅜in.).
174. See Michael Druitt, 'The Fascination of Decanter Labels', *The Wine Magazine,* annexed to 3 *WLCJ* 89.
175. See 1 *WLCJ* 78 (2nd edn.).
176. In 7 *WLCJ* 51.
177. Sold Sotheby's 3 Feb. 1972, lot 102 (illus.).
178. See 2 *WLCJ* 148 where the label is ascribed to him.
179. In 2 *WLCJ* 149.
180. See 1 *WLCJ* 92 (2nd edn.), illus. p.93.
181. Moss and Roe, *Highland Gold and Silversmiths*, p.50.
182. Illus. *op.cit.* p.50.
183. In 5 *WLCJ* 178 where the label is illus.
184. See 7 *WLCJ* 26. It is marked JH, king's head, castle.
185. Wine name not given in 10 *WLCJ* 107.
186. See 2 *WLCJ* 147 (2nd edn.).
187. No. 34 in the Frederick J. Anderson Collection (cat. R.J.E. Inglis).
188. Sold by Phillips 19 Jan. 1979, lot 188.
189. 7 *WLCJ* 28, nos 32, 33 and 34.
190. Sold by Sotheby's 11 Feb. 1971, lot 44.
191. See companion volume on *Sauce Labels.*
192. Sold by Sotheby's 11 Feb. 1971, lot 32, illus.
193. See 5 *WLCJ* 178.
194. Illus. in 4 *WLCJ* 7.
195. 7 *WLCJ* 28, no. 31.
196. Sold Sotheby's 8 Mar. 1973, lot 53.
197. Sold by Phillips on 16 Dec. 1977, lot 268.
198. Sold by Bonhams on 22 July 1980, lot 125.
199. Illus. in 2 *WLCJ* 148 (2nd edn.) at D5.
200. Illus. in 2 *WLCJ* 148 (2nd edn.) at C1.
201. Illus. in 2 *WLCJ* 148 (2nd edn.) at D1 and E1.
202. Illus. in 2 *WLCJ* 148 (2nd edn.) at C3.
203. Sold by Phillips 5 Feb. 1982, see 7 *WLCJ* 18.
204. Alex Cuthbert had eight of his labels in his collection, see 3 *WLCJ* 11.
205. In the Royal Museum of Scotland - see 10 *WLCJ* 45.
206. Illus. in 10 *WLCJ* 42.
207. See 7 *WLCJ* 28, nos 35 to 37.
208. See 7 *WLCJ* 30, nos 38 and 39.
209. See 7 *WLCJ* 30, nos 40 and 41.
210. Writing in the launch issue of the *Wine Label Circle Journal* in Apr. 1952, Jean Rhodes, its first editor, remarked on the exceptionally fine labels produced by Irish silversmiths. John Beecroft, her successor in the editorial chair in 1959, seems to have given practical endorsement to Mrs Rhodes' view by choosing to make Irish labels a particular speciality of his, and it is his seminal articles and comments on Irish labels over the years that constitute the foundations of this overview. See, for example, Beecroft, J. 'Irish Wine Labels and their Makers' in 3 *WLCJ* 19-29, 4 *WLCJ* 197-216.
211. Ticher, K., Delamer, I. and O'Sullivan, W. *Hallmarks on Dublin Silver 1730-72* (Dublin 1968).
212. See Chapter 2, Part 10; fig. 3. Walsh is believed to have made sauce labels in 1750 for the Powerscourt frame, see *Sauce Labels*, p.167 and fig. 110.
213. See Chapter 5, Part 2 and 4 *WLCJ* 208, F2 illus., and Penzer, pl.5.
214. O'Brien, C. 'Dean Swift's Labels', 9 *WLCJ* 54.
215. The mark 'IH'. John Hopkins (1752), John Hillery (1756-1787), John Haughton (1764-1768), John Humphris (1773-1787) and James Heyland (1781-1812) are recorded from Cork, and two more from Limerick, John Hackett (1770-1784) and John Hawley (1784). Specific allocation of the mark to any of these has not yet been possible.
216. See Chapter 2, Part 10.
217. This design, which is often called 'Irish Crescent', is somewhere between a crescent and a symmetrical scroll. It was developed exclusively by Irish silversmiths of this period. It is seen here in its basic form; other variations are known, and it is also found surmounted by goblet or plaque, supported by stays.
218. Chapter 2, Part 9.
219. O'Brien, C. 'Irish Wine Labels', 6 *WLCJ* 223.
220. See 10 *WLCJ* 24.
221. Sufficient information has not been accumulated to enable the various IT and JT marks found on Irish plate to be definitively identified. It is clear, however, from the assay records that both Teares were specialist makers of wine labels, and it is not unlikely that the son may have used his father's punches indiscriminately with his own. The records do not provide information supporting Jackson's attributions of any mark to either John Townsend or John Tweedie. It is, however, evident from a pewter plate used for recording marks occasionally from 1765 to 1814 that one of the Teares used both I and J as the initial for John: in a space clearly intended for one maker's marks, three marks are shown in a cluster - IT in a small oblong, JT in a slightly larger oblong, and another JT (with dot between) in a broader rectangle. The mark encountered on the earliest John Teare labels (*c.*1790) is JT in script. Pieces fully marked for the early 1800s are found with a characteristic JT mark showing the cross-bar of the T as a scroll. Another characteristic mark, occurring 1810-20 consists of I T in a shaped rectangular shield. Throughout the period of Teare labels other variations of JT and IT marks are found, but they are not amenable to chronological classification. An early label assayed in Dublin of unusual escutcheon design, engraved on a scroll for HOCK is illus. in 8 *WLCJ* 5.
222. Not noted in *Silver in the Channel Islands* by F. Cohen and N. Duquesne Bird at p.136.
223. See further *Channel Islands Silver* by R. Mayne p.48, where SOTERNE is described a a 'plain wine label'.
224. Bearing the mark shown on pl.116 of Mayne's book p.89.

Notes

Chapter 8

1. See Chapter 8, Part 2 for gilt-metal and silvered brass.
2. See further above, Chapter 4, Part 1.
3. Frederick Bradbury, London 1912, reprinted Sheffield, 1968.
4. See further 5 *WLCJ* 61, 8 *WLCJ* 112 and 8 *WLCJ* 217.
5. See patterns illus. in 8 *WLCJ* 209-10 (c.1785).
6. See patterns illus. in 5 *WLCJ* 61, 8 *WLCJ* 112 and 8 *WLCJ* 217.
7. Two examples similar to fig. 965 are shown by Stephen Helliwell in his *Understanding Antique Silver Plate*, Antique Collectors' Club, p.104, engraved for RASPBRANDY and NOYEO and said to be rather clumsy in appearance. They usually have most of their silver rubbed off, perhaps because they were thinly plated. He also illus. diamond shaped labels, c.1790, for W. PORT and RUM, and cushion floral shaped labels, c.1820, for PORT, CLARET, SHERRY and MADEIRA similar to fig. 961.
8. Three examples from Matthew Boulton's designs for wine labels, E 2060-1952, of around 1780 are shown in Jane Stancliffe's *Bottle Tickets* at p.46.
9. Three neck rings with shell and piercing decoration for PORT, CLARET and W. WINE are shown by Helliwell, op. cit., at p.105.
10. This method is described and illus. in the *Collectors Dictionary of Silver and Gold* by Michael Clayton, London, 1971, at p.256.
11. Explanation by Shirley Bury in *Victorian Electroplate*, London, 1971, at pp.24-25.
12. Explanation in Bradbury (see note 3, above) at p.178.
13. A collection of 114 OSP labels, all unmarked, was sold at Phillips 19 Oct. 1990. For particulars see 8 *WLCJ* 234-35.
14. See also 3 *WLCJ* 181. The crested gadrooned curved rectangles were even issued upside down, see 3 *WLCJ* 184 where SHERRY and MADEIRA are illus. See further John Beecroft's article in 4 *WLCJ* 160-66.
15. Heal Collection, British Museum, 85.33, and see Bertrand, Giulian, *Corkscrews of the 18th Century*, 1995, p.40.
16. 3 *WLCJ* 50.
17. Some vine leaf labels were made of fused plate in German silver. The Sheffield City Museum has a set of three for MADEIRA, PORT and SHERRY. This cheaper version of a good looking label has been illus. in the *Journal*. See also Pinn, Keith, *Paktong*, Woodbridge, 1999, pp.73-76.
18. Bury, Shirley, *Victorian Electroplate*, London, 1971, pp.24-25.
19. See 9 *WLCJ* 35.
20. This introduction was written by Sir Geoffrey Hutchinson, Q.C. and published in 3 *WLCJ* 32.
21. Bernard M. Watney and R.J. Charleston, 'Petitions for Patents concerning Porcelain, Glass and Enamels with special reference to Birmingham, "The Great Toyshop of Europe"', *Trans.* of English Ceramic Circle, vol. 6, part 2, 1966.
22. Described in 5 *WLCJ* 133 as being produced c.1755 or even earlier.
23. Eric Benton, 'John Brooks in Birmingham', *Trans.* of English Ceramic Circle, vol. 7, part 3, 1970. *Aris's Birmingham Gazette*, 27 Nov. 1952.
24. Catalogued as Staffordshire by Bernard Rackham in the *Schreiber Catalogue*, vol. 3 as early as 1924.
25. 'The Art and Artist of the Battersea Enamel Wine-Label', *Connoisseur*, Dec. 1952 and Mar. 1959.
26. 'Battersea Enamel Wine Labels', *Antique Collector*, June 1935.
27. In *The Book of the Wine Label*, 1947.
28. 'The Art and Artist of the Battersea Enamel Wine-Label', *Connoisseur*, Dec. 1952 and Mar. 1959.
29. *Trans.* of England Ceramic Circle, vol.3, pl.77.
30. Illus. in Benjamin, *English Enamel Boxes*, p.9.
31. The labels illus. have not all been photographed to the same scale. Battersea labels measure approximately 7.6 x 6.4cm (3 x 2⅜in.). See also the article by Jean Rhodes in 1 *WLCJ* 36-7, and design notes in 1 *WLCJ* 118.
32. Sold Phillips Son and Neale 23 Jan. 1968, Lot 104.
33. Sold Phillips Son and Neale 23 Jan. 1968, Lot 104.
34. See further 1 *WLCJ* 186, 2 *WLCJ* 25, 3 *WLCJ* 35 and 5 *WLCJ* 104. Confusingly, W. WINE also appears in design 13.
35. Huile is an Anjou White wine, but Huile de Venus is given in the *American Family Recipe Book*, London 1853, re-printed from the American edn., as a drink made from:
Wild Carrot Flowers   1 lb.
Proof Spirit   4 gallons
Distil or macrate, and add an equal quantity of Capillaire. Colour with cochineal.
Capillaire is a flavoured syrup, usually orange-flower or rose-water. Note 29 applies.
36. See further 2 *WLCJ* 25, 2 *WLCJ* 155.
37. Sold Phillips Son and Neale, 23 Jan. 1968, Lot 104.
38. The design was also used on a box. See 3 *WLCJ* 36.
39. See also 2 *WLCJ* 25 and 5 *WLCJ* 104.
40. With two putti, one stirring the punch and the other squeezing what appears to be a lemon into it, (in the City of Liverpool Museums). See further 9 *WLCJ* 282.
41. This label, together with PALME and TOQUAY, was illus. in Bernard Watney, 'English Enamels in the 18th Century', *Antiques International*, London, 1966. It was formerly in the collection of Eric Benton, who originally purchased it in Paris. The only other example of the RANCIE label is illus. by Lord Ilford, *Trans.* English Ceramic Circle, vol. 6, part 1, 1965, pl.31. It was considered there to be a contraction of Irancy, but this seems somewhat unlikely. The wines of the Pyrénées-Orientales include the Vins de Grenache - 'Ce sont des vins de dessert corsés, moelleux, fruités, au goût de Rancio' (Poulain and Jacqueline, *Vignes et Vins de France*, Paris 1960). Rancio implies matured in cask. There is an appellation contrôlée Clairette du Languedoc-Rancio, a white wine of 14°. Rancio is also sometimes added to the label for bottles of wine from this region, such as from Banyuls and Rivesaltes.
42. See 2 *WLCJ* 25.
43. See 1 *WLCJ* 186.
44. See 1 *WLCJ* 186, 2 *WLCJ* 155.
45. See 2 *WLCJ* 25, 3 *WLCJ* 35.
46. See 3 *WLCJ* 106.
47. See 3 *WLCJ* 35.
48. See 6 *WLCJ* 257.
49. See 1 *WLCJ* 186, 2 *WLCJ* 135, 3 *WLCJ* 35.
50. See 20 *WLCJ* 44. This label and the following label for CAPE are illus. and described in Susan Benjamin's *English Enamel Boxes* at pp.38-29.
51. See 1 *WLCJ* 186 and note 27, above.
52. See labels illus. in 1 *WLCJ* 76 for LISBON, ORANGE, ESPAGNE and RANCIO. See also the set of eight French shield labels for *(inter alia)* CHABLY, CAHORS and TORRIN also mentioned at p.76, the CHABLY illus. at p.77.
53. Penzer, N.M., 'The Bin Label', *The Antique Collector*, Dec. 1960, pp.221ff.
54. There are forty-one labels in the Cropper Collection at the Victoria and Albert Museum, including some interesting names. The York Museum and the Norwich Museum have sixteen labels each. A list of some surviving wine bin label names can be found in Appendix 2.
55. A set of five transfer-printed labels have SPODE on the back and the number 5 impressed - see 1 *WLCJ* 60.
56. Little appears to have been written about bin labels. There was a most excellent and well-illus. article, written by the late Dr. Penzer, which appeared in the Christmas number of *The Antique Collector* 1960. A chapter on bin labels, written by Mr Geoffrey Willis, appeared in vol. IV of *The Concise Encyclopaedia of Antiques*, 1959, and the late Lady Ruggles-Brise gave brief mention of bin labels in an article that appeared in *Country Life* in 1942. The late Reverend E.W. Whitworth included a chapter on bin labels in his book, *Wine Labels*. Harvey's Wine Museum at Bristol used to display most of the Delaforce Collection of some 110 bin labels. Worcester City Museum displays the contents of George Joseland's wine cellar (listed in 7 *WLCJ* 38).
57. Compiled by Jean Rhodes (see 1 *WLCJ* 121).
58. See 7 *WLCJ* 141.
59. See Keith Thacker's article in 7 *WCLJ*.
60. See further Colin Paul's article in 5 *WLCJ* 191-98, which is well illus.
61. George Richards Elkington and O.W. Barratt had already patented in 1838 a similar process - the first of its kind - for electroplating with zinc.
62. R.F. Bud and G.K. Roberts, *Science versus Practice: Chemistry in Victorian Britain*, Manchester 1984, p.68.
63. Nickel ore imported from Saxony had actually begun to be refined commercially in Britain a few years before 1830, particularly by one Percival Norton Johnson of London's Hatton Garden, who had founded there in 1822 the firm that was to develop into the country's chief supplier of precious metals, Johnson Matthey and Company.
64. Frederick Bradbury, *History of Old Sheffield Plate*, Sheffield, 1912.
65. William Ryland, in S Timmins, ed., *Birmingham and the Midland Hardware District*, London, 1866.
66. Walter Sissons, *Old Sheffield Plate*, London, n.d. (c.1900).
67. Sissons, op. cit., p.5.
68. Further details of the Elkington factory can be found in 2 *WLCJ* 104, presumably written by the then Editor.
69. N.M. Penzer, *Book of the Wine Label*, p.34.
70. See further *Antique Sheffield Plate*, G. Bernard Hughes, pp.31-32.
71. Victoria and Albert Museum, Print Room: Catalogue of John Green in 1792, (ref M64b); Library; Parker and Wakelin Ledgers, Catalogue of the Cropper Collection mentions only two, both are missing, Claret and Madeira (M1304/5). There are a small number of plated and mother-of-pearl labelled stoppers.
72. The Bowes Museum, Barnard Castle, Yorkshire, possesses a set of six corks with plain silver gilt mounts. The plain cap has an eye that holds loosely a plain ring - they are unmarked - see 8 *WLCJ* 186.
73. An example of the plated horse's head bottle cork is illus. in 1 *WLCJ* 10, p.145.
74. See further: *The Connoisseur*, Oct. 1922; Short article by P.J. Cropper with illus. of Champagne and Macon; *Antique Dealer and Collectors Guide*, Sept. 1986, pp.82-83. Article by Judith Banister mentions early 'decanter' corks and later cork stoppers for the period 1820-60. Note that the Ashmolean Museum, Marshall Collection, has only a few plated stoppers and that the London Museum, Brown Collection, has only a few plated stoppers.
75. See further 8 *WLCJ* 82-95, with further illus.
76. Grimwade 1311.
77. Sold by Phillips, 30 Apr. 1986, Lot 145.
78. This stopper is illus. in *The Connoisseur*, Oct. 1922, p.117, with note by P.J. Cooper (Note 3) probably by 'Ionadab Greaves'. Johanadab Greaves appears in Sketchley's Sheffield directory of 1774 (Bradbury page 442) of Church Lane, under the trade description of snuff box maker. See also 8 *WLCJ* 88 for illus.
79. Sold by Phillips 30 Apr. 1986, Lot 146.
80. In Phillips' sale, 19 Feb. 1988, Lot 74.

Notes

81. Illus. in *The Connoisseur,* Oct. 1922, p.117.
82. Appeared in the Goldsmith and the Grape Exhibition and shown in the catalogue on p.35, no. (iii).
83. Sold by Phillips 25 July 1984, Lot 233. See further 9 *WLCJ* 106.
84. Sold by Phillips 25 July 1984, Lot 233. See further 9 *WLCJ* 106.
85. Illus. in catalogue to the Goldsmith and the Grape exhibition, p.35 (x).
86. Sold Phillips 18 Mar. 1983, Lot 227. Illus. in 8 *WLCJ* 88.
87. See Cyprus Redding, *a history and description of modern wines*, London, 1833, p.10.
88. This paragraph is based on Dr Watney's note in 7 *WLCJ* 5.
89. Information kindly supplied by Mr Christopher Sykes of Woburn.
90. Stancliffe, pl.34, p.28.
91. Published by Birmingham City Museum, 1973, reference B279.
92. N.M. Penzer, *Book of the Wine Label,* p1.19, row 2.
93. There is a similar label in the Cropper collection, Victoria and Albert Museum, illus. in Stancliffe, pl.37, p.29.
94. Victoria and Albert Museum booklet, 1958, pl.23e.
95. See 9 *WLCJ* 43-47.
96. Jane Stancliffe, *Bottle Tickets,* Victoria and Albert Museum, pp.26 and 34 (illus. at p.10).

Chapter 9

1. Hawkins, John, Sydney, *Australian Silver*, 1973 p.23. All details of silversmiths and marks from Hawkins 1973 and 1990.
2. Busby, James, *Journal of a Tour through some of the Vineyards of Spain and France*, Sydney, 1833.
3. Johnson, Hugh, *Wine*, London, 1974, p.226.
4. Originally in the collection of the late Michael Partington Esq., they were gradually sold off during the 1970s and 1980s.
5. Hawkins, John, *Nineteenth Century Australian Silver*, Woodbridge, 1990, vol.2, p.270.
6. Private collection.
7. This is a pair with CLARET and was made in around 1865-70.
8. Hawkins, op. cit., Woodbridge, 1990, vol.2, p.158.
9. Christie's, Melbourne, 21 Mar. 1994, lot 536.
10. Bradbury, p.253.
11. Bradbury, p.167.
12. Penzer, p.80 and pl.24.
13. See further 4 *WLCJ* 73, 'Beauty and the Beast'.
14. All details of silversmiths and their marks from Langdon and Mackay.
15. See Mackay, Donald, *Silversmiths of the Atlantic Provinces*, Halifax, 1973, pl.28b.
16. This label is particularly interesting as it has been cut from an older, larger piece of silver that has the remnants of early eighteenth-century style engraving visible on the reverse side.
17. *Birmingham Gold and Silver*, exhibition catalogue, Birmingham, 1973, B279, Stancliffe, pl.38, p.28.
18. Penzer, pl.25, bottom and p.80. Illus. in fig. 902 for BRANDY in Woolley and Wallis sale catalogue for 30.4.2003 at p.117.
19. London, 1983, pp.106-07.
20. Erich Pontoppidan, *Den Danske Atlas*, Copenhagen, 1764, vol.II, p.202.
21. For a full explanation see 9 *WLCJ* 174.
22. Punch is well known, though rare, on English wine labels of the 1750s to 1770s and has been recorded on a Birmingham label of 1828 for MILK PUNCH.
23. 'Pope' is another form of punch, mixed to a different recipe, based on port.
24. See Chapter 9, Part 18.
25. *Punsch*, Wahlstr md Widstaard, Stockholm, 1973.
26. As published by Mrs Elsi Lindhal and recorded in Tardy, *International Hall Marks on Silver*, at p.111.
27. *Idem,* table on p.116.
28. 6 *WLCJ* 269.
29. Taken from a catalogue of 1838 by Tardy in *International Silver Marks* at p.210.
30. Illus. in 8 *WLCJ* 21, maker's mark a pair of scales, CC either side, in a lozenge hatchment.
31. 6 *WLCJ* 266.
32. Maker's mark JL with an animal above, Paris, c.1820.
33. 6 *WLCJ* 267.
34. 6 Idem.
35. 6 *WLCJ* 268.
36. 6 *WLCJ* 268, illus. in picture 6.
37. 6 *WLCJ* 268, illus. in picture 7.
38. See 8 *WLCJ* 68 for the set of eight and lot 296, Bonham's 21.3.03 for the Clérin labels.
39. The foregoing paragraphs were contributed by Vivian Lewis with editorial additions.
40. Illus. in 10 *WLCJ* 90.
41. See 10 *WLCJ* 93, Andrew Gilmour.
42. See 10 *WLCJ* 93, Ian Smart.
43. Illus. in 10 *WLCJ* 93.
44. Penzer, pl.24, middle. A *kukri* is an all-purpose Gurkha Army knife.
45. See 5 *WLCJ* 82 for further details.
46. Salter, John 'The silver of the Knights of St John', *Country Life*.
47. Denaro, V., *The Goldsmiths of Malta and their marks*, 1972.
48. Jackson, Sir Charles, *English Goldsmiths and their marks*, 1921.
49. 9 *WLCJ* 203.
50. See Penzer, pl.20, PORT. Fenech's warrant is dated 20 Oct. 1821.
51. See further 10 *WLCJ* 97.
52. Unfortunately this label can no longer be traced, so the correct interpretation of the marks cannot be guaranteed by the author of this section.
53. Beet, B. *The Silver Society Journal*, Autumn 1998, p.16
54. Wittewaal, B.W.G., *Nederlands Klein Zilver*, Amsterdam, 1987, p.152; 2nd edn. Acoude, 1994, pp.167-68.
55. Dutch maker's marks and all hallmarks of the period concerned are to be found in 'Netherlands Responsibility Marks since 1797' issued regularly (and then containing all new finds) by the Netherlands Assay Office, P.O. Box 1075, NL-2800 BB GOUDA, The Netherlands. A registered maker's mark from after the abolition of the guilds is published with a unique five-digit number with preceding M. The information on silversmiths given there also contains the town(s) where the silversmith/factory was established and the period during which a specific mark was used.
56. Baarsen a.o., R., *De Lelijke tijd, Pronkstukken van Nederlandse interieurkunst*, Amsterdam, 1995. The Rijksmuseum, Amsterdam, took the lead in a successful attempt to reappraise the second half of the nineteenth century, generally referred to in the Netherlands as The Age of Ugliness, by mounting an impressive exhibition on Dutch decorative arts dating from that specific period.
57. Penzer, N.M., *The Book of the Wine Label*, London, 1947, p.125, gives PORT A PORT as a probable mistake. This Dutch label proves the opposite but unfortunately does not reveal the exact nature of the substance. Could it be PORT from PORTO with the French prefix 'à' indicating an origin, but here written as a small capital A? (Compare the French 'Acheter quelque chose à quelqu'un', which translates as 'To buy something from somebody'. The label referred to by Dr Penzer and now in the Ashmolean Museum has the title in Roman capitals, done as one word in letters all of the same size on a single vine leaf design, which can be dated c.1860-70. The original name for the town of OPORTO at the mouth of the Douro was simply 'PORTO'.
58. The shape of this English Renaissance revival label is very similar to the one shown in the right-hand top corner of pl.20 in Penzer, 1947 and described as type 17, architectural. Other names noted in the Netherlands on labels of identical design and manufacture are BESSEN and GIN. *Citroen* is a lemon-geneva of yellow colour drunk by males of the lower classes and *bessen* is a red-berry-geneva even favoured by females slightly higher up the ladder. Gin, in this series of Dutch labels, in the author's opinion refers to the English gin as imitated in the Netherlands and certainly not to Dutch gin being the English name for straightforward geneva (old or young). The proper label name in this case would have been Hollandse Gin but to keep in line with the other labels 'Hollandse' was probably omitted.
59. In the KAAPSCHE SHERRIJ and KAAPSCHE PONTAC labels the word 'Kaapsche' means 'Caapisch' or 'from the Cape (of Good Hope)'. Sherrij refers to the Spanish wine from Jerez de la Frontera. Kaapsche Sherrij may mean a Cape wine similar to the Spanish wine. Kaapsche Pontac is, as explained in Part 17 above, most probably a South African wine originating from the Cape district of that name. It is unlikely to mean a white wine from the Bordeaux area as suggested by Penzer, 1947, p.124. If this assumption is correct, Kaapsche was probably added to keep in line with the other label. These Dutch labels provide evidence that Pontac was being exported from the Huguenot-founded vineyard of that name in the Drakensburg area. It is interesting, too, that the late years of the nineteenth century, when these labels were made, coincided with a low ebb in South African wine exports to England, because of high import duties and the advent of *phylloxera*. Cape Sherry was hardly known in England until after the First World War.
60. Corn and juniper are ingredients for geneva. Also the barrel fits into that picture. The distillery D (istilliert). E.V. has not yet been identified. It is thought to be a commemorative label. E.V. could refer to a method or style of distillation or to a particular standard.
61. SOYA and KAYEN are in the Collection 'Duivenvoorde Castle' and are unmarked except for a later Dutch control mark. The observed precise sterling standard (0.925) on the chains and on the KAYEN label after testing (only SOYA curiously enough was not more than 0.900) indicate an English origin (see further *Sauce Labels 1750-1950* for an illus.). Export wine labels are known such as a Hester Bateman label for an Austrian titled family.
62. King George III visited St Paul's Cathedral in London on 11 Oct. 1797 in honour of Lord Duncan's victory over the Dutch fleet on 10 Oct. 1797.
63. Although the 4th Dutch War took place as late as 1780-1784, both countries were united again at Waterloo for the final defeat of Napoleon. His end also meant the end of supremacy of French fashion and influence in the decorative arts. Dutch Empire, for instance, was only French in name, the Dutch silver then being very similar in shape and decoration to the earlier English Adam. The next 'Dutch' style was the Biedermeijer indicating a more German influence. The revival styles following Biedermeijer in around 1850 (the period in which the first Dutch labels appear to have been produced in some quantity) was again following the earlier trend set in England by the Prince Regent, looking backwards to pre-Napoleonic times and grandeur.
64. All photographs by Henrik Reeh, assistant professor at the University of Copenhagen.
65. Tyskland is mentioned by Jorunn Fossberg in

Norske Sølvstempler, Universitets Forlaget AS, 1994, p.178.
66. 'Svenskt Silversmide 1520-1850', *Guld-och Silverstämpler*, Stockholm, 1963, vol.IV, p.642, mark no. 8724.
67. *Guldsmede haandverket i Oslo og Kristiania*, Oslo, 1924, p.354.
68. *The Book of Wine Antiques*, pl.167, p.165.
69. See 9 *WLCJ* 181.
70. See above, Part 6, Denmark.
71. See 7 *WLCJ* 167 for front and back illus.
72. Illus. at 7 *WLCJ* 168, top left.
73. Illus. at 7 *WLCJ* 168, top right.
74. 7 *WLCJ* 168.
75. At page 115.
76. See Wilkinson, Wynyard, *Makers of Indian Colonial Silver*, 1987.
77. Compare Maltese labels, where the period of manufacture and popularity are within the same span.
78. See Hughes, Dave, *Wine Routes of the Cape*, Struik Publishers, Cape Town, 1991, p.6.
79. Tardy, *International Hallmarks on Silver*, Paris, 1981, p.107.
80. Tardy, op.cit., p.109.
81. The author of this Part was offered about 100 labels in response to advertising, see 6 *WLCJ* 67.
82. See also Part 5, above, for the popularity of punch and its different spelling in Denmark.
83. See also Chapter 6, Part 1.
84. See also Part 4, above.
85. See 9 *WLCJ* 196.
86. Sixteen are listed in 7 *WLCJ* 165.
87. For details, see 6 *WLCJ* 69 and 7 *WLCJ* 165.
88. See 10 *WLCJ* 105.
89. This information is derived from the research of Wilson R. Duprey and was published in 6 *WLCJ* 24.
90. Fales, Martha Gandy, *Joseph Richardson and family*, Middleton, Conn., 1974, p.196.
91. Belden, Louise Conway, *Marks of American Silversmiths*, Charlottesville, Virginia, 1980, p.4.
92. See 1 *WLCJ* 151 and 1 *WLCJ* 166. A visual inspection of this label in 1999 revealed a close resemblance to the 'Prince of Wales feathers style' label by Peter and William Bateman, and although the hallmark has undoubtedly that of Louis Boudo the label could have been imported from England. Fig. 1439 is reproduced by kind permission of the Metropolitan Museum of Art, New York, N.Y. 10028 from Negative Number 134162 tf. The label was an Anonymous Gift in 1945 (ref. 45.44).
93. 7 *WLCJ* 125, where the maker's mark SS within an oval is struck twice. Silas Sawin is not mentioned in Patricia Kane, *Colonial Massachussetts Silversmiths*, Yale, 1988, which is now regarded as the definitive work in this area. It has also been suggested that it could be an unrecorded mark of Sun Shing of Canton.
94. A set of ten, dispersed in London in around 1981, including some quite sophisticated titles such as Hermitage and St Peray.
95. See 9 *WLCJ* 189 for a full description.
96. The patron saint of Fortrose, often portrayed holding a single key, is shown on the arms of this royal burgh. The arms of Gibraltar incorporate a single key.
97. Bonham's sale number 312 03A, 18.7.2002, lot 240.
98. Ibid.
99. Ibid.
100. Attributed to Hugh Gordon in *Sauce Labels*.
101. Bonham's sale number 312 03A, 18.7.2002, lot 241.
102. Ibid.
103. Shown in fig. 111, *Sauce Labels*, at p.168.

Chapter 10

1. Dent, Herbert C., *Wine, Spirit & Sauce Labels of the 18th & 19th Centuries* (Norwich, H.W. Hunt, 1933).
2. Victoria and Albert Museum, Registry, Blythe House, Hammersmith, London.
3. Ibid. For Fitzhenry's collection see further 2 *WLCJ* 33-35.
4. Ibid.
5. Holbourne Museum and Craft Study Centre, Bath.
6. See further Wilson Duprey, 8 *WLCJ* 151, 179.
7. He also wrote a second article, 'Antique Decanter Labels', *The Connoisseur: A Magazine for Collectors* (vol. LXIV, no. 254, Oct. 1922), pp.88-96 (p.117 has a separate short note by Cropper entitled 'Stopper Labels', two of which are illustrated); 'Collecting Bottle-Labels', *The Bazaar* (1, 8 and 15 Apr. 1921); 'The Ticket Collector, *Antiques* (Boston) Part I (Mar. 1923) pp.124-27; Part II (Apr. 1923) pp.166-69. For Cropper's collection see further *WLCJ* 90-91, 175, 183, 185 and 2 *WLCJ* 33-35.
8. See N.M. Penzer, *The Book of the Wine Label*, 1947. A.G. Le Reek was an anagram of the author's true name, G.A. Keeler, who was editor of *The Wine and Spirit Trade Record*.
9. Marshall Papers, Ashmolean Museum, Oxford.
10. Sotheby's sale catalogue 12 Apr. 1995. For Weed's collection see further 1 *WLCJ* 50-51 and 2 *WLCJ* 33-35.
11. R.A. Weed, 'Silver Wine Labels', *The New York Historical Society Quarterly Bulletin* (July 1929), pp.46-67.
12. Marshall Papers, Ashmolean Museum Oxford; papers passed to Mrs Marshall from Sotheby's 1955.
13. Ibid.
14. Ibid.
15. 3 *WLCJ* 106.
16. Marshall Papers, Ashmolean Museum, Oxford.
17. Ibid. and see further 2 *WLCJ* 147-154.
18. Ibid.
19. Ibid.
20. Metalwork Department Library, Victoria and Albert Museum, London. For Anderson's collection see further 1 *WLCJ* 98, 100, 135, 181-182 and 2 *WLCJ* 89, 91.
21. Vintners' Co., London - Archive Papers.
22. Ibid.
23. Ruggles-Brise, S., 'Wines and Wine-Labels', *Country Life* (8 Aug. 1941), pp.244-45 and 'Wines and Wine-Labels - II', *Country Life* (23 Jan. 1942), pp.164-65.
24. Marshall Papers, Ashmolean Museum, Oxford.
25. John Beecroft, Notes and Recollections given in correspondence, 1995.
26. 2 *WLCJ* 206, 207.
27. Marshall Papers, Ashmolean Museum, Oxford.
28. 1 *WLCJ* 72-75. For Tait's collection see further 1 *WLCJ* 32-33, 81.
29. John Beecroft, Notes and Recollections given in correspondence, 1995.
30. 1 *WLCJ* 54; see also Michael Forster, 'The Puzzle of Wine Labels', *Tatler and Bystander*, 25 Feb. 1953, p.324 with illustration of part of the Ormond Blyth Collection. For Ormond Blyth's collection see further 1 *WLCJ* 79-80.
31. W. and A. Gilbey, *Three Quarters of a Century of Successful Trade*. Private publication, 1938.
32. Companies House, City Road, London. Annual returns of W. and A. Gilbey.
33. 7 *WLCJ* 185.
34. 1 *WLCJ* 148.
35. 2 *WLCJ* 66. For Sandeman's collection see further 1 *WLCJ* 69, 81, 94-95, 148, 170, 184 and 2 *WLCJ* 30-32, 42 and 81; described by G. Bernard Hughes in *Country Life Annual* 1955, pp.78-81 and in WLC catalogue, 1957.
36. 1 *WLCJ* 104-110.
37. Ruggles-Brise, S., 'Wines and Wine-Labels', *Country Life* (8 Aug. 1941), pp.244-45 and 'Wines and Wine-Labels - II', *Country Life* (23 Jan. 1942), pp.164-65.
38. N.M. Penzer, *The Book of the Wine Label*, 1947. For Cuthbert's collection see further 1 *WLCJ* 20, 41-43, 133, 171-172 and 3 *WLCJ* 4-12, 134-135, 180 and 201.
39. 1 *WLCJ* 141. For Pratt's collection see further 1 *WLCJ* 29, 114 and 141-144.
40. See further *A Guide to Harvey's Wine Museum* published by John Harvey and Sons Ltd of Harvey House, 12 Denmark Street, Bristol, BS99 7JE.
41. Dunham Massey is a property of the National Trust. The Dunham Massey papers are held in the John Rylands Library, Manchester University. See also 8 *WLCJ* 104-110, 196-205.
42. Extract from a contemporary letter from Mrs Bradshaw to the Countess of Suffolk.
43. 8 *WLCJ* 147.
44. Information from Mr C. Truman.
45. Christie's catalogues of 20 Apr. 1921 and 25 Feb. 1951, 'Plate from Sir John Foley Grey' (a descendant of the Earl of Stamford) contained no wine labels.
46. Dent, Herbert C. *Wine, Spirit & Sauce Labels of the 18th & 19th Centuries*, 1933, pp.5, 6 and pl1.
47. *Country Life*, 16 and 25 Jan. 1986 and 24 Mar. 1988. See also 6 *WLCJ* 165-173.
48. Sotheby's, 22 Mar. 1979.
49. See Chapter 2, Part 1.
50. See Chapter 7, Part 6.

INDEX

'Abbott's Bottle, The', 105
Abdy I, William, 46, 60, 64, 179
Abdy II, William, 57, 59
Aberdeen, 265, 266, 268
acanthus, 29, 32, 54
    leaf and dot, 73
account books, 23
Achilles, 162
acorns, 155
Acts of Parliament
    Duty, of 1784, 266
    Hallmarking, 136
    Marking of Silver Plate, 130, 173
    of 1701, 208
    of 1836, 266
    of 1860, 314
    Plate Offences, 126, 137, 326
    Scottish, of 1457, 266
    Single Bottle, 33
    Turnpike, of 1751, 266
Adam, Robert, 29, 62, 243
Adam style, 29, 145
Adams & Son, 212, 216, 218
Adams, Ann, 179, 216
Adcock, Thomas, 137
added labels, 123
Addinell, G., 235
Admiralty, Board of, 80
advertising, 38
Aesop's fables, 96
Agnew, 94
Ahlers, Oltman, 367
Aitcheson, Lawrence, 259, 265
Aitken, Peter, 72, 259, 263
Aldridge I, Edward, 181, 182
Alldridge, William, 182
ale, 191, 197
Allanson & Co., Wm., 249
'almude', 290
alpaca, 320, 362
alterations, 26
aluminium, 292
ambassadorial plate, 23, 100, 101, 155
American Revolution, 347
Amontillado, 197, 200
Amsterdam, 362
anchors, 43, 80-81
Anderson Collection, 54
Anderson, Frederic Joseph, 375, 379
Anderson, F. St J. Kevin, 379
Andrews, 94
'animal' designs, 334
Ansill and Gilbert, 24
Ansill, James, 23

anthemion, 29
apples, 151, 231, 283
apprentices, 137, 140
aquavit, 368
arabesques, 49
Arbroath, 265, 269-270
Arbuthnot family, 292
archery prize, 242
Archery Societies, 83
architectural styles, 33, 318, 362
'Argentan', 292, 316
armorial, 46, 57, 94-103, 141, 153, 156, 158, 159, 168, 225, 326
arms, coats of, 43, 45
Arnhem, 362
Arnoldi, Peter, 347
arrow, single, 242
Art Deco, 38, 361
Art Nouveau, 34, 38, 361, 363
Arts and Crafts movement, 34
Ash, J., 102
Ashforth & Co., Geo., 249
assay, 126
    masters, 266
    offices, 15, 18, 208
        ledgers, 232, 275
Astley, William, 233, 235, 236, 238, 239
Atkins, James, 157, 179
Atkins, John, 70
Atkins, Theodosia Ann, 179
Atlantic Isles, 186, 194
attaching methods, 116
Auld, William, 64, 248, 254
Australia, 342-343
Austria, 301, 372
Aynsley, 332
Ayr, 265

Bacchante, 78, 101
Bacchic revellers, 74-78
Bacchus, 76, 77, 353
Baddeley, John, 89
badge making, 153
badges, 122
Bailey, Edward Hodges, 164
Baksteen, Willem and Cornelis, 362
Ball, Captain Alexander, 357
Ballam, T., 61
balloon, 61, 82, 104
Banff, 70, 265, 266, 270
Banister, Judith, 15
bankrupts, 144
banners, 175, 351, 353

Barber & Whitwell, 235, 236
Barber, James, 72, 137, 138, 204, 230, 232, 239
Barclay and Goodwin, 265
Barker, Robert, 65, 94, 169
Barker, Susanna, 26, 50, 51, 54, 55, 57, 59, 60, 64, 78, 99, 140, 151, 169-175, 177, 179, 182, 183
barley, 283
Barlow, Tom, 4, 8, 9
Barnard brothers, 107
Barnard, E. and J., 36
Barnard and Co., Edward, 162
Barnard, Edward, 227
Barnard family, 57, 116, 180, 316, 330
Barnard, J., 72, 88, 94, 103, 137, 138, 204, 232, 332, 359
Barnard, W., 359
baronets, 26
barrel labels, 305-313, 359, 367
barrels, 60, 78-79, 149, 175, 320, 362
Barrett I, William, 54, 55, 57, 179
Barrington, Kevin, 8, 9
Barsac, 197
Barthes-Roberts, 307
Bas, Le, 292
Bass, James Le, 187, 275, 278
Bateman, Ann, 148, 179
Bateman, Hester, 30, 50, 53, 54, 55, 56, 59, 62, 64, 87, 90, 93, 100, 104, 137, 140, 144, 145, 153, 177, 179, 191, 204
Bateman, John, 144
Bateman, Jonathan, 146
Bateman, Peter, 146
Bateman, Peter and Ann, 30, 41, 58, 59, 61, 64, 94, 149
Bateman, Peter, Ann and William, 70, 77, 78, 106
Bateman I, William, 54, 101, 149, 163
Bateman II, William, 149, 162
Batemans, the, 55, 61, 62, 77, 115, 122, 144-149
Bath, 65, 221-223
bats, 98, 348-349
Battie, Howard & Hawksworth, 249
Baxter, Gwen, 8
Bayeux, 332
beading, 51, 52, 54, 60, 62, 68, 114, 146, 151, 153, 175, 248, 320
beaked point, 54
bearded faces, 74
Beattie, Miss, 378
Beckford, William, 175

435

Index

Beckwith, John, 230
Beecroft, John, 8, 169
beer, 191, 197
Beer, John, 216, 221, 223
Beet, Brian, 4, 8, 9
Begley, Slaney, 15
Beilby family, 28
Beilby, Ralph, 228
Beilby II, William, 225
Belfast, 358
Belgium, 39, 78, 344-345
Bell, James, 227
Bell, John, 234, 239
Bell, Sidney, 14
Bellingham, Samuel, 179
bending, 108
Bennett, William, 242
Bermuda, 374
Bertram, 94
Besier, Antonius Henricus, 362
Bettridge, John, 242
bevelled edge, 70
Bewick, Thomas, 228
Bewick, Robert, 229
Bickerton, Benjamin, 46, 49, 182
Bickerton, Henry, 45, 46, 49
'big cat' mask, 96
Bigge, Thomas, 162
Bilston, 298, 299
bin labels, 305-313, 353
    circular, 312
    pottery, 353
    shelf, 312, 353
Bingham, Thomas, 291
Binley, Margaret, 23, 24, 46, 49, 56, 61, 140, 141, 169, 177, 179, 182, 299
Binley, Richard, 45, 46, 49, 54, 137, 140, 149, 181, 182, 384
Binleys, the, 149-151
birds, exotic, 357
Birmingham, 30, 32, 34, 38, 49, 54, 57, 61, 240-245, 298, 322, 334, 362
    Assay Office, 204, 240
        Guardian, 244
        duty books, 242
        record daybook, 240
    'Ravenet', 298
bishop's bowl, 351
black bottle scandal, 196
black wax, 18, 124, 260, 341
blackamoor embracing a leopard, 297
Blackamoor's Head, 165
Blackett, Sir Walter Calverley, 225
Blackford, William, 219
blacking, 26
Blagden Hodson & Co., 249
Blagden, Thomas, 249
Blamire, 105
blanks, 116
blind, the, 191
Blount family, 64, 66, 177

Blount, Sir Walter, 94
Blyth, Ormond, 376, 380
boar tusks, 36
boar's head, 44, 96
Bolin, W.A., 369
Bond, William, 165, 182, 183
bone, 340
Bonello, Guiseppe, 359
Booth, G.B., 235
Booth, George, 269
Borås, 368
Boston, 374
bottle collars, 66-70, 159, 203, 334, 340
'bottle rings', 203
bottle-companion, 17
bottle-friend, 17
bottle-tickets, 15, 17, 18
bottles, 18, 22, 26, 33, 38, 54, 223
Boudo, Louis, 54, 137, 372
bought-in stock, 138
Boulsover, Thomas, 282
Boulton and Fothergill, 30, 54, 240
Boulton and Smith, 162
Boulton, Matthew, 115, 201, 231, 240, 242, 243, 286, 317
Bower, John, 242
Bowers, Robert, 207
bows, 147
box master, 266
'boy on a barrel', 157, 274
boys, 74
Boyton, Charles, 38
Bradley, Samuel, 169
Braennvin, 368
Braithwaite and Fisher, 162
Brancker, Benjamin, 204
brandy, 197
brass, 49, 290
    gilded, 290
    silvered, 290
Bridge, John, 66, 68, 101, 162
Bridge, John Gawler, 162
bridge suit markers, 204
bright-cutting, 54, 55, 58, 60, 68, 111, 114, 146, 153, 165, 248
Brind, Walter, 181
Bristol, 56, 221-223
    glass, 223
        blue, 332
Bristol, H.M.S., 107
Britannia standard, 125, 143
    marks, 135
    metal, 291, 317
British Airways, 39
'British Plate', 317
Bronte, 196, 197
    Duke of, 190
Brookes, Peter, 23
Brooks, John, 293, 295
Brown, Miss M.V., 375, 376

Bucellas, 197
Buckingham Palace, 99, 140
Buckle, Joseph, 228, 230
Buckle, Stephen, 48, 223, 228, 230, 239
bucklemakers, 19
bugles, 83
Bull, John, 22
Burbridge, James, 240
burgh arms, 268
Burgundy, 197
Burma, 98, 346
'Burmese Dancer', 346
Burrell, John, 230
Burrow, W. and J., 307
Burrows, Alice, 179
butler, 188
butterfly shape, 337
buttons, 64-65, 158
Byne, Thomas, 216, 220
Byres, William, 268, 270
Byron, Lord, 358

cable border, 68, 146, 155
cable design, 58
Cafe, William, 49, 150
Calcavella, 197
Calcutta, 90, 138, 366, 374
Calderwood, Robert, 57, 273
Caledonian Horticultural Society, 76, 106, 188
Cameron, Alexander, 270, 271
Campbell of Lochiel, 94
Canada, 347
cannons, 356
canoe shape, 247, 250
Canongate, 265, 270, 359
Canton, 348
Cape, 197, 366
Cape of Good Hope, 194
Cape Town, 366
Carden, J., 87
Cardigan, Lord, 196
care of, 124
Caribbean, 374
caricatures, 2, 20-23
Carlisle, 227
    Earl of, 26
Carlscrona, 371
Carlton House, 6, 20, 21-22, 31, 101
Carss, John, 8, 9
Carstens, Nicolai, 351
cartoons, 19-23
cartouches, 29, 57, 58, 72, 146, 164, 242, 247, 250, 318
casemakers, 19
casks, 22
    labels, 320
cast labels, large, 159
casting, 33, 53, 54, 59, 110, 112, 226, 320

Index

recasting, 122
sand, 113
'slush', 113
Cattell, William, 234, 235, 236, 238, 240
Cattle and Barber, 70, 235, 236, 239, 384
Cattle I, George, 232, 239
Cattle II, George, 233, 239
Cattle, Robert, 232, 235, 239
Cavendish-Bentinck, William Henry, 159
celluloid, 312, 331-332, 367
chain border, 61
chainmakers, 146
chains, 26, 108, 116, 286, 293, 351
    brass, 300
    hooked, 68
    ivory, 340
    marks, 352
    silk ribbon, 341
    slip, 101, 158
    steel, 301
    test, 303
    thick, 159
    tortoiseshell, 340
Champagne, 198
Chang, Lin, 348
Channel Islands, 281
Charleston, 54, 372
chart, 194-195
chaser's pitch, 111
chasing punch, 111
Chatterley, John B., 19
Chawner, Henry, 54, 60
Chawner, Mary, 179
Chawner, Thomas, 60
chemical acid test, 288
cherry brandy, 198
cherubs, 74, 75, 77
    harvesting barley, 297
    head, 157
    large, 149
Chester, 28, 56, 201-207
    City of, 103
    Duty Book, 204
chevron, 151, 201
china, 331-332
    bone, 331
China, 155, 337, 348-349
'China Trade', 348
chinoiserie, 28
Chippendale, Thomas, 36
Christensen, Nicolai, 351
Christofle and Cie, Charles, 316, 324, 352
circular shapes, 64
City Livery Company, 330
Clackmannanshire, 187
Clarence, Duke of, 159
claret, 198

Clark, Francis, 242
Clark, Frank, 43
Clark, Richard, 230, 239
Clarke family, of County Durham, 225
claws, 337-340, 356
cleaning, 124
clenched fist, 358
clergy, 26
Clérin, Jean-Baptiste-Lazare, 353
Coakley, John, 207
Coalport, 331
coasters, 13, 20, 111
coconut, 340
Codrington, Admiral, 104
Coffin II, Thomas, 218
Coke, Earl of Leicester, 94
Coleman, Edward, 157
collectors, 375-382
Collier, Edward, 211
Collier, Robert, 165
Collingwoods, 43
Collins, James, 211
colloquialisms, 187
colonial territories, 374
Combrick, Johannes, Senior, 367
commemorative, 38, 104-106
Commission of Investigation, 230
Commission on the Royal Burghs, 266
Commissioners of Stamps, 129
commissions, 211
Committee of Inspection, 233
compound titles, 185
Comyns, William, 68
Concorde, 39
condition, 119-122
Constable, John, 328
Constable, William, 270
Constable's Book, 181
Constantia, 198, 366
conversions, 122-123
Cook, Cyril, 296
Cooke, Elizabeth, 179
Cookson, Isaac, 47-48, 74, 223, 227, 230
Copeland, 305
    and Garrett, 306
copies, 123
copper
    core, 286
    disc, 223
    gilded, 290
copperbacks, 49, 64, 115, 191, 231, 283
cordials, 186
Cork, 276, 278, 280
corks, 26, 326-330
    decanter, 326
corkscrew, 156
Corn Laws, 104
corners
    cut, 50
    inward curving, 51

rounded, 51
sharp, 50
Cornfute, James, 268, 272
cornucopias, 33, 154
Coronation Service, 99
coronets, 68, 84, 226
Cote Roti, 198
Courtenay, John, 17
covering over, 119
cow, 96
Cox, Robert Albin, 150, 181, 384
crab in a lozenge, 353
Cradock, J., 89
craft, 325
Craven, Lord, 243
Crawford, David, 227
Crawshaw, James, 249
creamware, 305
Creasen, L., 235
crescents, 19, 21, 22, 30, 52, 57, 61-64, 140, 151, 165, 175, 221, 226, 232, 247, 284, 334, 354, 359, 372
    enclosed, 62, 147
    horse's hoof, 343
    'horseshoe', 334
    jagged lower edge, 334
    saw-tooth, 177, 221
Crespel II, Sebastian, 76
crests, 64, 65, 72, 73, 229
    garter, 155
    'out of a tower', 226
    phoenix, 224
Creswick, Richard, 246, 253
Crichton, L.A., 105
Critien, Emilio, 78, 359
Cropper Collection, 140
Cropper, Percy J., 375, 377
Crosbie, Richard, 82, 274
Crossley, Jonas, 234, 240
crouching beasts, 72
Crown Staffordshire, 331
crowns, 84
    'Irish', 274
Cruikshank, George, 20-22
Cruikshank, Isaac Robert, 119, 157
Cullen, Joseph, 268
Cumberland, Duke of, 26, 293
Cunliffe, Nicholas, 203, 207
Cunningham, Mrs Alexander, 256
Cunningham, Patrick, 256, 259
Cunningham, W., 256
Cunningham, W. and P., 72
Cupar, 265
Cupid, 75, 77, 156, 247, 295
    draws aside the veil, 297
    protecting a lamb, 297
    'two', 112
Curacoa, 198
cushion shape, 50, 54, 149, 151, 233, 247, 284
    domed, 54

437

Index

cusps, 62
cut-out, 119, 322
    letters, 70-73, 337
    words, 36, 70-73, 247
Cuthbert, Alexander, 381
cutting, 36, 110
Cyder, 191, 197

Daffron, J., 276
Daily Advertiser, 293
Dalder, Theo, 9
Dalkeith, 265
Dalton, Richard, 293
damage, 119
Damant, William, 250
Daniell (or Daniel), Thomas, 180, 183
Darling, David, 228
Datalis, J.G., 345
Davenport, 307
Davenport, William, 38
Davidson, Alexander, 270
Davie, W., 189
Davie, William, 61, 254
Davis, Jack, 9
deacons, 129, 266
    convener, 266
    initial punches, 266
Deakin and Francis, 107
dealers' licence, 129
decanters, 6, 13, 18, 19, 20, 22, 26, 28, 30, 33, 38, 43, 52, 54, 352
    glass, 225
    label, 18
    stands, 197
decorating, 108-117
Dee, H.W., 72
Delftware, 305
Delvaux, 300
demi-eagle, 94
Demouriez, General, 20
Den Bosch, 362
Denaro, Victor, 358
Denmark, 349-351
Dent, Major Herbert C., 296, 375, 378
designing, 108
development, 17-44
Devlin, Stuart, 38, 43
Dick and Macpherson, 256
Dick, Alexander, 342
Dick, Lexi, 43
Diderot's *Encyclopaedia*, 108
die-stamping, 30, 32, 33, 59, 62, 114, 138, 247, 259, 283, 286
    'double-die', 115
    machines, 240
Dilettanti, Society of, 11, 19
Dingwall, 265
Dinwiddie, James, 82
Dionysus, 28, 72, 75, 76, 77, 96, 164, 273
    infant, 273

'Reclining', 105, 155
discs, 158, 334, 340
Distillers, Worshipful Company of, 103
distillery, 187
distribution, 210
division of labour, 240
Dixon & Sons, 249
Dixon, James, 38
Dixon II, Joseph, 206
documentary evidence, 17-18
dolphin, 94, 98
'doming', 110
Donald, John A., 39
Dorrell, Jane, 179
Dorrell, William, 181
double dot, 201
Douglas, J., 64
Douglas, James, 254, 269
dove and olive branch, 250
Dove, Anthony, 8
dragon, 98, 107
Drakensburg, 366
drape, 62
drapery, 30, 149, 248
    festooned, 146, 164
Drennan, Dr William, 85
Dreyfous, 300, 354
drinks, 194
Drinkwater, Sandylands, 19, 26, 45, 46, 49, 54, 61, 66, 70, 74, 86, 94, 111, 115, 117, 126, 137, 139-143, 149, 180, 183
    trade card, 139
Driver, Michael, 43
Druitt and Co. Ltd., Michael Wyard, 38, 39, 41, 78, 292
Dublin, 273-280
    Company of Goldsmiths of, 43, 86
Dudley, 298
Duke I, Joseph, 206
Dumbarton, 265
Dumfries, 68, 265
Dundee, 64, 265, 270-271
Durbin, Leslie, 105
Dunsford, J.N., 213, 214, 215
Dutchmen, 78
duty, 24
    Act of 1784, 266
    additional, 130
    books, 19
    dodging, 126
    drawback, 129
        mark, 135
    increase, 130
    marks, 129-134, 258
        flattened base punch, 132
        incuse, 50, 51, 57, 62
        twice, 131

Eadon and Co., George, 192
Eadon, Kibbles & Co., 249

eagle, 334
earls, 26
East Devon Record Office, 208
East India, 305
Edinburgh, 34, 54, 57, 61, 254-256
    assay office records, 254
    goldsmiths' incorporation, 266
Edington, J.C., 93
Edmondson, A., 90
Edwards II, Edward, 84
Edwards, Jack, 9
Edwards, Thomas, 84, 90
Egan, John, 70
Egan, W. and Co., 104
Egan, William, 41
Egar, John, 276
Egerton family, 94, 384
Egyptian antiquity, 31, 32
Egyptian Service, 159
Elder and Co., 256
Elder, George, 270
elephants, 94, 154, 157
electroformed, 93
electroplate, 33, 68, 79, 84, 103, 117, 120, 123, 124, 243, 292, 314-325, 362
Electro-Plated Nickel Silver (EPNS), 292
Eley, William, 317
Elgin, 54, 265, 266, 271
Elizabeth II, Queen, 38
    Coronation, 38, 41, 105
    Golden Jubilee, 38, 44
    Silver Jubilee, 38, 39, 41, 105
Elkington and Co., 34, 38, 288
Elkington, George and Henry, 243
Elkington, George Richards, 314
Elkington, Henry, 314
Ellerby, William, 90
Elliot, Eric, 332
Elliott, William, 59, 64, 154, 328
Ellis Tucker & Co., 249
Elson, Anthony, 43, 44
embellishing, 108
emblems, 136
Emes and Barnard, 72, 88, 94, 103, 137, 138, 204, 232, 332, 359
Emes, John, 72, 88, 94, 103, 137, 138, 204, 232, 332, 359
Emes, Rebecca, 177, 179
Emmanuel, 38
enamels, 121, 224, 298-304, 353, 354, 372
    Battersea, 97, 121, 292-298
    coloured, 117
    non-Battersea, 298-304
    'stove-back', 300
engravers, 43
engraving, 50, 53, 57, 58, 111, 228
    machine, 318
    re-engraving, 119

Index

'scratch', 337
erasure, 119
Erskine, James, 268
escutcheons, 23, 28, 34, 45-49, 57, 140, 143, 150, 151, 153, 201, 211, 221, 224, 226, 232, 247, 273, 284, 294, 333
    domed, 302
    foliate, 155
    'smiling lip', 141
    triangular, 48, 274, 355, 383
    with lion's mask, 247
esquires, 26
Etherington, William, 61, 234, 240
Eton College Chapel, 163
Evans and Matthews, 322
Evans, Richard, 58, 137, 204
excise duties, 194
Exeter, 56, 65, 208-221
    Goldsmiths' Company, 208
    Museum, 212
eye shape, 57, 62, 175, 247, 250, 274
exhibitions
    Birmingham, 1849, 319
    Great, 1851, 316, 319
    International, 1862, 316, 320
    Manchester, 1845, 319
    Paris, 1834, 319
    Sydney, 1861, 342

face, marked on the, 242
facets, 64
faience, 332, 353
fakes, 122-123
families, 382-384
Fane, 94
Farr, John, 221
Farrell, Edward, 32, 77, 78, 94, 143, 154
Farrow, Charles, and Farrow and Jackson, 307
fashion, 194
Fearn, Thomas, 317
feather-edging, 46, 52, 55, 60, 61, 114, 140, 146
feathering, 49, 54, 150, 151, 153
feathers, 104
Fenech, Francesco, 70, 359
Fenton, Creswick & Co., 249
Fenton & Co., M., 249
Fenton, Matthew, 246, 253
Fenwick, George, 254
Ferguson, William Stephen, 54, 271, 272
Ferris, George, 212, 216, 217
Ferris, Richard, 208, 211, 216, 217
festoons, 29, 30, 33, 62, 284
Fielding, Owen, 210, 211, 212, 215, 216, 218
Field, Alexander, 59
figure-of-eight link, 248

Fillan, William, 269
filling-in, 119
finger ring, 326
finial, decorative, 326
Finland, 352
Fishmongers' Company, 143, 152, 154, 155, 156
Fitch, Daniel, 289
Fitzhenry, Joseph Henry, 375, 376
Fitzpatrick, M., 44
Fitzwalter, Earl, 18
five bar gates, 34, 154, 157, 233
flat chasing, 45, 111
flamingo, 328
Flavelle, Henry, 275, 276
Flaxman, John, 162, 164
Flitton, John, 41, 43
floral border, 70
flowerheads, 54, 60
flower petals, 64
flowers, 43
    national, 104
fluorescence, 302
Folcker, Gustaf, 371
Folcker, Gustaf Theodor, 371
font, gold, 159
Forbes, Thomas, 268
Ford, John, 221
Fortrose, 68, 374
Foster, George, 328
Foster I, John, 328
Fothergill, John, 240
Fowler, John, 212, 216, 219
foxes, 94, 96, 154, 334
    running, 96
    'singing', 96, 157
    sitting, 158
Fox, Charles James, 17
Fox, C.T. and G., 96
France, 301, 324, 332, 337, 344, 352-354
France, James, 203, 206
'François Premier', 320
Fraser, Donald, 271
fraud, 136
Fray, James, 276-277
Frazer, Robert, 256
Frederick VI, King, 351
Free Trade, 33, 104
French Empire style, 31
'French Plate', 290
'fretwork', 158
Frisbee, William, 159
Frontiniac, 198
Frost, T.W., 194, 196
fruit and vegetables, 43
Fuller, Brian L., 43, 97
Fulton, Joseph, 216, 221, 223
funnels, 13
Furniss, Poles & Co., 249

'GM', 221
gadrooning, 46, 60, 114, 284
Gainsford, Goodman, 235
Gainsford, Robert, 74, 90, 188, 247, 249, 252, 292
Gallais, J. de, 281
Gamble, James, 90
gaming counters, 122
'Gang Forward', 254
Garde, Phineas, 90
garlands, foliate, 146
Garrard and Co., 23, 105
Garrard, J., 94
Garrard, Robert, 23, 68, 72, 154
Garrard II, Robert, 78, 89, 96
Garrards, 38, 39, 101, 316
Garrick, David, 188
garter, 66
    motif, 99
Gaskell-Taylor, Patrick, 8, 9
Gauffin, 369
gauge
    light, 146
    thick, 175
geometrical shapes, 33
George III, King, Coronation Service, 177
George IV, King, 22, 33
'German silver', 292, 316
Germany, 301, 343, 355
Gerritsen, Johannes Albertus Adolf, 361
Gibraltar, 374
Gibson, Joseph, 276
Gibson, W., 107
Gilbert, John, 34, 36, 330, 362
Gilbert, Stephen, 23
gilding, 117-118
    electrolytic, 117
    fire, 117
Gill, Margaret A.V., 224, 226
Gillett, Nathaniel, 269
Gillray, James, 20-22
Gilmour, Andrew, 8
gilt labels, 28
gilt metal, 49, 289-290
gin, 187-188, 198
Glasgow, 54, 57, 256-265
    Goldsmiths' Company, 258
glass, 28, 331-332
Glassford, Charles, 316
glasshouses, 223
Glenisheen Collar, 104
glis-glis, 43, 97
goat, 96
goblets, 87, 146, 147
    and festoons, 284
Godfrey, Peter, 57
gold, 158, 288-289
    standard, 288
Golden Ball, 180

439

Index

Golden Salmon, The, 161
Goldsmith and the Grape exhibition, The, 38
Goldsmiths and Silversmiths Company, 38
Goldsmiths' Company, 102, 139, 165, 169, 221
Goldsmiths' Hall, 18, 126, 127, 129, 137, 175, 177, 179, 183, 342
Goode and Co. Ltd., T., 331
Goode and Sons, T., 331
Goodman & Co., Alex, 249
Goodrich, John, 226
Gordon, George, 356
Gordon, Hugh, 68, 374
Gordon, James, 268
Goss, Benjamin, 65, 214
Gothenburg, 368, 371, 372
gothic revival, 32, 34, 36
gouge marks, 320
gourmet at his table, 344
Govan, 265
grafting, 196
Grafton, 26
Graham and Willis, 65
Graham, Adam, 57
Graham, Thomas, 221
Grand Service, 89, 100, 159
Grape, 198
grapes, 32, 46, 54, 60
graver, 111
Graves, 198
Gray, David, 270
Gray, Malcolm, 43
Gray, Robert, 54, 256, 260
Gray and Son, Robert, 261
Gray and Sons, Robert, 72
Gray, William, 159, 256, 261
Green, John, 326, 328
Greenock, 256-265, 271
Greig, David, 270, 272
greyhound, 96
Grierson, Peter, 70
Grierson, Philip, 259, 262
Grimwade, Arthur G., 170, 180
Gruchy, T. de, 281
Grun, Jules Alexandre, 23
Grunbaum, H., 365
guarantee of quality, 137
Gubbins, Martin, 231
Guernsey, 281
Gwin, James, 293

'HF', 72
Haig, John, 189, 193
Hales family, 141
Halifax, 347
Hallmarking Act, 136
hallmarks, 125-138
    pseudo, 122, 125, 318, 348, 366
    single basal cusp, 131

    three-cusped, 130
    two-cusped, 130
Hamilton and Co., 90, 337, 356
Hamilton, Sir William, 19
Hammer, Christian, 372
Hammersley, 331
Hamon, Louis, 28, 46, 61, 111, 181
Hampston and Prince, 48, 54, 56, 61, 140, 230, 239, 384
Hampston, John, 239
Hampston, Prince and Cattles, 72, 239
Hancock, Joseph, 283
Hand and Coral, 139, 180
hand, open, 358
Hanger, Col., 17
Hannay, William, 89, 258, 272
Hardwick, William, 205
hare, 96
Harman, J., 214, 215, 223
harps, 43, 85-86, 104, 274
Harris, C.S., 107
Harris, Simon, 216, 218
Harvey and Sons, J., 38
Harvey, Anne, 144, 179
Harvey, John, 26, 28, 46, 74, 76, 117, 135, 143-144, 181, 190, 192, 383
Harvey II, John, 144
Harvey's Wine Museum, 14, 170
Harwood & Sons, T., 57
Haughton, Moses, 19
Hawksworth, Eyre & Co., 249
Hay, James, 254, 268, 271
Heal, Ambrose, 169, 175
hearts, 86, 142, 153
Helsby, John, 207
Helsinki, 352
Heming, Thomas, 26, 28, 70, 96, 191
Hendery, Robert, 347
Hennell, 183
Hennell, David, 183
Hennell, Robert, 183, 330
Hennell I, Robert, 183
Hennell, Samuel, 183
Henry, Guillaume, 48, 281
heraldic, 147
Hermitage, 198
Heron, John, 258, 268
Hewitt, Joseph, 203, 206
Hicks, Joseph, 210, 211, 212, 216, 217
High Victorian, 322
Hilliard and Thomason, 34, 36, 38, 244
Hills, T., 206
Hinchsliffe, Mark, 270
Hing, Wang, 348
hinges, 68
Hiort, Peter, 351
Hirsch, Mirjam, 43
hitting, 110
Hock, 199
Hockley, Daniel, 76, 122, 154, 155, 157, 366

Hodgson, Richard, 9
Hogarth, William, 19, 292
Hogrefe, Julius, 351
Holland, arms of, 94
Holland, Henry, 31
Holland, Margaret, 267
Holland, Thomas, 90
Hollands, 199
Hollebone, Herbert W., 375, 378
Holy and Co., Daniel, 248, 249, 252
Holy D., Wilkinson and Co., 288
Home, James, 254, 256
Hong Kong, 98, 348
hoop, 66
Hoorn, 360
Hope, William, 216, 218
hops, 283
'horns', 45, 61, 226
horse, 96
    head, 328
Horton, Samuel, 242
Horwood, Richard, 180
Hougham, Charles, 138
Hougham, Solomon, 59
hounds, 158
housekeeper, 188
Hoyland, John, 249
humped upper edge, 232
Humphrey, H., 20, 22, 23
Humphris, John, 46, 54, 182
Hunt and Roskell, 36
Hunt, J., 89
Hunt, J.S., 70
Hunt, John, 160
Hunt, John S., 36
Hunt, John Samuel, 160
hunting, 96
Huntingdon, Mary, 179, 207
Huntington, Thomas, 228
Huntsman, Benjamin, 110
Hurt, Henry, 161
husks, 275
Hutchinson, Geoffrey, 9
Hyde, James, 26, 30, 49, 50, 54, 55, 57, 58, 59, 60, 61, 62, 138, 152, 154, 182, 183, 384
Hyde, Mary, 153, 154, 179, 183
Hyde I, Thomas, 46, 86, 99, 143, 152, 181, 182, 183
Hyde II, Thomas, 46, 137, 152
Hyde family, the, 152-153

'IC', 68
'IH', 48
'I L' with star above, 45
'IR', 45, 49
'IT', 68
ibis, 326
Ilchester, Earl of, 188
illustration, contemporary, 2, 7, 11, 17, 19-22

Index

Imperial Crown, 84
Incorporation of Hammermen, 256
India, 36, 192, 337, 356, 366
individually designed labels, 38
industry, 325
Inner Temple, 103, 328
Inns of Court, 328
insignia, 122
intaglio (incuse), 129, 135
International Wine and Food Society, 39
inventories, 18
Inverness, 57, 265, 271
invoices, 243
Ireland, 48, 52, 57, 58, 60, 273-280
    EEC commemorative, 39-41, 104
    Irish Company of Goldsmiths, 103, 104
    levy, 131
    Society of United Irishmen, 85
Ironmongers, Worshipful Company of, 103
ivory, 66, 340, 353

Jackson, Sir Charles, 165, 175
Jackson, Edward, 234, 235, 236, 238, 239
Jackson, Joseph, 64, 66, 277
Jackson, Samuel, 68
Jacobean style, 123
Jacobite roses, 224
Jacobite wine glasses, 104
Jacobs, John, 45, 46
Jago, Mahala, 179
Jamieson and Naughton, 271
Jamieson, George, 269
Jamieson, William, 269
Janssen, Alderman Stephen Theodore, 293
Janssen, Delamain and Brooks, 293
'Japanned ware', 290
Jay, Edward, 81
Jenkins, Richard, 216
Jensen, 349
Jersey, 281
'jewels' (paste), 290
Johnson, Dr, 17, 184, 188
Johnson, T., 96
jokes, 187
Jones, Bruce, 8, 9, 211, 212
Jones I, Robert, 203, 204, 206
Jones II, Robert, 204, 206
Jones, Sarah, 43, 103
Jonssén, Carl Frederik, 372
Jorgensen, Christian Albrecht, 351
Judkins, Mathew, 143
jugs, 23
jump rings, 68, 116
Jupiter Ammon, 78, 101

Kalberg, Antonius Alphonsus, 362

Kavanagh, John, 277
Keay, R. and R., 189
Keay I, Robert, 272
Keay II, Robert, 272
Kehoe, Darby, 54, 277
Keith, John, 266
Kelso, 265
Kelty, Alexander, 84, 226, 227
kidney shape, 149, 151, 247, 317, 334
Kikkert, J.F., 79, 362
Kilmarnock, 265
King, Abstainando, 59, 77, 97
Kings Cup, 99, 177
Kingsteignton Wallpaper Book, 151
Kippax, Robert, 249, 250
Kirby, Waterhouse & Co., 249
Kirkby, Gregory & Co., 249
Kirkup, John, 223, 227
Kitchen and Walker, 249
Knight, George, 97, 104, 135
Knight, Samuel, 58, 97, 104
Knight, William, 97, 104
Knight II, William, 135
Knights, the, 68, 97, 104, 180
kukris, 356
Kyhl, Peter, 351

lacquer, 120, 124
ladder between wings, 155
Lady Bountiful, 77, 157
Lamb, James, 104, 224, 228
Lambert, Peter, 272
Lamerie, Paul de, 18, 28, 139
Lamont, Norman, 23
Lang, O., 213
Langdon, John W., 216, 220
Langford, James, 347
Langlands and Robertson, 47, 61, 62
Langlands, Dorothy, 54, 179, 226, 227
Langlands I, John, 47, 68, 70, 224, 226, 227, 229, 383
Langlands II, John, 226, 227
Langman, J., 107
Langwith, John, 228, 230
largeworkers, 19, 165
    register of, 146, 153
Larvik, 363
Latimer, Joseph, 228
Latin tags, 187
laurel wreaths, 29, 93
Law, James, 264
Law, John, 249, 256
Law, S., 274
Law & Co., Thomas, 64, 248, 249, 252
Law, William, 60, 61, 79, 274, 277
Lawrence and Co., 242
Laymont and Shaw, 38
lead, 305
Leader, Daniel, 249
Leader, T. and D., 249
Leader, Thomas, 51

Leader, William, 56
leather, 68, 341
leaves, 89-93
    apple, 231
    bamboo, 357
    fern, 93
    four-leaf clover, 93, 164
    ivy, 93
    'leaf covering the label end', 259
    oak, 158
    slanted, 60
    vine, 46, 89-93, 157, 242, 247, 320
        single, 34
        triple, 155
Lebrun, Gioacchino, 358
ledgers, 18
Ledsam, Vale and Wheeler, 242, 330
Leith, 265, 271
Leith, George, 267
leopards, 154
    pelt, 159. 164
Léoville, 157
Leslie, John, 268
letters, 77
    cut-out, 72, 158
    Cyrillic, 365
    gilt, 340
    gothic, 70, 72, 323, 340, 352
    initial, 70, 247
    italic, 72
    large initial capital, 232
    large silhouette, 232
    script, 70, 72, 232, 324, 332
    silhouette, 72
    single, 38, 70-73, 191
Levy, Emmanuel, 216, 218
Levy, Simon, 216, 219
Lewis & Wright, 65, 226, 227
Lewis, George, 227
Lewis, Kensington, 162
Lias brothers, 90
Lias, I. and H., 94
Liberty, 38
Limerick, 276
Lind, Gustav, 9
Lintveld, Harmanus, 360
Linwood I, Matthew, 88, 243
Linwood II, Matthew, 57, 88, 242, 243
Linwood III, Matthew, 243
lions, 346
    crowned, 96
    Imperial, 101
    Madrid, 368
    on a chapeau, 155
    passant, 94, 126, 128
        facing to sinister, 233
        guardant, 127
    pelt, 32
    rampant, 94
        on a bar, 156
'lipped' design, 46

Index

liqueurs, 197
liquors, 186
Lisbon, 199
Lister & Sons, 227
Lister, William, 227
'little sword', 360
Liverpool, 201, 298
Livingstone, Edward, 64, 270
locations, makers', 179-183
Lönberg, Peter Eduard, 368
London, 223, 298
   Society, The, 41
   Stock Exchange, 44
loops, 54
lost wax process, 112
Love and Co., John, 248, 249
Lowe I, George, 103, 203, 207
Lowe II, George, 203
Lowe, Margaret and John, 203, 289
Lowe, Robert, 207
Lowe, Thomas, 203
Lucas, Robert, 46
Lumley and Co. Ltd., L., 307
Lunel, 199
Lyberg, Hans, 368
Lymington, Lord, 18
Lyon, William, 372

MT., 93
Maarseveen, Petrus Franciscus van, 362
McDermid, J., 256
Macdonald and Reid, 263
MacDonald, David, 259
Macdonald, David, 256, 263
Macdonald, J., 75
McHattie, George, 72, 75, 76, 89, 90, 105, 254, 256
machines, 115
   rotary, 117
MacKay and Chisholm, 57
McKay, J., 72, 88, 96
MacKay, J., 57
Mackay (McKay), James, 254, 256, 265
Mackay, William, 256
McKenzie, Thomas, 256
Mackenzie, William, 256
Maclellan, Archibald, 258
McNab, Archie, 272
McOnie, Andrew, 258
Macord and Arch, 307
Macrae, Alexander, 330
Madeira, 199
Madras, 138
Madrid, 368
Maid's Head, The, 192-193
mailed arm, 94
Mair, John, 374
Maitland, Sir Thomas, 359
Makepeace, Robert, 223, 227
Makepeace II, Robert, 48
makers, 400

marks, 125, 136, 145
   new form, 127
making, 108-124
Malaysia, 98, 357
Malmstedt, Johan, 368, 371
Malta, 70, 90, 357-359
Malton, Earl of, 18
Manchester, 201
Manson, David, 270
Manton, Henry, 318
manufacturing patterns, 237
Mappin and Webb, 38
Mardon, Thomas, 215, 216
Marlborough, Duke of, 26
Marquand, Frederick, 372
Marsala, 199
Marshall and Sons, 36, 72
Marshall Collection, 170
Marshall, Mrs H.R. (Monica), 375, 379
Marshall, Wendy, 44
masks, 32
mass-produced items, 34
mass-produced labels, 38
Maw and Co., 307
Medlycott, Edmund, 28, 46, 54, 76, 180, 181, 182
Medway School of Art, 44
Melbourne (Australia), 324
Melbourne, Viscount, 26
Mercers Company, 102
Meriton, Samuel, 52
Meriton II, Samuel, 183
Merrett, Peter, 221
metal plates, 172
metals, 288-292
Methuen, 190
   Treaty, 190, 194
Middendorp, Johannes, 362
mildew, 196
military, 106-107, 356
mill, 110
milled edge, 60
Miller, 221
Mills, Nathaniel, 93, 322
Mills, William, 271-272
Milne and Campbell, 260
Minerva, 352
Minton, 307
mirror-smooth surface, 122
missing parts, 119
misspellings, 184
Mitchell and Son, 264
Mitchell II, Alexander, 259, 260, 263
Mitchell, J. and W., 265
Mitchell, John, 265
Mitchell, R., 242
Mitchison, John, 56, 226, 228
Moka, 93
Möllenborg, Gustaf, 368
Montreal, 347

Montrose, 265, 271-272
Moon, Miss Jennie, 256
Moore, John, 240
Mordan, Sampson, 33, 77, 104, 116, 204
Morley, Elizabeth, 30, 61, 70, 154, 179, 180
Morley, Thomas, , 54
Morris, William, 324
Mortimer and Hunt, 160
Mortimer, John, 89, 159-160
Morton and Co., R., 64, 249
Morton, Handley & Co., 249
Morton, Richard, 246, 250, 334
Moselle, 199
mother-of-pearl, 49, 61, 68, 333-337, 349, 353
motifs, 121
moulds
   cuttlefish, 113
   open, 113
   rigid closed, 112
Moulton IV, William, 373
Mount Etna, 186, 190
Mountain, 196, 199
mouse, 97
Muir, James, 259, 264
Murray, George, 227
Murray, John, 259, 263
musical instruments, 104
mythology, 32, 346

names, 286, 385-399
   foreign, 186-187
   regional, 185-186
   unusual, 184-191
Nangle, George, 60, 78, 79, 100, 274, 278
Napier, James, 316
Napoleon, 357
naturalism, 319
Naughton, Robert, 57, 271
naval, 106-107
Navarino, battle of, 104
navette shape, 384
neck rings, 66-70, 142, 247, 283, 341
   spring wire, 374
Nelson, Admiral Lord, 189, 357
neo-classical period/style, 28-31, 145, 225
neo-gothic, 123
Netherlands, the, 90, 360-62
New Caledonian nickel, 317
New York, 362, 372
Newburyport, 373
Newcastle, 28, 47, 54, 56, 61, 223-229, 230
   City of, 225
   Corporation of, 103, 226
   Goldsmiths' Company of, 223
   registers, 230

Index

Newlands, James, 262
Newlands, Luke Frazer, 262
Nicholson, Thomas, 292
nickel alloys, 291-292, 316, 320, 322
    hardness, 322
    white, 324
'Nickel Silver', 292
Nicolay, Peter, 188
niello, 18
Niner, James, 212, 215
Norblin and Co, 364
Nordbeck, Peter, 347
Norfolk, Duke of, 155
Norris, Henry M., 216, 220
North, Lord, 26
North, William, 233, 239
Norway, 349, 363
Nova Scotia, 347
Nowill & Kippax, 249
Nowill, Joseph, 249
Nowlan, Laurence, 278
Nowlan, William, 278
Noyau, 199

Oatridge and Marindin, 243
O'Brien, Conor, 8, 9, 18
octopus-type label, 61
off licences, 33
ogee, 45
Oidium tuckeri, 196
Old Sheffield plate (OSP), 56, 61, 62, 64, 66, 68, 87, 115, 120, 124, 140, 145, 191, 231, 247, 248, 250, 282-288, 344
    characteristics of, 286
    colour of, 286
Oliphant, Thomas, 137
Oliver Makower Trust, 44
Ollivant, John, 204
Ollivant, Thomas, 204
Olympia exhibition, 4, 14, 28
Onslow, Arthur, 26
openwork surmount, 226
Orange, 199
Order of St John, Knights of the, 357
organic materials, 337-341
ornamental plate, 31
Orr and Co., 337, 356
Orrery, Earl of, 18, 273
Osborne House, 156
Osborne, John, 79, 274, 278
Osborne, Jonas, 260
Osment, John, 213, 216, 218
ostrich, 94, 158
ovals, 57-61, 146, 149, 165, 226, 247, 286
    embellished, 57
    linked by swags, 60
    small, 60
    suspended, 58
overstriking, 137, 145

ovolo design, 114, 146, 150, 151
    conjoined, 60
owl, 147
Oyras, 155

Page, Thomas, 347
Paisley, 256-265, 272
paktong, 291
pales, 60, 68, 155, 159
palette, 121
palimpsests – *see* reversible
Palliser, Admiral Sir Hugh, 80
Palmgren, Pehr Fredrik, 372
Pan, 75
    mask of, 259
Panter, George W., 375, 377
panther, 77, 97, 104
paper labels, 19, 21, 23, 46
    printed, 33
parcels, 208, 237, 240
parchment, 27, 54
Parker and Wakelin, 18, 99, 328
Parker, John, 23
Parkin, Isaac, 56, 211, 212, 216, 219
Parkin and Co., Padley, 316
Parliamentary Commission, 230
Parliamentary List, 177
Parliamentary Select Committee record, 215
Parson & Co., John, 249
Parsons, Francis, 65, 214, 216, 217
patents, 293, 314, 316, 344
patina, 120
Patrick, John, 212, 216, 217
patronage, 44
    royal, 177
pattern books, 284
pattern of demand, 237
patterns, 112
Paul, Colin, 9
Paxarete, 199, 200
peacock, 94
    head, 292
Pearse, Wm, 213
Pearson, George, 59, 77, 154, 155, 330, 362
Pearson, Joseph, 68, 270
Pegasus, 103
pelican, 354
penalties, 129
Penzer, Norman M., 13, 14, 15, 26, 75, 161, 162, 169, 177, 184, 196, 376, 380
Pepys, Samuel, 17
Perry, John, 244
Perth, 57, 265, 272
pestilence, 194
petal border, 60
Peterhead, 265, 272
petition of silversmiths, 231
pewter, 290, 363

Philadelphia, 372
Phipps and Robinson, 50, 51, 56, 57, 58, 60, 61, 62, 64, 68, 70, 73, 74, 81, 87, 88, 93, 94, 99, 102, 137, 188, 191, 203
Phipps, Ann, 167
Phipps, Elizabeth, 167
Phipps family, 55, 165-169
Phipps, J., 54, 61, 104
Phipps, James, 54, 59-60, 61, 183
Phipps I, James, 85, 165, 182
Phipps II, James, 168
Phipps, Robinson and Phipps, 68, 76, 140
Phipps, T. and J., 49, 72, 102
Phipps, Thomas, 167, 183
phoenix, 224
phylloxera, 196
Pickett, William, 162
piercing, 36, 53, 108, 111, 153, 155, 159, 226
    double, 60
    saw, 110, 322
Piercy, Robert, 183
pig, 96
pinchbeck, 49, 290
Pinchbeck, Christopher, 289
Pinkney and Scott, 224
Pinkney, Robert, 226, 228
Pinnell, William, 165
Pitt, William, 20
Pittar and Co., 90, 356
plaques, 52, 56
plate, 353
platemakers, 19
plates, 18
platinum, 41, 292
plumed, 47
Plummer I, William, 183
Poland, 364
polishing, 26, 116
    'foam' polish, 124
political, 188
'polo' design, 65
Pontac, 366
'Pontypool ware', 290
Pope, Alexander, 221
Pope Society, The, 351
Pope, William, 214, 215, 216, 219
porcelain, 332, 353, 354
port, 199
    red, 200
    white, 200
Portland, Duke of, 159
Portugal, 190, 364
Poseidon, 88
'postage stamps', 70, 73, 337
Postans and Tye, 242
pottery, 331-332
pouncing, 111
Powell, F., 107

443

Index

Poynings' Law, 85
Prahl, Samuel, 351
Pratt, Edward J., 13, 14, 15, 375, 382
presses
   drop, 115
   fly, 115
   machine, 129
   screw, 115
   steam-powererd, 322
Price, Joseph, 362
prick dotting, 60
pricked edges, 151
Prime and Son, Thomas, 34, 36
Prince & Cattle, 235, 236
Prince and Cattles, 239
Prince, John, 239
Prince Regent, 119, 157, 159, 221
Prince Regent, 101, 107
Pringle, John, 272
Proctor and Co., Luke, 192, 248, 249
production, 210
Pugin, Augustus, 36, 72
Puginesque style, 323
Pugwash, 347
Pullan, Peggy, 4
punch, 188, 351
Punch, 72
   and Toby, 158
   Mr, 36
punching, 46, 60
putti, 74, 164
   'two', 26, 140, 143, 149, 224, 242, 248, 250, 355
putto, single, 143

Quakers, 159
quality, 223
quatrefoil, 164
Quebec, 347
Queen's Head, 181
Quesnel, Charles William, 281
'quiffed', 47, 224

'RE', 62
Rack, 362
Raisin, 199
Rait and Son, D.C., 264
Rait, David Crichton, 104, 259, 264
ram's head, 250
Ramsden, Omar, 38
Ramsey, Jonathan, 215, 216, 220
rate collectors' books, 180
'Rav, fecit, S.', 293
Ravenet, 14, 48, 298
Ravenet, François, 97
Ravenet, Simon Francis, 292-294
Rawlings and Summers, 36, 57, 68, 72, 84, 89, 93, 94, 102, 107, 289, 318, 322, 330
Rawlings, Charles, 34, 65, 70, 72, 76, 77, 89, 154, 157-159

rays, 64, 66
rear latching, 68
receipt, 129
rectangles, 22, 45, 49-54, 211, 247, 284, 286, 340
   berry bordered, 154
   broad, 140
   domed, 52, 232, 373
   fretted dome, 148
   narrow, 148, 334
   shaped, 146
Reece-Goldsworthy Studio, 43
reeding, 46, 52, 60, 61, 62, 146, 153, 175, 248
Reeh, Rasmus, 9
Regency period, 31-33, 117, 146
regiments, 158
   4th Lincolnshire, 107
   9th Bengal Native Infantry, 107
   22nd Foot (Cheshire), 93, 107
   38th Grenadiers, 107, 330
   77th Foot (East Middlesex), 107
   Light Infantry, 83
   Madras Artillery, 107
   Worcestershire, 86, 107
registers, 18
Reid and Sons, 226
Reid, C.K. & Sons, 228
Reid, Christian Ker, 54, 226, 228
Reid, David, 54, 227
Reid, W.K., 89, 93
Reid, William, 227
Reily and Storer, 34, 54, 70, 72, 93, 123, 157
Reily, Charles, 70, 89, 156
Reily, John, 49, 57, 68, 76, 89, 93, 96, 99, 107, 119, 154-157, 183, 299
Reily, M. and C., 94, 183
Reily, Richard, 154
repairs, 18
replacements, 158
re-plating, 120
repoussé work, 346
reproductions, 64, 123
responsibility, 137
restoration, 121
retail mark-up, 24
reversible (palimpsests), 192
revivals, 123, 361
Reynolds, Sir Joshua, 11, 19
Reynolds, William, 48, 274, 278
Rhodes, Mrs Jean, 14, 381
Rhodes, J.R., 38
rhodium, 120, 124
ribbons, 36, 320
Rich, John, 49, 52, 54, 59, 61, 62, 66, 70, 87, 99, 154, 175-177, 182, 384
Richards, Alison, 43, 81
Richardson, Joseph, 372
Richardson, Richard, 201
Richardson II, Richard, 46, 47, 78, 201-203, 205

Richardson III, Richard, 202-203, 205
Richardson IV, Richard, 203, 205
Ritchie, William, 57, 272
Rive Saltes, 200
Roberts and Belk, 39, 250, 253
Roberts & Hall, 249
Roberts and Slater, 249
Roberts Cadman and Co., 235, 249
Roberts, Samuel, 292, 316
Roberts, Smith & Co., S., 249
Robertson, Ann, 179, 225, 226, 228
Robertson, James, 256
Robertson I, John, 226, 228, 229
Robertson II, John, 226, 228
Robertson, Patrick, 254
Robins, John, 175, 180
Robinson, B.W., 175
Robinson, Edward, 166, 183
Robinson II, John, 181, 182
Rock, William, 159
rococo, 28, 32, 49, 50, 54, 111, 114, 117, 123, 140, 143, 165, 190, 273, 318, 322
   revival, 34, 362
   scrolls, 34
Rocyn-Jones, John, 8
Rodgers, Thos., 249
rolling, 110
Rooke & Son, B., 249
rope-work, 68
rosettes, 51, 54, 62, 275
Ross, Adam, 347
Ross, Thomas & Michael, 228
Rotterdam, J., 362
roundels, 54
Rousillon, 186
Rowbotham, John, 249
Rowell, Thomas, 222
Royal Academy, 293
Royal Collection, 159, 163
Royal College of Arms, 155
Royal crown, 100
Royal Family, 225
Royal Grafton, 332
Royal Inventory, 78, 89, 99
Royal Mint, 134, 135
   Chief Engraver, 134
Royal Society, 134
Royal Wedding, 1981, 39
Royal Wine Company, 194
Ruggles-Brise, Lady, 376, 380
rum, 200
Rundell, Bridge and Rundell, 32, 101, 161-164, 154, 159
Rundell, Philip, 78, 90, 101, 159, 162
Rush, Thomas, 28, 46
Russell, William, 259, 264
Russia, 365
   leather, 341
Ryland, William, 325

Index

Sachs, Lady, 43
Sachs, Sir Eric, 44, 165
Saddler and Green, 298
St Andrews, 265
St Benedict, 374
St Botolph, Aldersgate, 12
St Dunstan, 358
St Eloi, 358
St Helen, Confraternity of, 358
St Vedast, Foster Lane, 167
Salford, 201, 234
Salkeld, John, 99
salmon, naiant, 359
Salter, John, 8, 9, 15, 175
Samson, Emile, 296
Samson (of Paris), 121, 187, 296, 302
Sandeman, Ernest S., 381
Sandeman family, 381
Sandeman, Patrick, 14, 381
Sandeman, Tim, 381
Sandeman, W., 375
Sanders, Jimmy, 43
Sasseville, François, 347
Sathersten, E., 84, 324
saturnine mask, 317
satyrs, 74, 75, 247, 286, 295
Sauce Labels, 15
Sauternes, 200
Savannah, 372
saw-tooth border, 55, 62, 153, 221
Sawin, Silas, 374
Saxony nickel, 317
Schmidt, Jeremiah, 351
Schvart, Diedrich, 368, 371
Scofield, John, 175
Scotland, 48, 52, 54, 57, 61, 374
Scott, Digby, 32, 77, 101, 117, 118, 162, 163
Scott, Robert, 225, 226, 228
Scott, Sir Walter, 150, 189
Scott I, William, 270
Scottish provincial, 265-272
  incorporations, 129
script, 19, 27, 49
scroll borders, 29
scroll surmounts, 60
scrolls, 19, 22, 52, 54-57, 149, 151, 165, 175, 221, 222, 247, 250, 273
  'C', 57
  golden brown, 299
  'reed and tie', 155
  reverse 'C', 36
  rococo, 34
  Vitruvian, 60
sets, 25, 188, 211
Settle, J. & T., 249
Settle, John, 330
Settle, Jonathan, 249
Settle, Thomas, 249
Setubal, 290
Sewell, Thomas, 228

Shanghai, 98
Shapland, C., 38
sheep, 96
Sheffield, 30, 32, 34, 38, 38, 56, 61, 62, 246-253
shells, 32, 88-89, 154, 164
  double, 157
  pectens, 88
  scallop, 88, 275
  tridacna, 89
Sheridan, Richard Brinsley, 17
sherry, 200
Sherwin, James, 58, 82
Sherwin, John, 30, 60, 62, 87, 275, 278
shield, 45, 52, 56, 64
Shore & Rotherham, 249
Shrewsbury, 204
Shrewsbury, Marquess of, 96
Shrub, 196, 200
Sicily, 189, 194
Sid, John, 272
Silber and Fleming, 318
Silenus, 75
silk, 341
  ribbon, 341
silver, 126
Silver Dip, 120
Silver Lion, 180
silver-gilt, 68, 352, 353
Simon, André, 14, 184, 190, 379
Simpson & Son, T., 330
Simpson I, William, 70, 266, 268, 270
Singapore, 357
Sitges, 384
Sjöblom, Gustaf Magnus, 371
slang, 187
Slater, James, 46, 126, 181
Slaughter, Stephen, 19
Sledmere, 138, 231, 234, 383
Sloden, William, 56, 87, 221
slogan, 85
slot, 70, 344, 352, 355, 359
small brass plate, 230
smallness, 125
smallworkers, 19, 165
  ledger, 139
  register, 149, 153
Smart, Ian, 8, 9
Smiley, William, 36
Smith & Co., Nathaniel, 249
Smith and Gamble, 70, 73, 84, 275
Smith and Hayter, 57
Smith, Benjamin, 32, 36, 77, 89, 101, 117, 118, 154, 157, 162, 320
Smith II, Benjamin, 88, 93, 101, 162
Smith III, Benjamin, 90, 96
Smith III, James, 117, 163
Smith, John, 133
Smith, Knowles & Co., 249
Smith, Richard West, 90, 275, 279
Smith, S., 93

snake, 43
Snatt, Josiah, 180
Snatt, Sarah, 179
Sneyd, John, 20, 22
snuffboxes, 155
Sobey, William Rawlings, 210, 211, 213, 216, 219
Soho Factory, 240
soldering, 108, 119
Solomon, Francis, 228
South Africa, 332, 366-367
sovereign's head, 129
soy sauce, 73
Spain, 368
Speirs, Thomas, 256
Spencer, Lady Diana, 105
sphinx, 107
spirit decanters, 38
  frame, 34
spirits, 33, 73, 187, 197, 245
  Railway, 187
  rectified, 368
Spode, 307
sponsors, 232
  marks, 136-138
Spooner and Coles, 242
square, 49
squirrel, 97
Staffordshire, 298, 300
stag's head, 359
Stalker and Mitchison, 224
Stalker, William, 56, 226, 228
stamping, 53, 54, 115, 146
standards of silver
  Britannia, 125, 143
  French, 358
  Maltese, 358
  Roman, 358
  sterling, 126, 127
stars, 22, 64-65, 155, 175, 247, 286, 351
Stationers, Worshipful Company of, 103
  Hall, 194
stays, 52, 56, 58
steam engine, 145
Steiner, Henry, 186, 342
Stephenson, William, 326, 328
sterling standard, 126, 127
Steward II, Joseph, 384
Stewart, Alexander, 271
Stewart, Thomas, 271
Stirling, 265
Stockholm, 369, 371, 372
Stokes (Australasia) Ltd., 324
Stokes, Thomas, 324, 343
Stone, John, 216, 220
stoppers, 326
  flat top, 326
  mounted cork, 326
Storer, George, 70, 89, 156
stork, 354
Storr and Co., 36, 159, 162

445

Index

Storr and Mortimer, 160
Storr, Paul, 32, 38, 78, 88, 96, 101, 111, 117, 118, 140, 154, 159-161, 164
Story, J.W., 328
Stothard, Thomas, 164
'stub', 129
Styles, Alex, 39
sulphur, 196
Summers, Henry, 158
Summers, William, 36, 68, 72, 77, 89, 157-159
suns, 66
   in splendour, 65, 66, 94, 177
   radiant, 351
Sutherland, Daniel, 96, 259, 264
Sutton, William, 326
swags, 29, 52, 58, 60, 146, 147
swans, 43, 147, 225
Sweden, 324, 352, 368-372
   crown, 84
      jewels, 369
Sweet, Edward, 212, 216, 220
Sweet, John, 208, 212, 216, 217
Sweet, William, 216, 220
Swift, Dean Jonathan, 17, 18, 124, 125, 126, 273
Sydney Gazette, 342
Sykes family, 18, 138, 231
Sykes, Sir Richard, 383

'TW', 57
Tain, 265
Tait, Dr Greville, 380
Taitt, Benjamin, 30, 58, 61, 79, 82, 85, 100, 104, 274, 279
Talbot, 94
Talbot of Malahide, 94
tally marks, 138
tankards, 22
tantalus, 353
Tapley and Co., John, 162, 163
Tatham, Charles Heathcote, 31, 164
tavern club, 17, 21
Taylor and Perry, 34, 90, 242
Taylor, Alfred, 322
Taylor, John, 244
Taylor, Joseph, 87, 88, 242, 244
Taylor, Michael Angelo, 17
Taylor, William, 23
Teare, Henry, 279
Teare, John, 60, 61, 75, 78, 79, 88, 100, 274, 280
Teare, Samuel, 54, 274, 280
teeth, 337-340
   sharks', 340, 374
Tellander, Hans, 368
tendrils, 32, 34, 46, 54, 60
Teneriffe, 200
Tengstedt, Carl, 368, 372
Teniers, W., 78
Terrantez, 359

Terry, Carden, 280
test piece, 268
Thacker, Keith, 9
Theed, William, 161, 162, 164
Thomas, John, 208, 216, 217
Thomason, Sir Edward, 242
Thompson, Joseph, 347
Thompson, Samuel, 228
Thornton, John, 242
Thurso, 265
tick marks, 238
'tidying', 114
Tiffany and Co., 348, 362, 374
tiger, 97
   claws, 36
tin, 290
   alloys, 291
Titchfield, Marquis of, 159
toasts, 189
Toddy, 362
Tolekien, J., 276
toleware, 290
Tone, Theobald Wolfe, 86
tonic, 359
topers, 154
tortoiseshell, 340
'Touch, the', 126, 229
Townsend, John and Thomas, 366
Townshend, George, 20
tracery, 36
trade advertisements, 230
trade-in, 26
trademark, 137
'Trades' House', 256
tradesmen's ledgers, 15
Trayes, William, 154
trefoils, 36, 60
trellis, rectangular, 317
Trinity Hall, Cambridge, 102
Trist, Joshua (or Joseph), 212, 216, 218
Triton, 88
Troby, W., 61, 78
Troika Designs Ltd, 39
Trowbridge, Francis, 208, 216, 217
Truro Cathedral, 38
Tucker, Fenton & Co., 249
Tucker, William, 74
Tudor and Leader, 247, 249
Tudor & Co., Henry, 249
Tudor, Henry, 51, 56, 252
turned back edges, 286
Turner and Simpson, 38, 242
tusks, 337, 356
tutenag, 291
Twemlow, John, 207
Twemlow, William, 207
twentieth century, 38-44
Twentyman, Lawrence, 366
Twentyman, W.H., 356
Tyland and Son, Thomas, 242

Uddevalla, Carl Frederick, 372
Underdown, Wilkinson & Co., 248
Unite and Hilliard, 242
Unite, George, 34, 49, 83, 90, 123, 210, 242, 244
United States of America, 372-374
United Volunteer Movement, 85
universities, 102
unmarked labels, 127
urns, 29, 62, 147, 175
   festooned, 248
   lidded, 87

Valhalla, 105
Vanders, 38, 39, 44
Vansittart, 94
varietals, 186
vases, 29, 62
Venus and Cupid, 295
Verhoef, Manicus, 362
Vernon, Nathaniel, 372
Victoria, Queen, 33
   Golden Jubilee, 84
Victorian period, 33-38
Vidonia, 200
vine leaves, 46, 60, 89-93
vines, 32, 34
   fruiting, 53
vineyards, 186
Vintners, Worshipful Company of, 43, 102, 159, 170
Volta, 314

waiter, 196
Wakelin and Garrard, 162
Wakelin, Edward, 23, 24
Wakelin, John, 23
Wakelin Ledgers, 18, 23-26, 70, 80, 117, 137, 139, 150, 211, 326
   Gentlemen's, 23, 24, 25, 26
   Workmen's, 23, 24
Waldegrave, 26
Wales, Prince of, 6, 18, 20, 21-22, 26, 31, 99, 107, 203, 225
   feathers, 53, 100, 104, 149, 232, 274, 283, 372, 374
   Service, 99
Walker I, George, 203, 206
Walker I, John, 203, 207
Walker Knowles & Co., 249
Walker, Nelson, 347
Walker, Samuel, 249
Wallis and Hayne, 57, 59, 97, 233
Walley, Joseph, 48, 203, 205
Wallis, Thomas, 57, 83
Walsh, Stephen, 76, 273, 280
Walther, Herman John, 54
Walton, John, 228
Wardell and Kempson, 242
Warrington, Earl of, 18, 190, 382-383
wars, 194

Index

American War of Independence, 129
Napoleonic, 191, 194, 210, 374
Revolutionary, 194
Warszawa, 364
Warwick vase, 32, 159
washing, 124
Washington, George, 372
Waterhouse & Co., 249
Waterhouse, Hodson & Co., 249
Watney, Dr Bernard, 9, 291
Watson, Christopher, 234, 235, 236, 238, 239
Watson, John, 249
Watson, Thomas, 103, 226, 227, 228, 247, 248, 249
Watson, William, 253
waved borders, 60
waved concaved borders, 60
wear, 121
Webb, John, 216, 219
Wedgwood, 307, 331
Wedgwood, Josiah, 29, 243
Wednesbury, 298, 299
Weed, Raphael, 375, 377
Weir, Samuel, 256
Weir, Thomas, 43, 86, 103, 217
Welch, William, 65, 212, 216, 218
Wellington, Duke of, 159
Wells, Richard, 9
Wendt, Jochim Matthias, 343
West Country, 90
Westphaly, William, 18
wheat husk, 62
wheat sheaves, 33
Wheatley, Thomas, 227, 228
Whipham, Thomas, 139
whisky, 189, 200
White, 200
White, Robert, 139

Whitfords, the, 68
Whittingham, John, 51, 70
Whitwell, William, 233, 239
Whitworth, Eric, 9, 169
Wick, 265
Wickes, George, 18, 23, 24, 28, 137, 139
widows, 138
Wigan, Thomas, 56, 222
Wilkinson & Co., H., 249
Wilkinson & Co., Henry, 330
Wilkinson, Henry, 330
William IV, King, 163
Williams, J. and J., 212
Williams, James, 208, 214, 216, 221, 223
Williams, Jane, 87, 179
Williams, John, 221
Williams, Josiah, 208, 214, 216, 221, 223
Williams, Robert, 216, 220, 223
Willis, Jacob, 221
Willmore and Alston, 244
Willmore, Joseph, 72, 74, 77, 88, 242, 244
Willmore II, Joseph, 90
Willmore, Thomas, 242, 244
Windsor Castle, 99, 140
wine
  bottles, 13
  Cape (South African), 194
  currant, 106, 198
  fortified, 33, 197, 245
  funnels, 153
  gooseberry, 106
  quality of, 194
  siphons, 153
  South African, 186
  table, 197
Wine Label Circle, 8, 105

100th member, 39
Golden Jubilee, 44
Winter & Co., John, 246
Winter, John, 246
wire loop, 68
Wisting, Hans Petter, 363
Wittewaal, 360
women silversmiths, 178-179
Wood, Mrs., 243
Woodhouse family, 189, 196
Woodhouse, John, 194
Woodman, William, 210, 211, 212, 214, 215, 216, 219, 222
wool industry, 233
workmen, 137, 138
woven fabrics, 341
wriggle work, 60
Wright & Fairbairn, 249
Wright, Charles, 139
Wright, John, 227, 228
Wyatt, James, 243
Wyon, William, 134

Yapp and Woodward, 242
York, 48, 54, 56, 61, 229-240
  Goldsmiths' Guild of, 230
  Minster Library, 235
York, Duke of, 162
York House, Battersea, 293
Young, Walker, Kitchen and Co., 252
Younge & Co., J.T., 249
Younge & Co., John, 249
Younge & Co., S. & C., 249

Zeppelin, 43, 105, 292
Ziegler, Alex, 256
Ziegler, John, 256
Ziegler, W., 57
zigzags, 55, 146, 222